STRUTTING ON THIN AIR

Paths from Imperial Fantasy

Chris Benjamin

ISBN: 978-0-9561579-0-4

To chums and colleagues

CONTENTS

We're running out of Lucknow

LAST Christmas we mused on the Spirit of Recessions to Come. Today we're not sure we're out of the last one. So not much has changed. What ever does?

We tend to ourselves to historical parody — politicians daubing on their woad, prancing PR rituals, and sharpening flint-heads for the next tribal battle; the TUC displaying its neanderthal tendencies in condemning as "alien" the approach of perhaps the world's most efficient manufacturer; or our industrial barons, clanking with Ks and aspiring squires, heralding their advances, even if still leagues behind the forces of Attila and Hideoshi. Plenty of scope for fun.

But a more relevant historical perspective is that Britain will soon be the last outpost of the British Empire; even as Churchill foresaw it lasting a thousand years, its collapse within 20 years was writ. Still, attitudes and institutions hang on, if anything more tenaciously as the gap between accustomed rhetoric and the evidence of decline widens.

So we increasingly resemble the besieged garrison in the Lucknow Residency during the Indian Mutiny — continuous internal bickering, and redoubts crammed with communists and policy advisers to block the smallest shaft of reality breaking in. Yet the old arrogance struts on.

Did we really have the gall to preach free trade, while running the largest closed market in history? Did we really build the first railways of India and nearly half the world? Or set up education systems, universities, hospitals and legal structures around the world? And did we lead the world in industrial innovation? Totally improbable to a visitor trying to cross London, taking British Rail, glancing at our education statistics.

In vain does industry look for any perception of the realities of international markets in the corridors and lobbies of government. Proper administration needs detachment, impartiality, attention to broad policy, and concern only for the framework of fair market conditions — and decidedly not direct contact with the boxwallahs, babu merchants and maharajas. When confronted by baffled industrialists, one could only try to reassure them by explaining that the essential qualifications to partake in the ecstasies of policy were a proven ability to parse the gerund and a smattering of Adam Smith.

Some in the DTI have long concluded that the prevalence of Classical Greats (Latin and Greek) accounted for the Treasury's apparent belief that research is an activity best conducted in a bath, while Modern Greats (Politics, Philosophy and Economics) explained their conception of the economy as also most safely viewed from a tub.

So industry is treated as but one of the special interests begging at the gate, and the more reprehensible since it apparently wants special favours, dismissed by such graffiti terms as "subsidies", "intervention", "consistency" or "coherence". To be fair, the Central Statistical Office has been mounting sorties to make contact with native tribes — such as taxi drivers — to find out what everyone else knows. And some outpost agencies are being set up to strengthen the defences; under strictly limited discretion, of course — such as the ECGD.

The City stands as a further rampart against reality minting into the Residency compound. The excesses of its rajahs, nizams and nawabs — golden handshakes, golden parachutes, golden handcuffs, massive pay awards, and soon, no doubt, the latest from the US, golden coffins — are tolerated with, so long as the pretence of "efficient markets" avoids any onus for involvement, never mind its influence on competitive behaviour in the "real market".

But the rats have been getting at the sandbags lately, with odd remarks about the unacceptable faces of capitalism. The largest breach, however, has been the belated awareness of the rich vein of fantasy talent in the accountancy profession. As company accounts resemble episodes of Star Trek, "efficient markets" has become a surrogate term for a colloquium of Galaxy Award winners (with all their analysts, lawyers, agents, etc). Or the Crime Writers' Guild, judging by the case lists of the Serious Fraud Office and DTI investigations branch.

The system needs a steady flow of new recruits into the defences — the highest aims of our proudest institutions

The post-war Raj . . . odd couple only for lack of plumed hats

have been to produce young men equipped for long periods up-country (or in Arab prisons, according to one released hostage), and ultimately to become governors of Bengal. Imagine any post-war eminent Establishment person in a plumed hat, astride a grey, reviewing the sepoy divisions at Dum-Dum, and few would not appear more comfortable than in the job they were doing.

True, we established public schools overseas, where young nawabs could be conditioned to the games ethic — to lose with dignity — and so ensure they toed the line later. The least successful of our students were consigned to commerce, practising a straight bat and looking for even pitches.

Don't bother to compare our performance in producing engineers, technicians, linguistic skills, or practical commercial minds with that of our main competitors. That's never been the point, so long as education turned out enough — ideally, just enough — to perpetuate this system.

The "Raj still rules" model is plainly OK for some. But the Economist in September surveyed the Japanese community in Britain and, on their anxieties about social tensions, reported: "One acute young banker mused that he could see where Karl Marx got his idea of the class struggle from." I say, Carruthers, spotted the relief column yet?

Chris Benjamin is a former assistant secretary at the Department of Trade and Industry

Indicators

TODAY — UK: Building societies monthly figures (Nov).
GER: Cost of living (Oct).
UK: Trade figures (Nov).
US: Personal income (Nov).
US: Personal consumption (Nov).

TOMORROW — JP: Leading indicator (Oct)
FR: Trade balance (Nov)
US: Durable goods orders (Nov).
WEDNESDAY — Christmas Day.
THURSDAY — JP: Industrial production (Nov).
JP: Retail sales (Nov).
FRIDAY — JP: Consumer prices.
Source: Yamaichi International.

PROLOGUE

Over a mere five decades, or a single generation, Britain has gone from a leading force across technologies as wide as aviation, computers, nuclear power, electronics, ball bearings and motorbikes – commanding some 12% of the world's exports – to a negligible position in new technologies and barely more than a marginal presence in other industrial activities; with a trade deficit having exceeded £100bn a year (currently down to £80-90bn as recession has depressed demand) and a current account deficit having reached 5.7% of GDP, and this is only likely to increase as reliance on imported energy, foodstuffs and consumer products increases. No bother, apparently. Of late we hear only Panglossian views that the reliance of the economy on services is inevitable, or "natural and desirable".[1] Yet other nations, like Germany and Japan, with higher labour costs than Britain, have raised the level of their technologies to retain leading positions in higher-value-added products and run substantial trade and current-account surpluses.

Behind the conventional "rebalancing" of the economy, away from consumer profligacy to be achieved by a fall in the value of sterling – apparently relying upon some Archimedes in the heavens with levers and pulleys – there are occasional cries of "Revive manufacturing before it is too late".[2] Yet the structures, systems, institutions and attitudes that have presided over this decline are the least attuned to sustaining the growth of internationally competitive enterprises. Especially now that they are up against not just contestants from the old developed nations club, but also new protagonists from "the rest". So, without change, and it is still downhill all the way.

Studies of Britain's industrial decline petered out in the 1980s, along with most industries themselves – industry warrants barely an occasional glance in histories of modern Britain compared to the rise of the Beatles, the Rolling Stones and occasional riots.[i] The late Lord (Eric) Roll's 1995 monograph *Where Did We Go Wrong* was a last gasp.[3] Having hoofed extensively through Whitehall and the City looking back to 1925, he notes "only one possible catalyst" could account for "these unfortunate phases"... "a very imperfect adaptability to changes in circumstances of the magnitude that have occurred during this period. It is this almost

---

[i] Typical is Andrew Marr's *A History of Modern Britain* (Macmillan).

automatic reaction by traditional modes of thought and action to historically new demands that can account at one and the same time for a variety of mistakes." Among the symptoms of this malaise, he notes "failures of successive governments" to invest in infrastructure, skills, education and "turning away from manufacturing". Yet after this catalogue, his sharpest criticism is "even if the doctrines of economics provided a surer guide to public policy as they are as yet able to do, they would not be altogether safe in the hands of politicians", and his conclusion is that "the difficulty of prescription lies precisely in the varied nature of the causes, ranging from inadequate clinical observation and analysis to the stubborn persistence of almost Pavlovian reactions to problems."

As a diagnostic exercise, few could quibble. And its authenticity is guaranteed by the paean of "decades of under investment" continuing for many more decades to come.

Praying "a very imperfect adaptability to changes..." may carry a tinge of self-exoneration. After all, if the failings are socially systemic, the efforts of any individual against inherited structures are almost bound to be futile. Especially when the origins reach back into history with its accumulated baggage of status. And indeed they do go back to the latter half of the 19th century when the US and Germany responded more effectively to the organisational and investment demands of the new heavy industries of steel, electricity, and chemical processing. With Japan, after "catching up" in engineering, shipbuilding, railways etc, taking over dominance in textiles by the 1930s to earn the title "Manchester of the East".

All this happened while Britain was pursuing its absurd fantasy of a latter-day Roman Empire, demanding that the highest academic laurels for the ruling elite should be classics,[4] of absolutely no practical relevance save contributing to the cackhandedness with which the Empire was governed,[5] and as a device to secure an arrogant segregation – hence the status of the "Balliol Double-first". Perhaps the turning point was Thomas Huxley's failure in the 1870s to convince John Stuart Mill that sciences were as good a discipline for the mind as classics. By contrast, while Britain was preoccupied with Empire and its "world status", other major nations and "the rest" gave priority to technical skills and science as the essential foundation for their development. The current trumpeting of skills and higher education is a belated, and belated by some 150 years, response. Even worse, as Herodotus has fallen from the pinnacle of academic attainment, the entry ticket for the arrogant elite has shifted to selected quotations from Adam Smith, conveniently ignoring some of the old guy's most perceptive insights.[6] This has put the "buggered" into the formulation, "Balliol's buggered us" once muttered in the corridors of Whitehall.[7]

Most disquieting from Lord Roll's diagnosis for those who have been in the boiler room of industrial decline – Ministers, officials, managers, financiers, trade unions et al – is their complicity in a national myopia that persistently ignored the effectiveness of other idioms of economic development. Personally, to borrow Prospero's phrase, having a "dark backward" as a relic of the Raj and an "abysm" in Mrs Thatcher's DTI,[ii] one was unwittingly weaned into this complicity. And this mindset persisted in various Departments concerned with "industry" until the shock of the motorcycle industry collapse in the mid-70s, when names unquestionably accepted as being "world leaders" fell out of a seemingly sunny sky into bankruptcy and occasioned the first in-depth study of comparable industrial performance against international competitors. From which, the obsolescence of Britain's leading manufacturers became starkly apparent.

Typically, political debate at the time was confined to empty rhetorical gesturing on the merits of workers' cooperatives against the disciplines of the private sector. Yet had corresponding studies been made of other companies that flopped on the government's doorstep over the same period, virtually all would have been revealed to have fallen equally adrift of the competitive tempo set by international leaders. Though to be fair, the motorcycle industry analysis did convince Ministers to try to employ the available powers for industrial support to stimulate investment and modernisation, even if this has turned out to be only putting off the inevitable.

With impotence still all the rage, we have no want of seething: daily, columnists seethe at the never-ending flow of cock-ups, absurdities, and posturing that accompany our national governance. And there are enjoyable periodic polemics against this structure.[8] But all, whether consciously or by tutelage, are in an idiom of literary commentary that harks back to Joseph Addison, the early 18th century founder of *The Spectator*, with such essays as "Pleasures of the Imagination". All too easily dismissed as an amusing diversion by those imperviously closeted within the system, or by the glib political shrug in the sure knowledge that these outbursts are couched in a cultivated language that passes most of the public by.

Going back to the self-styled glories of Empire, from the perspective of

---

[ii] "What seest thou else/In the dark backward and abysm of time?" *A Winter's Tale* Act I sc.1

other countries it was "free-trade imperialism".[9] And they naturally, and entirely rationally, evolved structures, institutions and mechanisms to defend themselves against this form of hypocritical mercantilist coercion. Whereas for Britain, free trade was fine so long as it was accompanied by mercantile and financial superiority – backed by a few battalions of sepoys and the Royal Navy to capture market share. As these props have fallen away, the structures of other countries have shown themselves to be more resilient and adaptable to take on the challenges of new technologies and change. Leaving this country recycling outdated formulae of "free trade" and "open markets".

This leads naturally into the seething, reaching crescendo levels as the consequences of the "credit crunch" spread to the real economy, about the Government's subservience to the City. What's new? The driving concern behind foreign policy in the days of Empire was always the comforts and fortunes of denizens of the City.[10] Irrespective of their failings in providing competitive finance for industry. Latterly, our glorious "private sector disciplines" have contributed a self-debilitating rate of acquisitions and mergers, excessive dividends at the expense of sustaining investment to create future options for growth, and a culture obsessed by encapsulated contractual relations – at its most evident in the "outdoor relief" to lawyers, accountants and City finance houses provided by the public/private gimmickry of the Treasury's off-balance-sheet financing. Of course, the tradition of the Treasury being conned by the "private sector" is at least a century old, but now any concept of the "private sector" taking risks has been lost beneath byzantine contractual verbiage where, with a bit of creative accounting and use of tax-havens, risk equates with guaranteed excessive profits. If the City's justification is "creative destruction", the "destruction" is incontestable. But where's the "creativity? Inflated fees for investment bankers, and their trickle down to squaddies of analysts, lawyers and accountants? Impenetrable devices to increase the personal rewards of insiders?

If the sanctimonious facade of economics orthodoxy is showing cracks in the grease paint,[11] this is a relatively new phenomenon in Britain. Tomes have piled up, even by practitioners, depicting its malignant impact on developing countries and the inadequacy of its inherent assumptions. Yet largely unquestioned here, as Pavlov has proved dominant – nowhere more so than in the official corridors of Whitehall. Insulation from reality, pre-eminently in the Treasury but spreading elsewhere, is a natural legacy of the Raj mentality – "the *burrah sahibs* can't be wrong" – has been elevated to sustained fantasy. A colleague who transferred from the Ministry of Aviation to the Treasury characterises indoctrination into the latter as a "reality detox",[12] with copious injections of economics, on the grounds that to take on other Departments on the real merits of the case, the Treasury was bound to lose since others would always be better armed with real information.

"We're all intellectuals, really," remarked one senior DTI colleague, noted for chairing interminable meetings (all of those attending having drawn short straws), but by education, culture, and inclination ideally groomed for posting to the Legislative Department in New Delhi – in 1928. While so many of one's senior Whitehall colleagues had the effortless comportment for Governors of Bengal. Except we've run out of Bengals. Though the occasional one secures their perfect niche in our dwindling tasselled posts.

The main product of this "rounded amateur" tradition is the myth of "policy": a mystic phantasm of superior gobbledygook only attainable by indoctrination in some arcane discipline – the more arcane the better. The general essay in my Open Entry exam for the Administrative Class – "Silence is an attenuated form of prayer. Discuss." – should have been a klaxon warning. Approached by baffled industrial managers asking why we could not have "an industrial policy" like the French, Japanese and others, the conventional, "Not to interfere with the operation of free markets etcetera, etcetera, etcetera" would have been plain absurd. Because every other country interferes continuously. But we need do no more than glance around. The answer could only take the form, "Why should industry expect special treatment when no other facet of the nation has enjoyed such a privilege?"

Energy? What odds on blackouts in the next two decades? Rail infrastructure? We are just crawling out of a staggering self-inflicted shambles viewed with incredulous awe around the world: as originally devised, a uniquely British contraption demanding more lawyers than engine drivers to operate the system, or, in diagrammatic form, Heath Robinson discovers financial engineering. Road and aviation infrastructure? More vacillation between piles of paper; characterised by ad hoc spurts of investment only when capacity tolerances have disappeared, so that "an integrated transport policy" has morphed into "an integrated "congestion-charging policy". Water and drainage? Should we worry about future flooding when "South East has less water per person than Sudan"?[13] Education and skills? When have "skill shortages" not been a constant complaint, with the equally constant response of exhortation matched by inadequate focused investment? Health? Behind the endless repetition of the political mantra that "the National Health Service is the envy of the world", again a history of under investment and vacillation.

Among the spectral figures roaming the land are murky shapes addressed as "policymakers" – daily importuned, advised, urged, chastised, beseeched and summoned in newssheets and journals. Yet, bluntly, "Wot policies?" Of all the charges levelled against the Treasury, mostly justified, most heinous is a complete failure in routine housekeeping of the nation's assets: simple care and maintenance, capacity expansion and modernisation of what is generally regarded as public infrastructure. A policy "black hole" in any sense in which the term "policy" might be construed elsewhere. The new emphasis on "delivery" is an open admission of this hiatus. For a "policy" that fails in "delivery" must be entirely spurious. While even the new "disciplines" of "targets" devised to "deliver" have shown themselves to be either only marginally effective, or counterproductive, even if propagated by overarching arrogance.[14] Public disillusion with politicians is but a natural consequence of "policy" increasingly being perceived as simply a redundant rhetorical appendage.

One modest advantage from a career spent near the plimsoll line of Britain's foundering industrial competences is that one might lever off a few of the barnacles of subsequent myths. Notably, having been involved in activities berated by theoreticians as "picking winners" or "corporatism", as Lord Roll remarks, these have been "grossly exaggerated". You can say that again. Not least because Britain simply lacks the technocratic raw materials, mindset, and structures to produce "winners" – where, outside sectors dominated by government procurement like defence and health – Rolls-Royce, GSK – or resource industries established in the days of Empire – BP, Shell, RTZ – have UK markets picked even a good two-way bet, leave alone a winner? Courtaulds? GEC/Marconi? Hanson? ICI? Dowty? Hawker Siddeley? Dunlop? or Vickers? just to list the most obvious. Or why, bluntly, to toss in a sample of comparisons, not a single Honda, Toyota, Renault, Bosch, Siemens, Miele, Evergreen, Acer, Lucky Goldstar, Samsung, Sony, Nokia, Wipro, Embraer and so on? Or why have we failed to achieve the institutional coherence of the real post-World War II successes – France, Germany, Japan, South Korea, Taiwan, Singapore etc?

In reality, the "picking winners" dispute, even if it returns by Pavlovian repetition,[15] has been deliberately skewed into stupidity by a frenetic fervour to avoid any questioning that conventional "markets" are effective. Of course, "no system seems all that good at picking winners",[iii] least of all financial markets. And, of course, no country picks winners on an analogy with sticking pins into race cards on Ladies' Day – once

---

[iii] *The Wisdom of Crowds*: James Surowiecki (Little Brown).

hilariously confirmed by a unanimous show of hands when a vote was called in an OECD Industry Committee meeting. But taking the horse racing analogy, the real trick is breeding and rearing winners.[16] And contrary to the dogmatic economic proposition that "efficiency" is promoted by "flexibility" and "liquidity" of resources, the underlying essential for industrial success is "continuity". As any number of predominantly "foreign" examples attest, it is "continuity" that fosters consistent focus, expertise evolved over decades and pursuit of research, innovation and knowledge application to secure the feedback for "increasing returns". The annual DTI/BERR R&D Scoreboard is a regular audit of the relative performance of UK companies against contenders who have better sustained their "continuity". A more pertinent entry-exam essay would be "Why industrial decline in booming Britain and dynamic innovation in deflationary Japan?"[17]

An equally pertinent question over decades – assiduously ducked by the CBI, IoD, EEF, TUC, and indeed Government – has been why Britain, despite all the rhetoric about "entrepreneurs" and "enterprise", is incapable of evolving companies with the qualities of a Honda or Sony, which started from extremely small units in product areas that were ferociously contested both in their home market and internationally? Or why Japanese, German, French, Swiss, Mexican, Italian, Indian and Nordic companies have an ability to evolve successful operations in this country using the same resources of labour, suppliers, and infrastructure where British companies have lamentably failed? Yet the habitual strut goes on. If our corporate leadership, with a few rare exceptions, had spent but half the zeal employed on devising obscure devices to reward themselves on the essentials of sustaining businesses in the changing international competitive scene, we would not have suffered the continuing loss of industrial competence. Consequently, our business leadership, with a diminishing few companies measuring on any international scale, for all their airs are little more than overpaid bucket-shop bosses.[18] As some consolation, at least the band of foreign owners have demonstrated that, assuming committed owners and capable managers, in principle our national talents can exert skills to produce tradeable value-added products.

As a tail-note, the country does confront a debility of language to cope with new realities. Just as the term "policy" has been gutted, and as "efficient" in economic jargon distorted to a subversion of meaning, as but a small quibble with Lord Roll's critique, "manufacturing" could also be consigned to a Middle-English dictionary. "Manufacturing" plays into a folk memory of hordes of L.S. Lowry figures pouring out of blackened factory gates at the first sound of the 'ooter, "workers versus bosses", and reinforced by repetition of "dark satanic mills" – incidentally, a complete misreading of Blake's symbolism, whose real intent was a theological variant on "Balliol's buggered us". In this century, the trend in higher value-added products is best illustrated by facilities such as Toyota's Prius production line in Aichi, which is open as a tourist attraction, or plants run by the likes of Fanuc, Mazak, Canon and Kyocera that can run for prolonged periods without any "wear and tear of hands" at all – operations where skills, experience and accumulated knowledge of technology and processes are efficiently integrated. While the term has propagated a false dichotomy between "manufacturing" and "services".[19] The supreme irony is that many countries that have developed to leading status have done so through emulation of a Britain that we today no longer recognise.[20] While there is nothing in the spreading shambles of dysfunctional "celebrity chat show", "cookery" and "antiques-driven" "service" Britain today that is a model for emulation anywhere.

To help untangle the skeins of complicities, one has applied the old civil service form of a submission: Ministers were assumed to be busy, so brevity and a plain style were desirable, with any backup material in Notes and Appendices. Ideally, a text not more than two pages, and Notes – often more designed as a disclaimer that civil servants could not be fingered for failing to present a full picture. In this case, the convention allows reference to readily available material on how the world has moved on, systematically ignored in this country.

Beginning with a modestly biographical section has several merits: the national memory has a skittish superficiality whereby the immediately preceding four or five decades are consigned to museums, awaiting examination by academics as official records are researched, with recollection over the period confined to political biographies where posterity is sitting on the shoulder.[21] Sifting out the humdrum in the daily round also permits a more authentic account of the changing ethos: from the habitual swagger of Empire and Cold War illusions, the crazy swing from Tony Benn to Keith Joseph in the DTI – only otherwise possible in a banana republic – and the self-annihilating certainties of Thatcherism and its New Labour disciples. As well as some innocent merriment at a system totally unprepared for the realities of fast-moving technologies and a rapidly evolving international trade scene. Having bequeathed the "License Raj" to India, who are beginning to reap the benefits of its dismantling, the flame of byzantine bureaucracy still shines incandescently in the courts of Whitehall. Retrospection also permits a viewpoint outside the conventional "instant anachronism" of the British elite education system – public school/Oxbridge – and comfortable sinecures in hermetic boxes in the City, academia or quangos; and takes in a decade as an advisor to Itochu (Europe), a Japanese sogo shosha;[22] involvement in the Major Projects Association, a club of interested companies and experts; and as a Visiting Fellow at Sussex University running an Innovation Club.

The structure of this approach begins with the recognition that by upbringing and education one was a prime specimen of the "Instant Anachronisms" who have landed us in this pickle. A first section from earliest years is a necessary foundation, which varies from the model of most contemporaries only in having absorbed a basic scepticism of the competencies of "the British ruling caste" from observation at a height of less than 4'6" – a scepticism essential to retain sanity in a civil service career. This blissful state of unknowing persisted until becoming involved with the aerospace industry, where initially the tempo of farce was a diversion. But as direct contact with other countries increased, and, in posts avowedly supporting British industry – even though the rest of the system, and indeed companies themselves, were disinclined to acknowledge that most of the world was working on entirely different principles – one has been in close proximity to the demise of more industries than most. This account could only be entitled, "Fantasy to Scrap Heap".

If with a derisory outcome in terms of industrial performance, this experience at least provides the basis for a critical glance at this country's institutional thinking that is increasingly adrift of the real world. "An Obsolete Nation" is a rough audit of our relative national industrial standing, and the dysfunctionality of our antique economics ethos. "They Ain't Daft" attempts a brief Cook's tour, drawn from direct contacts and academic studies perused from natural curiosity, of how other nations have evolved from a very different set of premises, and whose resulting institutions and orientation have left them better equipped for the future. The sort of brief outlines that British Ministers should take on board before arriving blinking in other countries. More pertinently, rhetoric about "fitting the nation for the next century" is vacuous without recognition that most other countries have pursued an entirely different trajectory of economic development. "Get out the Shovels" attempts to illustrate the underlying basis of this ancient myopia, and to suggest some modest steps to correct the astonishing self-deception and arrogance that still persists.

As an editing point, instead of the reiteration of knighthoods an "*" will be used, since at the time the individuals were just "Bill", "Bob",

"Sam", "Dick", and so on. As for the customary expressions of appreciation, I have not sought to consult widely, since the numbers involved are impossible. Where an individual is identified, this arises primarily from the narrative, though occasionally there are unacknowledged characters among the hewers of rock and wielders of shovels who deserve more profile than they have been granted. Otherwise, I would be echoing many of my vintage of civil servants in thanking others for having contributed to a fun time, and mostly civilised companions, who, even in the natural inter-departmental clashes of Whitehall, have contributed to shared frustrations and entertainment – mostly the latter.

The conclusion is regrettably not far from Lord Roll's: the shortcomings have been so painfully obvious for so long with so little resolution to change that continuing decline – albeit with immaculate pretensions – is almost inevitable. By virtue of decades when "markets" have substituted for thought, the country's economic structure has been hazardously skewed towards reliance on services. If London as a world financial centre has provided comforting rhetoric for politicians, even if its flickering lustre is proving costly for the rest of the nation, in many fields of industry the country has lagged to the negligible or barely sustainable. The resulting dependence on an increasing range of foreign products, in addition to energy, foodstuffs, and clothing, has contributed to the rising trade deficit since 1986.

Reversing this trend poses a genuinely radical wrench from conventional approaches, ranging from the financing of corporate enterprises to the programming of an entirely new technocratic brand of *burrah sahibs*. The enormity of the task of converting the nation from worship of its ancient idols is approaching the insuperable. Even if all attempts fail, however, then at least our leaders should contain their insufferable predilection to preach to others. After all, strutting on thin air is hardly an elevated lectern.

For a second impression, whilst there have been significant changes – such as the collapse and rescue of General Motors, the growing global presence of China, India and Brazil – the essentials of Britain's implacable pursuit of "decline by aloof inadvertence" have continued unchanged. If "the ethic of cultivated ignorance" has been the guiding vision of the UK's governance, the frantic debate over increasingly fanciful economic projections heralds a new apogee of "accumulated ignorance". Meanwhile, out there beyond Dover, where merchandise goods and related logistics account for over three quarters of world trade, according to the latest IHS Global Insight survey, the UK manufacturing value-added output stands at $227bn (2.6% of 2009 world manufacturing output, down from 5.4% in 1980 and 3.6% in 2006), falling behind France, and only $13bn ahead of South Korea, $20bn in front of Russia and $22bn more than Brazil, with every prospect of falling out of the top ten manufacturing countries (*FT* 21.6.10). Updating is focused upon further examples of policies adopted by countries that take industry seriously.

---

[1] On the MG Rover collapse, *A tale of greed and gullibility* (*FT* 8/9.4.05). "Over the past two decades manufacturing output has grown by a third. But its relative importance has continued to shrink, as services have grown by 85 percent. This is natural and desirable."

[2] "Revive manufacturing before it's too late", Richard Wachman (*Observer* 9.9.07), with a plea: "It is no good for ministers to bang on about the merits of a knowledge-based economy, a phrase that has become meaningless over time. What the government must do is to declare its support for manufacturing and single out industries that could benefit from a new research and development programme that brings together the private and public sectors, the schools and universities. But we need to act fast, before our European and US competitors open a gap that will be impossible to close." Fair enough, except that gaps have also been opening up in Asia.

A flurry of interest followed Sir John Rose's call: "Britain needs an industrial route map" (*FT* 24.4.08), where the chief executive of Rolls-Royce acknowledges that financial services "generate almost one million well-paid jobs, large corporation tax revenues, and a positive balance of payments of about £20bn." But "unfortunately this does not offset over £70bn deficit in trade in manufactured goods". With a call for recognising the contribution of "high value-added manufacturing", and for the development of "a framework or 'roadmap' to set priorities for both public and private sector investment" though not "centralised industrial planning". While the rising trade deficit and widening implications of the credit crunch also stimulated "Why the future is made in Britain" (*Observer* 27.4.08): an anthology of current commentators ranging from benign hopes that the depreciation in Sterling will encourage niche and specialist manufacturers to scepticism that the country's increasing reliance on foreign ownership and supply makes Britain more dependent on imports of "technical expertise".

[3] Published by Faber. Eric Roll, Lord Roll of Ipsden (died 30 Mar 2005), after a distinguished academic career, served in the Ministry of Food and the Treasury, in London, Washington and Paris; and was involved in Lend-Lease, the Marshall Plan, NATO, and the initial negotiations for entry to the European Union. He ended his civil service career as Permanent Secretary of the short-lived Department of Economic Affairs, since when he had been active in the City becoming President of the Warburg Group. A useful compendium of vantage points.

[4] Just recall the entry examination requirements for Haileybury, the Indian Civil Service College: "Each candidate shall be examined in the four Gospels of the Greek Testament and shall not be deemed duly qualified for admission to Haileybury College, unless he be found to possess a competent knowledge thereof..... Not unless he is able to render into English some portion of the works of one of the following Greek authors: Homer, Herodotus, Xenophon, Thucydides, Sophocles, and Euripides.

"Nor unless he can render into English some portion of the works of one of the following Latin authors: Livy, Terence, Cicero, Tacitus, Virgil, and Horace; and this part of the examination will include questions in ancient history, geography, and philosophy." (*The Lion and the Tiger* by Dennis Judd (Oxford)).

With the consequence: "The British elite pored over Roman histories in part because of their fascination with a previous great empire, but also because they were looking for lessons in managing vast swathes of land on different continents. There was a demand, as it were, for people skilled in language, history, and imperial administration. This, however, ended up trumping the need to develop the engineers of the future." (*The Post-American World* by Fareed Zakaria (Allen Lane))

[5] A deliriously entertaining account of Britain's peculiar imperial ineptitude is provided by Piers Brendon in *The Decline and Fall of the British Empire 1781-1997* (Random House), which prompted one reviewer to muse, "The real wonder, after reading this book, is how Britain ever managed to have an empire at all."

[6] Just for starters, how about? "To buy in one market, in order to sell, with profit, in another, when there are many competitors in both; to watch over, not only the occasional variations in the demand, but the much greater and more frequent variations in the competition, or in the supply which the demand is likely to get from other people, and to suit with dexterity and judgment both the quantity and quality of each assortment of goods to all the circumstances, is a species of warfare of which the operations are continually changing, and which can scarce ever be conducted successfully, without such unremitting exertion of vigilance and attention, as cannot long be expected from the directors of a joint-stock company". Adam Smith, *The Wealth of Nations* vol II. Probably as good an epitaph to the decline of British industry as any.

[7] The quip "Balliol's buggered us" occurred when, in 1974, on learning that the banks were no longer ready to support British Leyland, a group of officials were poring over the company documents in an attempt to explain its catastrophic failure of management. One observant participant remarked that some member of the senior management had apparently been to Balliol, and, "That explains it" was a natural rejoinder. And the more general proposition, "Balliol's buggered us" was greeted with universal applause.

Without questioning that this institution must have produced some worthy citizens who have added genuine value to the nation, it is a convenient rubric for the bias of our most venerable educational bastions towards an output focused on filling slots in City legal, accountancy and financial offices, with some diverted to Whitehall – and politics, but who in all other respects are instant anachronisms.

A charming illustration of this ethos comes from an obituary recollection of Ted Heath (*Ted Heath and me* by Michael Cockerell (*Guardian* 19.07.05)): "Taking Heath back to Oxford to film him in Balliol – he had a won an organ scholarship to the college – put him into one of his jovial moods. In the grand dining hall we talked as we inspected the imposing portraits of old Balliol men who'd become prime ministers – Asquith, McMillan and Heath himself. Did he think Balliol gave some quality that helped in becoming prime minister? 'Oh yes, complete mental control – intellectual control.' What they called tranquil consciousness of effortless superiority, I said. 'Yes, absolutely it's the first thing, they teach that from the moment you get here.' And he felt that for the rest of his life? 'Yes, that's what caused so much trouble.' And he laughed."

The merits of "effortless superiority" depend rather on the value and relevance of what is imparted during this sojourn among the dreaming spires. But just to spread the metaphor a bit, whatever may have been the accomplishments of the Cambridge Economics faculty, they owe the nation a debt that will probably take several centuries to pay off for having produced the architect of the British Rail privatisation, perhaps the most monstrous act of government ineptitude in living memory. But the Oxford, and other, economic faculties must pay their share, since there must have been any number of their alumni in the Treasury whose equal divorce from reality failed to counter the sheer organisational lunacy of what was being proposed.

[8] *Britain's Power Elites – the Rebirth of a Ruling Class* (Constable) by Hywel Williams offers an entertaining catalogue of some of the more noteworthy cock-ups, and the impervious spirit of detached aplomb with which these are viewed by the perpetrators. While Simon Jenkins, whose *Accountable to None* (Penguin) is an engaging account of Mrs Thatcher's centralising tendencies, can be relied upon for regular outbursts of seething.

[9] *The Rise of the "the Rest"* by Alice Amsden (Oxford). The full quotation is: "As a catch-up strategy, free-trade appears to have been limited to Switzerland and Hong Kong. That is, whatever the historical time period, these are the only two obvious 'countries' that managed to achieve high per capita increases without tariff protection or export promotion. Therefore, despite free trade's appeal in terms of administrative simplicity, and despite its theoretical claim to 'pareto optimality' (assuming perfect knowledge), it's practical significance for latecomers was relatively small. The question then becomes, if free trade has so much to recommend it, why were its adherents so few?" (Page 185). And both Switzerland and Hong Kong had special circumstances: the former in being surrounded by vigorously industrialising countries, and with an extremely good technical education system; and the latter having the historic advantage of being the main entrepot for trade with China, and this synergetic link has been confirmed since the handover by largely shifting its industrial production 40km up the road into Guangdong. The same judgment comes over more crisply: "To

date, not one successful developing country has pursued a purely free-market approach to development." (Joseph Stiglitz and Andrew Charlton in *Fair Trade for All* (Oxford)).

[10] The historic dominance of finance in our imperial past is well documented in *British Imperialism* (2 Vols) by P. J. Cain and A.G. Hopkins (Longmans). A contemporary twist is that, whilst the tenets of the Washington Consensus hark back to the approach of "informal empire" employing the coercion of finance in Latin America during the 19th century as a substitute for territorial acquisition, today the financial beneficiaries are primarily American investment banks; so Britain finds itself expounding the "free trade" guff, with most of the rake-off going elsewhere.

[11] Things must be getting desperate when Martin Wolf, the *Financial Times* pre-eminent economics mullah, comes out with: "I now fear that the combination of the fragility of the financial system with the huge rewards it generates for insiders will destroy something even more important – the political legitimacy of the market economy itself – across the globe. So it is time to start thinking radical thoughts about how to fix the problems." (*FT* 16.1.08). The same journal followed up with a think piece "The fall of the financial model of capitalism" by Jean-Louis Beffa (Chairman of Saint-Gobain) and Xavier Ragot (Paris School of Economics) adding to the call for "greater transparency in order to prevent actions that offend business ethics, such as creeping takeovers and speculative strategies that undermine companies' long-term interests." (*FT* 22.2.08).

[12] Confirmation, if confirmation were needed, comes from John Kay, "How economics lost touch with reality" (*FT* 22.4.09).

[13] *FT* 17.5.06.

[14] Lord (Andrew) Turnbull's (Lord Turnbull was an ex-Permanent Secretary of the Treasury and retired as Cabinet Secretary) interview with the *Financial Times* (*FT* 20.3.07) may have gathered headlines for "the sheer Stalinist ruthlessness" with which the Treasury has enhanced its control, and its indirect reference to the reigning Chancellor of the Exchequer. The article followed, however, a mere 48 hours on from the second part of Adam Curtis's *The Trap*, with its punch line that the only people who behaved according to the rational self-interested economists' model were "economists themselves and psychopaths". Less remarked among the noble Lord's comments was his depiction of the Treasury's "more or less complete contempt with which other colleagues are held". Replete itself with economists, this tends to confirm that the equivalence with "psychopaths" is soundly based. With politicians reduced to mere ciphers.

[15] A recent resurgence is reported to have occurred in response to the call from Sir John Rose, Chief Executive of Rolls-Royce, the government should "not be frightened" to agree a strategy with industry for supporting technologies potentially decisive in future decades (*FT* 22.2.08).

---

[16] The "picking winners" argument is a typical piece of "straw-man" logic: the illusion is created of a detached, ignorant, and parochially self-interested agency wielding arbitrary authority. Bizarrely, a curiously accurate depiction of recent British governments when commanding a sizeable parliamentary majority. But in its theoretical outline, the straw man is an imbecilic dictator, contrasted with the wisdom of the invisible hand functioning magically through free markets.

In practice, elsewhere, confronted by the need to evolve new technologies, capabilities and essential infrastructure demanding substantial resources and with high risks, it has been standard practice to identify national agencies on which this effort is focused. In effect, rearing national champions. Techniques to carry legitimacy vary. But many countries have successfully followed practices of consultation and coordination. An exposition of Japan's mechanisms of "bureau pluralism" is provided by Tetsuji Okazaki in *The Government-firm Relationships in Post-war Japan: the Success and Failure of Bureau Pluralism* in *Rethinking the East Asian Miracle* (Oxford). While similar circumstances of stringency, including the use of Marshall Aid, compelled the elites of France, Italy and Germany to follow similar coordination mechanisms.

On the other hand, the role of the state has never been as neatly circumscribed as theoreticians might pretend in order to achieve the elysium of "economic efficiency". Just tot up the Pentagon funding (not to mention NASA) that has gone to establish the technological position of IBM, Boeing, GE, Pratt & Whitney, Raytheon and so on, and their subcontractors, systems suppliers, materials producers etc. Probably the largest economic distortion in real terms in industrial history. Or how about, "It is fashionable for Western economists to insist, 'government cannot pick winners'. Japanese governments have been picking winners for 100 years now, in two senses: *deciding* which industries to develop, and often also *predicting* which entrepreneurs and corporations would prove to be skilled enough to be worth supporting." (*Governing the Japanese Economy* by Kyoko Sheridan (Polity)). Or go through the list of "hot industries" identified by late-industrialising nations for special support measures, in general with substantial success, set out by Professor Amsden (ibid.). In practice, virtually everyone except Britain has been "breeding winners".

[17] To take a relevant contemporaneous test, on a comparison of the US Patent Office high-tech patent applications per million population (EU Innovation Scoreboard 2002), the UK figure was 14.4 compared to Japan's 80.2. The absolute difference?

[18] Under City conventions for leading Board appointments, an essential qualification for Chairmen appears to be the number of businesses that they have previously driven to the knacker's yard, or been taken over under their charge.

[19] Some belated applause, if belated by decades, should be granted to *The Economist* for its Pauline conversion in finally acknowledging the fatuousness of this facile distinction: "The division between manufacturing and services has become redundant. A more sensible split now is between low-skilled and high-skilled jobs. Neither manufacturing nor services is inherently better than the

other, they are interdependent." (1.10.05). Yet the sediment of this dumbing-down distinction and the systematic downplaying of "making things you can drop on your toe" has been absorbed into the rhetoric of purported policy discourse over decades to the point where it is an essential ligament of the arthritic British approach to industry. But just as the trend is towards products – like, as an example of modern manufacturing, Hitachi's latest RFID chip (Radio Frequency Identification, effectively a system of data signature, like barcodes, that can be interrogated by remote radio signals) which measures 0.075×0.075 mm (*Nikkei Weekly* 15.6.09) – that are too small to be picked up leave alone aimed accurately at a toe, so replacing one facile simplification with another i.e. between low and high-skilled jobs, is just as questionable. It may be comforting to assert that: "Developed economies comparative advantage is in knowledge-intensive activities, because they have so much skilled labour," but, given the relative output of graduates, especially in applied sciences and technical skills in China and India, following South Korea and Taiwan, this cushion – if indeed it ever existed – is deflating fast.

[20] "The island borrowed from every country of the Continent its skill in special branches of industry, and planted them on English soil, under the protection of her customs system," until "by practice, experience, and internal competition they readily obtained ability to equal in every respect the older productions of their foreign competitors." (*The National System of Political Economy*: Friedrich List - 1841).

[21] Inevitably, ex-Ministers have a natural tendency to present their actions as the best conceivable in difficult circumstances, without acknowledging the weakness of their guiding principles and perceptions. Official records – no need to instance the turmoil of the search for the origins of the Iraq escapade – have a tendency towards the bland. Even within the limited compass of one's own career there have been very controversial issues where the origins were obscure, even to searches by well-placed officials close to events: BOAC claimed that they had been "directed" to purchase the VC10 – "direction" being a formal device when nationalised industries were required by government to act contrary to their judgment, yet diligent searches of the papers of the time failed to unearth any such expression by the government. And repeated searches have never unearthed the rationale for the government's acceptance of a Treaty to develop Concorde with no "break clause".

[22] A privileged opportunity to join a highly talented and expert fellowship, with a global business perspective. A form of business that has never evolved in Britain.

PART I:

ON HER MAJESTY'S SERVICE

AN INSTANT ANACHRONISM

In retrospect, early upbringing, boarding schools, national service, Oxford University, entry to the civil service and the first years as an "assistant principal" can be run together as a typical, if less bedecked with primroses than many, pilgrimage towards the evolution of another "instant anachronism". Only tempered by a scepticism of the legitimacy of those in self-professed authority carried over from early years.

1933-46: EARLIEST YEARS

Maybe, under hypnosis, there is a Denton Welch narrative of growing up in the twilight years of the Raj. Arriving, by all accounts, unexpectedly in the Upper Class Waiting Room at Kurseong station – some four stops down the mountain railway line from Darjeeling, in 1933, up to return "home" early in 1946 was typical of an imperial childhood with an annual cycle of three consecutive terms at boarding schools interspersed by a two-month holiday break with parents wherever they happened to be posted.

With a father in the Bengal Service of the ICS, the first boarding establishment was Hastings House in Calcutta. Its faded 18th century paladin spaciousness was hardly chummy. Whatever learning may have been imparted, the lingering memory is of a large rubbish-hole usually filled with cuttings from the garden. But it was infested with a breed of minute frogs, which, prompted by a pinprick, could leap prodigious distances: this inevitably instigated competitive challenges of who could make the frogs jump furthest, often with high "dare" stakes for losers.

But when the rising flow of military vehicles, and Spitfires dispersed around the city *maidans*, signalled the prospect that the Japanese forces might break through in Burma, the children were relocated to "the hills", in my case to an improvised New School on a promontory facing the long-established St Paul's School in Darjeeling. Again the dominant memory is not of studious accomplishment but of our housemaster: as a quirky twist on the usual enthusiastic exemplar of muscular Christianity – he was a French ex-all-in-wrestler, a Mr Lamarro, whose party piece was tearing telephone directories into two with his bare hands and bending iron bars over his forearm. His wife by contrast was petite and acted the role of matron[1] keeping kindly control of a desultory rabble of schoolboys whose respect was undoubtedly reinforced by her husband's biceps.

With my father's posting to New Delhi, the family operated on the seasonal cycle of moves to Simla. And the next boarding school was Bishop Cotton School in Simla, first in the Preparatory School, and then to the junior forms of the main School.[2] This followed the formal structures of the British institutions on which the string of Indian "public schools" were modelled – suitable emphasis on the "in corpore sano" with regular physical jerks under an ex-military gym instructor, regular "runs" – quite an exercise at that altitude, and hockey and cricket played on a pitch carved out of the mountainside with high-wire netting to prevent balls disappearing into the valley below.

Otherwise, there was the conventional organisational form of "House", "prefects", blazers and the grey flannels, and "dormitories". With the difference that the school was multiracial, and the communal style created an entirely natural intercourse among the pupils. Notably, whatever may have been the academic attainments, the most developed skills attained were in marbles – instead of the prissy thumb-propelled approach of the "British tradition", the Indian technique uses the tip of the second finger pulled back by the other hand to produce a tension that releases the ball with immensely greater velocity, so that one objective of the game was to smash opponents to smithereens. Spinning tops was another art, where again the tops were hurled like a missile to break opponents into pieces.

The ultimate accomplishment of arms was the manufacture and mastery of the catapult. With a robust penknife, a couple of feet of quarter-inch square rubber strand, and some ferreting around the bazaar for leather rejects, a formidable portable weapon could be built. Indeed, in a variety optimised for particular functions – long-range, heavier missiles, firing buckshot, and so on. With ammunition plentifully to hand, most of us attained a high level of accuracy. And versatile. Keeping menacing pariah dogs at bay, sussing out any threatening bush and scrub, and a variety of contests: chestnut trees when the conkers were ripe to fall lent themselves to a test of how many could be brought down by a single shot. When the tree overhung a road, there was an elegant variation as three or four catapults trained ready for an approaching rickshaw could be fired simultaneously into the branches to release a shower of conkers on the incumbent – usually some official reading the latest copy of *The Times*, or one of the Raj-ladies travelling between bridge and mah-jong parties.

Between these periods of formalised routines, the life of a *chota-sahib* was one of extraordinary freedom. Beginning with early childhood benevolently supervised by an ayah, one frequented the bazaars, mastering local games, and gaining a taste for the delicious sweetmeats on display: if anything, Hindi was as much a first language as English. But once having mastered the bicycle, accomplished with the help of my father's head bearer, a striking Pathan figure, running alongside, the scope for roaming around Delhi was virtually unlimited. After the obligatory couple of hour's homework, from a launchpad of the Raj bungalow at 8, Hastings Road – now Krishamenon Maag – one could cycle in all directions. Following the horse-riding trails laid around Delhi, one ran along "The Ridge", famous from the relief of Delhi during "The Mutiny", but by straying only a few yards one could assemble a hoard of memorabilia: musket shot, breach mechanisms, bayonet blades, curved short-swords, buckles and buttons. Or a run just off the fairway of the golf course revealed scores of balls, smaller than today's variety, dropped by mongeese after realising that they were not birds' or snakes' eggs, and these could be sold on for a few annas each to supplement a tight pocket-money budget. Or a journey to the Purana Qila (Old Fort) whose battlements were an ideal launch-point for model gliders, even though the scope for this had been limited for a time when the internal area had been used to house prisoners of war.

As for the impact of such an upbringing on personal attitudes, one is probably the worst placed to judge. For there was an insidious element of imperial brainwashing, whether in the pattern of education;[3] in the reading to hand with comic-book heroes like Rockfist Rogan of the RAF, or the Hush-Hush Man of the Hindu-Kush, or through the dominant presence of novels by G.A. Henty, A.E.W. Mason, P.C. Wren or Sapper; or in the values gleaned unconsciously in the conversations of *burrah sahibs*.[4]

Set against such influences was a detached and sceptic eye, since one had an array of reference relationships outside the closed hermetic world of the senior levels of the ICS, for its absurdities and rituals. Those gymkhanas and garden parties, with their demands for immaculate grooming and "pukka" clobber, when there were far more interesting things to do on a bike. Dressing for "dinner", which seemed to demand an inordinate waste of time for the grown-ups: mercifully, *chota-sahibs* were relegated to "supper" at an earlier hour, though once a month we were required to go through the palaver of attending "dinner", presided over by the austere senior bungalow officer, Sir George Spence. Or "picnics" to the Kutub Minar, Fatehpur Sikri, Agra and other neighbouring historic sites, but "picnics" kitted out in a caravan-train comparable to Victorian equatorial expeditions.

Most influential, however, was the mythical domain called "home". This was a realm of order, cleanliness, high-principled inhabitants, properly educated in the classics, among communities of mutual support, and where everyone apparently played cricket in perfect attire with straight bats and natural adherence to rules. The first coherent memory of Britain had been during a "long leave" that was interrupted by the outbreak of War. The family had been parked in Weston-Super-Mare – Addiscombe Road rings in memory, where the sands were a natural place to keep children out of harm's way. But with the war and threat of invasion, we had the obligatory gas masks – in my case far-too-large – and slept under the dining room table. One recalls seeing the Crazy Gang perform *Run Rabbit* at the Bristol Hippodrome, and a shopping expedition to a large store where bills and payments zoomed around on a tangled network of wires or down mysterious tubes. Impressively high-tech at the time.

This brief intermission "home" was cut short by the family being despatched in 1940 on Convoy WS2[5] for troop shipments to Suez, and evacuees despatched to India and Empire outposts beyond. We were in the RMS Orion, which shortly after departure from Liverpool developed serious engine problems and diverted to Greenock for repairs. After a week of clanking and banging, the ship joined another convoy heading for Halifax, but once clear of the Western Approaches was detached to catch up with the original WS2 that was bound for Freetown and Cape Town. This was without protection other than an armed merchant cruiser, whose scant firepower of a single gun mounted at the stern did not seem to offer more than a morale-boosting presence. But this meant a journey with lifejackets permanently worn – bulky cork-slabs sewn into a canvas harness, yet of a standard size far-too-large for a 7-year-old. From Freetown to Cape Town, escort duties were taken on by real cruisers, which were majestic sights sailing alongside. On catching up with the convoy at Cape Town, and a rushed day of sightseeing, the Orion rejoined the convoy and arrived in Bombay on the 15th September. The family then returned to Delhi, and further expeditions by bike.

The next encounter with "home" was a return in early 1946, part of the mass evacuation of dependants before "independence". The ship, the Drottningholm, had been chartered from the Swedish-American Line, complete with its own crew. Without wartime restrictions, this was a more relaxed journey, passing through the Suez Canal, now freed for maritime use. There was plenty of scope for the younger passengers to dissipate their exuberance. The most traumatic moment was being hotly pursued in a rowdy game of tag: in desperation I ran down a stairwell into the crews' quarters, facing an interminable corridor with no other stairwells or doors for escape, and charged through the only remaining door. It turned out to be the ladies' shower. On a wet floor, breaking hard only landed me on my back, sliding along past screaming naked figures. They quickly recovered, picked me up by arms and legs and tossed me out. In an era when sex education was confined to surreptitious glances through *The National Geographic*, this experience imbued me temporarily with an instant authority among school contemporaries.

But this idyll came to a catastrophic halt as we berthed at Birkenhead at the end of February. In the gloomy dawn, sleet driven by a chill north wind was angling across the decks, gangway and railway platforms as the passengers huddled during the chaos of sorting the baggage. Then the ordeal of humping trunk-boxes to the right train. And the trains. Grimy, diminutive by comparison with the long-distance trains of India, and stinking of nicotine and soot. This was really "home". And a continuing scepticism with anything "British" was born.

There are surely passages of limpid prose to be inscribed on the ominous silence of sodden *khud*-sides as all of nature, from bugs to birds, senses that a landslide is imminent. On clouds of cicadas flying off the trunks of deodar trees when enough have been startled to trigger a swarming panic. On the tumult of ordered chaos at railway terminals and bazaars. On deserted rajput fortresses rising out of deserts. On mango ice cream supped on the veranda of Firpos, overlooking the Chowringhee Road in Calcutta – then with bleached white stucco, multicoloured awnings, and the continuous passage of black-hooded rickshaws. On the trek to Viceregal Lodge as part of the BCS choir to perform *The Messiah*. On the elusive shifts of prayer flags and shrines in the wafting mists on the hillsides around Darjeeling. Or on the multitude of memories offered by the sheer diversity of the country. But for a nation already impotent with nostalgia, this would only be another gulp of hemlock.

1946-52: SCHOOL YEARS

By family tradition, Monmouth School was the natural scholastic parking space as my parents deposited the children before returning to India for the final run-down of the Raj. Monmouth in this era can be depicted only in sepia shades: a sleepy market town, unmarked by the war; with its few local icons – Henry V, Rolls, and even Nelson – commemorated; on the confluence of the rivers Wye and the Monnow, with its picturesque Norman bridge; and with the scenic attractions of the Wye Valley and rolling countryside – only diminished by the scope offered for exacting cross-country runs. It was an idyllic setting for a seminary devoted to drumming learning into spirited youths in the tradition of "muscular Christianity". But frozen in memory by the narrow-gauge train puffing along the banks of the Wye from Ross, via Symonds Yat – where devout fishermen would disembark with rod and wicker basket, to pull themselves by boat ferry to the opposite bank – to Monmouth, and then downstream to Redbrook and Chepstow. Among the saddest casualties of Dr Beeching's culling of the railways.

The boys' School, with its sister girls School, was among the Haberdashers' portfolio, and had been founded by a Dick Whittington-type local lad who had made his fortune in London. When I arrived – the choice of school being dictated by family tradition, then immortalised by HDB, and KHB, carved on a lavatory door, to which CBB was dutifully added – the main hall was still in its original form with tiers of benches on three sides, classes being originally conducted simultaneously with clusters of students in separate "class" areas around these tiers, and a raised dais on the other. And the school complex also contained several small almshouses as part of its original foundation. Over my years the old hall was transformed into an auditorium, with a stage, and inaugurated a musical tradition beginning with *The Mikado* performed to a single piano, but within a few years graduating to *The Yeomen of the Guard* with an accomplished small orchestra.

The more surprising since the school has a robust "muscular" tradition, boasting an alumni of notable Welsh rugby heroes including "Bucket" Gwillam, who led Wales to their first clutch of Triple Crowns after the war, and Keith Jarrett of the solo runaway try from full-back against England. An abiding memory is the stroll, with boots slung over the shoulders by their laces, along the embankment beside the school's mock mediaeval facade, over the Wye Bridge to the playing fields on the other side – a plain formed by sediments over centuries by a wide bow of the river that could easily accommodate half a dozen rugby pitches.[i] But the pitch nearest the bridge, with the main pavilion, had the sanctity of "big side", and all sporting aspirations were to get into the 1st or 2nd Fifteens/Elevens to play on this sacred turf. The railway ran along one side, and it was common when a key rugby fixture was in full flow, or a cricket match in progress, for the train to stop for 20 minutes to allow

---

[i] Today, such a stroll has been blocked by the embankment road having been widened for a new A40.

passengers a privileged view.

The Spartan spirit was subjected to its most extreme test early in 1947 when the worst winter in living memory was followed by a big freeze. And a routine house rugby match, started on a sodden pitch thawed by an afternoon sun, extended into dusk, when the fall in temperature was so sudden that the players' kit and clogged mud froze into the texture of sandpaper. For us forwards, the rough-and-tumble at least kept the circulation going, but the centre and wing threequarters crouched in agony, wringing hands and flailing arms to keep mobile. And a few days later came the thaw, with the rivers flooding to historically unprecedented levels.[ii] The town was cut off except for access from the Welsh side, most day-pupils could not attend, and the rest of us engaged in emergency activities – such as paddling the cadet corps inflatable dinghies to rescue old ladies, children, cats and dogs from beleaguered cottages around the town.

With both parents in India for the final chaos of "handover", holidays for the first three years were spent with a maternal uncle on a farm at Acton Beauchamp on the Hereford/Worcestershire border. Another pastel period episode: taking the cart horse down to the local blacksmith, point-to-point meetings, bucolic adventures during hop picking when the farm was flooded by families on holiday from Cannock, hay-making by trampling the grass into ricks, and perilous cricket matches on uneven village greens.[6]

Somehow, out of all this, and in an ethos where "swot" denoted some genetic defect, one must have paid some attention to something, because one managed to score A-Levels in Maths, Physics and English: an unusual combination in those days, where enthusiasm for English came late and unexpectedly. With a School library stocked with the same old imperial standards of A. E.W. Mason, G.A. Henty, P.C. Wren and Sapper, perhaps the earliest sparks of real enthusiasm for literature came from *Songs of a Sourdough* by Robert Service in the parental collection. But in the background, especially through the radio, there was a lively dramatic scene – McNeice, Henry Reed, Christopher Fry – in an idiom where kitchen sinks had not taken over from imagination. While the London stage had a similar vein with regular productions of Anouilh, Sartre, Giraudoux and Shakespeare, with a galaxy of notable British actors in their prime. Perhaps these caught the interest, but the clincher was a quiet remark from the senior maths master, Mr Ellis – a remarkable guy, well

---

[ii] Perhaps the best historic record of this flood is the mark on one of the pillars of Dixton Church, a small Norman church on the banks of the Wye, where previous high-water marks are recorded.

over six feet tall, lean and fit from a daily routine of travelling from Redbrook, which entailed a 3-mile hike homewards from the station, usually with a knapsack, up the escarpment of Offa's Dyke – on going through some homework: "You're not really lazy enough to be cut out for mathematics." To be fair, he also included English Literature among his portfolio of subjects, and, with the main English master, Desmond Vowles, I was tutored up on the set texts. Enough at least to get me a place at Teddy Hall (St Edmund Hall).

1952-54: NATIONAL SERVICE

Even though coming up to the last of the intakes, taking a couple of years out of the learning cycle was viewed by many as a chore, and considerable efforts were taken to get out of national service. For myself it was simply within the expectations of the time to fulfil the "call-up" documents when they arrived. Reminders of the Cold War, Britain's "fighting retreat" from Empire, and echoes of what was done in "the War" were a continuous drumbeat to legitimise this call on the nation's youth. In my case, before gaining entry to Oxford, one option had been to join the RAF as a career, reflecting a long enthusiasm for flying models and kites, and one had even gained a civil flying licence with a "Flying Scholarship" through the school cadets. So, fair's fair, one could not avoid the obligation to do one's bit.

A boarding school career was probably the best grounding for the privations that accompanied the movement between "stations". Certainly, better attuned to the first frosty morning at Padgate, the RAF's square-bashing indoctrination centre, when in the gloom of a frosty dawn a glowing cigarette, which turned out to be a Corporal Jones, laid out the penalties for misdemeanours, including the ominous "latrine orderlies". The Officer Cadet Training Unit (OCTU) at Spittalgate, near Grantham, was the next stop, and having opted for the Fighter Control Branch, the next move was to the training centre at Middle Wallop on Salisbury Plain.

Setting aside the inevitably grimier moments, in retrospect it was mostly good fun, especially in the diversity of colleagues in the same boat: Roger Norrington of baton-wielding fame to the down-to-earth Rugby League veterans who contributed at OCTU to probably the most outstanding rugby side, including several national trialists, in which one had ever played.

"Postings" were apportioned by an impenetrable process against which it was fruitless to complain (a fair indoctrination for the civil service). While some colleagues were dispatched to comfortable Operation Centres and control units in the Home Counties and Germany, I found myself at a fighter control unit at El-Firdan in the Suez Canal Zone. The station itself, bounded on one side by the "sweet water canal" running beside the Ismalia/Cairo Road ("sweet" ironically demanding half a dozen injections for anyone who fell in) was a motor vehicle maintenance unit – a littered array of trucks and trailers being repaired and piles of old tyres.[7]

The Fighter Control Unit was a mile outside the main station around what had been the perimeter road and was equipped with wartime mobile equipment – Type 7, 8 and 15 radars, apparently designed for northern Europe, but under strain in coping with the extreme heat of the desert. Dogged with malfunctions, technicians struggled heroically in the servicing compartments in temperatures where occasionally plastic would be dripping off the cables. In hindsight, a typical experience of our military services being expected to operate "in anger" with clapped-out kit. In the post-Nasser Egyptian revolution era, political relations between Britain and Egypt were at high tension, and the Fighter Control Unit was, with the fighter squadrons – Meteor night fighters stationed at Kabrit (the original base of the SAS), and Vampire squadrons at Deversoir – in a continuous state of at least "alert" with occasional periods of "standby".

The security regime demanded continuous guards on watchtowers during the day, and armed patrols at night, while every journey on vulnerable roads could be undertaken only with an armed escort vehicle. In this context, the members of the Fighter Control Unit, who were inevitably closer to the "Ops" of real fighting, were distinguished from others on the station. But we all shared the same rigour of conditions – airmen in tents,[8] and NCOs and officers in "compounds" of mobile caravans. The cantonment social life reflected a closed community largely dependent on itself for entertainment, and offered an early introduction to the extraordinary psychological quirks that surface in such an isolated and stressed environment.

With this antique equipment, the actual job of controlling fighters became almost an art form: the aircraft identified by smudgy sausage-shaped "blips", where the actual position of the aircraft was at the middle inside edge. And the continuity of "target" and "fighter" tracks had to be marked by hand in chinagraph on the radar tube itself. Changes in direction of the "target" demanded three or four sweeps to be sure – a time lapse that could be critical, and those advanced in the art could spot such shifts in two sweeps.[9] If this were not tricky enough, the equipment did not contain the latest technology that cancelled out repeated identical returns, so that there was continuing clutter, and in certain meteorological conditions the Lebanese coastline covered half the screen.

1954-57: OXFORD UNIVERSITY

Teddy Hall – St Edmund Hall, after the rigours of the desert, was a haven, and, without elaboration, pure fun. The only initial discomfort was that if selecting English as a subject carried a presumption that it should be a soft option, the chore of getting through Prelims in two terms demanded a kiddable familiarity with Anglo-Saxon to cope with chunks of Beowulf and other texts, and, worse, study of a couple of plays by Corneille and Racine in the original French. More difficult, as the two years of RAF service had somewhat dented the habits of study.

The English faculty was an engaging triumvirate of some repute: Graham Midgley, at the time going through his preparations for the cloth, was a charming and astute guy with a specialty in 18th century literary figures – all those authors figuring in footnotes to *The Dunciad.* The easy wheeze in coping with set texts was to find a suitable commentary, without too much attention to the original. Graham had probably heard all these echoes before, and would, with a wry smile, draw attention to some features of the text that countered what such second-hand commentaries might have said.

Bruce Mitchell, a stocky Australian, studying some abstruse feature of Anglo-Saxon grammar for his doctorate, managed the almost impossible task of imbuing an interest in these ancient texts. And it is a continuing tribute that *The Dream of the Rood* is regularly drawn from the bookshelf. Contact with Reg Alton, the third of the faculty triumvirate, whose specialty of textual analysis did not impinge much on the student syllabus, arose mainly through turning out for the Oxford City weekend cricket teams. For which he would bowl at crafty medium pace off a long curved run.

1957-58: SUPPLY TEACHING, GILLINGHAM GRAMMAR SCHOOL

For all the fun and academic application, a 2nd in English was not an obvious qualification for anything. And the era of "recruiting rounds" by Accountancy and other firms had not begun. So a year's supply teaching offered scope to see whether teaching itself was attractive, but also to allow time to explore other options, with applying to the civil service as a reserve, though the more demanding for having to sit an entrance exam.

Despite a cheery and committed common room and the attractions of long school holidays, the prospect of teaching as a career was dampened by the tiresome chores – marking being the most prominent. And the continuing frustration that student performance, irrespective of innate talent, was so heavily conditioned by parental environment. The school catered for students from the "three towns" of Rochester, Gillingham and Chatham covering a diverse range of local society: children of solicitors, local government officials and military officers to the workforce at Chatham docks: most frustrating were parents employed in the Chatham docks complex, mostly salt-of-the-earth welders, electricians and other skilled trades, but imbuing their children with sadly little respect for the disciplines of learning beyond basic attainments.

One tried a number of major companies, none of whom seemed to offer much excitement, and sitting the Civil Service entrance exam loomed. Again an underestimate of the work required re-remembering all the stuff squeezed into the head for university finals. But one passed, and, even though the Foreign Office had been first choice, I obviously blew the interview when, in response to the question to suggest countries that would have a decisive influence on the future, I chose Asia and Latin America. My foresight was obviously half a century premature. So I finished up in my third choice.

1958-61: MINISTRY OF TRANSPORT AND CIVIL AVIATION

So a fairly typical progression for the usual round of post-university entrants to the Civil Service – sporting largely irrelevant degrees in history, law, classics, philosophy or economics, except perhaps in having been encumbered through national service and a spell of teaching with some experience of actually having done something in the real world. But, at the time, there was a strong group of colleagues who had suffered a break in their careers through military service during the War and brought with them the confidence and expertise of really having done something: the outstanding example was the Civil Aviation Operations Officer Class, which had the highest percentage of transfers to the Admin Class.

The first posting was to the Highways Division, housed in a converted fur warehouse in Hereford Road in the Notting Hill Gate area. A rather shabby outpost when the Department's headquarters were in Berkeley Square House. As a newly arrived Assistant Principal, the apprentice grade, the most striking feature was the vein of individual eccentricities among my new colleagues: opening a door, one could be greeted by the incumbent's feet, as he was standing on his head practising yoga; another might have his daughter, with fair flowing hair, practising her crayons while he was wrestling with some dispute over a bypass in Wales; and the head of Division, apparently an authority on Freudian analysis, was also a cricket fanatic, and during Test Matches, being before the day of the semiconductor, would park her car in the street with a portable wireless, while files were brought up-and-down stairs. And the first stage of the new M1 was in the charge of a striking figure, Terry Newman, who included organising supplies for the Chindits in his record, and whose approach was, "Let's build a road" to the extent of personally steering the line of the road, with adjustments where necessary, through direct contact with individual landowners – consequently the public inquiry phase was completed in record speed.

My *sensei* Principal, Tony Robertson, to all appearances a three-piece-suit and bowler-hatted conventional civil servant, turned out to be a railway fanatic, to the point where, instead of consulting Bradshaw's – the pre-Beeching comprehensive train timetable – the general practice was to "consult Tony". Every lunchtime, he would bring out of his draw two Ovaltine cans and pull out of them a series of small paper squares: after a few days, one inquired cautiously what lay behind this ritual, to be told that he was revising his mandarin, which he had learned while in a prisoner-of-war camp.

The workload, after a compulsory fortnight in "the Registry" to master the intricacies of a life depending upon the sanctity of "the file", was drafting responses to MPs letters, preparing briefs for delegations and taking the minutes. At the time, the government had authorised a spurt in expenditure to build new roads and modernise the existing trunk roads, so there was a constant flow of complaints about proposed new bypasses, local demands for roads to be widened, or claims that traffic warranted schemes where they did not get through the national criteria. As a then leader in Operational Research and the application of statistical techniques, the current forecast was a doubling in road traffic every six or eight years: so today's congestion, in the absence of intervening investment to keep pace with forecasts, has been long anticipated.

The most instructive case, offering a far better introduction to the civil service than the couple of weeks' indoctrination course – notable for having some extremely able Nigerian official trainees – was Selby Toll-bridge. A Yorkshire country town straddling the river Ouse. Historically, the river was navigable north of the town, and there were some craft building/repair yards. In the 1880s, as part of a wider national pattern, a wooden toll bridge was erected across the river on the route to Barlby, a nearby village, but the main road to York (currently the A19), with a swing-contraption to allow the passage of river traffic. There had been growing local pressure to have the bridge replaced, and the sitting MP, Sir Leonard Ropner, had asked his first Parliamentary Question in 1928, with scores of letters and Questions in subsequent years. After further representations, Ministers agreed to review the case, and all the files going back to the original Selby Toll-bridge Act of 1886 were dumped in the office, obliterating one wall, for me to "devil" the case.

The documents from the passing of the Act, which went through with no apparent debate, to the early 1920s were no more than an inch thick. Originally, all entries were in short texts inscribed in bold copperplate hand, presumably using quill pens. But then the typewriter, with its accomplice carbon paper arrived, and thereafter an inch of documents would barely cover six or eight months of exchanges.

Whereas most of this vintage of toll bridges had either sold out in the 30s as hard-pressed owners were prepared to get out at distressed prices, or commandeered during the war, or for the most obstinate undermined by building a parallel bridge alongside, the Selby Toll-bridge Act had some distinctive features. It conferred a monopoly for the owners on crossings of the river for 5 miles on either side of the bridge; the toll income was free of tax; and the concession was into perpetuity. All for minimal costs of maintenance to the original wooden structure, and running costs that were no more than the toll-collectors' remuneration. There were some 50 shares issued, obviously a highly desirable part of a gentleman's portfolio: similar terms would make even the craziest PFI/PPP give-away appear parsimonious. (One may have been remiss in not checking whether any of the copperplate script included the phrase, "there is no alternative".)

The tolls had originally been on a "per head" basis for human travellers, cattle, sheep, horses, pigs etc, and rates for carriages and carts. And then updated as forms of motorised transport emerged. In the view of the locals, on exorbitant terms. For, in one episode, the citizenry had deliberately crashed some barges into the bridge. But not inflicted any damage that could not be rectified by a few extra beams and planks, bolts and hammers. And the bridge was opened for business again in a matter of days.

The dilemma for the government was that the cost of buying out the owners, given the terms of the Act, was extremely steep: with revenues running at, say, £600,000 a year – virtually all profit, a representative valuation would double this to take account of the tax status, and allow 15 years in lieu of perpetuity – a valuation of some £18 million. At the same time, the monopoly right of way meant that a bypass would not come out much cheaper. And, given the relatively low volume of traffic by comparison with other schemes to improve trunk roads, these costs were way above what could be justified. In practice, the original Act could have been repealed or negated by a relatively simple procedure of "Laying an Order". Yet, repeatedly Ministers had decided against this course, and we could only surmise a common reluctance to set a precedent for "interfering with the rights of shareholders", or the political connections of some of the select band of shareholders.

At all events, the outcome of my research was a narrative of events, political declarations, and various legal opinions cross-referenced to the documents and key papers among the mountain of files duly flagged. The bundle was sent off to the Treasury Solicitors and must have been a lawyer's dream. At a last glimpse before my departure from this training stint was a legal opinion by one of the Hankey dynasty of civil servants running to more than 20 pages: achieved by the prevailing technological reversion to slave labour, a patient shorthand typist. [All this endeavour had its natural outcome of complete inertia, since glancing out of the window on a rail journey from Hull to London in the early 80s, deliberately chosen for travelling through Selby, this ancient wooden contraption was still standing. Subsequently, one gathers, the bridge was bought by the North Yorkshire Council in 1992 for £540,000, presumably because the owners were unwilling to contemplate the costs of rebuilding the bridge to cater for the increased weight of freight traffic. But there is currently a metal-arch swing bridge *and* a new bypass with its own swing-bridge across the Ouse.]

The next instalment of the AP apprenticeship was Marine Safety Division. The most interesting chunk of work was serving as secretary to an international group devising modifications to The Safety at Sea Convention to cater for the US Savannah – being developed as a nuclear-powered cargo vessel. In the event, there was reluctance among other countries to accept the vessel, and one suspects its economics were not commercial. But most refreshing was a move to Berkeley Square House, where the attractions of the locale were glamorously upmarket by comparison with Notting Hill Gate.

Airports Division, the next apprentice posting, was very active: the sell-off of Croydon land as airlines relocated their operations to the new Gatwick; with jet aircraft becoming more numerous, the issue of noise on local communities was becoming more vociferous, and evolving the procedures to control its impact were being explored. Heathrow was being expanded, and the new Terminal 3 under construction. Despite subsequent abortive debate about "an integrated transport policy", this was being actively pursued: with BOAC's headquarters at Victoria, the cross-Channel train service terminating at the station, the rail link to Gatwick, and the new Victoria Line in prospect, this seemed a natural hub for the capital's transport system. And a feasibility study was made of a direct rail link to Heathrow to complete the links. The only missing component was for BEA to locate their London office at Victoria with BOAC. But BEA doggedly refused and stuck to their independent office at Gloucester Road, perhaps the least convenient location in London. Yet again, Ministers were not prepared to bang the necessary heads.

While all this was going on, the Division was reassigned to the new Ministry of Aviation, along with the aerospace side of the Ministry of Supply. The culture shock was apparent the morning after the reorganisation. Virtually the entire Division found most of their files confiscated and with summons to appear before the security services. The civilised MTCA practice was to leave the office at the end of the day with the papers left on the desk as they were being worked ready to carry on the following morning, without much concern for the classification of files. While under the defence ethos of the Ministry of Supply, leaving papers marked "Confidential" openly accessible warranted confinement in the Tower of London.

It was also the era of aviation enthusiasm, and with visions of intercity VTOL (vertical takeoff and landing) travel, one served as secretary of a Committee to survey heliport locations in London. This is better treated in the next section, when, after these apprenticeship postings, dispatch to the Minister's Private Office was the final leg of the conventional civil service indentures.

Skipping through these reminiscences should offer a glimpse into the spirit of the times, and, more generally, the happy "rounded amateur" tenor of the nation's public governance.

---

[1] In the authority structures of traditional boarding schools, the house "matron" has a special sanctity: at some psychological level serving as a maternal substitute, she also had a pivotal role in instilling correct personal disciplines. From the regular administration of dietary supplements like cod liver oil and malt, to the precision of bed-making and clean space, to such hygienic demands as regular bathing, towelling including between the toes, and clean fingernails.

One arguable explanation for the craven behaviour of many of Maggie Thatcher's Cabinet Ministers lies in their previous conditioning through the Prep/Public School system. Just one quick glance at their fingernails as they entered Cabinet would have sufficed to reduce them to pre-pubescent jellies.

[2] "After the 1857 Uprising, the utility of these classes to the Empire in India was perceived. As one army officer wrote: those classes might, perhaps, ere it be too late, be worked up into the defensive system of a landwehr or reserve sub-vexillo." The backward educational state of the Anglo-Indians was the first

barrier to any such scheme. This concern spread to the ecclesiastical and government establishments and led to the creation of public schools in India.

The ethos of the English public school had been idealised by Thomas Hughes in his *Tom Brown's School Days*, published in 1858. The book gave a romantic account of the zeal with which the headmaster of rugby, Thomas Arnold, had inculcated what was seen to be the essentially English qualities into his boys. The public schools served as the breeding ground for the civil services. The Right Reverend C. E. L. Cotton, Bishop of Calcutta, had been assistant master at rugby under Dr Arnold. He planned three public schools in India which he hoped would "not be less secure and by God's blessing not less useful than Winchester, Rugby, and Marlborough." In 1866, Bishop Cotton was drowned a fortnight after the foundation stone of the school he had envisaged had been laid at Simla by John Lawrence.

Bishop Cotton School, meant to be a replica of an English public school, was founded in 1863 at Jutogh as a thanks-offering to God for His deliverance of the British people in India during 1857. It was shifted to its present site in Simla three years later. The school was designed to bridge the educational and the social gulf between the children of officials who came from England, most of whom sent their children to English schools, and the domiciled Europeans and Anglo-Indians.

The school was founded by public subscription and with financial assistance from the Government, which also had an active interest in the successful running of the school. On the Board of Governors, the four ex-officio members were the Lieutenant Governor of the Punjab, the Bishop of Lahore, the Commissioner of Delhi, and the Deputy Commissioner of Simla. There were also four elected governors who were to be residents of Simla. The Viceroy was the school's Visitor. The parents of the boys were largely clerks in Government service, and there were also many who belonged to the non-official classes. An official report proclaimed, "A European or Eurasian lad brought up and educated at Simla is, generally speaking, immeasurably superior to any lad brought up and educated in Calcutta or indeed anywhere in the plains." The Simla school was reputed the best. *Imperial Simla* by Pamela Kanwar (Oxford).

[3] An entertaining slant on the use of replica public schools to instil the correct attitudes among the future Indian, and indeed Imperial, national elite is depicted in *The Games Ethic and Imperialism* by J.A. Mangan (Viking). From Mayo College in Ajmere in 1885, a series of foundations were developed to produce "decent chaps" and replicas of disciplined "muscular Christianity". Typically, none of the early pioneers foresaw the time when national teams from the subcontinent would consistently trounce England at cricket.

[4] From this distance of time, it is impossible to imagine the stupendous and orchestrated machinery of Imperial brainwashing. Now exhaustively documented in *Propaganda and Empire* by John M. MacKenzie (Manchester University Press).

[5] This recollection is indebted to research by my brother, Kenneth Benjamin, on

the composition and movements of *"WINSTON'S SPECIAL – No 2" (Convoy Code "WS2")*. This is a detailed account of the trials of marshalling and escorting such a large vulnerable convoy in the early stages of World War II. One sad echo is the construction history of the vessels from a time when Britain was still the world's leading shipbuilding nation.

[6] As a callow youth of 15, taking advantage of natural double-joints, one developed the art of bowling slow but wide spinning leg breaks and googlies. With a recommendation from the sports master, this allowed me to join the Worcestershire team during early-season practice. Among the heroes! "Roley" Jenkins, Reg Perks, Don Kenyon, Dick Howarth, and "Laddie" Ootschorne – the first Sri Lankan cricketer in the first-class game, but remarkable for having an extremely heavy bat for a very small man. But an early lesson in the "Pro" approach to cricket: Dick Howarth – a left-arm spinner and lower-order batsmen, notable for occasioning mid-on and mid-off being pushed back to the boundary as he came down the pavilion steps, but whose best years were lost during the war – was batting in the nets. He was a left-handed batsman, and when it came to my turn to bowl, I managed to pitch a googly on his legs, which turned enough to bowl him. Perhaps he did not think such a youthful figure could have mastered this art, but as he patted the ball back, he smiled, "Well bowled, lad." My next ball, a perfectly spun orthodox leg break on his off-stump, with one stride was dispatched to the far corner of the ground for me to retrieve. Ever since, in wistful moments, particularly during interminable meetings, speculation has turned to an alternative lifestyle had one pursued a career in cricket.

[7] A crucial character in such a station was the Senior Equipment Officer, who, amongst the vast audit duties of keeping pace with the flow of bits and pieces, also held regular monthly auctions of surplus vehicle spares and old tyres. He recalled having asked one of the Egyptian merchants how he could make a profit on the prices paid for old tyres and drew the sage response, "You can sell sand in Cairo."

[8] Since the only equipment provided for housing airmen were rudimentary canvas tents, in themselves hardly suitable for protection against prolonged exposure to desert temperatures, sandstorms etc., the supreme British talent for DIY was put to a stern test. The term "tent" was in most instances notional, since beneath the canvas roof and sides supported by rigging to all appearances a conventional "tent", were roofed structures put together from whatever wood and panels that could be filched. And these were in effect boarded huts, and for the more advanced containing "extensions" and "storage rooms" built underground.

[9] The star virtuoso was Alan Redshaw, a Flying Officer, with the inevitable nickname "Red". Apart from an extraordinary ability to conceptualise the rudimentary radar information into a three-dimensional awareness of the situation from a pilot's viewpoint, occasionally, indeed, running three

interceptions at the same time, he was also an example of the quirky personal characteristics revealed by such a closed community. Apparently subsisting entirely on a diet of copious quantities of Tennants beer and chips, though these had to be immaculately browned.

FANTASY TO SCRAP HEAP – POST-IMPERIAL DINKY TOYS

The London Heliport Committee was a subset of the eldritch world of the British aircraft industry in the post-war period. At the time, there was a small platform on the south bank of the Thames at Battersea that served the occasional VIP use of helicopters. In Europe, with intercity transport still recovering from war disruption, Sabena was running a heavily subsidised helicopter network taking in Brussels, Paris and Rotterdam. So we, involved in administering London's airports, were taken aback by an apparently sudden Ministerial interest in helicopters as a solution to intercity and, indeed, London commuter travel. We could only put it down to a delayed reaction to seeing the black-and-white version of HG Wells' *The Shape of Things to Come*.

Given the high cost of helicopter operations, their safety requirements, the clearances demanded on the landing site if frequent flights were envisaged, and the necessary groundside services such as passenger handling, lounges, car parking and taxi ranks, the scheme seemed pretty harebrained. Duncan Sandys was insistent that we pursue this exercise, despite us on one occasion commissioning Freeman Fox to devise an outline drawing of a structure taking account of these requirements for helicopter movements every 20 minutes: the resulting drawing was a building well above the height of St Paul's. So a Committee was devised, with representatives of the LCC and British Rail, who owned several of the potential sites, and various aviation experts. The exercise was quite a model of its kind, where the "desiderata" – the ideal objectives to be met – were drawn up and applied to alternative sites.[1]

What lay behind this exercise emerged when we reviewed the potential range of aircraft for which such a heliport would have to cater. Amongst the array of Munchausen contraptions justified under the strategic imperatives of the Cold War, or in vain visions of leading the civil airliner market, was a machine called the Rotodyne. A prototype was being developed by Fairey at White Waltham near Maidenhead. It was one of the more imaginative attempts to meet the eternal military requirement for "rapid deployment". Mechanically it had a box-section fuselage – presumably to allow for ease of loading – in the prototype with space for a couple of dozen seats, and the Committee could boast to have been among the few who sampled this form of travel, albeit with gritted teeth against the extraordinary vibration – envisaged eventually to be stretched to 120-150 seats; stub wings with two Tyne turboprop engines; and a large four-blade rotor which would enable controlled steep landing and take-off, while rotating freely in level flight to function as an autogiro and augment the lift from the wings.

The really distinctive feature, however, was that the rotor was powered by ramjets at the tips of the blades. On start-up, this required the rotor to be spun from the power of the main engines until the tip-speed was fast enough to fire the jets. When this happened, and so long as the ramjets were in operation, the din was fantastic – if deafening the opposition was part of the operational requirement, it was spectacularly successful. It had been blithely assumed that a civil version would be a natural spin-off. But anyone listening from half a mile away to the rotor test-rig that had been erected at Farnborough before development was authorised would have realised that planting the noise footprint of a Boeing 707 at take-off in the heart of London was just not on.

The committee carried on surveying various sites: one has crawled over the roofs of most of the railway stations on the banks of the Thames, though ironically not Waterloo since, despite being Duncan Sandys' first preference, it transpired to have been built on tiers of Victorian brick arches that could not conceivably support the superstructure for a helicopter landing area. The LCC Planning staff were alarmed at the prospective noise and environmental detriment that were likely to result. But we had to have an actual flight of the Rotodyne to the Battersea Heliport, with noise monitoring equipment spread around the neighbouring areas of London – I was responsible for one monitoring device at Fulham Power Station – before it was eventually conceded that the aircraft would be intolerable in urban areas. And the project was cancelled at a development cost write-off of some £28 million. As for a London heliport, the site that was best against all the criteria was the Nine Elms goods yard, which subsequently became the relocated Covent Garden market. And the foundations were strengthened against any future technological breakthrough, or Ministerial flights of fancy, for a central London STOL operating station.

With periods in the Ministry of Aviation Private Office from Peter Thorneycroft to Roy Jenkins, and in the early Defence Sales organisation, one could vie for the accolade of having been in at the death of more millions of pounds worth of aerospace projects than anyone else. And with a subsequent spell on the Concorde project team, when it was always touch and go, my lead would have been out of sight had it been stopped.

With an introduction from the large volume of "aviation enthusiast" literature, this debris of misapplied resources, judging by enquiries for guidance, is now coming into the orbit of doctorate students looking for likely research topics. And there is vast scope for tracing through the vacillations and technological hysteria that lay behind this period of costly dinky toys.

The aerospace industry in the two decades after World War II still retained the capacities built up during hostilities and its production facilities were still largely intact. Consequently it was effectively the leading industry outside the United States. What should also have been a strength was the pioneering position in jet engine development, which was just moving into wider applications as the war ended. But for countries unable, or unwilling, to buy from the US, Britain was the leading source of aircraft purchases: notably China, to whom sales of the Viscount and Trident were made against US Trade restrictions, and military aircraft in Latin America.

The industry had a string of relatively effective military aircraft, which, under the conditions of war, had been produced in reasonable numbers: notably the Spitfire, Mosquito, and Canberra, the last increased in volume by licensing to the US. On the civil side, whilst the Viscount short/medium haul aircraft had hit the market at an opportune time when intercity air transport was developing to make up the deficiencies in rail travel, and sold more than 400, its earlier lineage of the Viking, Varsity and Valetta had not achieved significant sales, and its successor, the Vanguard, also had a disappointing sales record. Even less successful were attempts at longer-range transports – either failing in development, or when built unable to compete with the sheer scale of US purchases from Douglas, Lockheed and Boeing. Still, if imitation is the surest form of flattery, the Russians – the only country seriously attempting to vie with the US – found British industry a useful source of inspiration (if not direct copying) with both the Tupolev and Illyushin stables producing replica designs to such aircraft as the VC10 and the Trident.

Yet, despite its technological heritage, the corporate structure was still, as in so many other sectors, a fragmented cottage industry compared to the leading, predominantly US, companies. It would tax the memory of the most acknowledged enthusiast to list the companies that had pretensions to aviation competence in the 50s – at least a couple of dozen. But as a vivid example, the companies assembled for the Supersonic Transport Aircraft Committee (STAC) in 1956 ran: AV Roe, Sir WG Armstrong Whitworth Aircraft, Bristol Aircraft, English Electric, Fairey Aviation, De Haviland Aircraft, Handley Page, Short Brothers & Harland, Vickers

Armstrong, Armstrong Siddely Motors, Bristol Aero Engines, and Rolls-Royce. To this, devotees could toss in others such as Blackburn, Folland, Gloucester, Boulton Paul, Hawkers, Hunting, Dowty etc etc.[2]

Also as a consequence of the War, the industry had a tradition of funding by "cost-plus" since the pressure had continuously been on output without the scope for the government to act as a "tough customer". Moreover, the industrial mindset was one of looking to government for basic research, and then a "profit formula" for military projects, and on civil ventures some form of launch assistance for development, tooling and production.

Meanwhile, successive Governments still held a "great nation" vision in the immediate post-war dispensation, which demanded being a leading player in the Cold War, with the vestiges of global commitments extending to joint Defence pacts as far afield as Australia, the Gulf and the "spheres of influence" deals with the US. All against a strapped financial backdrop of stringency. Within this Whitehall capsule there were inter-service rivalries – the battle between the Royal Navy and Royal Air Force over the deterrent, at its peak in the Skybolt versus Polaris controversy, achieved the kindergarten intensities of "Who's got the nuke?" And the struggles tended to spill over into the stipulations for other Defence equipment. With perennial exasperation and impatience from the Treasury and other spending departments against budget-blowing increases in project estimates.

How these conflicting pretensions played out, with their succession of jerks and shifts, defies sequential narrative – most striking was the Duncan Sandys "no-manned aircraft" shift in 1957, in the belief that air defence could be assigned to rocketry, only to be reversed with the Lightning elevated from being a development aircraft to a front-line fighter – whatever its limitations, the Lightning retained a rate of climb superior to many subsequent types. There was also a subplot of "social" projects, notably to boost employment in Northern Ireland: the Belfast transport, sadly underpowered, and the Skyvan, a good idea for an aerial jeep that actually sold far better than Treasury expectations. And, lurking in the background, was the myth of a "light-aircraft" industry, with more lobbying than substance. And, of course, the saga was punctuated by a sequence of periodic "reviews", and a series of grand committees from "Brabazon" to "Plowden", with events invariably moving faster than their deliberations. If defying any attempt at a structurally coherent account, the period offers almost infinite scope for archivists and industrial archaeologists.

But at the coal face, the pace was never less than frenetic, with a continuous series of cost overruns on individual projects, leading to compensating "stretching" of development timescales, order reductions or cancellations; with conspiracies and deals in corridors, constant parliamentary noise, industrial lobbying and press interest. On the military side, the dominant concern was to evolve hardware to meet whatever seemed to be the trend of Soviet capabilities. Hence an ascendancy of the Operational Requirements (OR) outfits in the Ministry of Defence, who liased with US and other NATO intelligence agencies. Assessing the ability of industry to produce equipment to match these hypothetical threats and overseeing development of the resulting defence systems fell to the Ministry of Aviation, taking over from the Ministry of Supply, who drew on research at the "Establishments" – pre-eminently at the Royal Aircraft Establishment at Farnborough and the Radar Establishment at Malvern, and other specialist centres, for example for torpedo development etc. Industry was brought in through a series of consultative mechanisms on the feasibility of putting the potential of available technology into practice.

The skews within this system and its tiers of interfaces were complex. From the arrogance of the OR teams and Services, who reckoned they were doing "industry" a favour in providing them with orders. This was balanced by the willingness of industry at the other end of the process to go along with the system and play the "estimates game".[3] Because the military preoccupations were on future threat assessments, there was a corresponding focus on sustaining effective "design teams". Consequently, there were continuing pressures to dream up work – a barely disguised administrators' view, since they had the job of trying to manage these extravagant programmes and had to carry the brunt of briefing and appearances before the Public Accounts Committee, was that some of these cherished design teams should be exported to Lockheed, Boeing and Douglas. A typical example of this bias, demanding no hindsight, was the absurdity of having three medium/long-range "V" bombers – Victor, Valiant and Vulcan – when on the most optimistic assumptions, no more than 140 aircraft were in service.[4] And this was in an industry where wartime experience had discovered the "learning curve". But the pursuit of esoteric concepts devised to suit hypothetical situations, where no market existed beyond the perspectives of the British services, was endemic, and superseded any coherent approach to establishing a sustainable industry – as much among the companies as government – where continuous production runs dependent on orders beyond this country were imperative: witness the blank silence of officials when Roy Jenkins asked which of the projects that he had inherited had the best export prospects. As a consequence, production was in relatively short, or interrupted, runs, so that costs were "at the top of the learning curve".

Moreover, the peculiar British fixation of "rationalisation" was in train: basically, the use of "military" orders and offers of launch-aid for "civil" projects as bait to encourage mergers and acquisitions to reduce the number of gaping mouths. Whatever may be the theoretical advantages of gladiatorial competitive contests for purchasing similar products, once the number of contestants falls and specialist capabilities or technological expertise predominate, a contest morphs into "buggins turn", and, eventually when rationalised to a single UK source, into "muggins turn". The pretence that this can be efficient under a "quoted-company system" finishes up eventually as taxpayers' money being siphoned through companies into shareholders pockets – all early prototypes for the privatisation of British Rail. Other countries confront this dilemma without the baggage of the same theoretical upbringing of subservience to "markets", by extremely tough demands for "complementarity" and tight monitoring, dispensing with the pretence of arm's-length competitive bidding.

But the process was further complicated by the disparity between "military" programmes which were, in theory at least, predictable – within the vacillations of tussles with the Treasury, and shifts of government policy, and the "civil" side where demand was subject to the judgments of BOAC and BEA – both cussedly independent, and each with different traditions. For example, the first Comet, despite lacking transatlantic capability, was acceptable on old "imperial" routes, which at that time were BOAC's main revenue source. And, to his dying day, George Edwards* claimed that this "imperial" mindset led to the cancellation of the potentially transatlantic V1000, which would have beaten the Boeing 707 by several years. And the same recriminations resurfaced over the VC10, whose performance, the manufacturers claimed, was deliberately devised to suit BOAC's stipulation of operating out of the altitude of Johannesburg, then one of the airline's premium routes, which meant that it was less effective on the transatlantic service when BOAC shifted its priorities. While rocketry has its own clique of regretful reminiscence, from those involved in the development of Blue Streak, and the successful, if immediately cancelled, Black Knight/Arrow development, curtailed just as orbital satellite launchers were heralding the new age of space exploitation. And so on.

Even on the "military" side the overriding focus on meeting future hypothetical threats meant pushing the limits of technology and led to a succession of projects so specialised that sales beyond the British services were nonexistent, or ignored from the start. Consequently, the "aborted short run" syndrome was a constant, as was the "modification" culture as successive generations of OR staff, usually on 2 to 3-year postings, continuously "updated" their assessments, introducing new tweaks as development was under way.

The catalogue of projects that failed to meet expectations was extensive. When a Fighter Controller in the Canal Zone, we were frustrated by the limitations of the Meteor night-fighters, and heard of a "super" new aircraft due to enter service – the Javelin, which never quite got debugged. Or the Swift, whose danger to life and limb was such that the leader of the first formation squadron, Wing Commander "Twinkle" Storey, when subsequently a liaison officer to Abu Dhabi, was recommending a purchase of the Macchi 326, an Italian jet trainer powered by Rolls-Royce engines, on grounds that no British aircraft was worth buying. But the constant rush of developing new projects, tossing in variations of engines and electronic systems, led to the standing joke that the Ministry's development fleet based at Farnborough and the flight test centre at Boscombe Down was larger than many national air forces, except that every aircraft was different.

That there were missed opportunities was inevitable. And many old aviation salts will have their own recollection of such failures – the V1000, the Medway engine, extended versions of the BAC 1-11, and even the TSR 2.[5] And some did not need hindsight. My own choice examples were the Herald and a stretched version of the Hunter. Let it not be said that Whitehall is devoid of genuine emotion – an understandable view given the steady flow of sanctimonious self-righteousness peddled by politicians under the guise of convictions. As part of the "rationalisation" process, there was an RAF requirement for a medium-range tactical transport, an aircraft capable of operating out of unprepared or rudimentary strips. The two contenders were the Handley Page Herald and the Avro 746. Their configurations differed principally in that the former had a high-wing, with engines mounted to allow several feet of clearance between the propeller tips and the ground, while the latter was a low-wing design, which required the engines to be mounted on top of the wing to secure even a minimum clearance. And the former allowed more rapid access for troops and supplies. The RAF preference for the Herald was common knowledge.

The order was seen as leverage in "rationalising" the industry by making selection of the Herald dependent on Handley Page agreeing to become absorbed into the Hawker group. But Handley Page stood out against this pressure. And an arm-lock meeting was arranged with the

Minister. On the one side were the senior Hawker management, who included Sir Roy Dobson – maybe a lovely guy, but in all appearances the physical embodiment of caricatures of cigar-smoking "fat cats". And against these was old Sir Frederick (Freddie) Handley Page, with failing eyesight he lost his way on the second floor of Shell Mex House and had to be rescued by a search party from the Private Office. He doggedly stood his ground, unwilling to see the identity of the company that he had pioneered lost in an arbitrary merger. Peter Thorneycroft found the exercise extremely uncongenial. But in the end, the order went to the Avro 746.

Even without the launch of an RAF order, though in consolation and retrospectively in admission of its advantages a few were ordered for the Royal Flight, the Herald still managed a number of export orders. But the Fokker Friendship, with a similar configuration to the Herald, picked up several hundred orders around the world. And, with the backing of an RAF order, the Herald could have expected to compete in this category more effectively. The Avro 746/748 picked up a few orders – indeed, one of our craftiest applications of the Aid and Trade Provision was to help secure an order in Madagascar. And there were various ideas, not seriously pursued, for a stretched version. Yet another unexploited potential winner from the Handley Page stable was the Jetstream, which, under the Skybolt offset programme, won an order for a US Marine Corps communications aircraft in head-to-head competition with US manufacturers. That the process of rationalisation had been sub-optimal in securing market position could hardly be gainsaid.

The formation of Defence Sales, with its first "private sector" head – Ray Brown*,[6] was a belated recognition that the viability of the industry was dependent on overseas orders that required government involvement. The pace was being set by the US Military Sales Office, under the aggressive leadership of Henry Kuss, and an even more aggressive sidekick, MacDonald, a Brit who had happened to be in the US when the Vietnam call up took place. While the French were mounting an extremely bold export drive, where sophistications such as "credit-mixte" finance were posing entirely new problems. But, hitherto, on this side of the Pond, such dirty activities as commercial sales in a very distorted market were still a diversion from the true task of fighting hypothetical future wars. And Defence Sales were expected to make the best out of whatever hardware the military demanded: for example, if there was a lesson from the Six-Day War in 1967, it was the advantage of dispersing aircraft so that they would not be sitting ducks on airfields. And the ideal aircraft to meet this condition was the Harrier, which could be deployed away from conventional runways. A demonstration exercise was arranged in Cyprus inviting, separately, leading personalities from countries in the area. They were all impressed by the performance of the aircraft, but confounded by the price – "all we want is something to knock out the tanks over the hill" were typical judgments. About a fifth of the cost was the navigation/attack system, evolved to meet the RAF requirement of "reading a Welsh railway sign in a pea-soup fog", as summarised by one of Hawker's sales representatives. To replace it with a "bag of sand" by the time the resulting modifications were made and a flight-test programme conducted, the cost, spread out over a representative number of sales, was little different from the RAF version.

For old Defence Sales hands, there is an enjoyable irony in the justification of the present Ministry of Defence for overseas sales, replicating precisely the arguments that we were advancing against an unwilling military mind: spreading overheads, increasing operational feedback, continuity of production flows, defence and diplomatic links etc. But getting these points over in the early days was a Herculean task: to be entirely fair, the Ministry mindset was reinforced by the Treasury cash-based categorisation of budgetary discipline, where only expenditure and costs in aid of approved requirements were admissible – for example, when the Saudi Air Force requested some RAF training for their future Lightning pilots, the MOD's initial pricing was on a "full-cost" basis, where the resulting price for training a pilot was more than 40% of the cost of the aircraft. The Saudi Government had no option but to accept this at the time, but a senior RSAF Colonel remarked caustically, "You're worse than Arabs!"

But some headway was made when the Tornado was authorised, and the decision announced with the bland statement that the aircraft would have "a potential market of thousands", without consulting the Sales division. We protested at the wild enthusiasm of this guesstimate, and made a reasoned analysis of potential customers outside the consortium developing the aircraft, taking account of ties to other producers such as the US and Russia, their capability to buy such a complex aircraft, and their ability to operate/service either within their own skill levels or by employing imported expertise. And came out at a maximum sales potential of 60-70 aircraft, predominantly Saudi Arabia and any of the other Gulf States who might be able to afford it. A fair estimate as it has turned out.

Then when it came to deciding the new "advanced trainer" competition to take over from the Hunter, we were actively included in the decision process. There were some supporters for a more engineered contender from BAC Wharton, but the export market was clearly in favour of a simpler utility aircraft, and the decision went in favour of the Hawk. Again, events seem to have supported the sales judgment.

Meanwhile, though much time was taken up with monitoring the Saudi Arabian Defence Scheme, which had secured export orders for the Lightning and the BAC 146 trainer aircraft (and an extraordinarily complex "stack-beam" defence radar system), our bestseller was refurbished Hunters. Despite originally having been funded by Marshall Aid, and purchased in numbers by the RAF only when the Swift had been cancelled, the Hunter had secured orders from India and other Commonwealth countries, Nordic countries, Switzerland, Peru, Chile and Jordan so that for every aircraft phased out of the RAF, there was a queue of potential buyers for the refurbished aircraft to keep their squadrons up to strength, posing awkward diplomatic choices on how they should be apportioned. And, if further credentials were needed, there was even a very hush-hush approach from the Israeli Air Force, who admitted that it took three of their Mirage IIIs to see off even one Jordanian Hunter. In any other industry, having this level of market penetration should have prompted a follow-up model to hold, if not to expand, market share.

The appeal of the Hunter was its versatility: advanced trainer/ground attack/reconnaissance/battlefield air superiority. In fact, the Hunter replacement is a saga in its own right. To keep up with trends, however, it needed to have a supersonic capability. For example, the Mirage III could achieve this only with the use of a booster rocket, but enough to give it the cache of being "supersonic". And, indeed, Sidney Cam*, the legendary designer of the "H" line of fighter aircraft, had already built a prototype "slim wing" for the Hunter that was "leaning against a shed at Kingston", while there was a more powerful version of the engine, the 2000 series Avon, already being built for the Lightning at Rolls-Royce's factory at East Kilbride. The company estimated the cost of developing an uprated version as £18-20 million. OK, in those days a pound was a pound. But, pressing from the newly formed Defence Sales angle was an uphill task, since the Jaguar had been authorised, with the mystical "Wharton design-team" as part of the rationale. While Hawker themselves saw the RAF's preference as lying in the P1154, a "supersonic" Harrier under development – never built, but involving esoteric "plenum chamber burning" technology to add an afterburner to the rear pair of jet nozzles (Munchausen again!). Challenging Arnold Hall*[7] personally on why the company could not pursue a supersonic Hunter development privately, his response was that the idea had been dismissed several years earlier in the belief that with the end of the Korean War the US would be flooding the market with surplus Sabres. But he was unwilling to reopen the case without the MOD's support.

So, we lost perhaps the best chance to have "The Beetle" of military aviation. Ironically, this would also have gone a long way to meeting the original requirement of the Jaguar, which, one learns, Marcel Dassault dismissed as a "camel...designed by committee" (*FT* 17.7.04). But he should not have been so scathing. For it was the lack of a Hunter successor that opened up international markets for the Mirage III/V. In fact, while the French achievement in building up their aerospace industry is a notable national success, Britain fulfilled the role of Santa Claus.

On civil aircraft, Hawker Siddeley struck at an early alliance with Sud Aviation – indeed the nose section of the very successful Caravelle short haul jet airliner was a replica of the Comet. So successful that it far outsold the turboprop Vanguard, intended as the successor to the Viscount. But that BAE has a role in the Airbus goes back to this earlier relationship. On the military front, however, the generosity was even more marked: us conspiracy theorists noted the remarkable similarity between the wing-form of the Mirage III and the Fairey Delta research aircraft to suggest that cooperation between Farnborough scientists and their French opposite numbers was a shade too intense.

But one of the most generous contributions was the refusal to supply the Buccaneer to countries like Israel and South Africa. The Buccaneer was a rugged medium-range strike aircraft with a carrier capability designed for low-altitude flight and carrying initially a significant bomb load, and then the stand-off Blue Steel missile (which actually worked!). Inevitably, supplying such an aircraft to almost any country that might want to use it was hedged with political constraints, which Ministers were not prepared to countenance – another typical case of developing systems that no one else would be allowed to operate, at its extreme in the TSR 2, which could only have had a production run, probably diminishing as development costs rose, for the RAF.

But Dassault took quick advantage by unplugging unnecessary boxes on the Mirage III, installing extra fuel capacity and strong points under the wing to introduce the Mirage V on essentially the same airframe. Supplying the combination to Israel, with the "proven" operational success of the Six Day War, offered a platform for sales more widely. The only counter from British Industry was the modified Lightning – initially a very effective interceptor, and with a ground-attack pack developed for sales to Saudi Arabia and Kuwait. As if this wasn't enough, the Empire Test Pilot School based at Boscombe Down gave a very favourable evaluation of the Mirage, which Dassault gratefully added to their sales literature.

But the ultimate "coup" was Concorde: again obsessed by getting in first, the same motivation for the disastrous Comet saga, there was scant attempt at any real market analysis, particularly the impact of the sonic boom, and the project was approved as "an inevitable" progression of technology from military to civil applications. For all the controversy on this side of the Channel, the French showed little hesitation – only when it was too late to terminate did they acknowledge the hopeless sales prospects. But, whatever may have been their rationale, the wrangles over different systems signalled clearly that their prime concern was technology acquisition and building up the facilities at Toulouse – from a few Nissen huts to the leading aerospace centre of Europe was a transformation achieved largely through Concorde overheads. (One could note that the French have shown a similar adroitness in biasing European Space Launcher/Research activities towards building up their Ariane capabilities). If they have had their share of dodgy projects such as the Atlantique and Transall, the French have aggressively achieved a competitive helicopter manufacturing capability and produced the defining weapon of modern naval warfare, the Exocet.

The outcome of this process has been a steady departure of British industry from civil aviation. Perhaps the saddest consequence of the hubris of pretensions to be "among the leaders", and attempting to slug it out with the vastly larger – and vastly more subsidised – US producers, was the lack of focus on support for the more mundane "workhorse" markets of short/medium-range flexible aircraft. This would have followed on the success of the Viscount, and not that industry had been short of contenders – the Herald, Jetstream, Islander, Skyvan, Avro 748, the potential BAC 1-11 lineage, the DH 121/HS 125 executive jet (once a leader, but sold lock-stock-and-barrel to Lockheed), and finally the BAC 146 have all passed into the history books, latterly under the banner of enhancing "shareholder value".

Significantly, this is the sector in which newcomers have inevitably gained share. Embraer (Brazil), Bombardier (Canada), and Dassault, complementing its succession of military aircraft, have maintained a continuing presence through the Falcon/Mercure range. It is also the segment being targeted by Japan's aerospace group for their first wholly national civil aircraft since the failure of the earlier YS 11. Even Indonesia made an attempt, which for an archipelago of several thousand islands made sense – the programme was aborted by the 1997 financial crisis. But one retains the memory of a tour of their factory as part of Mrs Thatcher's delegation, conducted by Dr Habibie (whose technical apprenticeship in Germany was evidenced by several Messerschmitt-Bolkow helicopters on the airfield) – the entertainment enhanced by the dialogue with the Prime Minister being broadcast to the following retinue breaking down every time the head of the column turned a corner. But one could not help concluding that the Indonesian Government would have saved themselves a fortune had they licensed construction of the Islander, or, indeed, bought Britten-Norman outright a few years earlier.

The end result is that the stretched Hawk programme is the sole remaining British independent aircraft development – at least the lesson of the Hunter seems to have been learned, albeit four decades too late.

Such a modest exercise in industrial reminiscence suggests that aerospace – including the shambles of Blues and Reds in missilry – has been a spectacular example of confused objectives, industrial ineptitude, and misapplied resources that have contributed to a loss of comparative advantage and market position. While Brazil, Canada and Japan have industries rising to supplant Britain in this growing international market. Even if it is conceded that focussing on building up an industry is a relatively more straightforward task than rationalising, there was a persistent failure to recognise the crucial need for continuity of production, calling for products capable of winning sales in foreign markets, and that compromises to achieve a wider market would have benefited both the industry and its British military clients. (Another strength of the French was their readiness to tailor military demands and phasing of deliveries to exploit export markets). Meanwhile, it is questionable whether "mergers", when old rivalries between erstwhile arrogant managements persist, was an effective mechanism, as against supporting the company with the most competitive aircraft and leaving it to subcontract/acquire/invest in any additional capacity needed.

That Rolls-Royce should have survived this hurly-burly is little short of miraculous. But thereby hangs another tale. In 1971, Fred Corfield was doing his stint as Minister of Aviation, and as part of his duties was on a goodwill visit to Saudi Arabia in the early months to avoid the rigours of the summer heat. He scored an inter-departmental diplomatic triumph by remarking to Willie Morris, one of our pragmatic Arabists and our then Ambassador, that senior members of the Foreign Office were mostly, "jumped-up provincials". To which Willie replied, "Naht fuck'n likely." But everywhere he went, he was confronted by Saudi Ministers blaming the British companies in the consortium undertaking the Air Defence Scheme for any and every problem. And demanding that the British Government take steps to put these right. Our Minister robustly replied on each occasion, "It is not the policy of the British Government to stand in the shoes of industry". On arrival back at Heathrow, the moment the door was opened, a distraught private secretary rushed on and the Minister was whisked away before even completing customs clearance. And that afternoon he announced in the Commons that Rolls-Royce was going into receivership. This was the prelude to Rolls-Royce (71), a wholly government-owned company. A refinancing before privatisation and a few tranches of launch-aid later, the company has succeeded, with a range of alliances to share development costs, to hold second place in world airline orders. Ironically, the best-selling Trent engine retains the three-shaft configuration of the RB 211, whose development caused the company's collapse in 1971.

Still, scholars can have a field day poring over the entrails of this quintessentially British buggers-muddle. The bureaucracy was at least impeccable: submissions, reports, R&D Board minutes, and PAC hearings by the ton. Except for the occasional gap, such as the rationale for a Concorde Treaty with no break clause. But documents alone cannot capture the flaking imperial grandeur of this era. Gongs galore. The international durbars of Farnborough Air Shows. Or the tradition of country house banquets, or, in lieu of a few verdant fields, Lucas staged a full-day annual bash at a Park Lane hostelry, whose invitation list was the metier for anyone who pretended to be anyone, actually being someone. Perhaps the greatest spin-off benefactors from this era were Gilbey and Gordons, as gin seemed to provide most of the inspiration.

---

[1] The Committee was chaired by Ivor Morris, a somewhat academic and frustratingly pernickety draughtsman, and had Graham Hill, the Branch head, among its members. Graham was characterised by a wry wit and immaculate copperplate handwriting. He was also an adept doodler, with entertaining caricatures of Committee members and jottings. The most memorable, which has been validated over the years, arose from a series of definitions. "Committee = pooled ignorance". He subsequently transferred to the British Airport Authority on its formation and must have found plenty of scope for his talents.

[2] For those minded to gain a sense of these heroic golden years, a compilation of documentaries of the Farnborough Air Shows of the 1950s is contained in *Farnborough, the Glory, Glory Years* (DD2870), an era when the Show was exclusively British. Long-forgotten names roll through the commentary, but, typically, in 1950 there were 58 types of aircraft on show, and in 1951 49 types, of which 19 were new.

[3] The "estimates game" is inherent in any attempt to incorporate new technology into integrated systems, especially of the complexity of modern defence and

aviation products. And "procurement" involves a series of dilemmas inherently resistant to simple resolution. By definition, "cutting-edge" technology has no track record on which to base an estimate of cost, not just of the particular system, but how it interacts with other elements of the totality. Hence the historic trend of defence projects leading the introduction of new technologies, and invariably carrying the highest risk of cost escalation. At bottom, the eternal polarities are, if absolute certainty of costs is the prime driver, then buying off the nearest shelf is the solution, otherwise, if some enhancement of performance is needed, the risks of novelty have to be confronted. An "off the shelf" approach suits the predilection of the Treasury for neat boxes of expenditure and "competitive tendering". But this can hit the "assumption of surplus" fallacy at the core of competition theory as the options of competitive suppliers diminish, invariably arising from the increasing importance of specialist and technical competences. And then rather different mechanisms are required than reliance on the horny standby of "competitive bidding", or "markets" – as illustrated vividly by countries who have evolved their industries from a situation of "scarcity" of alternative suppliers, or developing technological competence from a less sophisticated base.

One of the ironies is that compromises in the interests of reducing costs by "uprating" an existing product with minimal additions of new systems can in practice, through integration problems and incompatibilities, have just as serious cost overruns. Such uncertainties vary in scale and impact with the form of product. The terrain between these polarities has been a fertile ground for the British propensity for Boy Scouts' badges, such as Project Managers, when internationally any other country handling this dilemma has relied upon individuals with accumulated and proven expertise in a particular field.

For new systems, however, any early estimate is bound to contain a high element of guesswork, and the saga of how to secure realistic initial estimates has probably been running for centuries, with a few more to go. We compared notes with the Pentagon at the time, and found that the difference between the initial estimates and final cost was best measured by multiplying the former by "Pi" – the universal constant. At an informal discussion with the NASA team boss for the "man on the moon programme", which is regarded as a case where the programme came out close to estimate, he admitted that this had been achieved by "multiplying the initial estimate by Pi".

The "game" comes when industry perceives an interest in some particular system on the part of the Services, and presents an estimate which they know full well is likely to be exceeded, but only when the programme will have reached the point where cancellation is difficult. The trick can be compounded by "international collaboration" where the freedom for unilateral decision is circumscribed by relations with other governments who will also have industrial lobbies having negotiated a share of the manufacture as a condition for contributing to development. Concorde to Eurofighter is a path of such projects being resilient against estimates escalation. Again, formulae to pass some of the escalation on to industry, or devices to share "pain and gain", as have been applied in other project areas, are continuously being explored but depend upon the scale of perceived uncertainty. But the "game" will surely go on, and on.

[4] A sad fond memory was a visit to a Handley Page plant in Cricklewood, North London, where a Victor was going through its final wiring and fitting, and in a corner within this vast space were some employees moulding and welding domestic household radiators, proudly displayed as an example of "diversification".

[5] A vivid flashback to the absurdities of the time is the video account, *TSR 2 – the Untold Story* (DD1092). All the standard constituents of the pantomime are on display:
– The doughty Operational Requirements Air Marshal justifying the specifications for the "Canberra Replacement" for an aircraft capable of a Mach 1.1 dash at 200 feet, combined with Mach 2 at 60,000 feet and a short-field takeoff and landing capability. A performance target way beyond the frontiers of then available technologies, and not attained by any aircraft subsequently.
– Inter-service rivalry, with the suggestion that the OR was approved as "compensation" for "the nuclear deterrent" being awarded to the Navy; and Lord Mountbatten, in his role as the most senior unguided missile, visiting Australia while the aircraft manufacturers were trying to persuade them to adopt the TSR 2 for their Canberra replacement, promoting the Buccaneer, the Navy's low-level strike aircraft.
– Wild vacillations in policy with the Duncan Sandys' decision in 1957 for "no-manned aircraft", leading to the industry being told that there was no certainty of any future aircraft projects, with the message "amalgamate or die".
– The heightened inter-company rivalries: the tensions between Vickers and English Electric over dividing responsibilities for the project; the optimum location for flight testing – whether at the Vickers airfield at Weybridge or the English Electric base at Wharton; and resentment at selection of the Bristol Siddeley "Olympus" when that company had already been awarded the contract for the "Pegasus" to power the P1127/1154 – until Rolls-Royce took over Bristol Siddeley.
– A bizarre project management structure, with the Ministry of Supply/Aviation being the coordinator, with a project committee of 58, which, after a call by the Chairman for "a significant reduction", became 61; with government control extending to the cockpit layout, which had to be completely revised when actual flying was in prospect.
The hero of the saga was the late Roland Beamont, English Electric's chief test pilot, whose downright professionalism and physical courage kept the project going. Among his choice, down-to-earth comments were: it was "absolutely crazy" to stipulate that the project should be done jointly by Vickers and English Electric, which led to "unnecessary complications", when the project should have been done by "one firm" with the best track record from previous projects, notably English Electric, who had developed the Canberra and the Lightning supersonic research aircraft, with additional tasks subcontracted. While the "Olympus" was an engine still under development, a wiser choice would have

been to select a proven engine when embarking on a demanding new airframe project – indeed, the Olympus test-bed had exploded, and there were continuing vibration problems deriving from the engine during taxi-trials of the prototype.

In undertaking the first flight in September 1964 under pressure to do so before the General Election on the 16th October, there were concerns over the engine's reliability, and Beamont did so with considerable professional reservations. In fact, the next test flight did not take place until the end of the year, and further trials encountered problems with the undercarriage, even to the point where on one occasion the observer in the rear seat was offered the option of ejecting before landing.

Roland Beamont's summary expresses regret that such a potentially superb aircraft should have been terminated, though admitting it was "very ambitious". Against this are interview extracts with Dennis Healey (then Chancellor of the Exchequer) and Roy Jenkins (Minister of Aviation at the time of cancellation) who indicated that the programme delays meant the aircraft was far behind the in-service target date, with development cost forecasts having tripled – with no assurance of not escalating further, and prospective future sales having been undermined by the Australian Government choosing the American F1-11.

A coda in the story was the decision to destroy all the jigs and semi-assembled aircraft. Both the Ministers denied any responsibility. But there should be no mystery: once the Treasury had secured the decision to cancel, it would be a natural triumphal stipulation at official level that "not another penny" should be spent beyond flogging off the remaining bits for scrap.

[6] Ray Brown, at the time with a record of having built up Racal Electronics from a component supplier in the 50s to a significant systems company, was brought in to the Ministry of Defence to head up the new Defence Sales organisation and add some entrepreneurial flair. His blunt and direct style clashed with the prevailing ethos and idiom. One recollection is a message from Willie Morris, then Ambassador to Saudi Arabia, "We cannot afford that bull in this china shop," following Ray's blunt expressions during an earlier visit. Yet he was a humane and genuine personality, and for several years held an annual lunch for senior Whitehall officials and industrialists – always a delight, and sparking lively controversy. If people are judged by those in whom they choose to confide, in contrast to the sycophants and crawlers hanging onto Mrs Thatcher's skirts, Ray picked out Ernie Harrison* at an early stage.

[7] Arnold Hall, given the spread of Hawker Siddeley activities, remained a continuing contact from aviation through to overseas projects and engineering – another personality who was warmer beneath an austere countenance.

VIGNETTES

DUNCAN SANDYS

It ever there was a Minister who warranted the title of "man of myth" it was Duncan Sandys, and a round robin to glean anecdotes from officials who worked for him would yield a bumper harvest.

A first official contact was indirect. While an Assistant Principal in Airports Division, I had been set the task of researching what scope there was in planning agreements and past policy for the expansion of Heathrow – another typical trainee job as the archives were dragged out and piled in the office, leaving little space to do anything else. Historically the decision to develop Heathrow as London's main airport was taken during the height of the war in 1942 – 43, including the cross-parallel runway layout, which ever since has meant an increasingly congested Central Area. And, in fact, a strip of land north of the "Old Bath Road" – the A4 – had originally been reserved for another runway, but was subsequently released for development. In the course of this research, Duncan Sandys, a junior Minister in the Air Ministry had been involved, and had addressed some suggestion in a minute to Churchill, to receive an extremely curt comment in reply – all the more intriguing since he was Churchill's son-in-law at the time.

The next contact was when Secretary of a group identifying sites for a prospective heliport in London – one of the fantasies of successive Ministers was a childlike dream that helicopters could transform London's commuting problems. The group contained permanent officials of the LCC, and as the selection of sites was narrowed down, there was a request from the Corporation for a meeting with the Minister. I was one of the team of officials who had a short briefing session on the likely LCC concerns – not inconsiderable given the racket that large helicopters like the Rotodyne would have brought to neighbouring communities. When the LCC delegation arrived, they asked for the meeting to be without officials, so we were dismissed – barely 10 minutes in the presence. But the next direct meeting was a few years later at the Farnborough Air Show when he was Commonwealth Secretary – Julian Amery treated these as aerospace durbars, and the President's Tent took on the aura of a Viceregal Pavilion – and all VIPs had to be greeted and glad-handed around. On one of my turns for the first handshake, up came Duncan Sandys with the greeting, "Hello. Mr Benjamin". Personal evidence of his remarkable mnemonic system for remembering faces – confirmed by checks with other officials.

Consistent with Julian's vision of Farnborough Air Show week as an assemblage of the aerospace Rajahs from around the globe, each VIP was accorded a different scale of entertainment corresponding to the number of gun salutes of the Raj – from the routine "call" in the office, to lunches in the week of varying degrees of formality, to a "show" with dinner afterwards for the top ranks. On this occasion, we only heard at the end of the previous weekend that an Australian delegation were coming – at that time, Britain still had pretensions to a missile and space-launching capability, of which Blue Streak was the last emblematic erection, which meant a continuing use for the Woomera test facilities, and continuing dispute with the Australian Government over the terms for doing so.

This put the Australian delegation in the top-salutes bracket. But, coming so late, the more popular range of theatrical entertainments – or those not already seen – had been booked. I told Julian that the options were extremely thin and suggested that some other form of evening entertainment might be in order. He suggested that I was not being imaginative enough, so he flicked to the Times' entertainment page. Within seconds he had spotted the Aldwych, the London base of the RSC at that time, showing Peter Brooks' production of *Marat/Sade*. "There you are," said Julian. "Marat – French Revolution – it must be good!" Any query that such an exotic piece may not have been quite appropriate to an antipodean delegation not accustomed to avant-garde theatre was brushed aside. So seats were booked, and Duncan Sandys – the Commonwealth Secretary – was invited to join the party, which he accepted.

The play, based on the premise of the Marquis de Sade having produced a drama on the death of Marat for performance by inmates of the lunatic asylum in which he had been confined, had nothing comparable to a linear plot. But an intriguing orchestration between twitching bodies and pandemonium, remarkable in hindsight for the young Glenda Jackson lashing the naked torso of an inmate with her tresses. Came the interval, as the party repaired to the balcony VIP suite for the "entr'acte" champagne and sandwiches, entering under the attentive obsequies of the manager, Sandys commented in a stentorian voice, "This is the worst play I have ever seen." The climax of the drama came when the play-within-a-play was over, and the inmates, deprived of their acting roles, reverted to bedlam. A breathtaking final few seconds of theatre, but, Julian had to admit, not ideal fare.

But the Sandys "myth" survived by recollections of many officials who worked for him – just a couple of examples from this subterranean pool of gossip:

– He was wont to work in the office to the early hours of the morning, especially when there was some crisis such as cancelling manned fighters, or rationalising the aircraft industry, and this demanded one of the Private Office staff staying on to deal with any actions that he wished to be followed up the next day. At some time around 3 a.m., as the Minister's suite were the only lights on in Shell Mex House, Sandys pressed the call button for the private secretary, and as the latter put his head around the door, he barked, "Coffee."

For some reason the tea/coffee equipment had been locked away. But as a young man keen to show initiative, the private secretary recalled that there was an all-night coffee stall open near the Embankment (then Charing Cross) Underground Station. Making his way along the darkened corridors, switching on lights as he went, awakening the Security staff to open the entrance, with instructions to keep it open for his return, jogging 300 yards along the Strand, turning left down Villiers Street to run downhill past the mainline Station until reaching the coffee stall, ordering a cup and carrying it back as rapidly as consistent with not spilling too much, he finally put it on Sandys' desk. Taking a preoccupied sip, he snorted, "Cold!"

– Like most other Ministers, he insisted upon a "private" telephone on his desk that did not go through his Private Office. In the course of a very tetchy meeting, where officials were no doubt tactfully pointing out that there were alternative courses without the same disadvantages to the one on which he was set, his "private" phone rang. Taking it up, "Call back" was his reply as he slammed it down. The meeting continued, but two minutes later, the "private"' phone rang again. Another curt "Call back".

Just as the meeting was getting underway again, sure enough the "private" phone rang yet again. This time it was picked up and slammed down without comment. But the private secretary was given a sharp instruction to get the line disconnected for the course of the meeting. Since the line was outside the Department's own switchboard, this entailed calling up the main BT exchange. Before this exercise could be completed, the "private" line rang again.

This time. No messing. Sandys strode across the room, pulled the telephone connections out of the wall, and returned to continue the meeting.

– That he had an impressive aura is borne out by the dispute over BOAC's order for VC10s: long after he had left the Ministry of Aviation, the airline wanted to cancel, or at least drastically reduce, its order in preference for the Boeing 707, and argued that they had been "directed" to buy the British aircraft. Researching the records for any evidence of a directive, the occasion when this might have occurred was at a meeting between Duncan Sandys and Sir Matthew Slattery, then BOAC's Chairman. There was nothing in the minutes to suggest even a reference, leave alone an explicit quotation, to support the airline's claim. When challenged, the Private Secretary in attendance at the meeting responded, "It was all done by atmosphere."

Whatever history may judge, his main political function appeared to be the shovel whenever there were especially difficult stables to be cleared out – the 1957 Defence Review, which saw a major downsizing and the end of National Service, the phasing out of manned-fighters – later reversed with the elevation of the Lightning from a research aircraft to an RAF front-line interceptor – or rationalising the aircraft industry, all roles demanding myopic fixation of purpose coupled with absolute imperviousness to counter argument. This may have been effective when there was an Augean stables to be cleared out but could be less so in other cases. Typically, the views of those who worked for him reflected this dichotomy.

He was also responsible, more than any other Minister, for the convention of submissions not exceeding two pages. In his case the rule was absolute. He would not countenance more than two pages, and that was it. Consequently his staff had to vet and précis every document to get it into the prescribed length.

Perhaps, however, his most permanent legacy is in the furnishing of Ministers' offices. Traditionally, Ministers worked behind desks of sombre Victorian or Edwardian vintage with separate conference tables. Duncan Sandys dispensed with the desk and used the table as a work surface with a bureau beside him carrying telephones, with stationery and other drawers. Julian Amery, who viewed Sandys as a model, insisted upon the same arrangement. When Roy Jenkins took over from Amery, he was attracted by this layout, and, as legend has it, took this preference with him on his subsequent Ministerial career. And, whether through laziness or preference, this layout has gained further supporters over the years.

PETER THORNEYCROFT

Peter Thorneycroft arrived as Minister of Aviation after earlier having resigned as Chancellor of the Exchequer. So twitching ambition, so often the preoccupation of politicians, was dormant. Yet he enjoyed a special relationship with Harold Macmillan; indeed, some regard the continued existence of the Ministry as a pretext to keep Peter involved in major issues, but with time to spare whenever the Prime Minister wanted an experienced and steady hand to deal with tricky issues between Departments. Or special jobs: he was selected to make the round of calls on the Commonwealth "east of Sri Lanka" to sell the prospects of Britain joining the European Community. But with his seasoned judgment, a sharp mind, relaxed wit, even temperament, and genuine humanity – despite a back complaint that required him to be trussed-up for set-piece Parliamentary debates, Peter was real fun to work with. Out of a few pocketfuls of recollections, just a couple of examples will illustrate his personal style.

Good for Mr Howell

A short summary of the Departmental machinery to approve expenditure would liken it to a long ladder – the ascent began as a functional Division or Research Establishment evolved proposals according to their future programme needs, checking these against their potential budget resources; the case would then be put to the Finance Division; out of this exchange would come a daft R&D Board submission, which after another round of checking with interested divisions would be submitted to the Board; and the Board's recommendations put to the Minister for approval.

The R&D Board was traditionally chaired by the Controller of Aircraft, with a galaxy of top officials, the Chief Scientist, Heads of the R&D Establishments – such as the Royal Aircraft Establishment at Farnborough and the Royal Radar Establishment at Malvern, senior representatives of RAF, Navy and Army etc, most of whom would have had minions involved in preparing the case during its progress. By the time a proposal had negotiated this snakes and ladders, the file was usually a couple of inches thick, with a few dozen "Enclosures" as variations of the paper evolved – all numbered in sequence, and several score more comments on the "Minutes" side of the file inside the left cover – all numbered in sequence.

On arriving with the Minister, the top "Enclosure" would be the R&D Board paper and recommendations, with a summary and comments on the left signed by the Division Head, or even Permanent Secretary if the scale of the case warranted. These were routinely put into the Minister's overnight box, in the expectation that, given this weight of deliberation, it would be returned the following morning with a dutiful "approved" and the Minister's signature or initials – a bold "PT" in Peter's case.

An early example was a plan to extend the helicopter proving area at Boscombe Down, the military aircraft flight test centre, involving new investment of a couple of million pounds. This submission came out of the overnight box with Peter's comment, "I endorse Mr Howell's proposal at Minute 4." Mr Howell was a junior Higher Executive Officer at Boscombe Down who had argued at a very early stage that there was an existing area of hard-standing that could be upgraded to do the job for less than £200,000. Despite officials' consternation and remonstrations, Peter, with a wry smile, firmly stood his ground.

Moral: Never let a good Minister have the complete file.

Go to Work on an Egg

At the other extreme, on a visit to Paris to meet M. Buron, the French Minister responsible during the early evolution of the Concorde, Peter, and I as duty private secretary, stayed at the "GB" – the Grande Bretagne – commonly used by Ministers because of its proximity to our Embassy. Obviously feeling a bit peckish, he ordered a poached egg for breakfast. Okay, it was a fairly expensive poached egg, as poached eggs go. But the Department refused to reimburse this cost on the grounds that it was more than the standard continental breakfast – since the private secretary was responsible for paying the bills, the shortfall would come out of my pocket. After five months of wrangling, the cost of which must have exceeded many scores of poached eggs, the Department finally gave way. I made a light-hearted aside to Peter when the saga was over, to be greeted with one of the very rare moments of annoyance. He must have mentioned this to Henry Hardman*, then Permanent Secretary, since I was subsequently taken aside and told gently that it was viewed as bad form to shop the Department.

Discretion

At a time when it was regarded as not insane to worry about those UK industries that still had a prospect of retaining a leading world position, close interest was taken in any moves involving co-operation between aerospace companies elsewhere in Europe. Peter was due to meet Herr Strauss, the German Defence Minister. The brief that came forward covered a raft of topics – the current position on jockeying NATO requirements, areas where there were suspicions that the Germans and French were getting together, potential collaboration between British and German companies, and so on. When officials had assembled for the briefing session, Peter flicked through the brief, remarking, "An extremely capable Minister can probably master three topics per meeting. I'm only average and can't manage more than two. Which are the two most

57

important? And I'll do my best." And sure enough, he played a good hand on these two points at the meeting, deferring any queries outside the chosen topics.

Commenting privately, he said that in the British system, political colleagues were brought up on a fodder of facile parliamentary exchanges, internal Party wrangling, arguing simplicities in electoral propaganda and were simply not trained to handle real issues. These were invariably complex, and in confronting opposite numbers from other countries, British politicians were invariably up against counterparts who could have been dealing with the topic for years. Discretion was always the better part of valour.

Other Titbits

But he was always a source of revealing asides, such as, "A good MP is one who will tell their constituents honestly that a complaint cannot stand up without putting it to a Minister in the sure knowledge of having it turned down." "Don't be surprised that Ministers always pay attention to cases involving individuals and small sums of expenditure," these always attract the greatest public attention.

You've Got Problems

A dominant personality on the "supply-side" of the Ministry of Aviation was Dennis Haviland, a curt Pooh-Bah who was obsessively focused on activities in his patch – a not uncommon experience was for him to accost officials in a lift or in the corridor and give them a sharp instruction irrespective of whether the official had any responsibility for the topic, leaving the official to sort out who in the Department should be dealing with it.

One morning, he barged through the Private Office and confronted Peter in extreme agitation, "Minister, we've got a serious problem..." – presumably a wing or something had dropped off one of the stream of Cold War Dinky Toys that were under development. Before he could say any more, Peter cut him short, "You've got problems. I've got problems. The Liberals have just won a Conservative marginal. And I'm in a marginal seat." (Eric Lubbock having the previous day won Orpington in the first Liberal by-election success for decades. While Peter's seat was Monmouth.)

He also had a charmingly chaotic domestic existence to which the Office had to adapt. Typically, he and his wife usually had their summer holidays on Capri. On one occasion, in the midst of the turmoil of clearing up urgent submissions, approvals and correspondence before he left on holiday, he remarked that Carla, his wife, was leaving that day to go on ahead to Capri but had some extra cases, and he asked if we could help to sort her through the airport. I was deputed, and he gave me a signed blank cheque to cover any excess baggage charges. Elphick, his driver – a stocky cheerful East-Londoner – and I turned up at his house to be greeted by a flustered Carla saying that there were just a few extra suitcases in the study, and asked us to load them into the car. There were four cases, but each so heavy that neither of us could lift them up, or could do so only at the risk of the a hernia or the handles coming off. Seeing our predicament, Carla explained that she had never got around to cataloguing the backlog of Peter's newspaper clippings and wanted to make a start during the holiday. Between us Elphick and I lugged them into the boot and unlugged them at the airport check-in. The excess baggage charge ran to several hundred quid – far beyond the customary transaction of a junior civil servant, to which Peter gave a resigned nod when told.

His farewell quip as, after Macmillan's "Night of the Long Knives" in July 1962, he packed up to take over from Harold Watkinson at Defence, was that the process had been so cursory that had the messenger walked in with a cup of coffee, he would have been appointed Foreign Secretary. After his spell at the Ministry of Defence, he retired from active politics, except for a spell at the dizzy heights of Chairman of the Conservative Party. But informal contacts continued intermittently right up to his time as Chairman of Pirelli UK – a titular activity that he very obviously enjoyed – and I was lucky enough to see him again at several of their functions. And I always enjoyed reminding him of treaties to develop joint projects with the French with no break clause.

JULIAN AMERY

To attempt any fair remembrance of Julian from a present perspective demands a heroic exercise of Prospero's plea to cast the mind into "the dark backward". And for myself a childhood conditioning of sceptical distance from the mores of the "ruling elite" was never more handy. With a father (Leo) a notable high Tory of the "Empire is good for you" school, and a member of Churchill's war administration – notable in legend for his call in 1940 to Neville Chamberlain, "In the name of God, go"; an elder brother convicted for high treason; and married to Catharine Macmillan, the psychological goulash of his family domain could only be guessed. But a more concentrated political upbringing could not be imagined, with stories of the young Julian assiduously going through *The Times* on the train journey to prep school. Still, "he had done something in the war", a phrase that was in common usage at the time for tolerance of all manner of vagaries.

As a Minister, however, he carried an extraordinary baggage of self-expectation, very different from his predecessor, Peter Thorneycroft. The Ministry of Aviation, without a formal seat at Cabinet, suited Peter and Macmillan in providing the Prime Minister with easy access to an experienced pragmatic colleague on tricky issues. For Julian, frustratingly, the seat was tantalisingly on the edge of real influence, but one where he had relatively little clout.

Initially as the Assistant Private Secretary, Julian's first impact was his tiresome, and for the functioning of the Department frustrating, daily regime: coming into the office at any time between 10-11 a.m., there was always a rush to get any "approvals" or "actions" in the overnight box around to those officials responsible, and he was wont to stay on in the office until 8:30 p.m., or later, requiring some Private Office staff and a typist to stay on.

His natural pace was always to put-off actions and decisions until the last minute, with its attendant disruption of meetings demanded at a half-hour's notice as officials trekked in from offices dispersed around a three-mile area of London.[i] When it came to Parliamentary speeches, this quirk was taken to an extreme: he would defer preparation of his speech until lunch hour and ordered a buffet from "Joe's", the office nickname for Fortnum and Mason, such as smoked salmon/caviar/game pie and claret. And he would sit munching while a secretary took pages to be typed on special 5"x8" sheets as they were completed. When pressed on this practice, his response was that he had seen too many political careers ruined by an error at the dispatch box, and he wanted to be sure that what he said was in tune with the preoccupations of the day. But it meant that his Ministerial speeches were invariably stilted and dull.

But this ran a risk of cutting things fine. On one occasion, as he was due to open a debate after "Questions" at 3 p.m., only half the speech had been typed by the time he had to leave the Ministry's office in the Strand, and a private secretary was to follow with the rest when it was typed. Encountering a traffic jam in Trafalgar Square, the secretary had to leg it down Whitehall to the "back of the Chair" in the Commons, where a distraught Anthony Royle,[i] his Parliamentary Private Secretary, was panicking to take the rest of the speech into the Chamber where the Minister was on his feet and on the last page of his available script.

Julian, at heart, had no real interest in the Department, and viewed the

---

[i] Anthony Royle was granted a life-peerage as Baron Fanshaw of Richmond.

multitude of projects being pursued as imperial totems not to be surrendered. Hence, any controversy turned into a dogged defence of ploughing on. Obstinacy may have been a noble virtue in negotiating with Archbishop Makarios over the leases of Britain's Cyprus bases, but where there were continuous shifts in "operational" demands and equally insistent pressures on public expenditure, a rather more adroit readiness to trade-off might have yielded better results. Consequently, on his attendance at Cabinet, or at Defence and other Committees, when invariably cancellation, or truncation, of programmes was on the agenda, he would put in one of his "dogged" performances, and equally invariably lost the argument. On return to the office, his own account was in the vein of having won concessions or forestalled a decision, and our golden rule was the supreme, "Always wait for the minutes." And occasionally he would be emboldened to challenge the recorded outcome with sulky exchanges with Ian Bancroft*, then Cabinet Secretary.

He, of course, had only the vaguest notion of what the bits sticking out of aircraft fuselages actually did,[2] and saw his own significance in a much wider political, if not global, context. Every Minister has the dilemma of handling the Press. At the time any quality journal had experienced aerospace correspondents, since the progress, or more frequently lack of progress, on a very extensive range of projects was barely out of the news. And Julian's approach was too blatantly self-exploitive for a corps of journalists well versed in sussing out the truth behind the proclaimed triumphs. Yet again, his style was counterproductive.

This is not to discount Julian's other attributes – a fluency in French, with a host of contacts across the Channel, and enough German to survive sitting through *The Ring*. A vast knowledge of political backstairs chitchat, an interest in other countries' political history, slogging out a biography of Joseph Chamberlain, and an authoritative interest in Persian miniatures. It was unfortunate that his Parliamentary performances were often so stilted by elaborate preparation because he could be a light-hearted raconteur with a fund of reminiscences about Churchill. But sadly afflicted by a growing dependency on the bottle.

By special dispensation he had obtained approval to see all incoming Foreign Office telegrams, which arrived daily in thick bundles that he assiduously went through. We had an arrangement with the FCO private office to pass on any comments that he made, not in any expectation that the Foreign Office would act on them, but to warn them that the point might arise as a result of Julian's private contacts with the Prime Minister and others. There was an enormous volume of these, and flitting through in idle moments, one stuck in memory, "Embassy on fire [garbled group]" from Jakarta, as a hangover from Britain having aligned herself with the Dutch in what is still regarded as the country's struggle for independence.

A Soviet Escapade

Only a matter of months after Julian's arrival, it was some relief to be moved from the Assistant Private Secretary seat into an active Division, which included in its functions the Department's interest in the control of strategic technology to the Soviet Union and its allies. When an invitation was received from the Soviet Government for a formal Ministry of Aviation visit, the chores of organising it was passed to my Branch. During the most frozen period of the Cold War, the chance to glean information on the real level of Soviet technology was a perennial concern, while at the same time avoiding any leakage of know-how where British industry was in the lead. But Julian's vision was more in the tradition of Francis Younghusband's expedition into the Pamirs during the Great Game: he insisted on an itinerary that took in Leningrad, Kiev, Tbilisi, Tashkent, Samarkand and Bokhara; and a delegation with the elite of "industry" – including Arnold Hall* (Hawker Siddeley), Denning Pearson* (Rolls-Royce), "Russ" Russell (BAC's design chief on Concorde), and a top Ministry team including Robert Cockburn* (Chief Scientist), Morien Morgan* (Controller of Aircraft), Dennis Haviland (Deputy Secretary, Industry), James Lighthill (Director, Farnborough), Air Marshal Chris Hartley* (whose appointment as Vice Chief was announced in the course of the visit), with Catherine Amery, Anthony Royle and his wife, Shirley.

Having spent most of the available time over several months sorting all this out, including special security briefing for delegation members – basically, it should be assumed that everyone was being bugged all the time, just a couple of days before departure, Ray Hibbert, who had taken over as Principal Private Secretary, suffered a stroke. And as a stopgap, while the Department sorted out a successor, I was deputed to take his place. This required a rapid shopping expedition to get kitted out for the climatic diversity of the trip, and attending final briefings on intelligence targets. But to complete the caravanserai, Julian insisted on copious reserves of three dozen crates of Scotch, three dozen of champagne, and a couple of dozen each of brandy and gin.[3] And to convey the whole expedition required a special aircraft to be chartered from BEA.

Inevitably, there were last-minute briefing documents, which in view of their "Secret" classification where carefully tagged together with string to make sure none went astray, to be issued and collected on the flight. And as bag carrier of all such documents, I went through the formalities of a "diplomatic courier" to negotiate customs controls.

The only fair way to depict this extraordinary expedition is by flashback:

– as Catherine Amery was making herself up for the opening Soviet reception, she complained that the lights were too dim. On returning to the hotel after the next day's programme, the room was festooned with lights.

– Julian's meeting with the British Ambassador, Humphrey Trevelyan* – the most elevated transfer from the old Indian Civil Service, but who had also been Ambassador in Cairo during the Suez Crisis – had what is technically termed "a certain frisson" in view of Amery's public pronouncements and whatever he had been up to behind the scenes.

– a Chekovian Sunday on old-man Tupolev's houseboat on the Moscow canals with his family and attendants in white-smocks. An engagingly non-political character who joked about the number of times he had been sent to prison, "but every time they wanted a new aircraft, they had to let me out."

– Kiev boasted a major aero-engine plant, and arriving in time for a formal lunch before touring the factory, a 20-stone Russian pulled Denning Pearson to the table, and within a minute had forced nine toasts in vodka down his throat. And, with the plant's chief designer taking the seat on the other side of Sir Denning, plied him with technical questions for the rest of the lunch. Since Denning's knowledge of turbine-blade geometry was comparable to Julian's mastery of the aspect ratio of the TSR 2, we could watch confident that no technological mysteries were being revealed.

Kiev also provided the most spectacular dinner of the visit, on a houseboat sailing down the Kneiper Delta, with successive courses being delivered by immaculately timed boats setting out from the banks. And the hardest drinking dinner on another evening, as our Air Attaché, an earnest Air Commodore, was passed a Mickey Finn, and after being put to bed muttering, "I must report this to the Embassy" was next visible in the early hours roaming the corridors in his underwear looking for a functioning telephone. If the local peppered vodka was powerful stuff for British palates, the locals seemed just as vulnerable to the less familiar powers of malt whisky, and some members of the British delegation were spotted dragging a couple of their hosts to their waiting official cars.

– Tbilisi, in Georgia, was a much less "Cold War" setting. A visit to the museum was an essential part of any official visit. The trouble was that its entire wall space was given over to images of St George. Julian enquired of the curator whether his collection included any Persian miniatures since over the centuries invaders and merchants must have carried many through the country. "Cellars full" was the response, with the apology that "the authorities" only permitted icons of St George to be displayed. So Julian disappeared into the basement with the curator, and the rest of the delegation were left to show an interest in infinite repetition. One observant member noticed, however, that the next call on the itinerary was "Visit to Brandy Factory". By common assent this seemed to hold out more potential, as well as the excuse that we were sticking more closely to the timetable.

So, leaving the Minister's car to follow, the delegation moved on to inspect rows of vats. The final scene was in the Director's office where everyone was seated with fourteen glasses in front of them, and, as discerning foreigners, we were invited to sample the product. So we went in fourteen sips from raw alcohol to Napoleon vintage: each sip was expected to be spat into a conveniently placed container, but inevitably several, especially among the riper vintages, were swallowed. Julian arrived just as this ritual had been completed and insisted on going through it again. So another fourteen sips all round.

Returning to the hotel to prepare for the formal Georgian government dinner, no one was entirely steady. And there followed a nightmare sequence as the delegation's simultaneous efforts to have a bath strained the hotel's plumbing – turning on a tap in one room had no effect, but triggered a gush of water into the bath three rooms down the corridor. Still, the delegation turned up late, but still flushed, for the dinner in a pavilion atop a hill overlooking the town. There were several courses, each served with Georgian wine, apparently among the choicest in Russia. The trouble was that it was served in hunting horns, which cannot be put down unless emptied. Then came the time for toasts, and every member of the delegation, alternating with one of our hosts, had to propose a toast – with vodka. The search for subjects became desperate, but James Lighthill distinguished himself by proposing his in Russian (he had bought a Gem dictionary at the airport and began by rehearsing the phonetics with an interpreter on the flight to Moscow). Finally, come Julian's turn, and swaying in delivery, he blathered on about Anglo-Russian relations, proclaimed his toast, everyone stood up and dutifully echoed his words, and downed their vodkas. As we slumping down, Julian turned and hurled his glass into the fireplace. The rest of the delegation, not wanting to leave the Minister isolated, followed suit, with the odd one being a few seconds late. After this shattering gesture, the delegation sat down to total silence. Not apparently shock at the destruction of the best plate-glass in Georgia, but, as one of the Russian interpreters leaned over and whispered to Julian, "That is a Czarist custom."

Then a band struck up, joined by local folk dancers – a style characterised by rapid deft foot movements. And the delegation were encouraged to join in. This was not the forte of the upper echelons of the British aircraft industry. So, out of consideration, the music turned to simpler waltzes and foxtrots. With the shortage of female partners, there were some odd pairings as Dennis Haviland waltzed with Arnold Hall. Our air attaché offered to teach our hosts Scottish dancing if they taught him Russian dancing: all went swimmingly until he pulled an Achilles tendon attempting a Cossack leap. He was taken to the local infirmary, while the rest of the delegation reeled into the convoy of cars as dawn rose.

– Tashkent was the staging point for the expedition to Samarkand and Bokhara. Again, a high-profile reception and dinner at the hotel for the Minister to meet local and party dignitaries. And Julian was once more embarrassingly late. I knocked firmly on the door of his suite, and heard a loud, "Come in." On entering, one immediately faced the lavatory, whose door was open and Catherine Amery seated with knickers down. I immediately went into the suite and, hiding fairly mixed emotions, confronted the Minister in as stern a voice as could be managed that his laggardness was far beyond any courteous excuse. And then left doggedly avoiding a glance at the loo. Julian actually turned up at the reception remarkably quickly thereafter.

The tours of Samarkand and Bokhara were disappointing, with our air attaché nobly hobbling a couple of hundred yards behind, as the historic buildings had been allowed to decay, with only a few tiles suggesting what they might have been in their prime. More spectacular were the transport arrangements. At Tashkent, those in the delegation interested in making the tour boarded two small Dakota-type VIP aircraft: the interiors were equipped with a sofa, two armchairs with a table between, and several other obviously temporary seats. Those in the armchairs facing forwards couldn't afford to relax, since in the centre of each table was a large bowl of flowers, which, on even the most primitive understanding of the physics of motion, were bound to slide towards the incumbent's lap on takeoff. As indeed they did. But the return journey was even more eventful. Leaving as the sun set, the delegation's two aircraft were diverted owing to bad weather at Tashkent. When the aircraft had stopped at the diversion airfield, the passengers were allowed out, but into total darkness – no runway lights, terminal buildings, or service facilities were visible. Except for a spectacular thunderstorm over Tashkent. Within minutes a couple of trucks crammed full of heavily armed troops arrived, and the only conclusion was that we had been diverted to a high-security military facility involved in missile/rocketry development.

When clearance came for the renewed return journey to Tashkent, one of the aircraft turned out to have a fault. So the delegation was crammed into the second, where there were not enough seats, and half the company had to sit on the floor. As the aircraft trundled along the runway, now thankfully lighted, it did nothing for confidence to see the old aviation-salts checking the second-hand of their watches since the plane must have been close to, if not well beyond, its maximum payload. But the flight was completed with passengers alternating in taking available seats to avoid cramp.

– In retrospect, the precise dates of this visit can be readily triangulated: the final farewell ceremony was delayed as the Russian Minister was held up by the celebrations for the successful mission of Ms Valentina Tereshkova, the first woman in space – 16th June 1963. Within a few days of arrival in Moscow, on the 5th of June, John Profumo had formally resigned after his initial "no impropriety whatsoever" denial when the scandal had broken in March. Julian had written him a personal note that he was handing over to the hotel clerk for dispatch when I reclaimed it, pointing out that whatever he might have said would be better conveyed by diplomatic bag than offered as a free gift to Soviet propaganda. Thirdly, after leaving Moscow, the next port of call was Paris, for the Air Show. Among those meeting us was Donald Grant, the Department's Press Officer: a normally ruddy cheery character, but quite ashen. After the obvious remark that he looked like I felt, he said that he had been under massive pressure, what with the Profumo press frenzy raging, to suppress disclosure that a BEA stewardess had found a "Secret" document tucked into a seat pocket in Moscow on the aircraft that the delegation had chartered – typical of the aerospace elite to detach a paper that had been meticulously tied to prevent just this happening. (In the subsequent inquiry, the document turned out to be no more than an intelligence report on a Soviet Air Show a couple of years earlier, and rightly should have been declassified).

Behind the public furore, the Cold War context of the visit and the sense of being permanently monitored conditioned one for a few days thereafter to carry on speaking in hushed tones. While at the security debriefing, Air Marshall Chris Hartley recounted how, according to the best espionage practice, he had made a point of leaning over workbenches at the various plants we visited, picking up metal filings on his palms, and then first distributing them in different pockets, and then into the socks in his suitcase that had been selected with a private colour code. It turned out on arrival in London that his clothes had been vacuumed of any trace of metal.

After the intelligence debriefing, and returning to my branch my first aim was to finish the notes and admin for the visit, and then sleep for two days. But instead I was summoned to Sam (Sir Richard) Way*, the Permanent Secretary, to be told that Julian had obstinately refused to accept other candidates for Private Secretary, and was sticking out for me. And put in a tone that suggested I had better accept. When I asked Julian subsequently why he had taken this line, his response was, "Anyone who sees Catherine in that condition and can pass it off with such aplomb must have all the attributes of the perfect Private Secretary."

Other Grand Tours

Other occasional Vice-regal tours followed: the precise aerospace pretext was not always blindingly obvious, usually confined to the fact that the country had purchased British aircraft, usually Hunters and Canberras, and to explore prospects for collaboration – the sheer number of workshop servicing plants visited was extraordinary. The most notable was to Peru and Mexico, with similar zany episodes. Just examples:

– in Peru, our accompanying Air Marshal had a heart attack in the course of our meeting with the Chief of the Peruvian Air Force. Consternation. And he was immediately rushed into an adjoining room complete with luxurious four-poster bed to await medical attention.

– in Cuzco, at the local government dinner, the mayor offered Julian a virgin each for the delegation: to which Julian, ever the one for the quick counter, responded that knowing the reputation of Peruvian men, he doubted whether there were any. There was professed outrage in the delegation when I reported this exchange, though at 8000 feet above sea level, and half the delegation dependent on puffs of oxygen to keep going, had this offer been taken up our invalid-list would have soared.

– in Acapulco, Ivor Morris, a senior official with most of his career in the civil aviation area, but noted for fiddling indeterminately with drafts and endlessly balancing the presentation of issues, who probably had not done anything approaching exercise for years, wrestled for more than three hours to land a six-foot barracuda. A close call whether the fish or Ivor would survive.

– Julian's propensity for honing time down to microseconds of tolerance escaped any serious diplomatic consequences largely through the ingenuity of others. Ironically, the nearest his tardiness came to a gaffe was not his fault.

Peru has its own legendary hero from the earliest days of aviation: an intrepid flyer who was the first to pilot an aircraft over the Andes.

Unfortunately, the feat concluded with a fatal crash on landing. But the achievement warranted a national monument, about twice the height of the Albert Memorial. And as Minister for Aviation, laying a wreath was a natural for his programme.

For once Julian was ready on time as we left for the ceremony scheduled in his programme for 10 a.m. On arrival, there were vast phalanxes of guards of honour from the three services on three sides of the Memorial, and a celebrities' stand on the other, containing the entire Peruvian general staff and sundry political figures. And greetings seemed a shade over-formal for the occasion, and with an exchange of national anthems, various commands and parade manoeuvres, the rituals were completed.

As we wound up, I noticed that several of the guards were fainting in the heat, and remarked in sympathy to one of the senior officers present that this happened even in the more moderate British climate. His response was that such frailty was hardly surprising since they had been standing in the heat for more than three hours. It turned out that the ceremony had been timed for 9 a.m., but through some bureaucratic mix-up had been put on the Minister's schedule for an hour later.

I cornered Julian before we left and suggested that some apologies might be in order. This he did, and among the Chief of Staff's comments one caught the term "gringo" uttered in menacing terms: our Escort Officer was a blonde Texan, whose presence in the Peruvian Air Force was a quandary, but who admitted to having been a cocktail-jockey in Las Vegas as part of his pilgrimage. Anyway, it was clear that, rightly or wrongly, he was being lined up as the fall guy for having kept the entire General Staff sweltering for a couple of hours. And, as we took off from Lima at the end of the visit, one had visions of him being hauled off to be pegged-out for the vultures in the Atacama Desert.

But a couple of other overseas jaunts are worthy of special mention.

High-Tech Intelligence

At the height of the battle for being the first to introduce a supersonic airliner, when both Russia and the US were professed to be developing their alternatives to Concorde, Julian was due to be visiting the States as a guest of Negeeb Halaby, Director of the Federal Aviation Agency, when the first, carefully disguised, pictures of the Lockheed Blackbird, a high-altitude Mach-3 surveillance aircraft, were released. This was seen as an indicator of the level of US technology, and on arrival in Washington Julian requested that his delegation be allowed to view the aircraft, with the intention of calling some experts from Farnborough to join the delegation and to inspect it more closely.

All things considered, Halaby did a persuasive job on the Pentagon in getting agreement that the Minister alone would be allowed to view the aircraft. So a couple of Farnborough experts, notably Handel Davies, were summoned to meet up with the Minister at Palm Springs before the visit to Edwards Air Force Base. The trip across the US in the FAA's Jetstar with Halaby at the controls, and accompanied by Alan Boyd, Chairman of the Civil Aeronautics Board, was an entertaining saga in itself. But we duly met up at a hotel in Palm Springs. By the swimming pool surrounded by bikini-clad lovelies and elderly retirees, the experts began briefing the Minister on the 50 key features that they wanted him to observe. One of Handel Davies' quirks was a gravely voice that was incapable of being pitched low. Consequently, the basking company around the pool could hardly avoid overhearing the technical issues on which Julian was expected to focus. Having compiled the list of questions, Julian retired for a couple of hours to memorise them.

On arrival at Edwards, we had some amusement at the shock of the US Air Force staff on seeing the drawings produced by the RAF Intelligence experts from the published photographs of their new aircraft – apart from the angle of the fins, remarkably accurate as it turned out. Then Julian departed for his inspection while the rest of us had a genuinely interesting hour of presentations and discussions with burly cigar-smoking colonels on other programmes being conducted at the Base. Debriefing took place on the Jetstar as we travelled from Edwards to San Francisco, where a visit to the Polaris program office at San Diego was next on the itinerary. Again, Handel Davies' voice carried above the ambient noise so that Alan Boyd, who had accompanied Julian on his inspection of the Blackbird, could listen with a wry smile. Apparently, Julian scored 9/10, with such accounts as the size of the air intakes depicted in forearm lengths, the colour of the leading edge metal as "dirty grey", and the wing planform "like a manta ray", and so on.

A Puff of Blue Streak

A legacy of the Sandys' "non-manned" defence bias was a pile of uncompleted rocketry, but most embarrassing was Blue Streak, originally intended as a long-range missile launcher but cancelled when it finally dawned on the experts that this would require silos to be dug around the British countryside. Eventually, Britain subscribed it as the first stage of the initial European Launcher Development programme. Even so, this face-saving gesture rather depended on the damn thing working.

As the first test launch was scheduled for Woomera, in Australia, within months of a prospective General Election, Julian insisted that he should be there to witness it. And managed to gain approval to make the visit, providing he was back to take Questions when the Department was First Order, allowing some ten days. We arrived in Adelaide as the staging post to go on to Woomera, and were put up in the Governor's splendid mansion – out-Bucking Buck-house, one had a personal butler who solemnly laid out one's M&S socks, underwear and shirts.

The then incumbent was a retired General, once in charge of the British sector of Berlin, with a most charming wife and a couple of youngsters, a companion/social secretary, and occasional A.D.Cs. We were expected to dress formally every evening for dinner, and Julian got on famously sitting next to our hostess, who spoke fluent French and had a cosmopolitan outlook. When the timing of the launch, and suitability of the weather, were confirmed, we flew on to Woomera, where the facilities were robustly Australian country-style.

We took our places to witness the great moment, and there was a hush as the countdown proceeded. And with "zero", there was a puff of smoke. But nothing happened. Expectations collapsed. And a French General, technical head of the programme, had tears pouring down his cheeks. The celebratory festivities readily transformed themselves into a wake, with a typically Australian "ham and eggs" served at 3.30 in the morning.

On return to Adelaide, we were due to be moving on to Sydney and Canberra. But Julian insisted that he stayed on for the rescheduled launch: this meant rejigging the rest of the programme, while there was a hiatus for the technical post-mortem and another break in the weather. So what had originally been planned as a two-day stay in Adelaide, dragged on day by day. As a variation for the dinner placement, Julian was seated next to the lady companion. Conversation dried up over the brown Windsor soup. So he glanced across the table at one of the A.D.Cs: "And what do you make of South Australian girls, young man?" The reply came, "Well, Sir" – sip – "You see, Sir" – sip – "I'm a bit inclined the other way". In an era when "coming out" was unknown, it was impressive how everyone continued placidly sipping their brown Windsor soup.[4]

Eventually it transpired that the technical checks would take a few more days and the next possible launch date coincided with the final day before we had booked the last BOAC flight that would have got him back to London a few hours before Questions. Julian still insisted that he should be present for the launch, and a truncated programme of calls at Sydney and Canberra was rescheduled, leaving him time to be taken back to Woomera. On this option, after the launch, courtesy of an Australian Air Force aircraft, Julian would be flown to pick up the scheduled BOAC flight at Darwin. The logistics worked fine up to this point, except that Blue Streak failed to get off the ground again.

But on arriving at Singapore, there was an aircraft ground handlers strike, and all departures were delayed indefinitely. And resigning ourselves to missing the deadline for Questions, we were just settling down to some sharks fin soup when it was announced that a Quantas flight for London was just leaving. Leaving our bags on the original aircraft we rushed aboard. The flight time, with refuelling stops, would still land the Minister too late to make it on his feet in the Commons. Explaining his dilemma to the Captain, Julian offered a couple of crates of champagne if the fight could make up time. With turn-rounds at Calcutta, Delhi, Tehran and Zurich cut to twenty minutes instead of the usual forty-five, Heathrow was reached with just over an hour to go. And with the office bringing out his PQ folder, Julian was just in time even if unshaven. He also did the honest thing in coughing up for the champagne to be sent to the crew.

Bare Ruin'd Choirs

Julian showed a less resolute side when the Ferranti scandal broke. In a nutshell, for defence purchases the overhead rate for a particular plant was applied as a multiplier to ongoing costs, and the company had been discovered as knowingly having allowed a higher rate to be applied to one of two programmes being conducted at the same plant. Because of the multiplier, this was worth a handy few million pounds of unjustified payments. Julian had controversially appointed Basil (Boz) Ferranti as one of his first junior Ministers, and shirked reprimanding the company himself: it was left for Sam (Sir Richard) Way* to suggest to Sebastian Ferranti that it was a stupid company that tried to cheat its main customer.

Julian attached the highest personal value to the TSR 2 and Concorde. The former was conceived as a medium-range strike aircraft capable of a low-level supersonic dash to get below the enemy radar, fitting neatly into Julian's "world power" fantasy. It was a formidable machine, with short solid wings to stand up to the buffeting, and one could not help have considerable admiration for Roland Beamont, the chief test pilot, being prepared to take the contraption into the air. But there was a panic to get its first flight in before the General Election, and this was just achieved in September 1964. Immediately after the election, however, the project was the Treasury's first "target for tonight" and was cancelled within six months.

Julian had signed the "Concorde Treaty" during my period out of the private office, but in those early days, buoyed by the manufacturers' euphoric visions of "at least 150" aircraft sales – even though there were little more than concept designs at the time – as a further celebration before the forthcoming Election, in July there was a fabulous gastronomic tour taking in Toulouse, Carcassonne, Avignon, Biarritz and M. Jacquet's constituency north of Paris – the lobster thermidor at Biarritz airport is a flavour never recaptured despite many attempts.

With the Wilson Government's Election success, Julian put in an appearance at the debate on Concorde immediately after. Thereafter, he disappeared from the aerospace scene. I had an informal lunch with him at his Eaton Square house while he was in the wilderness, but even this had a sad undertone as one noticed obvious gaps on the wallpaper where once rare Persian miniatures had been displayed. Our last indirect contact was in 1974, when he was Minister of State at the Foreign Office, and saw the commercial assessment of Concorde that we and the French had agreed – a maximum prospect of selling no more than 32, but with 16 the likeliest. This report was signed by myself and my French opposite number. But Julian fired off a sulky minute disagreeing with "Mr Benjamin's assessment" – a persistence of fantasy, since by then even the notional airline options had collapsed. Or perhaps a symptom of a fundamental failure to adjust perceptions to shifting realities. And Julian was far from alone in this.

IMPLACABLE DRAFTING

Drafting meetings have historically been a menial civil service chore. In particular, with the convention of "not more than two pages" being the standard for reconciling pressures of time and the lowest common denominator of perceived Ministerial intellectual competence, some officials have risen to surprising heights on little more than an ability to apply the skills of doing school précis. Hours spent swapping squiggles on successive drafts have probably consumed a sizeable chunk of most Whitehall careers, so that most of these hours merge into a forgotten sump.

That one such session should stand out in memory is all the more remarkable. The occasion was the announcement that BOAC were going to reduce their orders for the VC10. This had a fraught history going back into industrial folklore. For the manufacturers, the British Aircraft Corporation – of which Vickers had been a major element – blamed the airline's vacillation for the failure to launch the V1000, in their view the superior counter to the Boeing 707/DC 8 generation of large airliners. And having swallowed support for the VC10's development on an assured order from BOAC as one of the inducements to form the BAC group, they viewed this reversal as a betrayal; all the more so, since the alleged disadvantages of the VC10 against the Boeing 707 arose from BOAC's insistence that the aircraft should have a full payload performance at

Johannesburg, a relatively high airfield, which was one of the airline's main revenue routes.

For the airline, its new Chairman, Sir Giles Guthrie saw himself as having been appointed to get rid of the "gold-plated cutlery" tradition of the old Imperial Airways, and to bring financial concerns to a more significant position in management thinking. And to have the most economically efficient aircraft was seen as key to this transformation, rather than accept the VC10, which his colleagues claimed the airline had been "directed" to take.

The compromise of siphoning off the unwanted aircraft to the RAF was seen by the industry as effectively killing all future sales prospects, and the task of finding a public form-of-words to patch over these tensions and to buy off protests from one or the other of the factions was daunting. Julian Amery, who had been known to have advocated that the order should stand, was in sulking mood, and hardly the dispassionate authority to pull off preparing a text that reconciled these differing views: the Cabinet accordingly designated the Lord Chancellor to prepare a statement.

The Department was a bit disconcerted by this move, but sent the Lord Chancellor's Office background material and a draft, against a meeting of all sides fixed for the following evening, with the Parliamentary statement planned for the day after. His office indicated that no further briefing was required, and the meeting assembled in the Lord Chancellor's suite in the House of Lord's in the darkening gloom. Guthrie and the BOAC team on one side and Sir George Edwards with the BAC contingent glowered across at each other with Julian Amery, and other departmental officials perched around in studiously non-partisan positions.

Lord Manningham Buller moved his presence to the Chair, and announced to the assembled meeting that he had been over the papers and prepared a statement that met the concerns of all sides. This was then circulated to all present, and he said that he would wait to allow everyone to study the text. After a little more time than it took to read it through once, he made a cursory, "Let's begin." And turned to the opening line of the text, after which his conduct of the meeting went –

"The first word is 'The'. This is the customary form of the definite article, so I trust there is no disagreement."

"Next. 'Government'. There are several forms of reference to the State, but this is the usual term in Parliamentary statements. No questions?"

"'has reviewed'...."

And so on, word by word through the text. The glowering animosity of the facing factions began to drain away during the first sentence. And as the meeting dragged on, particularly among the manufacturers for whom reading and writing at any speed were not natural activities, the faculties to offer any amendments waned. A few grudging changes were made, but by the end of the second page both sides had been reduced to verbal acquiescence.

By the time the process was completed, the façade of the House of Lords was dark save for the Lord Chancellor's windows. It was left that the amended text would be circulated to interested Ministers within Whitehall, and to BAC and BOAC before the statement was due at 3 p.m. This meant returning to the office with the final text to put it ready for typing immediately the following morning, and, in the interests of speed, I left a short covering note to be typed on the lines of "Following a meeting under the Lord Chancellor at.....with.....present, attached is the agreed text of the statement to be made by the Minister of Aviation". The statement was duly typed in final form and circulated in time, only for me to get a message from the Lord Chancellor's Office that he was not happy that I had not recorded the nuances underlying particular phrases.

BORE 'EM TO DEATH

Coming up to the Summer Recess in 1964, with a sure prospect of a General Election before Parliament reassembled, in what should be the dog-days of a Parliament, the Labour opposition chose as their final "day" to debate the Ferranti scandal – where the company had effectively pulled a fiddle on overhead rates assuming no cross-comparisons would be made by the Department, and creamed off a few extra million pounds. Quite a good showpiece for the dubious merits of allowing the profit motive to rule unabated, and such a sitting duck that the Leader of the Opposition, Harold Wilson, was put down to open the debate.

The Whips came up with the deflationary counter-move of having the government's reply delivered by Neil Marten, a relatively lowly Parliamentary Secretary. Neil Marten suffered, like sadly too many politicians, from a misalignment between their self-esteem and their competence. But to be pitched against the Leader of the Opposition offered the vision of a political Thermopylae where his shining rhetoric would cleave apart the stoutest opponents. So, he drafted a speech glistening with shafts of pure Conservative doctrine – whatever it was at the time – and proudly circulated it for approval.

But he had wildly missed the purpose of the exercise – to bore the

House empty. So, on a hot summer evening in Julian Amery's study, with the windows open on Eaton Square, Neil, Julian and Sam Way* went over the draft. The original five pages were laboriously expanded with dull rituals of facts, references to previous statements, PAC quotes etc, and Neil Marten's private secretary shuttled between Eaton Square and the office in his vintage Rolls-Royce carrying redrafted pages to be typed as these rolled off and returning with retyped pages to be further amended. By the end of the session, the speech had been spun out to several times its original length with not more than a dozen sentences of the original surviving.

At the debate the following day, the effect was electric. After Harold Wilson's attack on the iniquities of rampant capitalism, within minutes of Neil Marten rising to his feet, the Chamber was down to a desultory few Members.

ROY JENKINS

To recall the mixture of enthusiasm, humour, caution and clarity of mind from Roy's first Ministerial appointment is always a delight. He arrived in "Aviation" as an unknown quantity, as indeed did probably all Ministers in the first Wilson Government in the autumn of 1964 after "13 years of Tory rule". Notable for well-regarded political biographies of Dilke and Asquith and a variety of essays for the quality dailies, his only obvious "aviation" connection had been an article in *The Observer* on the BOAC/VC10 controversy, and a brief but trenchant interjection in the House of Commons debate. If not welcomed across the Department, the balance of his commentaries highlighted the inherent tension between the "manufacturing" and "operating" components of the Ministry's domain.

If understandably tentative on the "technical" aspects of the usual daily round of material, he took genuine delight in the gritty casework, bringing to these a natural capacity for exploring the raw material and background and testing the balance of argument. In sharp contrast to his predecessor. No better illustration than the oscillating status of Richard Bullock, a prickly, but otherwise amiable, senior official who was madly overcompensating for some blot on his family public-service escutcheon. Richard was prone to write extremely long submissions, despite the injunction that these should be preceded by a summary of no more than two pages.[5] Julian Amery resolutely refused – in professed dedication to his Duncan Sandys's model, but as much as probably through mental lassitude – to read these. And a series of tetchy exchanges followed with Richard binding on at the Minister's tardiness, while the Private Office insisted that he should follow the proper form like everyone else. On one occasion, the Private Office ventured a draft summary for Richard, only to be berated that it was inadequate, with the inevitable rejoinder that he had better do his work for himself. Roy, however, lapped up Richard's vast tracts.

Roy displayed his pragmatism early – a quality highly prized by officials of their political masters. On the day the General Election had been announced, Julian was scheduled to have a meeting on support of one of our "independent airlines" for traffic rights on a new route. At that time, long before the current battle of "trading slots" at airports, scheduled airline services were negotiated in an esoteric game of "freedoms" and "rights" essentially trading capacity on major routes between national flag carriers. Britain virtually alone had a string of several "private" operators – Bamberg (Eagle) and Freddie Laker being typical examples – several having built up their operations from the Berlin Airlift: their main bread-and-butter business was charter flights, but occasionally these became sufficiently successful to warrant the airline demanding the right to run regular scheduled services. The problem was that negotiating these proposed schedules with other countries invariably led to the latter demanding concessions from the "rights" already enjoyed by Britain's national carriers; the latter inevitably objected, none more forcibly than BEA. On political orientation, the Conservatives were in favour of the "free enterprise" of the private operators – the archives will disclose epic meetings with Duncan Sandys, while Labour inclined towards the "national" carriers. In this instance, the balance of argument was on the private operator, having invested to build up traffic on the route, even if it left an aggrieved BEA. But Julian Amery accepted that since it would be declared in the inter-regnum period of the Election, a decision should be deferred. Inevitably, this case was among the first in the briefing sessions for Roy when he took over. What impressed was his adeptness at grasping the essential geometry of a topic that he could not conceivably have encountered before, and a readiness to take a balanced view without any dogmatic overlays. And the case was approved in favour of the "private" operator relatively quickly.

The same penetrating approach applied to the industrial area of the Department, albeit tinged with a scepticism that previous Governments had distorted the balance of resources going into the industry on projects that had insufficient long-term prospects of adding to national performance. Roy was somewhat taken aback by the extent to which this scepticism was shared among many senior officials (and junior, if one's own views could be added to the pile) and, rather than a dog-in-the-manger allegiance to industry lobbies, their readiness to cooperate with a questioning review process. But this had barely got underway before the Concorde storm hit. No Minister in modern times has had a tougher indoctrination than landing in a major diplomatic row with the French within a week of entering Office.

Over a chance meeting in Brook's Club, where Sam Way*, our Permanent Secretary, and Roy were members, Sam reported the rumour that the Cabinet were due next day to take a draft White Paper on expenditure which would effectively be advocating cancellation of Concorde. Roy's own account[ii] is a very fair reflection of the dilemma posed for a new Minister in a seat outside the Cabinet attempting to secure a more balanced view from colleagues, most of whom had already made up their minds. In particular, where we had assurances from the Foreign Office up the official chain that they would be cautioning against a peremptory declaration that could offend the French, in Cabinet the Foreign Secretary (the short-lease Gordon Walker) failed to stand his ground. Roy had identified George Brown, then angling for an economic supremo job with the Department of Economic Affairs, as leader of the pack and went out of his way to have a private word to get over both the diplomatic consequences, but also the risk of jeopardising manoeuvre on the project itself. But obviously to no avail. After the protracted Cabinet meeting which ran well into the evening, on Roy's return to the Office we had a personal call from George Brown, presumably with the intention of mollifying. In the prevailing political vernacular, George was "extremely tired", or more exactly "exhausted out of his skull", and after some incoherent mumbles put down the phone. After which Roy commented, "The trouble with George is that he doesn't realise we've won an election, and are not still fighting one."

The underlying situation was that the Concorde Treaty, triumphantly signed by Julian Amery a couple of years earlier, had two notable omissions: the absence of any "break clause", but equally serious a lack of any definition of the project beyond "a supersonic airliner". Consequently the period since signing the Treaty had been taken up by disputes between two sets of equally arrogant aerospace design engineers to come to a compromise between the different concepts on either side of the Channel. Anticipating the General Election, officials from both governments were preparing a joint report for the next British government – in fact, the previous Conservative government, despite the unqualified terms of the Treaty, had stipulated a review "in the autumn". While "if only..." scenarios must always be hedged, the process in train would have allowed

---

[ii] *A Life at the Centre* (Macmillan)

the British side, reflecting a more sceptical political stance, to demand some "trip wires" and "review points" – as would have applied in the normal run of projects – and to persuade the French to accept a more realistic view of the project. Not necessarily a well-founded assumption, for French motivation went beyond the straightforward manufacture of a particular aircraft. But at the very least, the options for striking a more balanced view in agreement with the French would have been kept open.

The nub of the issue posed by the draft White Paper was the expressed intention to undertake "a review of prestige projects". The debate boiled down to whether some such phrase as "such as the Concorde" should be added. If, almost surely to be interpreted by the French and the industry as tantamount to a declaration of intent to cancel, the proponents argued that without some specific "meat", the Paper would not carry conviction. The reference to Concorde was retained, and reactions to its publication, which took place only five days later, entirely as predicted. As a preparatory step Roy was required to go through the ritual of informing the British manufacturers beforehand – George Edwards* (BAC) and Reginald Verdon-Smith* (Bristol Siddeley), and a meeting was sought with the French to explain the British Government's position, in the event fixed for a couple of days later.

As usual, when confronted by buffoonery on this side of the Channel, the French played their hand coolly and effectively. From the moment of the White Paper's publication, all communications – on whatever subject – with the French were met politely but with a reluctance to enter into any dialogue by inference until the Concorde issue was settled. The same applied to official contacts between project officials, where before there had been very amicable relations. So when the time came for the visit to Paris two days later, it did not require any special briefing to forewarn that it was not going to be an easy encounter.

On arrival at the airport, there was a sea of photographers and journalists on the tarmac. As a slight amendment to Roy's recollection, understandably showing some pride at the moment when a new Minister faces the first call for brute physical bravery, he did not lead alone into the throng. In fact, contrary to the usual conventions of the Private Secretary carrying up the rear with the official boxes, on this occasion there was a uniform call from the entire British delegation, "After you, Chris," even though this meant me pushing past with boxes in a crowded aisle. And, whatever the original design specification for the traditional Ministerial red box, as I led the way, it proved an ideal weapon for scything, butting, and bashing out a path for Roy to follow, though not without suffering a fair amount of jostling.

The meeting with M. Jacquet, the French Minister, was handled by the French with superb theatre. Jacquet, and his accompanying officials, with whom greetings would usually have been cheerful handshakes and good wishes – especially since everyone had enjoyed an extraordinarily four days of French hospitality just a couple of months earlier – sat in stony silence, with barely a mark of recognition. Roy's line, given the Foreign Office legal advice on the potential costs of a unilateral breach of the Treaty, was inevitably to voice the new Labour Government's scepticism, but offering a readiness to explore options. M. Jacquet's response, polite and cool, was that the French Government would await the outcome of the British Government's deliberations. And the meeting closed. Roy paid a few more courtesy calls, again received politely, but all with a clearly orchestrated non-committal tone.

Roy thought the session went as well as could be expected, and we agreed that the French had been adroit in keeping the buck on the British side of the table, so that whatever manoeuvre his colleagues wanted to pursue, the British were inevitably in the weak position of being the demander. The annals will show that immediately preceding the decisive Cabinet meeting on the White Paper, Sam Way* had predicted this in a typically punchy note to the effect that if the government's intention was to withdraw from the project, they were proceeding in a manner least likely to achieve it.

A couple of days later, the Opposition chose to raise Concorde in the Debate on the Address. This is a House of Commons convention that allows the opposition to select issues, but with no formal vote to follow. Again, from the occasional backbenchers speech, to heading up the Government's position on a major controversy within a fortnight was a demanding test for a Minister-under-instruction. Roy confronted the challenge with a mixture of temerity, confidence and anticipation, since he was reasonably sure of his briefing and his ability to cope with the Opposition spokesman, Angus Maude. In contrast to his predecessor, who always left preparing his speeches to the last conceivable moment, Roy had spent a good few solitary hours preparing his, in neat manuscript for one who wrote so fast, and this was offered to a couple of confidants – Patrick Shovelton, who was heading up the Concorde administrative unit, and myself.

As Roy recalls, the debate was, in the political context of the time, a set-piece triumph, helped by jubilant backbench Labour cheers with every counter-blow landed on a Tory spokesman. And he felt that this initial success set in train his reputation as a Commons "big hitter". Yet, his most decisive blow was the outcome of a wrangle over the draft with officials:

his original manuscript had included the obvious debating point that it was the Conservatives who had landed successive Governments with a Treaty containing no break provisions. Given the priority of re-establishing dialogue with the French – on any topic whatsoever – it had been decided as prudent to have our Embassy in Paris deliver a copy of Roy's statement to coincide with the debate to avoid any possible suggestion that the British government were trying to bounce the French again. Pat and I argued hard that to include this point would almost certainly be interpreted as reinforcing the impression of an underlying intention to withdraw from the Treaty. Roy was reluctant to forgo this knockout blow, but was eventually persuaded, and the text as typed for presentation to the French excluded this reference. In the debate itself, however, Julian Amery joined the Opposition front bench and made a woolly and rambling interjection, which allowed Roy to retort that any comments from Amery sat ill with one who had personally been the signatory of a Treaty with no break clause, to tumultuous applause from Labour ranks. So, Roy got in his debating kick-in-the-crutch without offending the French.

Roy's recollection of subsequent events is curtailed to "the Concorde affair rumbled on for several months". This skims what was a tortuous process, as the French retained a polite but firm embargo on all contacts with Britain across the spectrum, while – one suspects unbeknown to the French – the Law Officers were advising that a unilateral breach of the Treaty could land the British Government in the Hague Court, with a downside risk of having to fund the French for half the development bill should the latter proceed with the project. Several bilateral gestures were tried with other governments, notably the US, to bring them into the project, but received the same blunt refusal as earlier exchanges since the Americans declared that they were in favour of a Mach 3 development.[6] And various compromise positions were kicked around internally by the government. But against a French position that the Treaty should be upheld; none seemed likely to be a realistic way out.

By December, the impasse in relations was so ominous that in desperation a highly covert lunch took place at Brown's in London with the leading French Concorde official, M. Robert Vernaud, who blandly held to the position that they were awaiting confirmation that the UK would stand by the Treaty. And he intimated that if the British government were ready to confirm this, a "confidential" meeting could be arranged. In effect, still demanding a full retraction on any intention to go back on the terms of the Treaty. By further informal contacts, this was scheduled for Bretigny on the 11th of January. It was essential that this should take place in complete secrecy: the French did not wish to give any hint that they may be open to British options; while the British government did not want to unleash unwarranted speculation. This put the Private Office in a quandary. For to use one of the Ministry's Dove aircraft – normally employed on calibrating navigational aids, but also available for the occasional Ministerial flight – would, even in filing a flight plan, lay open the possibility of the planned visit leaking to the press.

A week before, Roy was visiting the Hawker Siddeley factory at Kingston, where the P1127 was being developed – at the time the forerunner of the prospective supersonic P1154 – since he recognised that it would be politic to see the workers and management at the plants likely to be affected by the government's review of projects. Arnold Hall* was there, and, through sheer opportunism, I inquired whether the company would be prepared to release an HS125, a very competitive business jet just gaining market share, for a demonstration flight for the Minister. He agreed, and on the due day of the Bretigny meeting, the official party took off from the company's airfield at Hatfield for a French Air Force base – the pilot only knew of the destination an hour before take-off. This subterfuge was so successful that up to today none of the published Concorde histories refers to this visit.

In the event, after a half-hour journey through country lanes, we arrived at a delightfully antique chateau for Roy's second meeting with M. Jacquet. Roy raised several caveats, which the French politely brushed aside or responded that these could be taken up when the project was underway: but this was effectively a climb-down. And, after reporting back to Cabinet on 20th January Roy informed the Commons that the government would stand by its Treaty obligations. Historians may debate whether the phrase "such as the Concorde" was the most costly four words in a Government White Paper. But little did I suspect that the project would return to haunt me again.

A distinct pleasure of being Roy's private secretary was his frankness and readiness to tolerate argument. His background had given him sensitive antennae to the range of factions – political, trade unions and, less familiar, industrial – that had to be squared to achieve a more balanced approach to the aircraft industry. With the baggage of several projects that owed more to illusions of great-powerdom than commercial or economic logic, he reckoned the change would require a cross-party consensus, and he approached Lord Plowden – at the time, the universal factotum for inquiries where a mantle of rationality was required for more complex issues – to chair an assessment group, but not before lining up Austen Albu and Aubrey Jones to represent the main political parties. By the time the concept of a review had gone through the hoops, the committee had picked up a baggage load of "the great and the good" representing science, industry and finance.

At the level of projects, however, events could not await the deliberations of this grand accumulation of wisdom. Roy went out of his way to visit the main companies where the leading projects were being pursued – Kingston, Bristol and Wharton – and met both management and local unions. It was not the over-the-top flushed rush of a Tony Benn visit, with cup of tea and "you can feel the electricity" fervour – which in fact the locals viewed with some scepticism. But rather – despite his "claret" reputation – Roy had a very effective style of down-to-earth honestly to put over the wider context of the government's dilemma – a skewed budget, pressure on the balance of trade, narrow parliamentary majority etc – while also conveying genuine concern for the impact of decisions at the factory level.

Sorting out the future of the overhanging projects, however, was against very strong Treasury headwinds, especially having screwed up the attempt to cancel Concorde. The dilemma was to marshal a sensible basis for identifying which projects were worth saving. Without too much prompting from his Private Secretary, Roy sensed that the fundamental weakness was the virtual absence of any serious international sales prospects. When he queried assembled officials which projects had the best sales prospects, the studied silence in response was its own testimony – the AW 681, the P1154, and TSR 2 all had negligible prospective markets. I volunteered privately the P1127, which then existed only as a squadron being evaluated by an international team, and – adding the caveat that it should be kept simple – could match the pockets of most air forces. And the Harrier, as the P1127 became in its developed form, was the sole survivor.

The TSR 2, coming up to the sharply rising costs of production despite not fulfilling its stipulated performance envelope – in fact, the forward development estimate at the time was infinity, was the Treasury's primary "target for tonight". Some help came from the fact that the Australian Air Force had opted for the American F1-11 after an evaluation of both aircraft. But the project carried the highest weight of potential labour cuts, and with a Labour government on a narrow majority and under the shadow of overweening trade unions, there were some tricky corners.

Roy's informal view, imparted in contemplative moments, was that the British system was particularly immune to change. Attempts at consensus were bound to become entangled in well-intentioned consultations for a harmonious transition, which would inevitably run into the sands of inertia. The only way to achieve change was "to kick the bucket", however arbitrarily. And the TSR 2, more than any of the other hangover projects represented just such a target for a well-directed boot. One recalled his reasoning when, as Chancellor of the Exchequer, he subsequently pressed successfully for withdrawal of all defence commitments "East of Suez".

To prepare the way with the manufacturers, and to mute any substantive complaints, we developed the strategy of confronting the main contractor, BAC, with the absurdity of what continuation would entail. George Edwards* was invited for an informal exchange: Roy took the line that, with the increasing costs of production coming up, and still no limit on the rising development costs, it was impossible to mount a tenable argument to other Ministers. Was there any figure of development costs above which the company would share the costs? Predictably, George Edwards refused, arguing – admittedly with some justice – that if the Ministry of Defence were prepared to relax the stipulation for a low-altitude "supersonic dash", this would significantly reduce the system demands and the uncertainties of achieving the required performance. There could have been a further argument, but this response allowed the Government to have in its hip-pocket the response that even the company could not itself foresee a limit to the escalating development costs.

In the event, there was a substantial job loss at Wharton, and, whereas traditionally production jigs and tools were stored against future needs, in the case of the TSR 2, these were unceremoniously junked to make sure that this particular phoenix would remain a pile of ashes. Ironically, for all Roy's "kick the bucket" approach, with the Jaguar programme, work on Lightnings for Saudi Arabia and Kuwait, and then subsequently the Tornado, Wharton had within a few years been restored to a level of activity higher than at the time of the TSR 2 cancellation.

As Roy admits, he especially valued an intimate "no secrets barred confidante", which accounted for him taking David Dowler, my successor, as his private secretary from Aviation to his other Ministerial appointments – an extremely rare accomplishment in Whitehall. And, unwittingly, one had perhaps filled this role as Roy's first private secretary. For there were some enjoyable personal episodes.

For example, Roy's family had a weekend retreat on the Astor's country estate at Hatley in Cambridgeshire, and on one occasion he invited my wife and I to join them. We set off with Roy and Jennifer in his, even then, antiquated Armstrong Siddeley. And chunting up the A1 the big-end, or something, gave way and we were stranded on the Hatfield bypass (that confirms the vintage of the incident). Today's private secretaries no doubt have mobile phones to rescue them in such circumstances, but no such technology then. The nearest habitation was a farmhouse just visible over several fields about a mile away. So off I went, up the embankment, over the fence, and across the fields, and awoke a comfortably dozing farmer, who kindly allowed the use of his phone to call the office to make arrangements for rescue and an alternative vehicle to complete the journey. On my return to the breakdown, soaking from the knees down, the police had already arrived, and I was taken to join the rest of the group at the local constabulary headquarters. And the weekend was completed without further incident.

It was fairly clear that Roy was quite attached to this old jalopy, which had long passed out of production. I asked Arnold Hall*, then chief executive of Hawker Siddeley, whether out of the company's archives it would be feasible to find the original design documents and repair the car. He called back a few days later to say that it would make an ideal "apprentice" job since the old designs were still apparently available. Roy was visibly pleased. But we had a modest wrangle: Arnold had said the cost could be carried as a usual training expense, while we insisted that a reasonable charge should be paid to avoid any conceivable hint of partial treatment. So a "presentable" sum was negotiated, and payment went towards the apprentices' Christmas festivities. What happened to the car eventually is not recorded, but Roy seemed genuinely appreciative of the innovative flair that had rescued an otherwise written-off banger.

My proudest innovation, however, was to steer Roy to visit all his Department's London offices. As a Minister-under-instruction, on arrival we listed the routines that he should go through. Still with a tinge of conscience from Robbie Burns' early heart attack from rushing around to meet Julian Amery's erratic calls for meetings, I was determined that Roy should be aware of the demands on officials crossing central London, and the dilapidated conditions of many of the offices. This was, and one suspects still is, a rare ritual for Ministers. But it paid surprising dividends: both from colleagues who over the years have praised Roy's good sense of personnel relations, and for Roy as others subsequently recalled meeting him on his tour of the offices.

On the occasion of Churchill's State Funeral, I had arranged a TV and buffet in the previous Ministerial suite in Shell Mex House for Roy, family and friends, giving them a vantage point directly overlooking the pier at Waterloo, where the coffin was to be transferred to the train for its final journey to Blenheim. Having been lumbered with the job of "Usher" for the aircraft industry, presumably because one knew "the great and the good", I had been on duty at St Paul's since 6 a.m. It was a perishing morning and with no form of heating in the Cathedral. Despite two pairs of underwear interleaved with paper beneath the hired morning suit, by the end of the service there was a severe risk of frostbite. When I joined Roy's group, several stiff brandies were needed to start thawing out. One of the Jenkins' brood seized my Usher's baton and bumptiously asked if he could have it. Too frozen to argue, I gracefully allowed him to have it. So, somewhere in the Jenkins' archives is what should have been my memento of the Great Event.

After a few months, and with the Concorde crisis and fate of the overhang projects largely settled, Sam Way* pressed for me to be replaced as Private Secretary. Just as he had been insistent on me doing the job for Julian, he was equally insistent that my time with Roy should be curtailed. Sam, having worked his way up through the ranks – which had contributed to make him one of the most unfussy, pragmatic and effective dispatchers of business – may genuinely have felt that too long in proximity to the political level could be counterproductive. Anyway, I was aware of several private sessions as Sam strove to persuade Roy to select someone else. Neither Sam nor I appreciated the strength of Roy's attachment to having an alter ego, and, having established this relationship, his reluctance to let go.

Roy was taciturn over his exchanges, and I was summoned for a private session with Sam. Permanent Secretaries have an array of levers, many only implicit. But Sam pulled out a range of stops – detriment to future "career", the need to get experience of "the nitty-gritty" of real work, and even "good for the soul" – to suggest that I had spent too long already in the Private Office. Not ever a careerist, and certainly not in comparison to some of the more blatantly ambitious of some colleagues, one could not but be persuaded that Permanent Secretaries tend to have a more continuing influence and longer shelf life than passing Ministers .[7] So I had a session with Roy, indicating that there were pressures, and, having spent more than five years out of eight in Private Office, these were difficult to gainsay. And there were other talented guys who could do the job as well. He took this quietly, but, one suspects, this hardened his attitude to stand out for taking David Dowler, my successor, across to other Departments. Interestingly, in recording his eventual reluctance to part with David, Roy acknowledges that five years was probably about as long as it was reasonable to take an official out of the stream of Departmental work.

Subsequent direct meetings with Roy were scant and transitory. During his time at the European Commission, I had been in Brussels for some meeting or other and was checking in for my booking on the last flight back to London. Suddenly, Roy and Christopher Tugendhat turned up, all dressed up for some formal dinner in London, and demanded seats. I and my colleague from DTI were turned off to make way. Roy met my remark that his present office didn't seem to be as efficiently run as the Ministry of Aviation with a wry smile. Still, we had to doss down in the airport hotel, buying yet another shaver and toiletries for an unforeseen overnight stay.

In November 1998 there was a Conference organised by the Institute of Contemporary British History as a retrospective review of the Concorde project. Roy seemed in good form and we had an amusing retrospective of our own on the excitement of his first fortnight in office.

OUT DAMN'D TECHNOLOGY

It Could Be War!

One evening in early 1961 at the height of the Cold War – only a year away from the Cuban Missile crisis, just completing the chore of recording the minutes of the Minister's meetings that day, and putting them into the tray to be typed next morning, the Private Office was deserted except for myself and Mr Richardson, the head messenger, who was doing the final rounds of security checks. While putting the trays away in the safe, the phone rang. It was the Ministry of Defence Private Office to say that their Secretary of State, Harold Watkinson, wanted an urgent word with Peter Thorneycroft.

Peter had returned home to change for some dinner before going to the House for a vote at 10 p.m. I managed to reach him at his home number, and put the two Ministers in touch through the junction box on the Office desk. "Peter, the Cabinet have decided to test Soviet intentions by flying two BEA aircraft manned by the RAF outside the Berlin air corridor tonight." When Watkinson had put down the phone, Peter cheerfully quipped that I should have no problems arranging this.

After a few calls to BEA, I managed to reach Brian Shenstone, their head of operations, who greeted me, "the RAF are crawling all over me." When I had confirmed that this came from a Cabinet decision, he replied that he could not release the aircraft without his Chairman's approval. But we agreed that it would be more than our futures were worth for action to be suspended while he contacted his Chairman. So the practical arrangements were started. I reported this to Peter Thorneycroft, who admitted to taking the call in his underwear sitting on the stairs.

By now, Richardson, ever prompt at spotting likely bother, had made a bracing cup of tea. Allowing twenty minutes or so for BEA to have located their Chairman – Lord Sholto Douglas – I called Shenstone back to be told that his boss had not been located. Then the MoD's Private Office chased, complaining that BEA were not being fully cooperative, and after some wrangling accepted that it was not unreasonable for the airline to seek the approval of their Chairman. In fact, BEA were going as far as possible, short of releasing the actual Viscount aircraft, in preparing them and briefing the RAF aircrews. Trying to inject some urgency into the search for Lord Douglas, I contacted his private secretary, who was still trying out her contacts. And a call to his home was answered by an au pair with imperfect English who could make out only the letters "S-M-O-N" in the appointments book. Time passed, punctuated by chasing from the MoD and keeping in touch with Peter Thorneycroft, until the point was reached when the next opportunity for contact would be his House of Commons office at 9.30.

During this hiatus, Lord Douglas was located – playing bridge at the Smouhas, but he insisted upon speaking direct to the Minister. This meant coordinating a call to the House of Commons and to the "Smouhas" private number through the Office junction box: in those days, a box with four lines, each with a light to indicate whether the line was in use and each with a short lever with positions for "speak", "hold", "transfer" i.e. when two lines were linked, but allowed the operator to listen in undetected. Well, through this contraption, Peter from his Commons office was put through to Lord Douglas at the Smouhas. After Peter had summarised the Cabinet decision, Lord Douglas' curt response was, "I couldn't possibly agree to my airline's operations and aircraft being put at risk. And I doubt if you have the powers to direct me." Peter took this calmly and suggested that they meet later, to which Lord Douglas replied reluctantly that he would need to discuss the position with his people, and a time of 1 a.m. was fixed for the meeting at the Minister's office in Shell Mex House.

When Lord Douglas had put down his phone, Peter asked for a briefing session at 12.15 with the Foreign Secretary and Minister of Defence at the meeting, if possible, since it was important that someone present at the Cabinet meeting should attend. Thereafter, events were a blur. But on several occasions all four lights on the junction box were on, and Richardson manfully wielded one of the phones to keep contacts on the line – one phrase sticks in the memory, "Richardson, the Foreign Secretary is on 3. Just ask him to hang on." But, briefly, Watkinson was in transit somewhere and uncontactable, but the MoD were insistent they attend the briefing. And Lord Douglas-Home, then Foreign Secretary, we caught in his bath, and Peter persuaded him to attend. A key contact was Arnold Keen, the Department's legal expert on aviation law – against all the odds, the likeliest person to meet accidentally in airport transfer lounges around the world, having done so myself at Heathrow, Montreal, Tokyo and Singapore. But one could leave him to summon the other departmental experts needed. Not least were the practical problems of persuading the security staff at Shell Mex House to open the gates at this hour, man the entrance and turn on the lights for this high-powered gathering.

When officials turned up, there was a strong team of legal specialists, including the Attorney General's office. Peter Thorneycroft duly arrived, and then the Foreign Secretary – by now dried and dressed – and the briefing got under way. It quickly transpired that Lord Douglas was right – under the relevant Act, the government's powers to requisition aircraft were confined to circumstances of "great national emergency", and the legal view was that this went beyond a decision by the Government of the day, but implied approval by Parliament. Nor were the prospect of indemnities, with their financial implications, an easy topic of discussion in the early hours of the morning.

The BEA team was made up of Lord Douglas, his Chief Executive Tony Millward, and Brian Shenstone. Douglas was a stocky old "air dog" with a distinguished RAF career having taken over Fighter Command from Lord Dowding after the Battle of Britain, and the meeting began with Lord Douglas-Home giving a full account of the Cold War situation, what were seen as the issues at stake, and the rationale for the Cabinet decision. Lord Douglas responded firmly pointing up the impact that a loss of aircraft could have on the airline, and one was resigned to a dogged negotiation for several hours. But Alec Douglas-Home interjected, very gently, "Sholto. It could be war." Whatever may be the folklore about his economics competence being measured in matchsticks, this quiet gravity won a resigned nod from Lord Douglas, who asked his staff to put the arrangements in hand – by then, unbeknownst to him, the aircraft were on the tarmac, fully crewed, and with engines running.

With Richardson, we cleared away the debris of the meetings and left the office in the state it had been when we were about to leave the evening before. On arriving at the office later that morning at the normal time, having heard no news of a crisis over Berlin, there was only one good opening line: "Hasn't the Third World War started?" If but a small blip in post-war history, it was typical of the Whitehall farces increasingly played out behind the scenes as Britain has struggled to "punch above its weight" while holding up its togs.

Crossed Wires

Sometime later, I had another call, this time during normal working hours, from the Ministry of Defence private office to say that Harold Watkinson wanted a personal word with Peter Thorneycroft. Officials were gathering in the office for a meeting on the prospective supersonic airliner, eventually to be Concorde, but there were still several due to arrive, so there seemed time before the meeting could begin. Confident after my virtuoso performance on the telephone junction box in the previous episode, I checked with Peter that he would be ready to take the call, held the line open, confirmed with the Defence Department's Private Secretary that my Minister was on the line, and having my opposite number confirm that his boss was also on the line, I confidently pulled the appropriate lever on my junction box to connect them.

Maybe a modification of the box had been introduced – or I had simply forgotten, but I found that I had put Harold Watkinson through to a junior official in Labour Division. Watkinson, by repute, was a "good Minister" in that he was prepared to take a balanced view and practical in orientation, though extremely short of fuse. The exchange went roughly–

"Peter."

"This is Labour Division. If you could say who you are and what you want, I'll see if I can help."

"Peter! Peter!"

"If you could tell me your name, and..."

"Peter! Peter!" (Aside "What's going on?")

"Could you please let me know who..."

"Peter! Peter!..."

This impasse continued, with an ever more irate Watkinson and an increasingly exaggerated patience from our Labour Division colleague. In desperation, I asked if anyone in the office could sort out the crossed lines. Daphne Chapman, one of those eternally cheerful personalities without whom a busy private office could not function, came over and at one glance spotted the problem. "Chris. How many times have I told you to keep your knob up?" Immediate howls of laughter followed from the assembled officials.

But picking up the phone again, the exchange had reached the point–

"You realise who I am?"

"That's just what I've been asking for the past few minutes," came the painfully measured response.

"I'm the Secretary of State for Defence!"

"Yeah. And I'm Jack Sprat."

At which, one could only put down the phone and join in the hysteria.

Monitoring Conventions

Listening in on Ministerial telephone conversations is common practice for Private Secretaries – Julian Amery, always hyperconscious of being misquoted or misascribed, was insistent that this should be done, and even asked that one should tap into private conversations if these seemed to be going on too long: typical of the trivia overheard was during a conversation with Morea Wyatt, when it transpired that they were discussing one of the candidates for Profumo's vacant seat after his resignation, and she remarked, "But, Julian darling, he's an absolute sex maniac."

Roy Jenkins, moving into Aviation as his first Ministerial appointment in 1964, not just accepted the same regime, but welcomed another listener to discuss ambiguities, motives and possible alignments. And he took genuine delight in observing the nuances and twists that could be applied even in simple minutes recording meetings, and the interplay of arguments, the inevitable private office reconciliations, from the tensions within the Department. But his readiness to open up to baldly frank discussion was a welcome change from his predecessor, as was his attitude of exploring personalities and peculiarities of others – politicians, industrialists, trade unionists, as well as senior officials.

The most soul-wrenching occasion was when Harold Macmillan was stricken down while Prime Minister, and Julian Amery's office became the campaign headquarters for Quentin Hogg's bid to take over the Premiership. Actual work in the Department had to proceed on the basis that the Minister was on a temporary trip to Mars, as all manner of stray political personages flitted through, and phone calls were made to sundry shady figures. But Julian kept in touch with his father-in-law on his sickbed, since, it transpired, that Quentin Hogg was his own personal preference. But Quentin Hogg blew his chances with an eccentric exhibitionist performance at a Party occasion and alienated the waverers on whom so much attention was being lavished. There was real sadness in the old man's voice as he told Julian that it was no longer sensible to pursue the cause.

In the event, Lord Douglas-Home "emerged" after having been a rank outsider. And, by virtue of listening in, I was aware of this decision when the odds being quoted were 14-1. That one did not draw all one's savings and put them on a sure bet at the bookmakers across the Strand has left a lifelong quandary – was it probity or stupidity?

---

[1] Robbie Burns, one of our stalwart Deputy Secretaries, suffered a fatal heart attack after a period when Julian's erratic timetable had demanded a succession of rushes along the Embankment from his office in Shell Mex House to the Ministry of Defence. And one has always had a tinge of guilt that a more forceful obstruction of Julian's impatience might have put less pressure on Robbie's heart.

[2] The nigh-total ignorance among Britain's political elite of the technicalities of what lies within their ostensible sphere of responsibility can have positive advantages. At a reception in Washington, when the US was developing a supersonic competitor to Concorde, Julian was cornered by a Boeing Vice-President and plied with questions. The Vice-President subsequently remarked to me, "Your guy sure keeps his cards close to his chest."

[3] The vast consignment of booze turned out to be invaluable, not just as succour for the delegation. The Foreign Office advice on gifts – one rather ostentatious one, an onyx and gilt inkstand for Mr Dementiev, who was the official host; and a couple of lesser ones for his junior directors – turned out to be completely inadequate. Instead, at every port of call local dignitaries and party officials were expecting some formal gesture, and the ladies performed heroically in tearing up their underwear to make ribbons to attach to bottles of Scotch, gin, or brandy on each occasion.

[4] When Julian lost his Preston North seat in 1966 by a couple of dozen votes on the fifth recount, I took some mild pleasure in sending him a telegram, "Sorry. But they were a bit inclined the other way."

[5] The bureaucratic fetish of the "two-page summary", now given general currency in the convention of an "Executive Summary", possibly as a consequence of conventions seeping out of Whitehall, has several merits: for busy Ministers and their staff to gain a quick view of the relative significance of their queue of casework; a discipline on the Oxbridge tutorial essay tradition; and the practice of writing the summary first is a useful device for putting arguments in a coherent sequence. But on the other hand, it was, and probably remains, astonishing how many senior officials owed their elevation to no more than a polished skill in fifth-form précis writing. Not to mention the disasters that can result from action based on "It looks good on paper."

[6] The Concorde was designed as a Mach 2 (twice the speed of sound) aircraft, essentially because this speed could be achieved by conventional materials. The United States concept was a faster Mach 3 aircraft that required more sophisticated materials, such as titanium, to withstand the temperature and other conditions.

[7] Just before Sam's unfortunate heart attack while negotiating French road traffic

on his way to a holiday retreat, at an Aviation/Supply official's reunion lunch, he recalled that he had confronted a difficult time extricating me from Roy's private office. I could only respond that, given some of the detached fantasists among the senior levels of the civil service to whom one had been compelled to work, one could not detect any career advantage from having given up the post. While, as for my soul, the prospects of salvation didn't seem any more propitious either.

HUSH-HUSH TECHNOLOGY:

INTERNATIONAL ELECTRONICS DIVISION (IEL)

In the intermission between leaving the private office and being summoned back to serve as private secretary to Julian Amery, there was a stretch of 18 months in this specialist area.

There were a variety of international interfaces in the electronics field concerned with defence: the right to use, predominantly US, foreign technology; or vice versa, the terms of key UK know-how in radar, guided weapons systems, precision navigation etc being licensed or made available; negotiation of requirements for a NATO military and civil radar system (NADGE); and, my patch, the control of strategic electronic technology – particularly against leakage to the Soviet Union and its allies – through the international clearing system of COCOM. Much of the work was routine checking of the electronic content of products, the extent of its novelty and vulnerability to replication, drawing on the expertise of government agencies, such as the Admiralty's centre for valve technology at Bath. And a relative island of calm compared to the unpredictability of events in the Private Office.

As a sign of the times, however, when Vickers reported that they had secured a good prospect for selling a fleet of Viscount's – a short/medium range turbo-prop airliner – to China, the international tensions in strategic technology controls became dramatically evident. China was definitely off limits for the US. This would not have mattered except that under US technology controls their legislation demanded that any equipment containing restricted technology, whether components or intellectual property, could only be sold to anyone anywhere carrying a liability to criminal proceedings if this know-how found its way to forbidden hands. And conditional on this obligation being carried forward in the contract terms of any subsequent sale, and of any subsequent sales thereafter. There had, indeed, been cases of US court proceedings even when some item had been sold to Cuba sixth-hand.

The Viscount specification included STC equipment, for example, manufactured in this country under licence from its then parent company, ITT. Consequently, under the "extraterritoriality" of the US legislation, any US citizen employed by STC could face a prison sentence if he set foot in the States. This was only the most obvious instance, and we undertook a "technology" audit of the complete aircraft. The theoretical reach of the US legislation ran, at one extreme, to all transistors and semiconductors, which rested on Western Electric and RCA patents, to the main wing-spar of the aircraft, which also depended on US-derived patents.

A piecemeal approach to protect particular companies was impractical. And, given that the equipment was no more sophisticated than in any other civil aircraft, which assuming even a minimal espionage competence the Chinese could pick up in any maintenance shed in Asian airports, and given the prevailing political mood of "stuff the Americans", we had to devise a comprehensive solution. This was not difficult: we arranged a series of paper transactions whereby Vickers sold the aircraft to BEA, who then passed title to the Government, and we then sold them back to Vickers for onward sale to China.

This afforded the suppliers of equipment the let-out that, so far as they were aware, they were contributing to a routine supply to BEA. And, should some diligent American bulldog sniff along the chain of transmitted obligations, the scent would lead him to the British Government's door. Whereupon, the Government would be able to counter that such provisions were not consistent with Britain's trade policy. (Years later in DTI, the "Trade Policy" side produced a vast tract, replete with mountains of legal opinion, on "extraterritoriality". But not mentioning that this rather simple device had actually been employed.)

The Viscount sale went ahead, and began a long association with China in aerospace, including subsequent orders of the Trident, and a Rolls-Royce plant in Sian.

GOOD FOR THE SOUL:

ESTABLISHMENTS (PERSONNEL) DIVISION (1965-67)

The Civil Aviation Departmental Classes – embracing the technical skills for running the national aviation network, including navigational aids and local control of airports; the regulatory and safety regime; and handling operations, such as air traffic controllers – were a distinct category of employees with their own specialist needs. Within the Whitehall system, a distinct administrative cottage, apart from maintaining terms and conditions consistent with others in the government service: not to be underrated at a time of instability in labour and economic circumstances.

But, whatever merit for one's spiritual development, for most of the time 2 to 2½ days a week were taken up with chairing promotion boards for the diversity of professional classes. This activity was backed up by a team of 60 or more clerical staff sorting and updating personnel records – a "monstrous regimen of women" in the words of my predecessor. An extraordinary time-consuming exercise, often casting more light on the qualities of reporting staff than on individual candidates, but a fair run through the quirks and quiddities of human nature.

Perhaps the only warrant for mentioning this episode is that it offered the single instance in a civil service career when one personally solved a potential crisis. Extremely rare. Several of these classes, partially stimulated by their ingrained cliqueness, were among the most militant in the civil service. Before my arrival, the Air Traffic Control Officers, almost uniquely in service history, had gone on strike, and one inherited implementing an extraordinarily generous report that set out to address their grievances.

The Communications Officer Class, composed of cipher operators with a long history going back to the earliest days of telegraphy and a crucial role in the war, were being displaced in civil aviation by new technologies: transponders in aircraft were coding information in echoing radar signals, and increasing co-operation between national air traffic control authorities was speeding up direct information transfer. Consequently, the Class as a whole was due to be abolished over a few years with the loss of some 630 posts. Even their trade union, the

Institution of Professional Civil Servants, viewed the prospect with alarm, anticipating calls for the most generous redundancy terms, which the Treasury would almost certainly oppose. While the old formulae of "last-in first-out", "first-in last-out" etc held out only the prospect of some faction being dissatisfied and threatening industrial action.

At all events, the mixture appeared extremely volatile. So, I called upon my "regimen" to prepare a summary of the class – age, entry dates, promotion records, years of pensionable service – in tabular form. And packing this away in my briefcase, with ample sheets of working paper, I took the bundle home for the weekend. And spread them out on my study floor on a Sunday afternoon. One feature immediately stood out: seniority in the Class offered no basis for discrimination, since most had been appointed, or obtained transfers from military service, in the immediate aftermath of the War. And it was pure accident how many years they might have served previously in eligible pension service.

Going back to first principles, one plotted the date when the existing members of the Class would reach normal retirement. Surprise. The incidence of retirements roughly paralleled the run-down of posts, with a gap of no more than 35 in surplus staff. On Monday, checking with the Ministry of Defence, responsible for the GCHQ Communications Centre at Cheltenham, they confirmed that they were still recruiting cipher specialists and would be open to the transfer of 35 from the Civil Aviation Class.

Problem solved: 35 volunteers from the youngest members of the Class, irrespective of seniority, to transfer to MoD would allow retirements progressively to take care of the loss of posts. The simplicity shocked the trade union. But, if this forestalled another strike in the civil aviation area, as in most things in government, it came with a lead lining. Some years later, to Mrs Thatcher's chagrin, militant action occurred at Cheltenham, and one has suspected that this was probably a chip off the civil aviation block.

A MERCHANT OF DEATH (1967-71):

MILITARY AIRCRAFT SALES TO THE MIDDLE EAST

SAUDI ARABIAN AIR DEFENCE SCHEME

Yet again, the rationale of civil service postings defied reason: to put someone named "Benjamin" – even if derived from the familial nomenclature of some Welsh religious sect, to sell arms in the Middle East would not have been the first choice in most countries. But the main duties, and certainly the most demanding in time, was to monitor progress on the first Saudi Arabian Air Defence Scheme. It had been signed in December 1965, heralded as Britain's largest single export order,[1] and with all the fanfare of the subsequent State visit by King Faisal.

I arrived after the glory days of the initial triumph, secured, to no publicity, by a letter from John Stonehouse – he of the Victorian melodrama of leaving his clothes on the beach in Miami before living incognito out of the reach of his creditors and critics – on the best Ministerial paper, "We shall do all possible to ensure the contracts are completed to your entire satisfaction." Not a caveat. Not a qualification. Nor any reference to "co-operation", since introducing a modern high-tech defence system in the country as it then was, could only be accomplished with a massive complimentary effort from the Saudi government.

As usual, any subsequent searches for the culprit who had concocted this disastrous form of words were fruitless. But, crucially, no one had cleared the terms of this extravagant undertaking with the Ministry of Defence, who were inevitably the only source of expertise and resources to stand behind the implicit obligations. At that time, the ethos of that Ministry was to view "exporting" as a rather demeaning activity, and a positive distraction to the great tasks of preparing for hypothetical Soviet threats.

The first clash with this ethos came early. After the signature of the main contracts, but before the delivery of aircraft and facilities had begun, the Saudi government said that they were facing incursions on their southern border with the Yemen and requested some Lightnings to be flown out at short notice, with a simultaneously urgent request for training for Saudi pilots to fly them. These requests were conceded in the interests of not upsetting the major contracts, and the exercise was codenamed "Magic Carpet". Finding half a dozen or so Lightning aircraft that the RAF were prepared to release, and having them fitted out, was the easy part. When it came to the training of Saudi pilots, the Ministry of Defence insisted upon charging on a "full-cost" basis[2] as the only one on which they had authority from the Treasury. Consequently, the charge for training a Saudi pilot worked out at more than 40% of the cost of the aircraft. Despite remonstrations, there was no time to go through the bureaucratic wrangling to shift this mindset, and a senior RSAF Colonel was heard to remark informally, "You're worse than Arabs." After a heroic tussle with the MoD, this zany approach was eventually changed.

As with many projects, the scheme evolved into a closed system with its own logic and codes of normality. A common experience of those involved when asked by anyone in the familiar surrounds of Britain to describe what they had been doing was to encounter quizzical disbelief within minutes. For the official monitoring officer it imposed unique demands: for example, most of the Saudi pilots under training at Dhahran were related to the ruling family, and their flying always took place in the early hours of the morning since by 9 a.m. the temperature "soaked" by the Lightnings meant dehydration by the time the aircraft had taxied to the runway. But with Friday the equivalent of their weekend, they returned home and voiced their complaints about the performance of the aircraft. With metronomic regularity every Saturday morning there would be a telegram to the Prime Minister's office threatening that unless certain specified spares – citing a list of RAF specification numbers – were provided for the flying programme, diplomatic relations would be broken off. This was regularly passed on from Number 10, and the weekend was spent chasing BAC and the RAF supply organisation to have these items flown out.

After several months, the RAF complained that one of these consumable spares – some specialised clips used for retaining wires or internal panels that were regularly removed for maintenance – were being used at a rate 50 times greater than their normal consumption, even assuming that the RSAF Lightnings were being flown at the same intensity as those in the RAF. After several investigations at the flight maintenance depot at Dhahran, this extraordinary consumption remained a mystery. Until, during a visit to the local *suk,* one of the maintenance staff noticed a natty new line in necklaces on sale, made up of interlinked clips.

A typical instance of perverse logic arose, when under pressure from the Saudi authorities, we undertook an audit of the conduct of the contracts. Going through the current position was an exhaustive exercise, but the most glaring shortcoming on the Saudi side was the apparent failure to provide regular latrine collection: before the development of a comprehensive sewage system in Riyadh, many of the hastily built accommodation buildings still relied on the ancient methods of a "thunderbox" with a bucket that had to be replaced regularly. Despite being a fairly obvious shortcoming, the insistent advice of the Consortium Office was that this should not be taken up with the Saudi authorities. An explanation for this unhygienic tolerance was only revealed when it was explained informally that the "shit wagon" was the distribution system for bootleg *sidiki* distilled in a remarkably high-tech still stashed away in one of the garages (apparently, unless processed three times, the mixture can be lethal).

The happiest remembrance was during Dermot Boyle*'s introductory tour on taking over as Chairman of the Consortium. When in Riyadh, this coincided with an amateur production of *Lock Up Your Daughters*, a musical farce loosely based on Samuel Pepys diaries, by the ex-pat community. With the ingenuity of a stock of skilled trades, the set, built in the ballroom of a disused hotel, had beds flying out from every conceivable panel, and must have been one of the most sophisticated in any amateur production. And the community contained very passable performers. But the most dramatic moment was a power cut: the leading actor extemporised by torchlight for 20 minutes, but ran out of gags. He then invited Dermot to say a few words, and the audience were treated to a continuous flow of Irish humour until the lights came on an hour later, and many would have welcomed the darkness to have continued.

Even though the scheme appeared to progress on the brink of catastrophe, by gradually bringing in RAF expertise at crucial points, even achieving a liaison office in Riyadh, enough was achieved to establish confidence for the subsequent Al Yamamah contracts.[3]

HAWKER HUNTER REPLACEMENT SALES

By virtue of having been sold around the world, long after the production line closed, there was a continuing demand from the air forces for replacement aircraft. As these were phased out of RAF service, there was a continuing market – running in total into hundreds – for these aircraft when refurbished by Hawkers. And it was a continuing Solomon game, in which one was involved as a sideline to the Saudi escapades, to decide between demands of, say, India, Peru, Iraq, Jordan etc against the limited numbers coming available.

As recalled in the 'Dinky Toys' account, we even received an extremely low-key approach from the Israel procurement agency, who said they would be interested in acquiring at least 24 Hunter aircraft. They admitted that during the Six-Day War it had taken three Mirage IIIs to "see off" a single Jordanian Air Force Hunter, with no confirmed "kills". We could only say that the aircraft were available only in refurbished condition, and then only sporadically from the RAF, so that we could not consider their approach. But some tribute to the aircraft, and their Jordanian pilots.

SKYBOLT OFFSET

A diverting episode was involvement in the "offset" negotiations following the Prime Minister/President agreement to purchase Skybolt, the US airborne nuclear strike weapon. The US agreed in principle to purchase a percentage of the value in UK defence-related equipment, subject to competitive evaluation. The initial Pentagon list had covered products with a technical sophistication on a par with bootlaces. After representations that British companies should be allowed to bid for rather more technically demanding equipment, the next requirement to be opened for British supply was a communication aircraft for the Marine Corps. The Handley Page Jetstream won on price/performance despite the usual lobbying of Beech, Cessna and other US companies, and a project office was set up at the company. When Skybolt was cancelled, so was the Jetstream order, to the genuine regret of the Marine Corps Colonel in charge of the project, who said wistfully that he was sorry to say goodbye to "my beautiful bird".

---

[1] The cumulative value of the contracts was nearly some £180 million, historically Britain's largest export order and the extent of the scheme was remarkable:

– Supply of three squadrons of Lightnings, and sufficient additional aircraft for a conversion unit;

– A Flying Training School at Riyadh, with a complement of 36 BAC 167 trainer aircraft;

– A chain of AEI radars of probably the most advanced technology outside NATO. Iinstead of a separate installation scanning in vertical sweeps to indicate the altitude of a selected target, which needed to be rotated mechanically to align to the target, the Saudi radars had 13 "stacked" beams as it rotated through 360°, and the altitude of any particular target was computed by comparing the signal strengths of responses in the overlapping beams. This equipment demanded extremely fine tolerances in construction, erection and operational maintenance.

The most spectacular feature of the chain was the site of the Taif radar, atop the escarpment that marks the separation of the western coastal plain from the central plateau, with a view along the 2000-foot cliffs as they extended south and north;

– A sophisticated "troposcatter" communication system with massive aerial arrays which, as an extra feature, in the ambient weather focused the sun to achieve phenomenal temperatures that solidified the sand;

– A Technical Training College at Dhahran to build up a national skills base to support the system;

– Associated airfield developments at Riyadh, Dhahran and Ties, with a completely new military airfield at Tebuk.

The hardware and direct technical support were the responsibility of the manufacturers – BAC for the aircraft and AEI for the radars, and Airwork, predominantly through hiring ex-service personnel, to provide the professional services to run the system and the training centres, with a view eventually to hand these over to trained Saudi officers.

As a compromise with the Americans, the ground-to-air missiles to defend the installations were provided by batteries of Lockheed Hawks.

Coordination between the companies was ostensibly through a Consortium Office, based on a "Fourth Agreement" whereby the three principal companies – BAC, AEI (then latterly GEC, when they took over AEI) and Airwork would guarantee overall performance. This was effectively a binding "joint-and-several" guarantee, that meant each party was liable to pick up the liabilities from the failure of others – in British managerial ethos, the nearest to meeting Boris Karloff in a pitch-dark graveyard as the tombstones begin moving and hands claw their way out of the graves.

The first chairman of the Consortium was Lord Caldecote, then chairman of Metal Box, and he gave way to Air Marshal Dermot Boyle*, who had a distinguished service background in Fighter Command. The local Consortium team in Riyadh bore the brunt of the liaison role with the Royal Saudi Air Force. Inevitably with such a wide-ranging project in a relatively underdeveloped environment, controversy was continuous. And by happy chance, the Consortium recruited as their local Director Air Commodore "Paddy" Kiernan, an experienced RAF equipment and logistics hand, but also a fanatic glider pilot. Even more important, his happy Irish humour and delightful family provided excellent flak protection from the daily travails of aggressive criticism and of conciliation between different interests.

[2] The principles of Whitehall accounting were, even then, fairly arcane. Moreover, the Ministry of Defence had never before had to bother itself with tiresome issues of commercial relations and consequently responded immediately according to the Finance handbook for charging full costs. But to start with a simple "real cost" approach for training a Lightning pilot, there would be the actual cost of fuel, spares consumption, maintenance, instructors and time, and some allowance for the depreciation of the aircraft, that could be charged to the

job; at the other extreme was a "full cost", which would also add in the station overheads – fire and safety services, the security services to protect the airfield, air traffic control, electricity and other utility services, costs of maintaining roads, and so on. Moreover, the armed services were, in commercial terms, extremely inefficient with staff time taken up by parades, inspections, NAAFI breaks, sports afternoons etc. Tossing all these into the charge for training a pilot inflated it to exorbitant levels.

A more rational approach, to which, after endless disputes, we in Defence Sales finally secured agreement, was to adopt "marginal cost", which subtracted from the "full costs" all those charges that would have to be met irrespective of any training activities for non-RAF students. But no doubt this debate has continued to byzantine lengths subsequently.

[3] A few lessons emerged from working on the scheme:

– understand the client, beyond the strict terms of the contract. The RSAF had a relatively small core of trained and experienced officers. While the technologies and procedures of the system were unfamiliar. Yet they were also part of an autocratic system that put an arbitrary premium on delivery. Consequently, the pressures of "prestige" or "face" were as daunting as those in other very different societies.

– the optimal approach for a project in such contexts, if not more generally, is "to keep the buck on the other side of the table". Some investment is worthwhile to be in a position to point to outstanding obligations on the other side of the table.

– many of the controversies arose through suspicions that the suppliers were cutting corners, or raising false requirements. The value of being able to call upon direct expertise from the RAF helped to resolve these. But in offering this expertise there was often a measure of "making an offer that they cannot refuse", in the sense that, given the importance of "face", the RSAF staff were reluctant to have their own shortcomings – however understandable – being disclosed.

Trite, perhaps. But lessons that British industry, from observation of their behaviour in many overseas projects, has not themselves learned.

1971-74: CONCORDE DIVISION

It was a fairly rare experience to be present at the early exchanges between Peter Thorneycroft and M. Buron to set up the joint studies and collaboration contacts between Britain and France; observe the fracas of the Labour government's ham-fisted attempt in 1964 to get out of the project; then to be involved in the project team; and finally help to put together the BBC's obituary *Timewatch* to coincide with the aircraft's last flight.

There has never been a satisfactory published account of the project, though within the confines of time and popular appeal, the *Timewatch* account was an effective précis. Most accounts are caught by the undeniable glamour of the aircraft's shape and technical accomplishments, or by aviation enthusiasts bemoaning that the opportunity of a "fantastic future" was lost – despite there never having been a penny of genuine financial risk carried by the companies involved. For behind the tabloid depictions, there was a complex political/bureaucratic charade, often as complex as the technical intricacies, that had to be "engineered" for public presentation.[1]

My entry to the Division was by happen-chance, since at one lunch I found myself sitting next to Philip Jones*, then the Division's Under-Secretary, and I made some chance remark about acting as monitoring officer for the Saudi Air Defence scheme to the effect that industry spent more time trying to get government to bail them out of holes than avoiding the holes in the first place. This scepticism must have rung a bell, as I was deputed to join Concorde Division only a few weeks later.[2]

Yet again, an exercise in the absurd. A sketch of the main historical milestones is at Annex A. But the origins of the project typically derived from naïve simplicities. From the first presentation to a Ministerial committee chaired by Henry Brook*, George Edwards* of BAC had a simple depiction that there was an established progression of technical advances from military aircraft to civil aviation applications, and a supersonic airliner was a natural evolutionary step, especially in going for a Mach 2 aircraft that employed conventional materials. While, after all, the very success of civil jet aircraft confirmed "speed sells seats". And, after all, as Arnold Hall* and Dr Hooker of Bristol Siddeley pointed out, the Olympus engine was already under development for the TSR 2.

To be fair, this rational architecture was common to the time as both the US and Russia were planning their own supersonic transport programmes. Consequently, the political motives were a mixture of taking advantage of Britain's perceived leading position in aerospace – but unwilling to confront the development costs alone. Leading, first, to being rebuffed in seeking co-operation with the US, and then by joining with France to "show what Europe" collectively could do. And, within the Whitehall game, there was a defensive predilection among Ministers to establish a basis that would avoid the project falling under the Treasury's historic propensity to demand cancellation invariably when these were viewed as reaching fruition. Also, not to be ignored, was genuine scientific passion, immortalised by Morien Morgan's* mystical musings, "If God meant man to fly...."[3]

Reconciling these fantasies and aspirations was short-circuited by the transition from an agreement to undertake joint studies and establish the industrial structure for cooperation, which had been the theme of the Thornycroft/Buron exchanges in 1961, to a fully-fledged "Treaty" signed by Julian Amery on the 29th of November 1962 "to develop and produce jointly a civil supersonic transport aircraft" – a period while I was out of ongoing contacts with the project in IER Division. But the problem of the "Treaty" was less in what it said than what it did not.

THE TECHNICAL BOX OF TRICKS

There was no definition of the aircraft beyond "a civil supersonic transport aircraft", and the French and British had differing concepts for the target market. The French, after the success of their Caravelle, envisaged a successor aircraft with a range of no more than 2000 miles. And more than two years were spent on devising a design that married this concept with the British objective of a transatlantic aircraft. These exchanges were apparently fraught,[4] and it was not until 1964 that the medium-range variant was dropped and the decision taken to concentrate on a larger version with Atlantic range. One consequence was that the original pair of prototypes, on which work had started, were not representative of the eventual production aircraft and much test replication had to be done.

Far from the natural evolution originally propounded by the manufacturers, in practice the interdependent tolerances were incredibly fine. Without attempting rehearsal of the technical development saga, just as an illustration, the eventual aircraft had a gross weight of 400,000lbs, of which half represented fuel, and only 25,000lbs, or 6%, was payload i.e. the revenue earning capacity for paying passengers. At various stages in the programme, the "weight-growth" through development meant that either the range and/or payload could not be achieved, demanding changes in the aircraft's configuration – for example, extra weight demanded sturdier undercarriage and wheels, in turn demanding changes in wing dimensions, while the engine was undergoing continuous upgrading to match increased weight and performance demands.[5] In all, redesigns of the airframe and engines were equivalent to developing 3-3.5 aircraft.

These had an inevitable impact on prospective development costs – the initial estimate of £170 million turned out to be hopelessly wrong, with the full cost to government, including losses on production, at least 10 times this first guestimate. While the original date for certification (Certification of Airworthiness) to allow commercial operations slipped from 1971 to 1975. Not to discount the immense efforts of development, manufacturing and flight-testing staff in the companies, for many of whom the project became a way of life. But the whip end of all these trials and tribulations swung back to the project division, responsible for monitoring the programme, administering expenditure, liasing with the French government, and advising Ministers on options for the future and responding to the clamour of public debate.

A LEGAL MORASS

The essential dilemma stemmed from the second major omission of the "Treaty" – the absence of a break clause, or, indeed, any criteria to determine the merits of continuing with the project. Despite umpteen searches over the years, no satisfactory documentation has emerged to explain how Anglo-French discussions to explore the feasibility (against a Treasury limit of £50,000) became transformed into a full-blown unqualified "Treaty" to build an unspecified aircraft. All the more surprising when, from its initial conception, the Treasury had been firmly opposed. And, even after the 1964 cock-up to push for unilateral cancellation, maintained unrelenting pressure to seek a way out.

To bottle the legal issues, if agreement with the French could be achieved, fine. But for unilateral withdrawal the British side would have to establish "a fundamental change of circumstance", otherwise the French could reasonably press a case at the International Court for Britain to make good the finance either already committed, or necessary to complete the programme. Not only were the original "circumstances" so ill defined as to offer no firm basis for such an argument, but the corollary was that the UK side should not act in any manner to perpetrate what might be argued as "a fundamental change". This "double-bind" meant that for public presentation, we had to stick to the estimates of the manufacturers as agreed with the French, who were prone to accept the manufacturers' figures. Even though within Whitehall, the figures would be presented with sensitivities and adjustments from past experience. Contrary to suggestions by some commentators that officials continuously juggled figures with an optimistic slant, in fact Ministers were warned of enormous prospective losses going back at least to 1966.

An attempt was made in 1968, when Tony Benn was Minister of Technology, to define yardsticks – measured by such demonstrable criteria as estimated development cost, date of certification, market prospects – to justify a "fundamental change", and these were incorporated in the Benn-Chamant agreement. When, however, two of these were demonstrably breached, the political setting was one where Ministers concluded that positive relations with the French – given recollections of the 1964 ructions – was viewed as more important, and the opportunity allowed to lapse. Thereafter, the legal advice was that to resort to this agreement was nullified.[6] Yet, throughout the remainder of the programme, the option of unilateral withdrawal was one of those that had to be put before Ministers.

MANAGING CHAOS

Responding to the inevitable bucking bronco of technical development shifts, fielding a continuous flow of public and parliamentary criticism, and working with the French authorities posed a high-volume/high-pressure work scene. The project management structure was probably the most focused in government procurement history – a newly appointed Director General remarked in some admiration that within 20 yards of his office there was no question on the project to which he could not obtain an authoritative current reply. But this was built on a very diligent and committed programme team – with professional expertise drawn from across Departments and research establishments, and with teams at the British manufacturers' plants.[7]

The cost monitoring and formal estimating structures would be worth an essay in their own right. But instilling any worthwhile incentives in a "cost-plus" context was nigh impossible – indeed, we had to introduce incentives even to secure information on time. With such a broad range of key suppliers, and with many across the Channel, the application of such techniques as PERT (a Performance Evaluation Review Technique that had been evolved in the Pentagon for their programmes) was vitiated by the inability to have all inputs simultaneously updated.

However, a coherent picture can be painted in retrospect of the increase in UK development cost from the initial guestimate of £170m in

1962 to £1065m a decade later, and however sophisticated its allocation of causes, as the moving finger progressed, at times estimating had the quality of fantasy between optimism and realism.[8] Yet these "chores" demanded massive amounts of work from able staff. Moreover, as development proceeded, new materials and technology were continuously coming available, and there was constant pressure to attempt to incorporate these, though the costs of extended development – especially the fight testing that would be demanded – were potentially extremely high. And when it was decided "to freeze" design on the production model of 1972, there were even then more than £200m worth of "further refinements" on offer.

While all this activity was in progress in support of the technical development, the British side had to maintain as optimistic a public stance as possible, lest it be accused of having perpetrated circumstances that would inhibit any future prospects of withdrawal. For example, any pretence of a market rested on the "options" taken out by airlines – originally BOAC, Air France and Pan Am – in 1963, but reaching 74 from 16 airlines by 1967. Since no irrevocable payment was involved, these "options" reflected airlines taking protective moves in case the project turned out to have commercial significance. But some sophistry was demanded to keep up the pretence that these were "real". Not helped by George Edwards* pronouncing them to be "phoney orders".

ENVIRONMENT? EH?

When the project was conceived, the only environmental concern on the horizon was the take-off noise around airports. In practice, by adopting a steep take-off and throttling back before the ground monitoring points, Concorde could arguably meet the noise stipulations for the Boeing 707 generation. A crucial argument in gaining approval to operate in New York was that Concorde involved no more noise than that to which local residents had already been accustomed.

But, without apparent warning, the sonic boom emerged as a fundamental limitation, effectively curtailing the aircraft's supersonic operations to routes over water. Briefly, the intensity of the sonic boom is related to the mass of the aircraft: previous experience had been from military, usually relatively small, aircraft which, for example at Farnborough Air Shows, had been used as a crowd-thriller. But for the larger Concorde, the double-boom signature could have disturbing, and even potentially damaging effects.[9] We and the French worked hard in such fora as ICAO (The International Civil Aviation Organisation, based in Montréal) to avoid over-exaggeration of the sonic boom effects, to hold out against any bans on overland flying, but inevitably countries would retain discretion on whether they were prepared to tolerate such flights in defined corridors.

Even so, it was problematic whether any governments would readily allow such disturbance to their voting populace, especially since Britain itself banned overland supersonic flight. Or would do so at best exacting some major concessions in aviation rights, or other trade areas, compensation arrangements etc. And when, led by Pan Am and TWA, the 74 "options" evaporated in 1973, the absence of any sure routes for the aircraft, even if it achieved its design performance, became crucial.

Some of the romantically regretful reminiscence commentators are prone to argue that it was cancellation by the US of their SST program that sealed the fate of Concorde, since this robbed the US of any incentives to open supersonic routes. One wonders, however, even with its wide open spaces, whether any American administration would have risked the adverse reactions from exposure to sonic booms, especially since their proposed aircraft was larger and faster than Concorde. And, even so, it must have been questionable whether any other countries would have allowed overland supersonic flying, and hence offered any operating network to achieve economic use of the aircraft.

A curiosity of the project was that it triggered awareness of the ozone layer. So far as we could tell, the run-down of some Pentagon programmes in 1972 released some US scientists with nothing to do, and they seized upon the argument that Concorde might harm the ozone layer as a pretext for some research funding. The irony was that, at the time, knowledge of upper-atmospheric chemistry was sketchy, depending upon spasmodic testing by high-altitude balloons and occasional sampling fights by military aircraft, and it was the routine monitoring instrumentation on Concorde test flights that multiplied the detailed sampling.[10] In the event, a few dozen Concordes would have been no more than a marginal addition to the depletion from other sources. But this controversy brought the upper atmosphere issue into public perception for the first time.

THE MINISTERIAL PARADE

With a narrative running over at least three decades, and as departmental nomenclatures changed – Supply, Technology, Aviation, Industry, etc, there was a musical chairs progression of Ministers. All caught up in the game of bold pretence masking frustration at uncontrollable costs.

Invariably, the ratings from the standpoint of officials in the middle of continuous grind may vary somewhat from the self-inflated accounts in subsequent Ministerial biographies. From my time, we would accord the palm for a heroic contribution to Michael Heseltine, but not for the incidents that he chose to highlight in his own account of involvement with the project.[11]

Despite their never-failing optimism about future sales, when it came to financing the production aircraft, BAC resolutely refused to put up any of their own money. This meant that the government had to put through a Concorde Production Bill to provide loans for building aircraft destined for commercial sales, as distinct from the existing powers to fund the manufacture of development aircraft. The Committee stages of the Bill, which Heseltine had to steer through, allowed members to raise every conceivable criticism and concern about the project. Which they did. The final session was scheduled for after the Summer Recess, and reviewing the next steps we suggested that the only option was to give our Minister a series of replies to all the points that had been raised. And, as a tribute to his demeanour as a Minister, we did not appreciate that he had reading problems. But he managed the feat with a speech for the best part of an hour.

THE COOPERATIVE IDIOM

Playing a supporting role in France's ambition to build a leading aerospace industry was but one of the incidental pleasures, not least because several in the community of officials could see this was a process that would eventually deplete the UK's industrial capabilities.

The Anglo-French management structure followed a pyramid structure of a joint Concorde Directing Committee (CDC) composed of senior Departmental and Treasury officials, reporting to the responsible national Ministers. This was supported by a Concorde Management Board (CMB), whose membership was composed of officials from either side of the channel wholly devoted to the project, and this in turn had working groups as needed drawing also upon industrial and other expertise in special fields such as structures, noise, airworthiness, operational and commercial analyses. By convention the secretariat functions of preparing periodic reports for the CDC and Ministers alternated annually across the Channel. This structure was paralleled by joint groups among the airframe and engine manufacturers.

Much of the activity was grinding out common assessments of the current state of the project for periodic, usually six-monthly, Ministerial meetings for which the CDC submitted a report essentially drafted by the CMB. Where the French were most obstinate was in hanging on to the manufacturers' sales forecasts, despite continuing scepticism from the British side. Without being overtly stated, however, the underlying French objective, apart from completing the aircraft as a showcase of advanced aerospace competences and a "learning" process, became apparent in disputes over systems, where they also viewed the project as an exercise in technology acquisition. These exchanges could get quite heated, but the notable British success was to secure the undercarriage and braking system, one of the areas of genuine technology advance, for Dowty.[12] While, in the background, was the massive build-up of research, design and test facilities at Toulouse, much of it carried as "overheads" on the Concorde program: consequently, another area of occasionally heated dispute was the 50:50 sharing of developments costs set out in rudimentary terms in the "Treaty".

French officials and company staff were never less than good company. But most remarkable was the staggering difference in "democratic overheads":

– Just before leaving the Division in 1974, I had a rough count of the Parliamentary Questions that the project had generated, and this came to 860: since it continued as a subject of controversy for several years thereafter, the total PQ-count must have well-topped 1000. Over the same period, the French had answered 2 comparable questions.

– Whereas the British Concorde Division numbered up to 60 staff, not counting others in Procurement Executive who were monitoring the engine development, the French never had more than 4 staff engaged full-time on the project.

– There were, by 1974, seven Public Accounts Committee reviews of the project, and the accumulated volumes of papers and minutes called for a full-time archivist. Exceptionally, we insisted on a key official being promoted in his existing post, since he was the only one with command of the historical references.

– A routine internal exercise at each review point on the British side was meeting the Treasury's insistence on the forward estimates being "discounted" at whatever was the prevailing Treasury test-rate: a technique originally devised to compare the current values of different investment options, discounting has the impact of reducing future values the further away in the future. (Applied as an absolute measure, it is a technique to demonstrate that nothing is worth doing.) With all the different streams of costs, production assumptions, estimates of selling price, "learning effects" on different assumed production flows etc, this demanded the full-time efforts of several staff over a few days.

On one occasion, when it was the French turn to prepare the CDC submission, our Treasury representative demanded, in his wheedling tone, that the CDC estimates should be discounted. After the meeting, French officials admitted to be completely ignorant of what our Treasury delegate wanted, and we had to send one of our team, John Michell, to Paris to give them a day's teach-in. John reported a few days later that he'd had an ecstatic call from our French opposite numbers that the project was showing fantastic future returns – apparently, instead of discounting, they had inflated future values.

– Before each joint-Ministerial review, the British side had to insist that the material was ready at least four weeks in advance in order to go through the Whitehall hoops of circulating papers to official Cabinet Committees, and allowing Ministers to take whatever view they wished. The French were astonished, and their top official, Bernard Lathière[13] remarked that all he did, a couple of days before the Ministerial meeting was – gesturing with his hand – write a "dossier" for his Minister.

THE ADVENT OF REALISM

1973 was the turning point for several reasons. There were 16 aircraft under production, and with "orders" for BOAC and Air France at last a limit on the additional development could be set on an "in-service" version of the aircraft; Pan Am and TWA dropped their options, followed in succeeding months by other airlines; and, with the arrival of Jean Peyrelevade, then a junior member of the French aviation bureaucracy,[14] for the first time there was a responsive reaction on the French side to our scepticism about the aircraft's sales prospects.

To put the dilemma in the proverbial nutshell, it was highlighted by one of those cryptic – but testingly provocative – queries from Number 10, this time from Harold Macmillan: "Why not an aeroplane for millionaires?" On any reasonable commercial assumptions, the costs to be covered in charging passengers would include fuel, servicing and running costs, and amortisation of the costs of buying the aircraft. Taking all these into account, the fare would have to be higher than existing First-Class, and vast studies were pursued on the margin, eventually settling on 20%, that would be tolerable to attract potential First-Class travellers, and encourage a magical "slide-over" potential from Business Class who would be prepared to pay for saving time.

But as any air traveller can confirm, the number of First-Class seats on a typical long-haul flight is relatively small: a couple of dozen out of a total of 200-240 total passengers. Although small in number, a First-Class seat is the highest yield i.e. most profitable, for airlines. Consequently, putting on, say, a twice-daily Concorde service between London and New York, would, if successful, attract 200 First-Class travellers a day from other services: equivalent to the First-Class travellers on 10-12 normal long-haul flights. Higher Concorde frequencies would only increase the drain away from First-Class travellers from other flights. Not surprisingly, one of BOAC's main concerns about buying the aircraft was the damage it would inflict on returns from their other operations, assessed as "possibly by millions of pounds a year". Bluntly, to answer the query from Number 10, there were just not enough "millionaires" who wanted to travel simultaneously on the same route. Or, to generalise this rationale, Concorde was a unique product, in that the more successful it was, the less incentive there was for airlines to buy it.

SAVING A BIT OF FACE

For the first time, in 1973, the joint Commercial Working Group managed a report that cast doubt on the extravagant manufacturers' sales claims, even for aircraft incorporating further development. At the end of February 1974, after the miners strike – 3-day weeks, electricity rationing etc, and in a worsening economic setting, Harold Wilson's Labour Party were elected. And, as the fickle finger is liable to operate, our new Industry Minister was Tony Benn, whose constituency at the time was Bristol, where most of the UK Concorde work was based. "Gnats in pants", or some such, was his reaction to the bland, and, in our usual tradition, honest assessment of future costs that we submitted to our new Minister.

These ranged from losses of £80 million if production were immediately terminated, to, taking only the next four years, losses to public funds of £205 million if only 16 aircraft were built and all but 2 sold (in practice, the first 2 production aircraft were already engaged in completing the development flying in view of modifications introduced since the first prototypes), rising to £ 390 million if the manufacturers' proposed development and continued production took place, on the unlikely assumption that all aircraft would be sold. None of the estimates included prospective losses by BOAC from operating the aircraft.

Mr Benn's reaction was entertainingly adroit and unconventional. The only conclusion from these forecasts was that continuation in any form would involve very substantial costs for government, and it was obvious that Whitehall pressures would favour termination. In this situation, an early barnstorming visit to the manufacturers at Bristol was an obvious ploy, so that even if cancellation was the eventual conclusion of his Ministerial colleagues, at least he would be identified as a hero in adversity – this was in the pattern to which officials became all too accustomed: a grand meeting with the workforce and shop stewards without management, carefully handled press coverage, etc.

Less conventional was the protestation that the Department's submission was the first time that he, or indeed anyone else outside Whitehall, could be aware of the scale of costs involved. Since he had previously been involved in the project, and was fully aware that officials were bound to make corrections to company estimates – amply justified by subsequent events on the project itself, we could suspect only some delaying ploy. For, if anything, the figures would only fuel the strong counter-Concorde lobby. But he insisted that the estimates should be published.

There was a flurry whether we officials could defend our estimates: having been over and through these regularly in previous reviews, we could readily confirm that we could. Since any criticism was likely to come from the manufacturers, we produced two scholarly papers on the assumptions and adjustments that we had made to the airframe and engine estimates that they had submitted. Sure enough, Rolls-Royce called on the Department in high dudgeon, and we duly gave them the assumptions paper on the engine programme. They declared that they planned to line up with BAC to confront us. To this, we gave them BAC's estimates of production costs. This consisted of no more than a graph with a manuscript "bell curve", representing the theoretical model of costs being progressively exceeded from the proceeds of sales, always assuming that there were continuing sales.

The Division's trump card was John Webber, an even-headed production engineer, veteran of several military and air transport programs past, and we could cheerfully challenge Rolls-Royce to obtain better estimates of production costs from BAC than their manuscript doodle. Shortly thereafter, Rolls-Royce ruefully accepted that our estimate adjustments on the engine were not unreasonable, and confessed that BAC were unable to challenge the Division's figures.

Meanwhile, the swell of previous history pointed to only one outcome. The French, even if they now accepted that future sales prospects were close to negligible, were not going to lose face without a single production aircraft to show for their investment. And, after some Ministerial scuffles, in July the Prime Minister agreed with Giscard d'Estaing that no more than the 16 aircraft under construction would be completed. Tony Benn may have trumpeted this decision as a personal triumph, but the dynamics of the project moved the plates irresistibly to this conclusion.

Postscript – Saving a Bit More Face

Having a dozen aircraft in the hands of BOAC and Air France was pointless without any routes on which to operate them. A couple of trial services were opened up to Bahrain by BOAC and to Rio De Janeiro, via a stopover at a French Territory in the Caribbean by Air France. Neither of these carried the traffic beyond curiosity flights and insufficient to sustain a genuine scheduled service. For myself, having been kept on in the Division to provide continuity during the 1973/74 review, with the decision to stick to 16 aircraft, I was moved to the Industrial Development Unit: practice in coping with the completely zany accumulated through the years on the project proved an essential element of continuity.

The battle to get services admitted to New York – the transatlantic route between Paris/London and New York being the only one available offering sufficient "millionaires", or equivalents – was a saga in its own right. This was conducted by Ken Binning, who had taken over from Philip Jones, and the other Minister deserving of a "Concorde Palme d'Or", Gerald Kaufman.[15] This involved a demanding process of filing an environmental impact statement, rehearsals and a full hearing before the Secretary for Transportation – the limited number of flights and the argument that Concorde's noise was no greater than the generation of aircraft to which nearby residents had been accustomed, played their part in gaining approval. But the Port of New York Authority still refused entry, even though as a political manoeuvre, services to Washington had begun. And a US Supreme Court ruling – with all the Washington backstairs lobbying involved – was needed to quash their opposition to the Department of Transportation's clearance.

The aircraft was destined to carry a trail of headaches as various devices were employed to finance the operation, spares and maintenance support etc in a form that avoided accusations that airline services were being subsidised.

MYTHICAL SPIN-OFFS

There was unceasing pressure to identify spin-off gains from the development programme. But repeated exercises yielded negligible results. Because of the massive effort, especially in flight trials, to gain certification for civil operations, systems had to be frozen once their performance/safety/reliability had been established. Consequently, even though in flight performance the beautiful sleek shape might have been "decades in advance", its inherent technology was stuck in the 70s. An obvious example is the amount of wiring, weighing several tons, which today would be substantially reduced by computers and "fly-by-wire" systems. The use of advanced disk brakes in the undercarriage system was perhaps the closest to a "breakthrough" in technology.

Having gone through the fruitless exercise of looking for "spin-offs" many times, it was a pleasant surprise to learn that Renishaw, a specialist in high-precision measurement, evolved from work on the Olympus engine. But more generally, the project did establish that "modularity" i.e. breaking down the structure into elements produced at geographically different locations, was feasible for a complex integrated project. And it also demonstrated the inefficiencies of having two final assembly lines. Both lessons applied by the Airbus programme, indeed attributed by commentators as one of its main advantages over Boeing. While the latter has been progressively following a "modular" approach for its latest designs.

LESSONS

There are many obvious errors that stand out from the project's saga – a legally binding undertaking to collaborate on an undefined major project, a failure to establish thresholds or gateways for review, a failure to explore constraints from the operating context etc. Underlying these, however, was the fundamental discrepancy between the objectives of the French and British governments: the former saw the project as part of a deliberate effort to build an aerospace industry by setting up state-of-the-art facilities, acquiring technology and as a showpiece for industrial sophistication; to the British, the aim was narrowly to build a viable civil airliner. If the project dramatically highlighted this discrepancy, on lesser collaborative ventures it is worth an initial period of careful consultation to establish that the potential partners have an identity of objectives.

Postscript – Supersonic Strings

On a strictly personal note, one had suffered a moment of enforced frustration that prompted an existential challenge to face up to an aspiration that had never been pursued for one pretext of bad faith or another. Recalling adolescent wonderment while sitting a few feet away from a retired Professor of the Warsaw Conservatoire while he made the violin sing, I resolved to teach myself to play. From an initial purchase for a couple of quid of a knocked-about school violin, on a regime of spending 10 minutes a day, and working up to a Suzuki violin, one could eventually manage a passable tune.

But it was apparent from an early stage that the accomplishments of a Menuhin, Heifitz or Millstein were going to be out of reach. But the Concorde program offered the opportunity to be the first to play a violin faster than the speed of sound. And I have a certificate signed by Brian Trubshaw to prove it. Even if the performance was a bit of an anticlimax – the prototype had artificial weights to simulate a typical passenger loading, but more serious the internal vibrations completely swamped the sound of the instrument: while normally capable of generating complaints from a few hundred yards away, I couldn't even hear my rendition of Scheherazade myself.

Many years later, in Mrs Thatcher's glorious days, I was responsible for coordinating the "industry" brief for a meeting between her and her French opposite number. The French were proving slow in confirming the agenda, even to the point when late on a Friday afternoon the Prime Minister's Office were pressing for the briefing papers. Richard Evans* – later ambassador in Beijing – in the Paris Embassy was supposed to be chasing the French. So, in some impatience, I called the Paris Embassy and asked to be put through to Mr Evans. Some such phrase as, "What the hell's going on, Richard..." was hanging on the tongue, when a soft voice answered, "Mr Menuhin speaking..."

Quick gulp. "Sorry to trouble you, Maestro, but I was trying to contact Richard Evans," was the best I could manage, to which he responded that he was in Paris for a concert. But before he called off, I could not resist, "Speaking as a violinist myself..." and recounted my yarn of playing in Concorde. He replied that he had enjoyed flying in the aircraft several times, but not actually played in it.

Not the end of the story. Goes on like Mr Ponsonby. When Mrs Gandhi visited Britain, part of the formal ceremonies was a concert at the Festival Hall to be followed by a reception. Not attending the concert because of discussions on memoranda about future projects, we officials turned up for the reception before the concert was over. In the foyer, who should be there but Yehudi Menuhin and Ravi Shanker, who had earlier done a joint turn at the concert. One could boldly introduce myself, and happily recall our conversation about fiddling on Concorde.

ANNEX A

Concorde – Summary History up to New York Services

November 1962	Anglo-French Treaty
October 1964 - January 1965	Labour Government's failed attempt to withdraw
1967	Options total 74 from 16 airlines
1968	Benn/Chamant Agreement
1969	Prototypes 001 and 002 first flights
1972	Concorde Production Bill, with provision for loans of up to £350 million, approved.
	Production of 16 aircraft confirmed.
	BOAC orders 5, and Air France orders 4.
1973	Pan Am and TWA drop Concorde options, and other options also lapse.
1974	Harold Wilson and Giscard d'Estaing agree to complete only 16 Concordes, with no further development.
1975	Submission of US environmental impact statement.
1976	Experimental services begin to Bahrain and Rio de Janiero (later dropped as uneconomic).
	Secretary for transportation (Coleman) hearing approves Washington and New York services. But New York bans Concorde Washington service begins.
1977	New York Litigation begins/US Supreme Court overrules New York objections.
	London/Paris-New York service begins.

---

[1] The best summary of the complexities of the project was a seminar, held under confidentiality conventions, by the Major Projects Association at Templeton College, Oxford: *The Concorde Project – Proceedings of Seminar 9* in January 1983. The presentations had a fair cross-section of viewpoints from industry, airlines and government and presentations from leading personalities with direct personal involvement in the project.

A subsequent *Witness Seminar on Concorde* was held on 19th November 1998 under the auspices of the Institute of Contemporary British History, which will no doubt be published in due course. This had a wide attendance of personalities who had been involved, but inevitably lacked the orchestration and focus of the MPA event.

[2] An inevitable feature of having a very controversial task is for Whitehall to deploy some of its best talent. Jim (later Sir James) Hamilton was a scientist with a Farnborough background and had previously been project director on the Jaguar program before taking on the role of Director General Concorde when the Government's project organisation was set up. Jim was an embodiment of Huxley's argument that sciences could be as effective a discipline as Classics, or the liberal arts. He subsequently moved to the Cabinet Office, where he chaired the ad hoc group set up to vet the flow of Industry Act cases when Tony Benn was the Minister, and then to Permanent Secretary of the Department of Education.

Philip (later Sir Philip) Jones was the Under-Secretary, and a proud Classics double-first from Jesus. An extremely able, pragmatic and with an even temperament – though not without passion for Welsh rugby and tussles with the French – he went on to become Chairman of the Electricity Council and sadly died prematurely from an infection, but in time to save him any anguish at the Concorde disaster in Paris.

But the rest of the team, including engineering and program staff, were of high quality, and stood up to an almost continuous battering of PAC inquiries, public debate, CPRS examinations, while interacting continuously with the manufacturers and French counterparts.

[3] Morien Morgan (later Sir Morien), after a career in aviation development at Farnborough, became Controller of Aircraft (CA), and on retirement headed a Cambridge College. But other leading protagonists in the Concorde saga were Handel Davies, with the occasional Probert in the background at Farnborough, and there was a theory that the aircraft was some Welsh druidic plot.

[4] An illuminating vignette of technical exchanges with the French given by a senior BAC design engineer, with perhaps a shade too much condescension, runs, "The French, we found, in the main bright and very well trained, perhaps better trained than some British engineers, the cream of the Ecole Polytechnique. They did not have the background of the British team, but they had a great deal of talent and were quick to learn. They never missed a point, they were prepared to fight forever, and they were very well disciplined. A feature which does not seem to have been mentioned, but which was prominent in my world at least, was the

sudden unexpected change in relationship. Every French engineer at one time or another would, regardless of context, say something contradictory and negative leading to an increasingly acrimonious discussion, which usually ended up with de Gaulle. They would take up an unyielding position and huge charges of dynamite would be required to shift them."

[5] Put a group of Concorde technical old-salts in a room, and they will identify the air-intake, nozzle control and exhaust system as the most demanding feature of the development. A quirk of the design is that, while at take-off, the engines provide some 82% of the thrust, in supersonic cruise they provide only 8% of the thrust, with the rest deriving from the intake and nozzle. The air intakes have the prime function in supersonic flight to receive air at Mach 2.0 and slow it down to enter the engine at Mach 0.4 at the highest possible pressure and at a uniform air stream. Controlling these interactions for all the various modes of flight, including emergency conditions, consumed a major part of the development effort, involving protracted test flying in North Africa, Alaska, Caracas etc – and took expensive time.

Nor was this simply a question of technical gimmickry. There could be flight conditions where the pressure in the intake chamber could exceed the ability of the engine to digest it, in which event it spilled out in a "surge" and could trigger a similar reaction in the adjoining engine. As Brian Trubshaw, BAC's Chief Test Pilot, recalls, "In fact, the first time it went to Mach 2, I thought World War Three had started when I throttled back at the end of the first run and both right-hand engines surged." The French had no term for this effect, and we invented "pompage" as an addition to their vocabulary. But Brian adds, "The only experience of supersonic flight before Concorde was on military aeroplanes, which flew for relatively short times at supersonic speeds and were able to have a wide margin between the condition under which they were operating and the engine surge line, whereas on a long-range transport you have to operate as near the surge line as you dare. That was why we had to finely tune this aeroplane to the extent that we did. But of course, this is one of the facts which we now know about; nobody else whoever comes along to design a new SST has to start at the same point as we did."

A couple of other technical features of the box of tricks making up the aircraft: passengers on the many Concorde flights did not realise looking out of their windows that a few inches away the outside skin temperature could exceed 100°C, and the coolant to keep them comfortable in their shirt sleeves was the aircraft's fuel. This is circulated around the aircraft throughout its operation, and the flow adjusted to retain the centre of gravity within the critical limits of each phase of flight. As impressive as the aircraft itself was the fuel test rig at Filton that replicated the circulating system, and subjected it to the extremes of gravity and angular movement that might be encountered in practice. While the structural consequences of the widely fluctuating temperature conditions during operations were also tested by an even more spectacular facility at Farnborough, where a complete airframe were subjected to these temperature cycles many thousands in advance of any aircraft in service.

[6] In one of the more entertaining exchanges on the legal inhibitions against unilateral withdrawal, at a large review meeting the Treasury questioned whether, despite not having taken advantage at the time, it was still possible to use the breach of the Benn-Chamant criteria as an excuse to cancel. Jake Davies, an engaging Foreign Office lawyer (who sadly was killed with a number of other senior officials on a Tristar crash between Moscow and Paris), expounded the principle of *rebus sic stantibus*, or some such. Jim Hamilton, chairing the meeting, asked him to put this in terms that mere horny-handed men of toil could understand. Jake rose to the challenge. "Assume you came home and found your wife in bed with a buck-negro Top-Sergeant, and you threatened dire consequences should this happen again. And assume you came home a week later and found them in the same situation, but did not carry out your threat, 'your imprecations would be deemed to carry less force with each repetition'."

[7] In practice, the lines of communication within the official project structure were more rapid and honest than those within BAC, where, with their chieftain – Sir George Edwards – located at Weybridge and the development work carried out at Filton, the inevitable tendency to whitewash information as it flowed upwards was exacerbated by this geographic distance. And frequently officials would remark, "But, George…" tactfully attempting to point out that he was not up-to-date, or had not been adequately briefed.

[8] As a vivid example, in periods of testing for such crucial systems as the air-intake/engines, or while redesign was in progress, the predicted date for entry into service inevitably slipped. If, as was an inevitable consequence, it slipped uniformly with – and even occasionally faster than – real time, then on a straight extrapolation, the estimated development cost would be infinity.

[9] Another saga in its own right was the accumulation of experience of Concorde's sonic boom. However, many test runs to measure the distinctive "double-boom" signature, this could not illuminate the social dimensions of being subjected to this disruption. There was, however, a test-run course, starting beyond the Outer Hebrides and running down the Irish Sea with a spread of monitoring points principally to check flight performance. It didn't take much for the aircraft to run off course, and early on there were complaints of damage to windows, falling pictures etc.

This triggered a survey by Farnborough's Structural Department of buildings within a 50-mile corridor covering the test course to identify, and sometimes protect, vulnerable structures: for example, historic plate-glass windows. But most startling, we received expensive claims from mink farms: apparently, just prior to giving birth, if the animals are startled, they are prone either to ingest or eat their own young. Wiping out a generation of mink can be costly, and, for want of any counter-evidence, these claims had to be settled in some form. Subsequently, however, prior to every such test run, before the crack of dawn a message went to the vets in the vicinity of mink farms that might be affected so that they could observe directly what the effect was. A surprise was that there were as many as 8 to 10 such farms in the corridor.

Complaints from these test runs ranged from the farcical to the potentially tragic:

– The Belfast switchboard was jammed by reports of an outbreak of terrorist bombing;

– "I was just landing a 24lb salmon, when there was a sudden explosion. The fish jumped out of the water and snapped the line. Herewith enclosed a claim for..."

– From a crofter in one of the outlying islands, "My wife and I have three bairns, as many as we could afford. But six weeks ago, there was a terrible explosion, and my wife threw herself into my arms for comfort. We now have another bairn on the way. Please may we..."

There were more serious cases: a lady thrown from her startled horse, fortunately with no fatal or irreparable injuries; or, a slate was dislodged from a roof in Falmouth and fell, hitting the side of a pram with an infant inside a mere foot away.

Even after all this accumulated experience, there remained curious anomalies. Much of the supersonic test-flying program was carried out over approaches to the Channel, among the world's busiest sea-lanes, without generating a single complaint. Conversely, there could be a housing estate, largely unaffected, except one or two houses, which, through reflected reinforcement of the pressure waves, had all their windows smashed.

But in a project where spin-off benefits were difficult to find, this activity produced some examples: one enterprising engineer from Structures Department, after inspecting several cases of pictures falling from walls, concluded that the traditional method of hanging – by a single pin driven into plaster to support a hook, was inadequate since driving in the pin only weakened the plaster. So he devised a system of three or four shorter pins driven through a plastic base to which the hook was attached – now the standard method throughout most of Europe.

On another occasion, a structural expert was visiting Wells Cathedral to check the vulnerability of its windows and was invited by the verger to inspect one of the main columns that seemed to be corroding. With a naturally inquisitive mind, he ran a series of checks over months in his spare time and calculated that some pitch from the organ was echoed and amplified around the building and focused on this area of the column: thereafter, visitors will have noted that some baffles have been installed to dissipate this effect.

[10] As a period photograph on the eccentricities of Britain's democratic system, a question on Concorde's impact on the ozone layer was tabled in the House of Lords. Lord Denham was the Conservative spokesman on aviation: then a charming young man with some titular appointment to the Royal Household. For the briefing, our team included the Meteorological Office senior atmospheric chemist, and we assembled in the antique portals of the Lords' corridors before going into his allocated room. Quite understandably, there was nothing in our young spokesman's upbringing that touched even tangentially on the intricacies of the subject, and, as happens on these occasions, the exercise was one of

implanting phrases that at least were not misleading.

[11] In *Life in the Jungle* (Hodder and Stoughton), Michael elects to highlight his "sale" to the Shah of Iran, and the "sale" to British Airways, both equally bogus, though only the latter actually operated the aircraft.

[12] Even this was only a short-lived victory, since, as the current business title of Messier-Dowty implies, with the takeover of Dowty by Tube Investments (TI), the aviation undercarriage business was sold to a French company.

[13] If the Ecole Nationale d'Administration has a gallery of its more eccentric alumni, Bernard would deserve a high ranking. At the time, in his mid-30s, he had a field of responsibility covering that of three Deputy Secretaries in the British Departmental system. But his distinguishing traits were an ebullient self-confidence, matched by being heavily overweight, and with a gargantuan appetite – whoofing three stakes when most others could just cope with one. Intriguingly, comparing notes, he confessed to being born in Calcutta.

But a typical vignette was his recounting of an extremely weak shaggy-dog story about a Mr Ponsonby. We laughed politely. Before the next CDC meeting, we bet Jim Hamilton a bottle of champagne that he couldn't get Bernard to repeat his Mr Ponsonby story. Over lunch, Jim duly said, "Bernard, John Michell wasn't here at our last meeting and missed your Mr Ponsonby story." Bernard immediately dived into a repetition amid stifled laughs from the British delegation. Before the next meeting, we bet Jim two bottles of champagne that he couldn't get a further repetition of the story. So, at the next lunch, Jim began, "Bernard, John Fletcher (Air Marshal John Fletcher* had recently been appointed Controller of Aircraft) hasn't heard your Mr Ponsonby story, and I couldn't possibly do it justice..." And off went Bernard again, impervious to the roars of laughter that greeted his third retelling, or the anomaly of a joke that had greater impact with each repetition.

He subsequently moved to Aerospatiale, and Concorde old hands have speculated how many A300 series sales were achieved by Bernard simply gorging his customers into submission. Certainly, an unusual character.

[14] Jean betrayed a deft no-nonsense approach, being particularly severe on some of the ploys offered by the manufacturers to justify a dodgy commercial case: notably, there was a suggestion that load factors could be improved by "fag-ending" Concorde flights to New York by rebranding in Braniff colours to do a subsonic leg to Houston, which Jean shredded very sharply.

He subsequently moved through *Cabinets* of left-leaning Ministers to head Suez Finance and then given the invidious job of sorting out Crédit Lyonnais from past indiscretions. And he suffered cruelly from the routine bureaucratic gesture of initialling a fax message, since this was taken as evidence of implication in some dubious activities by his predecessors in California.

[15] Briefly referred to in *How to Be a Minister* by Gerald Kaufman (Sidgwick & Jackson) – an amusing, if partial, account of bumming around in the Department of Industry.

Vignette

Propensities for Arrogance

If the signature trait of top British management is arrogance – invariably inversely related to the performance of the businesses that they purport to run, this reaches its apogee when the company is dependent on the government for much of its business. One of the most luminous examples occurred during the Concorde project.

The project had started on the basis that the British and French governments would share the development costs, with the manufacturers financing production against the grand projections that they had offered of a vast potential market. After several £100 millions had been spent or committed by the UK taxpayer alone on development, the time came to begin series production.

Sir George Edwards, the British Aircraft Corporation's mystic man on the mountain was their Chairman, and he turned up to see the Minister accompanied by one of his sidekicks. Sir George declared that the company would not put up any finance for production. To drive the point home, the sidekick remarked "Isn't it time the Government put its money where its mouth is?" The sidekick was last observed on the board of Trafalgar House, probably the only appropriate business receptacle.

The pinnacle of native vacuous arrogance is probably beyond measure. The most successful assault on the summit yet has come from the "credit crunch", when City voices were accusing the Bank of England and the Government of "being behind the curve" in actually thinking before tossing tens of £billions into the morass created by incompetent financial management.

COLLAPSE OF OTHER INDUSTRIES

1974-78: THE INDUSTRIAL DEVELOPMENT UNIT

The Industrial Assistance provisions of the 1972 Industry Act have been variously interpreted: as an admission by the Heath government, despite the good times of the Barber boom, of the inadequacy of the financial system to provide the investment needed by industry to keep pace with rising competitors; a resurgence of the old spirit of George Brown's Department of Economic Affairs; or for free-market pundits a betrayal of the fundamental rules of the firmament, at least sufficient to prompt the resignation of Nicholas Ridley from a junior Ministerial post. Even in their most ghoulish nightmares, however, the instigators of the legislation could never have anticipated these powers in the hands of Tony Benn in his extreme left mode.

POWERS FOR FINANCIAL ASSISTANCE TO INDUSTRY

Whatever the origins, the dilemmas posed are not explicable without a summary of the key provisions of the Act. Apart from covering the designation of Development Areas, Industrial Development Certificates, support for the Textile Industry, support for shipbuilding and offshore construction etc, it also included provision for Regional Development Grants.[1]

Part II set out the powers for "Financial Assistance to Industry": the two main categories of assistance were Section 7, "to provide, maintain or safeguard employment in any part of assisted areas"; and Section 8 applicable "to benefit the economy" i.e. at any location, "in the national interest" that "cannot appropriately be so provided otherwise". The forms of permissible support were wide – "on any terms and conditions, and by any description of investment, or lending or guarantee, or by making grants". "Investment by acquisition of loan or share capital in any company" was allowed, but constrained as "not to be given... unless the Secretary of State is satisfied it cannot, or cannot appropriately, be so given in any other way", "not without the consent of the company", and disposed of "as soon as, in his opinion it is reasonably practicable to do so".

A curiosity was that these constraints applied to both Sections, but Section 8 had the added proviso "shall not acquire more than half, by nominal value, of the equity share capital of any company." Section 8 had two further constraints: the sums to "pay or undertake to pay… shall not exceed £5 million except... authorised by a resolution of the Commons"; and there was an overall limit for total assistance using these powers of £150 million which could not be increased by more than four tranches of £100 million.

If this seems dry old stuff, even with these limitations, these two Sections offered broad scope for support, and there must have been concerns about arbitrary use of these powers. Section 9, therefore, required an Industrial Development Advisory Board (IDAB) to be appointed "to advise" on the exercise of functions under Sections 7 and 8. The Board was to have a Chairman and 6 to 12 other members with "wide experience of, and to have shown capacity in, industry, banking, accounting and finance". "Advise" was given a sharp twist by the provision that if the Secretary of State "exercises his functions… contrary to their recommendation, he shall, if the Board so requests, lay a statement as to the matter before Parliament."

ADMINISTRATIVE STRUCTURE

As an organisational structure to implement these powers, there was a Departmental Minister, originally Christopher Chataway, given special responsibility for relations with the Board. The original IDAB was a mightily weighty outfit with the Governor of the Bank of England, Gordon Richardson*, in the Chair, and top industrial names like Arnold Hall* of Hawker Siddeley and Ray Brookes* of GKN (who seemed to have earned the nickname of "Batty"). The main IDAB was supported by a structure of Regional Industrial Development Boards located in the main Development Regions, who handled Section 7 cases up to a specified limit of assistance – initially £5 million – unless there were some overriding national concerns.

To support the Board, the Industrial Development Unit was set up with a predominantly "outside" staff, usually on 2 to 3-year secondments, from the private sector. This was Whitehall's first significant use of private sector secondments. A Director, originally Larry Tindale* on secondment from ICFC, was supported by 4 Deputy Directors usually of "senior partner" equivalent, but with a notional Under Secretary rank in the Department, and a number of "appraisal officers" with Principal rank. In addition, there was an Industrial Evaluation Section consisting of a couple of economists, a statistician and support staff whose main role was to identify activities where the UK had comparative advantages. The senior civil service post in the Unit was Secretary to the Board and general administrator for the Unit.

The structure was designed to provide professional and commercial expertise for appraisals and submissions to the Board, but had no budgetary responsibilities beyond its own running costs. Consequently, the Unit had to link closely with the Regional Policy Division on Section 7 cases, and the appropriate Industry Division for Section 8, though in practice there were often overlapping concerns including the Scottish and Welsh Offices who had devolved authority in regional aid cases. But the Unit maintained oversight on the use of these powers, coordinating the Annual Report to Parliament, and monitoring the commitments under Section 8.

The other admin to get out of the way is that it was not practice to "mix" the use of these powers. When Chrysler announced it was going to close its UK operations, for example, despite there being a considerable "regional" interest – not least the car plant at Linwood in Scotland – the case was handled under Section 8 since the predominant activities were outside assisted areas. The case also illustrates another quirk in that the total of assistance appeared a massive £184 million, but this included a tightly hedged guarantee of some £40 million which, however contingent, still counted as a "promise to pay".

Compared to the pace of activity subsequently, this system had barely been tested before I was put in to replace Peter Gregson* as Secretary to the Board.[2] There was very little case lore, and a conventional set of guidelines had been crafted about the powers being employed to correct "market imperfections", the importance of "viability", "externalities" that could be legitimately used to justify support etc. Coinciding with my arrival, it was all change as Gordon Richardson* was replaced by Bob Clark* of Hill Samuel, the departure of several leading industrial names from the Board, and "Rocky" Stone, by background a deft City share-juggler, who later went on to become Chairman of Manganese Bronze, became Director on Larry Tindale's departure. A matter of months later, he also left and was replaced by Graeme Odgers*, who was at the time an Industrial Adviser to the Department, after earlier appointments with the International Financial Corporation (IFC) and Barings.

BENN MEETS IDAB

It also seemed all change on the economy, as the 70s oil shock rippled through industry, leading to a rapidly rising caseload of "rescues" ranging from the "cooperatives", in which Tony Benn placed an obsessively professed ideological interest to major cases like Alfred Herbert, Ferranti, British Leyland, and Chrysler. Initial skirmishes where the Department were following Tony Benn's instructions to help the Meriden "sitting-in" workers to prepare a justification for assistance and the rumbling of other cases like Alfred Herbert were already in train in the months since Benn's arrival.

When Court Line informed the Department that it was in difficulty during June 1974, there was pressure of time – the company was a curious mixture, with a couple of holiday companies but also Appledore Shipbuilders and ship-repair yards in the North East. Tony Benn announced a readiness for the government to assist the shipbuilding interests: in the absence of any specific powers for nationalisation this had to be considered under Section 7. How far he may have implied an assurance for holidaymakers who had booked with the travel companies was the cause of an inquiry that rolled on for a couple of years. But this announcement hit the press on the morning when he was due to have an "getting to know you" dinner with IDAB in a private room at Lockets, a popular politicians' eating hole within "Division Bell" distance of the Commons.

This dinner, which from the outset had promised to be tricky – what with the extreme left-wing views that Tony Benn was propounding – turned out to be Siberian with Board members pulling out copies of the Act from their pockets. To a man they complained that it was assumed decisions to use the powers of Sections 7 and 8 would be with the advice of the Board, and they had not been consulted on Court Line. After some testy exchanges as the courses rolled by, a concordat was reached that the Minister would normally consult the Board, and, if he did not, this should be expressly stated. The drama had an added piquancy through the presence of Francis Cripps and Ms Frances Morrell, Tony Benn's political advisers, with the latter contributing to the atmosphere by smoking ostentatiously large cigars.

CASELOAD

To attempt a chronological account of the various cases would be impossible, since many were being pursued simultaneously as the Department became the first-call ambulance service for failing companies: the sequence of events on individual cases are recorded in the Regional or Industrial Division case files, and offer an enormous field for future archivists on Britain's industrial decline.

That the Department should have found itself in this role is in large measure a reflection of the absence of City mechanisms for refinancing companies in difficulty. There is quite a saga to be written about the City's evolution of procedures to handle rescue situations under the Bank of England eventually leading to the current "London Approach". At this time, however, the system had a mechanical simplicity where the dominant clearing bank, invariably with a fixed and floating charge, would limit its exposure to the write-down value of assets, and when a company's borrowing approached this limit, unless the company could show evidence of immediate improvement, a receiver was appointed. While the Department was coping with these cases, Sir Henry Benson, a senior accountancy figure, was active in exploring workable options, but none emerged in time to replace the DTI ambulance role. Finance For Industry (FFI) was one option, hardly effective at the time, which then became Invest in Industry (III), and now flying under the banner of *3i*, predominantly a venture capital fund (Larry Tindale was a linkman taking over the Chair at FFI and continuing with III).

Another consequence of this system was the position of the government in dealing with a failing company by virtue of the provisions of Section 332 of the then Company legislation, which held directors personally liable if acting in a manner that might jeopardise the interests of creditors. Whilst not directly applicable to Government, the Attorney General advised that the Government must behave as if it was. This "Caesar's Wife" ruling predisposed rescue cases to be handled by allowing the company into receivership, and then funding the receiver directly or by guarantee while the viable elements of the business could be sorted out. An added advantage lay in putting the company on a slab, where the, often bizarre, cross-guarantees and dodgy accounting practices could be dissected – there were plenty of predecessors to the manipulations of the Enron era.

FERRANTI

The Ferranti rescue, which occurred in September 1974, was typical of the deficiencies in the system. The procurement side of the Ministry of Defence approached the Department informally with concerns that they had been receiving ambivalent responses from the company in their normal contacts. I was deputed to make enquiries – tricky to make a blind approach. But speaking to the Company Secretary, I said that despite them having facilities in assisted areas, we had not received any approaches to help them invest. The response was that the company were concentrating on their existing business and were doing well. Less than ten days later, on a Friday morning, the Chief Advances Manager of the National Provincial asked to see Peter Carey*, the Permanent Secretary, and on entering the office said through clenched teeth, to quote the IDU case officer, that unless the government provided a guarantee, the company would be put into receivership that afternoon. Peter's response was a pointed speculation that however long it might have taken the bank to reach this conclusion, Ministers would have to consider the case in detail, and no response could be expected until the next week.

An initial assessment of the company's books was easy, since the Ferranti company headquarters was only a few floors above the IDU in Millbank Tower. So we made arrangements for an appraisal team and support staff to begin going through the company's books early on Saturday morning, with back-up staff to be brought in on Sunday to prepare an IDAB Paper to be taken by an emergency Board meeting on the Monday. Checking with the appraisal officer at midday on Saturday whether the back-up staff for Sunday would be sufficient, the response was that they would not be needed at all – once the company's performance was broken down to divisional level, its Trafford Park operations showed up as "a hole in the bucket" which had been allowed to run up large continuing losses over years, while other parts of the company seemed reasonably sound.

Apart from operations in assisted areas in the North West and Scotland, Ferranti was also involved in a number of priority defence programmes, and disruption would have had serious cost and delay implications. In the event, the Board agreed a guarantee for a receiver and the company was passed to the National Enterprise Board for restructuring and rejigging the management. That the weakness was disclosed after so simple a scrutiny was a commentary not only on the management – "after all, that's where it all started", was the excuse – but as much on the deficiency of the bank's scrutiny and disciplines. Subsequent calculations apparently indicated that the Government had made a return of some 25% on its guarantee, which suggests that a suitable mechanism to handle such cases should have been within the compass of the City.

The company's restructuring with Derek Alun-Jones, previously head of their plant near Edinburgh, as managing director, and the position of the "brothers" – Sebastian and Basil (Boz) – relegated out of executive roles, was generally accepted as a sensible "rescue". No one could have predicted the subsequent disasters that culminated in receivership in 1993.

BRITISH LEYLAND

So far as the Unit was concerned, the Ferranti case was the breaking of the floodgates, as the workload built up on the already very demanding legwork in pursuing Tony Benn's pet cooperatives, and other cases piled in. These ranged from complete no-hopers: for example, a small brick works in Wales employing about 30 locals was collapsing, and Eric Heffer – one of Benn's junior Ministers – was pressing for the Department to finance it, while at the time London Brick was accumulating brick stocks of tens of millions, to much larger cases with significant employment or technological/industrial implications.

Commonly the lights of the 7th and 8th floors of Millbank Tower would be on at 3 or 4 a.m. as appraisals, submissions and papers for Cabinet committees were being put together against extremely tight timescales. As an expression of the happy quality of human nature to respond with a closer community spirit when a small team is subjected to extreme pressure, the IDU developed its own cheery collegiate spirit, with the pent-up strains released in the wildest and most exuberant Christmas party experienced in a long career.

British Leyland was emblematic of the worst elements of British industry at the time. But the precarious state of the company was not more than dimly suspected: there had been earlier contacts with top management, with the latter not suggesting any concern except in funding their investment programme. In November 1974, Lord Stokes called on Benn to confirm that the company would require funding of some £200 million plus for its forward model development and investment needs, for which it would require some support from the government. And this was passed down to the Department to assess with the company. A review of the potential model replacement/upgrading options was prepared with the company, with estimates of cost, and with an assessment of possible levels of support, as the basis for more detailed discussions once there had been IDAB support in principle. The Board, with the odd caveat about the company's dismal production performance, were in general positive.

At the subsequent meeting with the company, the rather simple query was raised as to how the company would find the remainder of the funding for the programme beyond any Government support. By borrowing came the response. The bankers present said that this was the first that they had heard of a further extension of borrowing and doubted whether anything significant beyond current levels could be supported. A few questions later, it transpired that the company was facing a fundamental liquidity crisis.

The City had yet another opportunity to show its versatility. Lending to British Leyland had been on the basis of a "negative pledge" – a device for large companies where there was a presumption that they would not go bust (or be allowed to go bust) whereby, instead of bankers haggling over the scale and priority of their charge on assets, they all recognised that none would have primacy on the assumption that all would be equal in circumstances of default. Usually, one or two of the company's lead banks were deputed to keep an eye on the interests of the rest.

Well, you might have thought providing a guarantee to allow a company to continue operating would have been easy to negotiate since it would manifestly be in the interests of creditors. Not a bit of it. The meeting to negotiate terms of a government guarantee grew in scale to exceed any accommodation available to the Department in Millbank Tower, and we had to borrow Vickers' conference facilities on the top suite: a mere four Department officials were surrounded by nearly 200 representatives – from an astonishing array of banks – with their advisers, legal experts and sundry hangers-on, all peering at each other suspiciously.

Lord Ryder was appointed to make an appraisal of the future direction of BL, while operating under a guarantee under Section 8, and Bob Clark, as IDAB's chairman, was appointed to the Ryder Committee. When the Committee's proposals – essentially to retain the overall structure of the company with a large injection of new capital as equity to take ownership control by the government – were put again to the Board, to confirm the funding (and increase the level of guarantee) under the Industry Act, Bob Clarke had to stand down from the Chair and was present in a non-voting capacity. To say the outcome was a near-run-thing would be stretching the account, but there were certainly sharp queries whether sustaining the monolithic shambles resulting from earlier mergers and rationalisations that had created BL was in the best interests of the more viable elements of the business, and whether this approach was conducive to improving the history of fractious labour relations. One memorable quote was from Harry Irwin, a senior TGWU official on the Board, who commented, "If the workers were convinced that management were focused on getting new orders into the factory doors, you'd be amazed at the transformation that would follow." A phrase that returns whenever one reads of the success of foreign-owned companies where their erstwhile British predecessors are long defunct.

In retrospect, many commentators have been critical of the BL rescue. But in the context of the time, with a bleak economy, the company still accounted for more than 30% of the domestic car market; were major direct employers, and a significant, and in some instances, the sole customer for many subcontractors; consequently the social consequences of collapse were unpredictable. Some estimates put the consequential unemployment effect above 800,000. While the Government was coping with a militant left wing and with a parliamentary majority that was either negative or barely positive, any other outcome from the balance of tensions at the time would be difficult to envisage.

THE COOPERATIVES

At the other extreme from these major cases with high industrial significance, were a series of "cooperative" ventures, all spurred by workforce sit-ins when the business had collapsed. They therefore began in circumstances where their chances of sustainability were at their least likely, or downright hopeless, with the Department being expected to invent a pretext for providing financial support driven by a Ministerial head who idealised communist Chinese work practices. In terms of sheer physical IDU and official manpower, these cases consumed more resources than many others with real industrial relevance.

Each was a saga in itself, but to offer an official's perspective, the Meriden motorcycle cooperative was the one in which I was most closely involved, and the one with the widest subsequent influence.

THE MERIDEN COOPERATIVE

In historical accounts of Britain's post-war industrial decline, motorcycles these days rate barely a shrug – "BSA collapsed in 1975, although the remnants of the company survived for a few more years, with Government help, in the form of the worker-owned Meriden cooperative." (From Empire to Europe: Geoffrey Owen-Harper Collins pp192) or "over at Triumph, a workers' cooperative went belly up in 1973." (*Observer* 30 Jan 1994), or "the UK motorcycle industry was ruined by the invasion of cheap but sophisticated Japanese machines in the 1970s." (*FT* 27 February 2001) etc.

But it wasn't like that at the time. The machinations in setting up the cooperative, and coping with the pressures – whether real or inspired – for the entire industry to be nationalised involved a massive effort by relatively few officials, already under a range of demands in handling the impact of the early-70s recession on a largely unprepared industrial system. Nor do these retrospective views do justice to the motorcycle industry collapse as an exemplar in refocusing attention away from the "extreme left" preoccupations of "worker-power" to a more realistic awareness that international competitors had shifted the rules of the game, demanding a more complex, but equally radical, response.

The build up to the crisis had been a series of mergers and rationalisations through the 60s and early 70s that had seen the disappearance of such firms as Associated Motorcycles (AMC), J.D.Prestwich industrial engines and the disintegration of BSA under the extravagant indifference of "The Dockers". The remnants were consolidated, with the support of the then Conservative Government, in mid-1973, whereby under Manganese Bronze (perhaps best known as the traditional suppliers of London's Black Cabs), the BSA/Triumph motorbike interests were merged with Norton-Villiers (renamed NVT), and the non-motorcycle interests of BSA sold to Manganese Bronze. This seemed a balanced consolidation in the face of decline, especially since Dennis Poore, the chairman of Manganese Bronze – apart from being a businessman of the canny and deft variety – was a motorbike enthusiast, reportedly to be seen with sleeves rolled-up in the Norton pits on race days.

These moves brought together the three then existing plants – Wolverhampton, Small Heath (Birmingham) and Meriden (Coventry) – under single management. At the time of the merger, the BSA/Triumph motorcycle activities were continuing to lose money heavily, and the NVT management concluded that the only way to achieve efficiencies was to close Meriden and consolidate motorbike activities at Small Heath. This precipitated the sit-in at Meriden in September 1973, and a stock of completed motorbikes began piling up. This was in a national setting of the last year of the Heath government, with a weak economy, rumbling industrial unrest, the miners strike, three-day working week etc. If the Heath government dilemma was "who governs Britain", the Labour opposition were in a situation of accommodating a strong left-wing bias. In this hothouse atmosphere leading up to Heath calling an election in March 1974, the Meriden workers with braziers and picket-lines inevitably took on heroic status in standing up to the evils of capitalism, and thereby gained the backing of Jack Jones, one of the leading trade union figures of the day.

Almost immediately after the Election, with Harold Wilson running a minority government, and his appointment as Secretary of State for Industry – and before I had made the move from Concorde Division to the IDU – Tony Benn focused on Meriden. The Department cautioned against appearing to support illegal action, but an offer was made to provide expertise to help in preparing a case for viability, and to discourage NVT from taking steps to forestall the formation of the cooperative, with a public statement expressing readiness to view the position sympathetically and offering help to put forward a case for support. An early initiative was to persuade Dennis Poore, with some government financial assistance, to operate NVT with Meriden continuing as a managed cooperative within it. He declined, and, recognising the cooperative's lack of managerial skills, Geoffrey Robinson* – then MD of Jaguar (and before his subsequent career in the informal mortgage loan business) – was called in as an adviser.

The initial assessment of the case for the cooperative was bound to be hedged with serious doubts – the plant had been losing money heavily, and even if the workers' sacrifice of wages and purported efficiency savings could be secured, there were continuing challenges to be met. The models being made were losing market share against rising competition from Japanese producers vying against each other with new models; and to keep up a marketing drive in overseas markets, of which the US was the most critical, posed a major commitment of resources and expertise. The Department were, however, asked to put a "most favourable" case forward. On consulting IDAB about the outlines of the case, the Board were sceptical, but prepared to be non-committal, providing the management capability could be enhanced through Geoffrey Robinson and his command of Jaguar resources, and the competence to market in the US was secured. For even if competing bikes were far superior for most customers, there could be a residual "enthusiasts" market for a limited output of the Triumph brands, such as the Bonneville. (Subsequently, in evidence to the House of Commons Industry Committee, the IDAB Chairman indicated that of all the cooperative ventures pursued, Meriden had commanded the most sympathy.)

Despite reservations, Ministers (there was a special Cabinet Industrial Development Committee) gave assent in principle, "provided the arrangements were worked out in detail". Whilst this decision may have owed much to Tony Benn's eloquence and background lobbying by Jack Jones and others, it also owed something to the persuasion of officials to the Treasury that there might be a continuing "antiques" market for the output sufficient to sustain the venture for a few years, and that the costs could be contained to the £4.5-5.0 million ballpark. It was at this point that Graeme Odgers tossed the file to me with the remark, "All the appraisals have now been done, and it's just admin from now on." To be fair, the Unit was under increasing pressure as major company collapses and other cases were being pursued.

A blow-by-blow account of events would be impossible, but some of the key episodes were:

– Setting aside technicalities, a linchpin to establish the workers' cooperative as a genuine commercial operation was to have an adequate marketing system. The US market accounted for more than 60% of sales, but was sharply seasonal with virtually all sales being concentrated in the spring/early summer. Consequently, the usual supply cycle was to build up stocks progressively for the peak sales season, and this required funding supported by ECGD (The Export Credit Guarantee Department). These sums could be considerable – £8 million plus if a viable level of sales was to be maintained. But ECGD demanded some recourse against the exporter's assets as a safeguard against irresponsible over-extension of stocks. Under conventional banking arrangements, such contingent liabilities were charged against assets, and detracted from a company's borrowing limits.

Since it would have been impractical for the cooperative to set up a sales organisation from scratch, the only feasible route was to market the Meriden output through the established NVT network. Dennis Poore was extremely reluctant to penalise the rest of the NVT operations by conceding a charge against assets from which his business would not benefit. Conversely, with negligible margins in price to give NVT a worthwhile incentive fee, pressure to discharge this guarantee was the only leverage on NVT to make every effort to sell the Meriden output. After many a wriggle, and a series of discussions with Mr Poore, involving Harold (Lord) Lever – the Government's resident business contacts factotum, Joel Barnett – then Chief Secretary of the Treasury, Geoffrey Robinson, and Tony Benn, an accommodation was eventually reached with a still reluctant Dennis Poore (but not without an exceptional arrangement with the Treasury – see below).

– Harold Lever was called in on several occasions, even at one time trying to get Arnold Weinstock of GEC to put some money into the cooperative as "an experiment" to see what efficiencies could be gained by worker participation. But at his first meeting with officials, Lever made some apologetic remark that civil servants must be amazed at the lunatic propositions that we were expected to treat seriously – a fairly common challenge to officials attempting to support the Meriden case – to which the only response could be, "We're a philosophic bunch," or, "We're trying to give the operation the best chance." This response was even occasioned by an Exchequer and Audit clerk routinely going through the IDU files demanding an interview. (The Exchequer and Audit Department – now the National Audit Office – serves the Public Accounts Committee and its staff have an unrestricted right to call for any file.) Anticipating that despite all precautions, some irregularity might have been committed, I asked what his concern was, to which he shook his head in bewilderment, and murmured, "How do you cope?"

This ambience put the Department's officials in a bizarre situation: normally in Whitehall gatherings, officials dutifully plead the viewpoints of their respective Ministers, and usually there will be a measure of common ground between their different positions. But, with Benn, there was no supporting voice from anywhere – at most a few tolerant smiles as if we had swung in from some wildlife sanctuary, since he had apparently isolated himself in a minority of one.

– Dennis Poore had repeatedly made the point that the cooperative was viewed with animosity by his NVT workforce at other motorbike factories, who saw the offer of government support to Meriden – especially if it involved commitments from NVT – as a threat to the viability of their own jobs. Tony Benn, and indeed officials, had tended to interpret these remarks as part of Dennis Poore's negotiating tactics. But we had to modify this assessment somewhat.

The Small Heath/Wolverhampton workers sought a meeting with Tony Benn accompanied by their local MPs – Roy Hattersley and Dennis Howell, who had the distinction of being an ex-FA referee. It was led by the senior convener who did a masterly job of orchestrating the views of his delegates. At one point, a delegate, to all appearances a larger elder brother of Mike Tyson, half rose out of his seat with the threat, "Mr Benn! You're blackmailing us," to which the Convener gestured for him to sit down, and remarked, "You see, Minister, how strong feelings are." For officials, accustomed to seeing Tony Benn talk birds out of trees, it was a novelty to hear his best arguments capped by one or other of the MPs present with phrases like, "Come off it, Tony, you can't expect them to buy that." And the climax came with a peroration from Tony Benn pleading that the cooperative was close to "the heart of socialist principles" to which came the tart reply from a bespectacled voice at the left of the delegation, "You can't eat socialist principles."

It was left that the Minister would visit the plants to see for himself. Afterwards, chatting with Ken Griffin, an experienced Trade Union hand and the Department's industrial relations adviser, I remarked that of the many formal delegations one had seen, ranging from road schemes, shipbuilding, the aircraft industry and so on, the local convener had put on a tyro performance which should be worthy of accelerated promotion. To be met by the dispiriting response that there was no chance, and he would have to be content to slog his way up the Union hierarchy.

But this exchange was as nothing compared to Tony Benn's subsequent visit to Small Heath. As was the wont, Tony Benn had insisted on seeing only the shop stewards and the workforce. And, while Dennis Poore and the management had made all the arrangements, they did indeed stay scrupulously clear of the meetings. As usual, officials had turned up beforehand, and on arrival the Minister was shown into a small meeting room, crowded with shop stewards and union delegates, where the atmosphere was thick with cigarette smoke and heated abuse. Through this murky scene, the exchanges were so angry and insistent, with personal insults being thrown about, that it was difficult to make any coherent record.

The later visit to the plant was far from the usual turned-on cheery rush with a teacup and sandwiches. And the day concluded with a mass meeting with the entire workforce, a few hundred or more. Tony Benn switched on his most informal and familiar style, and sat down on the edge of the dais, with officials standing anxiously behind. If the early exchange with shop stewards had been tough, this was rowdily abusive – even the canteen ladies joined in. As the shouts became louder and more hostile, officials edged progressively further back on the stage, and Ken Griffin deserves credit for being the only one to hang within four feet of the embattled Minister. The conclusion was indicative as, after calls for silence and "hush", Tony Benn offered to sum up by saying that their message was on the lines that he had visited them that day, and "you want me to go back..." which, before he could go on, immediately provoked wild cheers and a bedlam of applause. And it took several minutes before he could carry on. But he suggested that it was now for him to find a solution to give them some greater assurance about their future with the cooperative running.

An unexpected and striking theme of the complaints were recollections of past feuds with the BSA factories, and Meriden in particular, suggesting that we had become embroiled in an ancient tribal war. There had apparently been occasions when the NVT plants had faced difficulties and found their approach to co-operate with Meriden turned down flat. From a perspective where Professor Michael Porter's concept of "clusters" as the most benign structure for industrial development has become the conventional wisdom, perhaps once the rivalry between brands like Matchless, Brough-Superior, Douglas, Rudge, Sunbeam, Scott, Thunderbird, Daytona, Bonneville, Enfield, Ariel, Commando etc predominantly made in Midlands factories may have stimulated a competitive dynamic that encouraged upgrading, driving for market share etc. But with decline this dynamic can transform itself into closed and defensive attitudes that make revival almost impossible; and perhaps the dynamics of declining "clusters" is to be Britain's current contribution to industrial history, and contrasts with such examples as the revival of the Swiss watch industry.

– Meanwhile. Back on the Meriden front, negotiations between the workers of the putative cooperative and NVT had reached a valuation for the assets and stocks that on monitoring appeared reasonable, and with a fair allowance for working capital for the plant to run for a few years (a minimum of three years was the yardstick for offering a chance of continued survival) came out at £4.95 million. Since Coventry was not in a designated Assisted Area, assistance had to be evaluated under Section 8, with the special proviso that assistance above £5.0 million could only be permitted with an Affirmative Resolution in the House of Commons – this requires the government to table a resolution to approve the particular use of the powers, so that the opposition could debate the case if they wished.

To the Treasury, the £4.95 million looked suspiciously like doctoring the figures to duck beneath the threshold for tabling a Resolution. After going through the figures and accepting that they were genuine estimates, Bill Ryrie*[3] protested, "I'm going to get that b...... to the 'bar' of the House, if it's the last thing I do." Surprising since Bill was one of the more pragmatic and equable of the Treasury clan. Excusable perhaps by frustration at being asked to swallow so many weird proposals from the Department of Industry in a short time. But he lighted on the need for an ECGD guarantee, and insisted that this should be counter-guaranteed by Section 8, taking the total of "funds paid or promised to be paid" above the £5.0 million threshold. There is a long-standing convention that one Whitehall Department cannot guarantee another, but this was thrown overboard. And if any successor Department wants to breach this convention, they have a precedent.

– Following the visit to Small Heath, and in response to the request to explore a wider package of support embracing all three motorcycle plants, officials had indicated a ball-park minimum of some £20-25 million, taking account of upgrading models and plant. But the Minister had to go back to colleagues at the Cabinet Industrial Development Committee because of the need for a Parliamentary resolution. And his suggestion of a new more comprehensive approach hit other Ministers like a brick wall. No doubt alarmed at the danger of the sit-in/cooperative pattern being seized as a precedent, they were sceptical of any industry-wide scheme to embrace the other factories. So, whilst agreeing the Meriden package, they insisted upon a thorough survey of the industry's prospects against the strength of Japanese competition.

For officials, who had repeatedly called attention to the strength of Japan's motorbike manufacturers, observable from the street – and not least from the numbers of Japanese bikes in the Meriden "enthusiasts" car park – this was a welcome note of realism. And within a fortnight, in March 1975, the Boston Consulting Group (BCG) had been commissioned to review options for a sustainable UK motorcycle industry – the selection was influenced by the strength of BCG's expertise in Japan.

– Negotiations between the cooperative and NVT continued, with Dennis Poore still uncomfortable with having to carry the obligation to market the cooperative's output without assurances that this would not have a negative impact on NVT. But, in March there was a debate on the Affirmative Resolution where the Conservative opposition focused on the sit-in as a justification for support with little attention to the more fundamental question of viability against international competition. In the following weeks the contractual details were negotiated between Manganese Bronze/NVT and the Meriden cooperative, and the Department's officials took an oversight position, expressly not to interfere, but to ensure that all the details were agreed so that the final signing ceremony could go off smoothly.

– A final session with Dennis Poore was also needed to clear the way for the Great Day of signature. Because he professed continued reluctance to accept the ECGD recourse requirements while Department of Industry officials were insistent that these should stand to keep the incentive on NVT to sell the Meriden output, the issue was referred to the Treasury to hold the ring. The meeting was chaired by Leo Pliatsky* – an archetypical example of that Treasury breed whose arrogance far outstrips any conceivable level of competence. And subsequently one of a string of Treasury *gauleiters* appointed to the upper reaches of DTI to ensure that the ivory slates were not allowed to slip off the Whitehall edifice. After an extraordinary opening flourish about being an administrator of long and outstanding experience who was confident that he could resolve any outstanding issues, following Mr Poore's explanation of his concern, Pliatsky conceded the point in two minutes on the grounds that the Department of Industry had agreed to a counter guarantee. How far this waving of leverage may have hastened the eventual closure of the cooperative is difficult to assess. But one recalls a phone call from Dennis Johnson, the leader of the cooperative team, some eighteen months later to say that he had managed to achieve an improved output the previous week, but the sad fact was that the bikes were just not selling.

– The Great Day arrived a few weeks later, and, with the preliminaries and documents all checked, the proceedings were expected to be completed by midday for some celebration drinks with the Minister and Jack Jones. Despite all precautions, the ceremony was bedevilled by a series of queries on annexes and schedules. From the Chair one was bound to give each a period for considered discussion and press for some compromise. For example, the cooperative had discovered that the number of "pallets" in the schedule was a figure like 87 short – for one whose only previous contact with the term had been in national service where it denoted a light straw-stuffed, and extremely uncomfortable, mattress, this required some elucidation. (It turned out to mean the wooden frames in which completed bikes were packed for shipment.) And the cooperative had made a detailed check of the mileage on the ancillary vans and disputed the value placed on them. As a result of reconciling a series of such disputes, punctuated by anxious calls from Benn's Office, the signature ceremony had to be deferred into late afternoon.

– Among the miscellany of personalities in the Meriden saga, Dennis Johnson, a quiet spoken and scrupulous guy, commanded a great deal of sympathy for holding his team together, but also because the company had suffered in the past from grotesquely bad management. If further confirmation were needed, it came unexpectedly some years later when at a routine internal meeting I was citing the motorbike manufacturers as typical of the parochial blindness of British industry in failing to realise the advances of their Japanese competitors, at which one of the officials present, Bill Morgan – a font of knowledge on manufacturing industry – seemed slightly put out. It transpired that he had been one of the small BSA team of design engineers, and he countered that they had reverse-engineered Hondas, Suzukis and Yamahas. And they were fully aware of the improved design, higher quality manufacture and performance, which could be matched only by a radical change with new models and tooling. But, summarising the attitude of the top management, "They just weren't interested."

But high on the honours list would be Alfred Suich, the Assistant Secretary assigned to the division responsible for motorbikes, who was one of those earnest, diligent and steady characters, rarely mentioned in dispatches, who hung in there despite the bizarre situations in which officials were placed. Ironically, he had previously been in the division responsible for shipbuilding at the time of the Upper Clyde Shipbuilders riots, and had been moved to the seat dealing with motorbikes as a rest area.

Among others in the shadows who made memorable contributions was

Bill Lapworth, a Coventry district TGWU official, who produced the prize quote that British workers had a right to continue making motorbikes by "knife and fork" methods irrespective of the competition.

– Harold Wilson reshuffled his government in June 1975, and Tony Benn was swapped with Eric Varley at the Department of Energy. The BCG report was submitted in July: given the amount of time, it was an outstanding and authoritative study, embracing detailed accounts of the Japanese and other producers against their British counterparts, their relative model ranges, scale and market penetration, and a diagnostic analysis of the collapse in the British industry's dominance of the US big-bike market a mere six years earlier. Although entitled "Strategy Alternatives for the British Motorcycle Industry", the obvious conclusion was that British manufacturers had fallen so far behind their competitors in innovation, market penetration, scale, financial strength and, above all, in productivity, where the difference was staggering, that there was no realistic option for a sustainable industry. (A summary of the study is reproduced in a lecture given subsequently – Appendix A.)

Consequently, among Eric Varley's first tasks was to attend a presentation by the BCG team to representatives of the Meriden cooperative, NVT and trade union representatives. Inevitably, the occasion was subdued, but one ghost laid to rest was the claim that Japan's success derived from "slave labour", where it was pointed out that on a comparable basis Japanese workers were paid considerably more than their British counterparts – the trick was their output of saleable bikes was vastly higher. But equally inevitably, perhaps, mutterings about "The Boston Stranglers" could be heard in the audience.

The report had been circulated to other Departments when it was received, and endorsed for publication. There was some consultation on deletions to protect commercially sensitive material, but the report, with an Appendix of detailed analyses, was published at the end of July 1975 (Cmnd 532 and 532-1). If not an instant bestseller, it was widely taken up by business, the trade unions and academia. Its conclusions were sufficiently clear that pressures for further government support to the industry subsided, but the established arrangements for the Meriden cooperative continued.

– The weaknesses identified in the motorcycle industry – essentially a failure to keep up with the rapid adoption of new technologies, production techniques and product innovations of international competitors in the previous two decades, were replicated in degree across industry. Vividly illustrated by the range of companies in nigh-cadaver condition confronting the government in the vehicle industry – in trucks as much as

BL and Chrysler, the struggling hulks of shipbuilding, machine tools, electronics etc. At the Chequers gathering of the CBI, Trade Unions and senior Ministers on the 5th of November that year, as recorded in rather surly terms by Tony Benn in his diaries[4] – in fact, a much more detailed account than the brief summary of conclusions passed down to officials, Dennis Healey, then Chancellor of the Exchequer, and others used the collapse of the motorcycle industry as a clear example of the malaise that was leading to the UK falling behind international competitors, and whose cure lay beyond ideological gimmickry. Instead, a pragmatic approach – expressly not "picking winners" – based on a sound analytic framework was commended. This reorientation was to be coordinated by the National Economic Development Office (NEDO),[5] and was supported by the CBI, even if an element in their thinking was that this approach was preferable to the threat of the National Enterprise Board being charged with a more acquisitive remit.

Whether the NEDO set-up, or indeed any system, stood a cat-in-hell's chance of success – against the confrontational mental programming of the major participants, the fragmented parochialism of the professions, and obsessional "arm's-length" relationships of Britain's industrial society – is debatable. For these separatist attitudes denied any prospect of the informal, cooperative and mutually supportive networks that underlay the success of Germany, Japan, France and Italy – all of whom had been experiencing their "miracles" in the 60s, irrespective of their different formal institutional structures. But it was at least reasonable for the government to look at these as potential models to reverse Britain's industrial decline on virtually every front. In the event, after the Chequers concordat, the focus of the Department of Industry shifted to attempt some constructive use of the Industry Act powers, albeit that there was still a steady flow of rescue cases, most spectacularly Chrysler (UK).

The period has, however, been mythologized as one of "national champions" – "Britain, then the sick man of Europe, was an arch-exponent of the strategy. It spawned a series of disasters of which British Leyland, the long defunct motor group, was perhaps the most prominent." ("No to champions", *FT* 26.5.04.) In fact, for those who bothered to follow events, it was an era when all pretensions of British industry being competitive on a world stage were dispelled, and when the collapse of the shipbuilding, motorbike, domestic vehicle industry, and other "lame ducks" served to demonstrate that British companies, and the maladaptive financing system behind them, were irredeemably decades adrift of the levels of investment, efficiency and innovation achieved in other countries – a fair number of whom had been successfully applying government measures to encourage the development of their leading companies.[6] The same fantasy-history recurs with the myth of "picking winners": when all the evidence was that Britain's national competences and institutions were incapable of generating winners, outside perhaps fields where the government was providing a steady stream of relatively soft orders.

THE OTHERS

– The Kirkby Manufacturing and Engineering (KME) cooperative was in facilities that had been left by a typical background of collapse, purchase and closure, but originally a subsidiary of Fisher-Bendix. At the time of its receivership it was employing some 1200 and Jack Spriggs, a robust local convener of the AWEU, pressed to have it saved. The Kirkby area was one of the saddest examples of dereliction, variously described as "a wasteland", "a battlefield", "devastation", and an emotional response of concern at the loss of jobs in the vicinity was understandable. Originally a body-pressing facility, the product mix had been "rationalised" into storage radiators and fruit juice, and it was nigh impossible to see any chance of a sustainable business.

Kenneth Cork*, an accountant who became the laureate of receivers, and by virtue of his contacts with the Department, almost worth a supernumerary appointment, was the receiver. His first reaction was that the business could not sustain more than 400-450 jobs. Yet the case was pursued, with the Department having a role of assisting the argument to be developed, and put to IDAB. While sympathetic to the social circumstances, the Board could not endorse any prospect of viability. Despite a negative assessment by the Board, Ministerial colleagues reluctantly agreed to a "once-for-all" grant of £3.9 million.

The case became the first – and one suspects still the only – instance where IDAB invoked the provisions of Section 9 in requiring the Minister to make a statement to Parliament. From a personal position, I had the dual-hat of drafting the Chairman's note to the Minister, and then the Minister's statement to the House.

Another side effect was to let loose a debate on the formalities of "an Accounting Officer Minute". By convention the ultimate defence of a Permanent Secretary, who is formally the Accounting Officer for the public funds used by the Department, is to inform his Minister that he will not be able to defend the use of funds if questioned by the Public Accounts Committee, and to copy this advice to the Auditor General. This has traditionally been a very rare resort. And Peter Carey* warned that he would apply this defence in the KME case given the lack of viability and

IDAB's views. Tony Benn's questioning lead to a review of this procedure and its formalities being redefined. (Its warming to see that DTI's Permanent Secretary must have been rustling through the old files in the case of Circatex – *Observer* 29 Jun 2003.)

An entertaining episode followed the arrival of a new young appraisal officer fresh from the cloistered tabernacles of Price Waterhouse. On arrival, he was told that he would be taking over the KME case from his predecessor, and given the latest appraisal to study in preparation for a meeting with the Minister that afternoon. He accompanied other officials to the meeting, which included Jack Spriggs and a belligerent delegation. Tony Benn, as was his habit, tossed the appraisal across to the visitors saying that this was his Department's assessment and invited them to comment. There followed a fairly blunt exchange, in which our new recruit acquitted himself with honours, as reported by others. On return to the Unit, he asked me whether this episode was typical, to which one could only comment, "Oh just another dull day at the office."

The business dragged on, but as the cash-flow allowance of the grant ran down, it began facing liquidity problems. A quirk of the story is that, just as it was confronting collapse, the hot summer in 1976 boosted sales of fruit juice to provide enough cash flow to just tide it over. But calls for further funding were up against the problems of having to renegotiate the Whitehall hoops again, since the decision had been "once-for-all". But not before a Whitehall economist, no doubt intent on displaying his adherence to prevailing policy, produced some calculations on a "resource" basis that continued subventions could be justified since the cost would be less than the level of providing unemployment benefit were the outfit to close – an argument which could in theory be applied to every business in the country hovering on the verge of collapse.

– Scottish Daily News in Glasgow pressed to be allowed to form a cooperative, again led by an energetic local convener, Alistair Mackie. This was perhaps the closest these "rescue cooperatives" came to a commercial proposition. Arthur Russell in the Regional Policy Division – another very capable and assiduous official who rarely gets mentioned in dispatches (and one with even worse handwriting than my own, often criticised for being too small: but Arthur managed to be illegible with a massive personal script of huge spidery scrawls) – held the line that viability would be extremely difficult to argue without some genuine risk sharing by the "owners", and a remarkably frank prospectus was prepared against which the workers put up a large part of their redundancy money.

Arthur had earlier served a long stretch in the Parliamentary Secretary's office in the Ministry of Aviation, with a string of Ministers including Geoffrey Rippon and "Monty" Woodhouse. But he had a rough time with his early submissions in the Benn regime: Eric Heffer had rejected one, with the rejection copied around the entire Department, on the grounds that he would only consider submissions in English, since Arthur had apparently used the term "pari passu". Another had been rejected by Tony Benn because it was too "Treasury", to which, Arthur, displaying true resourcefulness, revised the submission with a liberal sprinkling of phraseology from *The Daily Worker* and *The People*, to have it applauded as a model for what Departmental submissions should be. But his coup was to persuade Robert Maxwell, another great Labour charlatan, to put up £100,000 of his own money to support the Scottish Daily News.

The Scottish Daily News case duly scraped through a sceptical IDAB because of these financial contributions, and Ministers subsequently agreed a "once-for-all" contribution. With a business had been steadily losing money each month, and in the absence of any sharp rise in circulation, the operation closed within months of the assessment forecast. A boost to officials' morale came at a meeting with Len Murray, then head of the TUC, when Tony Benn complained that officials did not regard the case as viable, to which Murray replied, "You'd better listen to your officials."

Perhaps the most damaging consequence of these cooperative escapades lay in the false expectations under which employees were persuaded to put in their efforts, and indeed incomes, on ventures that had a negligible chance of success. The cooperative as a form of industrial structure – for example in such cases as Mondragon in Spain, or the artisan networks of Modena, or the structures evolved under "trust" arrangements elsewhere in Europe that encourage a collegiate unity of purpose – can be effective in operating quite large and diverse businesses. And in a country with stereotyped "equity" corporate structures, some variations in corporate form should be welcomed. But hardly likely to command much support by a track record of failure, and one sensed that Tony Benn might have begun to recognise the futility of encouraging cooperatives on the back of collapsed businesses. For one recalls a note – one of the strengths of the public service was the wide information spread of copies of notes of meetings, minutes identifying action etc – that he had seen a delegation from a Plessey plant confronting closure, and told them that achieving a viable cooperative was a difficult route.

OTHER CASES

With an active case list exceeding 200 at times, a detailed exposition for each can be left only to future academics picking through the entrails of Britain's industrial decline. And there would be plenty of revisionist material to be found in the records of IDAB meetings to counter fashionable panglossian accounts. But just a few flashes:

– Bear Brand employed some 500 manufacturing ladies' tights at a plant near Liverpool. As it confronted collapse, there was an irresistible political urge to save the jobs. The trouble was that the output went almost entirely to the UK market, where other producers were facing similar market pressures. Our economists came up with a blinding formulation, "displaced concreteness", whether invented on the spur of the moment, or from some arcane textbook: assuming the economy is modelled on tiddlers in a jam jar, assistance to support Bear Brand would only have the effect of putting extra pressure, with the prospect of further redundancies, on other tights producers (tiddlers) elsewhere in the UK. Eventually support was denied.

– The machine tools business of Kearney and Trecker Marwin was facing collapse. They had a reputation in some high precision products, and the view was that the business could be viable with some financial support to its development and marketing. There followed some negotiations where some funds under Section 8 were made available – the company was based near Brighton – with a view to securing a viable structure. The resulting deal was incredibly complex, with A, B, C classes of shares, preference shares and options – virtually every gimmick in the book. The trouble was that the appraisal officer, however adroit at manipulating these devices, was less than coherent at explaining their rationale. To meet queries from the PAC and elsewhere, the file was repeatedly returned to have this financial structure explained: having wrestled several times with this task, the best one could admit was a brief second or two of understanding that vanished the moment the file was shut. The firm was later sold to Vickers, but the site eventually closed in the 90s.

However, the appraisal officer subsequently atoned handsomely. He was one of the Department's team being interviewed by the House of Commons Industry Committee. Mr Maxwell-Hislop, notable for having pursued the "hybridity" attack on the Shipbuilding Nationalisation Bill, seemed to have developed a phobia against the Department – even, apocryphally, having accused the Department of showering him with water as he walked past its building in Victoria Street. In the case under discussion, he pointedly asked each official what they had done on hearing news of the impending company collapse: each in turn flannelled an answer, until it was the turn of the appraisal officer, who replied, "What a stupid question". A reply hanging on the lips of generations of civil servants appearing before Parliamentary Committees, but bitten back through conventions of deference.

– In the Chrysler rescue, the company had declared initially in November 1975 that it was planning to close all its UK operations, but subsequently said that it would keep these going with a suitable package of support. The internal government problem of achieving a balanced response, with the Scots as usual binding on about some unviable activities north of the border, was tricky enough. But then negotiations began with Messrs Ricardo and Iaccoca of Chrysler against a tight timetable. The company representatives probably knew to the nearest cent what they were after. As negotiations dragged on through Wednesday, through Thursday, and into Friday morning, one of the UK side said that he would have to leave early that evening because it was choir practice, and he was the only tenor available. Then the Chairman of the British team added that they couldn't reconvene negotiations until Saturday afternoon, because he was keeping goal for his local hockey club second eleven. But they did reconvene on the Sunday. The eventual rescue deal was very controversial. But again, in the familiar British way, the businesses were subsequently sold to Peugeot before being rationalised.

– Reconciling the disparity between Tony Benn's views and his Ministerial colleagues occasionally called for some deft handling of cases where departmental responsibility lay with the latter. On one occasion, a civil contractor was going bust on an important project, with severe implications for disruption and delay. Tony Benn's reaction was that we should secure some public ownership. But the last thing the Department concerned wanted was an equity stake in a construction company. Repairing an over-extended balance sheet usually demands a conversion of debt to equity, or an injection of new equity. In the context of the time, banks were reluctant to convert, and a government grant effectively stood in for new equity. The rescue package achieved this, but to meet Mr Benn's stipulation, there was provision for a further tranche of guaranteed loans to which a conversion option was attached – a sure incentive on the management not to draw down any of these loans.

– Some of the cases hit high farce: Fodens, a small quality truck manufacturer ran into cash-flow problems that arose, on examination, from having introduced a computer-controlled spares acquisition system. The trouble was that – in the words of the old rugger song – "there was no way of stopping it", and as demand collapsed, surplus spares began stacking up. This seemed a straightforward rescue where, with the support of a guarantee, the City could refinance the company and correct any management weakness. But this process took months, including a personal chase to Ron Artus, a notable investment guru of his day at the Pru, before the Department's guarantee could be discharged. This was accompanied by headlines in the financial press, "Saved from the clutches of Benn". The company was subsequently pocketed by Paccar, along with a few other bits and pieces of the truck industry.

– Gardner, the Rolls-Royce of diesel engines, was one of those grand old businesses where family members would make personal calls on international marinas to enquire whether the yachts used their engines, and whether there were any complaints. The appraisal visit was to respond to a suggestion that the company might expand, and typical phrases from the appraisal officer's account were on the lines:

"We only visit the bank to deposit money."

"We have three customers for every engine we produce."

Question: "If you're going to expand, won't you need more of these (pointing to stocks of components), and so more working capital?"

Answer: "Oh yes. But Jonathan looks after the shelves."

Question: "What about research and development?"

Answer: "Sh-sh-sh-sh-sh. Jack deals with that. You'll find him in the hut behind the main plant. But don't tell anyone else what he tells you!"

In the way of British industry, the business was merged with Hawker Siddeley's other diesel operations, such as Lister, and then taken over by BTR. And so on.

WHAT SYMPTOMS?

As the first rush of rescue cases struck just after Ferranti, the Unit conducted an analysis of possible symptoms that might help predict the casualties to which we would be expected to send our emergency medical teams. This was long before "Z ratings" or the multitude of accountancy formulae – all inevitably ineffective. And the staff researched the annual accounts of our existing A&E casebook to find common ailments in debt/equity shifts, levels of interest payments, stock levels, work in progress, and categories of liabilities etc. Not with much success, not least because the whims of top management, even among the most admired, rarely show up through the doctoring of accounts until it is too late.

One of our researchers, however, remarked that among the highest correlations was the award of knighthoods to the company board. The sort of formula he suggested was: a knighthood for the CEO means the knacker's yard within four years, and if the Chairman and CEO both have knighthoods, within three years. A formulation that has offered many a wry smile as British companies have passed into oblivion with benighted bosses cashing in share options and picking up their compensation packages, or on flicking through the periodic Honours Lists. More recent history suggests a variation: elevation to the Lords presages complete catatonic failure of his eminence's erstwhile business.

Perhaps the outstanding instance was the collapse of Dunlop, whose Board at the time read like a Messenger's speech from Henry V. Recalling a lunch with some of the directors beforehand, one boldly asserted, "We timed our rights issue to perfection, I thought" – another good anticipatory symptom that rigor mortis is setting in.

CORRALLING BENN

Independence of mind and a readiness to fight a corner are usually traits of all good Ministers. But it is unique to have a Ministerial head of a Department completely out of sync with his Cabinet colleagues, and tolerated as such. His fellow Ministers were clearly impatient at apparently being bounced on controversial cases, and concerned that discussions with workers and trade union representatives could shade into expectations that support would be provided. The criteria for assistance were put under close revision, and, in their final form published in the Industry Act Report for 1975, conveyed these qualms in such phrases as, "Departments will be at liberty to consult both management and workers in framing proposals for assistance. However, there must be no negotiations and no commitment to either party of any kind until a Government decision on assistance has been taken." An enduring testimony to the fact that his colleagues did not trust him further than they could throw him.

For purists against intervention, these criteria put a tight specification of viability as the essential hurdle, and companies were usually taken aback by the probing to which they were subjected during appraisal. Especially if they had been accustomed to the sort of scrutiny by banks and shareholders evidenced by Ferranti and British Leyland, and, at the back of appraisal officers' minds, was the knowledge that their assessments would be viewed by leading commercial figures on IDAB not renowned for being a soft touch.

But to be fair to other Departments, they were confronted, often at short notice, with demanding submissions seeking rapid decisions. And to process these a special Cabinet official group was set up to allow all interested Departments to send officials to go over forthcoming case submissions. This in turn called for submissions to take a defined form – a short summary of the IDU assessment, including the IDAB conclusion, and with the full appraisal attached. To this, the Minister would be free to put in his own paper making whatever recommendations he wished. But other Ministers would be fully briefed on the details of the case beforehand. Benn's officials were inevitably put under pressure, and responded "just on the facts", resisting all attempts, some occasionally quite hostile, to get them to offer a view distinct from the recommendations of their Minister.

These cross-examinations incidentally gave useful experience to the Unit's secondees, offering them another vantage point on the functioning of the Whitehall system. Even if their initial reaction was invariably one of shock at the size of meetings as officials from other "interested" Departments crowded in to ensure that their Ministers were not off-sided, but also one suspected for sheer entertainment.

ECONOMIC EVALUATION SECTION

While the maelstrom of controversial cases was building up, the Economic Evaluation Section was an oasis of calm. On taking up post, I had an early session with them to explore how their work fitted into the other activities of the Unit.

They occupied a corner room in Millbank Tower, with the other two walls covered in charts being continuously updated with statistics on the relative performance of Britain's industrial sectors against international comparisons. The most obvious feature was that the data was at least two years out of date, since the compilation of statistics by national and international agencies simply took time to collate. There were also confusions in the correspondence of different categories across national boundaries. And, for some countries – especially the rising economies of Asia, Russia and other bloc countries – the data itself was dodgy.

The stark message, despite these imperfections of information, was one of continuing decline in virtually all sectors. The only significant exception was chemicals, which included pharmaceuticals. Otherwise the material said nothing that was not fairly obvious. This introduction was also a useful lesson in how misleading statistics can be: the textile industry, carrying on a trend since the 30s, was in collapse on virtually all fronts. Except for socks, where for some reason market share was growing rapidly. Whether this anomaly has persisted, I'm not sure, but judging by supermarket shelves the evidence is sparse.

The immediate managerial reaction was that the outfit was the likeliest candidate for efficiency savings. But in civil service staffing conventions, it is always easier to make a case for reassigning an existing post than make the case for a new one. With rising workload pressures elsewhere, it was prudent not to sacrifice the posts prematurely. And the team carried on quietly compiling and updating their charts unnoticed.

But their day of glory came. We had an urgent call from Eric Varley's Office to ask whether we had any comparative material on the performance of British industry, since no one else in the Department appeared to have such stuff. We were able to respond with alacrity. The charts were pulled off the walls, and we took them to the Minister's office. After a briefing session with him to explain that, beyond showing almost universal adverse trends, the material had to be treated with care. But the charts were rolled up again. And Eric Varley disappeared into the November evening for a briefing session at Chequers, to all appearances a cowboy interior decorator.

A couple of days later, the charts were returned with the news that we now had an industrial policy, which would be adopting a strong sectoral approach.

STRUGGLES FOR RECONSTRUCTION

The post-Chequers scene marked a reorientation to what hindsightists have labelled "picking winners" (Economist 28.06.03) or the "old corporatism". Setting these interpretations from a post-Thatcherite correctness aside, at the time there was an abysmal industrial scene – Ministers had been right in identifying the failings of the motorbike industry collapse as endemic elsewhere; lack of sustained investment to match the rising generation of new competitors, whether in Europe or among the Tiger-cubs (Japan was then just emerging from being regarded as a developing country); a macho style of management that exacerbated the confrontational tradition in labour relations; and a financial system which, far from being an exemplar of dynamic markets, was daily showing itself incapable of applying either influence or resources to cure these faults, and lacking the mechanisms to handle major industrial restructuring – probably the most repeated phrase at IDAB as the parade of "rescue" cases passed across the table was, "The shareholders haven't done their job." What's changed?

The economic context was also bleak: IMF intervention was less than a year away, but the scenario was being set with a suicidal level of pay awards; inflation and interest rates clocking up into double figures; a collapsing balance of trade; the pound dropping below $2.00 for the first time; and unemployment exceeding one million for the first time since the 30s. Given available options, the NEDO "sectoral forum" approach held out some prospect of starting a process towards the cooperative structures that had been successful in the rising economies. On the other hand, the concept was dependent upon the participants – industrial and TUC representatives – having the consent and confidence of their constituencies. In the event, one or the other, or both, failed to deliver.

In this setting, earlier in the year, to counter the falling levels of investment, the Treasury agreed an experimental "Accelerated Projects Scheme" under Section 8, i.e. applying nationwide. To bias management decisions against the prevalent attitudes to defer worthwhile investment, the incentive structure was relatively simple: each case would be assessed by the IDU/IDAB; the investment eligible for support should be at least £2.5 million; the project should be a net addition to the company's existing capital investment programme; commercially viable and to be started within a tight deadline for applications of a year, but with a flexible definition for assistance "negotiated as the minimum necessary to bring each project forward".

ADDITIONALITY

This scheme gave birth to "additionality". At the meeting with Treasury to clear the scheme, John Lippitt – a very capable, rumbustious, if occasionally crass, Whitehall buccaneer, declared with confident aplomb that the Department's appraisal staff could readily assess "additionality". This was the first time anyone had heard the word, and his Departmental colleagues were far from clear what precisely it meant. But it seemed like a serviceable piece of extemporisation for the occasion.

It has since been refined and carried forward into the criteria for subsequent support schemes. Most spectacularly, following a presentation to OECD as part of the UK's contribution to a transparency exercise on State Aids, the term achieved international currency. And, presumably following normal linguistic rules, the meaning has adapted to circumstances: at a meeting a few years later in the Ministry of Finance in Delhi, the senior Indian official asked, "But is it additional?" And on querying what this meant, the answer was, "Do we get more aid?"

More generally, however, there are now virtually no government measures, whether in employment, training, health etc that are not subjected to the "additionality" test as part of all commentators' toolkits.

GETTING IT TO WORK

With a company in acute distress, or in receivership, the entrails of the business can be dissected on the slab, and the often-bizarre internal manipulations exposed with existing management sidelined. A genuine appraisal of "additionality" requires detailed discussions with management on a range of concerns that are usually reserved for the inner sanctum: their investment track record, their own internal thresholds, ordering of priorities, market position and trends, and eventually a judgment on the validity of the company's claim, and a negotiation of financial assistance to overcome what are judged to be genuine constraints.

An informal professional exchange between practitioners with mutual confidence and respect for commercial confidentiality could have expected to elicit a reasonable judgment. But the Scheme was introduced in April 1975, while the atmospherics were still laden with the shadows of Benn's "planning agreements", "worker participation", "consultation with trade unions" etc – hardly conducive to companies, particularly larger ones, coming forward with projects held over or deferred. Pitching the minimum threshold at a relatively high level was, therefore, focusing the scheme on precisely those companies most wary of approaching the Department. Moreover, in the economic climate of the time, many might have been hesitant to open up to scrutiny just how severe the impact of the recession had been. For a combination of such reasons, the initial response to the scheme was slow, consisting of no more than a number of tentative approaches.

Evidence, if any were required, to belie the conventional reinterpretation of the government "picking" – even though the term "selective" might be interpreted as carrying some flavour of "dirigism" – in practice the government possessed no powers of coercion. Use of these powers only followed on an initiative from companies, and were "selective" only in so far as the response would be discretionary. And, inherent in the legislation, then only under guidance of a Board of seasoned expertise, and augmented by published guidelines, with an annual report to Parliament.

The feedback from industry through IDAB, regional offices and other contacts with the Department was that the hesitancy to invest at the margin was most acute among small/medium-sized companies, particularly in modernisation of facilities where in depressed market conditions there was a tendency to soldier on with old kit. In November, the thresholds of the scheme were adjusted to a minimum project size of £0.5 million to admit modernisation and with the deadline deferred to September 1976.

The disappearance of the Benn overhang took time, but contributed to a marked shift in the response of industry. Applications over the period of the scheme reached 350, with 124 getting through the sieve of appraisal and receiving assistance. Outside the scheme, there were 27 proposals for investment in assisted areas that could be diverted to the normal criteria for Section 7. The rest were either withdrawn as the company realised that it could not get through the scrutiny, or rejected by the Board as not matching "additionality" and/or offering the gains envisaged by the scheme. But nearly all of those approved were projects that would have been eligible under the scheme as it stood before November.

There was always a strain of scepticism about the validity of judgments of "additionality". But, at its crudest, it was a very good scalpel for turning down cases where merits were doubtful. And the interplay of variables such as viability of the investment, the constraints claimed by the company, and negotiated levels of support, allowed the Board to take a rounded view of the merits and to challenge, often sending the case back to be renegotiated. At the extreme, for companies with an autocratic management style of a GEC, cases were challenged at managing director level.

Given its counter cyclical aims, the incidence of orders, completion of investments, and payments of support – paid on completion of staged investment – were monitored (see chart). Whilst commonplace for those actually in business, the timing and scale of orders generates the immediate impact on employment and economic activity, which, by virtue of linking support to investment, precedes the payment of subsidy. This needed some demonstration for economists who are prone to invent employment schemes – a notable example was the Temporary Employment Subsidy (TES) where cash was paid for each job sustained. Another outcome of this monitoring was that, even if the additionality effect was discounted by a margin to allow for conmanship, leverage of the scheme was still significant.

The Accelerated Projects Scheme was succeeded by a "Selective Investment Scheme" in December 1976 with a similar basic structure, but allowing greater latitude for non-manufacturing investment, and with the additionality component of the criteria expanded to encourage companies to propose projects with "a significant advancement in time", "a substantial increase in scale or efficiency", or "a desirable extension of product range or marketing". In effect, a further exploration of the mechanisms for assisting industry, from the relatively unsophisticated base of traditional attitudes to industry.

Appendix H—(cont.)

Phasing of Orders, Investment and Payments of Assistance (Estimates)

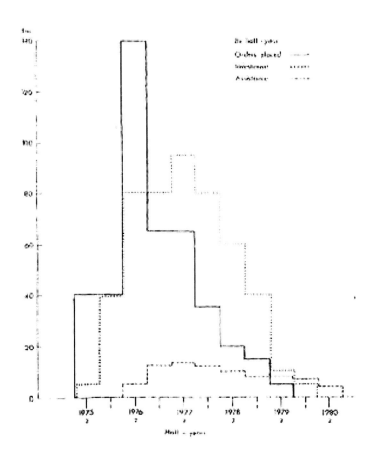

PHASING OF ORDERS INVESTMENT AND PAYMENTS OF ASSISTANCE (ESTIMATES)

SECTORAL SCHEMES

A conceptual consequence of the emphasis placed on the NEDO system was that its "sectoral" groups would identify underlying weaknesses, which could then be articulated into incentive measures to correct them. In practice, the first flow of such an approach took the form of "The Wool Textile Scheme" and "Clothing Industry Scheme" – knee-jerk responses to a continuing decline of the textiles/clothing industries over decades with "rationalisation" and "modernisation" performed in a corporate pantomime of clowns and villains, where names like Alliance, Djanogly, Hyman, Chambers, Kearton, Knight, Gartside, Hogg, Greenbury, Oates and Taylor oompahed across the stage. To no avail. Again, contrast with the vibrancy of the clusters around Milan and latterly Madrid.

The other constant standby was machine tools, which continuously since the war had some measure of special support, whether for investment, research, for customers to get over the "first order" risks, investment under defence procurement etc. And so a "Machine Tool Industry Scheme" was virtually inevitable. While decline continued equally inevitably.

The first fully researched scheme, however, with a thorough analytic approach was "The Ferrous Foundry Industry Scheme", where consultants had evaluated the impact of new techniques, automation and product refinements evolved by competitors and suggested the scale of investment necessary to counter these shifts in the market. The case submission was, at any event, an impressive wadge of paper. As an intermediate sector whose quality and efficiency impinged on a wide range of other activities, the scheme was approved: the pattern was to stimulate new investment/modernisation/innovation against a defined time limit, with a relatively straightforward structure of subsidy, but still requiring a test of viability through appraisal.

This basic package was readily replicable to other sectors identified for support. Not just in the purview of traditional Department of Industry sectors, but also within the scope of other Departments. A surprising source of pressure to introduce such schemes came from the Treasury – Dennis Healey's chancellorship was marked, apart from recourse to the IMF, by a series of mini-budgets, and the call came, as these were being framed, for a further sectoral scheme to be lined up for announcement.

Apart from drawing up a realistic rationale for such schemes was the need, since joining the Common Market, to clear them through the Commission. This demanded a sharp increase in the number of flights to Brussels for calls on Pierre Mathijsen, the senior official in DG4, the

Directorate concerned with State Aids. He was an urbane and cosmopolitan legal mind, author of the standard "Guide" to European Community Law, with a tolerant recognition of the diversity of industrial traditions within member states. Whatever the terminology of Articles 92 to 94 of the Treaty of Rome, from these discussions, and exchanges with European counterparts, the European tradition was more permissive of government assistance than the UK, rooted in the presumption that the private sector was an effective provider of finance for industry. The mindset of most other European countries had no such presumption, whether through historic tradition or through having intervened to stimulate post-war recovery, indeed regarding a legitimate role of the State to be the development and protection of key industries, and at a local community level the sustenance of key employers. By these standards the UK was a primitive novice.

Jumping the hurdles of permissible subsidies could be accomplished by steering clear of any hint of "operating subsidies" – a direct payment into the operating cash flow, by delineated clear objectives for the scheme, with a defined duration, and limited subsidy associated with a stipulation for viability. Mathijsen was gently sceptical about the ability of the UK to meet subsidy objectives, contrasting the example of shipbuilding support, where despite repeated applications of assistance, "nothing happened" in Britain: whereas the French would declare that a package of assistance would reduce "3 yards in Brest to 2" and 2 years later could demonstrate that this had been achieved.

Punctuated, therefore, by trips to Brussels, a series of schemes was introduced – The Printing Machinery, The Textile Machinery etc, but less remarked by commentators were those for other "industries": for example:

– The Poultry Processing Scheme

An EC directive on the standards of poultry processing hygiene, based mainly on the standards applied in Germany, required major augmentation of the facilities of British processors. These demanded a series of cleansing procedures – spraying, drying, temperature treatment – and it was alarming how deficient British operators actually were. And without support under the scheme, many would have been forced to close for want of being able to afford the investments needed to upgrade.

– The Energy Conservation Scheme

Following on the hike in oil prices and the coal pricing formula agreed to settle disruption in the mining industry, the Department of Energy had made a wide survey of the scope for improved energy efficiency, and the attitudes of management towards pursuing these. Their case was presented by Bernard Ingham before his Maggie-mouthpiece and Edwardian drama personae. And he did not have an easy job. There was massive scope for relatively small investments and modifications that would pay for themselves in 18-24 months. But these were not being pursued by management apparently because of "other priorities", concerns with reducing labour costs and trade union negotiations being the most frequently cited cause. (This contrasts sharply with the approach in other countries.[7])

For anyone with a professed belief in the effectiveness of private sector management, this was an absurd case. The scheme was approved, more in the spirit of resigned acknowledgement of the shortsightedness of management, and in the hope that it might encourage them to be more aware of the blindingly obvious.

The irony was that, when it came for all these schemes to be evaluated, those which gathered the highest marks from our economist adjudicators were those that had been dreamt up at short notice at the instigation of the Treasury, while those, like the Ferrous Foundry Scheme, which had been very thoroughly researched seemed to come out with lower marks.

IMPACT ON THE UNIT

With these new schemes, the number of cases requiring appraisal attention increased, on top of the occasional rescue, and Accelerated Projects Scheme cases with their bespoke assistance demands, which still demanded close attention by Deputy Directors and appraisal officers. Those arising under sectoral schemes with standard levels of grant support, were delegated to Industry Division staff to administer with an oversight role for the Deputy Director, who could expect a balanced portfolio of individual cases and monitoring one or two broad schemes. For the rest of the Department, this in turn forced officials out from behind their desks to hassle with companies on the justification for support, their prospects in their competitive contexts, and, at least, a first view on viability so that any doubts could be passed to the IDU appraisal officer for further assessment. In many instances, officials were out of the office for two or three days a week visiting companies enhancing both their understanding of the industry and sensitising their antennae for spotting conmen.

Nor should the impact on companies themselves be ignored. At its extreme, the Deputy Director with oversight of the Ferrous Foundry Scheme – a senior manager seconded from Shell, who turned up every Friday lunchtime with his weekend groceries purchased at the company's concessionary store across the Thames – became so alarmed at the absence of even rudimentary management accounting among the many small foundry operators that he took it as a personal crusade to re-educate them. This virtually tied up all his energies, and, indeed, the Scheme was extended, one factor being the sheer task of making coherent appraisals.

After the turbulence of the Benn era, the pattern of work stabilised on this portfolio, which offered an interesting mix, augmented in the later 70s by a rising incidence of major inward investment cases, ranging from a Ford engine plant in Wales to, more controversially, early assessments of assistance towards the Inmos semiconductor venture, on which a separate history could be written.

For the civil servants in the secretariat, we had become the design authority for Schemes and criteria. With a recurrent turnover in seconded staff, we also instituted an "IDU Handbook" that set out the format and coverage of appraisals, but also a summary of case lore on lessons learnt from earlier appraisals, forms of assistance, and pitfalls and requirements for guarantees. To build up to this accumulated recording of experience, we took advantage of the traditional Whitehall on-the-job training procedure of "assistant principals", who are moved around suitable posts at roughly six-monthly intervals, for whom this updating task gave them a quick understanding of the nature of the Unit's activities, while ensuring a continuing contact with real cases as they explored and recorded any special features with appraisal staff. Apart from its value for new entrants to the Unit, the Handbook was also taken by secondees back to their employers when they left the Unit, and, particularly for those secondees from clearing banks, provided the basis of their newly formed corporate units.

Even the humdrum monitoring of commitments had its moments: with the increased use of Section 8, the aggregate of potential of sums "paid or undertaken to play" approached the limit specified in the Act. We therefore had to seek an amendment to increase it. The text of the amendment was a straightforward change to Section 8 (7) to increase the totals specified. But, after an initial debate, the amendment went to Committee where, even on its narrow terms, there was scope for the Conservative opposition to philibuster and press for changes. Such committees are usually 13-strong, evenly divided between government and opposition backbenchers, with the Chairman, and his casting vote, from the government. Among the opposition members was Nicholas Ridley, who had resigned on the pretext of the original Act, and seemed intent on exacting some revenge. Even though he could not undermine the powers of Section 8, he sponsored a series of amendments which were outvoted. Discussion of another one dragged on, and the Chairman drew the session to a close, deferring a vote until the following morning. On reconvening, however, the government side was three members short, and junior whips were despatched to drag out the recalcitrant members. After waiting for what seemed a maximum tolerable time against increasing opposition jeers, the Chairman called for a vote. 6:3 in favour of the opposition on a show of hands. "Recount" called the government side. There were four "Recounts" as the occasional dishevelled Member sheepishly crept into the room, before the Chairman felt compelled to call a final vote even though the government side was still a couple of Members short. And the amendment was carried, even though the record suggests that our elected representatives have difficulty counting up to 6. As a result, the amended Act prohibits guarantees being provided to banks – no real impact on the use of the powers, since bailing out banks has traditionally been the preserve of the Bank of England and Treasury.

BALANCE SHEET

As an initial exercise in drawing upon private sector talents in areas where they added expertise beyond those of the civil service, the IDU/IDAB combination passed with flying colours. Especially in the difficult area of financial distress/rescue cases: beyond those which were in the national headlines, there were a string of testing cases ranging from Triang Toys, construction companies in difficulties on major contracts, to the *Observer* newspaper. A senior civil service colleague summed it up neatly, "Some outfits are good. Some are fast. But to be both good and fast is very rare."

The accountancy firms and banks did us proud in the calibre of their secondments. And Board members were unstinting in the time and commitment that they gave – including those personally nominated by Benn, who added a genuine new slant to the discussion, while recognising the essential demands of viability as the basis for support.

If always invidious to name individuals, much credit for the quality and balance of the Unit's output must go to its Directors: Graeme Odgers*, who made a wary start – understandable to get a measure of the Department, but the more so in the bizarre climate under Tony Benn. But his patient vetting of all IDAB case material kept up a high standard: in fact, we were proud that we had made him into the best civil servant in the Department, as no one left a meeting he chaired without acknowledging that all his points had been discussed, even if the balance of conclusions went against him. Raymond Bonham-Carter, who took over from Graeme in 1977, "a verray parfit gentil" guy, if ever there was one, brought with him from Warburgs a sharp sensitivity to the issues, a deft knowledge of City networks, and a personal concern for the team cohesion of the Unit.

Yet the fascination of observing the convulsions of a system, which still regarded industry as a grubby sub-species of trade, was matched by regret at the reluctance of old parochialisms to recognise the calls for radical change. The abiding lessons, however, after the Unit's crash-course in forensic accounting, was never to put credence in corporate accounts, borne out subsequently by the hyped growth scandals of the 80s,[8] as much as by the mirage accounting of the 90s. Whether formulaic accounting procedures can ever adequately depict the creativity, dynamism, or option and bequest values, leave alone Demming's "invisible numbers" – the qualities that distinguish the best businesses – is debatable. Any more than they can shore up the scope for monomaniacs to play ducks-and-drakes with any formal system. But this inherent fallibility of information has been so obvious for so long that the pretence of "rationality" or "efficiency" of financial markets must rate as the con of all cons, only sustainable by a network of complicity even now barely challenged.

Above all, the impact of the "motorcycle saga", and especially the session with "top industrialists" referred to in the Appendix, has been a sceptical template against which to judge whether British owned/managed companies have the essential qualities for survival in a competitive international environment. For example, there was a sporadic debate about the British "fork-lift truck" industry – then composed of Lancer Boss and Lansing Bagnall, both run by arrogant autocratic personalities, and the only conclusion was that they could not hope to survive against German and Japanese competitors (Toyota, apart from its strong position in autos, is also the world's largest fork-lift truck manufacturer): sure enough, the latter was taken over by Linde, and the former by Jungheirich, who found the inherent inefficiencies too great to turnaround. Or the interminable discussions at one time, "What can be done about Plessey?" "Nothing," was the only too obvious answer.

AN INTERNATIONAL DIMENSION

Apart from ritual visits to Brussels, the mechanism of an Industrial Development team under the guidance of leading businessmen occasioned interest from a number of other countries.

Among callers to have the system explained was a leading official from MITI. Japan was still viewed at the time as emerging from development status after the destruction of the war, despite having overtaken Britain as the world's leading shipbuilding nation in 1956. Part of the shock of the motorbike industry collapse was its evidence of astonishing productivity and quality gains against received perceptions. The question that hangs in memory was his casual query whether we had an "infant industry" policy. Neither I, nor to be fair any of my Unit colleagues present at the meeting, were familiar with this verboten terminology. Nor were we aware of the extent to which this approach was being implemented in Japan. Perhaps our perceptions were also clouded by the fact that most of the schemes and individual rescue cases were predominantly in the geriatric ward – though with hindsight these were merely the patients with the most advanced symptoms, and over following decades most of the industry "giants" would go the same way, including companies run by "the great and good" members of IDAB itself. Still, we managed a few responses on the lines that in viewing viability we were looking at businesses embracing new technologies, and in some areas, such as electronics, were focusing on encouraging research and innovation.

Another caller was from Malaysia, and they subsequently set up an Industrial Development Corporation. Having visited their offices, their track record in stimulating new industries, encouraging inward investment, and implementing a national bias in development has played a very positive role in the country's remarkable modernisation. Ironically, Japan has recently established an Industrial Revitalisation Corporation with a broadly similar structure of a permanent corps presided over by leading businessmen, though with mixed reviews so far. But the model is capable of adaptation elsewhere.

---

[1] Regional Development Grants (RDGs) have been surprisingly ignored in commentaries on industrial history. In practice, as *automatic* grants, tax-free, for capital investment in assisted areas they were equivalent to non-dividend equity, and range from 20-30% depending on the designation of the location i.e. between Development Area, Intermediate Area, or Special Development Area.

Their automatic status went unchallenged until development of the oil terminal facilities at Sullen Voe – in the highest designation area, these investments were bound to take place for the exploitation of North Sea oil, but commanded RDG payments of more than £800 million. Subsequently, RDGs were given an "additionally" stipulation, and then further modified. A further criticism was that they were biased towards manufacturing while many regional jobs could have benefited from an equivalent incentive for services relocation.

But while RDGs were in their heyday, Hans Leisner, the Department's Chief

Economist – a nice guy, but a sort of free-market nuncio who proclaimed his bull in vestments unsullied by contacts with reality – cited ICI as a company that did not seem to seek financial support. They did not need to: by virtue of their investments around Wilton in the North East and other assisted areas, flicking back just a few years ICI had received well over £60 million in RDGs – effectively "tax-free non-dividend paying equity". And judging by expressions at a meeting in ICI's Thames-side headquarters the day after the revision in RDGs was announced, the change was quite painful.

But Hans once grudgingly admitted at an internal meeting that the economists' theology became a bit wobbly if all countries were engaged in "distorting" practices – to a clamorous response, "They do." Or in reply to a remark about the outstanding adaptive qualities of Japanese companies, admitted, "I haven't looked at Japanese companies."

[2] Peter Gregson was despatched to join Alan Lord* and Ron Dearing* to work on the new Industrial Policy White Paper: this, in full form, envisaged planning agreements and an enhanced role for the National Enterprise Board, which industry viewed as being a potential lever for increasing government equity stakes in larger companies. In the event, despite all the wind and fury, these measures had virtually no practical impact, with only one planning agreement with a publicly owned outfit.

[3] Bill Ryrie's path and mine might have crossed long before our official contacts. He too was a relic of the Raj, and admitted to have gone to St Paul's School in Darjeeling. At the time, I was among the schoolchildren who had been evacuated from Calcutta at the threat of Japanese advances through Burma to an emergency school, the New School, on a promontory immediately opposite St Paul's. Since it was common practice for schools to raid each other in the night, it could have been that we had confronted each other in the dark with sand-filled socks. Even so, he was one of the more pragmatic of the Treasury clan, subsequently going on to head the International Finance Corporation and then picking up a sinecure at one of those, now defunct, merchant bank relics of gentlemanly capitalism. Sadly, his name will be long be associated with the "Ryrie Rules", one of the loonier formulations in the Treasury's unique approach to enhancing the nation's efficiency and productivity – continuous unimprovement. In effect making it extremely difficult, or impossible, for the private sector to finance infrastructure schemes: on a rationale described by a Number 10 Adviser as "pre-Gorbachev economics". But diametrically opposite to the wheeze of the Private Finance Initiative, once the Treasury discovered the gimmick of "off balance sheet" financing.

[4] Tony Benn: *Against the Tide – Diaries 1973-77* (Hutchinson) pp 455. A remarkably frank and self-revelatory account: probably more revelatory than the author perhaps realised. A suitable companion volume is *Self-Deception* by Herbert Fingarette (Routledge and Keegan Paul), on the philosophical paradox of who is deceiving whom. While there was inevitable discussion among senior officials as to what precisely was bugging Mr Benn, the quandary from dealing

with actual cases lay in the discrepancy between his acute intelligence, and the blindingly obvious weakness of the cases that he wished to support as a means of providing solid employment for employees.

[5] Institutional changes to encourage consensus and a more cohesive approach to industry had been kicking around across the political spectrum since the inter-war years. Indeed, NEDO itself dated from 1962, formed under a Conservative Government.

[6] In the current rewriting of industrial history, it is worth recalling that the recession of the mid-70s had just as serious an impact elsewhere. VW faced "the greatest crisis in its history", while at BMW, "the market collapse, which almost brought the car business to a standstill" (and they also suffered from the Japanese advance in motorbikes). (*The BMW Story* by Horst Mönnich – Sidgwick & Jackson). Yet the state banks of Saxony and Bavaria joined in steering the companies, with their house banks, out of crisis without the ballyhoo of British Leyland being dumped on the government. While Sumitomo Bank famously rescued Mazda, which was particularly vulnerable by virtue of the high fuel-consumption of the Wankel engine in its basic model.

[7] "For managers, the prime factor deciding the fate of their companies was how to respond to the rise in energy costs brought about by the oil crisis. This crisis mentality explains the approach taken by Japanese managers in deciding on R&D objectives." – *Japanese Style Management* – K.Hasegawa (Kodansha). Or try "Under intense pressure, Japanese companies invested heavily in energy-conserving technologies and moved toward higher value products. The Oil Shock was the catalyst for Japan's global leadership in energy conservation, which has benefited many industries. The Oil Shock was also the impetus for innovations that established Japan in advanced industries such as automobiles and consumer electronics. In TV sets, for example, the desire to reduce power consumption triggered Japanese producers' early move from vacuum tubes to transistors – a move that carried many other benefits in terms of the reliability, functionality, and manufacturability of products." – *Can Japan Compete?* by Porter, Takeuchi and Sakibara (Macmillan).

[8] *Accounting for Growth* – Terry Smith (Century). Prompted by the dodgy inflation of results in the 80s, but still a very useful reminder that Eden was despoiled long before Enron.

APPENDIX

THE MOTORCYCLE INDUSTRY

While public perception of the dire straits of the UK motorcycle manufacturers at the time had been buried under the political controversy over the Meriden workers sit-in, the prospects of this slipping into a call for nationalisation of the remnants of the industry prompted Ministers in February 1975 to call for a thorough analysis of the prospects for a viable UK industry. And within a few weeks the Boston Consulting Croup (BCG) were commissioned under these broad terms of reference. The choice was made mainly because of their acknowledged expertise on Japan's manufacturing industry (at the time Jim Abegglen, author of *Kaisha: The Japanese Corporation*, was head of their Tokyo office). Their report was submitted on the 22nd of July with a range of scenarios, all of which were viewed as unlikely to make up the gap that had developed between the residual British plants and the technology, production and the market strengths of their Japanese competitors.

These scenarios were backed up by a comprehensive analysis of the distinctive strengths of Japan's firms and an account of how their dominance, especially in the crucial US market, had been achieved. An edited version was subsequently published – Cmnd 532 and 532-1. Over the decades the study has prompted a maclstrom of dispute among academics and consultants, but passed with barely a glance by the British media, or by political or economic commentators.

Starkly, the issue was to explain how UK manufacturers had collapsed from commanding nearly 60% of the US big-bike market in 1968 to some 6% six years later. The study illuminated an idiom of competitive behaviour and management style radically different from the traditional "make-assets-sweat", "dishing out the dividends", and confrontational labour relations of so much contemporary British business. At a seminar later that autumn organised by BCG at a suitably agreeable Ascot hostelry, we made a joint presentation on the motorcycle industry to an assortment of the brightest and best of British top managers. One concluded, "It is inconceivable that my shareholders would allow me to do what Honda did." This resignation was echoed by other senior executives. To the question, "Can't you change their minds?" the response ranged from, "They wouldn't be interested," "They would just move their money," to a shrug of the shoulders. The moral was clear: if there were other companies in other industries that had even a modest share of the qualities of the Japanese motorcycle manufacturers, there wasn't much hope for any other British companies elsewhere.

As a continuing reminder, the BCG study has stayed on the bookshelf. It was pulled out when invited to lecture at a company "strategic weekend" to prompt discussion on radically different approaches to business. Prior to this, however, before participating in the financial negotiations for the Guangdong Nuclear Power in the early 80s, I had called on David Wilson*, then head of Far Eastern Department in the Foreign Office, and prior to his appointment as Governor of Hong Kong, to see if they had any briefing on negotiating with the Chinese, who had a reputation of being extremely difficult. He suggested that I immerse myself in Sun Tzu's *Art of War* and in Arthur Whaley's translations of Chinese verse. I could not get my hands of a copy of the latter before leaving – Helen Gardner's anthology of *The Metaphysical Poets* had to act as substitute, but this still remains the soundest counsel ever received from the Foreign Office. When I commended David on his advice, he responded by asking for a note on the commercial implications of Sun Tzu. So, preparing this lecture (attached) allowed me to deal with two birds at the same time.

There have been a number of management books purporting to draw lessons from this ancient Chinese text. Having read several, and flicked through many, though full of alleged applications of ruses and stratagems, none have done credit to the organisational precepts for creating the disciplines and suppleness to act decisively and successfully. The lecture attempts to depict something of the extraordinary dynamism and adaptability of Honda's development. Without shoehorning Honda into Sun Tzu, whether through a shared tradition of Confucian/Taoist thought, there is a resonance in the focus on fluidity, fuzzy categories, ambiguity, discipline, preparation and sensitivity to shifts in market context.

This effort is modest compared to the extensive analysis of Honda by Richard Pascale in *Managing on the Edge* (Viking). As a slight academic diversion, Pascale is primarily responsible for the view that Honda's successful entry to the US motorbike market was the outcome of "opportunistic learning" and "serendipity" – or "chance" as it is now interpreted. Viewing the controversy surrounding this view, a common feature is that academics, economists and consultants, with the occasional rare exception, have never produced anything other than verbiage.

My lecture appears to have been unintentionally revisionist in highlighting the extent to which the company's management prepared for their thrust to increase market-share. Earlier in their history, prior to achieving dominance in the Japanese home market, the company had used a period of booming demand to streamline production, line-up new models and sharpen distribution so that when a downturn occurred, it could strike aggressively.

One of the riskiest issues, however, for companies engaged in series production against tough competitors is the investment in new models and the production capacity necessary to launch them into the market. So, as they had done earlier in their history, it was a natural preparatory step for Honda to ensure that there was sufficient productive capacity for their Super Cub, their US breakthrough 50cc model (at a distance of time, it is difficult to appreciate the advance in power achieved for such a small engine). The company accordingly built a new plant to produce 30,000 bikes a month – 10 times the rate achieved for any other model. Even assuming success for this new bike in their domestic market, this facility still presupposed an exceptionally large continuing output to keep the plant viable. And, hence, a much larger target market than Japan. Simply, to drive for market share is impossible without the production capacity to back it.

This, rather, suggests that Fujisawa – Honda's commercial head (his *banto*, a professional manager brought into the traditional family-run business) – must have had an ambitious goal beyond the Japanese market, which could not just rely on "opportunistic learning". A crucial difference compared to their assault on their domestic market lay in the lack of a controlled marketing network in the US, where the scene was dominated by dealers specialising in the "macho" big bikes of the time. Consequently, unconventional outlets and catchy advertising had to be adopted, examples certainly of "opportunistic" tactics. But behind this lay the prior decision to invest in sufficient production capacity to meet the demand created by a successful market assault.

If further collateral were needed, as member of an informal Japan/British discussion group, grandly titled Benkyo-kai, we were on a visit to Cambridge hosted by another member, Nick Oliver of the Judge Institute, who had just completed an international benchmarking exercise on auto-equipment suppliers. Nick and I set off by punt along the Cam accompanied by the Chief Officer of Denso's UK operation at Telford. We Brits were put to shame by our Japanese companion immediately completing the quotation, "I stood in Venice on the Bridge of Sighs," while we were still rummaging through our sixth form English Literature recollections. But we fell to discussing the Pascale account of Honda's first entry to the US market, and the suggestion that their success had been the outcome of an opportunistic seizure of chance. Our Japanese companion listened politely and quietly shook his head. We took this to mean some disagreement, and queried why. To which he replied, "Fujisawa never left anything to chance."

This comment, from a senior manager of a leading Toyota group company, who for decades must have been watching with minute care the moves of their most aggressive domestic competitor, should be a clincher against the "opportunistic" or "chance" thesis. He confirmed that Fujisawa is still a legendary figure in Japan's industrial mythology. Apparently, with his love of western classical music – still recalled in the musical connotations of many of the company's models – he attended as many concerts as he could in the limited venues then available distinctively wearing traditional formal dress. Incidentally, at a seminar where Graham Day, who had been in charge of the Rover Group during their joint venture with Honda, was speaking, he remarked, "Fujisawa is the nearest the commercial world has come to a genius."

Perhaps the most resonant quotation attributed to Fujisawa is: "Japanese and American companies are 95% the same, but different in all important respects," – worth recalling as Honda, Toyota and leading Japanese companies continue to expand despite violating many of the norms of correct "capitalist" behaviour, while British companies continue their decline playing the "shareholder value" game and following the gimmicks of consultants. Nowadays, Honda registers in public perception mainly as a high-quality car manufacturer with a catchy-line in TV adverts (a marketing idiom reminiscent of their first assault on the US market), yet their strength in motorbikes has continued, with total annual sales, according to their 2005 Annual Report, of 10.48 million units. In a company updating (*FT* 21.7.05) on their three-year business plan ending in March 2008, they "projected motorcycle sales of 16 million units". In fact, the level of motorbike sales in 2009 was 14.9 million, no doubt influenced by depressed demand following the financial crisis.

ECHOES OF SUN TZU —

A COMMERCIAL PERSPECTIVE

ECHOES OF SUN TZU - A COMMERCIAL PERSPECTIVE

SUN WHO?

Sun Tzu's treatise on "The Art of War" was apparently written some-time around 400-200 years BC, and the Chinese profess to some amusement that Japanese businessmen should be such avid students of this (Annex A) - and another ancient text "the Romance of the Three Kingdoms" - as guidance on corporate strategy. In Samuel B Griffiths's edition of Sun Tzu*, indeed, it is noted that there have been more than a hundred commentaries on "The Art of War" in Japan, most recently on its commercial application.

But there also seems to be something of a Sun Tzu industry developing, with references in the film "Wall Street", in Coloroll's internal company guidance, and in such books as "The Corporate Warriors" which deals with some of the recent corporate struggles in the US and UK capital markets. But it is striking that the Japanese style of corporate development is very different from the market practices of Wall Street and the City of London, and their idiom of industrial development suggests that they are maybe taking a rather different interpretation.

Having browsed through Sun Tzu fairly regularly during some protracted negotiations in China, on reading "Honda Motor" by Tetsuo Sakiya** one could not help but be struck by some apparent echoes of Sun Tzu's thought. Since there is quite a lot of material about the motorcycle industry generally available, notably the study done by the Boston Consulting Group for the Department of Industry in July 1975***, it seemed worth testing how the idiom of the Japanese competitive approach reflected the principles of Sun Tzu. In any such analysis, inevitably, one is hardly likely to find evidence that every Honda executive sat with a copy of the ancient master at his elbow, but one might expect evidence of a general orientation of corporate behaviour.

One cannot pretend to be in any sense a student of Confucian teachings, and it is extremely difficult to compress Sun Tzu's pithy maxiums. But there does seem to be a consistent logic going through the Thirteen Chapters, which one might perhaps attempt to summarise.

I "For to win 100 victories in 100 battles is not the acme of skill. To subdue the enemy without fighting is the acme of skill." (III.3).

He starts from the view that the conduct of war, and actual engagement in particular, is very wasteful, and hence resources

---

* All quotations are from this edition, published by Oxford (Galaxy)
** Honda Motor by Tetsuo Sakiya, published by Kodansha International Ltd
*** Cmnd 532, and 532-1.

ACQAAA

should be closely defended and not put at risk unless sure of
success. It was part of the circumstances in which he was writing
that to expend resources for a protracted period on war against
one neighbouring state made one vulnerable to another,
"neighbouring rulers will take advantage of your distress to act"
(II.5), and the text is permeated with the themes of
unpredictability, fluidity and vulnerability, so that defence of
resources is a primary need but coupled with adaptablity and
manoeuvrability to bring a conflict to an end. "Invincibility
lies in the defence; the possibility of victory in the attack"
(IV.5).

II Thus, what is of supreme importance in war is "to attack the
enemy's strategy" (III.4). The concept of "Strategy" would seem
to go further than its customary "master-plan of campaign", but
also to embrace the underlying intentions of the Ruler. Sun Tzu
has a lot of concern about the ways in which this relationship can
enhance or jeopardise the freedom of the General to wage war
effectively.

III "War is based on deception" (VII.12) and "Creating a situation
to which he (the enemy) must conform" (V.20).

Deception has an infinity of guises, and in a world of such
vulnerability and change there is a need to maintain continuing
intelligence, a "Divine Skein" of agents (XII.6), not just against
the enemy but against all potential enemies; to convey
disinformation; to disguise intentions, so "keeping his officers
and men in ignorance of his plans" (XI.43); and to plan manoeuvres
to create enticements and be vigilant against them by the enemy.
Even in the mundane descriptions of terrain and manoeuvres, the
underlying thread is to create greater relative options and avoid
vulnerability, with the ultimate aim of maintaining a position of
dictating the play.

IV In practical terms, the general must make it impossible for the
enemy "to unite ..... to mutually co-operate ..... for good
troops to succour the poor ...... and for superiors and
subordinates to support each other" (XI.25). Sun Tzu gives
considerable weight to "moral influence" - "that which causes the
people to be in harmony with their leaders, so that they will
accompany them in life and unto death without fear of mortal
peril" (I.4).

V The General "seeks victory from the situation" (V.21), and "When
the enemy gives you an opening be swift as a hare and he will be
unable to withstand you" (XI.61). Consistent with the basic
premise of conserving resources and retaining them to assault only
when success is assured, there is a consistent theme of "adapting
to the situation" and striking suddenly with a well-prepared and
aimed force.

VI With such a premium on adaptability, movement and speed of
response, there are corresponding demands to maintain discipline,
a sound organisation, internal communications, to take advantage
of local provisioning, to avoid becoming over-extended and implied
is a highly professional task of manipulating large scale
resources in a theatre of constant manoevre.

2   ACQAAA

Such snippets cannot give a full sense of Sun Tzu, where the ambiguity of some of the maxims is itself an illustration of the theme: "To a surrounded enemy, you must leave a way of escape" (VII.31) is interpreted by one commentator to suggest that to show an opponent "There is a way to survival" is to encourage him to give up, which might be taken with Sun Tzu's earlier insistence that "To capture the enemy's army is better than to destroy it" (III.2) as a reasonably humane approach. Another commentator, however, remarks "Show him there is a road to safety, and so create in his mind the idea that there is an alternative to death. Then strike". Such differences in textual interpretation may be interesting for a scholar, but pose an uncomfortable dilemma for the encircled General - one with which anyone who has negotiated in China will have some sympathy. Similarly, the bland statement "There is no place where espionage is not used" (XIII.14) has been elevated by subsequent history to the level of a universal truth.

Time becomes a crucial player: at its most fundamental, there is a perennial need to sustain an immaculate defensive position, succour the troops, maintain morale, but above all keeping watchful vigilance and countermoves against all kinds of threats: the converse is to use this period to create advantage and bear down on the opponent's morale. At the same time the army must be poised for instantaneous and decisive deployment. Both extremes presuppose an organisation of the suppleness and latent power to adapt to these temporal extremes. Much of "the art" lies in creating and sustaining such a dynamic enterprise, and to protect and use it with the utmost effectiveness.

THE COMMERCIAL BATTLEFIELD

To illustrate something of the competitive ferocity that would reflect this style of thinking, it is worth looking at the Chapter on "The Kaisha as Competitor" in "Kaisha" by Abegglen and Stalk.*

Under the theme of "the winner's competitive cycle", the authors recall how Honda had previously been the Japanese market leader in motorcycles by the 1960s, when the 200 manufacturers of motorised two-wheel vehicles immediately after the war had reduced to four - Honda, Yamaha, Suzuki and Kawasaki.

The Chapter goes on to depict the situation when the market was more mature, and in the 1970s Honda were building their position in the motorcar market - even though MITI had pressed for rationalisation because substantial over-capacity existed. This move by Honda appeared to be guilty of Sun Tzu's cardinal fault of devoting undue resources to a protracted conflict against strong opponents, and by 1981, Honda's production share of the motorcycle market had declined from a high of 65% to 40%. Meanwhile, Yamaha

---

* Kaisha: The Japanese Corporation", Abegglen and Stalk(Harper an-Row).

ACQΛΛΛ

YAMAHA WO TSUBUSU

	HONDA	YAMAHA
1970 Share / Japanese Production	65%	10%
Models	35	18
1981 Share / Japanese Production	40%	35%
(Domestic Market Share)	38%	37%
Models	63	60
Profit / Sales	3%	3%
R.&D Expenditure / Sales	5%	1%
1981 Capacity (units)	3.8m	3.0m
With New Factory	3.8m	4.0m (60%)
Debt / Equity	1 : 1	3 : 1

"Yamaha wo tsubusu" translates as "Slaughter Yamaha".

YAMAHA WO TSUBUSU

JAN 1982 – MAY 1983	HONDA	YAMAHA
New Models	81	34
Changes (Discontinued Models)	113	37
Production Share	47%	27%
Domestic Market Share	43%	23%
Debt / Equity	0.6 : 1	7 : 1

YAMAHA	APRIL	JUNE
1983 Losses	¥ 4bn	¥ 20bn
Production Cut	1.5m	1.38m
Redundancies	700	2,700 (25%)

DEC 1983 – MAY 1984	HONDA	YAMAHA
Model Changes	39	23

had increased its share from less than 10% to 35% over the same period. Within Japan, Yamaha's market share had risen to 37%, almost catching up Honda at 38%.

Yamaha comforted by the thought that their "speciality" was solely in motorcycle production declared "If only we had enough capacity we could beat Honda", and announced plans to build a new motorcycle factory, with an annual capacity of one million units which would bring its total capacity to four million units, exceeding Honda's. At the time both companies had broadly comparable rates of profit, but Honda was spending some 5% of sales on R & D while Yamaha was running at some 1%, and in January 1982 Yamaha's President declared "In one year, we will be the domestic leader. And in two years, we will be number one in the world".

Yamaha had borrowed heavily to finance this expansion, pushing its debt/equity ratio to 3 : 1, while Honda stood at 1 : 1. By June 1982 Yamaha had announced historic records for sales and profits. Meanwhile Honda appeared to be still preoccupied with its car business, undertaking a major investment in the US. But Yamaha's declaration in 1982 had not gone unnoticed, and Honda responded. Over the next 18 months, Honda introduced 81 new models in Japan with increased promotion and sales stocks, coupled with price reductions of more than a third - "it was possible to buy a 50cc motorcycle (the large volume cycle in Japan) for less than the cost of a 10-speed bicycle". Yamaha could manage "only 34" new models. Yamaha's sales fell by more than 50%, and by early 1983, its unsold stocks in Japan were estimated as about half of the industry total, equivalent to a total year's production by Yamaha.

As a result Honda's production share increased from 40% to 47% while Yamaha's decreased from 35% to 27%. Honda increased its domestic market share from 38% to 43%, while Yamaha's share collapsed from 37% to 23% and financially Honda's position was strengthened by its success in motor vehicles. In 1983 Yamaha announced a half-year loss of Y4 billion, production plans were cut by 18%, and a reduction in workforce of 700 envisaged over two years. Finally, survival required a further sharp cut in production capacity and another 2,000 redundancies. Yamaha's President resigned, and the company sued for peace.

In Sun Tzu's terms, the battleground was the capture of demand - "relative market share"; and there had clearly been some very effective "deception" about the breadth of Honda's technology options, production flexiblity, and financial strength - "When capable, feign incapacity", and "Pretend inferiority and encourage his arrogance" (1.18 and 23). When Honda moved, it was with "divine swiftness" (XI.24) and "thus the momentum of one skilled in war is overwhelming, and his attack precisely regulated" (V.15). What is difficult to gauge is the extent to which Honda deliberately "lay in wait" (III.28) and "brought the enemy to the field of battle........ by offering him some advantage" (VI.213). But the President of Yamaha might well have been prudent to heed Sun Tzu on the fate of a general "unable to control his impatience" (III.9).

4   ACQAAA

175

However expressed, Yamaha's basic failing was to under estimate the latent energy in Honda's technology, scale and flexiblity of production, and financial resources. Again, there is a continuing theme in Sun Tzu about building up the potential for a sudden assault "as a hundred weight balanced against a grain" and "the effect of pent-up waters" (IV.19 and 20).

HONDA MOTOR - HISTORY

Inevitably, it is impossible in summary to do justice to Tetsuo Sakiya's account of Honda, which sets the story of the company in the context of Japan's post-war development and social changes, and is worth reading on that account alone. But at one level, Honda is a story of two engaging adventurers - one burnt down a forest trying to corner a bit of the turpentine-additive market when petrol was scarce, and on one occasion they entertained some bankers with such boisterousness that they were not given the full loan advance that they wanted. At another level, it is an example of outstanding technical advance, with the company's products reaching the levels of excellence to win both the Isle of Man TT Motorbike and the Formula I Grand Prix motor racing championships, with its engines powering many subsequent winners; and achieving a string of technological firsts in motorcycle and vehicle development, including fundamental work on combustion processes and ignition chamber design, the Overhead Valve Engine, the first manufacturer to meet US requirements for environmental control of emissions, and in design several innovations as in the use of plastics.

At the commercial level, the company has expanded from a small engine manufacturing unit, originally fitted to bicycles, moving into its first motorcycle design in 1949, with sales in 1950 of Y82m, to a turnover in 1986/87 of Y2,866,305m (with appreciation of the Yen over this period, in $ terms the growth would be more than doubled). Whilst still the world's largest motorcycle producer, cars and vans account for nearly 69%, motorcycles 10.5% and power products nearly 7% of turnover. Production facilities are spread from several factories in Japan, manufacturing installations in the US, China, Belgium, New Zealand and Yugoslavia, with association with several other manufacturers, such as Austin Rover. Each of these is adapted to the needs of the local market.

Perhaps Honda's most farsighted and adaptive move yet was to set up major facilities in Ohio, with their most modern manufacturing techniques, more integrated into US sources of supply, to build Civics and Accords. Most recently Honda have entered the US luxury car market with the Legend marketed under the separate Acura marque (in this category alone, Acura increased sales in the US in the first six months of 1988 by more than Jaguar's total US sales in this period - Sunday Times, 4 September).

Its US operation has a design facility to model cars for the US market, eg the Civic CRX and Accord 3-door versions are made exclusively in the US: currently, Honda envisages increasing exports from its US plant into Japan and other markets. Again, in its imaginative use of offshore production, Honda has been a leader of both Japanese motorcycle and vehicle producers.

5   ACQAAA

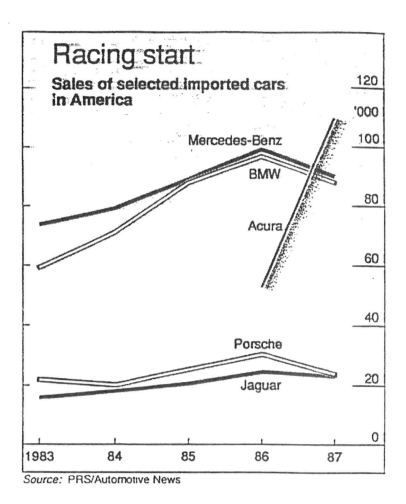

Racing start

Sales of selected imported cars in America

Mercedes-Benz

BMW

Acura

Porsche

Jaguar

120

'000

100

80

60

40

20

0

1983   84   85   86   87

Source: PRS/Automotive News

THE ECONOMIST SEPTEMBER 24 1988

ORGANISATION

The modern story of the company starts from an almost chance meeting between Soichiro Honda and Takaeo Fujisawa. Whilst Honda had built up a useful business in piston rings and sold out to Toyota before setting up the Honda Technical Research Institute, Fujisawa had worked in engineering and formed a Machine and Tools Research Institute. The two joined up in 1949, when the former was 42 and the latter 38. The nature of their understanding is recalled, "I looked for a financier in Hamamatsu, but all the potential investors want to recover their money quickly, and I don't like that", Honda said to Fujisawa, who replied "I don't have the money now, but I will find what you need to launch your technology". Undoubtedly the vision of "no end to the pursuit of technology" is uniquely Soichiro Honda's contribution.

For the commercial advancement of the company, perhaps it would be useful to cast Takeo Fujisawa in the role of Sun Tzu's "General". Whether he studied Sun Tzu during his period of service in the Imperial Army, he seems to have had a continuing interest in military thinking - apparently a close reader of Churchill's History of the Second World War, and was prone to resort to military concepts in visualising the structure and effectiveness of the company.

Fujisawa apparently often recalled the old Japanese saying "All is flux", and the company's story is essentially one of adapting to the changes in Japan and internationally. But not unreminiscent of Sun Tzu's maxim "As water has no constant form, there are in war no constant conditions" (VI.29) and just as Sun Tzu identifies factors of "organisation" as prerequisites to the conduct of war, it might be worth going over these features as they show in the history of Honda.

(a)   Alliances: Where Sun Tzu asserts that one of the first tasks of generalship is to "disrupt" an opponent's "alliances" (III.5) and "prevent allies from grouping" (XI.52), it follows that one of the first requirements to establish a sound defence is to have reliable allies. To a great extent, the capital structure of most Japanese companies is a creation of "alliances". Tetsuo Sakiya's account of Japanese corporate financing is a good thumb-nail sketch, as reproduced at Annex B. Rather than the traditional "arms' length" relationship of classical capital market economies, the Japanese company insulates itself against uncertain threats, such as takeovers, by apportioning its shares predominantly among those in whom it has shared obligations or mutual interests - in the case of Honda, Mitsubishi Bank, and 46.8% of the leverage of the top ten shareholders has been in hands of Mitsubishi Group". with other "benign" interests such as the Industrial Bank of Japan and insurance companies - and as with other companies, less than 30% of its shares are publicly tradeable even though it has been a "public" company since 1954: prior to that Fujusawa's view was that the company was not large enough. This effectively insulates the company from untoward or unexpected changes in ownership, and the management can focus attention undividedly on the growth of the business.

---

* Industrial Grouping in Japan 1982/3 (Dodwell) p.186.

ACQAAA

In turn, however, Honda has a shareholding in key subcontractors: BCG (Appendix II, Exhibit 12) identifies four cases where Honda has established such participation links, covering lights, shock absorber carburettors and engine parts. This has developed to the current structure shown at Annex C. In the same spirit, Honda's overseas manufacturing facilities are to a large extent extensions of the concept of "sure alliances", and Honda, like other Japanese manufacturers, has been wary of agreeing to local subcontracts until satisfied of reliability of product continuity and viability.

Throughout Honda's development, Fujisawa was also very "tough" in setting terms that assured prompt payment and secured the loyalty of distributors and agents, and ready to innovate with new distribution networks to achieve this. These various "alliances" were put to a test in 1954, when the company suffered labour problems which brought it close to bankruptcy. Fujisawa called on 300 subcontractors and asked them to continue supplies without an assurance of payment, and the subcontractors effectively carried the company for a period.

(b)   <u>Unity and Harmony</u>: Closely allied to the establishment of external "alliances" is the maintenance of "unity" within the enterprise: for, according to Sun Tzu, another cardinal principle is "When he is united, divide him" (I.25), and one of the most interesting features of the Honda story lies in its adaptive structures to ensure coordination and commitment across its operations. Sun Tzu in many contexts refers to "flexibility", "consistent principles", "authority", etc and his maxims underline the tensions between an effective military command structure and securing the loyalty of staff: neatly summarised in his description of the good General "wisdom, sincerity, humanity, courage and strictness" (I.7). (The disciplines for military situations in Sun Tzu's day were extreme, and some of the examples cited of his own behaviour suggest that "strictness" had a formidable edge - one story has it that a Ruler had to give up the heads of two of his favourite concubines to enable Sun Tzu to prove a point). At the one extreme "Because such a general regards his men as infants they will march with him into the deepest valleys. He treats them as his own beloved sons and they will die with him" (X.20), and at the other "Throw the troops into a position from which there is no escape and even when faced with death they will not flee" (XI.33).

In short, Sun Tzu's depiction of his optimal army confronting the extremes of battle, runs "Such troops need no encouragement to be vigilant. Without exhorting their support, the general obtains it; without inviting their affections, he gains it; without demanding their trust, he wins it" (XI.34).

If Fujisawa's vision of Honda Motor operating "so that employees would take their own initiatives in making judgements and taking specific actions" within "an organisational structure in which every human resource and skill would be utilised to the fullest extent" with "true leadership" becoming "doing nothing at all" is a mirror of Sun Tzu's view of the motivated autonomy of an army in battle, his earlier military service led him to the view that the hierarchical authority structure was inappropriate for a company such as Honda to achieve this.

7

(PART II)
(Mitsubishi)

Mitsubishi Group

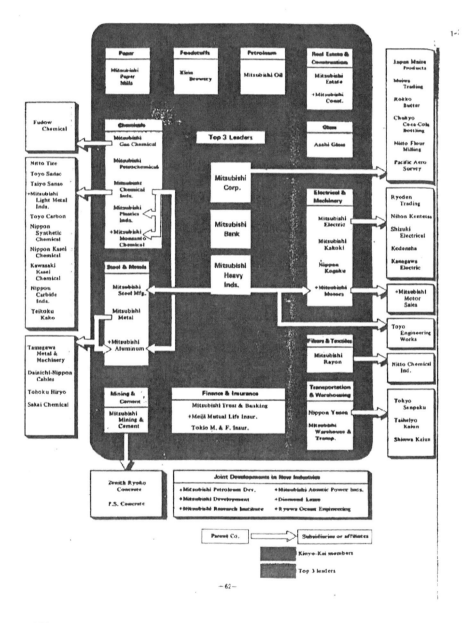

When Fujisawa talks of "the fundamental philosophy being understood and accepted by everyone" he is close to Sun Tzu's "moral influence, which causes the people to be in harmony with their leaders, so that they will accompany them in life and unto death" (1:4). One of the essential components of this "fundamental philosophy" seems to have been the underlying vulnerability of "those who flourish are destined to fall into decline", and, just as Honda Motor had achieved supremacy over many larger companies, so "he also knew that Honda Motor would sooner or later be governed by the same law". In effect, this generates a self-perpetuating dynamic of the more successful, the more vulnerable.

Consequently "Fujisawa came to feel that it was imperative to avoid corporate crises triggered with little regard for the long-range future of the company". From that point of view, the most dangerous situation was Honda Motor without Sochiro Honda. Fujisawa recalled that "we cannot be assured of continued corporate activity unless we have not just one but many Sochiro Hondas. We must foster experts in various fields. And we want to establish an organisational structure in which such experts can fully exercise their skills".

To see what his ideal meant, it is worth recalling Fujisawa's own views of his colleague's most outstanding qualities - "Did not seek quick results", "there was no end to his pursuit of technology", "a sense of satisfaction for Honda would come only when an independent individual meets a challenge without fear of failure and achieves his goal", "He possessed a grand dream", and the creation of Honda R&D Ltd was the first step.

The second was to revise the company's internal organisation: whereas the conventional corporate hierarchy would inhibit such "experts" climbing the ladder, and waste their efforts on managing subordinates, Fujisawa reasoned "There were fundamental differences between a research and development department, whose mission was to study advanced technologies and be prepared to face many trials and failures, and a production department, whose purpose was to mass-produce goods, accumulate profits, and not make mistakes. These two departments, he thought, cannot and must not be operated under the same financial or organisational structure". Under his new structure, research was an autonomous function with "any number of" chief engineers or executive engineers who could become directors on the grounds of their technical excellence alone. But, R&D engineers "can choose a research theme", and once approved, "pursue it alone". Rather than a system where "each employee is evaluated only by his immediate superior", Fujisawa's aim was to make experts out of as many company employees as possible", with the organisational links running "both sideways and vertically" to form "a spider's web". The system has apparently been developed to allow four grades of "expert".

This multi-dimensional flow of communication and responsibility lent itself naturally to the SED (Sales Engineering and Development) system for new products, where these three interests are linked into a project team. Equally, this structure stimulates the process of feedback from experience and the exploration of new ideas and technologies. Subsequently, there have been further

ACQAAA

changes in Honda's internal organisation eg to reflect its greater "global" operations, and broadening its product range up market in motor vehicles and other engineering products. But the basic drive is to avoid falling prey to "decline".

Honda's managerial innovations through its "experts" system have been extended to its US subsidiaries and emulated by other Japanese companies.

In the 1950s, Japanese industry was hit by widespread labour disputes as the new Trade Unions attempted to establish their position, and Honda were nearly reduced to bankruptcy. But Sochira Honda's own reaction was "One must create a workshop where everybody would enjoy working" and was concerned when three leading Trade Unionists were dismissed. The company has adopted a policy of fostering co-operative working relations, with job-rotation, quality circles - including the innovation of individual worker notebooks so that the originator of an idea can be identified; involvement in disciplinary procedures; and a scheme to allow workers to use plant facilities to experiment with any idea, however fantastic, to be rewarded from any subsequent use of it.

Behind these mechanisms, the company maintains a range of facilities for assisting its workforce - a stock-sharing plan, a deposit plan, a mutual aid system for purchasing houses, and a life insurance programme. The company also has such facilities as cafeterias, company apartments and dormitories, and vacation cottages. Most plants have athletic grounds, gymnasiums, swimming pools, exercise apparatus, libraries, study rooms and hobby workshops, with some having mini-motorcross fields. These measures encourage commitment and flexibility, since however necessary "harmony" is for military operations, it is equally necessary to exploit Total Quality Assurance methods, originally pioneered in Japan on the lines of Denning and Juran; for ensuring that improvements gained through experience are rapidly applied to improve efficiency and design; and for the integration of design with production.

(c)   Chariots and Provisioning: Assuming that the production facilities for making the product are an analogy with the provisioning of an army, one of the sharpest jolts at the time of the collapse of the UK motorcycle industry was the remarkable difference in productivity: Fujisawa had an earlier career in engineering, and instituted a continuing discipline to achieve improvements in cost, since price was such a vital element in the company's competitive strategy. When the company began, they were inevitably compelled to purchase production machinery, and it is recalled that they made visits to the US to acquire the best available and also learnt from Volkswagen's policies in production management. But Soichiro Honda seems to have been particularly concerned on seeing a piece of production machinery standing idle, and remarked "Don't you know these machines were made well before the instruction manuals were printed? Technology makes jumps every day. You must try to obtain a better performance than that given in the manual".

This basic approach lay behind the creation of the Honda Engineering Company as the focus for production engineering, innovating machine tool and factory equipment design and manufacture. By the early 70s it was employing 1,400 staff, roughly 10% of Honda's workforce. (BCG: II Apendix 12), and by then, Honda were operating manufacturing processes at the frontier of technology. And these were shrouded in as much commercial security as their R & D. Appendices 11 and 12 of the BCG Report outline some of the advances made in production and quality processes. It also underlines the company's investment in and relations with subcontractors, where at the Kumamoto plant, then under construction, Honda were establishing four affiliated parts makers within the factory site, each with highly automated plant, to provide wheels, crank case covers, silencers, handlebars, petrol tanks, mudguards, transmissions and crankshafts. In addition, 30 suppliers of other parts were required to establish factories in the nearby area.

The integration and unity of objectives with sub-contractors is remarkably close, even if not entirely comfortable: Honda is reported to have asked 200 plant makers to put together a three year plan covering productivity, R & D, quality control, marketing information, labour relations etc with a view to Honda guiding, and financing where necessary, implementation of such plans. Honda had also asked a number of part suppliers not to increase prices for the next five years, but was assisting them with the necessary design and rationalisation, and investment, to achieve this. Several British companies are now priding themselves on taking steps to introduce just-in-time production methods, but Honda was in the early 70s requiring "precisely timed deliveries........several times a day, timed to the minute", and other British companies are introducing Flexible Manufacturing Systems, where again Honda were reported as assembling "up to 50 models (of broadly similar sizes) on a single line........when Honda changed the model, the line is merely slowed down and the idle time required for rearrangement is of the order of 5-10 minutes" in the early 1970s.

(d)   Offensive Forces: In one of the closest echoes of Sun Tzu, Fujisawa draws a distinction between two categories of forces (TS p.172 ff) "Establishing the organisational structure of the head office and the factories should be a 'defensive' move rather than an 'offensive' move", but "I made the R & D centre an autonomous body as an 'offensive' measure. Technology is the driving force for the growth of Honda Motor, and R & D is the vanguard........setting up overseas subsidiaries like American Honda was also an 'offensive' move. For Honda Motor to expand its motorcycle exports and grow to become an international corporation, we could not be on the defensive". This has a strong echo of Sun Tzu's distinction "Generally, in battle, use the normal force to engage; use the extra ordinary to win" (V.5).

(e)   R & D and Secret Weapons: Whilst Honda surely did its share of "reverse engineering" to see how competitors' products were designed; kept abreast of technical change; and no doubt employed Mitsubishi Corporation - the Trading House - to keep track of innovation in other countries, it is striking that Honda - unlike many Japanese companies in the '50s and

ACQAAA

'60s - were so innovative in their own right - the string of
technological Firsts is a tribute to the meticulous and thorough
range of R & D undertaken. And the story crackles with
the excitement of improving technology and products, trying out new
solutions, etc.

So central was this to the "vision" of the company that Honda R & D
Co. was established as a distinct unit in 1954, and was employing
1,300 in the early '70s. Apart from the input into the Honda racing
activities, with direct spin-offs into motorcycles and cars, the
fact that it was a separate "centre" is misleading, since one of
Honda's special qualities was, to quote BCG, "A most effective
balance between the 'pure' engineering, production engineering, and
marketing requirements of the new project. Before design work is
started at all a preliminary cost assessment and commercial
evaluation is made. Precise programmes are then laid out for
research work, later development work and finally work actually to
get the completed design into production. Production engineers are
involved in the project team from the earliest stages, so there is
little fear of the needs of production being "overlooked" and before
the final commitment to production is made, another scrutiny is
undertaken by a cross-disciplinary team".

But beyond this, Honda was reported to have a "drawer" or
"refrigerator" in which it kept many design projects that had
reached an advanced stage of development, and were therefore ready
to bring to the market quickly when the situation demanded.

Consequently, their product cycle was 18 months, and in some cases
their rate of response could be even quicker.

(f)   Marketing and "Native Agents"

Almost Fujisawa's first act on joining the company was to secure
control over distributors: at this point, Honda were mainly making
small engines to be attached to bicycles, with the frame purchased
by distributors from another supplier. Fujisawa insisted, even
against Soichiro Honda's offering to help the frame-supplier, that
only complete machines would be purchased from Honda. With the
introduction of the first motor bicycle, he also demanded a system
of advance and prompt payment, which effectively funded the first
major factory expansion. Thereafter, the company showed
considerable ingenuity in entering markets, but constantly aimed to
secure a firm control over distributors and dealers. Some of the
steps were very innovatory - in the US, where motor bicycles had
been traditionally a male preserve, dealers tended to have greasy
overalls from servicing the machines, so Honda switched to marketing
through sporting goods shops, hobby stores etc; when entering the
domestic Japanese car market, most of the motor vehicle dealerships
were sewn up by Toyoto and Nissan, so Honda drew on the bicycle and
motorcycle agency network; later in the US, extension of product
range was viewed as a crucial move to gain "sole-dealerships" in
both motorcycles and cars; and for the special needs of the US
luxury car market, the Acura marque was set up with its own
distinct dealerships.

It is not quite clear how these fit into Sun Tzu's categories, whether "local guides" or "agents", but Honda's technique was to set up competitive pressures between their own dealers, and one remarked "I don't know why, but this company places an awful lot of emphasis on market share". At the same time, Honda established a strong spares support, financing, buy-back and marketing structure. Again demonstrating concern for "control" and "adaptability".

APPLIED ENERGY

Following Sun Tzu's distinction of the two types of forces, he has one of his more purple passages (V.7ff) "For they end and recommence; cyclical, as are the movements of the sun and moon. They die away and are reborne; recurrent, as are the passing seasons ..... for these two forces are mutually reproductive; their interaction as endless as that of interlocked rings. Who can determine where one ends and the other begins?"

Well, this process is well illustrated by Exhibit 4, and Appendix 9 of the BCG study. To summarise:

Honda Motor Company: gearing over time

Year	Debt/Equity ratio (net)	Comments
1954	3.5	Penetration of motorcycles
1959/60	0.3	Dominance in motorcycles
1964/5	0.7)	
	)	Penetration of cars
1969/70	1.6)	
1974/5	1.3	Consolidation "Pause"

During the '50s, when Honda was penetrating Japan's motorcycle industry, profits were held low, and growth financed by heavy use of debt. By 1960, dominance in small motorcycles was achieved, profits were very high, and debt was paid off. In 1963, Honda entered the car market for the first time, and in subsequent years debt was used again to finance penetration and growth, and profitability declined. Up to 1975, profits and gearing had stabilised, and this was undoubtedly a preparation for their further moves in setting up their manufacturing base in Ohio.

The behind-scenes story before the first surge is described by Tetsuo Sakiya. In 1955, the company launched a full scale programme to streamline production and "clerical work". Despite a buoyant market, Fujisawa's strategy was to reduce production costs without boosting production "If you seek to achieve simultaneously the three goals of streamlining production, elevating technical standards, and increasing production, you will end up not fully achieving any of these goals. That is why I dared to choose the most difficult path of reducing costs without increasing production". Again, the aim was to improve efficiency across the entire company's operations, and included the introduction of charts, tightening of supplies, inventories, etc. In addition, the constraint on supply was used by Fujisawa to cultivate distributors who were reliable and loyal, in that he stopped delivering goods to those who were in arrears. Then, while Japan was going through a tight-money regime, Fujisawa

12   ACQAAP

185

EXHIBIT 9.4

Honda motor company: gearing over time

Year	Debt/Equity Ratios Gross	Net	Comments
1954/5	4.6	3.5	Penetration of motorcycles.
1959/60	0.8	0.3	Dominance in motorcycles.
1964/5	1.2	0.7	Penetration of cars.
1969/70	1.8	1.6	
1974/5	1.4	1.3	Consolidation/'Pause' before resumed penetration of cars.

Notes: Gross debt is defined as all interest-bearing debt, ie long-term debt, short-term debt plus notes payable. In practice the company also has a significant amount in notes receivable against which a corresponding amount of notes payable may be regarded as secured. The effective gearing exposure of the company is thus best represented by net debt, which equals gross debt less notes receivable. Equity is, of course, simply total shareholders' equity. Note that all the data are for the parent companies; in Honda's case, consolidated figures are also available at a ratio of three times equity, in 1974.

Source: Annual Reports.

is reported to have called the salesmen to a conference and asked
them "The factories are now ready to increase production. Are you
ready now?" Maybe, he had recollections of Sun Tzu's further
comments about the two forces "When the strike of a hawk breaks the
body of its prey, it is because of timing ..... his potential is
that of a fully drawn crossbow; his timing the release of the
trigger" (V.12-16). Then, during the downturn in the Japanese economy,
Honda increased production, and captured 80% of the Japanese motorcycle market. With increased exports as well, between March 1953
and March 1958, the company's net sales doubled to Y14,188m, while
inventories were halved.

The thrust was achieved by the introduction of new models, or model
variants, with aggressive pricing - made possible by the
stringent cost improvements of the preparatory phase and the strike
timed for an opportune moment when increased competition could be
less readily absorbed by other producers.

THE AMERICAN CAMPAIGN

The BCG study of the options for the UK motor cycle industry, is
among the best product/market analyses available, not least because
it was prepared close to the events and not as a piece of academic
historical research. It presents a wealth of detail about the
evolution of the motor cycle market, the main competitors, and their
relative products and strengths.

But essentially, in the early 50s the US comprised 50% of total
world demand, and for the larger capacity machines over two-thirds.
The market was predominantly made up of the "leather jacketed" macho
consumer, with machines typified as large, dirty and dangerous. On
screen, Marlon Brando, Warren Beatty and Clint Eastwood were seen
astride bikes of the period, and the good guy image was the highway
cop of "Electra Glide in Blue". In this market, the British names
of Norton, BSA etc had a strong position - some 60-70% in the class
above 350cc, and close to 90% in the 400-700cc class, with Harley
Davidson and BMW in the super-bike class - initially sharing the
market above 700cc: a stable market with traditional products and
established client image.

Honda, by the mid-50s, had embarked on becoming the leading Japanese
producer. On the technical front, they were heavily committed in
attempting to win their first TT race, and after winning the team
prize in the 125cc and 250cc races in earlier years, they won both
classes in 1961. In 1956, Fujisawa is reported to have been looking
to the future, and appreciated that the level of affluence in Japan,
Europe and the US was rising and badgered Soichiro Honda to pursue a
lightweight high-powered machine "a bike powered by a 50cc engine on
which a young couple would start whistling happy melodies". A year
later, Soichiro Honda proudly showed him the prototype of the Super
Cub - revolutionary in its "step through" configuration and plastic
resin body. And by incorporating their experience of uprating their
TT series engines, the Super Club had a 50cc engine generating 4.5
horse power. Immediately the Suzuka factory was started, aimed at
producing 30,000 units a month, compared to the best selling
machines in Japan achieving only 2-3000 units per month.

EXHIBIT 9

Market shares of motorcycles ⩾440 cc
USA 1968–1974

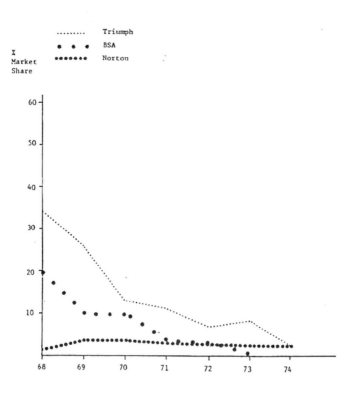

Source: R.L. Polk

Previously, Honda had undertaken its exporting through Trading
Houses, but Fujisawa recognised that serious exporting needed to
have a strong support presence in the overseas territory. There was
still a major choice of the market to be targetted, and a study
team, including advisers from Mitsubishi Corporation, surveyed the
world. They concluded that Europe and South East Asia, where many
countries were moving into the market for motor cycles, offered
the best prospects for Honda to expand, and of these South East
Asia appeared the better. The study team concluded that the US
market of 60,000 bikes a year was probably at saturation.

Against all this advice, apparently, Fujisawa insisted that the US
should be the target market, since it was clearly the most affluent,
and that products were more likely to be accepted elsewhere if they
had first been established in the US. After some problems with MITI
and the Ministry of Finance in gaining approval for the foreign
exchange to set up a subsidiary, American Honda Company was
established in 1960 as a wholly owned subsidary. At first, the
operation was not successful – it had begun by using existing motor
cycle outlets, who turned out to have the greasy overall approach,
so Honda developed its own network for the Super Cub through sports
goods stores, hobby shops etc. This change in distribution, coupled
with a major advertising campaign to present the image "You Meet the
Nicest People on a Honda" and "The Nicest Things Happen on a Honda"
achieved a major shift in the image of motor cycles. As a
consequence, with other Japanese producers following suit, Japanese
motor cycle exports to the US, some 6300 units in 1959 when American
Honda was founded, rose to 148,000 units in 1963.

The Adversaries.

BCG's bland description is that "Honda created the market – in the
US and elsewhere – for .. motor cycling as a fun activity". Instead
of the exclusively "macho" clientele, motor cycles widened their
social appeal to high school kids, young marrieds, working girls,
as small shopping vehicles, beach bikes etc. But before looking
at the subsequent battle, it is worth following Sun Tzu's guidance
of observing the "strategy" of the opposing forces.

(a) British Industry Strategy. The underlying approach of the
British manufacturers is described by BCG as "the fundamental
feature in this philosophy is its focus on model-by-model profit
levels. It is seen as essential that throughout its life cycle each
model, in each market where it is sold, should yield a margin of
profit over the costs incurred in bringing it to the market", and
from this it follows "products should be uprated or withdrawn
whenever the accounting system shows that they are unprofitable;
prices are set at the levels necessary to achieve profitability –
and will be raised higher if possible". "The cost of an effective
marketing system is only acceptable in markets where the British are
already established, and hence profitable. New markets will only be
opened up to the extent that their development will not mean
significant front-end expense investment in establishing selling
distribution systems ahead of sale"; and "plans and objectives are
primarily orientated to earning a profit on the existing business
and facilities of the company".

14

ACQAAA

189

(b)   Honda's Strategy.   To summarise the Honda approach, one can
recall Fujisawa's remarks on why the company had not sought funds in
the capital markets, "Honda Motor would lose its unique reputation
for putting technology first and become a company thinking about
'money first'," and had raised its battle standard in 1956 with
its new company motto "Maintaining an international viewpoint, we
are dedicated to supplying products of the highest efficiency at a
reasonable price for world-wide customer satisfaction".   This is
summarised by BCG as "Honda's basic strength in product design stems
from an extremely heavy commitment to R&D that ensures that its
products can be produced to meet the needs of any segment of the
market, and that these products remain in the forefront of technical
development.   Honda's pricing policy aims to introduce new products
at prices which are below those of comparable competitive models,
and that are designed to develop substantial sales volumes."

Product Policies - Manoeuvre

British manufacturers viewed motor cycles as a mature product -
"after all, their basic shape has not changed for 50 years" - and
"where the focus has been on pure design engineering considerations
rather than on designing products which were intrinsically low cost
to produce.   One result is that none of the existing British model
designs is suitable for manufacture using modern production
techniques". (BCG)

By contrast, Honda employed 1,300 staff in its R&D facilities and
another 1,400 on engineering and design, compared to British
companies' total R&D staff of 100.   But more fundamentally,
Fujisawa's approach was summed up, when he realised Honda had been
holding a particular model unchanged for too long in "the basic
theory that vehicles are fashions".

Also important to cost and flexibility was the sharp difference in
"organisation" - whereas Honda had links and co-ordination across
all phases of product evolution and manufacture, including subcontractors, British producers were relatively small purchasers from
sub-contractors such as GKN, Lucas etc, and took second place to
the latters' priorities for innovation (BCG page 63).

OFFENSIVE STRATEGY

Turning the US motor cycle market into a "fashion" business
required, in effect a series of sharp onslaughts on precisely the
lines described by Sun Tzu.   The customer loyalty of those
"captured" by a sale at one capacity, could be used to "induce"
them towards another purchase later of a larger sized machine.
Aggressive advertising, support, and "trade-in" terms linked to
the "assault" of a new model being introduced were further
"inducements" to the customer to buy at the next higher size of
motor bike.   This carry-over of sales to a new model then provided
the beachhead for attacking the rest of the market-segment.

As an example of this "offensive" technique, BCG say "Honda gained
their share (in the greater than 750 cc class) due to the
introduction of their new model, the CB750 in 1969, which caught the
market just at the time when previous riders of smaller Hondas were

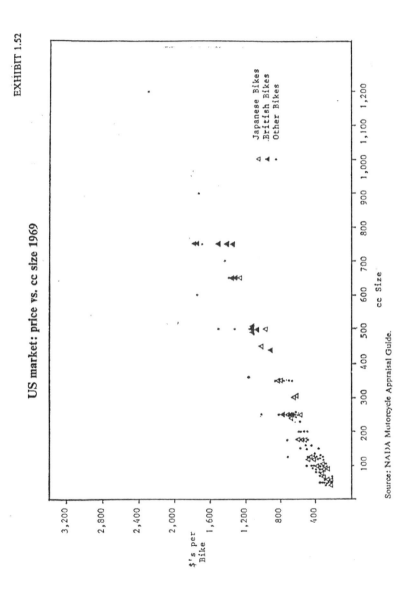

EXHIBIT 1.52

US market: price vs. cc size 1969

Source: NADA Motorcycle Appraisal Guide.

EXHIBIT 1.53

US market: price vs. cc size 1972

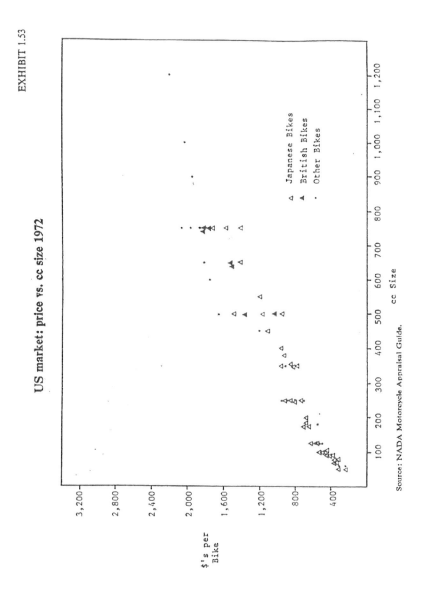

$'s per Bike

cc Size

△ Japanese Bikes
▲ British Bikes
· Other Bikes

Source: NADA Motorcycle Appraisal Guide.

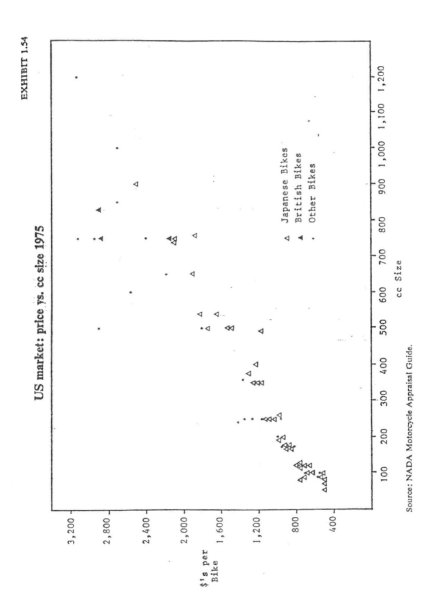

EXHIBIT 1.54

US market: price vs. cc size 1975

Source: NADA Motorcycle Appraisal Guide.

ready to trade up to a Honda Superbike".

By the mid-60s the pattern of "trading-up" was an established
feature of the market - BCG: Appendix 1: exhibit 10-13. The
percentage of repeat buyers going for a bigger bicycle was between
50 and 77 per cent in ranges up to 350 cc, and nearly 40 per cent in
the range 360-650 cc, and the period of customer ownership between
purchases reached the level where nearly 50 per cent repurchased
within 12 months, and 70 per cent within 24 months.

As a complement to the "capture" of new bike segments as the
customer generation moved up the capacity range, Honda were also
aggressive defenders of a sector position once gained, and amongst
examples given by BCG was a $200 discount on a 250 cc off-road bike
to meet Yamaha's introduction of a corresponding product, until a
better Honda version could be marketed: and quick moves into product
segments if it looked as though competitors were going to take a
lead position eg Honda's Elsinor model was quickly developed to
enter the developing moto-cross market.

As a consequence, the introduction of new models occurred at a
frequency that the British manufacturers could not match - by the
time of the BCG Study, the British manufacturers had made only one
engine upgrading in the period 1968-75, and in effect reduced their
models in the range above 440 cc from 8 to 3, whereas Japanese
producers had increased theirs from 3 to 13, of which Honda alone
accounted for 5.

Pricing

In Sun Tzu's model of engagement, where the aim is to achieve the
quickest route to victory, aggressive pricing supported aggressive
product introduction: new models were generally introduced at a
significant price discount against existing ones, or at comparable
prices if there were very substantial performance and quality
advantages as Honda moved up-market: BCG Appendix 1 52-54
illustrates graphically how Japanese prices under-pegged
competitors in individual segments as Japanese models were
introduced progressively up the displacement scale between 1969
and 1975.

Local guides and Agents

Rapid market penetration at each successive segment depended upon an
effective marketing network: Fujisawa rated the establishment of
American Honda as the decisive point in his strategy, and through
this office subsidiaries were set up in financing, buy-back, and to
handle stocks and spares; with a strong dealer support system -
including training mechanics, finance for the dealers and
development etc. Moreover, as in Honda's earlier market drive in
Japan, a premium was placed on "sole" distributors, who had the
loyalty to respond with the speed and flexibility needed for this
strategy.

But the market advance also strengthened the dealer coverage for
each stage: "Since 1962, the Honda franchise became more and more
desirable," as the range and quality of models grew. By 1974, Honda

ACQAAA

194

had built up nearly 2,000 dealers, 84 per cent of whom were sole distributors, whereas the British manufacturers had 400, of which only 7 per cent were exclusive. In addition (BCG Appendix 1) Honda offered very sharp incentives to secure sales volumes in time with their new-model introduction pattern, and the spread of dealers was designed to exploit competition between them.

Waging War

Over time, this tactical advance of succesively "offering one avenue of escape" - because of the British "strategy", only retreat, saw a progressive withdrawal of British manufacturers. The BCG despatch at the end of the campaign is sufficiently vivid to be quoted in its entirety:

"The Japanese began by developing volume and experience in small motor cycles in their domestic market during the 50s. Experience curve related cost reductions followed, leading to a highly competitive cost position which was used as a springboard for penetration of world markets. The British manufacturers tended to respond by withdrawing from the small bike segments of the market, which were being hotly contested by the Japanese with their superior cost. The Japanese progressively developed a greater volume and experience in even larger capacity ranges of motor cycles. As they did so, their relative cost position in these motor cycles also improved and their prices, which were brought down in line with costs, became increasingly difficult to match. The larger bike segments were therefore also withdrawn from over time in their turn, as the non-Japanese competitors and in particular the British, retreated to higher and higher displacement classes of motor cycle.

A useful strategic insight can be gained by examining the reasons which may have led to the failure of the British motor cycle industry to halt the advance of the Japanese during the 60s. In the early and mid-60s this was probably due at least in part to complacency and an erroneous belief that the Japanese were unlikely ever to be a threat in larger bikes, which were "more difficult to make". Although smaller manufacturers had been driven out of business, the largest company in the industry, BSA, was profitable through the 60s.

Given the tendency towards short-term profit orientation of the British industry, this continuing profitability no doubt encouraged any feelings of complacency to persist. In any case, profitability was not sufficiently high readily to permit investment at a rate comparable to that of the Japanese. The latter had achieved higher rates of profitability and this, combined with financial policies involving high gearing, enabled them internally to fund rapid rates of growth.

Continuing profitability for the British following this strategy depended critically on the growth in the motor cycle market being sufficient to offset their "segment retreat". This was in fact the case during the 60s so that although they were participating in narrower and narrower segments of the market, these segments were themselves growing rapidly. As a result, overall production volumes were broadly maintained at the 80,000 unit level throughout the period. This meant that the factories continued to be fairly busy, and because at any point in time the Japanese were not yet strong in the segment to which the British had retreated, the business remained profitable.

Strategies of this kind, in which competitors who are initially fairly strong and broadly based in the market progressively retreat over time to the lower volume and more specialised segments are frequently encountered in industry. They normally owe their origins to an excessive focus on short-term profitability and often do produce profits for quite long periods at a time, as with the British motor cycle industry. In the long run, however, they are almost always disastrous. The reason for this is that they allow the new competitors who are penetrating the higher volume segments of the market to become larger and more powerful over time, and - based on experience curve cost reductions - to develop high and secure profits in the segments which the retreating competitors have vacated.* This gives the new competitors a tremendous position of strength from which, ultimately, they can be expected to attempt to penetrate the last segments to which the smaller retreating competitor has withdrawn. And he now no longer has the resources to withstand this attack.

Only two possibilities can result in a segment strategy being successful commercially. The first is continued market growth such that the perpetual development of new segments creates a continuing avenue for retreat. These conditions rarely if ever persist indefinitely. In the case of the motor cycle industry they no longer exist, both because future market growth is likely to be slower and because the market appears to have reached a "natural" limit with respect to the sizes to which motor cycle engines can go without the machines becoming totally unmanageable on the road.

The second possibility involves calling a halt to the retreat and refusing to withdraw further. Commercial success will then depend on retaining a volume position within the segment such that your overall cost of manufacturing and selling products in the segment is as low or lower than the competitors'. Doing this is facilitated if "barriers to entry" exist making it difficult for larger competitors to penetrate the segment. This is only infrequently the case, and cetainly in motor cycles the Japanese have had little difficulty in taking a dominant share of the Superbike segment, which is effectively "the last Citadel of the British manufacturers". The heavy financial losses incurred by the British in the last few years may be directly attributed to their failure to retain at least a superior share of this segment relative to the Japanese competitors. Indeed it seems clear that these losses were effectively an inevitable long-term result of continuing with the essentially defensive strategic posture adopted by the British industry in the face of the emergent Japanese competition a decade or more before".

---

* This is called "winning a battle and becoming stronger" Sun Tsu 11: 20.

EXHIBIT 1.34

Market shares by manufacturers
450-749 cc, 1968 to 1974

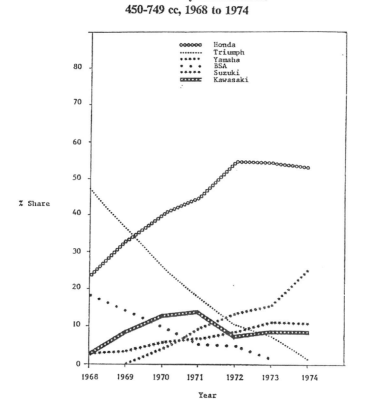

Source: R.L. Polk

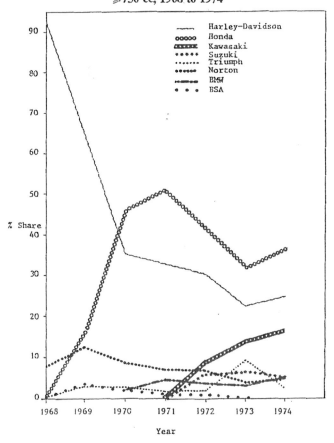

EXHIBIT 1.32

Market shares by manufacturers
≥750 cc, 1968 to 1974

Legend:
- Harley-Davidson
- Honda
- Kawasaki
- Suzuki
- Triumph
- Norton
- BMW
- BSA

% Share

Year

* Yamaha is removed for clarity. From zero in 1971
  it follows Triumph very closely.

Source: R. L. Polk

SURRENDER

At the end of this process, the situtation can be summarised:-

(a)   British bikes had fallen from a 65% share of the market above 440 cc to 4% between 1968 and 74;

(b)   Output per man year in the British factories was between 10 and 18, whereas Honda's company average was 106 bikes and 26 cars, with the Sazuka factory by itself having a figure of 350 bikes per man year;

(c)   From 1970, NVT were marginally profitable, but BSA/Triumph were showing continuing losses: Honda, on the same basis, were achieving profits of £50 million plus with an ROI of 12-24%.

The BCG study was itself part of a review on possible future strategies in response to pressure from the workforce, and the scale of investment required coupled with the extremely high risks of entering the market with such dominant and well placed competitors was more than either private or public sources would contemplate. Whilst the Government did provide some support to the Meriden Co-operative, it was only three years before both it and the remaining significant motor cycle capacity at NVT were closed.

One of the incidental advantages of the BCG study was to give the lie to various excuses: far from "sweated labour", Japanese workers were actually paid significantly more in real terms than British; there was no evidence of special "subsidies", indeed reading the Honda Motor story, MITI was probably more of a hindrance than a supporter - in their early days Honda received a loan from the newly-created Japan Development Bank, but beyond this MITI were not entirely helpful when the company wanted to move into cars, since at the time MITI were pressing for some merging of company structure; and when Honda wanted to set up their American subsidiary, they appeared to encounter some opposition as well. Moreover, the Japanese motor cycle market was so fiercely competitive that it is doubtful whether any administration would have confronted the problem of selecting one from another: Kawasaki, for example, are reputed to have lost money for several years before having a model with pre-eminent market appeal - an example of the difficulties of breaking into a market where the existing leader is rather more tenacious than the British manufacturers.

The contrast between the approaches of Honda and the British manufacturers has been treated as a paradigm for two different idioms of commercial style. It is fair to say, however, that, whilst Honda led the assault in the US, they were followed very aggressively by other Japanese producers. To this extent the US market became a battle ground for the Japanese "Warring States" to transfer their competitive battle into another market, with the British producers almost accidentally trodden underfoot. This fierce battle also had a damaging impact on other producers - both Harley Davidson and BMW went through serious financial difficulties and only survived after major restructuring. The

ACQAAA

199

final battle lines can be depicted by comparing the full number of Japanese models in the market in 1974 (79) against all other producers (18).

One might have thought that the process depicted by BCG would have been rather more closely remarked at the time. From the vantage point of involvement in the Industrial Development Unit, where fate put one in the Chair to set up the Meriden Co-operative, recent UK motorbike history had been "a series of mergers and acquisitions which took place during the 60s and 70s" - the generally beneficial process of "rationalisation": certainly, the margin-boys were busy fixing mergers and acquisitions, with the normal cart-loads of company lawyers and accountants; Clearers were appointing Receivers; consultants and accountants were appointed to define "strategies" for particular companies; the carpet-baggers moved into town to pick up the real estate of vacated factories at bargain prices; the jackals from the secondhand machinery market nosed around the debris; with redundancies and closures, there was continuing labour unrest, including sit-ins; and trade unionists, economists, trade associations and politicians preached and protested. A typical summer's afternoon in post-War industrial Britain you may say. Undoubtedly the wider benefits were equitably distributed - to each according to whatever-turns-him-on. But not much "harmony", and in Sun Tzu's terms, "a rout".

AFTERMATH

At the time, there were several features of Honda's approach that came as a shock, in bringing home the level of industrial performance achieved in Japan. The more important were:

A.   The extremely high level of "redundancy" that they were prepared to tolerate in their research - "on research projects, in which totally new designs had been developed as the basis for new product offerings, 99 per cent failure is permitted to achieve one per cent success", but at the same time, an extremely tight focus on production and efficiency "on subsequent development projects, which are directed towards the detailed development of products for production and sale, and which follow the research phase, not even one per cent failure is permitted" (BCG Appendix 11).

B.   Their outstanding production and cost performance, where scale/quality/flexibility were interrelated - indeed, previously "quality" had been seen as an optional addition eg finance for extra supervision, whereas Honda showed that high intensity production equipment, whilst obtaining marked reductions in cost, also had the advantage of higher precision and quality of manufacture.

C.   The combination of A and B into a single process of "developing for production" with continuous cross-functional links, and feedback vertically so that improvements derived from experience in the market and in improved production could be rapidly applied. If we could manage a German composite word, it would go research-to-develop-products-to-be-manufactured-most-efficiently-and-rapidly-adaptable-to-the-market, with the boundaries of the "organisation" extending from the source of finance to

20

ACQAAA

200

sub-contractors, and within a cultivated "unity" of purpose.

D.   This mechanism appeared to be driven by a concentration on "market-share" with very aggressive and innovative marketing through a subsidiary present in the market, and every advantage taken of volume sales to reinforce cost improvements.

Even with such a well-integrated force, the master stroke was to enter the US market at the small 50 cc bike level, and on establishing a beachhead to capture the market in successively larger models.   There may have been some intuition in this decision, but Fujisawa would hardly have made a massive investment to increase Honda's model capacity by ten times that of any previous model without a clear idea of the "situation". Fujisawa admits that "foresight" was among the characteristics of Churchill that he most admired, and he "lost no opportunity to discover the 'blind spots' of competitors".

Undoubtedly, Honda would have been aware of the technical performance of UK machines, whether by purchase and "reverse engineering" or through comparison while they were active in pursuing TT triumphs; they could hardly have failed to observe the industrial confusion; they would undoubtedly have obtained through Mitsubishi Corporation, the group trading house, continuing intelligence of the performance and behaviour of UK and other competitors; and it is not unreasonable that they might have tested competitors' tolerance to price-pressure elsewhere.

But, as Fujisawa and his Honda colleagues reviewed all this "foreknowledge", to decide on which model strategy - given the range open to them technically - to follow, maybe they recalled Sun Tzu's advice "now an army may be likened to water, for just as flowing water avoids the heights and hastens to the lowlands, so an army avoids strength and strikes weakness" (VI.27). For this is precisely what Honda did - capture the low ground of the small-bike market and advance up the higher "segment" slopes, and, as "those skilled at making the enemy move do so by creating a situation to which he must conform" (VI.20), achieved this by timed attacks of new models and sharp prices, which, given the "profit oriented" strategy of British manufacturers, left the latter with no option but to retreat up-market to the final isolated "citadel".

The account has followed Honda's motor-cycle development and there are probably many maxims of Sun Tzu that have been missed. But Honda goes on, and maybe there is another analysis to be made of their approach in motor-vehicles - they have shown the same qualities of moving from small displacement to the up-market ranges, and established overseas subsidiaries, joint ventures etc, adapting with acute flexibility to the particular "situation" of the market. Notably the major investments in Ohio, for a predominantly American manufactured range of cars, anticipated trade-friction and the changing Yen/Dollar value, and through their US operations Honda are now set to be one of America's largest individual exporters, notably to Japan. But it will be interesting to watch their other strategic plays now that there are new aggressive producers, such as Korea, coming into the market, and when Honda are on the defensive.

No doubt these future moves will also lend themselves to annotation
by the teachings of Sun Tzu. In the ultimate, however, it does not
really matter whether these references are more than the sheerest
chance, since the exploits of Soichiro Honda and Takeo Fujisawa have
passed into Japan's post-war industrial mythology. They both
retired on the same day in 1973, and handed the stewardship of the
company that they had built up to Kiyoshi Kawashima, who had joined
the company in 1947 when the company was building its first 50 cc
engine. But the characteristics shown in the organisation and
development of Honda have set a model for many other manufacturers
in Japan - indeed, Fujisawa's vision of "vehicles are fashions" has
been amply fulfilled: in 1987, Toyota sold 1.88 million cars in
Japan, of which there were no more than ten the same.

HORIZONS

The analogies between commercial and martial activity are fairly
obvious, and not new in management studies. But most of the
standard works using military analogies have tended to be focussed
on the fronts of marketing techniques or corporate acquisition.
Sun Tzu undoubtedly has many choice quotes to be jotted in
Filofaxes, to be trotted out as "paper entrepreneurs" ply their
buttons. But for the real world, Sun Tzu has a particular virtue in
posing challenging questions on "alliances", "internal unity",
"deception", "adaptability", "normal and extraordinary forces",
"drawing the bow", "speed and timing", and the acquisition of
"foreknowledge". Perhaps other masters on the art of war preached
similar themes, but Sun Tzu does have a remarkable brevity, and the
concepts elide to provoke us to query our apparently clear
distinctions and observe how often oppositions are infinitesimally
separated - "There is no distinction between attack and defence".

As Honda, and others have shown, Sun Tzu's idiom of thought does
have a special synergy with modern manufacturing in a global
context: "order" and "internal communications" are crucial to gain
the major efficiency advantages from the lessons of experience; to
sustain the cycle of innovation; and to integrate innovation,
production technology, and marketing. So making innovation and cost
the offensive weapons. And MITI, and other, studies indicate that
the essentials of Honda's approach are adopted across a wide range
of Japanese companies - not just in manufacturing - where the battle
is conceived in terms of gaining "market share" and thereby "winning
... and becoming stronger".

Nowhere is commercial activity discussed in metaphors of war more
than Japan, and, for example, the works of Lanchester are among the
best-sellers. But one is not for a moment suggesting that all my
Japanese friends are incipient war lords - quite the contrary.
Ronald Dore has remarked*, "the trouble with the Japanese is that
they have never really caught up with Adam Smith" - a lamentable
failing that they sadly share with Germany, Italy, France, Korea and
other rising industrial countries. Where the creation of a "market
system" is only a very recent overlay, it is not unnatural that,

---

*"Flexible Rigidities" - Althone Press

when confronted with problems of allocating and controlling resources, a traditional military model offers a good conceptual approach - Sun Tzu was, as a sideline, just as clearsighted on basic economic issues - "where the army is, prices are high; when prices rise the wealth of the people is exhausted. When wealth is exhausted the peasantry will be afflicted with urgent exactions" (11:12), a point rarely put as succintly. Maybe Sun Tzu's underlying sense of continuing uncertaintly and the precariousness of any fixed position finds a resonance in the Japanese sense of vulnerability. But the resulting virtues of order, harmony, foresight, constant vigilance, adaptability and the pursuit of security read across to commercial strategy - and there are commentators* who suggest that these are among Japan's national attributes.

On the other hand, one can have an amusing moment's speculation on how the Anglo-Saxon corporate system measures up to Sun Tzu's main requirements: if the "Ruler" is the "owner" of the company, whereas in Japan the company has a series of alliances to guard it against the wilfulness of unpredictable "private" shareholders, in the Anglo-Saxon tradition, the General is in a position where his Ruler will often see substantial gain in selling the army from under his feet. True, today, prudent Generals take steps to be sure they benefit from such a transaction, or, with the march of technology, have found a use for "parachutes" and other devices to soften their landings.

"Every man for himself" may offer many conveniences as a theoretical approach. But, in a military context, the command usually signals collapse of order and discipline eg the ship is foundering, or the line is broken. So it tends to operate in the commercial theatre: the General finds that his staff officers are ready to sell themselves to enemies for higher personal reward, or conversely he may be able to filch key staff from others. Not surprisingly, his troops are liable to threaten to lay down their arms, manoeuvre slowly etc in order to secure higher rewards.

Of course, "profit" is supposed to be the unifying and motivating principle. So, among the army, there is a continuing tussle as platoons plead "qualifications", "trade specialties", and other devices to create greater reward-leverage. And the General Staff can be so preoccupied with doing reports and valuations for the Ruler that they barely notice the enemy. There is also a resulting tendency for the General Staff to be heavily influenced by the inventory clerks of the Quartermaster's stores, where tallying the numbers of crossbows is more important in reporting to the Ruler than accounting for expeditions to find materials to increase the range of the bow, or than other activities such as training whose benefits cannot be immediately calculated. At all events, the chances of such a "mercenary" force in a global conflict against a force organised and deployed according to Sun Tzu's maxims where, like Honda, maximising profit is secondary to objectives of the

---

*"Japan - Strategy of the Unseen" - Michael Random (Crucible)

ACQAAA

longer term pursuit of technology and survival of the army, must be doubtful. Maybe the "mercenary" principle was ideally suited to financing privateers, slave-traders or wagon-trains, where a spirit comparable to Sun Tzu's army confronting death was ensured by the only escape being by drowning, being devoured by vultures, or getting scalped.

But in a world trading environment, where Sun Tzu's organisational and adaptive dynamism is becoming the condition of success, "profit-oriented management" can lead to the catatonic complacency and inertia of the British motorcycle manufacturers. Maybe not all British companies are like our erstwhile motor-bike constructors: and maybe not all Japanese companies have Honda's adaptive dynamism. There are, however, enough of the latter to have taken Japan to a position of world significance, as Paul Kennedy has remarked in "The Rise and Fall of the Great Powers", far beyond the expectations of the Japanese Imperial General Staff in 1940. Paradoxically, one might suggest, this has been achieved by them displaying the "acme of skill" depicted in "The Art of War".

POSTSCRIPT

I have tried to use my sources to illustrate how precepts, albeit of great antiquity, seem to have a direct commercial relevance today - not just in motorcycles, but similar patterns are discernible in other product areas where Japan has been successful: it is often amusing to set outraged City comments against the maxims of Sun Tzu. Because Honda have been, unlike many Japanese companies evolving in the immediate post-war period, relatively self-suffient in technology, this has not really allowed me to bring my favourite quotation from Sun Tzu into the text. But it does also illustrate another feature of the Japanese commercial style, so perhaps you will allow me the licence of self-indulgence. In Chapter 13 on "Employment of Secret Agents" he remarks (3 and 4).

"Now the reason the enlightened prince and the wise general conquer the enemy whenever they move and their achievements surpass those of ordinary men is foreknowledge.

What is called 'foreknowledge' cannot be elicited from spirits, nor from gods, nor by analogy with past events, nor from calculations. It must be obtained from men who know the enemy's situation".

True to form, Sun Tzu says more than the text: no truck for economists playing with their knobs and models; sages a 'babbling o' "the Invisible Hand" would have been buried up to their necks and left for the ants - or whatever was the appropriate Chinese punishment for those diverting the attention of the General. And, nowhere does Sun Tzu give instructions on levelling mountains to make "an even playing field" - rather, terrain, whatever its shape, is there to be exploited. In the realm of Sun Tzu, only reliable information in real time is a useful guide, and even then, as he goes on to comment, this has to checked through the use of "doubled agents" for whom "it is mandatory that they be treated with the utmost liberality" (21).

24

Perhaps the crucial difference between Honda and the British
motorcycle manufacturers lay in "the foresight" of the former, and
its apparent total absence from the latter. In short, the
"mercenary" principle tends to be relatively short-sighted. Whethe
"foresight" and "foreknowledge" are cognates, the first is dependen
on the second. Honda made use of Mitsubishi Corporation in its
earlier exporting to the US, but when it mounted its US campaign it
did so through forming a local subsidiary. Elsewhere it would have
used Mitsubishi Corporation for intelligence and data on local
conditions, as indeed it did in its marketing study of strategic
options. Mitsubishi Corporation is one of the Japanese general
trading houses, the Sogo Shosha, and these are unique in the modern
commercial scene: one of their prime functions is effectively a
"foreknowledge business": with a global geographical presence and
comprehensive information systems, they provide a continuous flow o
information on trade opportunities, changes in local "situations",
and developments. In particular, they have a close interest in the
licensing of technologies. Certainly, any UK company considering a
Japanese collaborator or competitor should assume that, well
before leaving Britain, he has been very carefully screened and
the information made available to the interested parties in Japan.
But beyond this, these companies fit almost ideally Sun Tzu's
description of an army "moving like water" as they amass huge
turnovers through filling in and mediating any trade gaps. One
could add point to this by quoting from the "Business Principles" of
one of the leading Sogo Shosha ".....shall manage its activities
with foresight and flexibility in order to cope effectively with the
changing times. Under no circumstances however shall it pursue easy
gains or act imprudently".

I hope to have put in a plug for all three of these texts as worth
close reading: the BCG analysis of the motorcycle industry is among
the best practical illustrations of the Japanese approach to
manufacturing; Honda Motor portrays the dynamism of creative
enterprise and adventure; and Sun Tzu offers a challenging account
of a particular approach to combative or competitive situations.
Inevitably, the last has the greatest resonance, posing searching
questions far beyond these spheres.

ACQAAA

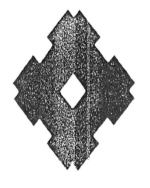

Our logo is a stylized form of a frame for wells in old Japan.
A distant ancestor of the House of Sumitomo is said
to have come from the town of Izumi, which means "well" in English.
The frame symbolizes water that gushes from a fountainhead
to form a river, which then flows into the ocean.

ANNEX A

PERSONALITY IN INDUSTRY: THE HUMAN SIDE OF THE JAPANESE
ENTERPRISE - HIROSHI TANAKA

Page 88 — "Now, more than ever, Onitsuka paid heed to the
teachings of Sun Tzu, a sixth century BC Chinese General and
military theorist. Sun Tzu's The Art of War, a sophisticated
treatise on strategy, tactics, logistics and espionage, had had
a profound influence throughout Chinese history and on Japanese
military thought; it is the source of Mao Tse Tung's strategic
theories and of the tactical doctrine of the Chinese armies.
Through the Mongol-Tartars, Sun Tzu's ideas were transmitted to
Russia and became a substantial part of her Oriental heritage.

The Art of War has been, and continues to be, widely read by
Japanese businessmen.

In "Offensive Strategy", the third chapter of the Art of War,
Sun Tzu states:

Those skilled in war subdue the enemy's army without battle.
They capture his cities without assaulting them and overthrow
his estate without protracted operations ..... Know the enemy
and know yourself; in a hundred battles you will never be in
peril. When you are ignorant of the enemy but know yourself,
your chances of winning or losing are equal. If ignorant both
of your enemy and of yourself, you are certain in every battle
to be in peril.

Onitsuka determined to arm himself with as much knowledge as
possible about the international market .....

ANNEX B

HONDA MOTOR — Page 193ff

Japanese corporations exist in an environment quite distinct from that of the United States and Europe. Theoretically under Japanese commercial law the stockholders are the owners of a joint stock company. In fact, these stockholders do not have a strong sense of ownership, and there is a widely held view in Japan that a company exists for the good of its employees. Virtually all members of the board of directors are chosen from among the employees of the company. These directors are of course obliged to improve corporate performance, pay dividends to the stockholders, and increase equity for the benefit of the stockholders. But their primary concern is to increase the company's market share (for which they are often willing to sacrifice short-term profits), to expand the scale of the company, to raise the salaries and improve the welfare of the employees, and to offer them sizeable bonuses in addition to their regular salaries. Although this bonus is classified as being part of past wages for accounting purposes, it is in fact a means of sharing profits with the employees.

/⁻The scale of such bonuses can range from the salary equivalent of 5.2 months in mining and manufacturing, 5.0 months in wholesale and retail, 4.6 months in the financial and insurance areas, and 4.4 months in the electric and gas industry._7

It should be noted that Japanese corporations were quite different before the end of World War II. During that period, Zaibatsu families controlled the holding companies. These companies were the major stockholders for many large corporations and absorbed a large share of their profits. In the pre-war days, there were four major Zaibatsu — Mitsui, Sumitomo, Mitsubishi and Yasuda — plus a number of smaller ones like Asano, Kawasaki, Furukawa and Nissan. Almost all major Japanese corporations were under the control of these Zaibatsu. Although the elite members of these corporations have a strong sense of loyalty, ordinary workers were paid low wages and felt little sense of unity with the company. A dramatic change in this situation came about immediately after the war, when the Occupation forces dismantled the Zaibatsu in a bid to deprive Japan of its ability to wage another war. They also liberated the farmers, destroying the landlord-tenant relationship that had been so detrimental to Japanese agriculture, and created owner-farmers. One reason for this measure was to further the demilitarisation of Japan, for the once formidable Japanese Imperial Army was made up almost entirely of tenant farmers. It was not long before the sons of these farmers, riding the tide of industrialisation, moved to big cities en masse, got jobs at factories, and infused industry with a spirit of agrarian co-operation. Thus, after the end of the war, a sense of unity gradually developed between management and blue-collar workers. Great progress was made in formulating the Japanese management system based on the spirit of unity, and the basis for a co-operative labour-management relationship was established. The success of the Japanese economy today, which

is rooted in this unique system of management, can be traced
back to the liberal post-war democratic reforms instituted by
the Occupation forces.

As in Europe and North America, the supreme decision making body
of a corporation in Japan is the stockholders' meeting.   In
Japan, however, the meeting is no more than a ceremony, an
understanding on all major issues having been reached between
the company and major shareholders beforehand.   Such meetings
are usually brief, and very seldom will an individual stock-
holder express objections to any item on the agenda.   This
spirit of harmony, in sharp contrast to the mêlées that sometimes
erupt at shareholders' meetings in the West, can be attributed
to the system of owning stocks in Japan.

Since 1947, holding companies that control corporations have
been illegal.   Instead, Japanese companies now tend to own each
other's stock.   For example, two companies that deal with each
other in business transactions will also exchange shares as a
means of cementing their relationship.   As a result, of the
total number of shares listed on the stock exchange, more than
70 per cent are owned by corporations and less than 30 per cent
by individual stockholders.

During the post-war era, companies that had belonged to a
Zaibatsu joined together again to establish new groups, such as
the Mitsui Group and the Mitsubishi Group.   A bank usually
forms the core of such a group, within which the member firms
will own each other's stock.   Under the Anti-Monopoly Law,
however, a financial institution such as a bank, a trust company,
an insurance firm, or a securities company is not permitted to
own more than 5 per cent of the issued shares of another company,
the purpose being to prevent a financial institution from
dominating an industry.   Thus within each "group", companies
can establish a close relationship through the mutual ownership
of stocks, without running the risk of being dominated by a
banking firm.   While there are cases where stocks are mutually
owned by companies belonging to different "groups", this is
more an exception than the rule.

In this system, the major stockholders of one corporation are
usually companies within the same "group", and these stockholders are quite familiar with the status of the company in
question.   Therefore it is rarely necessary for the stockholders
to be briefed at a formal stockholders' meeting.   Under this
system, the member firms within a group usually agree to keep
dividend rates low on a reciprocal basis, which in turn enables
them to allocate large portions of their profits to internal
reserves for further corporate growth.   The stockholders are
not in a position to receive generous short-term dividends, but
in the long run this is more than offset by the accumulation of
sizeable capital gains.   The system also enables the management
of an individual corporation to concentrate on long-range
strategies, without being bothered by pressure from stockholders
for quick returns.

In a Japanese corporation, the highest decision-making body is
the Board of Directors ..... includes very few non-executive,
outside members. As a result, the Board members are of the
same educational and social background, know each other well,
and find it relatively easy to reach a consensus. Moreover, it
is rarely the case that Board members will enter into a heated
discussion on any agenda item or vote to amend or reject any
proposal put to them. These members are classified into "ranks" --
the highest (at least in theory) being the Chairman, followed
by the President, one or more Executive Vice-Presidents, senior
Managing Directors, Managing Directors, and Directors. In
reality, the ultimate decision-making function of a Japanese
corporation rests in a meeting of senior members of the Board,
consisting of their Managing Directors or Senior Managing
Directors and those of higher rank.

The board of directors of a Japanese corporation not only
serves as the highest decision- and policy-making body, but
each member is a full-time executive in the company. Another
feature unique to Japan is that under commercial law, the
corporation must designate one or more members of its board of
directors as "representative directors", namely, those who have
the right to represent and make major commitments on behalf of
the company. In certain Japanese corporations, the Chairman is
vested with this right, but the chairmanship is usually no more
than an honorary position given to a retiring President. Unlike
most American companies, where the Chairman of the Board is
totally responsible for the affairs of the company, these
responsibilities within a Japanese corporation are generally
shared by a group of representative directors. For this
collective leadership to function well, there must obviously be
a strong sense of unity and mutual trust among the Board
members.

ANNEX C

The Honda Motor Group

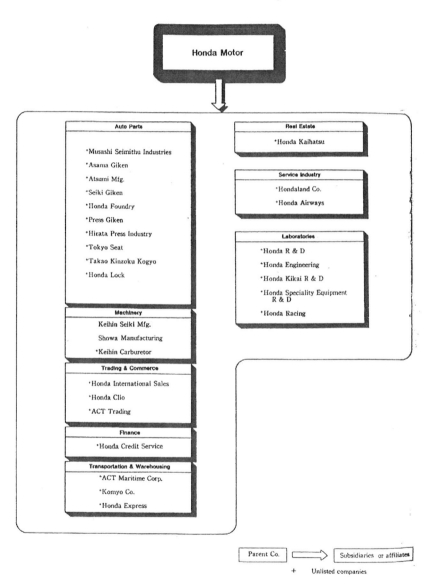

211

MAJOR SUBSIDIARIES AND AFFILIATES OF HONDA MOTOR

	Incli-nation	Annual Sales (¥ million)	Net Income (¥ million)	Paid-up Capital (¥ million)	Employees
1) TRANSPORTATION MACHINERY					
Automobiles & Auto Parts					
Honda Motor	****	1,400,340	23,138	60,628	30,487
+Asama Giken	***	14,629	494	800	738
+Atsumi Mfg.	***	14,851	N.A.	96	620
+Honda Foundry	***	16,000	N.A.	540	900
+Yachiyo Industry	***	115,441	243	1,700	2,041
+Press Giken	***	22,891	473	850	492
+Hirata Press Industry	**	26,081	98	350	885
+Tokyo Seat	**	101,296	2,118	1,200	1,100
+Tsuzuki Seisakusho	**	14,045	188	140	433
+Takao Kinzoku Kogyo	***	15,606	334	166	249
+Honda Lock	***	2,896	141	260	451
+Musashi Seimitsu Industries	**	22,139	218	780	736
		1,766,215	27,445	67,510	39,132
2) MACHINERY - GENERAL					
Showa Manufacturing	***	47,594	508	2,326	1,940
+Keihin Carburetor	***	18,558	429	400	950
Keihin Seiki Mfg.	***	31,927	325	1,442	1,640
		98,079	1,262	4,168	4,530
3) TRADING & COMMERCE					
Auto Sales					
+Honda International Sales Corp. (HISCO)	***	N.A.	N.A.	2,000	1,100
+Honda Clio Higashi Tokyo	***	3,500	N.A.	160	72
Others					
+ACT Trading Corp. (ACT-T)	***	54,036	N.A.	200	66
		57,536		2,360	1,238
4) FINANCE					
Leasing					
+Honda Credit Service	***	16,763	294	2,000	102
5) TRANSPORTATION & WAREHOUSING					
+ACT Maritime Corp.	***	N.A.	N.A.	50	N.A.
+Komyo Co.	***	8,088	N.A.	100	530
+Honda Express	***	31,420	268	900	1,524
		39,508	268	1,050	2,054
6) REAL ESTATE					
+Honda Kaihatsu	***	11,001	706	785	1,142
7) SERVICE INDUSTRY					
Amusement					
+Hondaland Co.	***	11,964	530	2,000	488
Others					
+Honda Airways	***	1,360	1	360	105
		13,324	531	2,360	593
8) LABORATORIES					
+Honda Engineering	***	51,697	61	1,200	2,000

INTERNATIONAL INDUSTRIAL CO-OPERATION (IIC) DIVISION: 1978-1981

The Division strapped together several functions involving international contacts previously spread around the Department of Industry – these generated a variety of activity streams unexpectedly complimentary and contrasting.

OVERSEAS POWER STATION PROJECTS

Nearest to the grease-under-fingernails real world was supporting overseas sales of power stations. This had begun when Lawrence Kadoorie[1] – head of one of the leading family groups in Hong Kong, which included China Light and Power, the power utility for Kowloon and the New Territories – called on Jim Callaghan at Number 10 with the proposition that he would be ready to order a power station for a new site at Castle Peak from British suppliers, providing the British government was ready to stand behind the order to vouch for its fairness. This proposition had been put to the Board of Trade, who, despite having an outfit with the resonant title of the Overseas Project Group, found proximity to the real commercial world uncongenial compared to pontification on trade policy. The question was then put to the Department of Industry, and John Lippit agreed to take on the job with an ad hoc team drawing predominantly on staff in the appropriate sponsor division.

This involvement with the dying throes of the power generation industry was to last for another eight years. The industry itself just after the mid-70s was the outcome of typically British bumbledum. There had been a saga of "consolidation" shrinking down to three main chunks: GEC with a dominant specialisation in steam turbines and control systems; Babcocks in boilers, coal handling and grinding; and NEI with a more comprehensive coverage of the systems of a classical coal-fired station. In effect, this left a dynastic polarity between GEC, who tended to favour Babcocks as an alliance to provide the bulk of the coal handling and boilers, and NEI. There was, particularly from the latter, continuous sniping against the other, with the piquancy that the companies' London headquarters were only a couple of hundred yards apart, with rather

213

different cultures: one in Stanhope Gate where the Weinstock ethos was proverbially penny-pinching, even apocryphally down to checking the make of the light bulbs: while NEI's London base was facing Park Lane, and the company ran a private jet service to connect to their main offices in Newcastle.

The CEGB was coming to the end of a major capital investment programme in new stations, which had effectively tied up British manufacturing capacity for more than a decade. These had been predominantly coal-fired, since the UK mining industry had historically been the dominant source of energy supplies, with a percentage of oil-fired and nuclear AGRs. This had produced enough generating capacity to "guarantee supply" – indeed the surplus capacity at the time of subsequent privatisation contributed to the UK avoiding the privatisation disaster in California. There was a political wish to introduce a larger nuclear-power component, but for coal-fired capacity no new stations were envisaged for at least another decade. If a more strategic view had been taken of the industry, it would have been sensible to phase this CEGB programme over a longer time frame. But the CEGB had its own historic problems: separate fiefdoms with barons vying for supremacy, where command of generating capacity was an insignia of power. At the practical operating level, however, the CEGB had a strong professional reputation, with among the highest level of consistent power availability.

With capacity tied up meeting domestic investment, British companies had not been motivated to try for international orders, with a result that many opportunities for following up on renewing or rebuilding plant originally purchased from Britain had been allowed to go uncontested – Australia being a notable example, where Japanese companies had successfully picked up a string of orders. Another feature of the UK was that the CEGB had retained design and project control, with a strong team of project engineers. Conversely, no British manufacturers had experience of being a lead contractor or taking overall project management of a complete power station.

The industrial background was characterised by decades of inter-firm rivalries and animosities; a network of relationships between suppliers and baronial domains within the CEGB, in turn giving rise to another tier of jealousies, recriminations over past shortcomings; and, to be fair, individual preferences for reliable previous performance. These frictions leaked into the political domain via MPs associated with manufacturing plants in their constituencies or direct contacts to Ministers. While, outside the defence field, the UK had no tradition of supporting British companies in contested project markets where competitors had an exactly opposite tradition and systems for the state to support their national companies. The Department's internal assessment was that 10 – 12 Gigawatts of orders were required to fill the gap in domestic orders, and that the odds were strongly against achieving this. Yet surely the continuing political concern was to avoid a sharp loss of employment, even though neither main party had disposed serious efforts to anticipating the situation, leave alone initiating the structures and mechanisms to meet it.

With this shambles backstage, maintaining a façade of confidence with clients was in itself a substantial exercise of theatre. But much of the pleasure of the job was relations with clients. CLP was a tight operation under Lawrence Kadoorie's group chairmanship. Lawrence has to rate high on the register of the most remarkable characters one has met: well into his 80s, he retained a razor-sharp shrewdness behind the most courteous and gentlest of manners. Wonderfully supported by his wife, Muriel, who kept close control of his diet – one of the delights was to see him negotiating agreement to order his favourite bread-and-butter pudding. One of his shrewdest moves was to recruit Bill Stones*as his General Manager from the domains of the CEGB, unquestionably one of their best operational managers who very obviously enjoyed the greater authority allowed by Lawrence. But the expansion of CLP's power capacity from the smoking chimneys visible from Kowloon in the mid-70s to one of the world's most efficient facilities at Castle Peak, and subsequently a joint venture with the Guangdong power authorities, is largely down to Bill Stones.

At the time of Lawrence's first approach, CLP, for its very slimness, lacked the depth of project engineering staff to take on a major new power station development on a coastal site, involving a spectacular chain of transmission lines. Leveraging such staff out of the CEGB for secondment to CLP at realistic rates was the main contribution that the Department could make. The choice of industrial participants was streamlined by Bill Stones' intimated preference for GEC turbines – put in effectively coded terms that it was for the Government to choose, "but…" Whether previous experience lay behind this nudge none of us knew, but it resolved one of the splitting headaches of dealing with the British industrial scene.

This was just the start. We still had the tradition of British companies being brought up on subcontracting to CEGB, who retained project leadership, thereby taking the overall risk of the venture being completed effectively, in the jargon, at the "owner's risk". The question of who should lead the British proposal demanded a series of meetings: GEC, under the Weinstock ethos, were concerned only with the pennies that led to a return to their own bottom line, and not a groat to be risked on liabilities beyond this; Balfour Beatty, the likeliest civil contractor by virtue of their experience on transmission lines, power station cabling, switchyards etc did not see their proportion of the work as sufficient to take the lead; and Babcocks, with interests confined to the boilers and coal-processing, were similarly reluctant. In typical British fashion, a consortium approach was impossible. Finally, largely on the grounds of not turning down the prospect of a string of turbine orders, GEC agreed to take the lead, but "lead" in a form where they would not have responsibility for the choice of suppliers outside their own specialisation. Consequently, negotiations involved taking several floors of the Hong Kong Hotel as alternative suppliers made their proposals to CLP: even though they had occasional gripes about the tough negotiating stance of CLP, GEC were fortunate in that this pattern married into the CEGB approach on which the project was being developed. And, to give credit where due, once their Rugby team had accumulated experience, with their own project programme systems built up, they became professionally confident to take on a coordinating function in subsequent projects.

Officials could stay reasonably clear of the negotiations, but there were a string of issues on the financing from security to back ECGD guarantees to wheezes on particular elements of the package. Here again, there were tensions, since Lazards were the lead bank chosen by GEC, while Lawrence Kadoorie was chairman of Schroders' Hong Kong operation.

In terms of Departmental structure, the branch concerned with power-generation, first under Alan Havelock and then Bob Dobbie, became the support team for pursuing overseas projects. But the "A" Station negotiations were concluded. And Gordon Manzie* took over from John Lippitt, on his departure to GEC, as "official top-gun", and negotiations moved on to the "B" and "C" Stations.

EUROPEAN INDUSTRY CONTACTS

There were regular EEC meetings of "Directors of Industry", and Peter Carey* found that, if there were useful informal contacts, the practice of a routine "tour de table" did not foster any real discussion to justify the time out for a day in Brussels. He deputed me to sit in, and his judgment was entirely correct in that the substance was less value than the personalities.

The form was an assembly for lunch, when Count Davignon, the appropriate Commissioner, occasionally put in an appearance, followed by an afternoon's roundtable session. Davignon, with an affable confident style, not always supported by clarity of judgment, was interesting as a product of a typically elitist industrial background – Belgium historically had effectively only one government controlled holding company, Sociètè Generale, with stakes in all other national businesses from Solvay to Tractabel. But by far the most impressive personality was Helga Steeg from the Federal German Economics Ministry: eloquent in English and formidable in articulating an argument, she was a first introduction to the German Rhinemaiden academy.

The nearest these occasions came to drama was offstage. At one lunch, both Davignon and Helga were conspicuously late. And then Helga entered with stern hauteur, to be followed a few minutes later by the Count whose usual ebullience was replaced by the demeanour of having had a passing encounter with a steamroller. Others present could only guess at what lay behind this clash: my own guess was that the French, who on the previous occasion had made a pitch against the Japanese – "The most frustrating thing about the Japanese is that they tell you in advance what they're going to do, and then still beat you to it," was a typical remark – might well have talked Davignon round to start the ball rolling for trade sanctions, to which the Germans were opposed. This was some years before the fashion of Voluntarily Restraint Agreements in the early 80s.

Beneath the EEC group, we had periodic bilateral exchanges with opposite numbers in individual States. The informal French view at the time was that Germany could afford to be more relaxed about Japanese imports, since they were already the most protected market in Europe by virtue of their insistence on DIN standards and their regulatory bureaucracy. And the French should know.

To impartial observers, however, this was the pot calling the kettle black. With each country we had a continuing series of complaints: for example, the French were blocking approval of the EMI body-scanner, the Decca Navigator system, and other British innovations. Equally, UK manufacturers could not get products like lawnmowers approved in Germany until they had passed all the hurdles of their domestic certification, while we had a standing line of humour about Germany keeping open coal-mining pits with costs several times higher than those of mines being closed in the UK as uneconomic – "But coal was where it all started," was the usual response.[2]

An entertaining facet of bilateral contacts was involvement with the Franco-British Association. Recollection is that this began through contacts with Derek Ezra*, then Chairman of British Coal (incidentally, also an old-boy of Monmouth School, one of its rare distinguished alumni beyond the rugger field). These involved a very lively Working Group at

Arundel, and being on the panel of conferences in Bordeaux and Avignon, spectacular as only the French can manage – the menu from the formal dinner at Bordeaux remains a treasured archive, with 7 white and 12 red wines, the only trouble being that there was pressure to recycle classes, so that any attempt to use one as a reference was dashed by the glass being whisked away.

Beyond the gastronomic memories, these exchanges left a fund of quotations to illustrate the disparity of cultures: just as examples:

– A French spokesman: "We believe you cannot have an entrepreneurial society without an entrepreneurial government." Something must have dropped off the ferry in translation across the Channel.

– A French "economist" introducing a working group session: "All our public corporations are doing well" – though he accepted that Bull had been a disaster. But when the British delegates were challenged on their industrial accomplishments, Douglas Wass*, since reference to the works of Ricardo would hardly have been appropriate, could only muster a reference to the funding of BL's new Metro production line.

– One British hit was when the French denied that they had any covert regulations against imports, and it was pointed out there was a section of their Ministry for Industry, at the time headed by a M. Marchand, to which companies wishing to import machine tools had to submit their applications to check that there was no suitable French alternative.

On another occasion, the French were challenged on the regulations required to divert shipments of VCRs to Poitiers. "No regulations", came the reply, "just extremely polite and quiet-spoken customs officers," who could find a pretext for delaying applications almost indefinitely.

OECD INDUSTRY COMMITTEE

Attending as the UK delegate was tossed into the pile of the new Division, rather on the assumption that it was an innocuous talking shop. In fact, it turned out to be a bureaucratic hoot.

The day before my first attendance, we had a gnomic message from the Treasury, having passed around several parts of the Department before finding the new Division responsible, to the effect that the US delegate – and the Committee Chairman – had called in on the Treasury to say that the US would be proposing an initiative to eliminate the "distorting" subsidies applied by European countries. Having just left the IDU, with its recent history of introducing a series of "industry schemes" and with a Labour government still in power, on checking around, the consensus of views from the Department was that a holding line should be adopted.

The original Agenda offered no clue on when the US delegate was going to launch his initiative, and it would have been useful to have agreed a line with other European representatives before starting. This was not possible, as the delegates from capitals turned up only a few minutes before the meeting was due to start. On arrival, we were confronted with a revised Agenda with the US initiative down as second, following approval of the draft annual report to Ministers: a compendium of standard economic platitudes, which, historically, apparently the Committee usually passed on the nod, confident that their respective governments would just carry on doing what they had done before. There was every chance that we would reach the US initiative before one could consult other EU delegations over coffee.

So, just as a ploy to slow the proceedings down until coffee, I picked on one of the standard formulaic phrases in the first paragraph that advocated the freest operation of "markets", and queried whether it was not time for the Committee to come into the real world and drop such jargon phraseology. Arguing that whilst product markets, such as machine tools, civil aircraft, commodities etc, or geographical markets like France, Germany or the US might have some analytic value, their common characteristic was that they were all imperfect, and in aggregate the term "markets" was meaningless. I did not realise how avant-garde this view apparently was, though, since Stiglitz's Nobel accolade for spelling this out in eco-lingo, it must by now be commonplace. (I drew my inspiration at the time from what I thought was an impeccable source, recalling that somewhere Adam Smith had said that the unfettered operation of markets was "chaos".)

But as a sop to the American position, and, to appear constructive, I suggested that every government adopted their own regulations to control markets, support for those disadvantaged by markets, and devices to counter the failure of markets, and a survey of these might be a better theme to commend to Ministers. The US Committee Chairman seemed a bit nonplussed. At the coffee break, the French delegate sidled up and commended my interjection as "absolutely correct", but queried why it was made on this occasion. I explained our advance notice of the prospective American initiative, to which his response was that we should demand that the US exposed their "distortions" before doing so ourselves.

But, talk about Pandora's box. What had been intended as a 10-minute holding operation turned out to take up the full day, and then the whole of the next day. And indeed the Committee had to be reconvened for another emergency meeting to clear the final report for Ministers. It became apparent that, having let this genie out of the bottle, many of the staff of the permanent delegations who were acting as national delegates were bored out of their skulls at the continuous repetition of economic slogans, and could not be restrained at the chance of "de-platituding" the text. We were still in the throes when the US Chairman said that he had to catch his flight back to Washington, and his place was taken by a redoubtable Austrian academic, Dr Zemsch. The phrase "picking winners" was solemnly put to the vote, with no hands raised for "those who pick winners" and a unanimous show of hands for "those not picking winners" – the attendance included Japan, France, Germany, and South Korea. After acting as an exemplary Chairman, Dr Zemsch, as we queued up to pick up our coats in the lobby, burst into roars of laughter, declaring that "nothing like this has happened at the OECD before". When I mentioned that my motive had been simply to encourage some discussion until coffee on the first day, he collapsed in helpless hysteria.

An amusing sideshow of committee politics was that the draft report had been prepared by the German Deputy Chairperson – another from the Rhinemaiden academy, whom even the German delegate referred to as Brunhilde, and who had aspirations to take over the Chairmanship. And my apparent criticism of the text was interpreted as a devious British manoeuvre to block her nomination.

In the midst of this debate, the Americans did manage to squeeze in their call for disclosure of "distorting" State Aids. And the French responded as they had indicated. Several other "Federal" countries were cautious, arguing that their central authorities had no powers to demand disclosure from their States. Informally, the German delegate confided that he would welcome this initiative since it would give the Federal authorities a pretext to find out what the Lander governments were up to. Eventually, with the French in the lead, a list of a dozen or so types of "distortion" were drawn up – subsidies to capital investment, reduced-rate loans, allowances for initial working capital, free provision of local transport and services infrastructure, assistance toward training costs, support for research etc. And the Committee presented this to the US for them to fill out before others would do their corresponding tally.

After a couple of months, a chastened US delegate, from their equivalent of the Rhinemaiden academy, presented a chart with the 51 States along the top, and the list of "distortions" on the left. There were no more than two boxes that did not have ticks in them. Thereafter, the "state-aids transparency" exercise continued with countries outlining their respective measures, but in a rather less doctrinal atmosphere. And the UK delegation unveiled a presentation on "additionality", which launched the term into the ether of international economic jargon.

In the midst of this exercise, the Thatcher government came to power. And we were able to respond with authority and alacrity to Keith Joseph's request for a paper on "Aid Disarmament", even indeed, with some modesty, claiming credit for having initiated the exercise. (The poor guy was chastised by his think-tank nuts for "going native" when all he was doing was facing up to the real world being a vastly dirtier place than theoreticians dare admit.)

Needless to remark, the programmed eco-lingo has carried on: incantation of "markets" becoming the highest aspiration of intelligent thought among many subsequent Ministers, while "picking winners" has continued its Pavlovian way as standard jargon of abhorrence among the doctrinally correct.

OECD COMMITTEE ON MULTINATIONAL ENTERPRISES/ UN COMMISSION ON TRANS-NATIONAL CORPORATIONS

Among the first stirrings of the "globalisation" controversy, international interest in the behaviour of multinationals had been ignited by the scandals in the early 70s as US corporations, with ITT under the mythical Geneen in the van, had been caught suborning governments in Latin America. The outcry from developing countries for restraints on the behaviour of such organisations could not be gainsaid, and the first conference under UN auspices had been staged in Lima. Anne Mueller* had been the UK delegate at what had been a fraught exercise in weathering the storm. Taking over from Anne, if in the main the job entailed a protracted series of meetings in London, Paris, New York, and even Mexico, in a continuous process of haggling over texts, each forum had its own peculiar dynamics.

As a result of this first gathering, the UN Centre for TNCs (Trans-National Corporations) was established, and a Commission of member countries was set up. The Centre, which had a tricky position between all the warring factions, performed a useful function in drawing up factual and analytic material on the activities and economic significance of multinationals: this was at a time when their full significance had barely been analysed, and the Centre did, and commissioned, a lot of valuable work to provide a sound basis for discussions. At the same time, there was a growing academic community looking at the issues, with such names as John Dunning and John Stopford. Apart from tensions surrounding work to devise restraints against a repetition of the ITT fiasco, there were also other related UN activities such as a group on "illicit payments".

The UN Commission broke down into "G" components[3]: for the purposes of discussions on multinationals, there were the G66, predominantly developing countries with a coterie of half a dozen around India as a leading protagonist; the Soviet "bloc" which, with the Cold War still very much alive, had a doctrinal motivation to exploit every opportunity to proclaim the "evils of capitalism"; and then the OECD group, which was viewed by the rest of the Commission membership as the multinationals' parents. Meetings of the Commission also had an "expert panel" of industrialists and trade union representatives, drawn up mainly by the International Chamber of Commerce (ICC) and the ILO (International Labour Organisation).

If these categories appear straightforward, to capture a real whiff of the times is extremely difficult, even if only a few decades ago. As ever, the real world is more complex than the stereotypes. ITT itself was seen even in the US as a dodgy totem of capitalism: its "conglomeration" started under Geneen with acquisitions of Avis, hotels and a string of other businesses at the expense of developing its inherent strengths, is viewed as an early casualty of the monocular pursuit of shareholder value. But for every ITT/Geneen outfit or for that matter Union Carbide of Bhopal fame, there were many multinationals, especially from Europe, with long traditions of operating in host countries, mindful that their interests coincided with the societies within which they operated. One recalls a visit to a Dunlop tyre subsidiary north of Calcutta, where the plant's medical centre served the local community, indeed boasting a leading world expert in the treatment of rabies.

But the ITT case undoubtedly triggered underlying frustrations in many countries, and it was a propaganda gift to Communist anti-capitalist voices. The UN, with a powerful developing world faction, albeit that many recognised the value to their economies of sustainable inward investment, and a "Cold War" Soviet bloc, was a volatile and unpredictable forum in which to have constraints debated, skewed by such a blatant transgression of responsible behaviour as demonstrated by ITT. Moreover, the phraseology that found its way into UN Conventions and Resolutions had wider legal implications, which in turn opened the scope for local interpretation and challenge.

Moreover, some issues could have far wider implications than first appeared. For example, the concept of "national treatment" may be unexceptionable – inward investments should observe the same local regulatory regimes as domestic businesses. But turn the card over, any stipulation that domestic companies should not receive any special support not equally available to inward investors leads into a debate – still raging now – about inhibiting countries from evolving their own indigenous industries. Or, itemising offensive practices overlapped other fora – "illicit payments" has also been a continuous topic over decades.

Among OECD members, even the most "laissez faire" recognised that oversight of the appropriate behaviour of companies registered in their countries could not be ducked, and that the international outcry demanded some formal response. Not being a regulatory body, any such mechanisms would have to be reliant on voluntary compliance and in a form that met international concerns while being workable within their own national commercial systems. On the UN Commission stage, therefore, there was coordination among OECD delegations to avoid, or temper, the prospect of hysterical demands, while at the working level within the OECD considered guidelines could be formulated as a response to international concerns.

There was a complex mix of pressures and tensions even within the OECD group ostensibly united by a common interest as the "parent" nations. These reflected very different national approaches to corporate regulation: for example, where the Nordics and Germany with established traditions of co-determination were more tolerant of extending consultation to local overseas operations, the US, if still inhibited by the obvious culpability of their corporations in triggering the row, was still inclined to hold out for terminology that allowed "management the freedom to manage".

The UK delegate was on shifting sands between these various tensions. The "brief" wobbled according to the political predispositions of the government of the day. Initially, the "position" had to reflect a Labour government contending with an extreme left-wing faction, to whom the multinationals were as much a stigma of "evil capitalism" as to the Soviet Union, albeit with a rather more balanced view elsewhere in the government. At this point, the UK delegate had to play some rhetoric for the former while recognising that the predominant Government approach was governed by the latter. Typical was a session chaired by Tony Benn – since he had moved out of the Department of Industry at the time, one cannot recall the formal status of the meeting, but with Edmund Dell*, then Secretary of State for Trade, also in attendance. As Benn and his groupies[4] worked themselves up about curtailing the iniquities of the multinationals, Dell appeared to be dozing off, while officials were left wondering where this lopsided debate was going to finish up. As the meeting came to a close, Dell suddenly galvanised and launched a blunt rebuttal of the tenor of the meeting to the effect that American vehicle, pharmaceuticals and other companies were among the most effective producers in the country, and the Government was not going to tolerate any manoeuvres that might discourage them from making their crucial contribution to the economy.

At the level of daily routine, there were periodic meetings with David Lea of the TUC, who effectively held the ILO watching brief. David, one sensed, had problems coping with the internal politics of the TUC, which was never quite as monomaniacal as the extreme left. While the ICC contact was an engaging, if rather fussy, Shell lawyer. Above this were the tiers of the OECD and UN Commission.

Steering workable texts through these conflicting interests, agendas and positions demanded a lot of trading drafts, meetings at OECD, group-coordination sessions, and inordinate gatherings in "corridors". With the conflicts in Ministerial attitude, one could honourably be prudently cautious, since the Commission had not got over the "position statement" stage at my first attendance in early 1979. The arrival of the Thatcher government, and Keith Joseph at DTI, at least had the advantage of sweeping out the ambiguities of the "UK position". After my "market-sceptic" stance at the OECD Industry Committee, it was now possible to adopt a rollicking "free-market" posture – the sort of guff that is usually confined to *FT* economics leaders. Not difficult, actually, if you assume that you have left half your brain on a Clapham omnibus. But one of my interjections prompted the US delegate, a Columbia law professor no less, to turn to his interns with the sharp question, "Why can't you guys write me stuff like this guy says?"

But each "tier" had its own idiom: the OECD meetings were smaller, and with increasing familiarity among delegates, increasingly informal. And spurred by a shared priority to achieve a balanced and workable set of guidelines that would anticipate, and ideally, set the pattern for, if not forestall, any corresponding UN formulation. With a reasonably stable membership, ready pooling of intelligence on the shifts in thinking among G66 countries, exchanges were remarkably frank and there were virtually no issues that came up at the UN Commission that had not already been kicked around within the OECD group. The UN Commission meetings by comparison were formally stereotyped, with a larger forum, held in public, and with the usual rhetorical conventions of, "The distinguished delegate of..." A useful lesson was the crucial importance of pace – with OECD countries mostly represented by delegates from their group, the OECD could usually time ahead of the game and liase on tactics.

An important player was the Swedish delegate, Sten Nicklasson: a ferocious fitness fanatic, an articulate and astute operator with a pleasant open personality. He took a distinctly liberal (open) position that allowed him on several issues to argue from a G66 position, and he was a very useful bridge whenever discussion appeared to be heading for a logjam – a stance that did not always endear him to all OECD colleagues. We even had occasions when Swedish business leaders lobbied us to discourage Sten from taking some line, which we met with the retort that he was the country's delegate and told Sten that this had happened. In fact, he seemed to have got on well with his country's leading businessmen, since, by pure chance, a few years later we bumped into each other at Geneva airport in transit to catch the same flight to Beijing. He was accompanied by a delegation of a dozen or so industrial barons, and I quipped whether he was taking the Swedish Davis Cup team – they had just won the Cup – on a tour. To which he replied that his delegation covered 95% of Swedish industry. That's a real corporate state.

Despite appearances of formalities in address, seating arrangements and alliances, there was plenty of scope for informal exchange. For example, in the UN Chamber in New York, by some curiosity the UK delegate was seated between the US and the Soviet Union, which allowed one to negotiate compromise wordings on occasional sensitive issues, and come up with "a perhaps helpful suggestion". And, as the only arena where a command of English confers any advantage, one could support a G66 proposed wording, especially from slightly pedantic Indian delegates, with the suggestion that a slight amendment would make it "better English", but tweaking the sense in a more favourable direction.

But one of the most satisfying byplays arose from a press report that the Moscow-Norodny Bank had been caught getting up to some irregularities in Singapore. This was too good a chance to miss, so the newspaper cutting was carefully preserved for the next Commission meeting. This was in Mexico, where in a theatre layout and using Spanish to determine seating, the Soviet delegate was seated immediately behind. When it was convenient, I began reading the account into the record, aiming for a final concluding remark that this was not the behaviour of a disreputable western bank, but that of the Russian-state foreign trading bank. One had barely got through the first sentence, before the Conference Chairman, Bernardo de Sepulveda (a Cambridge educated lawyer, who subsequently served a term as Mexican Ambassador in London) was gesticulating apparently in my direction. But on looking around I discovered that the Soviet delegate was waving his arms wildly to intervene. With some added pleasure, I completed reading the press account, and carried on to make the point.

Declaration of Mexico

To pretend that churning chunks of text is pleasurable, even to the ultimate bureaucratic mind, is difficult to sustain. On the other hand, it can involve some drama. Just for illustration, the pace of the UN Commission was disrupted during its session in Mexico City, in early summer of 1980, when the President declared that he wished to conclude the occasion, of which his government were the hosts, with a "Declaration". With a range of controversial issues still unresolved, such as legality, compulsion, scope, penalties for non-compliance, and appeal provisions, but at a point where texts and non-texts were being exchanged, the danger of hasty wording in a "Declaration" was sufficiently acute for the OECD group to shift focus to this exercise. Even if the informal reaction among the group were variations of, "Oh shit!" None more so than from Sten and I, who, by chance encounter in the canteen with two attractive local female staff and in response to our natural curiosity about the status of ladies in the national "macho" society, had been promised a "macho tour" of Mexico that evening. This had to be called off in the interests of drafting the "Declaration".

With four days to go, a "Declaration Group" assembled at 10.00 or 11.00 p.m. after the day's Commission proceedings, depending on whether there was some formal function, under the chairmanship of an East German banker – hardly impartial. The OECD team concluded that this was an occasion for a philibuster, and, on a tit-for-tat basis of exchanges with G66 and Soviet bloc speakers, both of whom pressed extreme demands for inclusion in the "declaration" invariably beyond the scope of the drafts before the Commission and impinging on the domain of other UN fora, the first aim of survival was to spin out the discussion. But with no predetermined time for concluding each session beyond the whim of the chairman and sheer exhaustion, this was extremely testing: a few of the OECD group took their turn and could not manage more than 30-40 minutes each, including our Columbia law professor. This just carried us through the first two nights.

With another two to go, we were extremely nervous whether the group had the resources to spin out time. But we need not have worried. The French delegate, one of their permanent UN staff, took up the baton. Fantastique! Speaking in French, with earnest countenance and conceding to positions that never existed, he drew distinctions and split hairs, which only the French language could distinguish. Within this dazzling display was a very effective account of the extent of other UN instruments that covered, or clashed with, various aspects of the concerns voiced by the G66 and the Soviet bloc, developing the argument that issues should be addressed in their appropriate context. This heroic performance, with occasional support from other OECD speakers, carried us through the night. But the moral is, if you want sustained convincing bullshit, call up the French.

As we came to the final evening of the Commission before the closing ceremony the next day, there were impatient calls from the President's office. Yet there was still no text on the table. And impasse. Sten made the suggestion that we should start with an entirely uncontroversial sentence, and then build up a statement to reflect the views of different participants. So, we began with the preamble expressing the Commission's appreciation for the hospitality of the Mexican Government. On this basis, the G66/Soviet bloc offered an assertion, to which the OECD delegates proposed a neutralising counter-phrase. And so it went on, until well-past midnight, and with an increasingly restive Mexican official. After leaving the room for a telephone call, he returned to say that the President wished to see a text within half-an-hour.

The Chairman insisted that the declaration had to conclude with a call for a Code to be "the most effective". After a few seconds, the Canadian delegate[5] – give him due honours – responded that this should be matched with "and most appropriate". It took only a glance between him, the French, the British and American delegates to anticipate the final move. The German delegate, a young Rhinemaiden, was on the point of speaking, but the British delegate ungallantly kicked her ankle to avoid any further intervention. With a nod to the French, the British delegate suggested that as a final concession, only to meet the concerns of the President's Office, and in the interests of achieving an agreed statement, we would be ready to drop "the most" before "appropriate". The Chairman nodded, and the Mexican official grasped the master draft. While our Columbia law professor muttered the famous quote of a US Senator on the conclusion of the Vietnam War, "Let's declare victory, and get the hell outta here."

The final text of half-a-dozen apparently anodyne lines was duly proclaimed in the closing session of the Commission. But for many years thereafter, there was a clique of officials, to the puzzlement of others assembled for whatever the occasion, who would praise each other's contributions as "most effective and appropriate". And my farewell rejoinder to Sten on our arrival in Beijing after our chance meeting in Geneva was the hope that his visit would prove "most effective and appropriate", to which he cheerfully reciprocated with the same formula.

Run-in to OECD Guidelines

The pressure was to complete the "formal OECD Guidelines" and the formalities were largely completed by early 1980. Indeed, the first test case under the appeal procedure of the Guidelines had been heard: this allowed a foreign subsidiary to complain if it had reason to question treatment by the parent company. The case involved a Swedish subsidiary of BOC who were pleading inadequate consultation before a "rationalisation" that had resulted in local redundancies, and a panel of OECD members was duly set up. The most striking feature of the panel hearing was the outstandingly articulate advocacy, in impeccable English, of the Swedish trade union Convener, a sharp contrast to earlier experience with British trade union officials in the era of Benn. In the event, the case was settled reasonably amicably. And the OECD could claim the effectiveness of the Guidelines in practice. The Guidelines were reviewed in 2000, as the globalisation debate was rising in intensity, and found to be robust enough to continue, except that the original did not encompass environmental issues: to be fair to the OECD group who so assiduously drew up the Guidelines, the "environment" as a topic had not been discovered at the time.[6]

CHINA LOOMS

Interleaved was a growing activity on "overseas projects" – the power generation interests had completed negotiations for the Castle Peak "B" station, and, in pursuit of orders to fill the capacity gap in domestic orders, the "sponsor" team had extended its activities to other options for coal-fired stations. These included rebuilding one in Nigeria, where coal supplies had been by overhead cable, and the whole facility long since derelict; and one of the world's eternal potential projects, exploiting some carbon deposits in the Sinai Peninsula, where one learned from braver personal accounts, the coal was only just off-white in colour.

Perhaps the longest-shot arose from contacts with CLP, where Lawrence Kadoorie suggested that there might be an opportunity for a nuclear power station in China, with Britain supplying at least the turbines. At the time, the departmental view was that this was an eccentric fantasy, but, since we were still in the course of negotiating the Castle Peak series, the only course was to lend such support as we could to his efforts, however unlikely the prospects. In fact, CLP had begun selling electricity across the border into Guangdong several years earlier, and had opened up a continuing dialogue with the provincial authorities. At the same time, Lawrence himself showed extraordinary energy in himself making contacts with party/provincial cadres in the course of visits to old family sites in Shanghai. Again, though, the tireless efforts to pursue this opportunity were down to Bill Stones*.

We had an active Franco-British Industrial Cooperation group as an avenue for exchanges, including a joint study of Japan's industry, meeting alternately on either side of the Channel, with each side responsible for arranging a visit to some point of interest. In France, this included a visit to Fos, and industrial development zone on the Mediterranean, and to Cadarache, the French nuclear research centre. While staying in the spectacularly modernised Chateau that served as the latter's visitors' lodge, we noted from the Visitors Book that the first Chinese delegation had visited in early 1978. So, at the time of Lawrence's visionary idea of a nuclear power station in China, the French were already launched on their campaign to secure orders there with a complete French nuclear and turbine proposal.

A Greek Episode

These "longshots" also included perhaps the best project that we never won. The Castle Peak development of a large coastal station with its own coal off-loading, storage and handling facilities, offered a good "reference", and GEC spotted the potential for a similar development in Greece. The scheme was presented to the Greek power department, and proposals were developed: meanwhile, a key element of the package was a guaranteed supply of coal, which was to be achieved by a long-term agreement with Shell to provide coal at ruling world-market rates, with a back-up guarantee from the NCB to provide short-term stocks against any potential disruption. Definition of the project and conditions continued in the Athens heat, including exchanges with some terse Dutchmen in Shell to tie up the coal-supply proposals. And it looked as though the project could be ready for a memorandum to be signed during Mrs Thatcher's forthcoming visit.

All was going well until the day before her arrival, when the Greek government had a cabinet reshuffle, replacing the Minister responsible for the power-portfolio with another who was reported to be more in favour of the French. There were also dark rumours of intimate connections between the French and Greek ruling dynasties. Anyway, when Maggie arrived, far from a laurel-strewn path to the Acropolis in honour of a major power project, the scheme was cancelled, with the Greek authorities giving the high price of NCB coal as the pretext. This was broken at a meeting in the Ambassador's residence – Venezelos' old house with a portrait of Byron on the wall. And she was livid.

We had a senior NCB official, a Welshman who must have been a

Davies, and she turned on him, berating the NCB for their inefficiencies, citing the pit-head prices of the more efficient mines, comparing these to others, challenging why the Board could not improve their performance to the best, and so on. This tirade was punctuated by the NCB official trying to get a word in with, "Ah but Prime Minister..." in a rolling Welsh baritone. But every interjection served only to ratchet up her fury. As the frustration notched-up, one looked around for our Ambassador to pour some soothing diplomatic oil on what looked like seething up into a tempest. Especially since he was of the Sutherland clan. But whatever the "Braveheart" tradition might have been, he was carefully out of sight behind a settee. And so, boldly, I volunteered, "Prime Minister, you are due to meet the Greek Prime Minister in twenty minutes. Shouldn't we consider the line to take?" At which she turned in my direction, "We haven't got a line," and directed her ire at me. This implanted a firm resolve never to try to do the Foreign Office's job. As Maggie disappeared for her meeting, I commiserated with our Welsh baritone, to which he replied, "The trouble is, she's right."

A couple of evenings later, after the formal Greek Government dinner, the British team was assembled in the Government's guesthouse – bow ties loosened, stays undone, and the Scotch and gin flowing, when Maggie turned to me, "What would President Giscard, have done in these circumstances?" While her cohorts watched eagerly in anticipation of another moth being pinned to the board, there seemed only one straight answer, "President Giscard would never have got into these circumstances. Long ago, he would have made an offer that couldn't be refused."

In earlier negotiations, the company had devised a code for communicating with their project team in Athens, in which "coal" was designated "sugar". A tricky issue had been the minimum period of back-up supplies to be provided by NCB: the initial period had been a month, but this was not regarded as sufficient, and the NCB agreed to double this guarantee. This was passed to GEC's Rugby Office, who conveyed it to their team in Athens. The next day appeared a headline in a prominent Greek daily newspaper, "Britain to double sugar supplies to Greece".

Visits to China

The period 1977-81 was a turning point in China's modernisation. On my first visit in 1978 as part of a delegation headed by Edmund Dell, we made our way on foot over the bridge at Shenzen. While the Chinese people were all wearing the mandatory tunic and trousers, with ladies allowed only two hairstyles, and we had to go through the obligatory queue for Mao's mausoleum. The industrial team included top managers

230

from Rolls-Royce, who were advanced in their engine joint venture at Sian, Lord Kindersley from Kleinwort's, and members of the "48 Group", a gaggle of businessmen who had heroically maintained contacts during the Maoist ascendancy. One of the successes at the time were coal-mining equipment manufacturers, where for once the dour tenacity of the Geordie and Yorkshire temperaments were ideally suited to the business environment.

A subsequent visit with Eric Varley – hosted by the State Planning Commission, notable in TV coverage for the sight of the delegation stuck in snowdrifts en route to the Great Wall, offered several star moments:

– Bill de Vigier of Acrow travelled with several large suitcases, turning up with one at every meeting, and, at the slightest provocation, would pour out models of his products on to the floor.

– Just before the visit, China had taken some military action on their border with Vietnam, and Eric Varley was briefed to express disquiet at such a potentially destabilising action. This he duly did at a meeting in the Great Hall of the People with a senior Vice-Premier, to be greeted by a torrent of outraged guttural noises, which the interpreter blandly translated, "But they dared to touch the arse of the tiger!"

– The cultural highlight was a concert where several artists of international repute in "Western" classical music, who had been suppressed during the Cultural Revolution, were allowed to perform publicly for the first time.

These delegations invariably included luminaries of the Sino-British Trade Committee, which, by some bizarre British quirk, has tended to have a Jardine personage as its Chairman, despite the Opium Wars having a formal position in Chinese history comparable to the Holocaust, or King Leopold's exploitation of the Congo. Italy, by contrast has been adept at exploiting its "Marco Polo card".[7]

As one of only four *gwilos*, I joined Hong Kong's first trade visit to Guangdong under David Wilson*, then Political Adviser to the Governor. The rest of the mission were Hong Kong "entrepreneurs", all probably billionaires by now. But the outstanding memory, apart from a personal experience of the astonishing curative effects of acupuncture in treating a sprained ankle, was the phenomenal transaction speeds of our Hong Kong colleagues. As we visited factories, then with relatively primitive "communist" equipment, a quick sketch of a pressing, simple fabrication, or whatever – an exchange about price and volume – passing over a card with the agreement scribbled on it – "my representative will call tomorrow to sort out details" – and the deal was done. Some members of the delegation were turning over a dozen such tricks a day. Historically, this was the start of Hong Kong's manufacturers shifting their production 40km into Guandong, and, followed by other investors, leading to an economic development of seven decades crammed into as many years. (Also staying at the same hotel in Shenzen was an Australian delegation pursuing co-operation in agriculture and food-processing, led by an official who had also been on the OECD Multinationals Committee – another "most effective and appropriate" exchange.)

A few years later, another visit with Peter Carey* attached to a Ministry of Defence delegation headed by Francis Pym carried on this routine.

The direct trade value is impossible to quantify, not least because deals in China were extremely difficult to schedule, or, if attempted, simply offered another lever to be used by the Chinese in negotiation. At this time, however, there was such a procession of national delegations that the UK had to be in the queue. But personally, such visits were valuable in imparting a sense of how the Chinese system at the time functioned, and as a background to the more protracted negotiations in which one was involved later.

Hong Kong Mass Transit

A Japanese consortium initially won the order to provide the rolling stock and systems for the first Hong Kong Mass transit development. But this broke down, and opened the opportunity for British companies to move in. The Mass Transit authority was chaired by Norman Thompson, a capable "can-do" guy, with a mercantile background and a sharp eye for costs. The authority was backed by the Hong Kong Government both by virtue of guarantees, but also through operating concessions and rights to revenues from commercial developments occasioned by the system's facilities. It happened that, with the opening of the Victoria Line, British rolling stock was arguably among the leading products, and there was a chance of picking up the order that had fallen off the Japanese tray.

The Mass Transit team were tough customers. Any illusions that Hong Kong was disposed to do favours for British companies should be immediately dispelled. The society is one in which money is measured in minute fractions, and any suggestion that the public is being charged over the odds leads inevitably to vociferous complaints. Consequently, there was pressure to devise a competitive package against the terms under which the Japanese had been originally given the job, which tested the customary accountancy mentality of the Laird Group, which owned MetroCam at the time. The company was not happy with the response that they were getting from the Department of Trade's Project Group (OPG), and hearing of the Department of Industry's successful support in winning the Castle Peak contracts asked for us to take a hand. This posed a problem since it was outside the power sector. We worked with the OPG, pursuing devices that would not otherwise have occurred to them, such as persuading the Department of Transport to bring forward payments to the company from London Transport, in return for a matching equivalent price reduction by the company.[8] When eventually the contracts were secured, we were modestly ready to allow the OPG to gather the glory.

Yet this brush with reality proved uncomfortable for the traditional Department of Trade ethos, which had already declined to take on the government role in securing the Castle Peak contracts in response to Lawrence Kadoorie's original approach, while various companies were complaining that "Industry" was giving them better support in overseas markets than "Trade". For connoisseurs of Whitehall reorganisations, the transmogrification of IIC into the Projects and Export Policy (PEP) Division was unusual in that it occurred as a compromise while the two Departments of Trade and Industry were separate. With completion of the first OECD Code on Multinationals, and passing other functions back elsewhere, there was capacity to merge with the Overseas Projects Group to form a single focus for support of overseas projects. To seal the merger of functions, one had the rare pleasure of drafting a minute to be sent from one Secretary of State to another, and having this sent down from the recipient to draft a reply, which was dispatched and returned from the first to be put on file.

---

[1] There is simply not enough space for an adequate appreciation of the CLP community. Lawrence Kadoorie and the group with the family name deserve a history in their own right. Lawrence had made a fortune twice, once in Shanghai before the Communist take over – he would wryly show pictures of the family house in Shanghai, under the then Chinese government, converted to a music college, and then with his diversified group in Hong Kong: this apart from CLP, included in its portfolio a range of businesses from the Peninsula Hotel to the Peak Tramway. Intensely loyal to his circle of colleagues, but renownedly a counter of pennies. A typical story told by Dean Barrett, a wan Australian who had been with Lawrence from Shanghai days: the company head offices were in St George's Building on Hong Kong island, whose power was provided by a rival utility, Hong Kong Electric. It was for long Lawrence's practice to personally approve all bill payments, which Dean routinely cleared with him. When it came to the electricity bill, Dean would recount, "That was the one that really hurt."

In negotiation, Lawrence was quiet but direct: he was wont to take off his watch and apparently fiddle around adjusting the setting. This was one of the cues that the next question was going to be extremely astute. He was subsequently made a Lord, and his home in Hong Kong was always a friendly respite from the hectic idiom of life in the city. His brother, Horace, was reticent where Lawrence was the entrepreneur, but an authority on classical Chinese ivory and jade, and active in a wide range of charities, notably a trust for Gurkhas and their dependants.

Bill Stones and his wife, Joy, also offered a very kind refuge for British contractors and officials either directly involved in CLP activities, or on the trail to and from Beijing, which until the mid-80s was still a relatively rare expedition. But others in the CLP team added their own trials and tribulations – "CK", a Taiwan born accountant, who like everyone in CLP seemed to have found some magic potion to keep the symptoms of age at bay, will always be remembered by the French, who admitted in the course of the Guandong nuclear plant negotiations that the combination of "CK" and the Chinese was the toughest negotiating opponents that they had ever encountered.

[2] An authoritative survey of the dynamic development of "combinations" in the evolution of the German coal industry is to be found in *The German Tradition of Organised Capitalism* by Martin Parnell (Clarendon Press Oxford). Particularly illuminating is the function of early joint-stock banks in the development of industry. For example, in 1853 the Darmstädter Bank declared its role as: "It is called upon to further large, sound enterprises by share ownership and investing external funds, and to do its utmost to share in the responsibility, arising from its clear insight into the total situation of German industry gained from its high vantage point, for directing entrepreneurial initiative and capital into appropriate channels, according to the needs of the moment." We ain't never had any of them.

[3] The "G" designation is a conventional label of group alliances formed in such international fora as the UN, WTO/GATT. It varies according to each context and as the geopolitical scene shifts, for example the break-up of the Soviet bloc, expansion of the EU, and new alignments generated by "globalisation" and bilateral trade agreements have dispersed the old structures. But it is at the top table that the obsession with "G-string" respectability encapsulated Britain's economic, trade, defence and foreign policies. Over a career, from the G4 of the post-World War II dispensation, Britain has been clinging by increasingly worn fingernails to what is now a G7/8, depending on the presence of the Soviet Union, with China, India and other rising nations becoming more dominant in the international economic scene. If this survival owes something to the courtesy of other countries not to drop a declining Britain, for national priorities "G-string" anxieties have forced dollops of resources into "nukes in handbags", nuclear submarines and other hardware in support of "our role in the world". More insidious has been the traffic between the Treasury, ODA and other economic departments and the sinecures of the World Bank/IMF, where dogmatic theory at its most simplistic was enunciated under the dominance of the US Treasury – a

dogma that the US would never have practised on itself. Not only since subservience to the IMF in 1975, but by continuous drip-feed since then through continuing Treasury and Ministerial contacts, the UK has become not just "Caesar's wife" in protesting these simplicities, but uniquely pursuing them in practice.

[4] One of the more nauseating experiences of civil servants, apparently reaching sickening proportions in recent years, is the habit of politicians to surround themselves with a coterie of sycophants. "Cronies" has probably been commandeered as a special title by Tony Blair's circus. "Groupie" seems appropriate for Tony Benn, since *The Sun* had a pungent reference to Brian Sedgemore MP as Benn's "parliamentary groupie". Other coteries no doubt deserve other sobriquets.

[5] The Canadian activism in this discussion was sufficiently striking for me to ask their delegate whence it arose: this was long before the overseas expansion of Bombardier. "Bata", was his quick reply. We tend to forget this remarkable paternalistic company was among the first truly global multinationals.

[6] OECD Guidelines for Multinational Enterprises: Revision 2000. ISBN 9264033971.

[7] The Chinese have difficulty in coping with the English pronunciation of "L" and "R". On one visit, I had an appointment with the Bank of China, with Ken Cotterell – a senior ECGD underwriter – due to be following me in an hour. The first 20 minutes of my session was taken up by rehearsing with Chinese officials how they should pronounce "Cotterell". "Col-l-lul" was their first attempt, and we went by careful repetition through several further attempts, "Cot-lul-lul", "Co-tel-lul", and so on, with "Cot-lel-lil" about as close as we could get.

I recounted this saga to some delegation colleagues just before a British Government dinner in our Embassy in Beijing. During the meal, as we sat at our table of four Chinese and four Brits, Derek Ezra* asked one of the Chinese guests, "How often do you have an election?" – to several strained faces among the British delegation.

[8] The saga of MetroCam is a perfect instance of the futility of assisting British industry. The Government's intention was to capitalise on the success of the Victoria Line as giving the country a good international reference to continue to develop mass transit rolling stock and increase market share against international competitors. In the event, such profits as were gained from the Hong Kong orders – and the company also picked up rolling-stock orders for the Hong Kong-Canton railway – went straight into the Laird Group accounts, with minimal investment in MetroCam's facilities. MetroCam was subsequently sold to GEC, and then consigned to Alstom, before being shut down in 2003. Throughout this game of passing the parcel, the manufacturing plant retained its essential qualities as a Hackney carriage works.

VIGNETTES

KEITH JOSEPH

Across a crowded room of sipping academics at a Templeton College ceremony, Keith Joseph – there as guest of honour – spotted me, raised a hand in recognition, and moved through the throng to greet me with a radiant smile. This was some years after he had left the Department of Industry, and judging by his beaming expression – so out of sync with his usually preoccupied countenance – one could only assume that he was delighted to find a pretext for getting out of the clutches of some nutty professors. Clutching my hand, he remarked "You polymath."

Subsequently, after checking that this was indeed a compliment, it still left one puzzled how this became the impression that Keith should have retained. Perhaps because during his tenure I was involved in issues under the general rubric of "international co-operation", with continuing contacts with representatives of other governments – the OECD and UN Groups on multinationals, OECD and EU Groups on industry, and overseas projects, where he was less confident of his experience and had a genuine interest. But one was conscious of having an easier ride than some others in the Department – some colleagues are still gnashing teeth at having fallen victim of his edict that no new recruitment should be allowed, one particularly aggrieved that his personal assistant had resigned and, denied a replacement, he was compelled to write all his submissions in manuscript.

Keith's arrival in the then Department of Industry was not a cloud-parting, thunderclaps and chariots of fire process. In fact, by comparison with the zany clattering of crockery occasioned by the Benn, Heffer, Meacher triumvirate a few years earlier, it was a slumberland transition. One of the crosses born in the 70s and 80s by a Department with "industry" in its title was that it became a totem of the extreme wing of whatever the political party when elected. And the first Ministerial appointment had to be an apostle for the most "way-out" rhetoric. The dilemma was how far these appointments to a "stigmata Department" really represented the policy thrust of the new government as a whole: just as the turmoil occasioned by Tony Benn's "Industry White Paper" and pursuit of Government stakes in "rescue cases" was conducted against all the evidence that his Cabinet colleagues didn't trust him further than they could throw him, in Keith's case all the doctrinal stuff of his "reading list" sat oddly against the feedback from elsewhere that the Thatcher agenda was no more than a crude approach of throwing North Sea Oil revenues, which in 1979 were just building up, into income-tax reductions in the fond expectation of being re-elected forever.

But elections are Indian summers for officials. After completing the usual round of briefings enclosed in different coloured folders according to what was in party manifestoes, activity during the election itself is in suspense – save in extreme circumstances – to avoid any decisions prejudicing the policies of whatever party is elected. And there is often quiet pleasure at the humiliations of the hustings on ex-Ministers whose style may have been unduly arrogant or insensitive.

When Keith's appointment to the Department was announced, to most officials he had the ambiguous aura of "a guru", and recollections of skimmed newspaper columns. The Whitehall tom-toms also gave mixed messages of "very good", "nice guy", "inclined to think too much", "slow", "gutsy"… My only previous experience had been hearing Keith address an HBS Alumni lunch, which I attended as a guest of Raymond Bonham-Carter. His line had been that all previous Ministers of whatever complexion, himself included, and all with the best of motives, had attempted too much, and should have relied more on the natural motives and abilities of agencies other than Government. This penitent line did not appear "the tooth and claw" version of free-market ideology. And in response to questions, he encouraged the predominantly business audience to participate more in the political process, irrespective of party allegiance, even going so far as to suggest that the Tories were the traditional party of capital and landowners, while the Liberals were the historic voice of commerce and business.

Even before confronting the Department with the much-publicised reading list (in practice, this was not the chore that commentators have suggested, since Peter Carey commissioned the Department's economists to provide a resume, which they managed in a dozen or so pages – Adam Smith on five sides – copies available for 20p), we were set a dozen or so general essays. And, as these were parcelled out, "Aid Disarmament" fell in my direction. It was not difficult to pen an agnostic survey of the scale and diversity of aid flows, the extent to which these had become a part of the international idiom, and the inextricably mixed motives – from the humanitarian proposition that resource transfers from the richer to the poorer were benign, to the more shady "national influence" dimension behind the programmes of the US, Japan, France and others. And concluding with an assessment of the obstacles to such a radical approach, and the practical problems of devising a regime that could be monitored effectively. Meetings were arranged to go over these several essays, and we turned up for our session anticipating a testing grilling, only for Keith to call off the meeting without discussion or explanation.

Another early encounter was Keith's first official visit to Paris to meet Andre Giraud, his French opposite number. As was usual practice, an agenda covering current issues was agreed through our Embassy, a date was set, and both sides prepared briefs against the agenda topics. Ministerial exchanges with the French – having suffered these rigours over a few years on the Concorde project – are traditionally very civilised: the meeting begins not before 10 a.m. in one of their splendid period venues, with a cultivated move through the agenda for a couple of hours, followed by an excellent lunch for another couple of hours.

A brief was duly put together, with the usual two-page summary and suggested line on each topic. Recognising that the issues would not be familiar, and in view of his reputation for thorough reading, each topic had a more detailed annex. The topics were typically diverse – reactions to prospective Brussels manoeuvres and directives, potential collaboration between industries, progress on actual programmes etc. His Office said that he did not require a briefing meeting. Without thinking further, I met him at the airport for an early flight to Paris – he was without the usual private secretary – and while waiting, I enquired whether there were any details of the briefing that he would like clarified, since one could always leave a message with the Duty Officer for subsequent material to be sent to the Paris Embassy. To this he responded, "I haven't read them. No Minister can be expected to know all that."

With Giraud the arch-French technocrat and the leading figure in building up their nuclear power industry, one could only reply lamely "I'm sure you'll find, Minister, that Monsieur Giraud does," which got the brusque retort, "I don't believe it." On the flight, he was preoccupied with going through a few pamphlets and books, leaving one trying hard not to speculate on the meeting in prospect.

A briefing chat had been fixed with Reg Hibbert, one of our saltier school of ambassadors, where a typical exchange was "What is Monsieur Giraud's constituency?" reply "I doubt if he's been elected to anything in his life." Anyway, we arrived at the meeting, and Giraud, always an affable host, greeted Keith with warm good cheer, inquiring after his health since we had notified in advance Keith's rather austere and limited dietary requirements. The meeting began with Giraud leading off on each topic almost exactly as the briefs projected, with Keith responding "Surely that's a matter for the companies to sort out?" "Why should governments be involved?" and so on. Civil servants, contrary to some views put around, actually do their best to avoid their Ministers getting into difficult corners, or try to bail them out if they do – some remark like "Perhaps the brief was not entirely clear on the point, but..." or, "The situation has changed slightly since you discussed this, but..." providing a tag to redirect the discussion, or offer the Minister a lead. But Keith's position was so detached that there was no scope to intervene.

As a result, the agenda was covered in just over half an hour. The final topic was Japanese investment in Europe – the French were at the time going through one of their paranoid phases on Japan, consigning video recorders to Poitiers, alleging that the UK was becoming a Japanese aircraft carrier, and so on. When Giraud asked, "And what about the Japanese?" Keith replied, "What's wrong with the Japanese?" And went on to suggest that they had a lot to teach European industry about productivity, efficiency and marketing. Even the most optimistic observer could only have concluded that dialogue was impossible.

The meeting came to end with more than an hour to spare before lunch. Keith and I strolled around the Tuileries Gardens. He seemed very agitated, taking it out on himself, muttering, "I just don't believe it." That evening, Reg Hibbert gave an informal dinner for the two Ministers, and Keith displayed a fluent command of French, completely at variance with his innocence about the way the French system works. On the return flight, he was noticeably more relaxed and intrigued to hear experiences of working with the French on Concorde, and their flamboyant credit mixte financing and other techniques in pursuing defence sales.

Keith subsequently held a "colloquium" on the French to explore why, despite their apparent disregard of most of the tenets of conventional Anglo-Saxon economics, their successes in several industrial areas could not be gainsaid. A quintessentially Keith question was, "But are they financially continent?" To this, Reg Hibbert offered the counter, "They certainly keep plenty of their money under the bed," which would normally be the feed line for a jokey rejoinder, but the tenor of the discussion was a shade too earnest.

Keith seemed equally at sea in other national industrial cultures. He had apparently at one time been an advocate of the German "social market" but again without apparently any awareness of the, by his standards, highly interventionist Federal/State support networks that underpin their style of capitalism. One was not present at the oft-quoted occasion when he asked a German Minister, "Why does your government intervene and try to pick industrial winners?" With the repost "Because it works." (A variant of this incident, or conceivably another, recounts Keith's inquiring of a Federal Science Minister, "How do you justify paying all those subsidies to large companies like Siemens?" With the rejoinder, "I don't. I just do it.")

Rather more frustrating was his national deprecation. He obviously had a standard line that the entrepreneurial spirit in Britain had been extinguished. When he tried this on Giraud, the latter responded that he could name a few industrialists who displayed these qualities in ample measure. And on visits to "niche companies" during a trip to Denmark he repeated this formula, only to meet amazed expressions as local managers instanced two or three aggressive UK competitors. (His trip to Denmark, despite his somewhat erratic public humour, produced an amusing opening gambit at the formal dinner, when he remarked that Denmark had regrettably elected Socialist governments since the war, but had shown the wisdom not to nationalise.)

The Department had become agnostic about its various Ministers – from Tony Benn to Keith Joseph in less than four years must be the ultimate test in ideological adaptation. But given the theoretical corner into which the Thatcher government had worked itself, it was inevitable that successive Ministers would be under pressure to demonstrate their ideological macho by offering up evermore of the Department's budget at successive expenditure reviews. On the other hand, if Keith was the prototype of this approach, he could be surprisingly pragmatic – at the time, I, like many colleagues, was unaware of his previous close involvement with Bovis – he readily acknowledged the heavy upfront costs and risks in trying to win overseas projects against competitors who had access to a wide range of government support and, if after some tortuous discussion on the technicalities of ECGD facilities, was ready to take timely decisions.

If there were voices from his ideological seminary critical that Keith had apparently been "swallowed up" by the Department, or "turned native", this is more a reflection of how detached such voices were from the real world of international business and industry than on Keith having to reconcile himself to such realities. In the common civil servants' game of drawing analogies to Ministerial personalities, in the Thatcher period an obvious parallel was Chaucer's pilgrims ranged around the Wife of Bath – Millers, Reeves, Pardoners, Summoners aplenty, but few would fail to cast Keith as a "gentil knight". Another oft-told tale was a meeting with some Australian State politician, who, referring to Keith's reputation as an acknowledged thinker, asked him to summarise "in a word" the crucial issue confronting politicians. With only a hint of the jocularity of "our hoste" or the wit of the Miller, he could have passed this off with a quick rejoinder. But not Keith. He apparently went into one of those periods of anguished thought, with his head clasped in both hands, and after the proverbial eternity, replied, "Expectations". Full marks, but was the effort worth it?

If his armour stood up to some episodes of downright physical abuse, leave alone the lonely battles with ideas that he must have suffered, it also seemed agonisingly fragile in other circumstances, taking a heavy toll in emotional and physical resources. Even a recollection, light-heartedly so one thought, of the recently completed OECD transparency exercise on State Aids where the US delegate had been compelled to admit that their own States operated as extensive an array of "distorting" mechanisms as those for which they were chastising European governments, caused an agonising preoccupation comparable to his first meeting with Giraud. Fortunately, he did not have many moments of close discussion with his opposite numbers from Japan, Taiwan, Singapore or South Korea!

Perhaps a better literary echo would be an adaptation of the tribute to Brutus, "all save only he did what they did..." with dodgy motives, while he genuinely believed that the application of "markets" would liberate animal spirits, a new spirit of enterprise, or whatever – even if, in the event, the result was no more than casting a cloak of respectability over the British tradition of rogues, charlatans and spivs. Still, long after the Templeton meeting, occasional correspondence with him always received a courteous and carefully thought-out response.

EXPORT DELUSIONS

IDAB during the Benn/Varley period was a fund of balanced good sense in testing commercial cases from sensational headline rescues, such as Ferranti, Alfred Herbert, the motorcycle industry and all the other industrial kippers that landed on the Department's doorstep at the time, to more routine assessments of viability and "additionality". Remarks often reflected the contrasting backgrounds of Board members – Kenneth Bond, one of the core triumvirate at GEC, could be guaranteed to deflate an overenthusiastic case presentation: anyone citing a Queen's Award for Technology would be greeted with "unrecovered R&D", or boasting the merits of a Queen's Award for Exports would be met with "under-pricing again".

But the high quality of comment and argument, from a broad range of industrial experience, was an education in itself. Out of the many hours, a phrase that has echoed over the years was Bill Barlow*'s remarks on a proposal to support a small company's investment plans which argued that it aimed to expand its sales into the US. "The liquidator's courts are littered with the bones of companies who tried to get 1% of the American market".

CORPORATE SURVIVAL

At some formal dinner, sitting opposite Ian MacGregor*, just before he took up his post as Chairman of British Steel, with no more than a reputation as a corporate turnaround specialist and controversy over his salary, I queried light-heartedly what was the secret. "No secret. A declining business is impossible to run," was his reply.

Characteristically terse and to the point. When asked the rejoinder, "What about a declining country?" his shrug was equally expressive.

Through several later contacts with him, if there was assuredly a vein of iron, his style was always one of wry understatement, humour and honesty. A meeting at which he robustly defended the professional quality of British Steel's management and workforce sticks in the memory, at a time when these were being pilloried in the press, and despite Union humour around variations of him gaining entry to heaven (or hell) for his record in closing down blast furnaces.

PROJECTS AND EXPORT POLICY DIVISION: 1980-87

Call it an unreconstructed "industry" view, but when the obsequies to Sterling come to be written, with its final demise marked by prospects of an ever-increasing trade deficit into perpetuity, it will be recorded in some such rhetoric as, "Never in the conduct of human affairs has so much verbiage been expended to so little purpose than 'Trade Policy'" – with the possible exception of "Energy Policy" as the lights flicker. If reshuffling Departments appears to be conducted on a blotting pad at Number 10, the process can involve a clash of cultures, never sharper than that between "industry" and "trade" at the formation of the Department of Trade and Industry.

Where the "industry" faction had come from an immediate tradition of trying to stimulate the potentially viable elements of companies contracting/collapsing in the face of tough economic conditions and foreign competitors unencumbered by the class-ridden antagonistic confrontations that had formed the bedrock of Britain's industrial heritage, in the best Victorian mode of Whitehall the "trade" faction had found the "invisible hand" the supreme pretext to "sit on hands"[1] and avoid any direct contact with real "trade".

There may have been a time when there was a real job negotiating bilateral trade treaties to secure terms that kept open, or prised open, opportunities for British producers to extend their comfortable position in imperial markets to other countries; or when lobbying in galleries of GATT justified a highly select few posts in Geneva – on diplomatic rates. But by the 80s, with entry to the Common Market, and these functions moving to Brussels, the old tradition hung on with diminishing real significance: by Pavlovian repetition "free trade" is still the battle cry which Britain, as a lone voice, preaches with the fervour of "First over the parapet!" The Deputy Secretary/Director General post on "Trade Policy" has apparently been abolished, presumably taking advantage of new technology: if the standard line since the Opium Wars has been "free trade is good for you", it is now more convenient, and cheaper, simply to press the "Repeat" button. Where "trade" now lies between the Treasury and the new BERR Department, succeeding DTI, is probably only a matter of locating the computer with the "trade" button.

In other respects, in the newly-formed DTI, the "trade" drive consisted of assistance measures for companies, overseen by the British Overseas Trade Board (as a modern descendant of the Board of Trade), invariably provided through trade associations and other agencies, to have a presence at stands in overseas trade fairs. There was a time when "British" pavilions at such affairs were quite grand, with a Royal Family presence, but on a declining scale ever since the "Great Exhibition", and one reads that the Japanese had to make a special effort to persuade the UK to have a pavilion at all for the 2005 Expo at Aichi. While an "Export Intelligence Service" (EIS) was provided, partially funded by subscriptions from companies, circulating reports of opportunities identified by the commercial branches of overseas diplomatic posts.[2] In addition, a range of "geographical" sections was focussing on developments affecting business prospects in the local scene of particular countries, giving suitable attention to visiting personalities, and arranging contacts with posts in their territories – at their best vigorous in following shifts that might impact on business in their patch, but often a routine contact function.

Implicit was the assumption that larger companies would probably have established local operations or agents. But this focusing on smaller companies came not from any rational analysis,[3] but from some amalgam of a public school ethos of "supporting the underdog", or the "Florres syndrome".[4] To be fair, industry itself was embedded in the tradition of "pith helmet" exporting.[5]

DIVISIONAL REENGINEERING

To set up the new "Projects and Export Policy" Division – the acronym "PEP" had a nice appeal, the "project" element of the erstwhile IIC of "Industry" was joined to the "Trade" Overseas Project Group, which, despite its metaphorical echoes of dashing heroes operating in the Western Desert, in tune with the "trade" ethos had a negligible record of success in the international project market, where any pretence of "free and fair" trade had long disappeared as France, Japan, Italy (and Germans in their own way) applied every gimmick, including the use of "aid" funds and political leverage, to win orders for capital goods, and, at the time, to secure advantage in fields of rising competition, as, for example, between national telecoms systems.

A first task was to reshape the structure of the Division: it had an Overseas Projects Board, whose chairman sat on the BOTB. But we progressively adjusted its membership under Roy Withers*, a seasoned hand from Davy, and a mix of members including merchant bankers and accountants deliberately aimed at establishing a forum whose judgment for "selective" support, on the model of IDAB, could stand against any accusations of preferential treatment, since the international competition marshalled their national resources around single lead companies. We also introduced the practice of several "secondments", particularly a merchant banker to serve as poacher turned gamekeeper. And the division of project specialities was divided among four Sections, not without some tensions, but with power projects still being handled by the "sponsor division" of the erstwhile Department of Industry. One of the continuing difficulties in a large bureaucracy is ensuring that the team has a reasonably high proportion of quality staff, and PEP was fortunate in having Section heads and staff, most of whom were subsequently promoted at least two ranks, or, in the DTI's contraction phase, secured good jobs with private companies.

Within the Division's armoury was an "Overseas Project Fund", an annual allocation of 2 to 3 million pounds, designed to contribute half of the bidding costs for overseas projects, to be repaid if the company was successful. Whilst this was a modest instrument compared to similar facilities among competitors, as previously operated it had not been exploited for real leverage.[6]

BRITISH INDUSTRIAL PLATOONS

The national ranks for engaging in the style of conflict being pursued by other countries were in some disarray – far from picking winners, it was a matter of making the best of what we had. The British tradition of maximising domestic competition in the belief that this by itself would secure efficient results was antithetical to an arena where other players, invariably seeing themselves as "starting from behind", building competences from scarce national resources, or "hanging on to some advantage" had devoted considerable resources to establishing their national capabilities and were intent on securing the continuity of orders to maintain the viability and development of their leading companies – part of the process of "nurturing" winners.

The "project" game was dominated by the provision of finance under government export-credit guarantees to leading developing countries, with several players mixing in various other "inducements" such as reduced premia, "aid" injections, "free" technical support/training etc. Even if unpractised at these devices, at the time the UK had some advantage in financial engineering through the merchant banks such as Morgan Grenfell, Lazards, Schroders, Kleinwort Benson (now all largely extinct in this activity, or entirely so in any activity, but even then an arrogant – and expensive – fag-end of Empire, and not wholly reliable since occasionally they turned up in the phalanx of our opponents). A less remarked strength, even if relatively inhibited by their founding legislation, were our nationalised industries – coal, power, telecoms, rail etc, that had a reputation for technical competence, and for being impartial: especially important when many projects were in the responsibility of corresponding state agencies.

On the commercial front, our line-up of domestic contractors was, however, slim.[7] Davy, John Brown, Simchem, Babcocks, and the general-purpose civil contractors, were relatively small and lacked the asset backing (or risk-tolerance afforded by State-participation) marshalled behind major competitors. There were UK subsidiaries of the main US contractors – Bechtel, Fluor, Brown & Root etc, several having increased their British presence for North Sea development work. And some manufacturers, notably in power-generation equipment, were coming to realise that their best chance of gaining orders was to take a lead in securing the overall project. Also in this category were STC, which had a traditionally strong undersea cabling arm built up through laying imperial links but was coming under pressure for new orders as French and Japanese companies were increasing their presence.

Our "consultants" were a very variable asset: several very successful by virtue of their expertise, but mostly gaining their international reputations by winning contracts under World Bank or International Aid Agencies' competitive tendering. From this standpoint, they took pains to demonstrate their "independence", in the view of many British suppliers by deliberately not advocating British equipment – and tensions between them and suppliers was such that we could never get them to co-operate. But the corollary was that since every other country's consultants were unabashedly advocating their own national suppliers, clients concluded that British suppliers must have been abysmal. Exceptionally, one consultant might show the flair to move into a contracting role, notably Bywaters, but extremely rare since this involved taking real risk rather than the comforts of fee income. But there was the occasional company surprise: Plessey, which had been under almost continuous criticism for some time on most scores before its takeover by GEC and Siemens, had a remarkably adventurous airport development project team which actually secured orders in Francophone, Africa, previously uncharted waters for British companies.

FINANCIAL MECHANISMS

Government-backed Export Finance

The first "British" response to such "cheating" or "distortive practices" – reflecting presumably the ascendancy of the "games ethic" and Boy Scouts in traditional upbringing – has been to devise new "rules" to inhibit such unfair behaviour. With the corollary that one cannot preach gentlemanly codes unless immaculate as an exemplar of good behaviour, with collars and cuffs properly starched. The leaders in this campaign were inevitably the Treasury because of a blind aversion to anything – like long-term credit guarantees – that is not neatly compatible with their piggy-bank cash budgeting system. Throughout the period trying to compete against government-backed project proposals by other governments, there was a continuing undertow in Britain of calculations of "net grant equivalent", reviews, reassessments, revisions of criteria etc.[8] Even this, however, had its occasional entertainment value: sometimes we had to take deliberate steps to slow down the overseas client's decision process to allow the Whitehall bureaucratic constipation to work through – this was invariably interpreted by competitors as some devious trick of diplomacy, since the image of "Perfidious Albion" seems to hang on.

None of which was even modestly replicated in other countries, but required a special training course for new entrants to the Division to handle the arcane algebra. If the Treasury pretended that this was part of some cleansing of "free trade", it was in effect an "industrial policy" by stealth, since chunks of industry, with no realistic prospect of business in "uncontaminated" markets and a period of decline in UK orders, could only survive by seeking business in "contaminated" arenas, albeit that the international market is irrevocably "contaminated". Failure to secure such business meant only closure. If the consequences were not immediately apparent, they are beginning to show as Britain's companies have lost continuity (if not extinguished) and the competences for building major projects such as power stations.

AID AND TRADE

Early on, we made a presentation to Ministers on the relative balance of national competences, drawing upon our earlier research from selective financial assistance on the incidence of employment benefits against any government payments, and upon NEDO studies which demonstrated that the country winning the lead of a project could expect to capture more than 80% of its value (as compared with 1.5% when other than a British company won). A review of the aid programme was set up to explore the scope for matching some of the techniques adopted by other countries. The review, and subsequent implementation of the Aid and Trade Provision (ATP) revealed a bizarre theology in the concepts behind overseas aid.

Development aid, at least in Britain, is tricky territory. Universal concern at the desperate poverty in parts of the world is matched by universal frustration that these imbalances are so resistant to cure. Aid is therefore the topic that most readily lends itself to sanctimonious speeches – especially for Ministers doing their turn at grand international conferences. Yet in concept, application, and outcomes the issues are dynamically complex. While the discrepancy between the sheer scale of the problem and resources that donor governments are prepared to make available in the context of national budgetary pressures raises dilemmas of priorities, administration, repairing the distortions of past misapplications of aid, coping with risks of corruption and maladministration, and the mixed motives of donors.[9]

Behind the debate, the crucial fault-line is "displacement", whereby funds applied ostensibly for purpose "A", however laudable and well-intentioned, can contribute to release a recipient's resources for purpose "B", which may have less worthy ends. This dynamic inevitably varies with the circumstances of recipients, but an obvious example is the volume of aid flows to India and Pakistan while each has been developing a national nuclear capability. Yet to avoid such siphoning of resources demands a level of scrutiny and enforced "conditionality" that donor nations have been reluctant to stipulate.

The distinctive British approach to aid comes from a "Maundy Money" tradition, tinged perhaps with some postcolonial guilt, where the act of transfer becomes the key ritual, with some reinforcement from inter-departmental turf protection. There was an extraordinary dialectic around the "purity" of aid whereby the most serene countenance is achieved if "aid" itself is in the form closest to a "gift" i.e. a 100% grant, but also free from any concerns beyond the esoteric criteria devised by departmental theology. Hence the aversion to "tying" to national products or interests. And the rhetoric surrounding the "quality" of aid – everyone else sees this as an inversion of the classic, "never mind the quality, feel the width", as British governments have traditionally been high on rhetoric but short on "the readies". And, of course, "quality" is a pretext for employing increasing numbers of economists.[10] But, despite occasional lip-service from others, in practice this is an exclusive British construct, when other – much larger – donors have adopted a principle of "mutual benefit", especially in the use of long-term low-interest loans for the bulk of their bilateral programmes invariably tied to their own national technologies and businesses.

Nonetheless, securing the "Aid and Trade Provision" (ATP) was quite a breakthrough by British standards. Essentially, it was an allocation of the aid budget to be available outside normal bilateral aid to particular countries, to be applied to opportunities to match the practices of other countries. In most instances it consisted of an element of grant to be added to normal ECGD credit, which, given the invariable practice of British financial authorities to maintain domestic interest rates higher than most other countries, involved a cost as payments were made to banks to make up the difference between domestic rates and those agreed internationally for long-term credit to categories of developing countries. It was, therefore, inevitably restricted to those countries eligible for ECGD export credit. The bureaucratic liaison mechanics with the Overseas Aid Department (ODA, then still a subsidiary Department to the Foreign Office with their own subsidiary Minister, though not in the Cabinet) to evolve methodologies that matched their internal theology, while still allowing scope to match the practices of other countries was in general amicable, though stretched to cope with the pragmatic demands of individual cases. In retrospect, all this controversy boils down to a storm over Whitehall turf-protection, as "Aid and Trade" is now signalled at G7 meetings as one of the main contributions towards enhancing the prospects of underdeveloped countries by improving their infrastructure – precisely the purpose that ATP was aimed to fulfil.

One of the incidental delights was meeting senior officials from the Finance Ministries of recipient countries, who had evolved a remarkable adroitness in handling the approaches of different bilateral donors: from negotiating "protocoles d'aide financière" with their allocations of "aide liee" with officials from France's DREE (Direction de Relations Economiques Exterieures); Japan's OECF officials allocating long-term loans to projects spread around their Sogo Shosha; and various agencies from Russia, Italy, Germany and Nordic countries, all with their distinct approaches. Britain's current approach apparently involves the Department for International Development seeking contracts for the likes of the Adam Smith Institute, PWC, KPMG et al, which must leave recipient officials in the quandary of wondering, "Whatever turns you on?" since other countries, whatever their lip-service, will not have changed their traditional methods. One understands, that current "aid policy" claims to have dropped the practice of preaching "bad theory" while offering aid finance as a coercive arm-lock to secure attention – the new sacred words are "country-led approaches where programs build on partner development priorities, where conditions of aid are jointly agreed and based on outcomes rather than activities, and where there is mutual accountability between donor and recipient." (Securing the future, HMSO March 2005). But still, how to employ those batteries of economists?

SOME POLITICAL BACKING

Most uncomfortable perhaps was the Treasury, for whom the diversity of mechanisms for mixing budget allocations with the financial and currency twists of the real world complicated their historic "cash-based" mentality. In practice, their knee-jerk reaction when confronted with the unfamiliar was to insist on cash payment, however bizarre the circumstances.[11] But the Treasury have always harboured an ambition to do away with Export Credit Guarantees,[12] and ECGD has been under almost continuous review since the 1980s. And the concept of mixing this mechanism with "aid" to match the demands of the international market seemed to them even more heinous. There was therefore a prospect of the Treasury adopting their usual ball-and-chain approach on every case.

Fortunately, Mrs Thatcher turned out to be an ally – perhaps, having experienced the disappointment in Athens, recognising the necessity of pragmatic speed; perhaps having picked up an indication of the Treasury's distaste; or perhaps intuitively grasping that the grandeur of "Sterling" depended upon sustaining a sound trade balance. Though the clincher came when, over the weekend preceding the G7 Heads of Government meeting in Cancun, Davy won the contract for the Sicartsa steel plant, beating the French.[13] But, at all events, she let it be known that any instance where "bureaucracy" was hindering action to counter competitors should be reported to her instantly. We never actually used this sanction, though there were a couple of instances when we suggested that discussion with Treasury and other Departments was heading in this direction, and the prospect of Mrs Thatcher chairing a meeting proved helpful in achieving consensus.

PROJECT CASEWORK

Without keeping a precise tally, by 1986 the Division had been involved in securing some £19 billion worth of overseas projects. This was not solely attributable to the Division's staff alone, since the function was to co-ordinate moves with ECGD, ODA, DTI geographical divisions, other Departments, diplomatic posts abroad, and nationalised industries in tune with moves by British companies or by their competitors. With a hit rate of around 1:4, the Division had been involved – win, lose, or draw – in some £80 billion worth of projects.

At any one time, there could be 200 projects on the books, covering a diverse array of industries such as power generation, mining, hydro schemes, water systems, telecoms and undersea cabling, bridges, rail systems, airports, and all at differing stages of gestation. Some projects hung on indefinitely – the vividly titled Cobra Swamp, a prospective airport in Thailand (now built) dragged along interminably, while there is a "coal-fired" potential power station in Sinai, where on direct personal report the "coal" is "white", which still presumably remains undeveloped. Some were deferred under local budgetary constraints, while others were lost either because the British contenders could not match competitors, or the project had effectively been earmarked by other countries' financial ties. Far from being "dirigiste", all projects with any chance of success depended upon motivated companies to do the technical and commercial groundwork effectively – a fairly rare combination.

LIBYAN MANMADE RIVER

The "war stories" of projects would take several volumes, especially since we often learned more from failures than successes. One of the most rapid successes came when the US introduced strategic sanctions against Libya, where Brown & Root was the contractor on a massive venture to draw water from desert artesian sources and route them to the coastal regions – engineering a return to the days when Libya was the granary of Rome. The Project Office, including Libyan liaison engineers, was in Houston. Under current US strategic sanctions legislation, all commercial activities were covered, so that all personnel involved were liable to legal penalties. By contrast, the approach of successive British governments was that strategic sanctions, which were also in force for Libya, should not interfere with normal trade activities – for example, those applied to apartheid South Africa. It needed only an inspired Parliamentary Question and Answer confirming this policy, which Alan Clark as Minister of Trade agreed after only a few minutes conversation, for Brown & Root to satisfy the Libyan authorities that the project could be continued if they shifted the project office to this country. Over the years, bringing more than £200 million of activity to the UK. But just for a couple of days work.

GUANGDONG NUCLEAR POWER STATION

At the other extreme was the marathon running from 1980 to 1986 as a carry-over from our contacts with China Light and Power, involving British and French companies and officials over a series of negotiating sessions in Europe and China, the latter invariably running weeks longer than had been expected. Over the years one had always had an ambition to visit Japan, and fitting in a visit after a negotiating session in China seemed the ideal, yet one never got beyond the transit lounge at Narita airport. Apart from sheer weariness at times, the saga had a continuing fascination as various strands of negotiations interacted; from the incessant grinding over the same issues in exchanges with China's financial negotiating team, the fun in liasing with our pragmatic French counterparts, keeping updated with the companies in their fraught negotiations, and orchestrating manoeuvres at political level.

If the stereotype of the British brand of civil servant is one of an upbringing in academic cloisters and devoid of any competence in the dirty world of real commerce, this example at least illustrates that the system is (was?) capable of adapting to one of the most demanding commercial contexts, and those on the team could rebut suggestions of being bureaucratically cloistered with the response, "When you've negotiated the financing of a nuclear power station in China, then we'll listen."

The dynamic balance of the negotiating structure began with the French having their earlier negotiations to supply a nuclear power station broken off in 1978 as China went into a retrenchment reflecting, among various concerns, fragility over foreign exchange balances, and the French were prepared to co-operate with the UK because the CLP/Guangdong joint venture provided a client with funding and receipts predominantly in foreign currency. Conversely, the only grounds for Britain being at the table derived from the continuity established by involvement in CLP's development of Castle Peak, and its preference for GEC as the turbine-system provider. Underlying our relationship with the French was the clear message from the latter that they were intent on securing the order, if necessary with a UK turbine-island, but always ready to substitute their usual Alsthom supply if the UK failed to keep up with the game. The UK position therefore depended heavily on bluff, especially in apparent influence over the Hong Kong government, who, in practice, had a robust "free-market" approach to sourcing their major infrastructure investments.

Before we could proceed with the French, however, in typically British style we had a blundering amateur intervention by Walter Marshall* – a nuclear scientist appointed as head of the CEGB. Whatever may have been his qualities, perception of international commercial realities were not among them, since he conceived that the Chinese might be prepared to select a PWR of the Sizewell B configuration when it had not yet been built, and when the US were opposed to transferring the Westinghouse technology on which it depended. For some bizarre reason he managed to gain the support of Kleinwort Benson, one of the City's "dead men walking" merchant banks, but with undue influence among the political classes. This blundering around by an apparently senior British personage disconcerted CLP, confused the Chinese, and the pantomime gained even greater absurdity when one of Marshall's engineers turned out to have a missionary zeal to convert Southern China to Christianity. If there might have been a negotiating card in the bluff that the UK could build a complete nuclear plant, this escapade rendered it unplayable.

Once this eccentric charade had been played out, we could recommence marshalling tactics with the French. One of the special pleasures, indeed, lay in reconciling the byzantine bureaucratic hoops of the British system with the pragmatic aplomb of our colleagues from the DREE (Directorat des Relations Économique Extérieur, in perhaps the sharpest distinction to the Whitehall system, a division of the French Finance Ministry). This became apparent at our first discussion in Paris to prepare a joint position for the forthcoming visit of a Bank of China delegation in December 1984. We had already achieved a dispensation from an increase in the internationally agreed thresholds for financing nuclear power stations on the grounds that the original memoranda setting out the Chinese government's "requirements" as the basis for negotiations had been agreed before the new higher "subsidy" threshold. When the French outlined their initial financial proposals, one of the DTI team new to dealing with the French, by Pavlovian conditioning pulled out his calculator and did a quick "net grant equivalent" calculation, and remarked that the French terms were even lower than the threshold of the special dispensation, to be met by the response, "It's not where you start that matters, but where you finish."

This contrast was a continuing counterpoint throughout the negotiations. Whereas DREE officials were well-practised in the finesse of financial juggling and the cost implications of "the grains of rice" necessary as concessions in protracted negotiations, the British side had secured delegation from the Treasury for a "maximum threshold of net grant equivalent" – any concessions under each of the potential areas that we might tolerate were calculated back to be counted against this base threshold. The trouble was that the calculations and interactions were so complex that they could be handled only on a computer, and, in the days before laptops, this required one of our ECGD colleagues to hump around a 2-feet-square box containing the computer with the "master program" sherpa-like during our travels, most spectacularly in a getting through the Immigration Gates at Shenzhen railway station in competition with several thousand of the local citizenry.

With separate French and British negotiations up against the formidable Chinese machine, we were acutely aware of the dangers of them playing each of us against the other. And we managed to harmonise moves, tricky when there were differences in financial mechanisms, and went out of our way to indicate to the Chinese that we were aware of what was taking place in each other's negotiating sessions. But at the start of the final run-in joint negotiations in Beijing, my French opposite number adopted the novel line of offering a concession, which inevitably the Chinese dismissed as inadequate, and then withdrawing it. The Bank of China concluded that the British offered a more congenial forum for negotiations, and consequently all the financial negotiations were focused on the British team. It made little practical difference, since we checked with our French partners throughout, except that the exhaustion burden fell unfairly.

A major element in such a protracted negotiating game is time, as "grains of rice" have to be eked out to match progress, or breakdowns, on other negotiating fronts. The situation could be desperate, and, on one occasion, turning to the Midland Bank delegate on our team, I inquired whether the finance experts had anything to add, hoping for at least a 10 to 15-minute respite during dissertations on some subtlety. Instead of which the response was, "No, I wouldn't have anything to add" – a banker who can't bullshit is hardly an asset in this game.[14] But salvation came when we expressed doubts about some outrageous new demand, and the Bank of China leading negotiator said that they had a saying in his country, "When a dying man is thirsting for melons, you do not give him sesame seeds." Andrew Seaton, our Mandarin-speaking FCO team member couldn't offer any counter proverb on the theme of making the best of small mercies, so one had to extemporise on the "melon" metaphor. And "melons" became the currency of negotiations, offering a reasonably courteous idiom to reject outrageous demands, and suggestions of possible slices where some movement might be tolerated. This reached the point when, at the wind-up "banquet" given by the Chinese for the French and British negotiating teams, there was a specially commissioned canvas on the wall of a sliced melon, and melon was served as the final course, with inevitable exchanges over who should have the final slice.

In negotiating in China, however, "final" has a transitory meaning, and the British and French each faced some "final final" negotiations in Beijing as the separate commercial contracts with the suppliers were completed and "clarification" agreed on details such as the premium mechanisms. The French went first, with a direct concordat between Madam Cresson, their Trade Minister at the time, and Li Peng, then head of the Chinese nuclear ministry – rather different from UK traditions, he was actually expert in nuclear technology. GEC's final negotiations were kept running over the Christmas holidays in 1985, with the implicit leverage that concessions would allow them home to enjoy the festivities with their families. For officials lined up to complete the final loan documents, we had a booking to Beijing for every day between the 23rd of December and the 2nd of January, since attempting immediate bookings over the holiday period would have been impossible, and a daily call was made to the Duty Officer to check whether the commercial negotiations had been completed. If not, the next day's booking was cancelled. This lasted until the 30th of December, when the response came that we were required on the 2nd of January – so we spent New Year's Eve in transit, starting with a China Airlines flight that broke down in Geneva requiring a transfer to a Swissair replacement.

On arrival, with an ambient temperature at -10°, Bob Davidson*, Managing Director of GEC's power division, greeted us with a beaming countenance, "It's all agreed. Except the Chinese want the British government to guarantee GEC's performance." Talk your way out of that. Which we did without a blunt negative. But negotiations are never over. As the "final" documents were made ready for the "final" signature, and shown to us an hour in advance, since they were predominantly concerned with technicalities in ECGD's sphere of expertise, I suggested that the ECGD staff might be prudent to make a quick check. Sure enough, in one of the appendices was a form of words that appeared to accept a point that had repeatedly been rejected in earlier negotiations. Under threat of deferring the signature ceremony, the Chinese side accepted that it should be set aside to allow the formal completion of documents to proceed, and it was only "finally" negotiated after another round of talks in London.

As a further entertainment in pursuing business in China, during the latter stages of the Guangdong nuclear negotiations, a new coal-fired power station at Loyang was identified for ATP support. Whether through ODA prompting, or lobbying by NEI, it was decided that this should be offered on the basis of competitive bidding. And a senior ODA delegation on a visit to Beijing told the Chinese that they welcomed the latter's readiness to follow the competitive tendering approach. As things happen in China, one first heard of this, subsequently confirmed by sight of a reporting telegram, during an informal call on Hutchinson's China unit – down a back alley in Hong Kong, and manned by a very sharp local businessman and a physically imposing Nordic gentleman. The turn of their remarks came barely short of suggesting that the British government was mad to put two of their companies, to mix a metaphor, into a bear pit with the world's most ruthless meat grinder.

As ever, when confronted by incredulity at the eccentricities of Britain's national imbecilities, one could only extemporise to the effect that it was not chance that Britain was the origin of most of the world's spectator sports. If the "games ethic" of our best public schools extolled, not winning, but "losing with dignity" and "the stiff upper lip", a side effect was to convince the more astute pupils that the only dignified, and comfortably civilised, position was to be among the spectators. Consequently, over generations, the educated elite have carried this preference to be among the spectators into Government, the City and Academia. To insist upon "competitive bidding", if at best only likely to achieve a marginal improvement in cost and at the risk of prices pared to levels where the cheapest alternative implies a sub-standard result, ensures a comfortable seat in the stands from which to observe the resulting shambles. (If you want a recent instance, imagine the delirium of those officials and Ministers who dreamt up the privatisation of British Rail.)

But, after the travails of negotiating the nuclear station financing, we could comfortably relax, offering no action to support one party against the other, and enjoy the spectacle with detached amusement. Reverting to the normal Whitehall posture. Bill Barlow*– an old chum from IDAB days, as Chairman of Balfour Beatty, who had teamed up with NEI, would turn up periodically to report that in the latest discussions he was convinced that the Chinese were holding out the prospect of them winning the order. One could only surmise the ploys being played by the Chinese negotiators, but, in the position of a dispassionate betting man, one was bound to conclude that GEC, with a team of at least a dozen staff permanently in Beijing for the nuclear station negotiations, would have been assiduously playing the "banquets" game and with a demonstration plant down the road at Castle Peak, would have some edge. And, in the event, the order went to GEC.

One consolation from the China experience has been the wry pleasure of reading accounts of major companies like BAT, Shell and, indeed, MG Rover, returning blooded from negotiations there. And some further consolation from comparing notes with senior staff in Japanese trading companies such as Marubeni that they also find China extremely frustrating.

INDIAN AUTUMN

For a variety of reasons India offered a relatively good opportunity for projects: the country was embarking on investment to enhance its infrastructure; it matched this potential with an overall financial competence that, unlike many other developing countries such as its neighbour Pakistan, still gave it a good rating with export credit agencies; and there was a range of other happy coincidences – from good personal relations between Mrs Thatcher and Mrs Gandhi, and extremely close contacts at official level through John Thompson*, the High Commissioner, and the Commercial Section headed by Roger Beetham, while in key areas like coal and power generation, Britain's nationalised industries had both a good reputation and maintained contacts with their Indian counterparts. By contrast, while other countries would express some exasperation at finding India a frustrating environment, Britain's secret weapon was that these frustrations were almost exact replicas of those in Whitehall. Evidenced by the extraordinary success of *Yes, Minister,* which could be anticipated by a 20% surge in Delhi electricity demand as kettles were put on for tea just before it was scheduled.

The range of project-activities embraced a broad field, not necessarily all successfully: a continuing liaison group on assisting India make the best use of longwall mining technology, in which Britain was a world leader; power and hydro schemes; steel; rail modernisation; IT; non-ferrous metals; gas and oil sectors etc. If the spectrum of official contacts were wide, these were enhanced by a natural shared style of exchange. For example, the practice of addressing top Departmental officials in the traditional terminology of "Secretary" gave dialogue a relaxed continuity, which combined with their natural wit and humour – and delight in the English language, offered a fair mixture of lighter moments.

Even the Longwall Steering Group, which over time was among the most satisfying in achieving a genuine transfer of expertise, had the occasional lighter moment – among the memorable phrases, Madame Bordia, a no-nonsense senior official in the Finance Ministry, expressed some frustration at being confronted by ODA's customary demand for "an appraisal" of the coal-development programme, with the curt rejoinder, "We all know what's wrong with the Indian coal industry, and the last thing we need is a bunch of academics. But we do need the coal."

RIHAND POWER STATION

The project began through liaison links between the CEGB and the National Thermal Power Corporation (NTPC). The NTPC had been set up by the Indian government against a background of continuing underperformance by State Electricity Boards, where power station output was erratic, often less than 40-50% (while a continuing problem had been losses through leakage as, at high risk to life, communities attempted to tap into power by throwing connections over transmission lines). The NTPC was viewed as an elite group to, first, increase capacity by new investment, and, equally important, as an exemplar to raise operating reliability and standards. There were good contacts between NTPC and CEGB, who by international standards had a high reputation for operating efficiencies of 95% plus, with substantial experience of coal-fired stations.

The Rihand Lake in Uttar Pradesh already had a small hydro-generating dam, but was viewed as a suitable locale for a cluster of power stations fed by development at nearby coalfields. One station on the lake perimeter was already under construction by a Japanese consortium. The concept of a new station designed with the operating disciplines of the CEGB was viewed as natural, and sensible, to carry forward the NTPC's remit. Pursuing this concept as an early ATP case required considerable negotiation within Whitehall, since the aim was to emulate competitors by establishing a platform of finance covering a comprehensive development of a power station (2×660 MW), with provision for a second similar stage, the associated coalmines and transmission system. And then clearance through the Delhi Departmental system. And then securing endorsement at political level, eventually with Prime Ministerial agreement.

This was an exhaustive process, and when finally we gained clearance to begin the real job of defining the specifications for the power station, the initial response, according to the ODA "manual", was to require competitive bidding. Except that the NTPC said that they did not want the job of choosing between Britain's suppliers. Given the historical background of the British companies having been "consolidated" into two main contenders (effectively GEC, mainly interested in securing orders for their Turbine Division, but tending to ally with Babcocks for the boiler and coal preparation processes; and the NEI Group, which contained the capability for supplying complete stations) in a situation where there was insufficient domestic workload to sustain them, and the traditional animosities between them, this was an even more uncomfortable choice for Government.

One option was to have a domestic competition, with full specifications and an evaluation of their current production and project engineering competencies, and to have the Overseas Projects Board adjudicate – precisely the purpose for which it had been re-jigged. This would have taken several months, and run the risk of momentum for the project running down and it being deferred. Any independent observer could judge that the likely outcome would be, on the basis of current track record – GEC, through experience with China Light and Power, having evolved a tested project team. NEI, perhaps sensing this, lobbied hard that to be fair they should be allowed leadership – a hangover of the "buggins turn" game to which CEGB domestic orders had been reduced in the interests of maintaining competition, but embellished with the rhetoric that they "weren't like the other lot", and would ensure that all the necessary resources were provided.

In the event, we had one of those rare, but treasured, meetings with the leading managements of NEI, GEC and Babcocks, where the dilemma was set out, where the pressures for Government to hold a competitive test were spelled out, unless the companies could come to an understanding on how to make a coordinated proposal. And they were dispatched to a separate room to sort themselves out. A bedraggled hour or so later, they emerged to confirm a settlement that GEC would be allocated the turbines, Babcocks the coal-grinding and related feed systems, and NEI the boiler, water filtration and circulating systems, with NEI taking on the project leadership.

Fortunately, out of the CEGB's permutations of 60-odd different coal-fired stations – another consequence of continuous "competitive bidding" – there was one that could be presented as reasonably reflecting this combination of suppliers. And a visit for the NTPC to see this "model" station could be arranged to satisfy them that this was a viable allocation. Phew!

Negotiations to establish an "intent" agreement were a saga in their own right, and the archives should yield a merry PhD thesis in years to come. Because the government was in the uncomfortable position of "sponsoring" the project, we could not avoid a presence. And to ensure professional expertise in international power projects among our ranks, we recruited Mike Durham, an experienced power-station engineer, from Ewbanks – one of a cluster of internationally recognised British consultants. And James Moon, then a Principal on secondment from ECGD (by now, long-buried among the telephone-number remunerations of the City), was given the job of coordinator, since there were parallel negotiations due on the coal-mining development to complement the power station.

As the date for these negotiations was fixed, we thought it prudent to have a session with NEI on their proposed approach since we did not want to become drawn into unprepared situations. The company representatives were not able to offer a coherent strategic approach to the forthcoming negotiations, even when we inquired about the total indicative project price that they would be offering. We asked Mike for an indication of what would be the international ballpark price for a comparable station, since this would be the datum to which NTPC would be working. Around £240 million, he replied, though inevitably the final figure would depend upon a range of factors, notably the coal-quality (the carbon-content would have a significant impact on the sheer scale, and steel required, of the boilers, specifications for grinding equipment, ash-disposal etc), transport and communications infrastructure. To take account of these, there seemed general agreement that an initial price indication of £295 million would be a reasonable opening shot.

As the DTI team settled into the flight to Delhi two days before the scheduled start of negotiations, James was going through his last-minute mail from the office and flourished a copy of NEI's telegram to the NTPC indicating an initial price of £395 million. We optimistically consoled ourselves that this must have been a typing error. But not so lucky. On arrival in Delhi, it turned out to be genuine, and we were greeted by a message from the NTPC that it was pointless to start negotiations on this basis. The only way to resolve the impasse was a personal call on the NTPC Chairman, Mr. Shah. He greeted me with remarkable calm in the circumstances: as the Falklands War was dominating the headlines, he suggested that we should have confined our bombs to the Argentineans. The only excuse one could offer was that, with some key issues still unresolved, the company had obviously added in contingency margins. But he left no doubt that without a more realistic price related to the scope of supply, there was no chance of negotiations starting.

Even inured to the cringe-inducing features of British management that could be laughed off as part of the absurd saga of the nation's industrial decline, this episode, completely disregarding the efforts right up to the Prime Minister, to secure the project opportunity, did occasion a heated exchange with the company. And with a revised opening offer of £305 million, to save some face, negotiations began. Apart from such an absurdly high initial price virtually destroying credibility, other weaknesses became apparent. But to risk injury by bending over as far as possible to be fair, the British system of the CEGB controlling "project design" and retaining the engineering responsibility, meant that British suppliers were by tradition brought up to produce hardware according to CEGB's specifications without any experience of the responsibilities – and risks – of putting a total power-station together. GEC had to go through a learning process – even though they complained about its rigour – at the hands of CLP. For NEI, India was their kindergarten, except that

NTPC were among the world's most professional and experienced power-generation clients.[15]

Consequently, NEI were up against a rigorous expertise on technical details, project planning and phasing, manpower estimates etc, albeit conducted in a good-humoured atmosphere. Such negotiations are bound to carry on over a period of weeks (if not months, and sometimes years), and NEI's team was sadly under resourced for even such rudimentary steps as taking routine notes that could be invaluable in sorting out subsequent differences of interpretation. And the NTPC naturally added the epithet "harried" in their informal depiction of the NEI team. For us observers, the empathetic humiliation was acute as we listened in awe to such remarkable statements as Mr Bami, the NTPC Finance Director and leader of their team, saying on one occasion, "We want to give you the order. Will you please help us?"

As the indicative price was steadily chipped down, at £245 million, we submitted a paper signed by Mike Durham to the effect that, for a power-station in conformity with CEGB standards, this represented a fair and reasonable price, and a further reduction could jeopardise attaining these standards. Despite this, in the event the final price against this concept was reduced by a few further millions of pounds, and what was essentially a letter of intent concluded.

Yet we could not duck subsequent involvement – chairing early review meetings between NTPC and the contractors, with the former naturally pressing for evidence that the necessary network planning, cabling design, and so on, was proceeding adequately; using our good offices with CLP to obtain an experienced power station engineer for NEI; while there were complaints in the other direction over communications, infrastructure, and so on, where liaison was required.[16]

Despite an almost continuous flow of complaints and recriminations, the marvel was that the project was completed, even to the point where for a time it was blazoned as a showcase. From an early visit to the site, when access was over the lake – the boat broke down, demanding an athletic leap to a replacement – to a final visit when the station, with an accompanying township, was nearing completion was evidence of this transition. Much of the credit must go, however, to Peter Lockton, recruited, after the failure of earlier appointments, as the local project coordinator, and who successfully combined commitment, humour and an open readiness to engage with all involved in the project.

A STEEL SIDESHOW

In parallel with the NTPC negotiations on Rihand, Davy had also been engaged in protracted negotiations for a steel plant at Daitari on the Orissa coast. Their competitor was Demag, the plant contractor linked to Mannesmann – the old heavy industry Mannesmann, who had done the initial feasibility study (having seen the report, it was an excellent model of such an analysis), and were aggrieved that Davy had been allowed in to contest the order.

An entertaining episode had occurred earlier when Prince Charles visited DTI and attendance at a meeting in PEP included in his programme. This was expected to be a genuine meeting to avoid any false theatrics, and the timing happened to coincide with one where we were reviewing the financial package to support Davy. The convention was that we should outline the context and purpose of the meeting, and then clarify any unusual terms or issues that arose. The first shock for our distinguished visitor was that GEC were part of the Demag package while Morgan Grenfell were their designated bankers. More infuriating, one of our bankers from Lazards, in disregard of the risks of being garrotted after the meeting, inquired whether we should offer a "switch option", which required a bit of explaining.

But the negotiations for Daitari were due to reach their culmination at the same time as those for Rihand. There was feedback from various quarters that Davy had not handled the exercise with much finesse. But there was a standing joke that India was littered with foundation stones for new steel plants as its political leaders had found this a convenient device for securing temporary local popularity. More seriously, comments from the compass of Departmental Permanent Secretaries were generally on the theme, "India needs a new steel plant like a hole in the head."

Still, Sir John Buckley, a suitably silver-haired Chairman personage and Graham Raper, Davy's chief executive, turned up in expectations. Immediately following the Indian Cabinet meeting, the Secretary of the Steel Ministry asked John Thompson* to call at his office, and I accompanied him. The Ministry was in one of Edwin Lutyens' red sandstone blocks, with a courtyard invariably filled with Mercedes or ominous black Russian limousines, and the Secretary's office was approached up a flight of worn steps. The Steel Secretary – probably one of the most thankless of Indian Departmental briefs – a Mr Gill, was a slight, immaculate figure, highly intelligent, who spoke in a low-key, but with a self-effacing style of English whose sense moved in parabolas of subtlety that required John's practised ear to follow. But he said that the Cabinet had decided not to proceed with the steel plant, with no prospect of it being reinstated in the foreseeable future,[17] and that he had been charged to inform the company. John replied that he should see the company representatives before the inevitable risks of leaks and convey the decision in unequivocal terms.

Later that day, the Davy team called on the High Commission to report the outcome of their meeting at the Steel Ministry and seemed remarkably cheerful, saying that Mr Gill had indicated that the company had the prospect of resubmitting revised proposals. We listened politely, not wishing to disclose that we were privy to the Cabinet conclusions before the company. But as soon as they had left, we rushed around to see Mr Gill: he was aghast that the company should have drawn this interpretation from what he had said, since he had spoken "in very plain terms" with no scope "to misconstrue". It was left that the best way to disabuse the company of any ambiguity would be for Mr Gill to send a short and polite note to them confirming in simple terms the conclusive nature of the government's decision. The company team appeared to have got the message and left shortly thereafter.

OTHER ADVENTURES

If Mr Gill was of the modest self-effacing school of the India Administrative Service, Mr Ganupati, first encountered when Secretary of the Minerals and Mines Ministry, was on the ebullient wing.[18] A burly figure and affable countenance, disguising a shrewd perception of the byways of the Delhi bureaucracy. At the first meeting, in the early days of ATP, with Roger Beetham, the Commercial Councillor, we inquired whether there were any likely projects in his area of responsibility. He immediately responded that he had two of the best investment cases, but was having difficulty persuading the Finance Ministry, though if he could indicate some support in the financing, perhaps this would get them through.

These two cases were the Bharat Aluminium Company (BALCO), where efficient operation was inhibited by the unreliability of electricity supplies and could be enhanced by a captive power station, with any surplus power fed into the grid. The second was Hindustan Zinc, where the smelter required an updating of technology. Putting these cases through the hoops, it was agreed to indicate an ATP grant with the remainder of the finance on ECGD terms, both inevitably subject to an ODA appraisal. Hindustan Zinc turned out to be ironically straightforward: the technology was from Lurgi, and to qualify for UK support we had to set up Davy as the titular contractor and they in turn had to come to an agreement with the German firm.

The BALCO power station also encountered a surprisingly easy passage, since NEI had their hands full in carrying out Rihand, GEC was the only realistic option. NTPC were to act as the Indian client, with whom there were already good relations. The project development went smoothly: GEC made presentations on design, technical options, settled the specifications, and proceeded to negotiate a price, while the ODA appraisal went through with ease. And Roger Beetham and I called on the Finance Department to confirm the financing terms. Since the project had proceeded so well, there seemed no grounds to go beyond the minimum ATP concession of "30% net grant equivalent", so preserving more of the ATP budget allocation for projects elsewhere. So we held to this figure on the concessionality that could be justified, and confirmed that the aid would be "additional"[19] to the normal bilateral program.

Any complacency at the project having proved so straightforward should have been tinged with the certainty that under the British bureaucratic approach, farce is an ever-present companion around the corner. In this case, literally so, as a couple of hundred yards away a junior ODA official was calling on his Indian opposite number to review the normal bilateral program. The latter apparently noted that the budget was heading for an underspend that year, and his suggestion that the BALCO power station should be funded by grants under the bilateral program was agreed by the ODA official.

The first shock was that this "routine" concession undermined what we had been saying at senior level to the Finance Ministry. But to move from a "30% grant" level to a "100% grant" on a project costed at over £100 million was an extra payment of at least £70 million. GEC, in whose culture a concession of £2000 was heinous, was stunned that a junior official in Government could glibly make such a concession. Excusable perhaps in the zany Whitehall budgetary logic where, "if you don't spend it, you won't get it next year", it illustrated vividly – as indeed did Rihand – that concessional finance was not a "subsidy" in that the commercial terms for the project itself were entirely unaffected, and competitively tough, irrespective of the "grant" element in the finance.[20]

But the British brand of "farce" has a continuity of its own, and the episode inevitably had a sequel. Westlands were competing against the French for an order for helicopters to service India's developing offshore energy activities. Working with Westlands, we were tactically "matching" whatever financial permutations the French were introducing. The French, however, whether deliberately or by accident, hit on the most vulnerable feature of British corporate funding – they began increasing the level of performance "bonds" to be offered.[21] A. "bond" is a surety note, usually from the company's main bank, to pay a penalty charge, usually expressed as a percentage of the bid price, in the event of failure to meet the contract conditions, notably in delayed completion. Under the usurious British system, the bank is delighted to provide an unqualified surety, charging a substantial fee to the company, but securing the value of the bond against the company's own assets – in effect, incurring no risk to the bank, but reducing the company's scope to borrow for its normal business. The French competitor, being government owned, suffered none of these constraints.

Anyway, as the bonding-level offered by the French reached 10%, then 12%, and moved higher, the brows of the Westland management became increasingly furrowed. But then, out of the blue – but one could guess not without prompting by an alert merchant banker with recollections of the BALCO case – the Indian government suggested that this order should be funded by a normal 100% grant from the bilateral program. This was, in any event, a difficult case for ODA, since the aircraft would in practice be operated by the Indian Air Force. On the other hand, the Treasury view was the case should be funded only on a 100% grant basis. This time, it was the French who were stunned.

OTHER CLIMES

Even though restricted to countries that were on-cover for ECGD credit – excluding virtually all Latin America (though Mexico hovered precariously between being on- and off-cover) and Africa (outside South Africa) – there were continuing dramas in the Philippines, Malaysia, Thailand, Indonesia, Morocco, Egypt, Sri Lanka, and Turkey with varying fortunes, but rarely without our ever-present spirit of farce. Just as examples:

– The MRICA hydro-scheme in Indonesia was an Anglo-Swedish joint proposal, with Balfour Beatty in alliance with Skanska and Bovings, a UK-based but Swedish owned manufacturer of hydro turbines. Owing to controversy over East Timor, Sweden had a self-denying ordinance not to provide aid to Indonesia: consequently, the normal UK ATP allocation required some sophisticated presentation. Yet again, we were competing with the French. At that time there was considerable volatility in exchange rates, and with every slip in the value of the Franc, the French submitted a reduced price. To compress the saga, in effect we won the project (contract value £126m with ATP support of £12m) four times, having lost it three times. Most awkwardly, the Royal Yacht Britannia was taking the

Queen on a state visit to Sweden, and for want of any other current examples, this project was presented during the "Business Day" as a successful Anglo-Swedish venture. The trouble was that, just before the presentation, we heard that we had "lost" the project for the second time.

– Typically frustrating, John Brown – an antique Scottish company going back to the glory days of shipbuilding – was manufacturing gas turbines as a licensee of General Electric (GE), and one of the more persistent candidates for ATP support. One Friday they called to say that they were pursuing an opportunity in Burma, with an indication that competitors were offering mixed-aid finance, and had to complete their submission by 9 a.m. the following morning. Given the tricky issues of trade policy towards Burma, the justification for such a matching case, and the fact that Friday is normally a day when Ministers are dotted around their constituencies, getting a decision was a tall order. But by 4.30 p.m. that day we had secured all the clearances, and called the company back. But all we could raise was a security watchman, who said that there was no one around since it was the company's annual golf competition. And he had no idea of how to contact the golf club.

But we also developed a keen sense of projects to avoid: the Hub Power Station in Pakistan, advanced as an early example of build-own-operate (BOO) on purportedly commercial terms, was one where we withstood pressures to become involved – one recalls questioning one of the British promoters, "Where in the developing world is electricity sold at a genuinely commercial price?" And the Lesotho Highlands scheme, where, however rational the concept of using trapped water for irrigation, seemed to offer undue scope for jiggery-pokery. But as a footnote, just to stand up to the accusations of history, on my last day in PEP I had a call from a company inquiring whether I was aware of a scheme to combine ATP support for a dam in Malaysia with some defence orders. My response was that, even if the French would have done this without a qualm, in the British system this was an extremely bad idea since ODA jealously defended their purity against any possible involvement in "military" aid. This subsequently turned out to be the Pergau Dam, which raised some controversy with ODA stimulating a World Bank appraisal which was unsurprisingly negative – not that World Bank appraisals have an untarnished track record, while hydro schemes in Malaysia had previously figured in the aid program. Indeed, Mrs Thatcher, had visited one on her visit to the country – but it set up a pretext to terminate ATP as a device for supporting British companies.

Sadly, however, this period was a threnody to this country having any substantial competence in international major projects, largely because the corporate entities on whose motivations such activities depend have disappeared:

– In power generation, NEI, for some unaccountable reason, were absorbed by Rolls-Royce; GEC merged their power business with Alsthom, at the time on the basis of having letters of intent for three new stations from CEGB, but with privatisation and the "dash for gas" these were terminated – to the chagrin of their French partners, and any remaining British competence in power-turbines eventually closed down.

– The undersea cabling unit of STC, with its demise, was sold initially to Nortel, and then to Alcatel. While Plessey has been dismantled, with bits, if they still exist, spread around Siemens.

– The civil contractors such as Balfour Beatty, despite having built up positions in Indonesia and Malaysia, swung resources back to the UK, enticed by the easy pickings of the Lawson boom, and then the even juicier fruits of PFI deals.

– Davy merged into Trafalgar House, disposing of their rolling-mill unit in Bournemouth to Voest Alpine, while Trafalgar House was eventually taken over by Skanska.

– John Brown has sunk without trace, probably unnoticed by its management still preoccupied with sharpening their short game.

– While even the coal-mining longwall machinery companies, Dowty and Gullick Dobson, first merged into Longwall Mining, and then taken over by Harnishfeger, as the coal-mining industry was run down in the UK. From an occasional glance over the years, one consolation is that Fenner, a manufacturer of conveyor systems, seems to have survived with pragmatic diversification.

A wistful regret is what might have happened if recognition of the real international market had permeated national thinking a few decades earlier, though even this presupposes that British companies were sufficiently focused to pursue exports outside the comfort zone of national procurement. If entertaining enough, it was a unique "theatre of the absurd". Maybe we saw some of the best of British management, but we most surely witnessed some of the worst. And the British system is further crippled by inadequate support from the financial sector, and a persistent desire to ignore reality within Government. But a real regret is that customers were buying equipment with a prospective life of decades, and might normally have expected, as would have applied had they ordered from Germany, Japan or France, the suppliers would be around to deal with modifications, spares and servicing over the full operational stretch.

Another, less observed, but nonetheless crucial, consequence of this collapse of industry from major infrastructure exports is the dissipation of supplying industries, and with this an inevitable contraction of opportunities for engineering and technical skills. And, ultimately, national competencies.

---

[1] An incidental pleasure from watching recent paroxysms in Whitehall is the spectacle of this entrenched heritage, where "policy" has been the acme of aspiration, invariably concluding that "sitting on hands" was the best way to allow "the invisible hand" to work, coming up against the increasingly frantic calls of Ministers for real action. Ministers are themselves caught in a nice double-bind, as political discourse has also been dominated over centuries by the compilation of meaningless verbiage to convey the illusion of reasoned "policy".

[2] One of the surest measures of the effectiveness of the "EIS", or whatever it may now be called, was that, in downturns it was among the first expenses that British companies elected to cut – just when it might have seemed that the need for new business was at its most critical. On one occasion, out of the blue, I had a call from a Dutch company inquiring the latest position on some reported export opportunity. Passing its name to the right Departmental branch, I also to took the trouble to find out its UK interests: it was merely a "brass plate" operation. So the efforts of commercial posts was being made available to competitors – one could sense frustration during calls to commercial offices in overseas posts that their diligent groundwork and reporting met with such a limited response from British companies, or a more rapid response by competitors. Apparently, this is now all on the Internet, so more readily available to all-comers, presumably as an enhanced stimulus to competitive free trade.

[3] When Lord (George) Jellicoe was chairman of the British Overseas Trade Board, having drawn attention to the findings of one of Japan's comprehensive White Papers on Smaller and Medium Enterprises (1984) that "only 5.5% directly export goods to foreign purchasers" (page 60), we speculated informally whether it might be worth suggesting that, since more than 80% of UK exports customarily came from the 100 largest exporters, assistance to help these raise their performance by 5% might be more effective than efforts to help the others, which invariably had sporadic results. But he concluded that such a radical idea would just not be a runner.

[4] Presumably, we could only speculate, a hangover of memory traces from early recitals of such Third Form lays as, "In Florres in the Azores, Sir Richard Granville lay..." recounting the exploits of one of our Elizabethan privateers in heroically besting a larger Spanish force; Horatius on the bridge; "the boy stood on the burning deck", and so on. But structurally very different from the more practical approaches in Germany (via strong Commercial Chambers), Italy (via

their Confindustria) etc.

[5] I owe "pith helmet" exporting to an ex-Hewlett-Packard executive brought in by GEC to manage the bit of Plessey that they acquired: it was his depiction of the mindset of inherited Plessey management. But a bull's-eye phrase to conjure up the managerial ethos of Empire, when "market share" was gained predominantly by the Royal Navy and a few battalions of sepoys. In this balmy tradition, every couple of years, top managers would summon the butler, "James, pack the khakis, gaiters and topee. Oh, and pull through the elephant gun," and, with the usual pile of cabin trunks, set off by P&O from Tilbury to make a round of calls, between hunting expeditions, to local agents. The traditional approach of "trade" officials was a perfect complement to this style, where the assumption was that all that was needed for export success was a distinct "product" and a "price" which could be matched up with notified opportunities from Britain's far-flung overseas posts. If some advance on the speed of the traditional package-boat, this ignores the disappearance of the "export houses", which provided a mediation function in the grand old days of Britain's trade significance.

[6] The Overseas Projects Fund (OPF) was a limited budget to assist with the upfront, and non-recoverable, bidding costs, but refundable if the British contender was successful. If allocated without regard to the potential total gains, it could be nugatory: for example, one contractor's representative admitted that to gain access to proprietary technology for a particular process plant, the contractor would have to undertake to make efforts to further exploit the know-how by pursuing other business – often, it was not judged prudent to pursue further business, and the OPF offered a 50% contribution for them to make gestures to fulfil this condition but with no serious intention of winning further work.

On the other hand, if applied more deliberately, the Fund could have tactical gains. There was a call for design proposals for the Baghdad Metro, a prospect presumably buried beneath piles of rubble no doubt, but this occasioned the usual rabble of competing British consultants all demanding OPF support: but insistence that support would be offered for only one contender compelled these factions to work together for a single proposal making the best of their respective skills (even if the project has not transpired in the event, several participants admitted that the process had been constructive). Or, for a waste-water scheme in Malaysia, it was possible to agree the terms of reference for the initial feasibility studies supported by OPF with the Overseas Development Agency in advance, to help the latter's subsequent developmental appraisal.

[7] Another economic agent ignored by the conventional British theology is the contractor: every project is the integration of a wide array of inputs – suppliers covering the hardware, expertise in the construction of facilities, process units, electrical and other systems. Some guy has to draw all these inputs together to provide the outcome that the customer wants. In some instances, such as the CEGB's power station purchasing system, the client is prepared to take on this coordination function himself, but for overseas projects invariably the client wants a single coordinating agent with whom to place the contract. Within this

totality, it is feasible for the contractor to demand that each supplier carries responsibility, and the potential financial liability, for their direct contribution. Yet there are invariably a range of other risks that cannot be clearly allocated to those supplying the inputs from the knock-on consequences of routine delays, transport mishaps, untimely weather etc. The capacity to absorb these risks is the fundamental dilemma for the contractor. Economic orthodoxy where "risks are covered in the price" breaks down against realities: in practice, even though the contractor may have a tough time hanging on to margins, suppliers may well be earning rosy profits. Or, when the contractor is all, or partially, state-owned, or has the backing of a concern with a major stake in the project, the financial consequences of such risks can be passed on to a balance sheet more able to carry them.

Invariably the issue boils down to "Who has sufficient to gain from the project to take on this residual risk?" Every industrial society has evolved its own structures for handling this dilemma:

– In Germany, there has been a long tradition of their major companies forming financial subsidiaries to work in consortia with their banks in securing projects e.g. in power and rail, indeed one of Deutsche Bank's first operations was a consortium with Siemens. But their tradition of "combinations" has evolved contractors/consultants that have a major group with a supply or other interests in the outcome of the project standing behind them. For example, Demag (Mannesmann in its old metal engineering form), Lahmeyer (long-linked to Siemens), Lurgi (a subsidiary of MG), Uhde (Hoechst) etc.

– Japan had a number of specialist contractors, but for the integration of supplies and finance, has the backing of its major Sogo Shosha.

– France was the arch practitioner of framing political and financial leverage behind their main companies, which invariably had an element of state holding, so that risks were carried through to the government. Entirely pragmatic in approach, but capable of pulling off remarkably large combined deals: one in India in the 80s embraced nuclear know-how, advanced fighters, and a telecom system (much to the chagrin of the Germans who believed that their contender had won a competitive tender). They could also wheel in their national utility expertise, as their terms of service included liability to serve outside metropolitan France, and a series of "Sofra..." groups could be deployed to enhance the quality of their bid and monitor progress on the government's behalf. Recognising that securing the "contractor" role was crucial in determining the flows of project work, equally characteristic was their approach in building up a "national" contractor, Technip, initially by scavenging contracts in markets such as Egypt when other countries were loathe to extend export credit cover, and biasing national procurement. (Bechtel admitted to having shut their Paris office in the early 80s, for want of gaining a fair opportunity.) As an exercise in modest speculation, it is worth contemplating how differently the French would have set about developing the UK's North Sea energy had it fallen within their geographic jurisdiction.

– The United States, whilst it had a series of major contractors such as Bechtel, Brown & Root, Fluor, Foster Wheeler etc, who had built up a strong expertise, these tended to operate as providers of technical and procurement expertise without a particular remit to source from America, save were special American aid finance was involved. For example, one of our successes involved providing a platform of finance for Bechtel conducting the Balikipapan refinery in Indonesia. But when the US government had a special interest, the Corps of Engineers were likely to turn up.

– South Korea was moving aggressively to secure major provisioning contracts, with extremely aggressive prices. One particular national device was offering their young people "overseas works service" as an alternative to military national service, hence creating a workforce paid on low military salaries.

These national approaches had been current for many years without any tangible UK response, whether in stimulating more effective industrial relationships, or in the provision of competitive finance.

[8] ECGD has in recent years been the butt of a continuous stream of uninformed criticism – for example, the scale of loans backed by their guarantees are regularly depicted by pressure groups as "subsidies". This lack of appreciation of the rationale for an export credit agency, and indeed the hostile manner in which its activities are reported, must be unique to Britain, since other countries have not embraced the de-industrialisation ethos that underlies what passes for "policy". Setting aside the issue of "subsidy" for treatment elsewhere – see Note 20, with an involvement with ECGD going back to the 60s, that Department has always been under pressure from different quarters: from the Treasury with their myopic version of cash-budgeting over the next 3 or 4 years, and indeed from industry for not making unjustified concessions on particular cases. In practice, the technicalities and risk-evaluation have required a high level of professionalism, and over the years the outfit has gained a high reputation with its confreres in the international trade finance community.

Its functions begin with potential instabilities that can arise from volatile and unpredictable causes, in particular shifts in political circumstances. Recalling a glance at ECGD's history, the first such guarantee goes back to a deal in the early 20s to the Balkans, when it must have occurred to even the dimmest in Whitehall that there was some recent track record of political volatility and where the traditional gunboats of the Pax Britannica might be liable more to inflame than offer security. Jokingly, one has suggested over the years that ECGD has been compensating for the decline of maritime power and empire.

But if the threat of nationalisation, sequestration, revolutionary political movements etc may not be what it was in the Cold War era, there are still wide popular movements against capitalism, instability from fundamentalist movements, local wars, contagious financial crises etc to make this a field of "political risk" that the normal insurance market remains unable to cover. Without going into the actuarial niceties, insurance depends upon an adequate "spread" where the volume of risks undertaken has a measure of predictability in the incidence of calls, such as vehicle and property insurance, to take obvious examples.

Setting aside the technicalities of "supplier" or "buyer" credit, variations in collateral and recourse requirements etc, medium-term fixed-rate credit is applicable to a wide range of manufactured exports under the heading of capital goods, from major integrated projects the guarantee will have a counterpart assurance from the recipient government. Even so, there can be defaults triggered by oil crises, financial collapse, and so on, which disrupt the flow of anticipated loan repayments, and the treatment of outstanding loans in such circumstances is coordinated among the national credit agencies and banks through the Paris Club.

ECGD, for this "insurance function", like other countries' corresponding agencies and export finance banks (the UK has no corresponding development banks to those in Germany, Japan, France and several Nordic countries, nor an Export-Import bank like the US and several other countries, which are guaranteed by the State to make concessionary loans) charges a premium. The national variations in the scale and mechanisms for charging such premia can become a contested area, and in practice ECGD's approach is among the most transparent.

Linked to this insurance function is a demanding professional field of judgment in deciding appropriate exposures to particular markets: again, involving international consultation to avoid national agencies suffering if one or a few build up unduly large exposures that might undermine the standing of others. In the event of guarantees being called in circumstances of default, there are mechanisms for rescheduling, refinancing etc involving payments being delayed and hence a more prolonged period of reduced income, or calls on reserves. All national agencies inevitably suffer similar financial pressures from major recessions or regional financial crises. On the other hand, there are countries, such as China, who have kept up a virtually impeccable record of loan repayments.

The form of long/medium-term fixed-interest loans to developing countries arises from the heavy upfront cost of capital goods and is part of the development-financing repertoire of all major countries. There was a time, indeed, within living memory when Britain's overseas aid was managed by three ECGD staff adopting special terms and adjustments to the nature of individual countries. Apart from variations in institutions among supplying countries, all offer an array of specialist facilities for exchange risks, investment risks, etc.

ECGD has been among the most professional of these agencies, with their specialist staff always in danger of being pinched by the City. But in recent years there has been a continuing Treasury fixation to limit their activities, and throughout the 80s and 90s ECGD was "under review", with each settlement being immediately undermined by yet another review exercise (see Note 12). This continuing shadow of uncertainty impacted on the willingness of companies to undertake the investment to establish market position without assurance that comparable backing to that offered to competitors by their governments would be available. (The current situation where ECGD appear to have become an agency for policing corrupt payments seems to demand a command of forensic accounting not entirely appropriate to their main function, and, whilst undoubtedly welcome to the Treasury as a mechanism for further inhibiting support for exporters, is unlikely to be replicated in the practices of other countries who actually place priority on sustaining the continuity of business for their domestic industries.)

The intricacies of export credit finance were complex enough but became even more contorted when adaptations were made to compete with the mechanisms employed by other governments. A full account of the abstruse logic would be too arcane for rational depiction, but there were some distinct levels:

– The interest rates for official export credits provided under ECGD guarantee were disciplined through the OECD Consensus, which covered the main exporting nations. At one time there had been a loose comparison of national rates, but by common agreement a "matrix" system was introduced, which set, by six monthly review, a standard (effectively the mean of different national interest rates) interest rate for long-term government guaranteed loans. UK interest rates were invariably above the international mean rate (as distinct from countries like Germany and Japan that had national rates continuously below the mean, and were designated as Low Interest Rate Currencies (LIRCs)). Consequently, successful orders secured with loans under ECGD terms have continuously involved "make-up payments" from the government to make good the difference between the rate received by UK banks under guaranteed credit and the cost of funds dictated by domestic interest rates. Conversely, LIRC country governments made no such "make-up payments".

– As a second tier, if elements of aid grant were added to the financing package – or adjustments made in ECGD terms, these and the make-up costs of the ECGD guaranteed loan were discounted, and added, to reflect the "net grant equivalent". This became the basis for seeking international disciplines on the premise of making such devices more expensive, with "minimum levels" of "net grant equivalent" being progressively increased by international agreement – from 20% to 30% over the period of PEP, and a similar regime of rising minima were agreed periodically for certain categories of project, notably nuclear power stations.

– A theological distinction was developed between "initiating" and "matching": on a presumption of "open competitive tendering" as the norm for international projects, a discipline was established where a country initiating a proposal involving terms more concessionary than the internationally agreed standard was required to notify others to give them the opportunity to "match". Since in practice the normal procedure adopted by most other countries was to set up a platform of special finance against a series of prospective projects, the point of reporting "initiation" could be deferred until a project had been negotiated to the point when funds were due to be drawn down. But by then, "matching" was far too late to have any influence. Hence the Department retained the formula of "matching the practices" of other countries, which would allow similar "initiation".

– Even then, there was a continuing bleat about "untying" aid, with Britain in the van. Whereas other leading donors traditionally adopted a "mutual advantage" approach in that, where there were national competences and expertise that could be usefully applied to the needs of developing countries, these should be encouraged. The British position has always seemed daft in ignoring its own history – in his thorough and balanced survey *Raj, the Making and Unmaking of*

British India (Little, Brown and Company) Lawrence James notes "infrastructure" as one of Britain's proudest legacies. Most obvious in the rail network, with bridges and viaducts, but in the mid-1980s, one of the gates of the Sukkur Barrage was replaced under our normal aid program: the first major repair to the barrage across the Indus, which for a century had irrigated hundreds of square miles of what is now Pakistan. And when the Rihand Power Station in India was completed, by British manufacturers and with CEGB involvement, a senior ODA official was heard to remark grudgingly, "This is what we should be doing" – sadly, with no British manufacturers left, and the accumulated expertise of the CEGB long dissipated, this would no longer be feasible.

Apart from reflecting the familiar Treasury technique of "bureaucratic constipation", this edifice of tripwires was not replicated by other countries. For every deadline to tighten the restraints, other countries would table proposals beforehand so that they could argue that they could not change undertakings already provided. And we had some instances of pure farce: a power station project fell off a line of finance offered by the French in Brazil since other projects had taken up the available sums, and we were told that we could have the order if we matched the French terms, but, on inspection, we found that the French "net grant equivalent" was half the current accepted minimum, and we had to "invent" a hypothetical coalmine to justify the level of aid to comply with the ruling minimum.

The interaction of these strands of bureaucratic demands, to which could be added, with rather more justification, an economic appraisal to suit ODA's internal budgetary criteria, meant that that virtually all cases carried a substantial burden of work for the Division's officials, to which inevitably some were more adept than others. But everyone deserves praise for struggling with these demands, usually against tight timescales.

[9] Becoming involved in a review of overseas aid opened the doors to a uniquely British maze of esoteric argument. Just to put this into a global context, on a world scale at the time, Britain was (and is) a relatively small contributor – some 4.5% of Development Assistance Committee countries' total aid, compared at the time with Japan (18.1%), US (21.3%), France (16.0%) and West Germany (10.7%) substantially larger donors. Moreover, historically there had been a time when the country's "aid" had been run by four staff in ECGD: the original basis of the concept of long-term fixed-interest loans underwritten by government derived from the motive to provide consistent finance for infrastructure and capital investment in less-developed countries. But with the creation of a distinct "Overseas Aid" department in the 1970s, it inevitably evolved its own theology, and to secure funds did so by huddling close to the prevailing Treasury ethos.

In practice, the rationale for overseas aid under the tenets of orthodox economic theory is pretty dodgy. As we discovered when, under Keith Joseph's instructions, we insisted that the views of Professor Peter Bauer (subsequently Lord Bauer) should be taken fully into account. This caused such consternation in the ODA ranks that we deputed one of our eco-lingo people to find out wherein his magic powers lay. (*The Economist* did a fulsome praise of Bauer on his award of the Milton Friedman prize – 4.4.02.) As an ODA colleague remarked, Bauer wouldn't admit more than Red Cross and charity aid going directly to the impoverished, since all other financial flows, especially between governments, were open to corruption, misapplication, and distortion of market incentives. And, one recalls, he fought his corner very effectively: at a lunch-time seminar the day after the tragic TV pictures that gave rise to "Band Aid", to an audience full of aid-protagonists, he stuck to his guns pointing out that of several $100 millions dispensed to Sudan in aid, none had been passed down to relieve the plight of the poorest.

It is only a shrug of economic logic to argue that aid should be dispensed to encourage (coerce) "market-supportive/conducive/opening/etc" programmes – infamously branded as "the Washington Consensus". Despite the disasters perpetrated in the name of this doctrine, the tattered banner still flies over Britain's aid programme, if not, indeed, domestic economic policies, since one of the prime purposes of Britain's aid programme is to retain seats on the World Bank/IMF and their agencies, which, as the justification on relative economic performance declines, relies increasingly on rehearsing the correct rhetoric.

Yet there has always been a high element of double-speak in discussions on aid. For example, the US range of activities under aid set out in *International Security and Economic Cooperation Programme* (US Department of State) embraces the conventional humanitarian areas of Development Assistance, Food for Peace, Refugee Assistance, Narcotics Control Assistance, Inter-American Foundation, Peace Corps, but also, under the heading of Security Assistance, foreign military sales, military assistance, bilateral military education and training, peacekeeping and antiterrorism assistance.

But in the wide world beyond the cubicle of the Whitehall village debate, other countries have evolved systems of development assistance on a premise of "economic co-operation", where an element of "national benefit" for the donor is a legitimate part of the equation. All donors have an element of their aid budgets devoted to "technical assistance", arguably the highest welfare leverage, where expertise is made available to encourage self-help. Inevitably such programmes can only be funded on the basis of being free for recipients by means of cash grants.

The sharpest difference, however, emerges in the financing of infrastructure. Obviously, and indisputably, crucial for raising economic performance. To quote a recent recognised pundit: "Aid is vital because meeting the millennium development goals require well-governed, systematic public investments in basic infrastructure (roads, power, ports, water, sanitation and ecosystem conservation) and in social services (health, education and nutrition). These investments not only save lives but are preconditions for functioning markets and attracting private foreign investment." (Jeffrey Sachs – *FT* 7.6.04.)

It is in this area of investment that the distinct institutional and policy orientations of donors can have a decisive impact. Everyone has their own "national" way of doing it. For example, the KfW combines its provision of concessionary loans abroad with its development function within Germany, and German companies, with an exporting tradition of support from their banks, make reasonably sure of capturing the orders that flow. While France can employ agencies originally evolved for financing their colonial territories, but again with an undisguised predisposition to ensure that the resulting business goes to their firms. The common feature is that most such funds are "tied" either explicitly, or even when purportedly "untied" "tied" by informal practice. The UK has led the way in an "untying" campaign, but even when "tying" was in vogue, we found that the Japanese content of their "untied" aid was higher than the UK content of British "tied" aid. Even the US, as we discovered in the disputes over reconstruction aid following the Iraq war, is disposed to "tying".

If apparently a reversion to hideous "mercantalist" behaviour, in fact the world has never ceased to be "mercantalist". Recipients themselves, however, recognise that if donor taxpayers are making a contribution, it is not unreasonable that they should seek some measure of benefit. (Paul Channon, while Minister of Trade, met his Thai opposite number, who asked why Britain could not emulate the Japanese approach to aid – apparently, in response to international calls for food aid to sub-Saharan Africa, since Japan had no food surpluses, the government had allocated several $100m to their trading companies to acquire supplies from around the world and convey these to the aid agencies. Part of this had apparently been applied to purchase Thai cereals on a counter-trade basis for electrical generation and transmission equipment.)

In fact, Japan's development assistance is a clear example of a national approach that has differed from the theory-bound British perspective. Amply demonstrated by a remarkably clear series of Annual White Papers, and academic studies (notably, *Japan's Economic Aid* by Alan Rix (Croom Helm), and *The Manner of Giving: Strategic Aid and Japanese Foreign Policy* by Dennis Yasutomo (Lexington Books)).

Evolving from payments of post-Pacific War preparations to Asian nations such as Burma, Philippines, Indonesia and South Vietnam, the economic co-operation programme expanded as Japan's economy grew over succeeding decades. From the mid-60s, under a combination of pressures, including US demands to take a greater share of the costs of stimulating investment and growth in developing countries on the periphery of Communist influence, such as South Korea and Thailand; from a national viewpoint to secure energy and other raw material supplies; and also as a strategic diplomatic instrument. From the late 70s, as industrialised nations suffered more acutely from the second oil crisis, Japan substantially increased the scale of its aid flows – from 8.1% of Development Aid Committee totals in 1983 to 25% by 1987. While the geographical coverage shifted: if still predominantly in the Asian area, China became a more significant recipients as aid to South Korea was run down, and the range extended to Latin America, the Middle East and Africa. With Africa now receiving priority attention as the "race for resources" – led by a resurgent China – gathers pace.

The internal debate in Japan has been extensive, starting from its "peace constitution" viewing "economic co-operation" as a means to stabilise its economic and foreign relations. Blended into this has been a distinct national assurance that the country itself offered an alternative "development model" to that implicitly leveraged into the rationale of Western aid donors, with, indeed, the argument that one of the strengths of Japanese economic assistance was that it did not impose an ideology or national philosophy on recipient countries (Gaiko Forum, December 1988). While there have been typical bureaucratic tensions between MITI, and the Ministries of Finance and Foreign Affairs, by British standards, a much higher priority has been given to national economic and industrial concerns.

There have been occasional accusations of "predatory" practices, though it is arguable that Japan's approach represents a more coherent and effective blend of support measures: its technical assistance under the Japan International Co-operation Agency (JICA) draws on agricultural and craft traditions that are compatible with many Asian neighbours. Its bilateral programmes for infrastructure, energy and essential services are paralleled by incentives for Japanese companies to make direct investments, carrying with them technical transfer, and scope for increasing recipients' exports (also, incidentally, increased market share for Japan's companies).

But from the viewpoint of a country like Britain, which has eschewed any coherent approach to industry, perhaps the most striking example was the rationalisation of Japan's aluminium industry following the oil shocks that made the energy costs of domestic smelting prohibitive. After some controversy, the Asahan Hydro development in Indonesia was approved as a "national project" in 1975, with 70% of the $880 million costs provided by OECF, JICA and Export-Import Bank with OECF also taking a 50% equity stake in a consortium of five aluminium companies and trading firms to build new smelting capacity drawing upon a share of the hydroelectric capacity created. Another aluminium smelter and refinery were included in a $300 million mixed soft-loan and commercial credit package for Brazil (which by a quirk of history has the largest ethnic Japanese population outside Japan) in 1976, along with a steel plant, a harbour and paper pulp mills.

Latterly, during the "deflationary" 90s, the overall programme was reduced, but under pressure from leading nations encouraging Japan to increase its level of aid the ODA Charter was revised in August 2003 to "provide aid more strategically to promote the national interest" (Nikkei Weekly 12.4.04). Just for a change.

A balanced retrospective view of Japan's ODA is given in *The Japanese Journal* (September 2004 – *ODA-Japan's way*). Recalling that Japan was "once a developing nation" Furuta Hajime, director general of the Economic Co-operation Bureau of the Ministry of Foreign Affairs, remarks, "Out of post-war devastation, Japan rebuilt itself and managed to achieve rapid economic growth. Japan has carried out ODA in a manner that has met the expectations of developing countries that want to capitalise on Japan's experience." In the post-World War II period, Japan was itself a major recipient of humanitarian aid, and its infrastructure – including the Shinkansen train and the Tomei Expressway were constructed after receiving aid loans that Japan continued to repay until the 1990s.

Based on its own experience, Japan's ODA has focused on "supporting self-help efforts" – "If a country works on developing itself based on the efforts of the people themselves, that leads to true economic independence for that country. The guiding principle of Japan's ODA is to support such efforts. However, rather than pushing Japanese principles and national policy, Japan's policy is one of gaining a firm understanding of other countries' requests and then cooperating accordingly."

In concrete terms, Yen loans have primarily been targeted at infrastructure development such as roads, harbours, power plants and water/sewage systems: "loans make it possible to give the borrower a sense of responsibility. I think this is of great significance in terms of encouraging self-help efforts." With a historic focus on East Asia, typical examples given are: 32% of expressways in Bangkok, 56% of sewage treatment facilities in South Korea, the Beijing International Airport and Beijing Subway, and a coastal industrial complex in eastern Thailand. In consequence both domestic and overseas companies can "develop their businesses efficiently", and their strong subsequent export performance has evolved from, "What ODA does is to create conditions that enable private companies to give full rein to their strengths."

In support of indigenous skills development technical and research exchanges over the last half-century, the number of Japan's experts dispatched through ODA has reached 70,000 and the number of researchers and technicians accepted from developing countries for training, 270,000. Examples offered are the development of Chile as the world's second-largest salmon producer, and sustainable fresh water supplies to over 100 locations in Senegal, and post-conflict support in Kosovo, Palestine, East Timor, Afghanistan and Iraq. But also contributing to economic activities in tension-states, such as Noritake (the Crown Derby of Japan) setting up a ceramic factory in Sri Lanka in 1972, now with an output of $11 million and employing 1,200.

In the current vogue of institution development, under the rubric of "Intellectual Support", the distinct Japanese approach is summarised as "the act of thinking and working in co-operation with people from recipient countries, and listening to what they have to say. We need to theorise or synthesise this unique Japanese method and spread the word around the world." As distinct from other approaches, "as if preaching to lost sheep". While the voluntary arm and corporation with NGOs has been among the highest of donor countries.

[10] At the time, the Foreign Office had been charged to put commercial considerations higher on their agenda, and there was a constant stream of telegrams from posts abroad complaining that progress in securing an advantage against international competitors was being hampered by ODA's insistence on an "appraisal", involving a caravanserai of economists and experts to assess the case when none of the Britain's competitors did so. One especially curt telegram concluded, "Brash", which, one queried, looked like a new Foreign Office code. But, it turned out that the then Ambassador in Jakarta was Bob (Robert) Brash.

The staff costs for all this "quality" of aid could be relatively high – in international comparisons it transpired that Japan ran an aid programme eight-times the size of Britain's with less than a fifth of the staff. But among the more entertaining "developmental appraisals" was for the power station to be built for the Bharat Aluminium Company (BALCO) by GEC. This had been inspired as an

ATP case i.e. with an aid contribution alongside conventional export credit. GEC had a meeting with the ODA appraisal staff, ostensibly to ascertain what information they would be called upon to provide: being from the real world, the economic gobbledygook was way beyond their ken, but they managed to ascertain the drift of desirable answers. Their agent in India apparently discovered the itinerary of the prospective ODA appraisal team, and GEC despatched their own briefing team in advance to those whom the appraisal team were due to visit. The subsequent appraisal report was full of self-congratulation at the excellence and comprehensiveness of the ODA team's study.

[11] A nice vignette to illustrate this Treasury predisposition occurred when the closing stages were approaching on the award of the ANZCAN undersea cable contract – an undersea telecommunications cable connecting Australia/New Zealand/America/Canada – which was being hotly contested between STC, the traditional British contractor, and, since it was a major flagship project, competing proposals from Japan and France. With government support STC had already managed to secure the undersea cable links between the Gulf and Mumbai, Madras and Singapore, and the Singapore/Indonesia extension. Consequently, STC had an edge on track record and links with the major telecoms customers, but the selection process was to be undertaken by a group of telecom operators balanced according to their options for take-up of capacity.

AT&T, one of the largest operators due to take a share of options, indicated at a late stage that they still had a few regulatory hurdles to accomplish, and hence would not be able to put money on the line by the due date, even though they had every intention of being a major user. The dilemma was whom AT&T would request to purchase their proposed stake and hold it while their regulatory process was completed. If, for example, Canada took this holding on temporarily, there was a high risk of their votes being used to select Alcatel, the French contender. Conversely, if BT could be persuaded to volunteer to hold the AT&T stake, then a more balanced decision to favour STC could be expected. The sum involved to take up the AT&T options was relatively low by major project standards – some £2 million.

BT's position was that they had no interest in paying this sum, even though they had a firm declaration from AT&T to take over the options. STC would have been the obvious agent, but they also said that this would be too onerous. Whilst impatient at yet another example of British industry's reluctance to take on a liability when they clearly stood to gain, as a compromise we proposed a guarantee to BT, but to avoid any accusation of subsidy – and admittedly also reflecting impatience with the company, we indicated a swingeing premium. When this had been through the Treasury hoops, we had a meeting with the companies that allowed us the rare opportunity to use the formula, "We have good news and bad news. The bad news is that we cannot approve a guarantee. But the good news is that you can have a grant." The companies found this inexplicable, but took the lolly. And, in the event, STC won the contract, AT&T took up their allocation so that the guarantee would not have been called, and we might even have made a few quid from the premium.

On the other hand, the Treasury were very co-operative when we were confronted by the insistence of countries like Indonesia and China on receiving aid in "long-term low-interest loans" on the pattern of other countries that had established development banks. Lacking a comparable agency, we had to evolve an "annuity" mechanism, where a sum of cash-aid was "invested" and the return applied to reduce the interest charged on an ECGD backed loan – not an entirely satisfactory device, but at least an innovative approach to meet a weakness in the UK institutional structure.

[12] Its official. Just see, "So far as Britain is concerned, if private bankers will not provide private capital, then capital is probably better not provided."... "If a right-wing Conservative government was not prepared to get rid of export credits," one official says, "how likely is it that a government of the centre-left will do so?" (Pp 237 ff *The Secret Treasury* by David Lipsey). No other country benefits from the disadvantage of putting their national interests in the hands of the criteria of City "private banks". Indeed, when have British bankers shown any interest in industry? In practice, however, political risk has been an area that the private insurance market has been unwilling to accept, understandably given the scale of potential liabilities and lack of spread. With the result that governments have accepted this role, and guarantees of export credit are an inherent part of the international market, with implications across many industrial sectors. Consequently, the Treasury approach has effectively been a "de-industrialisation policy" by default.

[13] To beat the French at their own game and spike their triumphalism on the occasion of a Heads of Government meeting undoubtedly played into Mrs Thatcher's combative instincts. We never – as is usual from our political leaders – received any accolades, but we could rely on a supportive attitude from Number 10 thereafter, directly opposed to the inherent bias of the Treasury and others in "Trade", so long as she was around. As a reverse tribute one can confirm that, having posed the bland question, "What's your impression of Mrs Thatcher?" in countries as diverse as China, Indonesia, Mexico, India and Sri Lanka, the response translated from the local vernacular was always, "The only Englishman with balls."

The credit for winning the Sicartsa project goes to Ranjit Mathrani. Something of a conundrum, Ranjit was the son of a senior Indian Government official, intelligent, alert, with a sharp wit, and adept at the intricacies of export finance. But his own worst enemy in an over-assertive style that ranged from bad "people management" to appearing rude. But with talents best expressed as a loner, Sicartsa was ideal. After the usual protracted period of companies submitting bids and skirmishing, Ranjit reported on the Friday afternoon before the G7 meeting the following Monday that the latest news from Mexico was that the French had moved in to make their final negotiating pitch.

Since events were liable to move fast – considerably faster than Whitehall's ability to "consult" over a weekend, and we were well aware of the limits of "support" agreed between Departments, we left it for Ranjit to act as events dictated with no more constraint than "to keep me in touch". Every French move was trumped. By Monday Davy had been awarded the contract. And furious complaints were levelled by the local French ambassador. The lesson for the French, and indeed other competitors, is that in the unlikely event of Britain ever being competitive in major projects again, if they had timed their final moves for Wednesday, the ability of Whitehall to respond would be so constipated that they would have won hands down.

There were subsequently newsreel pictures of the steel fabrications for Sicartsa being trundled around Britain's roads before being shipped. The eventual outcome of the project is still clouded, since the Sicartsa company was a victim of the Mexican financial crisis and required substantial restructuring.

[14] At the end of the final clearing-up negotiations, as we slumped exhausted into the airline seats bound for transit in Bangkok for London, our Banker friend remarked something to the effect that the negotiations had been tough – rich, since he had made no contribution, even to spinning out time, and no doubt got a whacking bonus on the strength of legwork by DTI and ECGD. Repitition of this situation was probably responsible for more defections from DTI and ECGD than any other.

[15] The NTPC, by the time of the Rihand negotiations, had built up a positive track record. Assembled from indigenous expertise of electrical and power engineers, with staff who themselves had participated in building stations in India, their command of the disciplines and technical intricacies was unimpeachable.
They had cut their teeth in acquiring stations from several international sources ranging from Italy to Japan. And the negotiations with NEI were jokingly labelled the "British experience", while their contrasts of different national styles was always entertaining – the Japanese were characterised by fielding a large team of 20 or more, would engage in very little direct oral exchanges, but would diligently note every question and submit immaculately detailed answers the following morning.

Most striking, however, was the high morale of the NTPC team under Mr Shah as Chairman, and Mr Bami, their Finance Director, and the bonds of mutual respect among all their staff. Their resilience and disciplines blended with a relaxed humour, and they had a sound judgment of crucial issues, and of the special demands of the Indian context. It is a passing tribute that ODA's appraisal acknowledged that a "negotiated" approach was as demanding – India some might argue, more so – as the conventional competitive bidding procedure.

[16] Probably the most impenetrable topic, whether in power station construction or anywhere else, is reconciling boiler specifications. Whereas the premise of the project was that CEGB standards and procedures would prevail, in the detailed contract negotiations following the "intent" agreement, NEI had apparently conceded that Indian standards could be accepted for the boiler. An assemblage of experts to elucidate the differences between Indian and CEGB boiler specifications, their origins and practical import produced a totally incomprehensible exchange of verbiage and mathematical formulae; totally

beyond the conciliation powers of any normal human being. And we could only surmise at the time and cost of sorting this out.

[17] It was reported in June 2005 that POSCO, the leading Korean steel producer, had been granted a concession to build and operate a steel plant in Orissa, and one is inclined to suspect that the old Daitari project study had been dusted off.

[18] When I last encountered the cheery Mr Ganupati, he had been made Permanent Secretary of the Ministry for Small Firms – among the most impossible of bureaucratic assignments and bound to test his humour. Since, under the Indian regulatory regime, small firms were not allowed to go bankrupt.

[19] Since its invention in the early days of the IDU, and Britain's presentation on the state aids at the OECD, the term "additionality" now has universal currency, being a standard element of the economic commentators' toolkit. But following the standard laws of linguistic development, its meaning has tended to be adapted to national or other contexts. For the purposes of discussions with the Indian Ministry of Finance, it meant, "more aid".

[20] Throughout the duration of PEP, despite DTI Ministers – from Keith Joseph through several successors, and indeed the Prime Minister – all acknowledging that free and fair trade was a desirable objective, but so long as leading exporting countries chose not to recognise this, unilateral disarmament was not a realistic response, there was consistent pressure "to review support for overseas projects". Many long and fruitless hours were wasted on this exercise – if modestly entertaining in disclosing the false rationale underlying the British school of economics – on comparing notes, none of our international opposite numbers were similarly afflicted, leave alone as a hobby from coping with a fast-moving commercial scene.

This Whitehall farce reached zany proportions with the Byatt Report, a document purporting to assess the costs and risks of support for capital goods exports. (Ian Byatt* was a senior economist in the Treasury, who later went on to become a Water Industry Regulator – we actually went to the same Oxford college, and Japanese colleagues when I was working with a major trading company were puzzled that instead of their convention of "–kai", or clubs of ex-colleagues from university, school etc, my experience was having spent most of one's career rubbishing my ex-colleague.) The first target was the "interest subsidy" arising from the difference between Sterling interest rates and the fixed-rate of the OECD Consensus. Not surprisingly, for a document emanating from the Treasury, the terminology had a high element of special pleading, if not, indeed, special semantics.

A "subsidy" is generally defined as payments or assurances from some state agency that distort prices: the most notable current examples are the Common Agricultural Policy of the EU, and subsidies paid to the US, Japanese and the farmers of other countries, which distort the market against produce from developing countries. The nonsense of adopting the term "subsidy" in the case of exports supported by ECGD is plain when all the suppliers, contractors and consultants allegedly benefiting from this "subsidy" would have been unanimous in calling for this "subsidy" to be reduced i.e. for Sterling interest rates to be reduced to a level proximate to the Consensus rate. Especially since, so far as companies engaged on negotiations with overseas clients, or indeed actually engaged on undertaking a project, are concerned, the "subsidy" can be increased or decreased without their involvement, and without affecting the commercial terms of their deal.

That there is a cost in the interest make-up payments is undeniable. But these costs arise from the setting of national interest rates: at the time, the then Chancellor, Nigel Lawson, was adamant that the setting of interest rates was in the Treasury's domain. It should have been part of good management for the Treasury to have a program on its computer to calculate how these interest make-up costs would vary with whatever juggling they wished to do with interest rates. And this should have been taken into account in the decision; presumably, this is now a factor for the Bank of England's Monetary Policy Committee to take into its calculations as it contemplates its next "Maradona" feint. But to attempt to shuffle off responsibility with the label of "subsidy" is rank dishonestly.

The galling feature of this continuing background rumble was that the DTI's own economists were tacit supporters of the Treasury argument. Whereas, under normal Whitehall conventions, a Department's officials are supposed to support their Ministerial position, which was continuously to follow a pragmatic line so long as a lack of transparency, multilateral agreement and discipline were lacking, the Department's economists apparently saw themselves as somehow exempt. If the popular view of economists is that, on an analogy with apocryphal accounts of Italian delegates at EU meetings, putting two in a room together would yield five different views, not in Whitehall. There they form some hybrid between Midwich Cuckoos and a zany mediaeval freemasonry, all resolutely committed to avoiding contact with reality.

The exercise culminated in a weird jamboree under the Public Finance Foundation in October 1984 (PFF Discussion Paper No 1) chaired by Edmund Dell, who had been if anything among the more pragmatic school of Ministers. The Treasury by no means carried the day, despite reinforcements from the *FT* in the shape of Martin Woolf, who was gracious enough to admit that he was "not in any way an expert on capital goods industries and make no claims to be so". But Ian Byatt delivered the ultimate Treasury maxim, "the market is only moderately imperfect" – one could question the semantics of this proposition, but its serves as an illustration of the Treasury view that it is apparently an adequate approximation to accept the assumption that the market is perfect. In practice, as everyone actually in the market knows only too well, and with mountains of studies from OECD and analyses of other countries' policies, the "market" is incurably vitiated.

At the conclusion of this barn dance, one suggested that industry should take the Byatt report as illustrative of the idiom of Whitehall debate, and evidence that this country "is unique in having so little community of conception" between central government and the realities of business in global markets.

[21] A less remarked instance, but not less insidious for that, of the "unrivalled services of the City" that conspire to screw up all attempts by British companies to match international competition, is the treatment of "bonds". If in practice a subset of a nationally conservative treatment of "contingent liabilities" (Why is the Treasury so reluctant to accept guarantees that are routine in the financing of public goods in other countries?), in commercial impact, this is up there with "short-termism". And like "short-termism", industry has been loath to stick its head above the parapet, except for the occasional outburst from Lord Weir. Despite a continuing flow of complaints from contractors, matched only by their reluctance to take up the issue with their banks, we put Patrick Hodgson – a secondment from Schroders – to analyse the issues.

He produced an excellent analysis, no doubt somewhere in the archives. But the scam goes back to the days when Saudi Arabia was embarking on an investment programme to apply its oil revenues to upgrade the country – there were a large number of projects, which attracted the interest of suppliers and contractors worldwide. And competitive bidding threw up a slew of tenders that were so low as to be irresponsible – there are still remnants of projects where the contractor ran out of funds dotted around the kingdom. To impose some discipline on this unruly process, the Saudi authorities were persuaded – there is apparently some evidence that the idea was coined by some imaginative British banks – to demand "bid bonds", usually set as a percentage, 5%-10%, of the tender price. These "bonds" would be an unqualified promise to pay this sum if the bidder failed to proceed if selected. The "bond" would have to be signed by a reputable financial agency, in the case of British companies, by their banks.

For British banks this was "money for old rope", since it cost little beyond ink and paper to write an "undertaking to pay", and they could eliminate all risks themselves by "charging" the value of the bond against the company's assets. And for this excellent service, the banks charged a premium – ranging on inspection from 0.8 % to 1.8%, and sometimes higher, of the bond value. All for no risk. For the company, however, under Britain's ancient banking conventions, with overdrafts and loans limited to the write-down value of assets, the "charge" exacted by the banks reduced the scope for the company to borrow to finance its normal ongoing business.

The practice of "bonds" spread to "performance bonds" that could reach levels of 10% of total project value, ostensibly to ensure adequate completion of the contract. But, if, for example, delayed completion might provide an obvious pretext, in practice the causes of delay could be complex, and may indeed have arisen from failures of the client. So, for banks, an excellent opportunity to maximise their returns "for old rope", but the unqualified nature of the bond in theory allowing it to be called irrespective of antecedent causes, left companies even more exposed. At one CBI conference on bonding, indeed, a company representative, after remarking that they viewed their bank as a bigger threat than their international competitors, said that it adopted the practice of providing the client with a signed undated cheque, on the basis that they could halt a capricious attempt to cash a cheque more readily than its bank's "reputational" concern to pay immediately according to the open terms of its bond.

Other features of this abstruse area was the practice of banks, on the argument that the bond was an unlimited promise to pay, retaining the demand on companies to pay premia long after the pretext of the bond itself had transpired. Even better than "old rope". And even better still was a "cascade" effect: the company in the lead on the contract would understandably lay off these liabilities on to subcontractors, demanding counter guarantees, and the subcontractors in turn would seek backing from their bank. But there was no "netting off" as these back-to-back arrangements took place, even when it was the same bank involved for the contractor and the subcontractor. Consequently, the "cascade" could in aggregate place charges on company assets by values as high as 150%, and more, of the original bond.

A vivid illustration of the real impact of this practice was a call from an ex-employee of Fletcher Smith – one of the great old names of British industry going back over 150 years, which had at one time built virtually all the world's sugar plants. He reported that under the pressure of outstanding bonds, the Finance Director had forbidden the company to take on any new orders. Clearly, if a company desists from its leading activity, contraction must result, and, from informal inquiries and contacts through my Itochu process-plant colleagues, the company has become a design and engineering specialist: first, as part of Booker, relying on Japanese traders to carry out the plant-purchasing and contracting, and then, with the dismantling of Booker, sold to a French company, Fives Cail.

Unravelling this skein led us to the sacred cloisters of the Bank of England; since the convenient get out for the banks was that their practice reflected the reserve requirements imposed on them by the Bank. Presentations to the BOTB, and separate seminars, occasioned outrage, exasperation, frustration, and all varieties of ums and ahs. Not least because in reality the chances of a bond being called capriciously were minute – the only instance in current memory was Libya following their revolution in the late 60s. In other words, the remuneration squeezed out of companies by banks was wholly disproportional to the reality of risk, quite apart from the resulting restriction on corporate activity.

Needless to add, this whole charade was an exclusively British preoccupation: as the Westland case in India illustrated, French companies, often with state participation, did not have to go through these convolutions. While German and Japanese companies treat these transitory liabilities as obligations to be discarded, if performance of a contract is carried through, and if so, then with a low or negligible probability of being called. They are also, perhaps, less accustomed to pursuing "money for old rope".

VIGNETTES

WINNING BUSINESS

Among our round of contacts with significant companies involved in overseas projects, at one review session with Bechtel, I inquired how they got business. "With great difficulty," came back as the standard response. But with the rejoinder, "One thing's for sure. By the time you hear about it, it's too late."

MAGGIE'S LOT

Between Keith Joseph and David Young, who in their own ways challenged the extremes of human intellectual capacities, there was a bewildering sequence of other figures rushing in and out of DTI's Ministerial suites.

One of John Prescott's more memorable political quotes comes from his time as Shadow Transport Secretary in the Thatcher years: "We have had eight Secretaries of State for Transport in twelve years... It is the only part of this government's transport policy where you can truthfully say: 'Don't worry, there will be another one along in a minute.'" On the same analogy, Trade/Industry/DTI were the Keystone Cops on location at Clapham Junction. As the Jenkins, Lamonts, Clarkes (and Clarks), Maudes, Hamiltons, Cockfields, Hoggs, Lucas's, Notts, Atkins's, Bakers, Biffens, Brittans, Ridleys, Channons, Parkinsons and a cast beyond recollection rushed between platforms.

Even the most vainglorious would find it taxing to identify any accomplishments that could have made a lasting positive contribution to the nation's industrial future, adaptability or trade performance. And the most that are left as signatures are recollections of some more entertaining moments. Where to begin?

John Biffen

No one can recall his place in the queue, but he was among the more pragmatic of our senior Ministers. Attending his first NEDO Council meeting where the subject of overseas projects was on the agenda, he kept passing notes back to his accompanying officials. To the assembled quorum of "the greatest and the goodest" this appeared as a diligent Minister seeking clarification from his officials: in practice, the notes were in the vein – "He's been saying that for 20 years" – "I thought he'd died" – "Now I know he did".

On the way back to the office, in painfully exasperated voice, he inquired how many of these rituals he would have to attend. When told Council meetings occurred every three months, he audibly groaned. A bright official, in an attempt at consolation, said that the next meeting was due to be taking a paper on "quality" inspired by his predecessor, which elicited the response, "Knowing my predecessor (John Nott), I'm surprised that he inspired anything, leave alone on quality."

Kenneth Baker

He subsequently moved on to Education and for a period attained the dizzy heights of Chairman of the Conservative Party, in DTI had a functionary title involving "Science". But he was also given to enjoying "promotional" overseas visits. On the other hand, the convention had developed, largely from Cecil Parkinson's time in the seat, for the Minister of Trade to lead delegations of industrialists to overseas markets. From the viewpoint of pursuing projects, the least helpful setting was to be part of a gaggle of industrialists – all expecting prima donna attention – when each project in a country was at a different level of evolution and required individual treatment. So Kenneth Baker was an ideal coach on which to ride postilion and gain access to key Ministerial personalities. As a sideline were some "tourist" escapades like being nearly drowned under a waterfall in the Philippines, and a helicopter flight over the crater of Krakatoa. He had expressed an interest in visiting a Himalayan hill station, and suggested Simla as the first choice. I cajoled him into choosing Darjeeling as a less frequented alternative, not least because of my own early childhood connections.

Before the journey to Darjeeling, a few days were scheduled in Calcutta to visit the head officials of Coal India, with whom we had a running aid programme to assist in introducing longwall mining techniques, pursue power projects, and visit Durgapur, where there was a 50's-vintage steel plant originally built by the British but in need of refurbishment. The outward leg to Durgapur was by road – just before the monsoon season with both temperature and humidity close to 100 – and the tour of the plant included a view of the blast furnace in operation from underneath: with flames leaking from its base, and in a Stygian gloom there were sundry figures moving about apparently knee-deep in pig iron, Kenneth had the grace to remark, "Chris, you do take me to some extraordinary places." This excursion was followed by refreshments at a Dunlop tire factory, where the steam within the plant gave us yet another sauna experience, so that our suits had to be squeezed out like flannels when, forewarned, we changed into fresh clothing at the Dunlop guesthouse. The factory, now presumably owned by Sumitomo, boasted one of the leading clinics and experts on the treatment of rabies and served not just the workforce but was a medical centre for the local area. Then we returned on the "coal express" to Calcutta with the luxury of dinner on board.

On arrival in Darjeeling, Kenneth Baker was the first British Minister to set foot there for nearly five decades. And everyone left messages pleading for his time. It required advice from the local political agent to work out an itinerary that satisfied most of the competing claims over a weekend. This included a trip to Gum monastery, where, because we were outside the tourist season, two dishevelled monks were rustled up to perform on their immense Tibetan trumpets; a visit to a tea plantation lower in one of the valleys, which had a sophisticated array of equipment to receive TV and ensure continuous backup power, which the proprietor boasted allowed uninterrupted reception of Test Matches around the world; Sunday lunch at the Planters Club, to which the prefects from St Paul's School still turned up in blazers and grey flannels; and a visit to the Tenzing Mountaineering Institute, which was conveniently placed to take in a visit to the zoo.

When we came to the zoo, a gate into a wide area of fenced hillside, Kenneth asked what particularly he should see. The curator replied that their prize inhabitants were a pair of Siberian tigers that had been given to Mrs Gandhi by Mr Khrushchev, and Darjeeling had been the location closest to their natural habitat. After twenty minutes wandering about, we asked about the tigers and were taken to an area surrounded by an obviously more robust enclosure. After peering around, with an exclamation and a pointed finger, something with stripes could just be spotted through some bushes. "That's one. Where's the other?" asked Kenneth. The curator pointed to a hut on the edge of the enclosure, and, waving his hands around his head, explained, "Pugla! Pugla!" – one of the few remaining words from an infant mastery of the language, I translated, "Mad".

"Really. We must see this," and Kenneth strode towards the hut. Facing outside the enclosure was a window, closed by two solid wood panels, and these were swung open. And there, a foot away behind some bars were the bloodshot eyes and slavering jaws of a demented Siberian tiger. "Rather reminiscent of the Prime Minister?" I suggested. "Mild by comparison," replied Kenneth.

The saddest echo of the past was not the setting, for, apart from the large numbers of four-wheel drive vehicles that had become a standard form of transport, the view did not disappoint memory, including the Everest Hotel and the spectacular sight of Kanchenjunga at dawn before the monsoon mist rose to obscure the mountain. But that the resident "Brits" were down to two. One, a stalwart imperial lady with immense vigour for advanced years having survived husbands in Kenya and Asia, was running the Planters Club – she sadly passed on a few months after the visit. And the other was a retired engineer who supported himself by servicing the old diesel units on tea plantations – we obtained a list of his most critical spares, and the British companies supplied a batch of these subsequently for free.

The visit, however, had a sequel. Kenneth Baker had remarked on my desert boots – light suede with thick rubber soles, left over from my Saudi Arabian Defence Scheme days. He was told that a pair could be made for him locally. The shoemaker duly turned up at the hotel with an exercise book and catalogue; with a pencil he traced around each of the Minister's feet placed on facing pages, and noted his name. Kenneth ordered a similar suede shoe from the catalogue, but also seemed taken by several other designs and ordered these as well. Inevitably, these were not delivered by the time the visit concluded. A few months later, on a routine visit to Delhi, I was told that there was a parcel in the High Commission – the package with a half-dozen pairs of shoes had apparently made its way from Darjeeling to Calcutta, and then by next convenient journey to Delhi – with an outstanding bill. This I paid, and the excess baggage charge to take it back to London. Delivering the package with invoice to Kenneth Baker's office, it turned out the shoes didn't fit.

Cecil Parkinson

He turned up originally as Minister of Trade, and almost his first session began with, "How can we get rid of all the trade-distorting practices of the previous government?" Officials gazed at each other blankly, and one volunteered that the last time Britain had breached its international trade obligations had probably been in the 1930s. A perfect illustration of the invariable absence of knowledge accumulated in opposition, and their resulting tendency to believe their own propaganda.

He popped sporadically in and out of the Department, but his most remarkable quote was when he had an "Energy" hat on. He apparently takes some pride in the privatisation of electricity – the jury must remain out whether, as the surplus 20% of generating capacity at the time is sweated out, we may confront brownouts, though investment bankers fees and top management remuneration have hit undreamt of heights as ownership has changed more often than consumers could conceivably follow. But just before the great day, he addressed a lunchtime meeting with power-generating manufacturers with the assurance, "There'll be plenty of orders for all of you." Since British industry's capacity had historically been focused on coal-fired stations, whereas privatisation was bound to lead to the "dash" for gas-fired combined cycle stations, this declaration should have been accompanied by his only immortal utterance – "You're supposed to laugh," at a Conference when he too was at the dizzy heights of Chairman of the Conservative Party.

Norman Tebbit

By far the best of the lot – his most perverse quality is the pains to which he goes to create "the bovver boy" image, which disguises what a nice guy he actually is. He had done apprenticeships on short tours in junior Ministerial posts in Trade and Industry, before becoming Secretary of State DTI in 1983. But it was in the two previous years at Employment that he had steered the adroit campaign on Trade Union reform to "return the unions to their members" which remains probably the only lasting national gain from the Thatcher years.[1] Sharp, sure. And a ready knack to spot the jugular in opposing arguments, and quick at going for it. Which made him a very good Departmental Minister, testing officials on the one hand, and, when settled on a line, taking on other Ministers with a more than fair chance of winning.

One of the more charming episodes was a meeting with his French opposite number in London. Again, as usual, we consulted our counterpart French officials on an agenda. Since we were co-operating to secure the Daya Bay nuclear station, a review of the current state of negotiations was an obvious item. Also, the umpteenth dispute with the US whether Airbus was getting any unfair support, compared to the vast cost-plus contracts trowelled out to Boeing, GE others etc. And, more contentiously, a helicopter order in India, for which Westland was competing against a French contender, where we had been matching French concessions in finance from the ATP provision as they progressively raised the level of concession (subsidy). With a couple more topics, this barely seemed enough to fill a meeting scheduled for an hour. "Don't worry," responded my French colleague.

The day duly arrived, and Edith Cresson turned up with a couple of French officials. The nuclear power exchange was disposed of quickly, since we were in virtually continuous touch with the French, and so too the well-worn arguments with the Americans over civil aircraft subsidies.

Even the helicopter issue was settled in minutes, since before the meeting, to meet further French moves which pushed the discounted subsidy above one of their agreed minima, the Treasury had insisted that the aid should be provided as a grant i.e. 100% concessionality/subsidy, on the zany principle that this somehow imbued the transaction with "purity". So, whatever deals the French may have been ready to propose were immediately scuppered, and all they could do was gasp, "100%!" and no doubt drew extraordinary conclusions that there was some special British political or industrial rationale. So, in fact, the agenda ran out even earlier.

But, with the merest narrowing of an eye, fluttering of an eyelash and a whisp of a smile, Edith Cresson switched it on. And Norman responded, if not quite like a teenager on his first date, but into a sort of badinage not usually encountered in official meetings. My French opposite number winked, with the suggestion of a gesture of confirmation.

Norman, of course, also went on to the dizzy heights of Chairman of the Conservative Party.

Other engaging members of the passing throng were Paul Channon, whose background was comfortable enough to insulate him from the more extreme passions of political ambition. But also less dependent on Prime Ministerial graces and favours: notably, while Minister of Trade, he held on tenaciously to a position under Thatcherite attack, and perhaps even earned promotion as a result. Alan Clark was a distinctly different Minister from the usual run, and quite a challenge as he posed a rather unconventional line of questioning, especially when bridling at the more obviously public school/Oxbridge brand of official. Neither, nor indeed David Young, quite made it to the dizzy heights of Chairman of the Conservative Party.

How these compare with Blair's bunch, one has not had the proximity to judge. Though the latter have watched with equanimity an even more serious decline in trade and industrial performance.

David (Lord) Young

The only safe thing to say about David Young is nothing. On personal experience of his handling of a submission, checking elsewhere in the Department, no one could offer any evidence that he had read anything. When Michael Heseltine was surprised that "strategy" was a forbidden word in DTI, this followed a tradition established by David Young where any symptom of intelligent thought beyond "who–.o–o–o–o–o–sh" was a treasonable offence.

Correction: In response to a question from Lord Jenkins on the 29th of June 1988, Lord Young responded, "When an economy is growing as fast as ours is growing, it is quite likely there will be temporary imbalances and periods in which imports will exceed exports." With the trade deficit having topped £100bn, albeit in the current recession running at an annual rate of £ 80-90bn, and no prospect of balance being attained for several generations, if ever, this will ring down the ages as an exemplar of the level of economic wisdom attained by the Thatcherite gospel.

WE HAVE A PROBLEM

In the mid-Eighties, David Hardy, then Chairman of DTI's Engineering Advisory Board, invited me along to an Economist "Meet the Gurus" seminar to hear Kenichi Ohmae. After a typically crisp and well-articulated account of his "borderless world", when it came to questions I posed the query why, in many industries where British companies had spectacularly failed, Japanese companies were able to employ the same resources of British labour, managers and suppliers with outstanding success.

His reply was on the lines that Japanese companies found the British workforce reliable and adaptable, and the managers steady and professional. "But," he added, "you seem to have a class problem at the top of your companies."

There must be something in this. Shortly after, chairing a session on one or other of David Young's "Initiatives" – on skills, probably – I recalled this anecdote in summing up. The audience of a couple of hundred middle managers, by now mostly nodding off after realising that "Initiative" meant anything except money, instantly burst into clamorous cheers and whoops comparable to England winning the World Cup. DTI wasn't picking up many plaudits from anywhere at the time, and numbers of fellow officials from nearby offices peered cautiously through the Conference Room door to see what could conceivably have caused such boisterous applause.

Now, probably, the same scenario would provoke a riot.

DOES MARKET SHARE MATTER?

High on the list of absurd utterances, but equally among the most revealing, occurred at a meeting with John Hoskyns, self-styled Thatcher guru, but at the time Director General of the Institute of Directors.

Andrew Duguid, an ex-DTI colleague who had meandered into the seat of being his adviser, had prompted the meeting presumably on the pretext that I had paid more attention than most to the competitive strengths of Japanese companies. Hoskyns, apparently seriously, asked this question. A polite reply would have been difficult, since, whereas even the best companies such as Honda can have periods of annual losses – as indeed they did in the 90s recession – they can recover; but without any "market share" the only future for a business is the knacker's yard.

ARNOLD WEINSTOCK

The first of several brushes with Arnold Weinstock occurred when the "the young" Weinstock had taken over AEI, and while I was monitoring officer of the "first" Saudi Arabian Air Defence Scheme.

When signed in the early 60s, this was Britain's largest ever single export order – on a current value basis, it still is – encompassing three squadrons of Lightnings, a Flying-training School with BAC146 trainers, a Lightning conversion unit, a Technical College, communications systems, and a series of complex "stack-beam" early warning and interception radars with a related command centre. There were three main contractors: BAC (now the Wharton division of BAe), Airwork, responsible for the initial manning and training, and AEI for the radars. At Saudi Government insistence, a prerequisite for gaining the order was a Fourth Agreement, effectively a joint-and-several undertaking whereby each contractor undertook to make good any deficiencies in the performance of any one of the others. (The only time you will see British management break into a run is at the mention of "joint-and-several" as they rush for the nearest exit.)

Anyway, Weinstock's appraisal of AEI before he took them over had obviously not revealed this obligation. But on learning of it, he immediately demanded that AEI should withdraw from the Fourth Agreement. This would have removed the linchpin for the whole complex structure, and inevitably led to the Saudi Government cancelling the contracts and handing the order to the US, who were at best unwilling partners to the deal – there had been a fully-fledged US competing bid involving Lockheed, Raytheon, and others, out of which, as a compromise, they were awarded the air defence missiles. Unbundling this deal was therefore viewed with consternation by the other companies and the government.

But at the meeting with the Minister of Aviation of the day, Arnold opened with the quintessential statement, "Minister, I don't like any of my pennies in anyone else's pocket." In the event, the government stood against withdrawal from the Fourth Agreement. But the stronger argument was that such a course would lay GEC open to action by the other consortium partners who had expended considerable resources to secure the contracts. It was left for GEC to reach an accommodation with its partners, insisting upon whatever protections it could achieve without jeopardising the Agreement.

Even when only a shadowy figure, the Weinstock spirit could be influential. Later, during the Benn episode at the Department of Industry, Kent Instruments – one of those heraldic "British" firms – was being targeted for takeover by Brown Boveri (the BB of ABB). And the workforce appealed against this "Swiss invasion". Benn charged us to find another option. The only company that showed any interest, and that no more than mildly lukewarm, was GEC. But their image among the workforce was akin to Attila, yet they came around to support a competing bid. How serious the effort, we don't know, but when BB had raised their offer and won, Michael Lewis, the company secretary and one of the Weinstock triumvirate, sent the Department a bill for legal fees. (Not paid!)

More vividly, under the terms for examining "selective financial assistance" applications for regional or special support from industry, the test of "additionality" was introduced as a basic hurdle in appraising individual cases: in short, it was an assessment whether the subsidy would achieve a genuine incremental shift in the company's activities. Given the eccentricities of GEC's management style, the only final test could be by a direct exchange with Arnold himself – so periodically there were sessions between a group of officials and Arnold to review the cases from different bits of GEC. Then these were reported back to the Industrial Development Advisory Board for their decision.

A typical exchange might involve a couple of cases where officials would point out that heavy investment already in some product or facility suggested that additional investment was an incremental addition essential to secure returns from what had been done until then, and after a few minutes of cut and thrust he would accept "a draw", and set them to one side. On another, he would pull out the infamous chart of "Bond ratios" from the bottom drawer of his desk and point to the funding that had already been approved without generating any returns, with the conclusion, "If they asked for more money, they wouldn't get it. But if they say that some more money will get them a contribution from government, that's different." In this case, officials would call it "a draw".

In one such case, the GEC Division's managing director had obviously lost patience with the appraisal process and written to say that unless he had a response by a particular date, he would proceed anyway. Probably the worst argument for "additionality" – when officials pointed this out, Arnold asked to see the letter, and the manager concerned was awoken from his afternoon musing by a curt Arnold on the telephone, "Dougie, I've got the Ministry people here" – he was never clear on Whitehall nomenclature – "What are you doing writing them letters that prevent them giving me money?"

At least you knew where Arnold was coming from! Unlike many other "top" industrialists, who professed all manner of higher motives. And his tight cash controls created a consistently strong discipline – on a visit to GEC's management training centre, it was proudly remarked that the vegetable plot had an internal rate of return of 15%. But it also produced one of the most professional "project teams" at the Rugby division for securing power station projects in difficult overseas markets.

The tragedy was that, whilst any good company needs a bit of Weinstock – Toyota's continuing emphasis on eliminating "waste" would be analogous – this bread alone is not enough, and needs to be complemented by the drive for new momentum and new markets to advance against international competitors. GEC was actually more innovative than many commentators allow, but it was that ugly 3 to 4-year gap of development and proving with no tangible returns that always balked the cash-driven approach.

Yet one of his human failings was a sense of humour – one recalls a session when I was apparently being "carpeted" for some incursion by officialdom into an area that Arnold considered the exclusive preserve of business, where the moment he had been brought to a smile, the atmosphere collapsed. One of his less-remarked contributions was the numbers of ex-GEC managers who contributed to many other businesses struggling through successive recessions of the 70s and 80s. A few years apprenticeship in Weinstock's GEC was probably worth any number of MBAs.

RETURN TO INDIA

Suffering a near-miss in finding a pretext to return to India when Concorde's prototype world tour was forced to divert from Delhi because of an early monsoon, a real justification for visits a few times a year came in the 80s when responsible for supporting overseas projects. The range of projects being pursued – power stations, hydro schemes, rail modernisation, steel and minerals, coal mining and IT – offered many opportunities to meet a wide spectrum of Indian officials and industrialists.

On one occasion, while in Delhi staying with the Commercial Councillor, Roger Beetham, we learned that a delegation was in town from British Rail to meet their opposite numbers. Rail India is historically a major government agency, sufficiently powerful to have its own separate budget. Doubting whether the delegation could spot or respond appropriately to any signs of commercial opportunities, we joined the introductory dinner. The British Rail delegation, their burly rail tradition disguised in immaculate lounge suits, were more than matched by their Rail India hosts, who were equally robust and immaculately attired, but since most were Sikhs, with perfectly crisped turbans and rolled beards.

As their eyes met, inhibitions were cast aside, and they hurled arms around each other in impassioned bear hugs. This euphoria persisted as we sat down to dinner with much back-slapping, nudges and protestations, "Once a rail man, always a rail man" – yes, Britain even had rail men at one time – or "One rail man can always tell another rail man" to the point where the rest of the assembled company were in danger of being excluded.

So I chipped in, "So far as I can tell, you look more like a bunch of bank managers." Instant outrage. Cries of "Bank managers!" and "Bank managers! You, a civil servant, dare to call us bank managers!" To which I responded with the best aloofness that I could manage, "How many of you were born on a railway, leave alone on an Indian railway?" For the evening at any rate, I was voted an "honorary Indian rail man".

Out of a bagful of recollections, perhaps the most historic was attending, with Peter Carey and Sir John Thomson – our then High Commissioner – the farewell lunch for the last survivor of the Indian Civil Service. Assembled were a couple of score of present and past Permanent Secretaries of the Indian Administrative Service (IAS), the successor to the ICS. This allowed Peter, at his next PermSecs get-together at Sunningdale, to make some upmanship remarks about the paltry size of the British gathering. At the lunch, I managed to hold my own with the admission of having a father in the Legislative Department of the ICS, and memories of pre-partition India, like the myriads of darting, coloured kites flying over every maidan, but now, except for special rallies, down to a sad few.

Perhaps the most distressing 20 minutes of an entire career – as much as any reasonable person could stand – was listening to an Overseas Development official churning out recycled IMF formulae to Indian officials. (I had been invited to "sit in" on a donors' conference.) The destitution of mind on the part of the spokesman was understandable, since there is nothing in Britain's post-1947 economic performance that could sensibly be advanced as a model for anyone. But more galling was the sanctimonious coercion behind such utterances when the audience had to restrain counterargument against the implicit threat of reducing the "justification" for further aid funds. And it's not as though India lacks notable practitioners of the economics arts, and these indisputably better grounded in the realities of securing human necessities in extremely adverse circumstances: Manmohan Singh, at that time Secretary of the Planning Commission but who subsequently took on the task of introducing greater liberalisation in the 90s, and then appointed Prime Minister, just as an example – one of the clearest signals that a project for a new steel plant, then hotly contested between groups led by Davy and Demag, was not going to be approved was his gentle remark that new steel capacity stood far behind improved communications for rural areas in India's national priorities.

For the quality of the senior cadres of the IAS is remarkably high given the context in which they have to function – the sheer intractability of the nation's problems, and the insidious presence of corruption – if they have taken anarchy of the file to extreme limits, this is an understandable reaction within the dynamics of the British civil service tradition in such an environment. One of the most tangible symptoms of the continuing institutional tradition was the rise in Delhi's electricity demand by nearly 20% in the half-hour preceding the showing of *Yes, Minister* on local TV. And, while my French and German counterparts confessed to difficulty in communicating with Indian officials, for us Brits the simple use of "Secretary", which was the natural style in Whitehall, created an immediate common wavelength.

But they have retained the ICS State-cadres system where indentures are served in the administration at regional level, with exposure to real – in most cases extremely taxing – issues, with "flyers" sent to Delhi, either to return to senior State roles or posts among Indian delegations at international agencies. But the IAS has a more comprehensive central school of administration, and, a quirk perhaps borrowed from the French, a system of Departmental Finance Officers who are Finance Ministry officials within functioning departments.

On the pursuit of projects themselves, the score was mixed: competitors like France, Germany and Japan had traditional, if each somewhat different, links between companies, finance and government, whereas for Britain this was a novel, and, to established Whitehall economic theology, an almost reprehensible activity in which to be involved. At the same time, the industrial companies varied in their awareness and expertise of exporting, or doing business in India. The largest project was a coal-fired power station, which illustrated these weaknesses most acutely.

Perhaps the most rewarding activity was a continuing joint Working Group to assist Indian coal producers to introduce the latest longwall mining techniques, in which the National Coal Board was among the leading exponents, and specialist equipment for opencast mining. The Group met six monthly alternating between Delhi and London, with aid assistance for early purchases of equipment and technical expertise, but with the aim of progressively reducing the aid element so that Indian producers could continue these techniques by themselves. Meetings themselves were fraught with continuing tensions – over monitored production data, where rivalry between Coal India, the State-owned operator, and privately owned operators continuously showed uncomfortable comparisons; the inevitable tendency of performance failure to be attributed to the equipment rather than to the manner in which it was being operated; disputes between manufacturers and the bureaucracy as essential spares seemed to be held-up, despite a special arrangement for bonded stocks – indeed, it was not unknown for manufacturers to take key spares as part of their private luggage to deal with emergencies; and the quality of staffing, training and professional procedures – not least, the tendency to move key managers who had become proficient before they had established the continuity of practice necessary for efficient operations. To be fair, the Indian coal-mining scene is mired in cultural clashes of religion, cast, and mass politics, and holding the ring between all these cross-tensions was hard work, but rewarding in painstaking success, and interspersed with enjoyable personal contacts and fun. Here are just a couple of examples.

– One of the manufacturers' representatives was from "up t'north", which meant that his firsthand experience of mining technology was probably several generations old. But, however well-intentioned, his accent tended to bamboozle the Indian audience, and, to be honest, a few of the British delegation as well, so that we introduced a "Ray Horsfield Award" for the most confusing interjection at each Working Group meeting. On one occasion, there was some hold up in the Indian authorities approving funds for some specialist equipment, and since one of the advantages of an aid contribution was to speed up the Indian decision process, it was suggested that some Aid allocation might be applied. The Overseas Development official in the Working Group responded, "We would not exclude the possibility of bearing in mind..." but could not finish the sentence as everyone present immediately recognised this recital of official prevarication and either burst into laughter or offered alternatives to complete his sentence, such as "this proposal to take into account in ordering priorities." This won the Award hands down.

– At one of the informal chats between meetings, conversation turned to theories explaining bureaucratic behaviour. One official on the Indian team suggested a very complex application of relativity theory, so complex, we argued from the British side, that it could only have been devised by a bureaucrat. A counter suggestion from the British was Newton's Third Law, that for every force there is an equal and opposite force, so ensuring that nothing happens. This was dismissed by the Indian side as being far too simple. "How about Peter's Principle?" responded the British – this postulates that in large organisations everyone is promoted to their ultimate level of incompetence. To which an Indian spokesman blandly replied, "Peter's Principle has absolutely no relevance in India." There were several polite queries from the British side, since most could recall instances where apparently straightforward issues took an inordinate amount of time to clear. "Absolutely not!" was the repeated reply to these queries. "Are you quite sure?" the British side persisted. "Absolutely. The IAS has been promoting people far beyond their ultimate level of incompetence for years," came the confident rejoinder. Snap! But at least we should grant self-awareness as one of the essential strengths of the IAS compared to its British counterpart.

---

[1] Though the "Thatcher affect" should acknowledge the complimentary "Hammond affect" – as Eric Hammond, General Secretary of the EEPTU (Electrical, Electronic, Telecommunications and Plumbing Union) led the contentious moves to break down the antique traditional trade union structures. A rather underrated guy: always a source of down-to-earth sense on the Industrial Development Advisory Board, and as Chairman of the Electronics EDC at NEDO, it was that committee's report raising the prospect of protection against Japanese electronic imports that presaged Sony's first – and Japan's first – British plant.

A CLOSING CHAPTER

ENGINEERING MARKETS: 1987-1990

After Mrs Thatcher's "fantastic triumph" of being elected for a third term in May 1987, in a day that should be remarked in the annals of something, Lord Young arrived as Secretary of State, wreathed in laurels for having proffered winning "solutions". Almost immediately on arrival, however, Dr Mahathir, the Prime Minister of Malaysia, was reported to be in London on an informal visit, and a private meeting was arranged where a couple of officials accompanied the new Secretary of State to the Prime Minister's suite at the Hyde Park Hotel. In contrast to the formal attire of his reception of Mrs Thatcher, Dr Mahathir was in sports jacket and slacks, and plainly in relaxed mood. To his query about how the British economy was shaping up, Lord Young, still flushed with electoral success, responded that forecasters were predicting, "Three and a half percent growth as far as the eye could see," and that there was "a wall of Japanese money just waiting to pour into Britain." To this, Mahathir smiled, and replied, "You don't get Japanese money for nothing." The implications flew over Lord Young's head, and he carried on to extol the advantages that would flow from the new freedom to rely more fully on "markets".

We deduced that the belief in the magical powers of incanting "markets" must have come from a habit he had picked up from his time in Keith Joseph's Policy Studies Centre. But industrial historians will see this as the apogee of Britain's ersatz Reagonomics, where "enterprise" as proselytised by George Gilder became the natural rejoinder to "markets".[1] With a vocabulary narrowed to two words, it was inevitable that there should be a campaign marked by "wh-o-o-o-o-sh" and "z-o-o-o-m", and a semi-erect insignia for the new subtitled "Department of Enterprise". Elsewhere, this was the era of "yuppies" and the "wealth creators" – a bigger bunch of spivs not seen since the heyday of the nabobs.

Apocryphally, at a Permanent Secretary's meeting, an injudicious remark was recorded as, "The Department should consider..." Someone must have read this to Lord Young, since there followed an injunction from his office that no such symptoms of thought would be tolerated. Whether this illustrated his understanding of how organisations actually function, it set the tone for the permitted intellectual sweep of the

301

Department. In these degraded dimensions of "policy", this boiled down to "flog it no matter what the cost", as occurred when Rover group was sold to BAe with a "sweetener" that the EC subsequently demanded should be repaid.

This was, of course, merely a subset of the naïve wholesale "privatisation" drive of the late Thatcher/Major era: "If you knock-down prices far enough or even pay people to take something, you can sell anything to anyone." Scarcely likely to gain even primary school passes in the souks at Marrakesh or Dhahran, but the ultimate triumph of formulaic liberalism, siphoning huge gains into the pockets of investment bankers and managements ready to exploit information asymmetries.

Beneath this high philosophy, and the occasional mass meeting where the troops were addressed, with some chutzpah since he betrayed no knowledge of industry in any sense of the word, the projects scene continued. Visits to Rihand confirmed that despite its fraught origins, the project was moving with greater harmony with the NTPC, largely thanks to the contribution of Peter Lockton – another ex-GEC manager – as the project was approaching its final form, with effectively a new township growing around it: now generally praised, even by some ODA officials in hushed voices and contrasted with the initial "mountains of the moon" of the foundation preparation. While the Indian coal programme continued with its mixture of grudging successes and grumbles. And GEC's BALCO station was also proceeding well. (It is worth adding in hindsight, since both this and Rihand were completed after my departure from the projects scene, that both confronted a major problem in hand-over, as the Indian operators faced the responsibility of taking on full operation. In effect, both Rihand and BALCO went through a period when the companies were running the stations, making an input to the power grid for free.)

Lord Young's entry to the projects arena arose during a visit he made to China. Clive Palmer, a PEP official – subsequently to join GEC – who was accompanying Lord Young, phoned from some airport in China to say that our Secretary of State wanted to make an offer of ATP for the sale of some John Brown gas turbines: since we had repeatedly assisted the company, including in China, they were probably the worst case to demonstrate the proposition of "follow-on orders without aid". Even so, we managed to clear an offer in time. But Lord Young fell prey to two common failings: Ministers have a tendency, after one visit to China, to become "instant experts", whereas in practice it is one of the most complex societies to understand; and, having secured popularity by giving away public funds – the fact that we had managed to clear the ATP hurdles may have contributed, this seemed a route to eternal popularity.

Following on his visit, he called a meeting on the possibility of extending ATP support to Small and Medium Enterprises to set up in China. The sheer administrative hurdles would have been enough in themselves, but this was directly contrary to the concept of the scheme to counter the soft finance techniques of other countries. While, if there was an instrument for some "equity" support of this kind, there were other more suitable options, such as the Commonwealth Development Fund (CDC), or use of tax breaks to cover initial losses (on the model of Japan, Taiwan etc).

This was fairly tricky stuff to put to our Secretary of State, so that one had to concentrate on hard cases. China, even now after WTO entry, is an extremely difficult market, where auto and electronics companies with joint ventures and production facilities are mounting special defences against plagiarism and pirating. But in the late 80s, this was an even greater risk, and the Department was always cautious in advising companies about striking a balance between acknowledging the potentially vast opportunities, but also underlining the risks. One could demonstrate at the meeting a couple of current examples: Gullick Dobson, one of Britain's manufacturers of mining roof supports, had recalled that they had been faced with warranty claims from Pakistan, except that they had never sold anything in Pakistan – on inspection, it turned out that this equipment was a reverse-built exact replica, including the company name, manufactured from inferior materials in China. And, only a few days earlier, at a meeting with the then owners of Massey Ferguson, they had recalled selling a batch of 200 tractors to China in the hope of leading to a joint venture, only to find defective replicas popping up in Africa and Asia. These examples were enough to avoid an unnecessary flurry of bureaucracy.

Early in 1988, I was posted to what had been the Division responsible for "sponsoring" the Engineering Industry. The term "sponsoring" had been taboo for a few years, though simply as an organisational title consistent with industrial classifications, the term "engineering" had persisted. My arrival was to coincide with a restructuring at this part of the Department, and discussion ensued on how this should be accomplished. Ken Clarke, on a brief stint as Minister for Trade and Industry – depicted as on the moderate flank of the Tory party – was a strong abolitionist, and this Division, along with others, survived only because Lord Young was concerned that their abolition might give the impression of a loss of interest in manufacturing. But what to call these Divisions? You've guessed it, "Markets".

ENGINEERING MARKETS DIVISION

Like others, "Engineering Markets" had an elaborate new format. Some provisions for R&D support were packed away in a separate Division. But the Division was allowed a limited budget for studies and consultancies. And each "markets" Division was allowed its own tame economist and statistician – the latter said he quite enjoyed the freedom to use new presentation techniques and a varied focus of interest. And we all had a series of "Initiatives" to pursue, essentially presentations/discussions with industry on the basis of material published by the Department, on such themes as "The European Single Market", "Skills and Training". If direct contact with individual companies was discouraged, at least these got officials out of their offices and sharpened their "presentational" skills. And an "Advisory Board" was set up, in our case a lively mix with David Hardy* (then with Global Investments), and a varied group of members from industry, such as Tony Thatcher (Dowty), and others such as Keith Pavitt (SPRU).

Attempting to achieve some constructive edge to this new menu, we deliberately tried to slant our "initiatives" to challenge some of industry's traditional weaknesses. For example, on "Skills and Training" we chose inward investors like Komatsu as exemplars, since their approach to integrate with their local communities left traditional British companies standing. While British industry could always be guaranteed for a few laughs on the same theme. For example, when a "British" delegate repeated the eternal industrial bleat that the government had failed to provide a school output with basic competences, under questioning he admitted to being from Pilkington – that same morning the company had announced several hundred redundancies from plants in Scotland, which we pointed out did not suggest much husbandry of experienced skill resources, to which we had a lame "That's how it is" in response. (He was obviously anticipating the CBI's rallying call of "flexible labour".)

But on "supplier relationships", we managed to elicit a typically British admission from a Hawker Siddeley spokesman that they had driven such a tough bargain on price in one instance that they had to go "with a bag of gold" to save a key supplier from bankruptcy. Or, following on the rise of Japanese plants set up in the early 80s, we had a string of complaints from suppliers on how "unreasonable" these foreign outfits were. In the past, suppliers took it as a matter of course that every year they "updated" their prices by jacking them up according to whatever the inflation rate had been, but these new guys dismissed this approach with the argument that, for the orders that suppliers had received, they should have learnt how to make efficiency savings greater than the rate of inflation. Or, on another occasion, when we asked what was the biggest problem being confronted by an audience of varied companies, one volunteered, "IBM's approach to just-in-time, by which they mean, 'Whatever we want just when we want it.'"

Beneath these "initiatives", there was the more immediate task of the "flog it..." policy, in that there were still a couple of stragglers among British Shipbuilders' yards not already disposed of. It was to this function that Lord Young suggested that I might be relieved to be "doing something useful" compared with previous involvement in projects, where we had a role in securing getting on for some £19 billion of exports.

FLOGGING THE LAST YARDS

David Coates was the Assistant Secretary who had been involved in earlier disposals: one must confess to having harboured doubts whether, as an economist by upbringing, he was entirely adaptable to the real world. But he put in a tyro performance, especially in the sale of Govan to Kvaerner, where he showed an outstanding "propensity to consume" to match that of Nordic management, and still keep the "inducements" within the EEC limits for aids to shipbuilding.

John Lister, a pragmatic ex-ICI warhorse, had been appointed Chairman of British Shipbuilders: as a native Geordie, he had presumed that the aim was to make the remaining yards viable, whereas the government's approach was sale or closure. North East Shipbuilders (NESL) in Sunderland was the last remaining yard, and had earlier received substantial support to modernise, including covered yards. To gain an impartial view on its prospects of being sold as a going concern, David and John hotfooted to Japan and obtained the agreement of one of their major builders to make an audit.

In view of local sensitivities, this exercise had to be handled extremely carefully. Even so, the presence of the Japanese audit team leaked, with local headlines to the effect that "The Japanese come to Sunderland to learn about making ships". Not quite. For the same sensitivities, the conclusions were passed through an intermediary, an ebullient Japanese character who had lived in Britain as a consultant for more than a decade. In short, the quality of facilities and equipment, and the skills level of the workforce, notably welders, were competitive, but the audit was extremely critical of the flow of work – phrases like, "too much walking", "blocks standing unfinished and idle", "too many different activities in a confined area" were typical. But a striking feature was the comment on the greater use of computers at NESL, "Sometimes human brain better than computer". The final conclusion was that NESL used nearly three times the man-hours, with a 30% cost disadvantage, for comparable vessels against Japanese performance. Whilst there might have been scope for some continuing co-operation, the view was that these deficiencies could not be rectified within a reasonable period, and the yard was closed with inevitable local controversy. (There was reported to have been a welcome resurgence in shipbuilding in this historic area, led by a robust Dutch approach at the old Swan Hunter yard. But 2009 saw the last crane dismantled and shipped off to India.)

An amusing sidelight occurred when David gave our Japanese consultant a copy of my lecture on Honda. A few days later I received an excited call, commending the paper, but going on to recall that our Japanese friend had been one of Honda's advance guard when they were planning to enter the Isle of Man motorbike TT race for the first time. This team had apparently measured every bend and incline on the course so that Honda could design the optimum frame for their racing entries. Yet another angle on thorough foresight.

David was promoted to be the Department's Economic Advisor with these last remnants of British Shipbuilders "flogged off". But there was an old sore: some years earlier, Trafalgar House had purchased a yard with an oilrig partially under construction and had managed to lose a substantial sum. They were suing the Department for damages for a figure, including interest, well in excess of £300 million. Moving into a long-running case is always awkward, but on looking back over the papers, there seemed no substance in their case, since, given the "flog it…" ethos of the time, in response to the company's approach, the Department had not made any attempt to haggle, but rather took the line that the books were entirely open so long as the company made a defensible offer. Consequently there had been no let or hindrance to the company completing its own due diligence.

The company were going through a "discovery" process clocking up legal fees of the order of £200-400,000 a month, and it was envisaged that in due course the Department would have to go through the same exercise. This was a first experience of the absurd level of legal costs, and to placidly await our turn seemed absurd. Another factor was that the Department was still keeping key ex-BS staff on a retainer: having met them, with no suggestion that they might have been culpable of anything, one was just a bit nervous of how they might stand up to forensic grilling on details of some antiquity. Surprisingly, our legal advisers also thought so and suggested an explanatory informal conversation to sound out how far the company was prepared to go. Talking informally to the company's senior management, one questioned whether it was really prudent to embark on a legal action against a major potential future customer when the grounds were so questionable, but also pointing out that the Treasury was a peculiar animal. If occasionally slow, they did have deeper pockets than most, and had the quirk, well-displayed in the current privatisations, of being prepared to pay large sums to avoid continuing or larger liabilities. So that a deal where the company claimed "X" against the government's "Y" would be protracted and costly, and by no means sure that the government would be willing to "split-the-difference": in short, this was not going to run according to the customary civil contractor's game of clocking up "claims" against a final haggle with the client.

In the event, to give some credibility to this line, we managed to secure a £20 million provision in the next year's BS budget against contingent legal costs. The case dragged on beyond my time in the Department, since with the arrival of Nicholas Ridley in a few months the Division had been closed. But from subsequent contacts the case was settled out of court with a notional contribution to costs, vastly less than had the process been carried through.

Nicholas Ridley, who earned probably the most brilliant sobriquet in political history – Norman St John-Stevas' "He was one of us before we were" – must have harboured some old grudge from his resignation in the early 1970s over the forthcoming Industry Act. Intelligent, but with assumptions that admitted only occasional logical chinks, he was surprisingly open. A session on the theme of "City short-termism" turned out to be a lively, not to say blunt, exchange. At the time the Innovation Advisory Board had completed their draft report, subsequently published in 1990, still one of the best analyses of this haggard subject. Everyone chipped in – my own input was a note on British banks' reluctance to have any equity or direct involvement in companies, whereas "sticking to their last" could have disastrous consequences as in Midland's purchase of Crocker Bank where "they would have been better off doing anything else with the money, including burning it". After a remarkably sharp altercation, Nicholas Ridley disarmed the meeting by admitting that the City compared very badly in its support for industry with German and Japanese banks. But he doubted whether making a speech would do anything to influence its behaviour.

It was not long before the closure of the Division, and with no further posts of the equivalent rank it was suggested that I should volunteer to leave. Without haggling over terms, this seemed fair since the effectiveness of the system, including the innate ineptitudes of industry, were beyond any constructive contribution. Various companies had trailed coats, including Hawker Siddeley.[2] But one could never be convinced of their viability. Intriguingly, one Friday I had a mysterious call asking whether I would be prepared to consider some executive assistant post to an active Chief Executive: on inquiring the name of the company, the reply was "Guinness": I asked for the weekend to think it over, but on the Monday, the Saunders prosecution hit the headlines.

With less than two months notice before closure of the Division, surveying the options, with knowledge of the Japanese general trading companies and from direct contacts appreciation of the high quality of their management, they suggested a breadth, interest and novelty unmatched by any British outfits, and contacting the European General Manager of C.Itoh, as Itochu were then called, I was lucky enough to be offered an advisory post.

There were others who were "supernumerary" as a consequence of the restructuring, and once satisfied that they had found reasonable alternative jobs, it remained only to tidy away the office before taking outstanding leave. In the spare hours, I thought a valedictory piece would be appropriate, taking up one of the quotations from Adam Smith that our Departmental economists had tossed around in the shadow of Keith Joseph. This was circulated as an internal note, mainly to point out the anachronism of applying an 18th century mindset to the realities of the world 200 years later. But it must have leaked, since it led to an *Observer* citation in the *Financial Times*:

"SMITH OUT, LIST IN"

"Chris Benjamin, recently departed from the Department of Trade and Industry to the Japanese trading house, C.Itoh, has left behind a valedictory headed Minute to an Unknown Economist. It is an attack on Adam Smith and the reading list once recommended to the Department by the now Lord Joseph.

"Benjamin was held in high regard by Britain's exporters during his period at the project and export policy division, when he looked like convincing Ministers that the pursuit of free trade must be laced with Japanese-style government realism in chasing contracts. Then he moved to head the engineering markets division, since disbanded by Nicholas Ridley, the Trade and Industry Secretary.

"In the course of his economic researches, Benjamin came across Friedrich List whose ideas, a Swiss colleague told him, were behind the superior German economic performance. Only one copy of List's *The*

National System of Political Economy could be found. It was in the Bank of England library and held together by Sellotape and rubber bands. Thus Benjamin thinks that there must have been a subversive campaign against List by the economic establishment. When he mentioned List to a Treasury knight, the response was: "Ugh, protectionism!"

"Benjamin describes Sir Douglas Wass, the former Permanent Secretary at the Treasury as "undoubtedly a good Treasury chap," but one who virtually dismissed industry in his Reith lectures on "Government and the Governed".

"A lecture by Sir Robin Butler, the Cabinet Secretary, on the Government's new approach to business is dismissed as follows: "Maybe he was just reiterating a standard Treasury brief. But if such crashing condescension goes down OK with a British audience, in Frankfurt or Osaka these remarks would probably gather no more than the polite applause accorded to a talking polar bear."

"They must be glad he's gone."

Among other spin-offs, my new employers, like most Japanese companies averse to inadvertent publicity, must have looked a bit askance at taking the mickey out of the head of the civil service. But erstwhile colleagues have continuously prompted approaches for me to release copies, not in recognition for actually having ploughed through Adam Smith, but to answer baffled queries about the mysteries of Treasury psychology. From a present viewpoint, the "surrogate reality" of the Treasury ethos seems to have become even more pervasive, while the nation is pursuing its asymptotic convergence with the Motihori tribe of South America even more vigorously.

---

[1] George Gilder's *The Spirit of Enterprise* came out in 1985, just in time for at least one word in this long title to lodge in memory. And it's a near run thing that we didn't have a sub-title, "The Department of Spirit". The sequel to this mad guff, spelt out vividly in *One Market Under God* by Thomas Frank (Vintage), led inexorably to the financial scandals of the dot.com era, Enron, the implosion of pension funds, and chaos of the credit crunch. Sadly, with the slow-rate of rhetorical renewal in Britain, New Labour seems to have got stuck in the same "markets" groove.

[2] Arnold Hall*, whom one had known since Julian Amery days, then Chairman of Hawker Siddeley in his rather imperious curt style had an informal dinner, and approached me in the style of a done deal to join the company. Having visited

several of their plants, and in the knowledge that they were involved in financing the first stage of the Hub power project in Pakistan – as it has turned out, one of the most notorious ways of losing money, I had to suggest gently that I did not think his company could survive. His response was somewhat quizzical: maybe he thought I was trying to drive a hard bargain, or perhaps just unaccustomed to having opinions expressed forthrightly by others. Nor did I fully realise that one of the surest routes to scionacracy in British business is to have been in at the death of at least one, and preferably more than three, companies.

PART II:

AN OBSOLETE NATION

If a career marked less as a sweeping panorama than a floundering chronicle, invariably on the cusp of farce, under the comic banner of "supporting" industry. While British industry managed only to sink, in most instances out of sight, with a few exceptions still puffing away at their water wings to keep heads above water. If only the buoyancy of the drowned could have reflected the inflated egos of their top managements, they would have swept the oceans. But it would be unfair to single out British management, excremental though it has been. For scapegoats are all too aplenty in the national amalgam of ineptitude and parochialism. Within the battered flagship of Whitehall, including the assorted procession of politicians on the poop, "rounded amateurs" have bounced about with no practical competences beyond "a proven ability to parse the gerund and a smattering of Adam Smith". All, even the zaniest, avowedly well intentioned. All locked into an implacable conviction that traditional nostrums were still for the best. And all bearing the gene of imperial governance: that aloofness and detachment only gained from sipping pink gins on verandas in far-flung climes. But the consistent undertow has been myopia, and a moderately honest comparative audit should be in order.

ENDICTMENT

There have been a multitude of tracts on Britain's industrial decline. [1]And still flowing; albeit now at a funereal pace as industries have died, and their advocates have expired. Indeed, one of the few strengths of the country is as a source of archival material, with cautionary lessons for others, since the country itself seems incapable of learning from its own history. There have been periodic cacophonies of self-righteous myopias by politicians, trade unionists and industrialists as shipbuilding and the British motor industry collapsed. But the passing, or contraction, of the power generation, coal-mining machinery, civil aircraft and electronics industries has been accompanied by barely a whimper. Even when there was a luminously vivid audit of Britain's competitiveness at the collapse of the motorbike industry, debate was diverted to the irrelevances of whether workers' cooperatives were viable, ignoring the stark evidence that there was an idiom of corporate behaviour with a cohesiveness, flexibility, technical focus and efficiency dimensions beyond Britain's traditional patterns. This prompted no resolve to face up to the fundamental changes demanded. Even in the late 80s, a series of "competitiveness studies" of sectors such as pumps and valves, printing machinery, machine tools etc confirmed, with a few exceptions, the same dominant symptoms of fragmentation, under investment, and loss of markets in higher quality/technology products. Unsurprisingly, Britain's post-war corporate history, and including those arrogant dregs of gentlemanly capitalism in our now defunct merchant banks, has been a pilgrimage of dead men walking, with extinction only delayed to allow senior executives to stash up cosseted retirements in country haunts extending from the West Country to Florida and the South of France.

Measured by trade performance, the decline could not be sharper viewed from a career in proximity to industry. In the 60s, while in Peter Thorneycroft's Office, a distraught Permanent Secretary – Henry Hardman* – bustled in and reported in agitation that he had just returned from a meeting where it had been disclosed that the current trade account had turned negative by £10 million the previous month.

With the trade deficit today oscillating above £100 billion a year, give or take the occasional statistical aberration, a mere £10 million would barely cover the imports of PlayStation consoles. And can we even be confident of this figure, setting aside "that the recent revival of UK exports largely reflects the activities of fraudsters rather than genuine business" (*FT* 24.7.06), under the heading of "balancing items" where really invisible "invisibles" are hidden, we can expect to include money-laundering, "people trading", illegal drug imports (Did anyone realise that the British consumer was providing 70% of the Taliban's funding?), imports of firearms etc?

Yet a nation's success in prevailing against imports and exporting against international competitors is still as good a guide to competitive economic performance as any other, or at least it is regarded as so in most other countries. Moreover, since the capture of available world GNP has been, and still is, the driver for many countries to enhance their own living standards – export-led growth, in conventional jargon,[2] it is also a measure of how the UK's general performance has stood up over time. If this leads to accusations of "mercantilism" from trade theorists, the fact is the world has never ceased to be "mercantilist".

Just to remind ourselves, between 1899 and 1929, Britain's share of exports of manufactures from amongst the eleven main industrial countries dropped from 32.2% to 22.9% and, inflated in the inter-war years by imperial preference, protectionism and a relatively strong post-war industry, was running at 25.4% by 1950. But it declined to 7.6% in 1984 (House of Lords Report 1985). Since then, despite the occasional yodelling of economists of a resurgence in UK exports on the basis of OECD figures, in fact the fall in share has continued if the "new exporters", notably China, are placed in the picture,[3] now according to 2005 data down to 3.9%.

As an illustrative sideshow, in the 80s, there was a celebration to mark the centenary, or bicentenary, of the Board of Trade: somewhere among the DTI/BERR's antiquaries is the actual chair of the President! The occasion was marked by representatives of all the original official members, including the Archbishop of Canterbury. Maggie Thatcher was invited as well. It finally occurred to someone that there were no officials who had actually met her. Since I had been part of the supporting officials on her whistle-stop tour of the Far East, I was deputed to make the initial introductions. After having completed this chore, I could see no reason to hang around to celebrate an outfit that had presided over a 90% fall in Britain's trade influence.

Whilst the nihilism "Does it matter?" was the acme of policy discourse during the Thatcher/Lawson years, we had a comic interlude as David Young pressed to eliminate trade statistics – a natural sequel to his earlier "solutions" where any bad news could be obscured by altering the basis of statistics to the point where, indeed, unemployment data became unintelligible. Now the conventional wisdom is that at less than "x"% of GDP, there's nothing to worry about in the current account deficit (where "x" is an infinitely variable variable). Fortunately, the UK has secured a good proportion of foreign-owned production plants, some indeed resuscitated from the rubble created by British management, with their own international marketing networks. But with the depletion of the North Sea energy stocks, rundown of the coal industry, and the corresponding increased dependence on imported energy, we can expect to test the tolerance of "x".

NON-PRODUCTIVITY OF KNOWLEDGE

Unbeknown to custodians of "policy", a continuing literature in the US, largely unreported in this country, has been on the theme of how to avoid going down the same tubes as Britain. One of their sage commentators, (the late) Peter Drucker concludes: "According to its production of scientific and technical knowledge, Britain should have been the world's economic leader in the post-World War II era. Antibiotics, the jet engine, the body scanner, even the computer, were British developments. But Britain did not succeed in turning these knowledge-achievements into successful products and services, into jobs, into exports, into market standing. The non-productivity of its knowledge, more than anything else, is at the root of the slow and steady erosion of the British economy."[4]

Almost anyone could add to Drucker's list. My own favourite recalls a visit to the Royal Radar Establishment, Malvern in 1964, when the scientists proudly showed us among their recent accomplishments one of the first flat-screen applications of liquid crystal displays (LCD), aimed at eliminating the vagaries of mechanical instrumentation – also among the innovative gizmos was one of the first power lasers, demonstrated with pride as capable of knocking a minute hole in a razor blade. One learnt later that RRE held the original LCD patents for this application with RCA. This, and a good few other examples, suggest that the US itself is not immune to this malaise.

At the time there were at least half a dozen significant UK companies involved in civil and military electronic display technologies that might have taken up further exploitation. Instead, Sharp and other Japanese producers took the boom in electronic calculators in the late-60s and mid-70s as a basis for building up their expertise in LCDs, from which they developed to their current sophistication, with Samsung and Taiwan firms aggressive followers.[5] Yet the world market today for LCDs – ubiquitous in new generation TVs, laptops, handheld PCs, mobile phones, cameras, instrumentation etc – is running at scores of billions of dollars a year, and with the application of new technologies such as carbon nanotubes and organic displays evolving new generations of products, in which UK companies have no perceptible position. And to illustrate the difficulty of attempting to return to a product area once opted out, the capital outlay for a factory to build the next generation of liquid-crystal display panels runs to more than $900 million (Nikkei Weekly-9.8.04), far beyond the rate of return thresholds of any British companies, even if they had sustained the expertise, market position, and advances in technologies and processes.

COMPUTERS

Drucker even suggests one of the causes, recalling the critical stage in the evolution of the computer, "It was then pure accident, however, that it became an American development – the accident of World War II which made the American military willing to spend enormous sums on developing (quite unsuccessfully, by the way, until well after World War II) machines to calculate at high-speed the position of fast-moving aircraft overhead and of fast-moving enemy ships. Otherwise the computer would probably have become a British development. Indeed, an English company, the food producer and restaurant owner J. Lyons & Co., in the 1940s actually developed the first computer for commercial purposes that really worked, the "Leo" – Lyons just couldn't raise the money to compete with the Pentagon and had to abandon its working and successful (and very much cheaper) machine." The saga of the UK computer industry offers yet another pantomime of players like Ferranti, British Tabulating Machine Company, GEC, EMI, ICT, English Electric, Plessey, and Elliott-Automation, with bosses combining the classic British traits of arrogance and myopia. The resulting bits and bobs were merged into ICL.

The sale of a controlling interest in ICL to Fujitsu in 1990 had a number of ironies. By the end of the 50s, when Ferranti and others, drawing on wartime expertise, were world leaders in the field, Fujitsu was still predominantly a telecoms company with computing being pursued by a group of young engineers – "the crazy bunch" – led by the eccentric Dr Toshio Ikeda under "paternalistic tolerance". If in a different field, the evolution of Fujitsu is as much a story of innovative organisation and technology as Honda.[i] Their first attempt at a commercial computer, for the Tokyo Stock Exchange, was lost to Univac. They persisted with a series of Fancom computers that were viewed as technologically successful. But the

---

[i] *Japanese Business Success* edited by Takeshi Yuzawa (Routledge 1994).

company had no production facilities concentrated on computers, with manufacture instead spread around their Kawasaki plant where communications equipment, still the company's main business, was built. It was only in 1960 the company was rationalised into two divisions – telecoms and electronics, and not until 1962 that a separate computing department was established. And with this came the commercial focus to treat computers as a profit driver rather than "playing with expensive toys". Eventually, its Fancom-230 series more than matched IBM's 360 series.

As remarkable as this evolution was, there was a continuing pattern of government support. (Unlike Honda, whom MITI actively discouraged from moving into car manufacturing!)[6] In contrast to Britain, Japan at least had a real conception of what was involved in competing with the Pentagon "picking winners" and its "buy-American" bias. By the 80s, the government was providing some 25% of computer-related R&D, usually through cooperative research projects (up to the mid-70s, R&D funded by Fujitsu, Hitachi and NEC combined was less than half IBM's total research spending); assistance to domestic purchasers – by a joint venture among the seven manufacturers backed by the Japan Development Bank – for leasing computers; tax allowances to cover the mark-down on trade-in models as new ones were introduced, concessions to local Chambers of Commerce to buy traded-in models for supply at cut prices to smaller companies, and special depreciation allowances; and direct and indirect forms of market protection, to discourage foreign purchases if a local offering met the specification.

Even though formal protection devices have lapsed, Japanese companies still command 60% of the domestic market, and 90% of public sector purchases. While Japan is slugging it out with the US for the world's most powerful supercomputer – NEC's Earth Simulator has been pipped by IBM's Blue Gene/L, yet a Japanese consortium is evolving a machine aiming to be three times as fast as these current models. IBM Japan is now a significant local player, but still has to go toe to toe with competitive local suppliers even for the latest advances.[7] But this is yet another growing multibillion-dollar market from which the UK has copped out, and where the re-entry demands of investment, integrated technologies and marketing coverage are increasing. It is not that the threat of IBM was not perceived, but the scale and range of effort were comparable to playing bowls on Plymouth Hoe against the major-league baseball of the Pentagon's patronage. Patronage by itself, of course, may not be sufficient protection against management complacency, and there are several accounts of how IBM "blew it".[8]

But are we any better placed today to capitalise on our knowledge strengths? The shambles of our rail system is a continual reminder of our capacity for being led by "the invisible hand" to create chaos on ostensibly "rational", if entirely lunatic, pretexts. Perhaps the purest example of the unique British talent for dis-integration. But it is worth recalling that it was British Rail who were the early leaders in developing the tilting-train concept, now with Italy and the Nordics in the lead, and the early experimentation on a maglev system was begun in this country. So the gap between innovation and exploitation is still there, and indeed potentially wider as the range of viable enterprises has depleted.

WHERE HAVE ALL THE FLOWERS GONE?

As remarkable as its early buccaneering flair is Honda's growth to a leading multinational enterprise: by February 2004, with 120 manufacturing facilities in 29 countries. And achieved while retaining its ethos and integrity. But demanding a continuing focus to retain their market presence, to sustain the dynamic flexibility to meet competitive threats, and powers of renewal to adapt to diverse local customs and economic changes. The same could be said of Sony (like Honda, with less than a couple of dozen employees when they started), NEC, Fujitsu, Canon, Sharp or a string of others. Britain can boast no companies in the post-war era that have sustained a similar evolution: our system has been incapable of squaring up to the fundamental challenge of embracing change with continuity. Rather a progression of relative decline, fruitless mergers and acquisitions, exit or foreign takeover – Dunlop, GEC, NEI, Ferranti, Plessey, Hawker Siddeley, Dowty, Blue Circle, Trafalgar House, Davy, John Brown, Courtaulds.... And without enterprises with a continuing motivation to succeed in international contests, all the huffing and puffing of governments, flag-waving of strengths in science, calls for efforts to increase skills, marginal subsidies etc, are unlikely to do more than, as in the past, run into the ground.

To check progress, we are regularly reminded of the paucity of Britain's international corporate standing by the annual R&D Scoreboard. Its main purpose may be to compare research and related investment internationally within broadly comparable categories, but by comparison of sales, it is also a good ready reckoner of the position of British companies. The table from the Scoreboard compares the scale of the leading British companies by level of sales against their international competitors, and an indication of the number of international companies larger than the leading British companies can be drawn.[9]

Our industrial structure still has a post-imperial overhang; strong in

317

resource industries – BP, Shell and Rio Tinto have maintained a global strength from origins in the days of Empire – unlike Cable and Wireless, which has blown its historic position. Even in manufacturing relatively strong in primary processors – grub, booze, fags and drugs; notably Unilever retains its high position among food processors, another example of the quirky durability of Dutch/British joint ownership. In telecoms, BT survives despite a chequered past, and Vodafone has used paper effectively to reach a global position, bar the occasional debt write-off. And Rolls-Royce has struggled remarkably after a refinancing and some competitive launch support. Like BAe, and a cluster of smaller companies in the circuit of military defence purchasing, such as Meggitt, GKN and Cobham, they have also benefited from an ersatz-Pentagon purchasing approach. And relatively active in the tertiary sector, even if national ownership has also eroded.

Yet the presence of a few British companies sprouting on the higher slopes should not disguise the virtual absence of a significant presence in traditional manufacturing, and, more vividly, in the new technologies of electronics/mechatronics/optics/new materials which are evolving rapidly as the applications focus of micro miniaturisation and nanotechnologies approaches. And even among those fields where there are leading British players, these are not ones where the "value-added" derives predominantly from this country, indeed in the resource industries of energy and minerals the bulk of their turnover is outside the UK.

It would be trite in any other country to make the obvious point that size matters: one recalls a leading French enarque remarking, "David only beats Goliath in the Bible." But size is not simply a measure of competitive élan. For such companies will only have achieved scale and continuing success by integrating knowledge and resources effectively. Not only internally generated technology and processes, but also building the financial strength to respond to market demands and secure options for the future. But equally important also serving as a nexus for inputs from suppliers, subcontractors, financial sources and marketing outlets, with feedback in disciplining these to maintain the competitive edge of its own activities. In short, successful international companies are a prime transforming agent for converting Drucker's "knowledge" into value-added, both for themselves and their networks.

Fairly rare in Britain these days, since "shareholder value" does not figure significantly in the contours of these successful foreign relationships. The practices of a few companies like JCB, the efforts of Ian Gibson* and his team – and successors – at Nissan's Sunderland plant to develop such linkages, and similar efforts by other foreign transplants, are as near as we have got. But there is ample literature on Toyota in Chubu prefecture, and firms like Bosch in Baden Wurttenberg as examples of other national approaches.

No one is preaching gigantism for its own sake. But whatever the "economically correct" theory of the firm,[10] in countries not subject to the tyranny of stereotyped economic thinking, it is in this transformational function – with its inherent mutual obligations to sustain success for its people and networks – that lies the legitimacy for corporate existence. But to achieve and sustain this international presence is no mean feat. And its demands are the source of the multitude of "management potions" that purport to offer elixirs for quick enhancement. This evolutionary process is, however, essentially incremental with wary perception of changes and the suppleness to adapt more rapidly than rivals – the Honda story is as good an exemplar as any.

Sure, the world is getting more global. With new competences blossoming out all over the place. Software in India, ironically gaining an influx of experienced talent from the collapse of Silicon Valley. Semiconductors in South Korea and Taiwan, stimulating restructuring in Japan and in the US. Mechatronics and computers in China. And vehicle production in Malaysia, Thailand, Indonesia, and China. Yet again, it is the established international companies, those that have continuously invested on the frontiers of evolving technologies, process facilities, generated expertise and market presence who will be best placed to interact successfully with; to respond and to adapt to these new players; and to take advantage of these shifts. Moreover, given a choice of models to follow, these new upstart enterprises will tend to see the successful integrative corporate approaches as the ones to adapt to their own cultural and institutional systems. In short, no emerging country could sensibly find any feature of the British model worth emulating.

ANY WATTS ANYWHERE?

With so much pop-history, pop-empire, pop-steam power, pop-science, and pop-industrial revolution, the fairytale style gives no excuse for not knowing the names of heroes like Watt, Brunel, Telford, Kay, Stephenson et al. But this approach does scarce justice to the reality that all these names were embedded in a context of lively innovation across many related fields, including predecessors whose ideas they elaborated – or pinched; communities of trades, artisans, fabricators and other practical interests; and "webs of credit" – for example, the Stockton-Darlington Railway was predominantly financed through the Quaker network.[ii] A scene where "co-operation" was not viewed as weakness, but in essentials similar to the contexts of Toyota, Bosch, Honda etc today.

Even if this supportive national context has been eroded, the tradition of individual innovators lives on: having for several years chaired the sifting committee for the Queen's Awards, it is remarkable what some small companies have done. And some smaller enterprises like ARM, Meggitt, Ultra and Renishaw do fight on. But there is a sad formula that has been resistant to change over decades: 2 out of 5 start-ups will fail within two years, and 4 out of 5 within five years. Market pundits are prone to regard this as "healthy". Yet it remains an open question whether in a different institutional setting some of these failures might not have evolved the resilience of Mittelstand or smaller Japanese companies, who will not uncommonly boast 40-60% of world market share for some specialised range of products.

The decay of such supportive communities and interests is the stuff of archival scholarship, but not least has been the unwiring of local financial networks by the centralisation of financial services in the City – could Parsons have developed the steam turbine under the scrutiny of the advances bureaucracies of NatWest, Barclays etc? So, today, when the individual inventor still twinkles successfully, the supportive infrastructure is very different.

To take a recent example from involvement in an Innovation Club, which included a variety of companies and academic centres: on a Club visit to the Welding Institute (TWI), the Institute were justly proud of the breakthrough technique of Friction Stir Welding,[iii] which has overcome a problem of achieving high integrity welds that has bedevilled metalworking industries for centuries, and is currently being developed for an increasing range of applications. Yet the instigator, a cheery Welshman, will relate how he had to do the early tests in the proverbial garage before convincing sceptical colleagues that his idea was worth pursuing. It is possible to draw the analogy of the Institute as effectively a "society of friends", except that the acquaintances are so international that many would find it difficult to cope with a Geordie accent. Consequently, as the process applies predominantly to traditional industries from which British companies have withdrawn, the main value-added gains in product quality and efficiency of manufacture are being taken by such names as Boeing, ABB, Toshiba, Mitsubishi Heavy with others joining the beneficiaries as applications develop.

[ii] *Family Capitalism* edited by Geoffrey Jones and Mary Rose (Frank Cass).
[iii] See TWI website: www.twi.org.uk

If this is the sad fate of "new knowledge" in industries that the UK has exited, the situation is if anything more serious in those technologies where British companies have opted out of the research and investment necessary to stay among the leaders. We can be confident that some scientists in the same Malvern laboratories (The Royal Radar Establishment is now part of QinetiQ, the privatised research wing of the Ministry of Defence) in which their predecessors evolved the principles of liquid crystal displays will have some unique gizmo. But the prospect of British industry capturing the value-added are probably more remote than they were at the time of the LCD breakthrough.[11]

PATENT TESTS

The depletion of a crucial tier of industry has fed back into the UK's performance in research more generally. Despite proclamations of Britain's strengths in science, a recent snapshot of the UK's patent registrations (US Patent Office high-tech patent applications per million of population) shows the UK as just above the EU average, if behind Norway, Sweden and Netherlands, but way behind the US and Japan.[12] In overall terms, the UK's share of US patent registrations has fallen from 3.97% in 1977 to 2.2% in 2007, and on recent figures falling behind Taiwan and South Korea.

The most striking shift has been the rise of Japan, which, on a corresponding basis for the years 1963-80 had a per-capita rate one quarter that of the UK, is now running five times higher than the UK. (Since Japan's population is over twice that of the UK, the absolute figure is approaching 8-10 times as many patent filings as the UK.)

It may be unfashionable to refer to Japan, to whom references in the British press appear to be confined to problem loans and deflation, while they themselves are indefatigably gloomy about their prospects. No apologies, since this reporting bias merely disguises the paradox of innovative dynamism in "deflationary" Japan compared to industrial decline in "booming" Britain.

For all the dudgeon occasioned by the decision of Dyson to move production of its vacuum cleaners to Malaysia, and the prospect of manufacturing falling in Britain to some 10% of GNP,[13] "hollowing out" has been a concern in Japan for more than two decades as they have seen rising competitors in South Korea and Taiwan, and the threat from the flood of investment into China.

Having themselves "caught up" twice – once in the period from 1868 to the First World War, and then post-World War II – leading Japanese companies are well aware of the weaknesses among the erstwhile leaders that allowed them to do it. Their response, even among relatively smaller companies, has been to shift low-end products and assembly to lower-labour-cost countries, judiciously to ensure that the process is compatible with local skills, while also looking to exploit growth in local demand (again, Honda offers a good example).[14] But matching such moves with increased development investment to keep at the technological edge, create options for new products, and speed up the cycle for new products to forestall competitors. And the pursuit of new processes whereby labour-cost differentials can be neutralised, (a few of Honda's examples are more environmental/efficient engine configurations, robotic systems, onboard IT, aero-engines, light aircraft, and small jet engine/passenger aircraft) coupled with tightening company controls against leakages of technology.

Overall, on recent reports major Japanese companies are increasing R&D for the seventh consecutive year, with new international patents surging. And, as another indicator, Japan has chalked up four Nobel Prizes since 2000 in applied sciences such as conductive polymers, asymmetric catalysts, proteomics, and neutrino astronomy. A country where industry is still taken seriously, and where inevitable decline is not viewed as the likeliest outcome, nor indeed as inevitable. Rather, in Drucker's terms, having absorbed knowledge from elsewhere – yes, including computing and liquid crystal displays – during their post-World War II advance up the value-added industries, the current emphasis is on creating its own knowledge in a manner where their companies can appropriate the competitive gains.

OH DR PORTER

If confirmation were needed, a convenient audit can be made by comparing Professor Michael Porter's recent analyses of the UK and Japan. The former,[iv] published in May 2003, was greeted with a lukewarm response for stating what we already knew. But, even if there's always suspicion since the Hutton inquiry of "sexing up" and the document has a fair amount of padding on the nature of "clusters", the Professor identifies a constant theme of under investment: -

– "UK manufacturing companies are reported to spend less of their turnover on innovation...."

– "current levels of UK innovation are insufficient to drive UK

[iv] *UK Competitiveness: Moving to the Next Stage* by Professor Michael Porter and Christian Ketels (DTI Economic Report May 2003)

productivity growth and close the UK productivity gap...."

– in "physical infrastructure", including railways (gosh!), "port infrastructure" and even "telecommunications infrastructure"

– in education, with "lower marks" on "quality of schools", "maths and sciences" and "skills", "low GCR marks on the availability of scientists and engineers" and "lagging financing of the university and public research sector"

– public sector R&D spending "has worsened"

– while UK companies "are operating with lower levels of capital intensity" and "invest significantly less in R&D" than international competitors.

Indeed, according to the study, of the top 25 UK companies securing US patents in 1997-2001, more than half were foreign-owned. On a sectoral comparison of export performance, defence equipment – even if showing a relative decline, personal and healthcare products and services are the only fields of significant strength.

The Japan study,[v] if critically received by many in the country, still lists a range of sectors where Japanese companies remain competitive with strong supporting industries – automobiles, cameras, car audio, carbon fibres, continuous synthetic weaves, fax machines, forklift trucks, home air conditioners, home audio equipment, microwave and satellite communications equipment, pianos, robotics, semiconductors, sewing machines, soya sauce, tires, trucks, typewriters, VCR/DVD players, and video games. Even this ignores some of the horizontal capabilities such as computing, materials, precision fabrication, membranes etc. And the trains run on time. But such strengths are indicative of levels of continuous investment across areas where the UK has been deficient.

We can congratulate ourselves, as indeed we never hesitate to do periodically, on the strengths of British "science" – we regularly revisit the "white heat" rhetoric as governments search for some panacea that doesn't cost too much.[15] But, in the absence of a stratum of companies with a vision to renew themselves, the major value-added transformation into commercial products, apart from royalties and licensing fees, will go to foreign companies. For decades the excuse has been that in a "global" world it is not possible to appropriate this value-added. Again, Japan is an instructive contrast, now belatedly pursuing a policy of pushing its universities to open

---

[v] *Can Japan Compete?* by Michael Porter, Hirotaka Takeuchi & Mariko Sakakibara (Macmillan Press), 2000

up their research. But with the crucial difference that their academic centres are surrounded by an infrastructure of significant international players with their own advanced research facilities, expertise and developed transformational competences. And all motivated to ensure that the leading edge will be sharpened into competitive products within their walls. (While, of course, the massive research and development budget of the Pentagon remains predominantly focussed on exploitation by US companies.)

Professor Porter's analysis is incongruously titled "Can Japan Compete?", with a positive verdict. Had the UK study been similarly titled, any such conclusion would be problematic – "companies need to move to new types of strategies, investment priorities must change, and new institutions must be developed" is the boldest forecast. There is little to suggest that a similar comparison of capabilities with Germany, France or the Nordics would yield a much different result, as much as with Taiwan, South Korea and other rising Asian countries as their paths cross Britain's decline.

BRAGGADOCIO ENOUGH

Nothing in this is novel. When DTI was formed, an exasperated Foreign Office official said at some meeting, "Why can't you industry people simmer down and leave us to decline with dignity?" an echo of the wizened Lord Armstrong's apocryphal Treasury vision of the 60s that the governance of Britain was "the orderly management of decline". There is nothing dignified nor orderly in decline. And least dignified has been the posturing of post-Thatcherite leaders on the international stage: we have gone far beyond Paul Kennedy's "imperial overstretch"[vi] into the domain of "pretensional overstretch". Maybe, this braggadocio has been puffed up by North Sea energy revenues, but these too are declining. And soon there might even be old-fashioned concerns that somehow the nation needs to earn enough for the energy, food and manufactures that it will have to import to sustain its standard of living.

WHAT SERVICES?

As one of the symptoms of "parochial fragmentation", what passes for economic discourse in the UK uniquely segregates "Services" from "Manufacturing": an artificial dichotomy peculiar to the binary mentality of this country. In practice, in most other countries it would be a source of wonder to query what services could exist without a relationship with

---

[vi] *The Rise and Fall of the Great Powers* by Paul Kennedy (Unwin Hyman), 1986.

manufacture – the sogo shosha of Japan have a comprehensive trading (service) function, organisations the like of which the UK has long lost, embracing raw materials, foodstuffs, energy resources, to logistics, machinery, fashion, IT services, retailing etc, all interfacing with manufacturing. Such "trade" services and manufacturing each call for their own expertise and disciplines, but in any other country are viewed as complimentary, interdependent, and mutually reinforcing.

As a simplifying mantra "Services" is a package term embracing a wide gaggle of retailers – mostly selling other countries' output – financial intermediaries, transportation, hostelries, lawyers, take-away pizzas, estate agents, the flesh-trades, drug trafficking, the guff industries of politics, economics, protest, commentating etc. How far these by themselves can be a viable source of national renewal and tradable value-added must be open to question, as also their immunity to being hollowed out under the influence of information technology advances and the shifting global focus of economic activity. Don't hold your breath![16]

In short, "adjustment British-style" has seen a continuation of some post-imperial enterprises, but an institutional bias (with some rare exceptions like Roll-Royce, JCB, Renishaw, etc) to vacate, or duck out of, those industries where continuing investment in expertise, tailored facilities and innovative thrust are prerequisites to stay with international competitors. To have followed this path on such a massive scale and with such consistency suggests a fundamental flaw in national conceptions of the dynamics of adjustment.

---

[1] Lamentation and wailing at Britain's industrial decline used to be a fairly popular activity, tracing origins back to the latter period of the 19th century. But the consistent pattern has been occasional, sporadic and inadvertent, as behoves a nation that made itself an international laughing stock by having an "industry year" in the 1990s. And invariably ignored.

Readily available accounts are *The Decline of the British Economy* edited by Bernard Elbaum and William Lazonick (Oxford) consisting of a range of essays on sectors such as cotton, steel, shipbuilding and motor vehicles, and broader themes of education, research, finance and the role of the state. The early 80s, perhaps in response to avowed Thatcherite policy declarations to eschew any interest in industry, prompted a rush of such output as *Why Are the British Bad at Manufacturing?* By Williams, Williams and Thomas (Routledge & Kegan Paul), *Whatever Happened to Britain?* by John Eatwell (BBC), and *The British Economic Crisis* by Keith Smith (Penguin) – the last containing a jolly introduction to the never-stabilising-interacting-equilibria game of modish economics. In 1985, the House of Lords issued a report from their Select Committee on Overseas Trade

(HMSO), strident given its origins, but also largely ignored.

Britain's Economic Performance, edited by Buxton, Chapman and Temple (Routledge) – 1994, is among the most useful for recent historic comparisons, being a valedictory set of essays by NEDO staff following closure of the office in 1992. *From Empire to Europe* by Geoffrey Owen seems to be a Panglossian product of the *FT* research office, with the overlay that the declining share of Britain's trade outside the EU and relative growth of that with the EU presages a shift of perspective: an equally plausible explanation might be the loss of British-owned companies' competitiveness in world markets, compensated by the growth of the UK as a base for international companies to pursue sales in the EU.

The Decline of Industrial Britain 1870-1980 by Michael Dintenfass (Routledge) is an attractive monograph surveying the main attributable causes, including useful summaries of the country's relative failure to develop skills and technological adaptability, and relative historic weaknesses in marketing – for example, losing market share for agricultural equipment in Imperial markets like Australia. But, as all too many academic studies conclude, "There is a great deal of work to be done".

More recently have been a series of DTI pamphlets and initiatives on productivity, though statistical comparisons seem to suggest not so far yielding results to narrow the "productivity gap" with leading EU countries and the US. And in 2003 we have had the IPPR report on *Manufacturing in the UK*, perhaps the ultimate expression of the academisation of Britain, with a comfortable "relax and enjoy it" message about continuing industrial decline.

But as a sub-motif to all these analyses is Martin Wiener's *English Culture and the Decline of the Industrial Spirit* (Penguin) with its dominant theme that siphoning talent through public schools and Oxbridge was the surest way to ensure that it is neutered for any practical contribution to sustaining industrial competitiveness. Even W.D. Rubenstein's counterblast *Capitalism Culture & Decline in Britain: 1750 – 1990* ironically makes the same point in arguing that the elite has historically been attracted to the greater relative security of finance and commerce. A flick through David Kynaston's sagas of *The City* confirms that the development of British industry has historically been barely perceptible beyond a guilty afterthought.

Most devastating, Correlli Barnett's *The Audit of War* (Macmillan) with its documented saga of Britain's relative failure over generations to give technology any priority at all levels of education, fragmented structures of industry, the surly ghetto mentality conditioned into the workforce, and inept "practical" mindset of management. All the more powerful in fairly depicting the state of industry across virtually all sectors as they lamentably failed to match the rising competitive challenge in the 60s-80s from companies in other countries as they recovered from World War II. And subsequent volumes have followed these themes, but none with quite the impact of this account.

[2] Conveniently, a delightful vignette of the dilemma posed to countries with a persistent current account deficit was given in the *Financial Times* editorial of the 27th May 2002: "British citizens have been spending but, as so often, the money has flowed abroad boosting economic growth in other countries, not at home.

"In the first quarter, the rise in household spending alone would have generated 0.5 percent economic growth. If an increase in government consumption and the bounce in the inventory cycle is added, the rise in first-quarter domestic demand was 0.9 percent. But that healthy demand growth was entirely eliminated by falling exports and an increasing share of expenditure devoted to imports.

"Surveys show business confidence is improving. But until output growth exceeds that of domestic demand, GDP figures will continue to disappoint."

[3] Economic commentators consoled themselves on the strength of OECD data how well Britain's exports were holding up.

British share of world exports of manufactures

	1960*	1970*	1980	1986	1990	1991
Total (£ million)	*18,700*	*64,300*	*361,993*	*720,327*	*993,152*	*1,023,000*
Percentage shares						
Germany	19.3	19.9	19.8	20.6	20.4	19.9
United States	21.6	18.6	17.5	14.7	16.9	17.7
Japan	6.9	11.7	14.8	19.2	15.7	16.8
France	9.7	8.8	10.0	8.7	9.3	9.2
United Kingdom	16.3	10.6	9.6	7.6	8.5	8.4
Italy	5.2	7.2	7.8	8.1	8.5	8.4
Belgium-Luxembourg	5.9	6.2	5.7	4.9	5.4	5.2
Netherlands	4.0	4.4	4.5	4.4	4.8	4.7
Canada	4.8	6.2	4.0	5.3	4.4	4.3
Switzerland	3.3	3.0	3.3	3.4	3.4	3.2
Sweden	3.1	3.4	2.9	3.0	2.8	2.6

Excluding eastern Germany
Source: *The Economist*.

Yet, outside the comfortable OECD club, Far Eastern exporters were growing at multiples greater rates than the United Kingdom.

Far East export growth 1980-9091 (non-OECD)

	$ million		% increase
Country	*1980*	*1991*	*91/80*
China	18,099	70,451	389
Hong Kong	19,752	98,577	499
Indonesia	21,909	29,142	133
South Korea	17,505	71,897	410
Malaysia	12,958	34,440	266
Singapore	19,376	59,025	305
Taiwan	19,786	76,104	385
Thailand	6,505	28,407	437
(Total)	(135,890)	(468,043)	(344)
United Kingdom	**110,167**	**185,466**	**168**

Source: *The Economist*.

[4] *Post-Capitalist Society* by Peter Drucker, (Butterworth Heinemann 1993). As a more detailed summary of his thesis, still perhaps one of the best quick guides to Britain's historic contribution is the survey published by Central Office of Information in 1987, *British Achievements in Science and Technology*. Even then, the document was a PR disaster since all the ludorum lists contrasted sharply with the country's declining position in virtually all the industries covered by the survey. Today, sadly, the national status in many sectors is non-existent, and becoming relatively miniscule in most others.

But. Yippee. Look out. "A British success in technology transfer" pronounced the *Financial Times* (28.7.06) at news that "Britain's university professors are licensing more patents to business but starting fewer companies" on an analogy with the licensing "spin out" practices in the US. With the challenge, "Now British industry must follow through. It takes an average seven years to go from "patent to profit", but by the end of the decade new computer chips and medicines should be on the market. The challenge will be to turn products into world-leading companies, which has not always happened…. Britain, though, is showing what can be done when the lab coats and the pinstripes work together." Aye. There's the rub. A more honest comment would substitute for "not always happened", with "hardly ever happened". For our "pinstripes" have never shown the least inclination, competence or vision to stimulate corporate development to sustained international success. More likely the patents will be taken up by more adventurous international competitors. While the next day, the same journal reported a study by Cambridge University's Centre for Business Research that "a single US scheme, the Small Business Innovation Research programme, has been at least as important in value terms as venture capital as a source for early-stage finance for American start-ups. The SBIR program, which was established in 1982, is the world's largest seed capital programme for science and technology businesses. Each year it makes more than 4000 awards, amounting to $2 bn (£1.07 bn)." (US businesses "get more aid" than UK: *FT* 29.7.06.)

[5] An account of Sharp's evolution through successively more sophisticated applications of LCDs is provided on pages 56-58 of *Emerging Patterns of Innovation* by Fumio Kodama (Harvard Business School Press). On the next page is another example, "…carbon fibre was not recognised as a new material until Great Britain's Royal Aircraft Establishment discovered that a high-strength, high-modulus carbon fibre can be created from acrylonitrile fibre because the graphite crystal generated in the carbonising process is sintered under tension and arranged in the direction of the fibre. Rolls-Royce became interested in carbon fibres and tried to develop a jet-engine (RB211) that used composite materials reinforced with carbon fibres for its engine blades. However, the development of the engine was fraught with difficulties and led to financial crises for both Rolls-Royce and Lockheed Aircraft Co…"

Subsequently, no British companies, including Courtaulds and ICI, were prepared to invest in developing this composite technology. Yet, "In 1970, Toray invested ¥1.5 billion in a pilot plant. At the time, there was little demand for carbon fibre anywhere in the world. The market required barely one to two tons per month, while the pilot plant had a capacity of five tons per month. Toray, however, took the risk, recognising that composite materials reinforced with carbon fibre could be used in place of steel and light metals as a structural material. The properties of the carbon fibre obtained at the experimental stage were, however, uneven. After two years of developing its manufacturing technology, Toray's pilot plant produced carbon fibre with extremely little unevenness. The fibre was highly rated by the market, and Toray received many inquiries from customers around the world.

"....There was no aircraft aerospace market, the would-be primary market for the material, in Japan". But the golf and sports equipment market offered an opening for the new material, and by the late 1970s was growing rapidly. Currently, Toray is the world leader in carbon fibre composites, with its material used in Airbus and selected for surfacing the new Boeing 787.

But yet another industrial irony: to retain a role for Filton as part of the rationalised Airbus production structure requires investment in a facility to fabricate composite panels for future wing construction. And hence the rush around to find one of the diminishing array of British companies with an interest in such an investment (GKN is in the running "to take over part of the site and build a £100m composites plant there" – "Weak dollar costs GKN £90m in sales" (*FT* 3.8.07)).

[6] *Japanese Industrial Policy* by Ira Magaziner and Thomas Hout (PSI pamphlet No: 585 – 1988) An account of the robust steps taken to "nurture this rose" is in *Nippon* by William Horsley & Roger Buckley (BBC Books) pp 141 ff. A remarkably well-researched narrative of the evolution of Fujitsu and other Japanese computer manufacturers within the context of "controlled competition" is given in *Japan's Computer and Communications Industry* by Martin Fransman (Oxford).

Having a tradition of government working with industry, even if the mythological powers of MITI have been diminished, there remains a willingness to undertake concerted effort to meet prospective constraints in supplies of rare-earth metals. Japan's industries are leaders in digital TVs, laptops, handsets, hybrid vehicles, electric vehicles and batteries, solar panels and components that share a reliance on rare-earth metals. China, by virtue of its own resources and investment in extraction/isolation processes, produces some 97% of world supplies. In response to a worldwide scramble to secure supplies and reduce dependence on China – notably competition for refining rights for Bolivian deposits of lithium, Japan has adopted a range of interlinked policies.

Under a METI (the successor to MITI) report in July 2009, entitled "Strategy for Ensuring Stable Supplies of Rare Metals" a campaign to recycle crucial rare metals in cell phones and home appliances was introduced, and over the rest of the year more than 200,000 units had been collected. A special appropriation of ¥600 million was allocated for new recycling technologies. Studies by The National Institute for Materials Science suggests that such "urban mining" could extract about 1500 tonnes of iridium, some 40% of the world's reserves, while 16% of gold reserves already lie in "urban mines".

Dowa Holdings built a recycling smelter in 2008, and Nippon Mining and Metals is set to launch a recycling business in 2011 for lithium-ion batteries with a capacity to extract about 30 tons of lithium and manganese a month from recycled batteries.

Other prongs of the METI approach covers stockpiling, securing overseas resources, and developing alternative materials:

– Stockpiling: efforts already underway, with additional rare metals – including iridium, gallium, cobalt and tungsten – added to the mandatory list. The aim is to have 60 days domestic consumption available.

– Securing new sources: examples: – Toyota Tsusho Corp, the trading wing of Toyota, has signed a joint venture agreement to develop a rare earth mine in Vietnam that had been investigated by a Japanese government agency. The aim is to begin production in 2012, at a rate sufficient to supply one million hybrid cars. A yen loan is being offered for water supply and road infrastructure around the mine.

– The Japanese government and Sumitomo Corporation agreed with Kazakhstan's atomic energy agency a joint venture for collecting rare-earth metals from uranium extracted ore, with a prospect of producing an annual 3000 metric tons, nearly 10% of Japan's imports.

– Elsewhere, Mitsubishi Corp has gone into Brazil for rare-earth deposits; Mitsui has secured lithium from Canada; and Itochu Corp has begun prospecting for nickel and platinum in Canada. Japanese companies are also in the running for lithium deposits in Bolivia.

– Among the lines of research being pursued is development of zinc oxide as a substitute for iridium in electrodes: already having prototyped a 20 inch LCD TV that uses 40% less iridium, the aim is to achieve a complete substitution. Nanotechnology is being applied to widen the use of iron, relatively abundant: Mitsubishi Electric Corp has developed a high output motor for cars with only an iron-based ferrite magnet, so eliminating the use of neodymium. Combined with stored braking energy, the motor converts electrical energy to motive power with an efficiency of 93-94%, "good enough for use in hybrid and electric cars". Another line of research is the use of iron as a catalyst for the synthesis of medical compounds and liquid crystal materials instead of the usual cobalt, nickel and rare metals like palladium. (*Nikkei Weekly* 1 and 8.3.10)

[7] Extract from *Nikkei Weekly* – 4 August 2003

"Low-Priced Supercomputers Promise to Broaden Market

Fujitsu Ltd and IBM Japan Ltd had separately succeeded in developing low-cost supercomputers priced at around 10% of conventional models.

In both cases, the companies were able to develop machines with high computational power, achieved by using the Linux open-source operating system and stringing together a large number of commodity-grade microprocessors – widely used in personal computers. Conventional supercomputers use specialised operating systems and microprocessors.

Fujitsu has received an order from the Institute of Physical and Chemical Research, known as Riken, and IBM Japan received one from the National Institute of Advanced Industrial Science and Technology. Both government-affiliated institutes will begin using the computers next spring for nanotechnology and biotechnology projects, including analysis of the human genome.

Fujitsu's leasing agreement with Riken is for five years with monthly fees of ¥ 60 million ($504,200). IBM Japan's deal is worth a total ¥ 1.19 billion.

Fujitsu's supercomputer uses 2048 Intel Corp. microprocessors. In theory, the machine is capable of 12.4 teraflops (trillion floating-point operations per second). IBM Japan's model uses 2636 microprocessors from Advanced Micro Devices Inc. and has a computational capacity of 11.2 teraflops.

Supercomputers with similar configurations of operating systems and microprocessors have in the past reached computational capacities of about 11 teraflops. Fujitsu claims that its product is the world's fastest among similarly configured machines.

Among conventional supercomputers, a model jointly developed in 2002 by NEC Corp. and other entities, including the National Space Development Agency, set a world-record speed of around 41 teraflops. While the new supercomputers marketed by Fujitsu and IBM Japan are about one-third is fast, both companies expect to generate demand on a competitive price basis.

The global supercomputer market in 2002 was worth about ¥ 430 billion, according to high tech research firm Gartner Japan Ltd. Due to high costs, supercomputers have largely been limited to public research institutes. Both firms now plan on targeting their relatively inexpensive supercomputers at the research divisions of automobile and drug makers."

[8] Several narrative versions of how Bill Gates put it over on IBM are available, such as *Big Blues* by Paul Carroll. A more analytic account is provided in *Design Rules – the Power of Modularity* by Carliss Baldwin and Kim Clark (MIT Press 2000), illustrating how IBM failed to increase its in-house design effort to capture the modularity options of the System 360, thus leaving profitable modular design opportunities for software and peripherals on the table to be exploited by others. Subsequently, all credit, IBM has recovered by incorporating more of the "soft" potential while still maintaining a leading role in the evolution of technology. But still not the dominant position that it enjoyed in the 1970s.

[9] If the annual DTI R&D Scoreboard has the avowed purpose of comparing international levels of R&D investment, it also offers a convenient tabular comparison of sales by leading corporate contenders: inevitably there are classification ambiguities as these have changed, and increasing the scope from 600 International Competitors in 2001 to 1250 in 2005 affects rankings. Even so, as a general indication of the ranking of international competitors it serves as an indicator of Britain's relative industrial strengths and weaknesses.

Sales of Leading UK Companies vs. International Competitors (£m sales) – 2001[2005]
(From ranking of top 600 [1250] international companies by R&D investment)

Sector	Leading UK Companies			Leading International companies			No of Lager Int'l Cos	
Aerospace & Defence	BAe Systems	(9814)	[11,019]	Boeing	(40,181)	[31,946]	8	[7]
	Rolls-Royce	(6328)	[6603]	EADS	(18,751)	[23,503]	10	[10]
	Smiths	(4958)	[3017]	United Technologies	(18,977)	[24,886]	10	[13]
	Cobham		[1090]					[19]
	Meggitt		[616]					[21]
Automotive & Parts	GKN	(3432)	[3645]	Robert Bosch	(20,718)	[28,869]	30	[36]
				Delphi	(18,012)	[15,606]		
				Denso	(10,633)	[13,818]		
				Visteon	(12,319)	[9888]		
				Valeo	(6231)	[6625]		
Beverages	Diageo	(12,821)	[----]	Kirin Brewery	(5792)	[6094]	0	[-]
Chemicals	ICI	(6425)	[5812]	Bayer	(18,432)	[18,815]	7	[15]
				DuPont	(17,071)	[15,517]		
				BASF	(19,787)	[29,370]		
				Dow	(19,197)	[26,973]		
Construction	Pilkington* [NSG UK]	(2507)	[2582]	St-Gobain	(18,502)	[24,124]	6	[14]
Diversified Industrials	Tomkins	(3374)	[3182]	Tyco	(23,499)	[24,338]	20	[16]
	Cookson		[1635]	GE	(86,771)	[87,195]		[56]
Electricity	BNFL [British Nuclear Group]	(2146)	[2564]	Tokyo Electric	(27,668)	[24,909]	9	[14]
				EDF	(23,224)	[35,077]		
Electronic & Electrical	Invensys	(6472)	[2713]	Siemens	(52,968)	[51,838]	14	[30]
	Spectris		[656]	Canon	(15,301)	[18,525]		[73]
	Renishaw		[176]					[97]
Engineering (Industrial)	IMI		[1578]	MHI	(16,024)	[12,786]		[39]
	JCB Service		[1100]	Caterpillar	(14,119)	[20,179]		[56]
				Komatsu		[8399]		
Food Processing	Unilever	(31,363)	[27,258]	Nestle	(34,824)	[40,252]	1	[1]
				Kellog	(6112)	[5928]		
				Danone	(8810)	[9099]		
				Ajinomoto	(4781)	[5295]		
Forestry & Paper				Int' Paper	(18,201)	[14,036]		[--]
				Stora Enso	(8225)	[9061]		
				Svenska Cellulosa	(5378)	[7056]		
Gas Utilities	National Grid	(9361)		Gazprom	(12,226)	[28,040]		[5]
				Osaka Gas	(5010)	[4813]		
General Retail	GUS	(6475)	[7915]	Amazon.com	(2156)	[4945]	0	[1]
				eBay	(517)	[2175]		
Health**	Amersham(GE)	(1515)	[--]	Medtronic		[6577]	11	[--]
	Smith & Nephew	(1205)	[1407]	Fresenius		[5421]	19	[16]
Household goods	Coats*	(1247)	[--]	Electrolux	(8866)	[9476]	16	[--]
	Dyson*	(226)	[465]					[24]
IT(Technology) Hardware**	Marconi	(4310)	[1337]	Hitachi	(42,066)	[46,710]	24	[51]
	Spirent	(862)	[465]	Fujitsu	(28,801)	[23,505]	70	[98]

Leisure Goods	Pace Micro		[253]	Matsushita Sony Phillips		[43,985] [34,268] [20,884]		[27]
Media	Reuters Reed Elsevier	(3885)	[2885] [5160]	Time Warner Vivendi		[25,426] [8941]	6	[6] [5]
Oil & Gas	BP Shell	(119,117) (93,352)	[145,308] [178,664]	Exxon Mobile	(129,460)	[184,879]	1 2	[1] [1]
Services	Hunting*	(1035)	[1522]	Halliburton Schlumberger Technip	(8933) (9480)	[12,229] [8335] [3695]	3	[8]
Personal Goods	Reckitt Benckiser	(3439)	[3498]	P & G L'Oreal Kimberley Clark	(27,085)	[33,050] [9985] [9268]	7	[8]
Pharma'cals & Biotech	GSK Astra Zeneca Merial Shire Phm Skye Pharma	(20,489)	[21,660] [13,950] [1152] [932] [61]	Merck Pfizer Abbott Labs	(32,944) (22,272) (11,224)	[12,821] [29,912] [13,011]	3	[2] [6] [37] [45] [110]
Software & IT Services	Amdocs Misys Sage Logica Symbian	(1059) (859) (484) (1133)	[1187] [985] [777] [1836] [115]	IBM Microsoft Oracle SAP	(59,283) (17,465) (7488) (4469)	[53,084] [25,793] [8376] [5849]	13 25 31	[17] [20] [24] [13] [95]
Industrial Metals**	Corus	(7699)	[10,140]	Alcoa JFE POSCO	(15,782)	[15,329] [13,837] [15,716]	4	[6]
Telecoms	Vodafone BT	(22,845) (20,559)	[36,616] [19,514]	NTT DeutscheTel France Tel	(59,612) (29,412) (26,195)	[53,329] [40,954] [33,694]	4 5	[2] [5]
Tobacco**	BAT	(11,371)	[9325]	Philip Morris/ Altria Japan Tobacco	(50,362) (23,689)	[23,020]	2	[2]

Where there are more than 1 UK company in the 600 [1250] List, the figure in the right hand column indicates the number of larger international companies for each.

* Indicates where there is no UK company in the 600 top international companies in the list, but is the largest British company in the category. It follows that there will be many more larger companies than those in the international list.

** There has been major subsequent restructuring in this sector so that the order of companies by scale will have changed.

The category of "Support Services" has been omitted since it represents too broad a spread to allow comparison.

(Rather than revise the table for the latest R&D Scoreboard, the figures in square brackets indicate the comparable figure in the 2005/6 Scoreboard where ascertainable.)

[10] "The Theory of the Firm" is one of the zanier branches of economics. The standard sourcebook is apparently the assembly of papers in *The Nature of the Firm* edited by Williamson and Winter (Oxford), and it is just possible to have an interesting time chugging through discussions of "transaction costs", "nexus of contracts", "internal labour markets", "incentive intensity", and so on. None of which appears to have the remotest relationship to how real, and really successful, firms actually function. Alarmingly, this guff is earnestly being imparted to

undergraduates at our more prestigious universities as part of their concerted effort to maintain the output of "instant anachronisms".

Unsurprisingly, a work by John Roberts, an academic economist at Stanford University, *The Modern Firm* (Oxford) won plaudits in *The Economist*, "With an economist's disciplines, the author introduces the reader as gently as possible to some demanding and stimulating ideas, ones that have already been tested by the likes of BP. Nobody, it can now be said, is fully fit to run a modern firm until they have read "The Modern Firm". Sadly, this runs into the peculiar Anglo-Saxon ailment of "the curse of excellence" as "BP has called in Bain, the consulting group, to find ways to simplify the complex organisational structure that the oil major blames in part for its recent problems.... it's not difficult to find examples where our complexity has driven inefficiencies, negatively impacting performance..." (BP calls in Bain to simplify the structure (*FT* 4/5 .8.07)).

Closer to the real world are such works as *Business Organisation and the Myth of the Market Economy* by William Lazonick (Cambridge). It draws on Alfred Chandler's research into the evolution of management structures in the late 19th century, where managerial coordination in structured organisations – "The Visible Hand" – effectively commandeered the allocation of resources from free market mechanisms. And it suggests that the development of this style of business operation, in Germany as well, proved more effective at exploiting the new technologies in the latter half of the 19th century than the proprietary form of organisation which stimulated Britain's early industrial advances. While Japan's "collective capitalism" introduces a further evolutionary shift. Caveats to such an overlay certainly, but the image of the firm as an organising agency for creating value, innovation, learning and continuing development is a major step in the pilgrimage of economics towards reality. And his Laocoonian struggle with the economic theorists deserves at least a couple of statues.

But there are still "more things in heaven and earth" in the dimensions of the real world. On the narrow issue of the implied weakness of "proprietary" capitalist forms i.e. family owned, to the extent that this implies a reliance on traditional craft and manual skills, identifying its limitations against the "Springfield" progress of mass production and the new heavy engineering industries of the late 19th century may be fair. On the other hand, the "proprietary" style of family succession and relationships has a continuing viability. For example, Toyota recently rescued Tomen, one of the weaker of Japan's trading houses. Whilst there must have been some commercial justification, one element was that the founder of Tomen was related to a contemporaneous senior figure in Toyota.

But the "family enterprise" has shown a remarkable resilience. In the German mittelstand, where companies with family control can become significant world players, Robert Bosch and BMW might be the most visible, but many others remain largely unnoticed (*Hidden Champions* by Hermann Simon (HBS)); the family component continues to be an influence in the corporate functioning of Japan (*A History of Top Management in Japan* by H. Morikawa (Oxford)); and the family dynasties of India, and South Korea's Chaebol, despite recent moves to limit the latter's influence. A more elusive variant is the "network" enterprise – typically, the Chinese diaspora (*The Spirit of Chinese Capitalism* by Gordon Redding (de Gruyter)), which has historically been dominant in workshop-type businesses, but now boasts examples of major world-scale operations, for example Li Ka-shing's Hutchinson, with interests ranging from port infrastructure in China and Panama to telecoms, retail and perfumery. But the form would also embrace Acer and the semiconductor fabs of Taiwan.

An even more obscure form is the centuries-old tradition of merchant networks, such as the Arab tradition (*The Merchants* by Michael Field (Overlook Press) portrays some of the more visible contemporary dynasties, if anything narrowed by oil wealth in comparison with the corresponding networks of past centuries) where co-operating cells may be spread geographically very widely. In the shadows, even less discernible shapes are the forms evolving as China modernises without the structural conventions of established Anglo-Saxon institutions – the variations between erstwhile "military" facilities turned to commercial use, the Town and Village Enterprises (TVEs), where "ownership" has a communal and often unwritten form, and as these become linked to the flair of Chinese businessmen in Hong Kong, Malaysia, Singapore, Indonesia and Taiwan (*Asia Rising* by Jim Rohwer (Nicholas Brewley)), with Vietnam also evolving in a similarly fluid manner.

A crucial feature of these unconventional idioms of capitalism lies in their reliance on informal relationships, where trust has a higher valency than "contracts", and consequently have a more opaque style of interaction. But a style where speed and efficiency of transactions confers advantages.

Forefend that economists should venture into the real world. After all, Adam Smith's account of a pin factory (though it transpires he never actually stepped in the door of such a facility) set in train centuries of disastrous oversimplification. But the literature is not lacking in accounts of these diverse forms, and indeed also the diversity of relations between business and the state. To illustrate how freakish Britain has become, it is worth recalling Peter Drucker's recent reminder: "With the exception of the US and UK, no developed country believes that the corporation exists for the sake of the shareholder. This is a totally alien idea. Corporations exist in most countries for the sake of social harmony, for employment. In Japan the social reality is that employees come first. In Germany, too."

But without getting out of their ivory towers, economists could try a diet of company histories to satisfy themselves of the irrelevance of their precepts. Apart from Honda, some candidates might be:

Mitsui: Three Centuries of Japanese Business by John Roberts (Weatherhill). Apart from being virtually a history of modern Japan, the account also illustrates the extent to which family and managerial capitalism can co-evolve. While the antiquity of the zaibatsu is probably unique for corporate durability: when Adam Smith refers to Japan's silver being traded in the streets of London, he is referring to the activities of Sumitomo, another of this genre.

The Nokia Revolution by Dan Steinbok (Anacom). A startling reminder that growth to world contention can emerge from unexpected sources, where a third of the nation seems involved in the company's success.

Sony – the Private Life by John Nathan (Harper Collins); *Toshiba* by Robert Cutts (Penguin); *Toyota* by Edwin Reingold (Penguin); *The Rise of NEC* by K.Kobayashi (Blackwell); *Personality in Industry* by H.Tanaka (Pinter).

All illustrate the dynamic questing and questioning of the best international companies, and the spirited individuals – entrepreneurs, in our terminology, for want of anything else – who carried them forward. But with many a puzzling query: for example, Toshiba competes fiercely with Sony in laptops, home electronics, DVD formats etc, yet makes the key microprocessor for PlayStation (an anomaly only recently resolved by Sony selling its stake in the joint venture to Toshiba).

If the stuff of MBA case studies, a continuing question is why such enterprises remain unattainable through Britain's corporate system, even though an increasing share of economic activity in this country derives from their operations within our shores. Rolls-Royce is perhaps the only British candidate in this fellowship, though not without some timely government intervention.

Beyond the Firm Ed Takeo Shiba and Masahiro Shimotani (Oxford) offers a series of portraits of differing national group structures, with timely reminders that the forms most suited to adaptation to shifting patterns of technology and development are not from the market-allocative tradition. But more later.

[11] How about?

"GPS chip shrunk to fit anything

Semiconductor designer C&N Inc. has developed a tiny chip with built-in Global Positioning System functions that measures just 18 mm square and weighs just 7 grams.

Given a power source, the chip can be built into just about any product, such as watches and pedometers, to provide a means of tracking location, as well as nursing products for the elderly and items for children.

The chip runs software that determines location using signals from GPS satellites with an accuracy of 3 m. Combined with digital map information, precision can be increased to the level of several centimetres.

The Tokyo company uses basic GPS technologies from QinetiQ Ltd., a British defence firm, and modified chip circuitry to simultaneously receive satellite signals and convert them into digital signals.

C&N also uses proprietary software to extract only the necessary information from the GPS satellite feeds. The result is a GPS chip that is not only small but also fast, displaying locational information in only around one second, compared to the usual eight seconds.

C&N has priced the chip at ¥15,000." (*Nikkei Weekly* 14.8.06)

[12] UK Relative R&D Performance

If only an imperfect measure of "innovation" in its broadest sense, the level of patents applications is generally regarded as a rough surrogate for depicting relative R&D success. Again, there are banks of comparative data, but a useful starting point is the comparison of US patents per million population in *Britain's Economic Performance*. The third column draws on a survey of high-tech US patents for 2002 on the same basis.

	1963-80	1980-85	2002*
UK	44	40	14.4
Germany	55	97	14.4**
France	27	39	13.3
Italy	8	14	4
Japan	10	79	80.2
US	236	158	84.3

*Compiled on the basis of high-tech patents from an update presented to a Cambridge/MIT Institute seminar on 19 Nov 2002 drawn from the EU Innovation Scoreboard 2002.

**Includes the previous East Germany

There may well be some statistical categorisation differences in the update, but the purpose is narrowly to indicate relative country differences. Not shown is the rise of Finland (35.9), Sweden (29.5), Netherlands (19.6) and Denmark (17.3) above the UK in 2002.

A general indication of international shifts in national technology significance can be drawn from taking five-yearly comparisons of all patent types registrations by the US Patent and Trademark office:

	1977	1982	1987	1992	1997	2002	2007
US Origin	45049	37704	47916	58791	69923	97125	93691
Japan	6500	8656	17294	23164	24191	36339	35942
Germany	5653	5621	8093	7605	7292	11957	10012
UK	2774	2280	2967	2637	2906	4202	4031
France	2195	2075	2990	3282	3202	4421	3720
Taiwan	53	99	411	1253	2597	6730	7491
Canada	1335	1158	1770	2218	2817	2857	3970
South Korea	7	18	105	586	1965	4009	7264
Sweden	945	804	1089	727	970	1824	1278
Netherlands	733	651	998	974	895	1681	1596
Isreal	95	116	257	350	577	1108	1219

China has historically been excluded from international comparisons, but is targeting 2% of GDP on R&D by 2010 having reached 1.42% of GDP in 2006. The country's objectives have a comprehensive reach across energy, minerals, agriculture, manufacturing, transport, IT, health and national security, and 16 "megaprojects", deploying a range of tax incentives. In high and medium technologies, China and India have patent growth higher than the US and Japan. (OECD Science, Technology and Industry Report 2008)

One of the refreshing pleasures of following Japan's industrial evolution is the reporting of the Nikkei, more thorough and analytical on their companies' activities than could be found in the cursory, heavily stock-market biased, coverage of even UK quality journals. And Japanese companies have not fallen prey to the "analysts' tyranny" of sticking to narrow sectors of activities, rather recognising that their competences can permit sensible diversification where there are viable interfaces. There has, admittedly, in the past been a tendency for some Japanese companies to extend the range of diversification over-aggressively, the cause of much restructuring in recent years. To keep up the story of Japan's R&D investment, "Combined R&D spending by 264 major corporations in Japan will rise by 6.37% on the year to ¥11.84 trillion ($97.8 billion) for fiscal 2007, increasing for the eighth straight year, according to a Nikkei survey." (*Nikkei Weekly* 30.7.07)

At a more specific level, *The Nikkei Weekly* (25.10.04) noted that shipments by chemical corporations in 2003 totalled some $333 billion, second in value to automobiles but with the highest in value-added. In materials for semiconductors world market share of Japanese companies was in excess of 70% (ranging from 61% for Photoresists, 75% for silicon wafers to 100% for ceramic boards), and over 70% in materials for LCDs (ranging from 49% for ceramic boards, 78% for deflecting plates to 100% for TAC and wide-view films). In more specialised fields, Zeon Corp supplies nearly 100% of the lens materials for camera-equipped cellular phones; Toray has become the dominant supplier of carbon-fibres for next-generation aircraft from Boeing and Airbus; while Kuraray supplied a Vectran fibre airbag for the US Mars probe; and Teijin has a line of advanced functional fibres, including one that produces a sheen comparable to butterfly wings. Such in-house technologies allow their unique proprietary knowledge to be better protected than others, and their incorporation in other product fields is such that electronics and machinery manufacturers are increasing their chemical expertise.

Perhaps because of their strong tradition of company-centred research and innovation, Japan has been relatively backward compared to the US in spinning technology out of their universities. In the past decade various measures have been taken to stimulate venture capital start-ups, and the leading technology universities now have a cluster of incubating companies.

As a further move to exploit the research strengths of their universities, the last LDP government set up a ¥100bn ($1.05bn) FIRST (Funding Program for World Leading Innovative R&D in Science and Technology) fund to run for the next four years. This has been confirmed by the new Democratic Party government. The fund is allocated to leading researchers, both corporate and academic, in their respective fields to assemble the various disciplinary teams drawing upon both universities and leading related companies to prove commercial applications.

Examples of the current allocations cover extending performance of atomic resolution holography electron microscopes (¥5.0bn); green nanotechronics (¥4.6bn); disease diagnosis by mass spectrometry (¥3.4bn); reverse-osmosis membranes for desalination (¥2.9bn); regenerative medicine with induced pluripotent stem (iPS) cells (¥5.0bn); nano-satellites (¥4.1bn); plastic optical fibres (¥4.0bn); fastest database engine (¥3.9bn); photonic-electronic integration system (¥3.9bn); fluoroscopic real-time tracking radiotherapy for removing organ tumours (¥3.6bn). (*Nikkei Weekly* 1 and 8.3.10)

[13] *Manufacturing in the UK* by Richard Brooks and Peter Robinson (IPPR 2003). In projecting the longer run future the authors conclude, "There is no reason to believe that the long-trends for the manufacturing sector to shrink as a proportion of the advanced industrial economies will halt or reverse, and achieving such a reverse should not in any case be a goal of public policy." The long-term trend suggests "a UK manufacturing sector accounting for some 10% of output and less than 5% of employment by 2050."

There is a curiously elliptical conclusion that such a prospect could only be faced with equanimity "if such a transition can be managed smoothly, without harmful impacts on particular regions where manufacturing is concentrated, without any sudden worsening of the current account balance, and without unacceptable negative effects on the high return activities related to manufacturing such as research and development." (Page 25)

The outstanding feature of this rationale is that it illustrates the main attraction of the "invisible hand", a wonderful excuse for "sitting on hands". Later, there is a justification that "uncertainty" is a rational pretext for firms "to wait and see" before investing (Page 34). More "sitting on hands". There is even a bow to the favourite industrial excuse, "much depends upon external factors such as the trade weighted sterling exchange rate". Come off it. Just compare: Honda, Toyota, Sony and other Japanese companies have had to contend with a yen/US$ exchange rate that has moved from 360 to 100/120, even down to 90 at one point. While German companies have had to cope with a strong Deutschmark for decades. Meanwhile, sterling has devalued over the same period from 2.40 to 1.70/1.80 to the US$, briefly falling to parity in the 1980s. With such reinforcement for inertia, the projection of manufacturing accounting for 10% of output by 2050 could be too high and/or reached much earlier.

This is a rationale for completing the national cop-out for any significant world economic presence. For manufacturing and product-related services still comprise more than three-quarters of world trade, and this is likely to persist. And none of the provisos for managing the transition smoothly have been adequately tested.

[14] Extract from *Nikkei Weekly* – 18 August 2003

"Honda kick-starts bike R&D

Honda Motor Co. has set up research and development bases in India and Vietnam to increase local motorcycle development and sales.

In India, a subsidiary of Honda R&D Co. has launched a wholly owned motorcycle R&D unit in a New Daily suburb. The lab, with some 10 staff members, will initially research motorcycle colours popular with Indian consumers to reflect them in new motorcycle models.

The Indian motorcycle market is expected to grow 10 percent from a year earlier to 25.5 million units in 2003.

In Hanoi, Honda has established a representative office to promote motorcycle R&D. The office will also do research on what types of motorcycles are favoured by local consumers. The units in India and Vietnam have raised the number of Honda R&D bases in Asia to five, together with those in China, Indonesia and Thailand.

According to Honda, combined motorcycle sales in five Southeast Asian countries – the Philippines, Malaysia, Thailand, Vietnam and Indonesia – plus China and India stood at 21.72 million units in 2002, up 18% from the previous year. The company said it grabbed a 26% share of the market that year."

[15] The Government's trailed "blueprint to boost science" in the 2004 was yet another prance around a very tattered maypole, and barely enough to make good years of under-investment. Even before the "white heat of technology", there had been a series of efforts, under such banners as the Advisory Committee on Scientific Policy, Department of Scientific and Industrial Research (DSIR), National Research and Development Council (NRDC) – well catalogued in Correlli Barnet's *The Verdict of Peace* (Macmillan). Since when there has been a continuous stream of "Schemes" and "Initiatives" to stimulate academic research, industrial exploitation, and R&D by industry.

Consistent with the "dodgy insurance salesman" society that has evolved from the dominance given to "service sector" industries, you have got to look at the Treasury small print. All credit to *Observer* (*FT* 17.3.04) for spotting, under the heading "Dismal Science": "Footnote of the week – and possibly the year – came yesterday from the Treasury, in its paper on science and innovation."

Beginning with a paean to the government's grand intentions for a "10-year investment framework for science", the report rather let itself down with Footnote 1.

"'Science' is used throughout this document in its broadest sense, to encompass all aspects of engineering, technology, mathematics, design, social sciences and the arts and humanities," it reads.

Perhaps a revolutionary new holistic vision of science. More likely, as *Observer* suggests, a pretext for extending the Treasury's role as the sole remaining patron of economics faculties, by making "the dismal science" eligible. Still more likely, on past form, this is a device to create a funding heading that can absorb other budgets e.g. Arts Council to save expenditure, or, conversely, if proposals for genuine science are not forthcoming from the nation's depleted research base, the expenditure figures can be topped-up with other activities to spin a semblance of success.

[16] Even as the curtain rose on the Savoyard Opera of Britain's future lying primarily in services, the Bank of England concluded (Quarterly Bulletin: September 1985 – Services in the UK Economy): "The United Kingdom has lost share in the value of world exports in services at a rate similar to that at which it has lost share in the value of world exports of manufacturers".

THE ADJUSTMENT DILEMMA

A consistent theme in critiques of Britain's industrial history is "the failure to adjust", "failure to adapt...", and many hours in whatever Department had an interest in industry have been spent, and probably still are, on discussions around this theme. These are spiced periodically by whatever is the latest guru snake oil – "competences", "clusters", "supply chain management", "entrepreneurial spirit", "networking" and the latest variations on "knowledge/innovation". Each amplified by academics and consultants bandwagoning. Tossed into the perennial debate are the "inhibitors" of change – "labour intransigence/managerial incompetence", "short-termism", "relatively high interest rates", "over-regulation", "infrastructure neglect", and so on. Out of this melee has come the inevitable ascendancy of the resignationists "does it matter?", "can we have an economy that relies solely on services?" – especially prevalent in Keith Joseph's day, when there was shocked horror at the realisation that even Luxembourg was home to Arbed, one of Europe's historic steel companies, the "Ar" of Arcelor. Or, "Don't worry, we can rely on the returns from our overseas investments". Or, "inward investment will save us".

Despite this morass of verbiage, and, of course, periods of brilliant macroeconomic management – invariably followed by a "bust" – the underlying process of decline has been inexorable. This should have suggested by now that there is a fundamental flaw in the architecture that has defined the national response to change.

To get a handle on this theme, it might be instructive to look at the conventional wisdom on industrial change. In their edition of the 20th of February 1999 *The Economist* included a survey on *Innovation in Industry*.[1] If in typically smart-arse style, and, if in the euphoria of the time, it instanced Lucent – one of the most catastrophic collapses of the dot.com bubble – as one of the dynamic centres of innovation, it sets out the now-conventional orthodoxy. In a section with the catchy title *Catch the wave*, with a snappy headline *The long cycles of industrial innovation are becoming shorter* over a cartoon of a fish being drawn out of a high-rise office block, the argument goes, "Think of innovation as 'x' in the economic-growth equation – a factor that clearly matters but no-one is quite sure how much... from Adam Smith to Karl Marx, economists have struggled to understand productivity growth. But it was not until after the Second World War that the beginnings of an explanation emerged. The theory now generally accepted stems from work done on the so-called 'production function' by Robert Solow of the Massachusetts Institute of Technology. This says, reasonably enough, that the output of an economy depends on its inputs – in short, capital and labour. Double the inputs and you get twice the output. To the basic theory, economists have added a rider to account for embarrassing quirks such as the law of diminishing returns. In the revised version, if you add more and more capital to a given labour force, or an increasing number of workers to a fixed amount of capital, the result will be successively smaller increases in output....

Unfortunately, the real world works rather differently. For instance, if the law of diminishing returns operates as it is supposed to, why have returns on investment in America, Europe and Japan been higher in the second half of the 20th century than in the first half? Why, for that matter, has the gap between the world's rich and poor countries widened rather than narrowed? The theory says that where the stock of capital is rising faster than the workforce – as has clearly been true in the industrial countries since the Second World War – the return on each additional unit of capital should fall over time. Instead, it has risen over the decades rather than fallen, so something is amiss.

For want of a better explanation, that "something" is now reckoned to be technological progress plus other forms of new knowledge – in short, innovation. In this scheme of things, innovation accounts for any growth that cannot be explained by increases in capital and labour. And although the return on investment may decline as more capital is added to the economy, any deceleration in growth is more than offset by the leveraging effects of innovation. This explains why rates of return have stayed high in rich countries, and why poorer countries have not caught up.

There the economists tend to leave the argument, as if technological progress – along with other new knowledge – was simply to be taken for granted, as free as air. However, experience shows that technological know-how, manufacturing experience and market research are not free; they have to be acquired at considerable cost. And once acquired, such proprietary knowledge tends to be hoarded as trade secrets or hedged in by patents and other intellectual-property rights. To ignore such quibbles might be justified if innovation contributed only marginally to economic growth. Yet, maddeningly, this residual, intangible and largely ignored factor seems to account for more than half of all growth. Thus, if this reading is correct, it is innovation – more than the application of capital or labour – that makes the world go round.

All attempts to understand the effects of technological progress on economic growth pay homage to Joseph Schumpeter, an Austrian economist best remembered for his views on the "creative destruction" associated with industrial cycles 50 – 60 years long. Arguably the most radical economist of the 20th century, Schumpeter was the first to challenge classical economics as it sought (and still seeks) to optimise existing resources within a stable environment – treating any disruption as an external force on a par with plagues, politics and the weather. Into this intellectual drawing room, Schumpeter introduced the raucous entrepreneur and his rumbustious behaviour. As Schumpeter saw it, a normal, healthy economy was not one in equilibrium, but one that was constantly being "disrupted" by technological innovation." This is summarised in the chart reproduced in Figure 1 below.

Figure 1

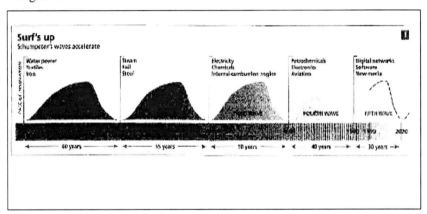

Some might argue that this is a somewhat muted account of the disruptive consequences of Schumpeter's reasoning. But this rationale seems to lie behind the search for "the next big thing" that entices investors to blow bubbles – a rationale that *The Economist* itself tends to promote. But it has also been the underpinning of that simplistic school of policy which boils down to "out with the old" – the "smoke stack", "rust belt", "metal-bashing" – and "in with the new".

Notwithstanding the mountains of tracts in the "literature" on "revolutions", as a depiction of the realities of industrial change, only a short period of reflection should be enough to recognise that it is not only inadequate, but plain wrong. Just to take one of the earliest "wave" industries, textiles. It has been in a continuous state of evolution. For example, a Tsuzuki plant, by virtue of innovations in sensing, control, feedback and spinning processes may have a capacity for spinning cotton comparable to the whole of the historic Lancashire industry in its prime with nigh-immaculate quality and a wide range of counts.[2] The advent of artificial fibres – nylon, Terylene, rayon, polyesters etc – set in train a further interaction of technologies. Toray, as its name implies, began as a licensee of rayon patents, but is currently producing fibres in nano-dimensions, and consumers now have a range of blended and composite fibres, particularly evident in new weatherproof wear, not to mention ladies swimsuits that avoid the damp after-presence of water. The same technology has applications in nano-aperture membranes (Toray is also a leading producer of carbon-fibres). While dynamic change is continuing under the pressures of "fast fashions" and further innovations such as "intelligent" materials. In reality, "textiles" has continued to be a vibrant and innovative industry, interacting with technologies in apparently unrelated fields.

The "steel" story is the same – not only such process innovations as basic oxygen furnaces (BOF), gas recovery (OC) systems, continuous casting (CC), and arc-furnaces, but with improved sensors, control systems and integration, and new laminates, composites, surfacing technologies etc, we learn that 70% of the steel used in new cars did not exist ten years ago. Indeed, the 2005 update of the Honda Legend has a steel/aluminium alloy for its bodywork, a technological feat long regarded as impossible owing to the incompatibility of the two metals. And further innovations in energy-saving, enhanced precision and materials are being evolved. Someone has clearly omitted to tell POSCO, Nippon Steel and others that they are "rust belt".[3] Or, to recall my visit to TWI, Mitsubishi Heavy (MHI) recently boasted that their new MJ civil jet aircraft will be the first to employ "friction stir welding" – in fact, BAe are using this technology in their production of the wings of the new A 380. Or, "rail", "electricity", "chemicals", "internal combustion engines", or any of the other "waves". All show the same characteristics of the "old" being revitalised by the "new".

As *The Economist* author suggests, and as implied by the depiction of compressed sine-waves, economic orthodoxy is predisposed towards the imaginary domain of equilibria. This ducks one of fundamental tensions posed by Schumpeter, in that change by its nature is directed at disrupting equilibria. But the author goes on to note, "In real life, the innovation process is a cat's cradle of inter-relationships, a network of feedback connections." That the transition from innovation to market impact involves a range of interactions is indisputable. But industrial adjustment is a continuous process, with continuous turbulence, continuous interactions, continuous feedback and continuous destruction. The term "technology fusion" seems as fair a depiction as any of the dynamic interaction between these diverse flows of technology and knowledge.[4]

It did not require any "wave" of new technology for the Japanese motorcycle manufactures to destroy the British industry. That there are periodic breakthroughs that have greater dynamic impact may be true. Even so, the Archimedes-bath model is not necessarily the norm: for example, the Light Emitting Diode (LED) is more efficient, has longer life, and is potentially much less expensive to manufacture than the luminescent bulb, yet the costs of replacing installed systems will delay its widespread adoption.[5] Or, while the technology for the fuel-cell goes back to the late 19th century, it has taken a combination of new materials, refinements in precision engineering, new systems for isolating hydrogen and controlling the interaction, and pressures for more environmentally acceptable forms of power to bring the development to potential application.

Moreover, beyond the creative interaction of particular technologies, there are continuing trends and pressures for change. Optics is not usually included in the conventional "waves", yet it was the innovations in glass and lenses that opened the horizons for the scientific and engineering advances of the 17th and 18th centuries,[6] and continuing advances in refining discrimination through the microscope, magnetic field scanning, speed of photography and control systems are opening the way to micro-manufacturing. A symbiotic pressure has been the demand to make products more manipulable and portable, evidenced today in the increasing compression of computing and electronic gadgets, and systems for sensing and transmitting real-time performance in aero engines and airframes, as much as in the compact vanity boxes of Victorian ladies and rice-paper *Crudens* for missionaries. In this progression, "manufacturing" is moving into wholly new dimensions where components and modules of successive generations are demanding ever-increasing precision, quality and speed of fabrication, and, indeed, imposing the same demands on the "machines to make the machines".[7] Far beyond any labelling of "metal-bashing".

Equally, to select "rail", "internal combustion engine", and "aircraft" ignores other innovations such as the "telegraph" and "wireless" in the continuum of communications enhancement. This strand includes an outstanding example of a transparent innovation that managers must have been tripping-over for generations: the concept of "containerisation" has been inherent in the nursery toy of placing wooden cubes into an oblong cart that goes back at least to Victorian times. For all the obvious efficiencies in dock handling, loading and stability against "slipping cargoes", that in all the decades when Britain ruled the waves our maritime marine did not exploit this obvious technology further than the "tea chest" is some tribute to the myopic path-dependency of management, even in those days. While videoconferencing as a substitute for physical travel is merely one of the latest manifestations of this strand of feedback.

To attempt a graphic presentation of a dynamic process is bound to simplify, but *The Economist* illustration should be recast on the lines of Figure 2.

Figure 2

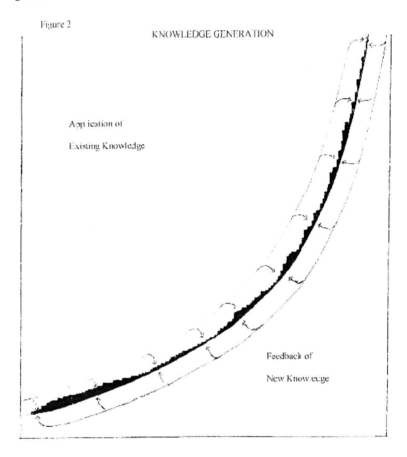

Figure 2

KNOWLEDGE GENERATION

Application of
Existing Knowledge

Feedback of
New Knowledge

This suggests many more "waves", of varying impact, but with the "new" drawing continuously on the knowledge of the "past", with "new" innovations feeding back to existing expertise. Not only a better depiction of reality. But also a better reflection of what Schumpeter actually said, "capitalism... is by nature a form or method of economic change and not only never is but never can be stationary", and confronting "the perennial gale of creative destruction".[8] And incidentally reflects Sun Tzu's "there are no constant conditions". In effect, if *The Economist* author makes passing reference to "feedback" he fails to feed this into modifying his sine curve model.

The appropriate organisational response – whether of the firm, institution or society – has to embrace the dilemma of sustaining continuity to carry forward the experience and knowledge of the past, and generating the resources – human as much as physical and financial – and suppleness to exploit the opportunities flowing from new knowledge. One of the most perilous distinctions drawn in the academic literature is between "radical/disruptive" and "incremental" innovation. Invariably the former demands the latter to be exploited commercially, or, more pointedly, it is those companies that have an established capability of feeding-back experience and knowledge that will have evolved a context where the potential of a "radical/disruptive" innovation can be applied. But this dilemma is sharpened by the ambiguities flowing from change, when disciplines, competences and structures once successful can become rigidities.[9] And a clear lesson is that, once falling off the curve of knowledge enhancement it is more difficult to return: to take another of Britain's "smokestack" industries from which it has largely exited, leading producers today knock off a 60,000-ton ship in two months.[10]

But to make the shift in perspective from the economists' customary vantage point on the moon to the realities of knowledge flows and interaction also demands realignment of much of the customary jargon – for example, "catching up". In conventional application, a stage through which underdeveloped countries have to pass en route to "developed" status. In reality, all enterprises and economies confront the constant challenge to "catch up" with shifts in technology and processes, and their impact on existing activities. Ironically, there is a tendency for "catching up" enterprises and economies to overshoot those previously rated as "leaders". In the former, once having evolved organisations and structures honed to capturing technology and with the dynamism to overtake the "front-runners", this dynamic persists. Aided, certainly in the saga of British industry, by the complacency that derives from the satisfactions (and rewards) of providing "shareholder value", even though the underlying business is in relative decline.[11]

But that orthodox economics can be so far adrift poses the question whether it may itself not be one of the prime culprits distorting efforts at successful adaptation. Indeed, if there is a sect in Britain more deserving of being buried in a shower of conkers, if not worse, it is economists. And it would be worth firing a few pebbles into the chestnut tree to see what happens. But to follow the due rigours of scientific method, a hypothesis should be erected, and then tested. How about, "Economics is Bollocks" as a starting hypothesis?

---

[1] While acting as Programme Director of an Innovation Club run mainly from the Science Policy Research Unit at Sussex University, this article was drawn to my attention. The Club's activities involved exchanges about corporate approaches to innovation from a diversity of companies such as Rolls-Royce, BT, Procter & Gamble, Sharp, Skoda, Ove Arup and Balfour Beatty: in the real world of real competition the last thing on any company's mind is "waves".

[2] The rise of the "new spinners", of which Tsuzuki was among the technology leaders, is summarised in Chapter 6 of *Technology and Industrial Development in Japan* by Hiroyuki Odagiri and Akira Goto (Oxford).

[3] The diversity of products under the heading "steel" is such that several manufacturers still see their future in terms of specialised products rather than in the economies of scale that have influenced major restructuring in the industry. Examples are Voestalpine of Austria, that sees its "focus on specialist products give us plenty of opportunities for growth"; Rautaruukki, a Finish producer, that focuses on parts for construction as well as esoteric types of high-value steel, "in this specific part of the steel industry the need is to give a better service to customers, and to introduce new and specialist grades of steel, not the idea of getting economies of scale"; or Böhler Uddeholm of Vienna, the world's biggest maker of high-value steel for use in cutting tools, "In our field, the steel we make and sell can cost up to €3500 a tonne [roughly 7 times higher than the price for conventional steel]. We consider ourselves more like a pharmacy than a steelmaker, shipping orders to customers around the world in small quantities. We would not want to lose this focus on quality and technological improvement that almost certainly would be threatened if we were to merge with another company with a different philosophy." (Steel might shy away from partnerships: *FT* 9.10.06.) Or the subsequent comments of the Vienna-based company, "We sell to 100,000 customers and in many ways are more like a pharmacist than a steelmaker: we have to get out material to customers at the right time and in the right formulation." (Dawn of steel's flexible future: *FT* 24.11.06.)
    But is "steel" always going to be "steel"? With volatile raw material/steel prices and supply constraints – indeed, Nissan having had to shut down production for a week through shortage of steel, and under pressures to make vehicles lighter Nissin Kagyo, a major supplier of brake parts, has made a new nanocomposite material as light as aluminium but as strong and heat resistant as cast-iron.
    "The Honda Motor Co affiliate is studying applications of the new material to brake systems, which must endure one of the most hostile environments of vehicle components. It has already created some prototype brake parts using the new composite.

A carbon nanotube is a hollow cylinder of molecules with a diameter about 1-10,000th of a human hair. The tubes are 400 to 1000 times tougher than aluminium and have twice the thermal conductivity of a diamond.

In 2003, the Ueda, Nagano Prefecture, firm began research into creating a material with the benefits of both carbon nanotubes and aluminium. That goal had been hampered by the difficulty of disbursing nanotubes evenly within aluminium. After numerous failed attempts, the company has finally developed a way to mix the two....... The new material is 30% stronger than steel and can withstand a comparable level of heat. It also features 30% higher thermal conductivity than aluminium and is just as corrosion resistant.

Initially, the biggest hurdle for commercialisation was the high price of carbon nanotubes. But as their applications spread to other areas, the costs of certain types have fallen to around ¥10 (9 cents) per gram from thousands of yen, bringing the innovation closer to the marketplace." (*Nikkei Weekly*: 27.6.05)

[4] "Technological fusion" figures in *Emerging Patterns of Innovation* by Fumio Kodama (Harvard Business School Press) denoting the diverse streams of technology and processes that have to be integrated in the formation of a successful marketable product.

This fusion defies academic classification, and pretensions for managing "knowledge", "innovation", "breakthroughs" or whatever should be treated with caution. The real mystery lies within the dynamics of companies and their cohesion and drive. Which will vary beyond neat classification. Some glimpse of the contemporary realm of innovation might be to take an account of the early innovators, such as *The Industrial Revolutionaries* by Gavin Weightman (Atlantic Books), with all of the happenstance and diversity of origins, and multiply the pace a hundred fold.

[5] Light Emitting Diodes (LEDs) resurrect Alexander Bell. "Communications via light began 125 years ago. In 1880, Alexander Graham Bell sent the first wireless message on what he called a photophone. In the trial, the photophone converted a sender's voice into vibrations of a thin mirror. The reflected, vibrating beam of sunlight then reached a second mirror 200 m away, whose vibrations in turn reproduced the message for a receiver.

Unfortunately for Bell, the photophone was prone to interference from factors such as clouds. The century-old technology lay dormant until (Prof Masao) Nakagawa shed new light on it in 1998.

That was when a new light source, the LED, drew Nakagawa's attention for its ability to blink millions of times a second. Traditional light sources such as fluorescent bulbs are limited in link frequency, which ruled them out as a means of transmitting data in amounts large enough to be practical. Nakagawa's team formed the Visible Light Communications Consortium (VLCC) to set standards for the technology".

If initially industry was cool on taking up the concept, at a trade show in October 2004 the technology amazed visitors with the ability to listen to music and see pictures coming from light fixtures. Among applications being developed is a cellphone that receives train timetables from lights on station platforms, to provide information on museum exhibits, simultaneous translation services with languages distinguished by streams of data in different colours of transmitted light, and conveying travel directions from streetlights." (*Nikkei Weekly* 24.10.05)

[6] *The Glass Bathyscaphe* by Alan MacFarlane and Gerry Martin (Profile Books) offers a fascinating insight into the role played by advances in glass formation in stimulating the ascendancy of North West Europe in sciences and technology in the 15th to 18th centuries. If the Industrial Revolution was characterised by the fervour of ideas and "entrepreneurial" spirits so vividly illustrated by Jenny Uglow's *The Lunar Men* (Faber), it is at least arguable that this dynamism was underwritten by the scope of inquiry opened up by this evolution of glass technology (and the private "surpluses" generated by the privateer/slave/plantation industries – see next section).

[7] With the thrust to miniaturisation, working in micro-and nano-dimensions, processes and materials seem to have gained a more crucial role. For example, cleaning old-fashioned screws for manufacturing Hard Disk Drives (HDD) – ubiquitous in CD/DVD/mobile music players – to avoid any granules being released that might interfere with the drive and sensitive sensing systems has become a closely guarded technological secret: even more protected as the trend is for HDDs to become smaller. (Takumi avoids filing patents to keep edge, controls 70% of global market – *Nikkei weekly* 18.7.05.)

Or, take capacitors, devices to store electrical charges and regulate current flow, which go back as far as Edison. To make them in dimensions of $0.4 \times 0.2 \times 0.2$mm for the latest trends in mobile phones, LCD TVs and laptops really separates the men from the boys, with Murata and TDK tussling to become the world market leaders, both of whose strength lies in developing their own machines to layer multiple ceramic sheets as thin as several microns. (Murata capacitors are backbone of global electronics industry – *Nikkei Weekly*, 28.1.08.)

[8] Joseph Schumpeter *Capitalism, Socialism, and Democracy* (Harper & Row). Douglass North – *Understanding the Process of Economic Change* (Princeton) – is refreshingly frank on the limitations of economic orthodoxy to measure up to the complexities, uncertainties and interdependencies underlying the process of beneficial economic development: "The complex interdependent structure of our modern political economies has evolved its modern form over time and usually without deliberate planning. As a result we have very imperfect understanding of the structure essential to their performance. But as soon as we attempt to improve the performance of poorly performing economies we become very conscious of what complex problems result from this interdependence. The integration of the dispersed knowledge requires more than a price system for its accomplishment."

Recognising that "the growth in the stock of knowledge is the fundamental underlying determinant of the upper bound of human well-being," its evolution is characterised by an "intricate mixture of new knowledge, applied knowledge, and techniques... integrated together by institutions and organisations to realise the potential of this knowledge." And he illustrates the exponential growth of technology since the 18th century by the incidence of scientific periodicals and the escalation in new technologies and applications, particularly in the last century.

The sine curve depiction of "waves" of technologies simply fails to acknowledge the diversity of interactions, and, left to themselves to examine "knowledge", economists naturally emulate angelic salsas on pinheads: typical is *The Economics of Knowledge* by Dominique Foray (MIT), where the pastime of mutual citations among an esoteric clique is played out with scant reference to the real world.

[9] The dilemma of being poised on the cusp between exploiting existing knowledge, including that which is tacitly held within the organisation, and being alert and accommodating to the new – if a happy hunting ground for "witch doctors" – is more in the nature of a continuing existential choice, where the validity of response will be specific to each organisation in its particular situation. The more challenging of the management analyses tend, therefore, to counsel a continuing questioning of choices, sensitivities, attitudes and abilities. Among better examples on these lines are *The Knowledge-Creating Company* by I.Nonaka and H.Takeuchi (Oxford); *Wellsprings of Knowledge* by Dorothy Leonard (HBS Press); and *Competing for the Future* by Gary Hamel and C.K.Prahalad (HBS Press).

A striking recent example of superiority becoming a rigidity springs from "lean production", which allowed Toyota to make rapid strides of efficiency, quality and product cycle timescales ahead of other, notably US, rivals. It also allowed greater product flexibility on the production line, and one recalls stunning the NEDO Manufacturing Committee in the early-80s with a newspaper cutting that Toyota had produced 1.4 million cars in Japan with only 10 the same. In a period when demand was booming during "the bubble", the flexibility to offer customers variants was a competitive strength. But, as Takahiro Fujimoto illustrates in *Innovation in Japan*, edited A.Goto and H.Odagiri (Oxford), in a situation of falling demand and a depressed market, this can become "fat design" when the focus shifts to cutting costs through common components, shared platforms etc. A question still outstanding is what advantages flow from having mastered such flexibility of product specification, even when austerity may have "slimmed design".

[10] "Kobe Shipyard & Machinery Works of Mitsubishi Heavy Industries specialises in building container vessels. It only takes two months to build a 60,000-tonne vessel at the shipyard, a fraction of the time traditionally required. The bow section, engine section, crew quarters and other blocks of a ship are built at nearby work sites, and only assembly work is done at the shipyard itself. Each block weighs between 1000 and 5000 tons, and unless each block is built to a high degree of accuracy, deviations amounting to several decimetres to more than one meter can result when blocks are laid out on the shipyard and welded together. At Kobe Shipyard & Machinery Works, the error has always been less than a centimetre. There are hidden innovations in the technologies used to cut iron plates, to process and weld them accurately and to control schedules, enabling errors after welding several tons of iron for assembly to be kept to within a few millimetres." (*Look Japan* Mar 2004.)

[11] An entertaining sideshow came with the breakdown of negotiations between the US and EU on the long-running dispute over civil-aircraft subsidies, occasioned by claim and counter-claim over "launch aid" for the A380, and the US and Japanese subsidies to the Boeing 787 Dreamliner. Sure enough, *The Economist* boldly asserted, "Airbus... is no longer an infant industry and ought to be weaned off soft government loans". (26.3.05). Echoing, sure enough, the *Financial Times* Leader (22.3.05) – both journals are subsidiaries of the Pearson Group, "State support for private companies, even those with long lead times and big development costs, becomes indefensible as they mature. Infant industries must grow up," in rather stern Victorian parental tones.

Firstly, if Britain can boast of any contribution to industrial development, it lies in having tested beyond the limit what financial markets and "shareholder value" can handle. Eurotunnel – a relatively modest project by the standards of integrating technology and systems in a modern airliner – has produced a continuing spate of disputes over outstanding loans; British Rail privatisation has been among the most spectacular shambles in pursuit of "sharing risk", while allowing private financiers to reap disproportionate returns; and the London Underground PPP, only among the starkest. While continuously, if less spectacularly, the failure of British companies to invest at competitive levels in the new technologies has driven a steady decline of significance and increased dependence. Second, despite the cries of purists, sadly the civil-aircraft market – like all other markets – is fundamentally vitiated – not least by the number of countries vying to gain or retain a position in it. Japan, apart from its involvement in the 787, is undertaking the development of its own civil aircraft programme, to which can be added existing or potential players such as Brazil, China, Canada, Russia, India etc. And all can draw solace from the decline of earlier British leading companies.

Third, there is a continuing dilemma in assessing the timescale of such "hormonal" or "steroid" treatment on infants. Boeing's 747 – for many years effectively the monopoly leader for long-haul travel – had its development wholly funded by the Pentagon in a competition with Lockheed for a large capacity long-range transport, won by Lockheed with its C5 (Galaxy). But the "profit" advantage has been immense over the years. While Boeing still receives doses of support, injected through the variety of its business limbs.

Given the rate of changing technologies/processes that impinge on aircraft development, is "maturity" a desirable, or achievable condition? Certainly, if Britain is an exemplar of this rationale, as it has been under Treasury/*FT* theology, the transition from "infant" is straight to "premature senility". Perhaps the ideal condition is continuous adolescence, with occasional visits to the surgery for injections. But this dispute is bound to go on and on, offering scope for even more miles of fruitless copy, as other countries come to stretch their aerospace ambitions, by when, by way of example, Britain's industrial capability will have passed on.

But this is nothing compared to economic commentators' use of metaphorical language in other contexts. Companies have become "slimmer and fitter", which again on British experience seems to mean, "anorexic". Or, how about, "squeezing out" inflation – are we dealing with toothpaste or acne? And so on.

"FREE YOUR MIND OF CANT" (DR SAMUEL JOHNSON)

"There is no invisible hand," declared Joseph Stiglitz, a 2001 Nobel economics laureate (*Guardian* 20.12.02). You know, that what's-it that's supposed to "advance the interest of society" through "the gratification of vain and insatiable desires"[1] in a free market. Now they tell us. After decades of Thatcherite and New Labour zombies, spivs, acolytes, groupies and sycophants prattling on about "markets" as a substitute for thought, we learn that it is all a bloody great con. Oh, Doctor, did England ever need you more!

For all the theoretical garbage, the mantra "markets" was never more than a no-brain proxy for passing national governance to the financial services of the City, where there is another mythical panjandrum called "efficient markets".[2] "Efficiencies" recently displayed vividly by the history of pensions miss-selling, endowment policy scandals, split-level investment trusts, precipice bonds, leasing scams, tax-fiddles, dodgy derivatives, "boiler rooms", and "soft commissions", with mismanagement of a large segment of the nation's savings as investment managers followed the herd, "rationally" of course, into the dot.com and IT fantasy world. Not to mention the widespread casualties from the will-o'-the-wisp financing through off-balance sheet derivatives and structured investment vehicles that even the originators did not know how to value. And all the intermediaries, in the best traditions of "gentlemanly capitalism" – fund managers, analysts, researchers, trustee managers, lawyers and accountants – still pocketing fees, commissions, premia and the other "invisible" gains. If the Wall Street scandals, epitomised by Enron, WorldCom etc, all of which gave a whole new meaning to "creative destruction", could be shrugged off with the response that these practices could not happen here (Marconi notwithstanding), the complicity of the City in the dud assets of mortgage miss-selling, and the resulting "credit crunch" cannot be gainsaid.

Consequently, despite nigh-catastrophic outcomes, the myths of economics, which may have served the nation with useful hypocrisies during our imperial past, are now among the wellsprings of our nostalgic impotence. For all the column-miles contributed to our media daily by declared practitioners, the passport to profundity is to quote ancient authors at least 200 years old. A clever wheeze to make entry to the sect dependent on wading through otherwise unreadable (and irrelevant) tracts to ensure exclusivity among the priesthood. That so many of these sages were somewhere between weirdoes and lunatics is conveniently ignored.[3]

A MODEST DECONSTRUCTION

The most striking feature of economics is that, if approached from a starting point in the real world, it immediately translates into nonsense. Compelled to peer into this mad world with the arrival of Keith Joseph and his reading list, reinforced by the Department's economists seizing on his arrival as open season for tossing around quotations from Adam Smith, it was only too apparent that this miraculous fantasy world was sustainable only on a foundation of "cultivated ignorance". When challenged on the absence of any correlation between concept and reality, Milton Friedman's excuse to avoid "the pretence of knowledge" (quoted in the *FT* 13.2.04) must be the emblematic formulaic excuse: as, indeed, it has been the ritual cop-out of juju men since the dawn of time.

One possible excuse is that economics is usually inculcated into impressionable minds at a young age, and that it is feasible to progress into academic cloisters or the British Treasury without any intervening congress with reality. Thereafter, reality can be kept at bay with elaborations of increasing complexity and esoteric speculation, perhaps the ideal case of de Bono's "intelligent trap", but in direct lineal descent from the medieval scholastics.

Having been badgered to hand out copies of my valedictory essay, prompted by ex-DTI colleagues, for its depiction of the "surrogate reality" within which the Treasury functions, the diagnosis still seems germane. The pernicious consequences of this "surrogate reality" are evident all around our national scene. But no more vividly than in the mad shambles of the British Rail privatisation, where from the various "robust models" littering the Treasury floor "to shed risk", it's just unfortunate that they picked the one with square wheels. The direct and indirect costs of correcting this aberration were, and remain, incalculable. And equally miraculous is that apparently sane Ministers should have presented such lunacy as rational.

It is not too soon to apply a shovel to shift some of the sods supporting this weird national eccentricity.

FLEXIBLE LABOUR MARKETS

Most commentators excuse Adam Smith's most obvious irrelevances as "of his time", so that partial quotation can become a respectable pre-requisite for economic discourse. The "invisible hand" is a typical example. Taken by the enterprists as licence that anything goes in the pursuit of self-interest since this will still "advance the interest of society" – it now turns out to be a typically humourless Scottish joke.[4] But the most significant feature "of his time" was the slave trade: the publication of *The Wealth of Nations* in 1776 in fact coincided with the peak of the slave trade.

With my own schooling overshadowed by imperial jingoism, as it must have been for generations since Victorian times, one cannot recall the slave trade having any significance. Not surprising, therefore, that the raw precepts of economics have only been questioned in whispers under blankets. But now, with a rising tide of studies, TV series on Britain's Slave Trade, Stephen Schama's *History of Britain* could not avoid "King Sugar".[5] And, eventually, the country has sidled shiftily to recognise the bicentenary of the abolition of the slave trade, and the subject is to be included in the national education syllabus with a number of local museums.

There are a growing number of recent studies synthesising earlier research that illuminate the scale and extent of the slave and plantation trades' penetration of the metropolitan economy – a contemporary economic commentator, Malachy Postlethwayt, apparently remarked that the slave trade was "the first principle and foundation of all the rest, the mainspring of the machine which sets every wheel in motion": from the plantation colonies as markets for British goods, such as cottons, linens and metal products; the cash-flow gains from the continuing provisioning demands of slave traders for textiles, iron billets, nails etc (a "cash-cow" part of their portfolios, in current management jargon); the cycling of returns from the slave trade and plantations – notably sugar, cotton and tobacco – into infrastructure investment such as canals, harbours, docks, drainage, shipping etc linked to overseas trade; to providing a source of raw materials – a lively sugar refining industry evolved around Bristol, and over a longer term for the textiles industry. This activity in turn contributed to stimulating new technologies/innovation through increased demand, and indeed through financial networks – "it was from money gained from the West Indies trade that capital was found to finance Watt." And, large slugs sluicing into the rising "merchant houses", the granddaddies of "gentlemanly capitalism".

With so many of the upper reaches of society involved in the matrix of slavery-related activities – the shareholders of The Royal African Company and The South Sea Company included many of the nation's elite – Adam Smith, not averse to rubbing shoulders with notable Scottish slave captains, was no abolitionist, "Slavery… has hardly any possibility of being abolished… (it) has been universal in the beginnings of society, and the love of dominion and authority over others will probably make it perpetual." Consequently, he was, at best, relatively muted in his comments – "the work done by freemen comes cheaper in the end than that performed by slaves" and the output of the latter could be enhanced if they were given more opportunity "to better their condition". The sting is "in the end" since the life expectancy – "wastage" in current management-speak – of landed slaves, subjected to the "just-in-time" demands of processing sugar before it began decomposing, made any comparison with "freemen" odious. But maybe not surprising in a society where, like Jane Austen's account of spirited-girl-made-good in *Mansfield Park*, what went on in the estates in Antigua was mostly out-of-mind.[6]

Moreover, the conditions of labour in the rising new industries of the day were barbarous by modern standards. For it was a time of "wear and tear of hands", indeed "wear and tear of slaves", and Smith could blandly reason, "…the demand for men, like that for any other commodity…". But perhaps the most ruinous legacy of his "commodity" approach is the equivalence of "…withdraw a part of their labour or stock from this employment" as a means of reducing output when "effective demand" falls. And rolled over through generations of management and reinforced by continuous repetition, even today by financial commentators, this maxim has steadily eroded Britain's manufacturing industries.

Observed from DTI over the years, a consistent mechanism in the chronicles of post-50s British industrial decline has been the "ratchet effect". For products, particularly those liable to a cyclical pattern of demand, with every downturn British companies have traditionally responded by "withdrawing labour and stock", cutting back on investment and development (invariably accompanied by maintaining dividends levels as a signal of "confidence" – apparently the investment world still has to catch up with semaphore) to keep prices down. But dastardly foreign competitors – usually from Japan, Taiwan or, more recently, China – seem to have a different textbook: cutting prices even more aggressively, increasing output, offering generous financing, and even introducing new models. With each upturn, British companies found themselves with less capacity to respond, with customers having defected to competitors, and with every repetition of the cycle market share has been lost.

These competitors demonstrate that businesses focused on applying their own "knowledge" to secure their futures, and exploiting the creative talent behind "the hands" of their members, paradoxically foster an adaptive and flexible labour force by mitigating the continual threat of "withdrawing labour".[7] A typical example closer to home came when meeting Ian Gibson*, then managing director, during a visit to Nissan's Sunderland plant when he was sharply critical – expletives tactfully deleted – of other European car manufacturers trying to recruit his members virtually at the factory gates. The young Geordies that joined the company and took part in the evolution of routines and practices and building relationships with suppliers were creative assets not to be readily surrendered. Or from the viewpoint of "labour", if a few members have an idea how a job could be done by 3 instead of 6 of their colleagues, are they going to suggest a change if they sense that the likeliest outcome will be "the withdrawal" of three jobs? In short, there is an evident conflict between "flexible labour markets" and achieving a "flexible labour force" within the company. Underlying this dichotomy is the "commodity" view of labour deriving from the "division of labour" and "specialisation" that flowed from the new energy/extractive/capital intensive demands of the Industrial Revolution, as compared with the "industrious" revolution that took place in other countries – notably Japan – before embracing the new "industrial" system.[8]

That the CBI should declare that "labour market flexibility has been a jewel in the crown of the UK economy for 20 years" (1.9.2003), confirms that "British" management has hardly moved on from the 18th century, while the abysmal performance of "British" managed businesses over recent decades suggests a trip a couple of stops down the Central Line, if its running, to Hatton Garden might be in order to check they haven't been sold a paste job. From a trade surplus of £2 billion in 1982 to a deficit of £22 billion in 2002 is hardly a saga of doughty Horatius's parrying the surge of imports with new products, nor many intrepid adventurers slicing out international markets with devastating technology. And the thousands of destitute pensioners short-changed by their company schemes doesn't offer many credentials for management's human concerns.[9] While our political classes could prudently avoid strident lectures to the rest of Europe, whose industries have shown a remarkably better facility to adjust to remain competitive than our national breed.

At the level of "In the end we are all dead", "flexible labour markets" stands as a trite formula. For an avowedly management organisation to honk on repeating the phrase suggests an attempt to create the presumption that no job is "firm". But in most other countries it is precisely the role of management to make the jobs in its trust as firm as possible, and, by engaging its people, to achieve this by being more competitive: Toyota has plainly succeeded in making its jobs firmer than those in General Motors, just as the most obvious example.

Moreover, formulaic phrases like "flexible labour markets" carry a load of presumptions: for example, Britain's locational rigidities are high through regional disparities in housing, education, infrastructure etc. But most crucially, variations depending on skills and expertise: the higher these are, the greater the scope for flexibility across national boundaries. Consequently, assumptions about friction-free movement within a defined national market, say the UK, are invariably questionable. Researched case studies are rare: Arnold Weinstock famously, to counter accusations about his approach destroying jobs, had his own study in the bottom drawer to show that the unemployment from a closure in Woolwich had been resettled within the year – but no indication whether the process involved a waste of skills or losses through emigration; and there was a study made following cancellation of the TSR 2, where some 18%, all the highest skilled, had left for Australia and South Africa, ironically to assemble Mirages under licence.

"Flexible labour markets" should, therefore, come with a health warning. For, in practice, there is no shortage of "flexible markets" as the nation's talent, especially in research and technical expertise, continues to drain to the best-supported facilities internationally.[10] While even Silicon Valley is being outsourced to India, Russia and East Asia; financial houses are increasingly putting back-office functions abroad; and, apparently, UK telephone directory enquiries can be sourced from the Philippines. Bluntly, the dilemma for this country is to generate and sustain activities that offer the best of our talent the security and prospects to prevent them seeking these elsewhere.

WHAT'S FREE ABOUT TRADE?

As if recognising the dodgy origins of much of the "wealth" that Adam Smith saw about him, and the distinctly "unfree" element of liberal trade at the time, economists have dreamed up a new halcyon age of free trade. "The world of July 1914, far more than is the case today, was one of free trade, free capital movements, and free migration and travel. For all these reasons, the pattern of transactions was, in many respects at any rate, less affected by the existence of international boundaries."[11]

The equanimity to express such sanguine sentiments depends a bit on where you are sitting. For the decades prior to the First World War saw the carving up of Africa; the Russian expansion of Empire eastwards; the "unfair treaties" to open up China and Japan; while a sixth of the Government of India's revenues came from state-sponsored opium sales; the "informal Empire" in Latin America established by British mercantile finance; by 1910, there were 100 international cartels and a dozen shipping chambers to share spoils and keep newcomers out; despite the self-righteous abolition of slavery, the practise continued through indentured Indian coolies shipped as labour to the sugar plantations of British Guyana, and to Fiji, Mauritius, and South Africa until after the First World War; and so on.[12] A rather different read on this period emerges when "a Japanese diplomat in Paris asks: "Why should we be nice to them when they walked all over us in the 19th century in the name of free trade?" – a natural reaction to "free trade imperialism."[13]

It's not as though "free trade" and laissez faire have been much better received elsewhere. Germany and France have historically been sceptical or downright hostile, as have most of Europe's "neo-corporatist" states. While the US in its industrial and imperial expansion (colonisation westwards was just as much an expansion of Empire as Russia's eastwards – the oft ignored "water fallacy"), despite echoes of Adam Smith in its Declaration, has been notable more in the breach than the observance. And more recently Japan, South Korea and other Asian emulators seem to have developed remarkably well without much attention to the sacred texts.[14]

This has left Britain virtually alone in waving arms and shouting from the pulpit. For a century or more, "Trade Policy" officials in whatever Department was responsible have enjoyed the unique luxury of continuously recycling the same Ministerial briefs and speeches – "to create fair and open markets at home and abroad" – though, with a careful eye on the plum jobs in GATT/WTO in Geneva or the OECD in Paris on much-prized diplomatic rates. Among the recycled nostrums is the rhetorical: "You can hardly preach free trade without practising it." Fine in those halcyon days of Empire, when we could boast a couple of gunboats in the bay, land a brigade of sepoys, or when we had imperial preference (which in fact persisted beyond the founding of GATT). But now the capacity to exploit such hypocrisies has virtually collapsed, leaving us, in the spirit of "first over the parapet", still recycling platitudes. The prudent step would be to stop preaching and relieve others at international fora, and the British public, of further tedium.

No dispute that increased exchange within and between nations should be good for everyone. And a rulebook is useful so long as everyone plays the game. But as WTO Ministerial gatherings since Seattle in 1999 have demonstrated, more than platitudes are needed to convince that the sentiments of the Japanese diplomat are not equally justified by the behaviour of leading industrial countries today. For when has free-trade not involved exploitation even from its origins? A shade more recognition is needed of the right of countries to evolve their own political economies, if necessary with similar policy instruments to those previously used by nations now prone to preach.

WHITHER ADVANTAGES?

A subset of trade dogma is another fantasy of "comparative advantage". As depicted in Samuelson's *Economics*, sufficient to consign his tome to the darkest recesses of the attic. As expounded, the thesis rests on simple products "food" or "clothing" and postulates different levels of efficiency in producing these between "America" and "Europe", with the mutual advantage of exchanging these argued in terms "America's problem is...." Firstly, this presupposes totalitarian regimes with powers to "manage trade", and, second, an assumption that relative advantage will persist in a static world.

In practice neither holds: even the mighty MITI had problems corralling Japanese car manufacturers when the US and Europe demanded Voluntary Restraints Agreements (VRAs) limiting imports in the 1980s. Among a variety of perverse outcomes, this gave MITI added clout just when complaints about Japan's allegedly distorting government policies were at their height; customers were denied the outstanding mini-cars made in Japan because their producers concentrated on exporting higher value-added brands; and the restraints stimulated the rise of "transplants" that have been putting increasing pressure on American and European domestic producers ever since.

As for the persistence of "advantages" – even in the "modified" form now enunciated (a special feature of economics is that as each platitude is finally acknowledged as rubbish, hordes of academics justify themselves in "modifications" to attempt to reconcile the faith with reality in a neo-Copernican dispute) – maybe if land and climate are benign for foodstuffs, say in the corn belts of America and Canada, or the fruit and veg industries of California (augmented by a continuing supply of illegal subsistence labour), the relative efficiencies may persist. But in virtually any other activity, advantages are transitory. Raw materials are finite, witness the disused collieries and "heritage" mine workings of this country – and look forward to "heritage" offshore oil rigs in a few years. While in products, "advantages" can be overturned with increasing speed.

"Catching-up" is no longer decades, but "leapfrogging": witness South Korea overtaking Japan in memory chips with massive investment and deliberate accumulation of technology and skills; or the Taiwan Semiconductor Manufacturing Corporation becoming the world's largest contract chip maker, again with massive investment, supported by an equity injection from the government's Cabinet Development Fund.[15] While China is evolving rapidly across a range of products from white goods, machine tools to computers.

The desperation to find some British "comparative advantages" can reach extreme lengths: it was once seriously debated in DTI whether English could be exploited as a national strength.[16] But "comparative advantage" tends to be pulled out of the hat whenever a bit of special pleading is demanded: the City, universities, etc. Yet "advantage" in services is as vulnerable to technology, sustaining competitive infrastructure, efficient costs and adaptive speed, as much as for any tangible product. For example, the increasing risks of climate change leading to premature failures in the Thames Barrage or the necessity to restructure the London Underground against rising ambient summer temperatures have barely been recognised among the "threats" to the City. And just hark a leading Indian software and services company manager, "The goal is to suck out knowledge from customers".[17] Unless "advantage" is renewed it will always be vulnerable to competitive shifts: though judging by the City's performance and influence in recent years, it is questionable whether this is an "advantage" worth retaining. If some antique authority is necessary, Edmund Spenser's *Two Cantos of Mutabilitie* would be rather more beneficial reading than anything in economic textbooks.

PANTOMIME LOGIC

High among the most ludicrous, most touted and most destructive gobbets from the Adam Smith canon has been, "Consumption is the sole and end purpose of all production; and the interests of the producer should be attended to only so far as it may be necessary for promoting that of the consumer." At its most literal, it is trite in that no producer could survive unless its output satisfied sufficient consumers to sustain a viable use of assets and skills. But in suggesting a simplistic polarity between "the consumer" and "the producer" it is creating a false antithesis. Folded into national class prejudices, the arrogant superiority of gentlemanly capitalism, and preoccupations of status in the managerial class, this has resonated with a cultural predilection for adversarial binary stupidities. The result is an insidious antithetical logic – Services vs. Manufacturing,

Labour vs. Capital, Workers vs. Bosses, and so on – that has stereotyped national, and especially political, debate.

But Smith was merely employing personification, a standard rhetorical device of his day: just glance at the bits of Gary's *Elegy* that everyone forgets. Statuesque no doubt, but hardly a rational idiom of thought. Indeed, taken to its limit, a society where "the consumer" was dominant without any "producers" would be comparable to drought-ridden sub-Saharan Africa. In Britain, we are especially disadvantaged in having to produce at least enough to support our population of economists, who, by definition, produce nothing.[18] While, in addition to the "unproductive labour" noted by Smith, Britain has been fecund in evolving a large force of "counterproductive labour" – politicians, lawyers, accountants, consultants, advisers, and so on.

Yet economists seem incorrigible. The Entrepreneur is another mystical idol,[19] where ancient alchemaic practices still persist. Presumably blending the essences of Honda, Branson, Li Ka-shing, Gates, Ford, Dell et al, with a tincture of Smith, would yield an elixir, so that we can all demand "an ounce of entrepreneur, good apothecary".

To play out this rhetorical charade, we have to seat ourselves amongst the audience for the Chester Miracle plays – or Christmas pantomimes. Enter stage right (the goodies), "The Consumer". Enter stage left (the baddies), "The Producer". Then, centre stage, they meet and Punch-and-Judy like, bop each other over the head. "The Consumer" has only the motive to satisfy "vain and insatiable desires". Of course, other personae that might interfere with this simplistic slugging match, such as "The Parent", "The Intelligent", "The Human" etc, are kept safely out of sight in the wings. But "insatiable" is tricky because "The Producer" has to come up with some variations. So, with a puff of smoke, swinging from the rafters by wire attached to his jockstraps, arrives "The Entrepreneur" to offer "The Consumer" exotic new "vain" delights.

For societies that have evolved uncontaminated by this medieval garbage, propensities to consume and to produce are viewed as mutually interdependent, and, indeed, the exercise of consumption carries an obligation to produce. Maybe, in Smith's day, "the sneaking arts of underling tradesmen" were a threat to a largely uneducated mass of consumers, and landowners who were too dim to know where their self-interest lay. But the world has moved on from Smith's "cobblers", "tailors" and "bakers" to the point where, even in routine "products" there is a diversity of "producer/consumer" relations.

Yet if we glance at reality, this false dichotomy has proved disastrous:

hence the rundown "producer" regions of Britain, whether agriculture, mining, steel, shipbuilding or engineering, with their high levels of social deprivation that, for all attempts at regeneration, will remain welfare-dependent for a generation or more. Contrast this with areas such as Aichi, the home province of Toyota, which has enjoyed growth levels above 3% while the national economy has been depressed. Or the application of Britain's "North Sea bonanza" to "The Consumer" via tax reductions (on the brilliant logical extension that "The Consumer" is "The Voter"), with continuing under investment in transport infrastructure, health, education etc. The only sane course is to consign such economists' nostrums to their medieval origins, and place Adam Smith's outpourings alongside those of the Venerable Bede.

UNIVERSAL ROBOTS

Fair's fair. Economists have long anticipated Honda's ASIMO humanoid robot. Except that economists have assumed that human beings are robots, with the latest supercomputers plugged into their heads, a memory encompassing the *Encyclopaedia Britannica*, and with fantastic crystal balls continuously calculating all the inputs to maximise utility, optimise the risks and "discounted present value" of competing benefits, and so on, under "rational expectations". While selfish "fear and greed" are programmed as good approximations for the sum of human aspirations. That those not members of the faith have always accepted foibles and lack of rationality as natural human traits, their protests have been dismissed as "common sense".

Now it turns out, from 2002's Nobel laureates, that "rationality" isn't quite what it was cracked up to be. That human beings actually behave in perverse ways – except apparently economists who are the most prone to selfish responses. This has led into a sectarian dispute between "behaviourists" and fundamentalists. And we even have "neuroeconomics" in pursuit of biological determinants to reduce human activities to predictably mechanical dimensions for economic analysis.[20]

WOT'S GOING ON?

Estimates of the UK's "informal/shadow/grey" economy run at 5-12% of GDP. The range of the estimate is testament to its elusiveness. But even at the lower limit it is very substantial. These cover activities from the common practice of payment to decorators and fence-menders in cash, getting fags through customs, to drug and immigrant trafficking, pornography, skin trades, money-laundering – all in our burgeoning service sector.

Elsewhere, there is a similar black hole in measured economic activity – from recent studies, around 9% of US GDP in 1994 – some $650 billion. Or, by a different measure, in 1998 apparently the federal tax shortfall was some $200 billion, or some $1.5 trillion of undeclared personal income, not including earnings from criminal activity. Similar estimates run to 27% of GDP in Italy (where tax evasion is virtually a national sport); in ex-Soviet Union countries in a range of 31-51% of GDP; Bolivia 65% and Nigeria 76% of GDP.[21] And in a sample of Asian countries informal credit accounts for between a fifth and two-thirds of total rural credit, and about half of urban credit.[22] While in China, statistics are notoriously questionable because of such untraceable exchanges.

In trade, there are more black holes between recorded transactions totting up to many $billions on a world scale – a global current account deficit estimated at $180 billion in 2003 by the IMF, where the distribution of this gap could radically upset the scene presented by conventional figures.[23] If there is now recognition that financial flows are notoriously elusive with the search for terrorist funds focusing on hawalas networks, the diversity of informal mechanisms has a history running to centuries among the diaspora of China, India, Arab nations and other Asian countries where transactions carry a high-trust component and a minimal system for recording obligations.[24] The rise in Foreign Direct Investment (FDI) in recent decades, especially in Asia, has taken an increasing network form predominantly by smaller firms relying on relational links, which in aggregate can be very large – for example, Taiwan companies are among the leading investors in Vietnam, but again there are wide discrepancies in reported statistics.[25]

When even marginal percentage changes in conventional measures such as stock-market moves or trade flows can occasion twitches, these movements may in reality be relatively small compared to shifts in the shadow world. Moreover, the informal and formal worlds overlap, where the transaction speed and efficiencies of the former can impact on the rate of product change, cooperative innovation, and cost reductions. Particularly in comparison to sclerotic systems locked into formal legal contracts and the bureaucracies of financial markets.[26]

Oh shit, we've just found another vast black hole of "shadow finance", where the uncharted and incalculable liabilities through Structured Investment Vehicles (SIVs), Credit Default Swaps (CDSs) etc are threatening the global economy.

WHAT'S A PRICE?

Price determined by the intersection of supply and demand curves, however elegant on a textbook page, becomes an increasingly dodgy concept the further from local produce and commodities. After all, "asymmetric information" – the difference in the quality of information between parties to a transaction – has crept into the canon: despite being a common experience of any citizen buying insurance, a mortgage or a second-hand car. The credit crunch has taken this to new heights by creating "toxic assets" for which no price can be determined, presumably a consequence of "symmetric ignorance".

For more complex products, the outcome of a tier of multiple inputs, mechanisms that create confidence between suppliers to eliminate the usual "margining up" of arm's-length subcontracting, and capture continuing feedback to achieve increasing efficiencies in processes and product innovation can yield startling gains in production costs. To the point of pitching prices in anticipation of continuing cost reductions. One of the sharpest lessons of the motorbike industry collapse was scoffing that such an apparent pursuit of "market share" was to the detriment of "profit". Yet Honda, and the other warring Japanese producers, have survived reasonably well, several indeed having become competitive in autos and other products, so that they must have been generating surpluses to sustain R&D and capital investment in order to grow. The same applies in other product areas such as machine tools, TVs and home electronics, cameras, copiers etc.

In practice, this apparently perverse disregard of profit, derives from a sustainable commercial logic: prices are struck competitively to ensure sales, with costs then reduced to match the price by feeding back innovation and process experience as "volume and velocity of throughput" are maintained, and profits achieved. Effectively reversing the classic formula "cost + profit = price" to "price" determining "cost" and then "profit" achieved through improved efficiencies. Over time, there are continuing feedback gains from multi-skilling, flexible manufacturing, coherent routines for capturing accumulated experience – both within the firm and with suppliers, and evolving expertise in relevant technologies, now augmented by selective application of IT. With the dynamic outcome of increasing, not diminishing, returns.[27] The crucial linchpin is absolute confidence that such an outfit, embracing suppliers as well, will continue to deliver efficiency and innovation gains. Without this, the practice would be suicidal.

In this idiom, rather than a "commodity" price being set by clearing to achieve a magical equilibrium, the innovative firm's primary aim is to disrupt equilibria, and price/product innovation becomes a tactical weapon to take advantage of market circumstances: most vividly, a downturn becomes the aggressive competitor's killing ground.[28] And a special twist is that this approach depends upon, not just "learning" – economists have just got around to acknowledging "learning by doing" – but also interactions from "learning by using", "learning by decomposing", "learning by making" etc reflecting the "creativity" behind Adam Smith's "hands", or, in normal language, it's amazing what people can do if they work and think together.

A wider consequence is that commercial systems are becoming increasingly fluid, with cooperative network variations to enhance creativity, integrate expertise to exploit shifts in rapidly evolving technologies, achieve international efficiencies in product design and production, sharing risks etc. So fluid, indeed, that they escape stereotypes whether of academic theory, accountancy conventions, or institutional forms. And hanging onto these stereotypes only hastens obsolescence.

"Price" is also being recognised as having rather more complex dimensions than the theory conceives from the customer's viewpoint. Whether in networks of mutual co-operation, in capital projects as much as in manufacturing for series production, an obligational/social component is crucial in gaining an order or sustaining an ongoing relationship. While in some markets where customers are rather more demanding even fairly common products have to fulfil expectations beyond the most obvious perceptions of price and quality.[29]

Among the more facile consequences of the "commodity" view of price is that "the pounds sliding (against other currencies) makes firms' goods cheaper in foreign markets": on this premise, the yen's appreciation from 360 to 90-100 to the US dollar should have annihilated Japan's exports, yet the country has sustained a trade surplus; while the UK pound has depreciated from 2.40 to 1.50-1.60 (even falling for a time to parity) against the US dollar, with a steadily rising UK trade deficit.

IT'S RAIN DANCING

In its purest form, the "neo-liberal", "market fundamentalism" or "Washington Consensus" simplistic model – to borrow Joseph Stiglitz's formulation "the competitive equilibrium model, in which Adam Smith's invisible hand works, and works perfectly" with "no need for government", turns out to be a form of conceptual pornography: a fantasy world of friction-free movement with lubricated pneumatic resources that slither around reality. As Joseph Stiglitz points out, this fantasy is extremely precarious: "The theory says that an efficient market economy requires that *all* of the assumptions be satisfied": even more fantastical, this congealed sludge – the economy – is supposed to slush around towards an "equilibrium" dictated by shifting patterns of supply and demand, except that all the varieties of glug have their own cycles of supply and demand and are all mixed together. And, believe it or not, they've dreamt up mathematical models for this slurping around.[30] The ferocious dishonesty thrown into defence of this fantasy world should come as no surprise, as for example in the World Bank report on the *The East Asian Miracle*.[31]

That Thatcherism should have latched onto this extreme variant derives from a variety of sources: maybe too frequent congress with the IMF/World Bank through the coterie of snake-oil advisers, sycophants and official Treasury contacts – remembering that Britain had to go on its knees to the IMF in 1976, or simply too much browsing the top-shelf magazines of the Oxford and Cambridge Economics faculties. Or bowing to the calls of the City, which has been adept at exploiting asymmetries of information under the pretence of its "efficient markets". But the delights of fantasy seem to have seduced New Labour as well. And Britain stands fair to become the exemplar of the resulting chaos.

But don't worry, chaps. It's all under control. As one of the Monetary Policy Committee confessed to the Commons Treasury Select Committee, "We do not have perfect foresight. But we do not have perfect hindsight either." This prompted the realisation of one Member, "It's a rain dance". At least one penny's dropped. Since when it seems the pursuit of eldritch fantasy is ensconced as a prime duty of the Governor of the Bank, as Mervyn King has propounded the "Maradona theory of interest rates"[32]. Though what's concealed under the carpets of the Governor of the Bank of England's sumptuous suite from past MPC rituals doesn't bear thinking about.[33]

DIMINISHING OR INCREASING RETURNS?

Among the sacred tablets, the Law of Diminishing Returns is inscribed in Samuelsaic terms, as "An increase in some inputs relative to other comparatively fixed inputs will cause total output to increase. But after a point the extra output resulting from the same additions of extra inputs will become less and less. This falling off of extra returns is a consequence of the fact that the new "doses" of the varying resources have less and less of the fixed resources to work with." That's simple. After a certain point, extra dollops of labour and capital have progressively less impact – negative feedback.

But how to account for such staggering progressive enhancements in efficiency, productivity, technology applications and growth exemplified by Toyota, Honda, et al. with, at times, incrementally low, or negligible, increases in manpower and capital plant? Or, indeed, the extraordinary growth levels attained by Japan and some other Pacific Asian countries in the post-World War II era. After a process of erudite squabbling that leaves medieval scholastics in the shade, we now have the staggering admission, "Knowledge of how to do or make things can raise the productivity of the other two factors (labour and capital).... Investment in capital and knowledge can stimulate and reinforce one another in a 'virtuous circle' of cumulative causation so that acceleration in the rate of capital investment can raise the long-term growth in per capita income.... Thus, whereas neo-classical theory predicts that the rate of long-term growth will decline because of diminishing returns, the new theory postulates that the possibility of increasing returns means that the growth rate need not decline."[34] – positive feedback. Hooray, at last!

But "knowledge" is a tricky "commodity" to handle. Not just difficult to measure. But more varieties than baked beans.[35] If the new emphasis on stimulating university research to be transferred to industry reflects this "new growth theory" it is still in the mode of a "teaspoon" of leading-edge research being added to industry's capital and labour. But the fizz from such potions depends on the recipient enterprise having a dynamic mixture of ingredients for continuous regeneration. More elusive, therefore, is the stimulation of knowledge generated within an enterprise and its suppliers: the deliberate process of drawing feedback from the creative potential of ongoing experience. When the Boston Consulting Group devised the concept of the "experience curve" in the 70s, it fell into disrepute because companies assumed it was just another "invisible hand-job" – jack up output and enjoy it. But the "experience curve" has survived in the Japanese process of kaizen – generating "increased returns" by drawing out efficiencies from within the company itself and in its relations with suppliers.[36]

The mutual reinforcement of these strands of knowledge, and achieving increasing returns, is inhibited by other features of the conventional economics tool kit. How far is the continuity and focus needed for effective "experience feedback" achievable within a context dominated by "withdrawing labour", "flexible labour markets", and disruptions of direction and ownership from "efficient markets"? Or, is it surprising the pursuit of "maximising competition", "shedding risk" or whatever economic gobbledygook, while ignoring the costs of disrupting the knowledge routines of an integrated business, should have the catastrophic outcomes of the privatisation of British Rail? Contrast with the German approach to modernising their railways whose customers are mercifully free of the dogmatic absurdities in Britain.

More fundamentally, as one economic practitioner has concluded, increasing returns results in "the wreckage of the greater part of economic theory".[37] Surely the clincher?

Q.E.D.

PS: We have been lucky to have had the late J. K. Galbraith's *The Economics of Innocent Fraud* (Allen Lane), whose delicious irony supports much of the above. But just like Eric Roll's elegance of phrase, liable to pass many by. Galbraith aside, if there is a hardcore of pedagogic practitioners, for whom any perversion is justified, there are others who have taken the pains to ascertain how real economic activity is conducted. And when they clash, expect a few entertaining sparks.[38] In fact, there are piles of heretical texts by practitioners, prompted by recognition of the fantasy of the theory's underlying assumptions, or the damage that can flow from blind adherence to the runes. While others have noted that societies can evolve viable and effective structures for economic development in disregard of these precepts.

Bewilderment across the pond at how the US could have fallen prey to the extremes of simplistic theory may be gathering pace. But this has not really been matched by any similar disquiet on this side at Britain's idolatry of the "mythical" US and of these same perversions. That they suit financial markets may be common, but this country has the reinforcement of centuries of unthinking hypocritical imperial rhetoric. But how to free ourselves from this rationale of decline?[39]

---

[1] In economist lingo: "more recent advances in economic theory...have shown that whenever information is imperfect and markets incomplete, which is to say always....then the invisible hand works most imperfectly." From *Globalisation and Its Discontents* (Penguin), a scalpel dissection of the consequences of applying the narrow prescriptive approach of the IMF/World Bank to the problems of developing countries, which has been influential in modifying this bias to the point where we read, "The Washington Consensus Fades into History" (*Financial Times* 4.8.03) – except in Britain, where the IMF has been a dominant influence since their intervention in 1976. But through paperback sales Professor Stiglitz has reached an audience that would not normally be enlightened on the formulaics of economic dogma. Still, be cautious on the persistence of change,

since, with academia still churning out economists drilled on old textbooks, Pavlov is a more decisive an influence on the flexibility of economic thought than Adam Smith.

Although, perhaps, perhaps, this programmed ossification of mind may be coming under irresistible attack through Eric Beinhocker's *The Origin of Wealth* (Random House), which offers an incisive critique of the assumptions underlying "traditional economics" – the guff that has been the staple of academic teaching, and political rhetoric in the post-Thatcher era.

[2] The archetypal declaration of subservience came from Mrs Thatcher: "There is no way in which you can buck the market." No doubt, in pursuit of ensuring Britain stood out as unique, since every other country sees government as an exercise precisely in "bucking" the destructive influences of the market. The widespread impact of Britain's subjection to this adage is crisply spelt out in *City State* by Richard Roberts and David Kyneston (Profile Books).

Unsurprisingly "efficient markets" guff has been coming in for some clobbering since the credit crunch set in – "The use of such euphemisms (referring to inflation as commodity price rises) encourages the denial of past errors and increases the risk of their repetition. It is favoured by those responsible for the errors, such as the Greenspan Fed and by those who wish to preserve the discredited Efficient Market Hypothesis, according to which bubbles are impossible as assets can never be mispriced": Andrew Smithers in "Lessons from the turmoil" (BEST OF FT.COM: *FT* 28.7.08).

Going through any account of the financial crisis – for example, *The Myth of the Rational Market* by Justin Fox (Harriman House) – the only conclusion is that the ethos of the Salem witch trials has become embedded in the US national consciousness, as a gaggle of bogus economic divines in universities and business schools pursued an alchemic fantasy of "beating the markets".

[3] *Dr Strangelove's Game* by Paul Strathern (Hamish Hamilton) is an entertaining jaunt through the cavalcade of oddballs who have contributed to the canon of economic thought.

[4] Everyone now seems to be jumping on the rubbishing bandwagon, despite for so long having tacitly gone along with facile interpretations. In its entirety the quotation from Adam Smith runs, "In spite of their natural selfishness and rapacity, though they mean only their own conveniency, though the sole end which they purpose from the labours of all the thousands they employ, be the gratification of their own vain and insatiable desires... they are led by an invisible hand... and without intending it, without knowing it, advance the interest of society."

Rather than a licence for "tooth and claw" pursuit of self-interested profit, or underwriting "infectious greed", or an imprimatur of Providence deigning that nothing should be done to interfere with the rigours of free-markets – connotations that the phrase seems to have carried at one time or another, it has apparently even been suggested that Adam Smith intended it as an ironic joke (Emma Rothschild), from Macbeth's plea to darkness to hide his crimes "with thy bloody and invisible hand". This reference is also followed by John Kay (*Financial Times* 24.9.03) who concludes, "The moral of Macbeth, and of Smith's magnum opus, is not that selfish behaviour works for the public good. It concerns the foolishness of human ambition and the failure of grand designs."

Humour, however, hardly seems Smith's forte. At all events, a rather different take on the central prominence that the phrase commands in conventional textbooks: "Adam Smith... was thrilled by the recognition of an order in the economic system. Smith proclaimed the principle of the 'invisible hand'" – *Economics* by Paul Samuelson.

But, having worked through his *Wealth of Nations*, the prospect of facing even a part of the rest of his massive output was more than spirit could bear. So as a shortcut *Adam Smith and His Legacy for Modern Capitalism* by Patricia Werhane (Oxford) seemed a handy alternative – only 180 pages. What was surprising was that "the invisible hand" was not expanded further in his mountain of verbiage, so that interpretations have been really piling selective weight on this single phrase. Equally surprising is the emergence of phrases "fellow feeling", "not to hurt or disturb in any respect the happiness of our neighbour", "sympathy", "a desire of the welfare and preservation of society", and even "the benevolent principle".

Or, how about? "In the theory, compensation only needs to be possible – it is not imperative to provide it. There is a macho appeal to this rhetoric of rugged self-reliance. It legitimises ego preferences (and property rights) as the only arbiters of desert. As Hume expressed it sarcastically – 'it is not contrary to reason to prefer the destruction of the whole world to the scratching of my little finger.' What protects this view from dismissal as mere barbarism is the doctrine of the 'invisible hand', that the self-seeking of individuals adds up to maximise the welfare of society. In this extreme version, the 'invisible hand' doctrine is simply an article of faith. It was not held by Adam Smith himself. Despite more than two centuries of effort, it has never been proved theoretically except under the most stringent and artificial restrictions and qualifications.

"Adam Smith actually had a different view. He understood that our well-being depended on the sympathy of others and suggested a code of conduct that could *earn* their esteem. Each individual earns sympathy by being worthy of sympathy. She follows the guidance of the 'impartial spectator', an inner voice that simulates the norms of society. That is quite similar to my own understanding of how well-being is achieved in the 'economy of regard'. Under reciprocity, the regard of others is earned by providing them with our own regard, directly or indirectly." (*The Challenge of Affluence* by Avner Offer (Oxford))

The guy really does seem to have been shafted in his treatment by successors. The final collapse of fantasy must surely have been signalled by Alan Greenspan's admission on the 23rd of October 2008 to the US House Oversight Committee: "I made a mistake in presuming that the self-interest of organisations, specifically banks and others, were such that they were best capable of protecting their own shareholders and their equity in the firms."

[5] "In the 1780s the slave trade, indeed, was not only restored, but attained its

highest levels.... So in the ten years between 1780 and 1790 at least 750,000 slaves were carried across the Atlantic: perhaps 325,000 by Britain, Liverpool being as ever the dominant city." *The Slave Trade* by Hugh Thomas (Picador). See also the historic table at page 510 of *The Making of New World Slavery* by Robin Blackburn (Verso).

These studies synthesise a massive weight of research. The former depicting perhaps most vividly the inhumanities of slave exploitation. It leaves a distressing open question on the development of "complimentary" economies to service the demand for slaves, and the extent to which this tradition of "commodification" has contributed to the genocidal tribal conflicts of subsequent African history.

The latter is a more cosmopolitan survey of the differing styles of slave exploitation by the European powers, focuses on the evolving technology of plantations, and contains a fuller analysis of the economic ramifications of the slave/plantation activities. It also provides a fascinating account of the sophistry of theologians in justifying the slave trade – matched only by the arguments of extreme advocates of unfettered globalisation.

An indirect indication of the pervasive influence of slave-related activities illustrated by both studies is the enumeration of interests that opposed abolition. Reinforced by Adam Hochschild's account in *Bury the Chains* (Macmillan) of the abolitionist movement. But there is a sequel in the US "secondary market" as slaves were sold "down the river" to the Southern plantations, which, long after abolition in Britain, still provided much of the raw materials for Lancashire's cotton industry. While Britain, after the sanctimonious triumph of abolishing the slave trade in 1830, substituted indentured Indian coolie labour shipped from Calcutta to the Demerara plantations of British Guyana, to Fiji, Mauritius and other imperial territories, but notably to South Africa for rail construction and mining until Ghandi took up their cause – *Coolies: How Britain Re-invented Slavery* (BBC). Hardly surprising that Adam Smith, on the basis of selective quotation, should be most reverentially treated in the two nations with dominant traditions of exploiting slave labour.

[6] "Yet most cultural historians, and certainly all literary scholars, have failed to remark the geographical notation, the theoretical mapping and charting of territory that underlies Western fiction, historical writing, and philosophical discourse of the time. There is first the authority of the European observer – traveller, merchant, scholar, historian, novelist. Then there is the hierarchy of spaces by which the metropolitan centre and, gradually, the metropolitan economy are seen as dependent upon an overseas system of territorial control, economic exploitation and a socio-cultural vision; without these stability and prosperity at home – "home" being a word with extremely potent resonances – would not be possible. The perfect example of what I mean is to be found in Jane Austen's Mansfield Park in which Thomas Bertram's slave plantation in Antigua is mysteriously necessary to the poise and the beauty of Mansfield Park, a place described in moral and aesthetic terms well before the scramble for Africa, or before the age of Empire officially began. As John Stuart Mill puts it in the Principles of Political Economy:

These [outlying possessions of ours] are hardly to be looked upon as countries.... but more properly as outlying agricultural or manufacturing estates belonging to a larger community. Our West Indian colonies, for example, cannot be regarded as countries with a productive capital of their own.... [but are rather] the place where England finds it convenient to carry on the production of sugar, coffee and a few other tropical commodities.

Read this extraordinary passage together with Jane Austen, and a much less benign picture stands forth than the usual one of cultural formations in the pre-imperialist age. In Mill we have the ruthless proprietary tones of the white master used to effacing the reality, work, and suffering of millions of slaves, transported across the middle passage, reduced only to an incorporated status 'for the benefit of the proprietors'!" .*Culture & Imperialism* by Edward W. Said (Chatto & Windus)

[7] Extract from interview with Fujio Mitarai, President of Canon – *Financial Times* 24 September 2003.

"Mr Mitarai has come up with a different management model. 'It has become a hybrid, it's true. On the technical side of things – finance, investment strategy, marketing and research and development – [Canon is] international in terms of management style. But in respect of personnel policy, I believe my management style is quite local. It's not that I intentionally pursue a Japanese management style. I am merely pursuing what is the most rational style for my employees.'

The US labour market, he says, is determined by supply and demand, where workers and companies are constantly jostling for personal advantage. 'Workers are trying to improve and be hired by a better company. If you go to leading US companies, you will always find a stack of applications on the personnel manager's desk.'

When Mr Mitarai was in the US, 'that was how we operated, too. But it happens right now that I'm in Japan, so I'm implementing the Japanese system.'

What is lost in flexibility, he says, is gained in employee loyalty and the ability to pour resources into workers' training without fear of their defecting. He says the stable environment created, where researchers can plan years ahead, is responsible for Canon's high number of US patents, second only to International Business Machines last year."

[8] *Flexible Rigidities* by Ronald Dore (Athlone). One of the cultural antecedents to this discrepancy is traced back to the evolution of the European Industrial Revolution, led by Britain, with its basis in energy/raw material extractive/capital intensive and specialisation/division/saving of labour, while Asian countries who came late to this style of industrialisation – China in the 18th and early 19th centuries and Japan in the Tokogawa period – remained essentially agrarian, yet still managed significant growth. Within the relatively stable societies of the latter, efficiencies were achieved by an "industrious revolution" involving local co-operation to enhance the rice and other yields, diversification into artisan skills and development of merchant networks. Their subsequent adoption of industrial modes of activity were influenced by this different social ethos, in many fields leading to competitive performance exceeding the industrial originators. (This

rationale is explored more fully in *The Resurgence of East Asia* ed. Giovanni Arrighi,Takeshi Hamashita and Mark Selden (Routledge), and particularly the contribution by Kaoru Sugihara, "The East Asian path of economic development: a long-term perspective".)

In practice, the tension between "flexibility" in its usual economist jargon as implying "liquidity" in labour markets, and the real "flexibility" attained by creating flexible internal skills and problem-solving supplier relationships, in large measure aimed at overcoming the inefficiencies of "spot" transactions, is vividly explored in *Strategic Industrial Sourcing* by Toshihiro Nishiguchi (Oxford). Indeed, the latter increasingly appears a crucial prerequisite for success in complex high-value products.

While interpretations of Japan's "lifetime employment" have typically reflected our tradition of binary thinking – in practice there are no such individual contracts, but a general acceptance that for core employees there will be a "lifetime commitment" – companies will also have a "temporary" margin of employees. Toyota, and indeed other Japanese companies, are adjusting the balance between different categories of employees according to prospective shifts in the global distribution of activities, availability of future talented recruits, or, more recently, to reemploy experienced retirees. But none will readily give up the accumulated gains of experience, expertise, and sustained relationships with suppliers that will continue to enable them to adapt more rapidly and efficiently than competitors.

But no need to reason why the "bosses organisation" should hang grimly onto "flexible labour markets". After all, as their friendly *Economist* argues (Let the fight begin – Give shareholders a vote on pay; but don't let others interfere: 14.6.08), "Whereas workers' pay depends on the labour market (and has been kept down by the huge numbers of people joining the global economy), managers' bonuses are chiefly tied to returns on capital" as justification for "managers' pay has grown faster than workers' pay". No prizes for spotting the weaknesses in this simplistic logic. If perhaps ignoring the contribution of "labour" to achieving "returns on capital", particularly in high-value-added products and processes, no need to look further for the source of the disjunction of the heart of the decline of British companies. And confirmation that economic thought has not moved on from the 18th century "...and the demand for men, like that for other commodities..."

[9] Among the most eloquent expressions of outrage at British industry's treatment of employee pensions comes from Martin Wolf, "A shameful pensions confidence trick" (*FT* 1.7.05). Commenting on the decline of private sector defined pension benefits schemes, and the prospects of them disappearing altogether in a few years, he goes on, "Predictably, as the schemes disappear, the supply of self-serving, self-exculpation from managements and those who speak for them soars"... "What we have been watching is the unwinding of what was – in effect, if not in the intention – a confidence trick known as "bait and switch": offer something attractive and then switch it for something else when the customer comes to collect."

If governments cannot avoid being implicated in this sorry tale, "In a nutshell, companies pretended to make promises they were unable to keep, while governments were determined to force companies to keep the promises they pretended to make. This is a classic British game of hoping for the best. What kept the confidence trick in play was the stock market bubble...." And after the lame excuses of "people are living so much longer than expected. Does anybody believe that rising longevity is a surprise?", "stock market returns have been low", and "regulation is onerous", the conclusion is, "Companies have played the bait and switch game: now comes the switch. Everybody involved should feel thoroughly ashamed of themselves." Presumably, someone has discovered a deficit in the *FT* pension scheme.

[10] THE BEST OF FT.COM, (5.2.07) notes under the heading "Worrying aspect of the brain drain" that "56 per cent of the UK-born elite scientists have left the United Kingdom and currently live abroad. This figure was reached by analysing the proportion of the world's 250 most-cited scientists who were born in the UK."

While the OECD study on international patterns of migration (*FT* 21.2.08) noted, "The UK and Germany had the highest number of highly skilled emigrants – 1.1m and 860,000 – leaving for other OECD countries." The relative pool of skilled talent from which this drain is taking place is much smaller in the UK than Germany. While a more vivid conclusion from this report is, "the UK is leaching professionals on a far bigger scale than any comparable country; more than one million skilled graduates live abroad, 319,000 of them with degrees in science and engineering... we have waved goodbye to one in 10 of our most skilled compatriots." (Forget non-doms: we face a real brain drain – *Observer* 24.02.08)

[11] From *The World Economy: Towards Integration* by David Henderson in *Beyond 2000: a Sourcebook for Major Projects* (MPA 1994). A convenient summary from one of the leading economic fantasists, one time head of the Economics and Statistics Department of OECD, and variously in and out of the Treasury. Yet the myth persists, carried forward by Pavlovian repetition, as a more recent example, "Today, much of the global financial sector is as liberalised as it was a century ago, just before the First World War." ("The new capitalism" by Martin Wolf (*FT* 19.6.07))

[12] No great scholarship is required of the economics fraternity: just try:
The Race to Fashoda by David Levering Lewis (Bloomsbury), which conveniently summarises the carving up of Africa at the turn of the 19th century with a before-and-after pair of maps for 1890 and 1900.

Any reasonable account of Britain's Empire: for example, *British Imperialism* (2 vols) by P.J.Cain and A.G.Hopkins.

Or the neat summary that between 1870 and 1900, European nations seized control of some 10 million square miles of territory on which 150 million people lived. See *The Unconquerable World: Power, Nonviolence and the Will of the People* by Jonathan Schell (Allen Lane).

[13] The reference to the Japanese diplomat comes from *The Sun at Noon* by Dick Wilson (Hamish Hamilton) – still one of the sharpest quick introductions to

Japan's post-Pacific War orientation, by an experienced "Asia hand". The term "imperialism of free trade" is referred to in *The Rise of the "the Rest"* by Alice Amsden (Oxford) p 70 – "China and the Ottoman Empire experienced an 'imperialism of free trade', or forced market opening by European powers". But, after surveying the development approaches of a range of countries from the US to Asia and South America, she queries pointedly, "Therefore, despite free trade's appeal in terms of administrative simplicity, and despite its theoretical claim to "pareto optimality" (assuming perfect knowledge), its practical significance for latecomers was relatively small. The question thus becomes, *if free trade has so much to recommend it, why were its adherents so few?*" With only Switzerland and Hong Kong, and each of these with special circumstances, as examples.

[14] Laissez Faire. Où?
Just a quick survey of how the tattered principles of economics have been followed around the world. A fuller Cook's Tour is provided later in the section "They Ain't Daft".

In Germany, industrial evolution since Friedrich Wilhelm I in the mid-18th century began his reforms in Prussia has embraced the concept that the state, even if extensively debated for the next century, had a role in the national economy (*The Spirit of Capitalism* by Liah Greenfeld (Harvard) pp 171ff). Later Freidich List (1789-1846), in the face of a fashionable surge in calls for "liberalisation" recalled that in fact Britain was among the first nations to employ protection, promotion of infant industries, acquiring technology from others, and preferential development of a merchant marine etc, concludes with his comment: "It is a very common clever device that when anyone has attained the summit of greatness, he kicks away the ladder by which he has climbed up, in order to deprive others of the means of climbing up after him." In this lies the secret of the cosmopolitan doctrine of Adam Smith, and of the cosmopolitan tendencies of his great contemporary William Pitt, and of all his successors in the British Government administrations.

"Any nation which by means of protective duties and restrictions on navigation has raised her manufacturing power and her navigation to such a degree of development that no other nation can sustain free competition with her, can do nothing wiser than to throw away these ladders of her greatness, to preach to other nations the benefits of free trade, and to declare in penitent tones that she has hitherto wandered in the paths of error, and has now for the first time succeeded in discovering the truth." (The National System Political Economy)

List's rationale – more later – was persuasive in Germany: indeed Bismarck is reported to have had a copy permanently on his desk. And this wasn't, apparently, for fun. This can be illustrated from *Gold and Iron* by Fritz Stern (Penguin), an enthralling account of the backstairs in Bismarck's Germany, "To make sure that free traders would suffer for their sins, Bismarck insisted that none of them "should be proposed for a decoration." The protectionist stalwarts, Tiedemann and Varnbüler, on the other hand, received appropriate orders. In the new phase of the Reich, Conservatives garnered most of the honours.

In spirit and substance, the new economic programme marked Germany's departure from its brief, liberal course. In the 1850s and 1860s laissez faire thought had been popular among educated and commercial classes, but the veneration of the state was an older, stronger habit, and Germans never really adopted the liberal suspicion of the state. Unification had vindicated the authoritarian state; and the boom, bust, and corruption in the early 1870s were quickly interpreted as a moral judgment on liberals. Interest groups clamoured for "national" protection; influential academics, organised in a League for Social Reform, demanded an end to Manchesterism and a new activist state. The older liberalism was declining – even in England – and Bismarck came to believe that a programme of what he called state socialism would forestall revolutionary or democratic socialism." (Page 208)

And German industrial development has since evolved in a distinct idiom of combinations and structures of co-operation within regional contexts. Today, in conversation with German businessmen, references to Adam Smith are liable to be met with some such rejoinder as, "There's more to life than making pins".

France has a history of state involvement going back to Colbert, and, whilst well versed in the doctrines of the laissez faire school, has chosen a markedly pragmatic style. One of the delightful ironies is that the term originates from Vincent de Gournay (1712-59), a leader of the physiocratic school of economic theorists, with the doctrine summarised "laissez faire, laissez passer". On the other hand, a textbook depiction would be: "French industrial policy has also not been dosed with the nostrums of classical economics. Instead of focusing on short-term profitability or regarding as axiomatically correct the decisions of the market, it has taken a much more structural view of French industry.... One factor of great importance is differing ideology between France on the one hand and Britain and the United States on the other. In the first place, faith in the ability of market forces to allocate investment funds optimally has, at least until now, been weaker in France than in the USA or Britain. A separate but related ideological factor has been the greater faith in the state in France than in Anglo-American democracies... French governments have been able to evoke a tradition of regarding the state as a servant or guarantor of the long-term public interest, that which citizens pursuing what Rousseau had termed the 'General Will' would favour, that has found little support in British or American intellectual life. The market is seen as less intelligent and the state as wiser than in Anglo-American thought. The argument that the state needs to promote economic growth is therefore more readily accepted." *Business and Politics* by Graham Wilson (Macmillan) – a crisp introduction to national variations.

Typically, a French official asked incredulously whether DTI had in fact been told to study Adam Smith. "Not only that," was my response, "we even have him quoted by our economists." "But that was two hundred years ago," my French companion said aghast. To which there was only one reply, "Steady up. You don't think we rely solely on Adam Smith. We also have Pliny and Herodotus."

Or, more crisply, at a Franco-British Association Conference in Bordeaux, a leading French official declared, "The greatest service *Le Bon Dieu* did for France was to make Adam Smith and Keynes Englishmen." Of many personal experiences of their sharp pragmatism in marshalling trade support, one might serve as an illustration. In 1985, David Henderson's Reith Lectures *Innocence and Design* was circulated within DTI as a summary of scriptural wisdom. Literally, pages of *The Listener* had been solemnly collected, photostatted, and bundled together with string. Given a normally busy daily routine, this bundle lay unread in the pending tray against the time when there would be absolutely nothing better to do.

The opportunity came during a typical stage in a protracted negotiation in China where the French were our partners. The only sure prediction in any major negotiation in China in the early 80s was that there would be interminable longuers to offer the ideal context of absolutely nothing else to do. The leading DREE official and I were sitting in our hotel lobby during one of these periods when I finally finished reading the homework. Seeing him dozing off, having exhausted all the available periodicals, I handed the bundle over to him expressing the mischievous hope that he might find them interesting to while away the time. For the next three hours, he religiously applied himself to the text. And then tossed it aside with the remark, "We wouldn't waste airtime on that in France."

After this round of negotiations, while packing to return to Hong Kong, I realised that the bundle of sacred scrolls must have been left where my French colleague had thrown it. On arriving in Hong Kong, I thought to replace my lost scrolls with a copy of the printed version. None of the bookshops near the Commercial Counsellor's office admitted to knowing of such an author. But just before leaving, I chanced to be flicking through to find some in-flight reading when one of the attendants to whom I had spoken earlier said that a book by this author had just arrived and "was selling like hot cakes". This seemed a bit unlikely. And sure enough it was *The Logic of Business Strategy* by Bruce Henderson, founder of the Boston Consulting Group – whom I had met in the days of the motorbike saga. Since copies were indeed going fast, and it had the brevity suitable for a long-haul flight, I got a copy before the shelf emptied.

His views on economics were hardly flattering, "...Economists have provided little or no insight into the realities of competition. Their assumptions do not match reality nor have they been confirmed by observation. Their view of competitive interaction is simplistic. The myth of the perfect market has been preserved in the fantasy of identical small competitors competing in a commodity market without inhibitions. This is not real. Nor is it useful as a concept for decision rule formulation." So, among the livewire business community of Hong Kong, market share, the experience curve etc might expect to carry a bit more clout than economic precepts.

As for America, the land of the free etc, it has a negligible record of practising free trade: a brief commentary from a native American, "Advocates of the free market... must confront the fact that Adam Smith's invisible hand has always been celebrated far more in theory than in practice. Alexander Hamilton's *Report on Manufactures*, an early blueprint for America's commercial development, praised Smith's thoughts on specialisation but ignored his faith in the free market. On the contrary, Hamilton urged the federal government to play an activist role in creating an urban, industrial society. The railroad construction that later provided the foundation for nineteenth-century economic growth was subsidised by massive federal land grants, as was the settlement of the American West. The

378

tariff that protected American manufacturers for decades after the Civil War had more in common with mercantalism than with any of Smith's notions about free trade. The economic history of the twentieth century continued along the same lines: the New Deal rescue of capitalism, direct government investments in industry during the Second World War, the highway-building of the Eisenhower era, the military spending responsible for our current dominance of the aerospace, computer, and software industries. For some reason these facts are not mentioned in current debates over economic policy. The period of America's greatest economic supremacy – from the early 1950s until the late 1960s – was marked by high income taxes, rigorous anti-trust enforcement, and unprecedented levels of union membership. No period of American history has remotely resembled the free market ideal described in *The Wealth of Nations*. Even Adam Smith was more concerned about the harmful influences of concentrated economic power than are many of his contemporary followers." *Reefer Madness* by Eric Schlosser (Penguin), just as one of many examples.

More recently, President Bush Jnr's hike in agricultural subsidies, tariffs on steel imports etc are but the latest in a history of US "trade" distortions – the dispute over export subsidies, even before its guise as the Foreign Sales Corporation (FSC) programme, has been running for decades unchecked.

There are too many studies of Japan to attempt invidious selection: *Nippon* by William Horsley and Roger Buckley, published to accompany a BBC series is a very readable overview. While *Kaisha* by Jim Abegglen (Harper & Row) is a vivid insight into the competitive environment that has generated their distinctive leading companies. Or the increasing number of studies by Japanese authors – *Japan's Capitalism: Creative Defeat and Beyond* by Shigeto Tsuru (Cambridge), or titles in the Japan Business and Economics series published by Oxford University Press.

As a personal anecdote, when a senior manager in Itochu admitted to having read economics at university, I enquired which authors he had studied. "Marx and Keynes," was his reply. "Not Adam Smith?" I asked. He shrugged, "Oh, we know all about indivisible hands," with only the barest wisp of a smile.

For confirmatory material of what others have been up to in the course of their industrial development, Alice Amsden's *Asia's Next Giant* (Oxford) is a lucid study of South Korea's early advance, with an account of the country's deliberate approach of "getting prices wrong", while Robert Wade's study of Taiwan's development, *Governing the Market* (Princeton) is a further illustration of how the state, apart from investing in the high-risk capital intensive industries, set the context and responded sensitively to the rapid evolution of a thriving small business community. And they haven't gone to sleep – the Taiwan government plans the sale of a third of its 7.4% stake, through its Cabinet Development Fund, in Taiwan Semiconductor Manufacturing (TSMC) – the world's largest chip fabricator – for $1.39 billion. "These include 600 million TSMC shares. After the sale, the fund will still have roughly one billion shares." (*FT* 30.9.2003)

While the context of the neo-corporate countries of Europe, where "the market" has traditionally been circumscribed, can be sampled in *European Business Systems* edited by Richard Whitley (Sage).

[15] Perhaps the outstanding example of a "static" view of comparative advantage is the unfortunate Mr Naoto Ichimada, Governor of the Bank of Japan in 1952, who expressed the view, "The attempt to foster a car industry in Japan is futile. This is the age of the international division of labour. Since America can produce cheap, high-quality cars, shouldn't we depend on them?" (*Nippon* page 155). With the US-owned car manufacturers currently toppling against a loss of share in their own market comparable to that of British manufacturers in their domestic market during the mid-70s, mostly a consequence of the higher quality and better value of Japanese makes, the remark deserves to be inscribed on some memorial shrine somewhere.

[16] Marubeni, one of the Japanese general trading companies, produced a booklet *The Unique World of the Sogo Shosha*, which included an account of selling communications equipment in Libya: neither side had a Japanese/Arabic translator, but both had an interpreter into English, so the negotiations took place in English. In fact, English has become an international mediator of business with many "foreigners" having a better mastery of the language than most native speakers. If anything, the language therefore confers advantages to others. While the relative backwardness of British businessmen, with a few notable exceptions, to master other languages compounds the disadvantage.

Gordon Brown, as Chancellor of the Exchequer, picked up this theme during his visit to China in Feb 2005, presumably briefed by Treasury officials drawing on their customary "cultivated ignorance". Someone closer to Britain's historic links with China might have reminded him that, during the 1980s – while I was in the process of negotiating in partnership with the French – the Chinese government had asked Britain to set up a British Council centre in Beijing. The British Council, presumably under some Treasury constraints, was dithering in providing a response. The French, on hearing of this hesitancy, had offered to set up an English Institute immediately.

Moreover, latest studies suggest that far from being a comparative advantage, the mono- (if not partial-) lingual Brit is likely to be seriously disadvantaged in the commercial world of the 21st century. *English Next*, a lucid study of current trends in English studies, by David Graddol under the aegis of the British Council, charts the increasing use of English as a business transaction code, and the sharply rising drive to instil it in foreign education. But "global English" as it is evolving will be utilitarian, with foreign students preferring to learn from their national teachers, and a developing trend for foreign universities to offer specialist and technical courses in English.

[17] A quotation from "The next leap for India's knowledge economy" by Guy de Jonquieres (*FT* 29.3.05). The article reflects discussions with management at Wipro and Infosys, two of India's leading software services companies, who both saw a continuing expansion in their activities. "India's ambitions seem to know no bounds" is a summary of their intentions. For a more comprehensive treatment of this trend, a flick through *The World Is Flat* by Thomas L. Friedman (Farrar, Straus and Giroux) might prompt more than a few doubts on the stability of any comparative advantage in services.

Financial services, indeed, have never ceased to proclaim their natural superiority for "the highly paid and skilled jobs they generate" – typical, *Asia seeks financial future in field of dreams* (*FT* 18.4.06). But, with applause from developmental economists, evidence is piling up that these can increasingly be outsourced to locations less "highly paid": for example, the legal work associated with due diligence in M&A activities, one of the best screws for City legal firms (*Legal work in pastures new* (*FT* 12.4.06)). The level of legal process outsourcing (LPO) to India is expected to grow from $146m in 2006, to $440m in 2010 and reach $1.1bn in 2014, flowing from the costs of English/American legally literate staff being 1/8 of the hourly rates ($400) charged by UK legal firms (*The Economist*, Passage to India – 26.6. 2010).

[18] Moments of honesty are fairly rare among the economist clan: but Frank Knight, by all accounts a bit of maverick, deserves the palm for admitting, "It beats working for a living". Quoted in *Against the Gods* by Peter L. Bernstein (Wiley).

[19] *Entrepreneurs and Managers* by Peter Temin in *Favourites of Fortune* (Harvard). Judging by the references following the essay, a few thousand hours must already have been spent in mixing potions. But it is even debated periodically whether economics is comparable to religion: obviously, any theological pretensions would need a sounder ethical foundation than "vain and insatiable desires" to be a serious contender. Typically the publication of Robert Nelson's *Economics As Religion* (Penn State Press – 2001) triggered some commentaries, such as Michael Prowse (*FT* 26/27.1.02). If any codicil were needed, we have the sentiment, "The sensible pursuit of self-interest, so far from being a crude prescription for personal enrichment, is in fact a subtle doctrine, perhaps too subtle for this world" – Yea. Verily it passeth all understanding... (*The subtle doctrine of self-interest* – Samuel Brittan (*FT* 27.8.04), commenting on a pamphlet by David Henderson, *The Role of Business in the Modern World* (Institute of Economic Affairs). Surely alchemy – or quackery – is probably the closest economics comes to this fantasy?

Spare a thought for Prof Avner Offer, who must be living in constant terror looking over his shoulder for figures in long pointed hats. As one of "the profession", though apparently contaminated by an earlier career as a soldier, farmer and conservation officer, he dared in *The Challenge of Affluence – Self-Control and Well-Being in the United States and Britain since 1950* (Oxford) to argue that far from optimal rational beings most of us are myopic creatures vulnerable to the lures of immediate satisfaction, and with less interest in the longer term as affluence increases. For this he received a stern rebuke from the counsel of the Grand Inquisitor that the new move to "behavioural economics" is preferable "as a set of exceptions that modifies but leaves intact the canonical model of rational choice, not least since it is irrational to suppose that people in general behave irrationally." (*The Economist* 29.4.06.)

This really does put us back among the gargoyles and mediaeval chop-logic: for history is replete with crazed cults and demagogues who have persuaded millions of devotees on avowedly "rational" grounds to support ludicrous, and occasionally lunatic, causes. Surely, it must be "rational" to be sceptical of any purportedly "rational" postulates without questioning the validity of their assumptions. And, in practice, the new vogue for "happiness" and "behavioural economics" attest, if anything, to the questionable relevance of economic orthodoxy to real behaviour and aspirations.

If "quackery" seems a bit harsh, a lively flow of descriptive analogies for "financial economics" was let loose by Nassim Nicolas Taleb's article "The pseudo-science hurting markets" (*FT* 24.10.07) as the consequences of the "credit crunch" rippled through markets. He had achieved some celebrity as the author of *The Black Swan: the Impact of the Highly Improbable* on the theme of the inherent failure of conventional economic formulae to cope with, if not exacerbate, uncertainty. He remarks that, "Modern Portfolio Theory" (MPT) may have earned Nobel recognition, but is "incompatible with the possibility of those consequential rare events I call "black swans". Yet, in practice, "MPT has the empirical and scientific validity of astrology." With a sequence of examples, where laureate blessings were disposed on equally dodgy "formulae", "The environment in financial economics is reminiscent of mediaeval medicine... while economic models, it has been shown, work hardly better than random guesses or the intuition of cab drivers." Amongst the entertaining stream of metaphors released into the correspondence columns subsequently was the suggestion that "mediaeval medicine" should be replaced by "a circus sideshow" ("Financial economics more like a circus sideshow" (*FT* 30.10.07)).

[20] "To Have and to Hold" (*The Economist* 30.8.03)

"There Is No Invisible Hand" (Joseph Stiglitz *Guardian* 20.12.02)

"Neuroeconomics – In Search of the Inside Story of Economics" (*Financial Times* 20.9.03)

Even, so help us, "The 'dismal science' turns its attention to the question of happiness" (*Financial Times* 10.1.05).

The sophistry, and admirable adroitness, of economists maintaining the credo even when undermined could hardly be better illustrated than in absorbing "behavioural economics". If the "behaviouralist's" essential insight is that human beings have a fundamental flaw in perversely acting contrary to rational self-interest, which should be sufficient to junk the theology, it becomes admissible to apply incentives/disincentives even in subliminal forms to bias such foolhardy behaviour towards the appropriate rational response. All entertainingly sketched out in "The new paternalism – The avuncular state" (*The Economist* 8.4.06), covering such fields as gambling, smoking addiction, insurance and inadequate savings provision. But before too much applause that commonsense appears to be seeping into the canon, introducing some of the social mechanisms that other societies over millennia have evolved through kinship, community and cultural networks, just beware the multiplication of jargon – "intimate contest for self-command", and "Just as one individual can inflict an externality on another, so one side of a person's nature can inflict an "internality" on another". Blimey. We'll be having "existential economics" next!

Yet not to despair. Some of these contortions represent a genuine attempt to twist the propositions of traditional economics to recognise its inherent fallacies. Perhaps the most stunning annihilation of several (or most) of the fundamental tenets of "Traditional Economics" is offered by Eric Beinhocker in *The Origin of Wealth* (Random House), drawing upon work at the Santa Fe Institute. The paradox is how avowedly rational economists could have bought in so uncritically to the bunkum of "rationality".

In a field normally characterised by overweening arrogance mea culpas are rare, if not non-existent. So John Kay's "How economics lost sight of the real world" (*FT* 22.4.09) comes as a shaft of rare honesty. "Economists, like physicists, have been searching for a theory of everything. If there were to be such an economic theory, there is really only one candidate, based on extreme rationality and market efficiency. Any other theory would have to account for the evolution of individual beliefs and the advance of human knowledge, and no one imagines that there could be a single theory of all human behaviour. Not quite no one: a few deranged practitioners of the project believe that their theory really does account for all human behaviour, and that concepts such as goodness, beauty and truth are sloppy sociological constructs. But these people discredit themselves by opening their mouths." For the pretensions to "rigour" are based on "the self-referential criteria of modern academic life." He concludes by recalling Keynes' cautionary observation that economic understanding required "an amalgam of logic and intuition and a wide knowledge of facts, most of which are not precise."

[21] *Reefer Madness* by Eric Schlosser (Penguin). Apart from its frankness in admitting that America has never subscribed in practice to the dogma of Adam Smith, this is an illuminating survey of the marijuana, pornography and illegal immigrant underground economies in the United States.

But an elegant probing of the vacuous data on "business services" in the UK is offered by Chris Giles "Lies, damn lies and befuddlement" (*FT* 27.7.07). Despite grandiloquent forecasts that "business services will exceed 40% of the economy by the end of the decade... we do not really know with any certainty what is going on. The statistics on business services are rather like a cheap sausage; alluring on the outside, but the more you delve into the ingredients, the more queesy you feel." Examples include, "most of the £83bn contribution to the UK economy in 2004 is the ONS's (Office for National Statistics) estimate of how much it would cost property owners to rent their own homes.... in estimating this huge adjustment, the ONS has to guess the notional private sector rental value of every UK home using some heroic assumptions. The upshot is that if planning restrictions damage the UK economy and force rents up, measured GDP increases, improving Britain's apparent productivity performance relative to other countries." While, "even bigger problems lie in differentiating real growth from changes in prices... banks have traditionally used interest rate rises to improve margins by jacking up interest rates on loans by more than on deposits. This is clearly inflation, but the measurement of inflation-adjusted interest rate spreads are so difficult that under the ONS's chosen methodology, it will be recorded as an increase in banking activity and productivity." "Or take lawyers... law firms had increased their hourly rates by 6 to 10 per cent. That is inflation. But it will appear as increased output in the index of services, because data shortages force the ONS to adjust law firms' turnover for inflation using an index of the wages of estate agents, among others. In other words, pay a lawyer 10 per cent more and Britain's output and productivity rises. But pay a doctor 10 per cent more and it is inflation, because output in health services is measured by the amount doctors do".

[22] *Informal Finance – Some Findings from Asia* – Asian Development Bank (Oxford). Admirable for the depth of the survey, and a fascinating account of the diversity of mechanisms at the informal level of a tontine character to make finance available at a rational price.

An unexpected consequence from the high percentages of "informal" activities in developing economies lies in their relative dependence on tariffs as their more reliable sources of government revenues. This plays into their reluctance to concede tariffs in trade rounds, apart from any natural preference for retaining protective differentials to lever their domestic markets to secure technologies and build up their own capabilities. (No deal may be better than Doha deal on the table – Kevin P. Gallagher, Department of International Relations, Boston University: *FT* Correspondence 15/16.4.06.) This draws the comparison between estimates of projected benefits of current proposals under the Doha Round and the tariff losses that would result:

"Projections of the economic benefits of the deal on the table range from $6.7 bn to $20.5 bn for developing countries – or less than a penny a day per head. In contrast, Unctad, the United Nations Conference on Trade and Development, has published estimates of projected tariff revenue losses under the manufacturing negotiations.

Total tariff losses for developing countries could be $63.4 bn or 3 to 10 times the benefit. Many developing countries rely on tariffs for more than one quarter of their tax revenue. For smaller nations with little diversification in their economies, tariff revenues provide the core of government budgets."

Nor does this take account of the astounding levels of 'dead capital' i.e. unrecorded individual capital holdings, in the developing world identified by Hernando de Soto's research teams depicted in *The Mystery of Capital* (Black Swan). Nor the financial flows across borders arising from tax evasion, organised crime and corruption, 'The World Bank estimates annual cross-border flows from criminal activities, corruption and tax evasion at $1000bn-$1600bn (£504bn-£806bn), of which half comes from developing and transitional economies.'" (*FT* 5.3.08.) And the gap continues as "UN warns of gangs' global muscle" (*FT* 18.6 .10) depicting the value of illegal trafficking at an annual rate of $130bn.

Black holes in economic data go back a long way: the trade and capital flows from the slave/plantation trades are amenable to estimation from contemporary records of shipping operators, merchants, estates etc. The loot extracted by the East India Company nabobs, however, defies records (*The Industrial Revolution and British Overseas Trade* by Ralph Davis (Lancaster University Press)). If Baron Clive of Plassey could boldly proclaim to a Parliamentary Inquiry, "By God, Mr. Chairman, at this moment I stand astonished at my own moderation", it must be mute whether such modest claims could be echoed by other ranks in The Honourable Company.

[23] Under the banner of the Engineering Markets Division in DTI, we set up a conference in the late 1980s to explore opportunities in the ASEAN area. As one of the position papers, the Division's statistician was asked to prepare a note on the development of trade flows in the area, one purpose of which was to examine how far it was evolving as a self-sufficient bloc. He returned a bit worried pointing out that there were a "lot of $billions" missing between the national trade statistics of the countries involved. He mentioned this to his colleagues in the national statistical office, and shortly afterwards there was a flurry of concern about the "lot of lot of $billions" slipping through international trade data. One suspects that we are now in the dimensions of a "lot of lot of lot of...". A global trade deficit estimated at $180bn. in 2003 according to the IMF, but a topic thrown into relief by the US/China dispute over the latter's trade surplus: even here estimates can vary from $43bn. to $148bn., depending on allowances for Hong Kong re-exports. *A truer measure of China's trade surplus* (*FT* 30.10.03). Closer to home, we have had the comic interlude of "Fraud could account for 10% of UK exports" (*Guardian* 11.5.06), when "Trade deficit on goods hits record despite improvement in exports" (*FT* 11.5.06), which prompted one commentator to remark, "The data really show a rapid surge in the UK's tax evasion industry."

And now that "globalisation" is becoming the theme of the day, we have the reassuring conclusion from the Federal Reserve's annual junket at Jackson Hole (*FT* 28.8.06), "But figures showing the human costs and benefits of globalisation, which cannot be adequately captured by mainstream economic data, are some way off. Debate on the pros and cons of globalisation looks set to continue in largely evidence-free fashion."

[24] There has been growing interest in the "networking" structures of informal corporate relations and trade: just a few useful anthologies:
Overseas Chinese Business Networks by Michael Beckman (Australian government). A well-researched and revealing study of the provincial ties between China and countries in South East Asia.

Asian Business Networks, edited Gary C. Hamilton (de Gruyter). Detailed analyses of networks in Hong Kong, Taiwan, Japan and South Korea, particularly illuminating on Taiwan – for example, underground investment companies and groups of related enterprises, with some questioning essays on the validity of conventional economic characterisations of "the company".

Networks, Markets and the Pacific Rim – Studies in Strategy, edited W. Mark Fruin (Oxford). An attractively diverse series of essays, analysing the functioning of networks from a traditional fishmarket to internal procedures for innovation.

Underlying these patterns of informal networks is the premise of co-operation. Whilst the theologians of economics having given priority to competition, and arm's-length contests as an insurance against parties acting "against the public interest" and in the pursuit of efficient prices (how realistic such assumptions may be in practice is debatable), co-operation is at least as natural a human response against uncertainty and as a basis for reducing transaction costs. A truly seminal work – taking this much-overused term, was *The Evolution of Co-operation* by Robert Axelrod (Penguin) which took the test case of the "iterative prisoners' dilemma" to indicate that in many circumstances co-operation evolves as a natural series of choices when "zero-sum" individual advantage turns out to be unfavourable for both parties. Among the striking examples that he cites are the codes adopted in the brutal confrontation of the First World War frontlines for each side to alert the other about forthcoming bombardments. But in an industrial context, such relationship structures are inherent in the "common-interest" groups that have evolved in some countries, and in the group patterns of Asian corporate forms. Needless to say, economists have seized on this work as fodder for their twist on "game theory".

[25] *Taiwanese Firms in Southeast Asia – Networking Across Borders*, edited Tain-Jy Chen (Edward Elgar). For example, between 1980-95 reported Taiwanese investment in Vietnam was US$3,578 million, or 17% of the total, exceeding Japan and Hong Kong (p 217).

[26] A fascinating account of Toshiba working with other companies to develop a high-density smart card is contained in *Knowledge Works* by Mark Fruin (Oxford). Even though each participant was committing substantial development resources, this was conducted at surprising speed – faster than any competitors – without contractual wrangling.

From personal experience, the President of a medium-sized Japanese company, when faced with an inch-thick legal joint-venture agreement with a leading British company, negotiated over nearly a year, flicked it disparagingly with the remark, "If anyone expects me to sign this, it can only mean he doesn't trust me. In Japan, we'd have agreed on four pages what we were going to do. And we'd be rolling out the first prototypes by now."

[27] "Setting the Sales Price
The same considerations (how fast and precise a response to the immediate situation can be made) applied to the distinctive way prices are set in Japanese companies. In the great majority of cases, "cost-plus-profit = price" is not the recognised formula. Instead, management's first step is to set the selling price and then to see how costs can be brought into line.

The selling price is dictated by competition with the other companies in the same industry. The urgent need to reconcile costs with the selling price is the driving force behind Japanese marketing efforts. If a company fails in this, it will run into the red and head for bankruptcy.

This method of setting the selling price makes the sales division extremely powerful. It is responsible for devising means to beat the competition, and its main method is ultimately a low price.

When top management agrees to the selling price, the production division is presented with a target for cost cuts. The production division may provide the sales division with cost figures as a rough guide, but it is not permitted to dictate what it considers a reasonable price.

In the unlikely event that pressure is applied by the production people, the sales division may well ignore it. Most information concerning production costs is gathered not at official conferences but through unofficial channels, by means of nemawashi (informal consultation). But even though the sales division is fully aware of production costs, it often has to disregard them to meet the competition.

This is why the cost-plus-profit concept, recognised as the basis of many modern management methods, just does not apply in Japan. The corollary is that rises in costs, whatever their cause, can be reflected in the selling price only with extreme difficulty.

One offshoot of the Japanese pricing formula is the strategy of aggressively setting low prices to win domination of a market and then rapidly improving production to bring costs in line with prices... how dynamic the corporate response can be is illustrated by a major automobile company. When the yen reached 150 against the dollar, Nissan ordered its R&D division to reduce costs by 10 percent. The R&D division asked for suggestions from all of the companies' production divisions – and received two hundred thousand responses." *Japanese Style Management* by Keitaro Hasegawa (Kodansha).

Try this approach on the finance director of a company focused on "shareholder value"! A crucial difference in perception lies in the lack of confidence among British companies to deliver consistently the level of cost savings necessary to compete on this basis. But over time, the continuing drive to reduce costs has been the motivating dynamic of Toyota's distinct production system that has only evolved over several decades, and is still being adapted for further cost reduction: see *The Evolution of a Manufacturing System at Toyota* by Takahiro Fujimoto (Oxford).

[28] Recall Honda's drive for market dominance in Japan. Or look at Dell's prices in the post-IT collapse period just after 2000! But *The New Competition – Institutions of Industrial Restructuring* by Michael H. Best (Polity Press) is a lucid account of the collapse of economic orthodoxies against new forms of corporate organisation.

[29] The distinction between "economic exchange" and "social exchange" relations is touched on in Werner Pascha's essay *On the Analysis of Change and Continuity in Japan's Socio-Economy* in *Japan's Socio-Economic Evolution*, edited by Sarah Metzger-Court and Werner Pascha (Curzon Press). Or, from a marketing viewpoint, in *Consumer Behaviour in Asia* by Hellmut Schütte and Deanna Carlante (Macmillan).

[30] *Globalisation and Its Discontents* by Joseph Stiglitz (Penguin) p74. An entertaining critique of the nonsense perpetrated by economics in pursuit of the myth of equilibrium is offered in *The Origin of Wealth* op. cit pp 45ff, as indeed one of the more enlightened members of the clan admits, "To be sure, economics has evolved a highly sophisticated body of mathematical laws, but for the most part these laws bear a rather distant relation to empirical phenomena, and usually imply only qualitative relations among observables." Drawing the inevitable rejoinder, "Traditional Economics is built on a shaky foundation of assumptions that has led to equally shaky conclusions."

[31] A gentle rebuke of the sheer intellectual dishonesty of the prevailing dominant economic ethos of the time.

REVIEW ARTICLE
The East Asian Miracle

CHRIS BENJAMIN

WORLD BANK, *The East Asian Miracle: Economic Growth and Public Policy* (Oxford University Press, 1993. Pp.xvii + 389. £14.99)

Typically, this study of the high performing Asian economies (HPAEs) – Japan, S. Korea, Taiwan, Hong Kong, Indonesia, Malaysia and Thailand – shows the scars of drafting by Committee. But rarely can the result appear to be by separate hands – the A Team for the Overview and final section, and a B Team for the main study. The crunch was bound to come when orthodox neo-classicism collided with successful intervention. When the A Team asserts 'our assessment of these major uses of intervention is that promotion of specific industries did not work', the B Team concludes 'more selective interventions – forced savings, tax policies to promote (sometimes very specific) investment, sharing risks, restricting capital outflow, and repressing interest rates also appear to have succeeded in some HPAEs, especially Japan, Korea, Singapore and Taiwan, China'. The assidious reader could play volley-ball with counter-quotations for some time. But this underlying disparity is worth noting at the start, since the shock to anyone familiar with the area from reading the A Team's economically correct 'overview' could put them off the B Team's useful compilations.

The essentials of the 'miracle' are well summarised:

- combining high and sustained growth (4–7 per cent average GDP growth between 1960 and 1985), with declining income inequality and reduced poverty – 'shared growth';
- continuing high savings and investment;
- rapid increases in primary and secondary education enrolment rates;
- sustained productivity growth;
- superior export performance – as a group moving from 9.4 per cent to 21.3 per cent of world manufactured exports between 1965 and 1990, with Japan individually expanding from 7.8 per cent to 11.8 per cent, and the Four Tigers (Korea, Hong Kong, Singapore and Taiwan) from 1.5 per cent to 7.9 per cent over the same period.

The B Team provides a useful compendium of the wide diversity of techniques followed to develop human capital, agricultural reform and social support, establishing financial and savings institutions, instruments and policies for selective intervention, developing a sound and technocratic public service, encouraging technology acquisition, export support, sharing risks, and supportive/responsive macro-policies. The report notes that the predominant approach was to rely on private companies (save, ironically, in Taiwan, where performance is usually attributed to its lively smaller companies, but whose public ownership of heavy and primary industries is the largest of the group, and instances such as Korea and Malaysia where the state has retained dominant ownership in capital-intensive industries, notably steel). Applause is granted by the A Team for pragmatic flexibility in adapting policies, even if their final prescription is getting 'the basics right', 'to accept the growing integration with global financial markets', and pursuit of 'export push' within the prevailing GATT system.

Chris Benjamin, Itochu Europe plc

Journal of Far Eastern Business, Vol.1, No.2 (1994), pp.86–90
PUBLISHED BY FRANK CASS, LONDON

Not surprisingly the Report has hit a fair amount of flak, not just for internal inconsistencies, but on a range of technical aspects, such as inadequate presentation of the extent of 'getting prices wrong' during early interventionist phases of development. More worrying, however, is the inadequacy of the basic axioms to do justice to the reality that they purport to describe. For example, when the B Team concedes 'more interventionist policies have the potential to contribute to growth in cases where they address economic coordination problems, but to succeed, they must combine the benefits of cooperation with competitive discipline by creating "contests"', the concept of 'Contests' with 'Rules' and official 'Referees' is introduced, believe it or not, on an analogy with children's games.

Really? Professor Shigeto Tsuru[1] uses the term 'paternalistic guidance' to describe Japan's officialdom. But remarks 'episodes abound in the post war history of Japan's industrial policy where clever use of administrative powers enabled specific industries to tide over difficult conjunctures of events', such as the allocation of import permits for sugar to exporting shipbuilders so that prices could be reduced by 20–30 per cent during the 1953–54 recession. Other instances he cites are JETRO's manoeuvres to gain entry of sewing machines into Europe, capacity coordination in the steel and shipbuilding industries, subsidies for importing machine tools and developing domestic substitutes. A more recent study by Harvard Business School[2] concludes that in semiconductors 'Japan demonstrated that, under the right conditions, infant industry protection works'. If the number of regulatory cartels is now 69, there were 1,079 in the 1960s. Examples could be multiplied, but on a 'games' analogy, Japan's officials were closer to the base of the scrum than blowing whistles. While in South Korea, a military metaphor would better depict the marshalling of resources behind the *chaebols* for 'forced growth'. The world as a fantasy game is a recurrent image – 'why should governments interfere with the level playing field created by the international market?' is posed apparently without any trace of humour.

So, perhaps unsurprisingly, the Report recalls how 'Adam Smith's invisible hand paradigm argues that each individual in pursuing his or her self-interest, also maximises the common welfare: cooperation is therefore unnecessary', and justifies 'a greater role for government to create institutions and facilitate cooperation'. This may be a heroic concession from economic correctness, but as long ago as 1842 the point was countered by Frederick List: 'the whole social state of a nation will be chiefly determined by the principle of the variety and division of occupations, and the cooperation of its productive powers'. Concerned with how Germany could counter Britain's dominance in commerce and trade, his prescription – no games – is echoed throughout the Report in the approaches of the leading East Asian economies – development of 'mental capital', 'accumulation of all discoveries', 'perfection of transport', support for 'infant industries', 'moderate protection', 'continuity', 'self-improvement and cooperation in the improvement of others', pursuit of 'invention and discovery', to 'raise herself to an equal position with the most advanced manufacturing nation'.[3]

And economic miracles have happened before: List's approach underlay the German 'miracle' of 'organised capitalism' that surpassed Britain in the later 19th Century in metals, chemicals and manufacturing. Translated into Japanese in the 1870s,[4] within a few years of Adam Smith, it is easy enough to see that List's concepts were more in tune with Japan's Confucian tradition, while Germany's success in 'catching up' was a vivid practical illustration of their effectiveness. His approach thus provided Japan with a workable, and proven, framework for its first 'miracle' industrialisation. The post-World War II 'miracles' of Japan and Germany built on their earlier industrial and institutional structures, while the post-war French 'miracle' also took a similar interventionist form, though they would naturally cite Colbert as their mentor. America had also followed its share of protectionist policies during its first industrialisation (and after, some would say). Japan in turn offered a model for Korea, and others. So List's 'catching up' programme has a successful pedigree. Consequently, the underlying tension of the Report is less between 'neo-classical' and 'revisionist' views, as between distinct capitalist traditions as much evident in European tensions today as in East Asia.

Against this background some of the Report's terminology could do with variation: instead of the neo-classical neutral 'openness to foreign technology', the reality could better be expressed as 'vigorous pursuit of imported technology', as any company confronting conditional demands for technology transfer can attest. The Report also omits reference, apart from US rehabilitation aid to Korea and Taiwan, to the large sums of ODA provided to several economies: these provided subsidised funds and strengthened the allocative leverage of the state (as did Marshall Aid in Europe).

A more serious omission, however, is the admission, 'the more informal mechanisms . . . are impossible to measure systematically'. To set aside the 'informal sector' in any account of Asia is tantamount to going on the pitch with bat, stick or racket sawn in half. A recent study by the Asian Development Bank[5] surveys the diverse, ingenuous and flexible forms of informal finance in a sample of countries, concluding that informal credit accounts for between a fifth and above two-thirds of total rural credit, and about half of total urban credit. And one recalls 'kerb' credit in Korea described as 'massive'. These mechanisms rest on a basis of community and familiar relationships: if an ideal training ground for entrepreneurs, these systems are still only one facet of the informal business idiom.

For the informal is the pre-eminent idiom of commercial transactions in East Asia: with differing patterns of corporate law, accountancy systems – or effectively none in some regions – transactions inevitably rely on mutual trust, observance of obligation, and 'face'. The tradition is notably unlitigious, where compacts for major deals can be sealed on the back of menus or by chit – starkly, where alternative dispute mediation (ADM) (that is no lawyers) is seen as a management breakthrough in 'advanced societies', ADM is the norm in Asia. Particularly confusing for Western businessmen are the skeins of relational networks behind the apparently familiar formal institutions of finance and regulation, even those as well developed as Hong Kong and Japan. Whilst shares in companies tend to be organised as a protective system against takeover or unwelcome shareholder intrusions into the priorities of the business for fulfilling its obligations.

The distinct idiom of the ethnic Chinese diaspora is simply noted in the Report, and one has to look to Professor Gordon Redding's pioneering study[6] to sense its scale and influence: to summarise a few of the features, enterprises can range from the small family concern, found in myriads, but with familial links across national boundaries in many cases, to dynastic diversified combines with hundreds of affiliates and combined turnovers reaching more than $8 billion; spread across virtually all the economies of East Asia; generally characterised by high turnover against assets; and their dynamic impact can be gauged by their investment flows into Asian countries, including China, matching or exceeding the combined investment from Japan and USA. This fluid style of capitalism, evolving through linkages of trust, combines an astonishing freedom of manoeuvre across national boundaries – no one has any historic quarrels with the ethnic Chinese – and high transaction efficiencies. And, since they tend to be patriarchial in management form, one can envisage meetings in any of the luxury hotels in the region – usually owned by one or other of these groups – with no more than half-a-dozen present, whose combined turnover may exceed $50 billion, and can settle informally on mutual plans to develop new regions, joint investments, marketing and so on, and how the plans will be implemented.

To take in more recent trends, with relaxation of Cold-War barriers and continuing rapid growth, a cascade effect is taking place as one-time leaders find that their success has led to relatively high costs, and capacity is relocated to lower income countries. The process is moving much faster than institutional reform, so that traditional distinctions between public and private are increasingly blurred: at one extreme, erstwhile military establishments are turning into thriving businesses ('in a speech to a military trade union in Hanoi in September, the Communist Party politburo member Vu Oanh warned the military not to let the rush for riches obscure its military purpose") or, at the other, state-backed corporations like Citic are evolving rapidly into major multinationals with commercial links around the globe. In effect, transitions that may have taken other countries decades of adaptation are being telescoped into a few years.

This unprecedented dynamism is exciting and fascinating, but slices through the stereotypes on which the Report is based. In its apologia for an active public policy, the B Team remarks 'A primary function of markets is coordination. The price system is a mechanism by which the production decisions of the myriad firms that make up the economy is coordinated . . . institutional arrangements for cooperation and information exchange in developing economies are weaker than in industrial economies, yet the need for these forms of coordination are undoubtedly greater'. Can we be so sure in the case of East Asian economies? Markets may transmit price signals, and, by tortuous reasoning, stock markets may pretend to signal companies likeliest to generate profits.

But for enterprises whose prime concern is to perpetuate corporate or familial lineage by organic growth, markets still have to catch up with semaphore compared to the 'cooperation and information' on the real options, risks, methods – indeed behaviour of international competitors – available through East Asia's informal network. Did it not occur, indeed, to the World Bank authors that one of the prime reasons why the interventions of some countries have been so markedly successful may well lie in the information that these mechanisms provide to government for sensible policy formulation where both the state and private industry share a common-aim of raising themselves to 'an equal position with the most advanced manufacturing nation', and act jointly as a consequence. (Korea would be a notable exception, lacking the same scale of international informal links as some other countries, so making its achievement in modernisation all the more outstanding.)

Given their resources and scope of contacts the Report is disappointing: maybe the World Bank also has problems of 'face' by virtue of its received orthodoxies having been pummelled into decades of exchanges with other developing countries. Its tone is liable to be condescending – to conclude 'they got the basics right' carries the risks of provoking the same reaction as 'basics' did recently in Britain; especially to an Asian audience – *the Analects* would cover a fair number of the 'basics', and to take a populist example, none of the 'classical' economic texts ever put the point as vividly or cogently as 'where the army is, prices are high; when prices rise the wealth of the people is exhausted. When wealth is exhausted the peasantry will be afflicted with urgent exactions' a few hundred years BC.[*]

But the Report's final message, in effect 'Sorry guys – miracles are over', when all the leading economies have embraced interventionist policies in their rise to eminence (indeed the US seems to be thumbing through its Listian textbooks at present) can only ring of 'intellectual imperialism', to borrow a phrase, or hypocrisy of the kind that Britain made uniquely its own during the days of Empire. At all events, there is no sign of the Report curtailing the enthusiasm or number of officials from CIS, central European and developing countries visiting Tokyo, Seoul and other capitals to pursue these successful national models.

If pressed for a recommendation on the Report, it could only be 'sell', despite the B Team's sterling work. And 'buy' instead a copy of Frederick List – a real test since no English translation is readily in print; Gordon Redding's study of the Chinese style of business; or, if irretrievably conditioned to the neo-classical, then

Planning for Change by James Vestal (OUP), which is a rather more balanced assessment from this standpoint of Japan's industrial policies.

NOTES

1. Shigeto Tsuru, *Japan's Capitalism: Creative Defeat and Beyond* (Cambridge, 1993).
2. David Yoffre (ed.), *Beyond Free Trade* (Harvard Business School, 1993).
3. Frederick List (trans. Samson S. Lloyd), *The National System of Political Economy* (Longmans, Green and Co., 1904).
4. Tessa Morris-Suzuki, *A History of Japanese Economic Thought* (Routledge, 1991).
5. Asian Development Bank, *Informal Finance – Some Findings from Asia* (Oxford University Press).
6. S. Gordon Redding, *The Spirit of Chinese Capitalism* (de Gruyter, 1990).
7. *Far Eastern Economic Review*, 23 Dec. 1993.
8. Sun Tzu (trans. Samuel B. Griffith), *The Art of War* (OUP).

[32] Simon Hoggart – *The Answer Is "Don't Know". Now What's the Question?* (*Guardian* 1.3.2000). Mervyn King's flight of fancy came in the Mais lecture (*FT* 18.5.05), "Maradona ran 60 yards from inside his own half, beating five players before placing the ball in the English goal. The truly remarkable thing, however, is that Maradona ran virtually in a straight line. How can you beat five players by running in a straight line?" With the analogy, "Likewise, according to Mr King's theory, the movement in financial market expectations of interest rates is often sufficient to stabilise demand without official rates having to change." Effectively admitting that the MPC is simply a player in the "expectations" game of financial markets, even to the point of spread-betting books being run on the voting behaviour of its members. This prompted a further series of variations in the following day's *FT* Notebook, including "The Gazza principle", "The match-fixing rule", and "Beckham's first and second law of economics", and so on. A further elaboration was Mervyn King's declaration (11.8.05) that he would "play each ball on its merits" – emulating Maradona with pads and abdominal box is a spectral fantasy that we await at a high pitch of anticipation.

But the profession of ignorance has now attained heroic proportions, as economic pundits line up to applaud the Bank's manipulation of interest rates: "Not only can the MPC not be sure where the economy is now or, peering through the windscreen, where it is heading but now the GDP revisions mean that the rear-view mirror is misted up, meaning the Bank cannot even be sure of what is behind it. The governor of the Bank, Mervyn King, has likened himself to a pilot steering through turbulence, so you get the idea.

"Constant uncertainty is what the MPC is dealing with. Given that, I think it has steered an incredibly steady course for inflation and the economy in recent years. Also admirable is Mr King's honesty when he tells us he doesn't know where the economy is going." *A difficult drive through the mist* – Ashley Seager (*Guardian* 1.8.05). While the persistence of glitches in statistical data that could have influenced MPC decision-making goes on – *How an attempt to fix a small problem created a bigger one* (*FT* 28.9.06).

[33] The declaration of independence to the Bank of England in setting interest rates under the Monetary Policy Committee was heralded as an analogy to the Bundesbank. You must be joking. David Marsh's acclaimed study of *The Bundesbank* (Heineman) lists in an Appendix the generations of Council and directorate members – predominantly Lander central bank chiefs. Each of them, though a further Appendix would be needed, linked to State political and business networks – that awkward word again – not least through the development function of their own banks. The Council thus has a continuing direct feedback from business activities and sentiment across the country. If probably few, if any, would pass the test of "economics literacy" – a view Eddie George* expressed to shrug-off any suggestion that membership of the MPC priesthood be opened to an industrialist – the Council has a continuing feedback at least of what is going on, and an accumulated input from an internationally oriented business community.

Moreover, the sanctity awarded to interest rates as the universal regulator seems to rest on a wobbly logical basis: the first order effects of an interest rate rise, for example, must be to raise borrowing costs in a system heavily dependent on short-term debt, which most would regard as inflationary. However suitably disguised by juggling definitions of price indices – "The all items index includes mortgage payments, and I seem to recall that one of the historical reasons for introducing the other indices was the effort somehow to overcome the unfortunate fact that increases in interest rates, designed to cool the economy down and reduce inflation, have the perverse immediate effects of raising the all-items index and making the inflation picture worse." (MPC's self-fulfilling prophecy: William Keegan (*Observer* 12.11.06.)

But, it takes time, obviously, for interest rate changes "to work through" – a typical statement of the platitude is, "However, the MPC seeks to curb future rather than current inflation. This is because a rise in interest rates takes about a year to slow the economy and then another year for that slowdown to have its maximum impact in breaking inflation." (*The Economist* 7.5.05.) But the longer the time, the greater the scope for any of a variety of other inputs to inflation to change: and, at long last – at very long last – economics appears to have caught up with commonplace knowledge. In *A foreign affair* – Inflation is increasingly determined by global rather than local economic forces (*The Economist* 22.10.05); the conclusion is "Globalisation does not relieve central bankers of their responsibility for maintaining price stability. But it may require them to steer policy by a different compass: one that takes much more account of developments abroad." How this might affect all the modelling frenzy in the Treasury and the City is difficult to predict, but one obvious conclusion is that the MPC should reserve some time on the Met. Office's new supercomputer.

As one of DTI's economists (John Barber) remarked, for which he was apparently chastised by his brethren, all the inputs to inflation have not been clearly discerned, nor how they interact – though he can draw consolation from entering that extremely select band of the half-dozen or so "honest" economists. Simon Hoggart's perceptive conclusion on witnessing the MPC in action reads, "Apparently, the Governor spends his life adrift on a vast, unfathomable sea of ignorance. Now and again he sights a hard statistic or an incontrovertible fact, but, as he shouts and waves his shirt, it disappears over the horizon".

Moreover, history hardly supports the rationale for the interest-rate golf club. One regrettable consequence of establishing the Euro has been to narrow the range of currencies covered by the OECD Consensus agreement to adjust export credit rates according to a comparison of differing national interest rates. From continuing observance over a career since the 60s involved in exporting, the consistent pattern has been: Sterling interest rates have always been in the upper quartile of OECD currencies. If the theory holds, UK inflation rates should have been among the lowest, even for short periods. Yet UK inflation has also remained persistently in the upper quartile.

Juggling interest rates is, at any event, a highly discriminatory form of intervention: on the one hand, delivering gratuitous gifts to lenders, who can "lead" and "lag" passing on increases/reductions to borrowers – "Most lenders fail to pass on interest rate cut in full" (*FT* 13.8.05) or "Savers hit by sharpest rate cuts in two years" (*FT* 3.9.05) being typical headlines. While, on the other, introducing instability for businesses having to invest to keep up with competitors with stable and invariably lower domestic interest rates. Consequently, rather than higher interest rates depressing inflationary trends, the coincidence of relatively high inflation and relatively high interest rates has continuously undermined the readiness of industry to invest, while the volatility of rate movements – wider and more frequent than other countries – has added to uncertainty, even if giving our banks opportunities for gratuitous gains. Truth be told, behind the mumbo-jumbo has been a continuing anxiety, going back to the Sterling crises of the 70s, to avoid the flight of hot money parked in Sterling accounts.

[34] Page 113 of *Global Political Economy* by Robert Gilpin (Princeton). The work is a magisterial synthesis of the social, cultural and national components that condition development, and a sharp critique of the pretensions, analytic validity, and limitations of normative economic prescriptions.

[35] An amusing debate has been occasioned by *The Economist's* declaration of "The Death of Distance", "The death of distance as a determinant of the cost of communications will probably be the single most economic force shaping society in the first half of the (21st century)." Certainly, the costs of transmitting information have been radically reduced, with obvious implications for such activities as financial flows, data transmission between suppliers and customers, etc. Yet on a more comprehensive definition of "knowledge", including the largely unexplored realm of "tacit" and product-specific knowledge, the "distance" between British industry and their leading Japanese competitors in autos, machinery, electronics, shipbuilding, transport machinery and so on, has probably doubled, not least because the latter can exploit the gains of "information flows" in a more "knowledgeable" context. And some "knowledge" has a tendency to be "sticky" in geographic locations or areas or, increasingly, within corporate structures (*Globalisation and Knowledge Flows* by Michael Storper in *Regions, Globalisation and the Knowledge-Based Economy* edited by John H. Dunning (Oxford)).

[36] My first actual encounter with an economist, who, prior to Thatcherism, had a status in Whitehall comparable to the elves, was in preparing a Ministerial paper on the options for handing the collapse of Ferranti. One was to allow the company to go into receivership without any government support for an entirely "private sector" restructuring. Since this would have involved a freezing or interruption of ongoing programmes, particularly in the defence field, with the risk of key staff leaving to find other jobs, suspension of contracts etc, it seemed only fair to point out that one of the consequences would be a disruption of the "learning/experience" gains already achieved. Out of the elvish domain some economist fired-off a comment that these were still "unsubstantiated hypotheses". Having just moved from a job where many man-hours had been spent projecting the costs of alternative scenarios of hypothetical Concord sales, drawing upon the production know-how of previous programmes, assessments of the "learning" effects were commonplace. It was infra dig in then civil service conventions to

put personal comments in writing, so I phoned him to suggest in the most measured terms possible that had he made this statement in briefing a Permanent Secretary before a Public Accounts Committee hearing, his testicles would have been served for breakfast in Brixton Prison.

A weakness in much of economists' output is that they don't seem to have been in proximity to anything approaching real work since Adam Smith's account, apparently second-hand, of a pin factory. Consequently, "division of labour", "specialisation", "wear and tear of hands" etc have continued as the rudimentary foundation on which their pinnacles of professed profundity are built. To be fair, at the time of the Concord/Ferranti collapse, "learning" was still assumed to arise predominantly from increasing familiarity and dexterity.

Yet process techniques have moved dimensions over a couple of centuries in exploiting feedback to achieve "increasing returns". And, as the motorbike industry collapse illustrated vividly, even at the time of the Ferranti debacle, British industry was way adrift of the levels of efficiency and dynamism of leading competitors. But, apart from such concrete examples, it's not as though there isn't plenty of literature on the evolution of techniques where innovation and experience feedback are harnessed for remarkable competitive gains.

Even here, however, some caution is needed. "Lean manufacturing" may have attained a high rating in the jargon of snake-oil salesmen, yet the "increasing returns" are in practice very "asset/product/process-specific", to drop into the jargon, evolving organically from the individual idiom of an enterprise. Notably, the Toyota system, despite a raft-load of literature, is extremely difficult to replicate owing to such factors as the geographical proximity of its suppliers, and the decades of evolving routines and practices both within the company and with suppliers (*The Evolution of a Manufacturing System at Toyota* by Takahiro Fujimoto (Oxford)).

Consequently, simply applying a formulaic approach can actually be counterproductive. One recent quintessentially British example occurred when the Head of the Civil Service, a typical Sir Wot-not nurtured in the Treasury's ivory towers, in arguing for greater professional qualifications at senior levels applauded the cost savings achieved by the Ministry of Defence in its logistics by applying "just-in-time" – to be followed in a matter of days by an Audit Office report concluding that provisioning for the Iraqi invasion had been "too-damn'd-late".

The scope for "increasing returns" by recycling experience through the inherent intelligence and creative potential of the human talent within an enterprise is illustrated by the variety of examples in *Kaizen* by Masaaki Imai (McGraw-Hill): just a few:

– "Our members provide 1.5 million suggestions a year, and 95% of them are put to practical use." Or more than 540,000 improvement ideas from its Japanese employees in 2005. (Toyota)

– In one year "employees submitted a total of 390,000 suggestions with an estimated worth of $US 84 million. Total expenditures on the suggestions system were $US 1.08 million, meaning that the payback was 77-fold." (Canon)

– Applying Total Productive Maintenance (TPM) disciplines, over three years the improvements were "Labour productivity: up 32% – Number of Equipment Breakdowns: down 81% – Tool-replacement time: down 50-70% – Equipment operating ratio: up 11% – Costs of defectives: down 58% – Inventory-turnover rates: up 50%." (Topy)

Whilst the elements of this approach can be itemised: multi-skilled and committed workforce; cross-functional interaction; integration of design, innovation, and production processes; iterative recycling of improvements; continuous measuring and feedback routines etc, the blend and effectiveness of such practices varies with the context of a particular business.

Cooperative interaction is also extended along the strands of suppliers: again Honda is a good example, "as a result of such efforts for improvement" over four years the company's suppliers achieved "Average sales: up 60% to 80% – Number of employees: almost the same or fewer – Per-capita added value: up 60% to 70% – Breakeven point: down more than 15%."

The practice has been extended by the company to their worldwide operations through a "BP programme," (*Powered by Honda* by Nelson, Mayo and Moody (Wiley)). But with varying results depending upon the attitudes of suppliers (*Remade in America* edited Likert, Fruin, Adler Page (Oxford) – see pp 158 ff).

Japan figures mainly because its management methodologies for "increasing returns" have been most heavily documented – at one time obsessively so. But these techniques have been emulated and transferred, though with differing success and variations. And it is inconceivable that companies such as German mittelstand, French auto-manufacturers, Italian textile-machinery manufacturers, or the durable Nordic enterprises can have adapted so continuously to changes in competitive conditions without their own comparable mechanisms, albeit less the subject of academic analysis. In essence, "increasing returns" has been part of a good business's basic competences around the world, long before its grudging acknowledgement by economics practitioners.

But the challenge to conventional economic categories is becoming even more acute as products move into micro-fabrication: to recall Akio Morita's neat summary, "things are getting too small for the human finger". Already companies like Fanuc, Mazak, Canon, and Kyocera are running plants with "no labour" over periods of several weeks manufacturing at sub-micron accuracies. In effect, "the knowledge of how to make things" has largely supplanted labour. As the dominance of micro-manufacture grows, the components of the production process are shifting to make traditional economic categories even less meaningful. In this domain, knowledge substitution expands throughout the supply network. The final product is achieved by an integration of highly precise processes, which require highly precise machining, which in turn require highly precise machining for their manufacture, and so on. And this trend is replicated in the processing of materials and components. Equally, development and design must embrace and integrate the knowledge and systems in these processes.

[37] Gilpin op sit. Page 133. But Pavlov reigns supreme, just like as, "For on the excellent classical principle of diminishing returns, they (western nations) have reached the stage where marginal additions to real take-home pay have a

diminishing impact on welfare." Samuel Brittan – *The subtle doctrine of self-interest (FT* 27.8.04).

[38] "David Henderson (The Myth of MITI – Fortune 80 Aug 1983) claims that 'the real explanation for the Japanese economic miracle is the country's laissez faire policies on taxes, anti-trust, banking and labour', which prompts Chalmers Johnson to wonder whether Henderson understands French." Footnote from *Governing the Market*.

[39] There are an increasing number of heretics, but a good flavour can be gained from just a few:

Paul Ormerod's *The Death of Economics* (Faber) is an effective critique of "the empty box", all the more telling from his experience as a Henley forecaster. Typically, countering the proposition: "Today, the general equilibrium model is not the exclusive province of the high-tech theorists; rather, it is a basic part of the professional economist's tool bag, and one that is increasingly used" his response is, "The performance in fact resembles the revellers in Edgar Alan Poe's story *The Masque of the Red Death*. Everyone is having a splendid time, indulging 'joyfully in virulently esoteric chat'." And this was before the market debacle of the late 90s. While his conclusion is that current economic theory be "abandoned or at least suspended until it can find a sounder economic base." His subsequent *Butterfly Economics* (Faber) follows this theme in exploring the insights of other sciences to provide a better understanding of how societies actually work. While in *Why Most Things Fail* (Faber) he shares his delightful pastime of pulling off the legs and wings of the sacred scarabs of Economics as taught.

The Market Experience by Robert E. Lane (Cambridge) draws in a vast array of expertise to question the real, and often perverse, consequences of the premises of economic theory – work as a source of satisfaction and esteem, rather than a disutility; the misaligned value attached to money; and so on.

John Kay *The Truth about Markets* (Penguin) and Will Hutton, whose *The State We're In* (Jonathan Cape) was such a roaring success that there must be a sediment of scepticism among the public: both are consistent commentators on the perversity of outcomes from dogmatic prescriptions. While Richard Layard, after a profuse career of propagating economic fantasies, on his elevation to the Lords, admits, "many of the most important things that touch us do not reach us through voluntary exchange." *Happiness* (Allen Lane).

While *The Challenge of Affluence – Self-Control and Well-Being in the United States and Britain since 1950* (Oxford) by Avner Offer is a rollicking assault on the underlying presumptions of rationality in economic orthodoxy.

Governing the Market by Robert Wade (Princeton), focusing mainly on the development of Taiwan, has been followed by a continuing concern that developing countries should be allowed the scope to evolve their own social mechanisms for economic development without the imposition of structures that reflect the interests of industries in currently advanced nations.

Alice Amsden, since her *Asia's Next Giant* (Oxford) – which has a high personal rating as the first economic analysis one had read that came close to depicting reality as actually experienced – has continued swinging away at the hydra of dogmatic economics with impeccable scholarship, including a contribution to *The Market Meets Its Match* (Harvard) on the shambles of enforced market prescriptions in post-Soviet Eastern Europe, and *The Rise of the Rest* (Oxford) which sets out the repertoire followed by successful late industrialised nations – "getting prices wrong" and "picking winners" to allow national enterprises to evolve the comprehensive knowledge and expertise to compete internationally, reciprocal interactions with the State etc, with a cautionary contrast in the performance of those who "opened" prematurely.

Both Joseph Stiglitz – *The Roaring Nineties* (Allen Lane), and Paul Krugman – *The Great Unravelling* (Allen Lane), have voiced concern at the skewed outcomes of adherence to a narrow economic agenda in the US over recent decades.

But one of the most eloquent critiques comes from Jane Jacobs – an author much admired by Sir Keith Joseph – in her introduction to *Cities and the Wealth of Nations* (Penguin), "macroeconomics – large-scale economics – is a branch of learning entrusted with the theory and practice of understanding and fostering national and international economies. It is a shambles. Its undoing was the good fortune of having been believed in and acted upon in a big way. We think of the experiments of particle physics and space explorers as being extraordinarily expensive, and so they are. But the costs are as nothing compared with the incomprehensibly huge resources that banks, industries, governments and international institutions like the World Bank, the IMF and the United Nations have poured into tests of macroeconomics theory. Never has a science, or any supposed science, been so generously indulged. And never have experiments left in their wake more wreckage, unpleasant surprises, blasted hopes and confusion, to the point that the question seriously arises whether the wreckage is reparable."

More recently, however, there is further evidence of a welcome fight back by common sense in Douglass North's approach of "institutional economics", which has none of the traditional arrogance of abstracted myopia. Rather, a recognition of its limitations: typical sideswipes from *Understanding the Process of Economic Change* (Princeton University Press):

"The economic paradigm – neo-classical theory – was not created to explain the process of economic change. We live in an uncertain and ever-changing world that is continually evolving in new and novel ways. Standard theories are of little help in this context."

"The rationality assumption underlies economic (and increasingly other social science) theory. There is an immense literature on both the usefulness and limitations of this behavioural assumption. The substantive rationality assumption of the economist works well in competitive posted-price markets... but as soon as we move away from this simple competitive model and the price depends on the behaviour of other buyers and sellers the complexity of the decision increases and we need to delve much more deeply into the cognitive process. In particular we must take account of the ubiquitous existence of uncertainty...."

"The new institutional economics, focusing as it does on the incentive

399

structure humans construct, should provide a much deeper understanding than we currently possess of the complex interlinks involved in the interdependent economic, political, and social world we have constructed. Formal (neo-classical) economic theory ignores this structure and therefore is of limited value for coming to grips with these issues. Information networks developed by sociologists explore the complex interlinks essential to undertaking all kinds of economic activity. The complex information channels developed in the Silicon Valley to realise the potential of the computer revolution go far beyond the formal structure of firms and markets developed in standard economics.

Economists of a libertarian persuasion have for some time laboured under the delusion that there is something called laissez-faire and that once there are in place 'efficient' property rights and the rule of law the economy will perform well without further adjustment. The scandals involving Enron, Dynegy, WorldCom, and others in 2001-2002 should have laid such a delusion to rest. In fact, not only must factor and product markets be structured at a moment of time to get the players to compete via price and quality (rather than by killing each other or engaging in other kinds of anti-social activities) but the conditions for maintaining market efficiency will vary over time with changes in technology, human capital, market conditions, and information costs."

He pursues, instead, a more eclectic synthesis of socially relevant sciences, posing questions beyond the hermetic mindset of conventional economics, and admitting that most of the answers to most of the important questions are still unclear.

After her erudite and enlightening survey of political economies leading up to their respective "take-offs" Prof Liah Greenfeld offers a brief assessment of the value of economic sciences: "Secluded in their ivory towers, high above – or, at the very least, far away from – the wheeling-and-dealing world of business, before long the economists were talking mostly to themselves, for what they said had meaning only to the initiated. A distinguished member of the group, George Stigler, wrote in 1984 that the profession was producing "a literature that no person could possibly read – the limits imposed by sanity are stricter than those imposed by time. Indeed, it is a literature that perhaps is read by a number of economists only moderately larger than the number of writers. The best memories can recall only a tiny fraction of this literature, and if the literature were irrevocably destroyed, most of it would utterly perish from human knowledge.

"This development resulted in a paradox. The more exclusive economists became as a group, the more special grew their skills and the more formalised and abstract their theories, the surer became their hold on their chosen identity, for the society at large concurred with them in the idea of science as formal, quantitative, and inherently incomprehensible to laymen. The surer became their identity, the greater was their authority as a science. And the greater their authority as a science, the more often highly credentialed economists exchanged mathematical modelling for social preaching and parlayed their technical proficiency into positions of generalised opinion leaders... And yet physicists and biologists have a relatively clear grasp of their subject matters and, as a result, have been able to manipulate them for the benefit of humanity – an achievement that has, so far,

400

escaped economists." (*The Spirit of Capitalism* op. cit.).

No better exposition of Professor Greenfeld's image of an "ivory tower" than *Knowledge and the Wealth of Nations* by David Warsh (Norton). Except a more appropriate setting would be a mediaeval monastery, like the film set for *The Name of the Rose*, with convocations, schools, sects and schisms in protracted dispute within a parallel universe where "economists" vainly pursue pretensions of being a "science" or a "profession". An extraordinary feature is that "modelling" is the ultimate truth, and what cannot be modelled according to the prevailing orthodoxy does not exist. Hence, extraordinary semantic tropes, such as public/non-rival/indivisible/intermediate/substitute/.... goods/products, and acrostics to reduce issues to calculable formulae. And for what? Apparently a "new growth model" deriving from an arcane formulation under the heading "Endogenous Technological Change" propounded in 1990. The scribe, Paul Romer, deserves some applause for common sense in discerning that the previous orthodoxy was rubbish. But far from a stunning moment of enlightenment, this was simply an extremely belated recognition of what other countries, uncorrupted by this sect of economists, have been pursuing for more than a century. Ironically, the United States has been at the forefront of massively subsidising new technologies. As John Kay, a good exemplar of the commonsense of school of economists, remarks, "Endogenous growth is a rather pretentious description of the idea that technological advance does not happen by chance but is the result of investment, is dependent on the scale of economic activity and needs to be embodied in new equipment.... It will rarely, if ever, be the case in economics that an old account of the world will be shown to be simply wrong, like the mediaeval account of planetary motion, or the phlogiston theory of heat. Empirical tests in social sciences are never decisive, as they sometimes are in natural sciences. Nor are new explanations of economic affairs ever so compelling that they exclude all others."

If a clincher were needed, we can return to Sir Eric Roll – the dion of Establishment dions – as he confesses in *Where Did We Go Wrong?* (Faber), "the effective contribution made by economic science to the solution of these (economic) problems over this long period (70 years) is not a glorious one. It is idle to speculate whether this is primarily due to the imperfect state of the science, though this cannot be entirely set aside." Scraping away the layers of Ming Dynasty enamel, this is tantamount to "economics is bollocks". Sir Eric offers no solution beyond the overriding diagnosis of a failure to adapt, "Our inertia in action was unfortunately rooted in a similar disinclination to think in fresh terms." But economics has been the rubric whereby this country has viewed the options for action!

AND SO?

So, what is the received wisdom of economics for businesses confronting the dilemma of dynamic change: a world where "there are no constant conditions"? A recent report purporting to draw on the latest literature and on the advice of the current clutch of economic divines is the IPPR study on *Manufacturing in the UK* (2003) – "P" as a designation usually implies the highest density of economists: two "Ps" presumably implies twice the highest density.

The role of uncertainty in this analysis goes:

"The economic literature attempting to explain investment behaviour is extremely complex and has somewhat limited predictive power. However, it is worth pausing to discuss the stream of work which highlights the role of uncertainty in investment decisions. Most capital investment is at least partially irreversible: plant cannot usually be sold at its purchase price if it turns out to be unneeded. Thus in the presence of uncertainty there is a value to firms in waiting to gain more information about the factors that will affect project returns. The key result is that uncertainty means firms will not invest when the net present value of an investment just not only exceeds its cost: the option value of waiting means that the returns must be greater than the costs by some extent."

And follows this theme in *What Drives R&D Investment?*

"From the firm's perspective, R&D is essentially a form of investment, although much of the expenditure will be on the salaries of skilled workers rather than on capital goods. We would expect that a firm's decision about whether to perform R&D would be similar in structure to the decision to proceed with an ordinary investment, involving an analysis of the costs and likely returns from the investment. The factors identified earlier as affecting general investment are likely to play a role in the level of R&D: current and expected demand, the tax regime, external factors such as the exchange rate, uncertainty, credit constraints and the availability of skilled labour."

On this basic analysis, there is an apparently "rational option" to "wait-and-see". In practice, it is precisely this rationale, reinforced by the orientation to "withdraw labour", that has generated the British pattern of "ratchet decline". This has been further reinforced by the "takeover market", where it is apparently a "rational option" to "wait and buy" capabilities that the business has not itself developed.

But, in an environment of change that "not only never is but never can be stationary", "to wait" is "to see" competitors not curtailed by this rationale move out of sight. And, when "waiting" leads inevitably to dropping out, what of the resources previously employed. Of course, "ting-a-ling", the invisible hand will magically transfer them to other activities with higher value. There is also, equally of course, a high probability that other potential employers will also have been "waiting" to "see". But when did Honda "wait-and-see"? If anything, "see" what might be coming and develop the options to beat the other guys.

So, rather than recycling orthodoxies of decline, let's glance at the model of a country that has managed to catch up in the high-value-added industries, not once, but twice, and skim through the conclusion *What can we learn from the past?* from *Technology and Industrial Development in Japan* (H. Odagiri and A. Goto (Oxford)):

"It has been more than three decades since Nelson (1959) and Arrow (1962) elucidated the peculiarities of technology (or, more broadly, information) as economic goods. Most importantly, they emphasised the presence of non-rivalry in consumption and the difficulty in fully appropriating the returns. And Arrow (1962) also discussed the "interdependence" of inventive activities, which reinforces the difficulties in achieving an optimum allocation of the results. Information is not only the product of inventive activity, it is also an input – in some sense, the major input apart from the talent of the inventor.

This last observation implies that the interdependence of inventive activity takes place both spatially and intertemporarlly, because it should be the information accumulated up to now that would be utilised as an input into the current inventive activity.

This intertemporal interdependence is exactly what we found to be the conspicuous nature of science and technology. How much technology a nation can absorb and how much it can generate are dependent in a crucial way upon the accumulated quantity and quality of technological capabilities. Some of these capabilities may be consciously created through innovation and education, while some may be acquired rather by chance, as the adoption of the QWERTY keyboard player illustrates. Consequently, the process of technological progress in economic change is *path-dependent*. The presence of sunk investment reinforces this dependence....

A very important consequence of this path-dependence, shown in many of our case studies, is that technology is not just something to be imported and implemented. In order to make use of imported technology, a high level of capabilities is needed. It is not just the so-called "absorbtive" capacity, that is, the capacity to *absorb* and *assimilate* the imported technology, that is needed. Certainly, making a product based on an imported blueprint or copying an imported product is difficult enough, because not only scientific and technological understanding but also a sufficient level of know-how in production management and labour skills are needed.

Still, copying foreign technologies is only a first step. One has to *adapt* and *modify* them,.... Usually, technologies have to be adapted in order for them to be effective in an environment physically or socially different from that of the country that originated them. Such adaptation requires a high level of technological capabilities on the part of the nation that imports them.

A similarly high level of capability is needed even to *select* appropriate technologies, because the right selection can only be made with a sufficient understanding of both the technologies themselves and the environment in which they are to be utilised.

Without first having such capabilities, one would never be able to proceed further to the stage of creating capabilities to *invent* new technologies. A corollary to this thesis is that a discontinuous jump in technological level is difficult to achieve, even if the country receives advanced technologies and finance. Unless it has sufficient capabilities, as well as a strong will to absorb and adapt the granted technology, it would never be able to utilise technology fully efficiently....

Technological capabilities are accumulated partly through conscious efforts, such as education and training. In the main, however, they can be gained only through the process of trial and error, and learning-by-doing. For, unless one experiences the technology in all its aspects, including the drawbacks, one would never really understand its potential as well as its limitations. This learning process can and must take place at every level of the firm from managers and engineers to shop floor workers. Managers, in other words, have to provide the workers with opportunities to learn from the new technology. It can be risky, particularly if the new technology has to be used at the site of actual production rather than within laboratories. Such risk-taking is an important function of entrepreneurship....

To be more precise, the adoption of the new technology may create a disequilibrium which begets an opportunity or a need for more new technology...

The presence of such complementarity in technologies also implies that timing can be very important. A new technology may function effectively only when complimentary technological and other conditions are met. More broadly, a new technology can be fully assimilated only when sufficient capabilities have been developed...

The process of technological development is neither a smooth one nor the consequence of well-calculated planning. It may accelerate in certain periods and certain industries, and stagnate in others. For development may take place in an unforeseen direction. An obscure and forgotten technology may become prominent when the surrounding conditions change.

The nature of technology itself is hardly stationary. Many technologies have become more science-based, illustrated most typically by pharmaceuticals research. On the other hand, learning through experience may appear to have become less and less important. So, will the past accumulation of technological capabilities become less relevant? We do not think so. In many industries, learning through experience is still important and will remain so. Even in science-based sectors, accumulated scientific knowledge and the know-how in doing research are imperative. Therefore, the process of technological development will never cease to be path-dependent."

No sign of "wait and see" in the scenario. Instead preoccupation with establishing the knowledge base to assimilate and select new technology, building up the expertise throughout the organisation to make the most of known technology, to disseminate the techniques to handle the new, to advance into complimentary technologies, and to match market needs.

This tradition has rolled forward to a persistent and focused attention to evolve increasing efficiencies in production,[1] both to ensure that the momentum of accumulated experience continues and to secure sales to generate the flow for further efficiencies to be pursued: all with a view to sustaining the surpluses to finance future options of new models and products. After all, when you have secured the efficiency advantages of the Japanese motorbike manufacturers over their British counterparts, or the 30% cost advantage disclosed in the NESL audit, or the evolutionary enhancements in efficiency and flexibility of Toyota, then there is greater latitude to confront the "trial and error" of innovation and absorbing new technologies. And, when proximate competitors are all pursuing this dynamic, the pressures on costs and refreshing products is even greater – reflected in the historically high levels of company R&D (85% plus) of Japan's national R&D effort.[2]

While this process of knowledge feedback[3] and its reinforcing dynamic of "increasing returns" is in progress, the rational British competitor is apparently locked into increasing intensities of DCF calculations. Mercifully, there are still some British companies who lack the benefit of economic wisdom.[4]

So, to come to the fundamental weakness of an economics founded on a presumed dynamic of price equilibria from a multitude of quick-trick transactions: if, with some heavy caveats, this analytic approach may be appropriate to commodities, or products where the process of production has been reduced to (largely) routine components, it is wholly inappropriate, or downright wrong, when attempting to encompass processes deriving from human creativity, co-operation or mutual interaction, and above all, vision. Or the qualities of "absorb", "assimilate", "adapt", "modify", or "select".

To put this into a real context, to take my favourite exemplar, Honda signed an agreement with General Electric to jointly develop and produce a small jet engine based on Honda's HF118, already installed in Honda's "Cub" six-seater executive jet prototype. The engine is apparently 10% more efficient than competitors. The company is also setting up another joint venture to produce a water-cooled engine for small propeller planes. In conventional management-speak these would no doubt be interpreted as a natural extension of the company's "core competences" in motive units, as evidenced in motorbikes, cars, lawnmowers and racing engines.

A jet turbine engine, however, has a variety of unique demands. For example, materials required to function close to, or indeed beyond, their normal melting point, control systems for adjusting fuel flows, and integration, and so on. There may be expertise from other motor engineering that reads across, but development of the HF118 must have entailed a continuing effort over decades, quite apart from designing and building their small executive jet. The "vision" explanation is that "old-man" Honda, himself from the Japanese aircraft industry, in forming the original company recruited some other colleagues from the aircraft industry, which had been closed down by the Occupation authorities. (Other aircraft industry migrants also went into the vehicle industry with other manufacturers.) He apparently enticed them with the promise that the company would return to aviation – a pretty extravagant dream for an outfit with only a few dozen employees at the time.

Yet, whatever weight might be given by commentators to this folk legend, the importance of the move into the jet-engine business was expressed by the company's current President, Takao Fukui: "Over 20 to 30 years it should make a major contribution to our earnings." (*Nikkei*

Weekly: 23.2.04) – the preservation of continuity. And a prospectus to the company's members that it has a continuing vision. The magic ingredients in this account are "excitement" and "growth", qualities knackered by decisions dictated by "when the net present value of an investment just marginally exceeds...."[5]

---

[1] The rubric of "continuous improvement" is now part of the standard text of all management handbooks. Yet the prerequisite is continuity, and for this a steady flow of throughput is essential. Even in one of the better management textbooks – *What Management is* by Joan Magnetta (Harper Collins) continuous improvement is expressed in terms of "benchmarking" and "best practice". This may be applicable in service industries like finance, retail or restaurants, where operations are relatively open to competitors, and where disruptions in throughput are rarely so sharp as to threaten survival. In manufacturing, as the motorcycle saga demonstrates, the cusp of continuing viability can be sharp. And leading competitors have their own "way" to evolve continuously the special strengths that they view as crucial for their future. For example, even if essential elements of the Toyota system are well documented, it is virtually impossible to replicate the accumulation of interactions, both within the organisation and with suppliers, evolved over decades.

[2] This is not solely the R&D effort of larger Japanese companies, since the country's industrial structure has a remarkably low concentration. Of the 1.6 million corporations in Japan, 99% are small and mid-size firms (of which the majority is controlled by families. Among listed firms, it is estimated that about 10% are managed by founding families) – *Nikkei Weekly* 29.12.03.
One of Japan's traditional strengths has, indeed, been its smaller craft and specialist companies. The monthly *Look Japan* regularly runs a portrait of one of these Japanese mittelstand companies, a random dozen would be (the employment figures are current as of the date of the article):
Takako Industries: with less than 200 employees, the world's leading supplier of rotary groups, which forms the central part of axial piston pumps, and an array of other ultra-high-precision products.
Nippon Ceramic Co: 290 employees, focused on ceramic sensors and ferrite – with 60-70% of global market share in automatic vehicle security applications; 60-70% for infrared automatic human proximity switches; and 80-90% for infrared security sensors. With an increasing range of new products.
Takenaka Seisakusho Co: 155 employees. Main products are fluoride-coated rust-free bolts and nuts for uses ranging from tunnels and bridges to oil refineries and deceleration plant. After acceptance by Exxon in 1984, the company has achieved a domestic market share of 90%, and 60% internationally. An active development programme is continuing.
Yasda Precision Tools: 250 employees. Micro-precision machine tools on a

customised basis for printing machines, injection and metal mould manufacturing, and currently moving into semi-conductor and nano-order technologies.

Strapack Corporation: 277 employees. Automatic strapping machines with a domestic market share of 40% and 10% global share.

Gosen Co: 230 employees. Achieves 60% domestic and 50% world market share of high-grade artificial gut used by professionals in racket sports. Products also include threads for fishing lines, clothing and medical uses.

Takemoto Oil and Fat: 432 employees. A traditional supplier of sesame oil, but the world leading supplier of surfactants for textile production, and manufactures surface-active agents for agrochemicals, construction and electronics industries, with development under way into organic synthesis.

Almedia Inc: 160 employees. Has achieved an 80% share of the global market for test media for video/cassette tapes, MD, CD-ROM and DVD producers.

Mitutoyo Corporation: 2249 employees in Japan, 1863 overseas. Manufactures precision machinery, with 95% domestic and 45% global markets for micrometers and callipers; and for three-dimensional measuring equipment 60% and 30% respectively, with a line-up of 5000 types of precision measuring products.

KGS Corporation: 64 employees. Building on its strengths in electromagnetic actuators and solenoids, the company has developed a range of products for the visually impaired. Holding 70% of the world market for Braille cells, products include printing devices, portable memos, PC attachments for Braille, including co-operation to set up an Internet Braille newspaper, and other applications such as space-tracking.

Alpha Electronics: 160 employees. Manufacture of precision resistors, gauges etc. Gained recognition with supplies to NASA, and its products are used in highly demanding environments such as satellites, Saturn-explorer probe, particle accelerators, and with a leading world share in MRI and CT scanning equipment.

Mitaka Kohki Co: 30 employees. Manufacture of high-precision astronomical telescopes and microscopes, including monitoring cameras for NASA, 3-D noncontact nanometer measuring devices, surgical microscopes etc.

Typical of the current crop of small niche market leaders (*Nikkei Weekly* 15.3.10) are:–

Daiichi Kigenso Kagaku Kogyo Co: a specialist in developing zirconium compounds, whose resistance to high temperatures have wide ranging applications in catalysts to remove toxic elements in auto-emissions and as a material in high output fuel cells. With a 50% share of the global market for zirconium – used in catalytic converters, the company develops its market by offering bespoke variants to clients, with continuous research embracing university and company contacts.

Tsubakimoto Chain Co: the world's top manufacturer of commercial chains from escalators to conveyors for sushi restaurants. Its marketing teams embed with client automakers and other potential clients as soon as an opportunity occurs, and maintain continuing contact over the product life.

Shoei Co: holds a 50% global share for quality premium helmets, particularly international auto racing professionals. Client contacts are maintained to adapt the product to individual needs.

Jeol Ltd.: a global leader in electron microscopes, also produces analytic instruments to investigate protein and other structures. Founded in 1949, it builds up contacts with overseas research institutes, and maintains continuing contacts with academic and research centres through highly qualified representatives to meet specific customer demands.

Suzumo Machinery Co: a specialist robot manufacturer of cutting edge robots for sushi-preparation, with 60% domestic market share, has extended this range to other traditional dishes like sushi-rolls, rice balls, to other specialties like rice-burgers and rice pizzas. In the US it supplies robots for California rolls, with an aim to increase overseas sales to 20% of turnover.

Taikisha Ltd.: the company moved from air conditioning technology to auto-painting systems, embracing painting plants, ovens and waste management, and the management of the overall system. Overseas sales account for 70% of turnover. Continuing development into new technologies is focused on reducing carbon dioxide emissions.

Nippon Shokubai Co.: the company has grown super absorbent polymers into a mainstay business with 30% global market share, supplying all leading diaper manufacturers, and with varying additions offers a range of up to 30 product types. With rising global demand, it is investing in new equipment at its Hyogo Prefecture plant to produce 60,000 metric tons of specialist polymer a year, while its production capacity in the US, China and Belgium will be increased by 15%.

[3] In the burgeoning literature on "knowledge" – of which, let's recall, the highest accolade of economics is to eschew any "pretence" – the distinctive approach of Japanese companies are among the primary sources through such works as *Knowledge Works* by Mark Fruin, and Ikujiro Nonaka's contributions in such works as *The Knowledge-Creating Company*, and *Knowledge Emergence*. These are published in Oxford's outstanding series on Japan, but have not apparently penetrated the University's economics faculty.

[4] Perhaps the most vivid illustration of this discrepancy in perception is given in Felicity Marsh's report on *Japanese Overseas Investment* (EIU Special Report No 142, April 1983)

"The typical Japanese manufacturing company has priorities which are very different from those of its Western counterparts, particularly in the short run. Nowhere is this better illustrated than in a joint venture between a Japanese and a Western enterprise. The example of the GEC-Hitachi television plant in Wales provides some fascinating insights into the conflicting priorities and methods of the two companies and how they have meshed together. The joint venture is 50-50 owned by each company and there are four directors from each on the board. Previously, the factory had been an unprofitable wholly owned GEC subsidiary, which was in danger of being closed down because it could not compete with cheaper and more reliable Japanese imports.

The managing director, Robert Shove, summed up the pressures pulling in different, and sometimes opposite, directions: "My Japanese directors look at the company as a long-term investment which gives them a European manufacturing base. This overcomes their problems of quotas and ensures their penetration of the European colour TV market. Their main concern is that we supply their sales companies with high-quality sets in the volumes they need. They stress this in preference to looking at the profitability of the joint venture. GEC, on the other hand, looks at this company purely as a business. Its main concern is the return on the money it gets for capital employed. It happens at the moment that we supply GEC Radio and Television Ltd with all of its colour TV set requirements, but if you can buy these sets cheaper from Taiwan or the Philippines it will." Any proposals for further capital expenditure outside the budget produce very different responses. Shove again: "Hitachi will ask if it is necessary for efficiency, and, once satisfied that it is, it will get immediate approval. GEC is more interested in the payback period. It wants to know the profits generated by the improvements in productivity and how long it takes to payback the investment. Anything over 18 months is tough going."

So far, the joint venture has emphasised Hitachi's priorities: Hitachi technology has been brought in and about $7 million has been spent on new equipment over three years, most of it to increase automation and reduce the human error element. About one-third of the workforce is engaged in quality control of one sort or another. The cost of achieving Hitachi's quality standards has been high: the factory suffered a $5.3 million accumulated loss during its first two years under joint ownership, before moving into the black. Criticism of the joint venture's performance today by its two partners further underlined their basic differences of approach. Although the GEC-Hitachi sets meet the quality and standards set by Hitachi for its main Yokohama plant, Hitachi is still not pleased with the factory's final quality test reject rate of 1.5% which is three times higher than in Japan; and GEC, on the other hand, is critical of the joint venture's profit performance."

One has occasionally speculated about the psychological impact on the redoubtable Mr Shove, and how he survived. Perhaps he could be found roaming the Welsh valleys talking to trees, or reciting the lays of Taliesin in wayside pubs.

But Hitachi seems to have survived the risk of contamination from contact with GEC: like all "heavy engineering" companies, they have been rebalancing their activities in response to shifts in technology and markets, but are still struggling by on sales of $68.2 billion (2003), with still active units in Wales. But where's GEC?

[5] Having slogged one's time through net-present-value calculations, these are totally ineffective for handling time horizons beyond 3 to 4 years: first, because net-present-values beyond this horizon, depending on the discount rate used, become insignificant. Consequently, activities that might be essential to maintain competitive options against competitors who do not go through this process will be "discounted out", or, indeed, options that may be crucial to establish further opportunities will be similarly stillborn. But, second, equally important, uncertainties over the period before returns can be attained will always be such as to demand wide sensitivities to be applied. The financial community in PFI/PPP deals under the gimmick phrase of "risk premia" has of course, capitalised upon the extent of such sensitivities mercilessly. But they are likely to confuse, rather than clarify, decisions to move "up" the adjustment process.

THE ASCENDANCY OF IMPOTENCE

If the acme of "PP" economics is so hooked on the path dependencies of "financial" disciplines that have contributed to the continuous erosion of productive capacity as not to acknowledge the essential disciplines and dimensions of "increasing returns", then the continuing saga of "opting out", the practical consequences of "wait-and-see", is unlikely to change. A national curiosity is how such an ethos can be advanced in the expectation of being taken seriously, against a recent history of its continuing failure. Or how the nation has apparently foregone any consistent challenge, outside the rhetorical platform of "globalisation", on the score of simple economic malfunction. After all, the public equivalent of "wait-and-see" has been decades of "make-do-and-mend" with the inevitable outcome of persistent "too-little-too-late".

For the essentials of "increasing returns" are applicable as much to fields such as transport infrastructure, power generation, health and educational services. To take the obvious example of rail transport, in contrast to the traditional British approach of making assets sweat, in Japan, France and Germany there has been a continuous process of upgrading with manufacturers and operators naturally in continuous dialogue on improvements derived from working experience, the introduction of new technologies, and planning these into the system. Consequently, operators and manufacturers are continuously improving performance for the public, but equally enhancing the competitiveness of products in world markets. The British failure underlies the areas of under investment in Professor Porter's diagnosis.

The pervasiveness of this continuing system failure takes some explaining: whether there was indeed a shared underlying acceptance of "Keynesian" perceptions in most of the post-World War II period,[1] is a question one can safely leave to the Balliol school of common room debate. For there were few Ministers, with the possible exception of Roy Jenkins' gang, who were capable of articulating in such terms. In practice, most of the time was spent fire-fighting potential calamities – the obsessional grip of the Cold War, unbundling an empire, propping up Sterling, and so on. And this scurrying about spanned party political boundaries: for example, "nationalisation" of Rolls-Royce fell to a

Conservative government. In hindsight, it is all-too-easy to dismiss the mindset of governments as obsessed with illusory pretensions.[2] But, sadly, it is fair to say that all-too-often such calamities were self-inflicted, as in the running sore of industrial relations and barmy pay settlements. And, for fair measure, such situations were confronted by a government system nurtured on "parsing the gerund and a smattering of Adam Smith", without previous relevant experience, knowledge or technocratic competences.

Governments of whatever complexion were grappling for consensus with institutions, structures, attitudes and modes of thoughts rutted with "path dependencies" where reconciliation, leave alone concerted action, was impossible. This process was predominantly introverted and parochial, with perceptions still under the shadows of Empire. So that, for example, when Japan's manufacturers took over the world leadership in shipbuilding from Britain in 1956, or indeed knocking out the motorbike industry in the late 60s, such collapses came as complete shocks with British structures lacking any agility to respond competitively – amply demonstrating the "wait-and-see" ethos, and nigh-extinction was compressed into just a few years. The same fustian attitudes have inhibited adjustment into competitive performance in computing, electronics, machinery, power generation, aviation and surface transport products, even if this loss of capacity has occurred without any of the evident concern of earlier failures.

Over most of the period, for those with any proximity to the real world, economics was recognised as being responsible for some weird phrases that used to crop up in missives from the Treasury, and generally recognised as part of their armoury for inducing bureaucratic delays. More tiresome was (and is) the number of Treasury tits wired through to the *FT* editorial desk, even to the point of anticipating Cabinet agendas: for any other Department there would have been a continuous leak inquiry. Instead, all Departments have evolved techniques for last-minute additions to Ministerial briefs on the lines of "more balls from Brittan". And narks who would preach endlessly from the sidelines on the glories of "free trade" – the biggest imperial hangover of all, when no one else in the world understands what it means, leave alone follows its precepts.[3] There was, indeed, the sad trauma of Keith Joseph's epiphany that the world was ineluctably unclean.

Otherwise, working Departments could assume that, like proverbial Italian delegations at EU meetings, for every two economists there would be six different views. So how did this sterile surrogate reality guff come to permeate a "noble and puissant nation", despite relative economic performance steadily declining? All the more astonishing since the economics "profession" had moved into the pursuit of ever more esoteric "models" and theoretical calculation to allow its practitioners to dismiss lesser mortals as "not technically qualified". After all, a well-proven shamanite ritual, with computers replacing bongo drums.

The cleverest gimmick of all was the "very common clever device" to produce a *Blue Peter* version. Again, Joseph Stiglitz can help us lesser mortals out, "trade liberalisation, deregulation, and privatisation" have the merit of "simplicity" as an "intellectual doctrine".[4] So simple, indeed, that it could be mastered by rote in half an hour by any five-year-old. If now, after the World Bank/IMF inspired disasters of the late 90s, a cult that dare not speak its name, the "Washington Consensus" had already taken over Britain's political elite.

An obvious advantage of "simplicity" is that it naturally lends itself to "conviction" – the blue-riband of Westminster political rhetoric. "The world is flat, but..." just ain't got that ring of "conviction". Maggie Thatcher mastered this trick. With the ultimate, "There is no alternative". With occasional bizarre consequences. One recalls a purportedly "working" lunch with senior Indonesian Ministers: Ali Wardana, their Finance Minister-cum-Deputy President, a cheerful urbane guy, suggested that since this was in effect the Indonesian Cabinet without the President, perhaps Maggie would like to conduct it in the President's stead. So she did, and no one else got in a word. But every balloon tossed in the air she bounded after like a puppy, to the barely disguised amusement of Indonesian Ministers. Then one asked about the oil situation, Indonesia being a leading OPEC member. To this Maggie responded, "It all comes down to supply and demand..." and continued with a dissertation of roughly O-level economics: this to an audience that included at least four PhDs in Economics (the Indonesian Cabinet were nicknamed "The Berkeley Boys" at the time). At least she had the grace to admit afterwards that she had messed up the meeting.

But so successful was Maggie in the "conviction" stakes that both other political parties immediately took over the jargon. With some even more bizarre results. Clare Short MP at the Department of International Development, from a looney-left moth suddenly burst forth berating others for "stupid, economically illiterate" untruths (*FT* 8.8.02). Bystanders could only surmise at some secret laying-on of hands by Tim Lankester* (Perm Sec at ODA and ex-World Bank economist), or by one of his disciples.

Or Gordon Brown's over-weaning lectures to European neighbours on the self-styled excellence of Britain's economic performance, politely clobbered by Chris Patten among his final salvos as an EU Commissioner.[5] About the same time, *The Economist,* echoing the Bank of England, remarked that growth/wealth based on rising house prices was "phoney".[6] Of course, that's OK so long as the statistics can be massaged to tell the right story.

But more seriously, the shared "conviction" in "simplicity" plays into the surrogate reality of the Treasury. Despite popular caricatures of Maggie Thatcher, Treasury officials would admit informally at the time that, apart from being a "bit unreliable" on projects, she was the ideal Treasury Barbie Doll – a case of mutually shared simplicities. And the tyranny of this ethos has been extended throughout the political elite: one of Gore Vidal's bull's-eye observations was that Britain's politicians were "interchangeable careerists" so that a shared foundation of "simplicities" is the ideal laxative to lubricate an effortless passage in and out of office.

An entertaining sideshow follows from these shared "simplicities" as political debate has been diverted into a frantic search for other "convictions" to distinguish the main political parties. And the electorate is presented with a contest in "sincerities", with increasing scepticism whether these are more than synthetic "sincerities". Or, as a *reductio ad absurdum*, both main parties trading facile exchanges about "choice" in health and education despite the recent horrors of inadequately regulated "choice" in pensions and rail, and ignoring the vastly increased capacities necessary to proffer real "choice": yet another reinforcement for electoral cynicism.[7]

Yet, these simplicities endorse a system – a composite embracing ethos, institutions, disciplines and resulting managerial attitudes – that has been adept at adjusting "out" of productive activities, but totally inept at adjusting "up" the progression of continuously generating extra value from exploiting existing knowledge and creating, and absorbing the feedback of, new technology. For, as Joseph Stiglitz reminds us, things "are, unfortunately, not so simple". And the blunt application of these simplicities can be dysfunctional: even though he addressed his remarks mainly to those classed as developing countries, such categorising is itself distortive, since all nations are confronted with the continuous challenge of transformation, not least Britain. He identifies a range of other factors, notably education, technology transfer, knowledge acquisition and diffusion – precisely the components crucial to facing up to the adjustment dilemma. Government rhetoric and pamphlets may even recognise these components, even though they have been evident through the performance of other countries for decades. But the competence of the British system to adjust "up" rather than "out" is still unproven.

The extent of Britain's lag was trumpeted by the declining Maths and Sciences take up among "A" level students.[8] And international comparisons put Britain slipping behind such countries as South Korea, Taiwan, India and China in the output of skills and technical qualifications to flow into the knowledge-creation process. The maxim, "There is no alternative", whatever its merits as conviction-fodder betrays rather a fundamental sterility in recognising options that other countries have pursued to adjust to change more effectively.

If the national vision is a reversion to some Chaucerian idyll, fine. But with the run-down of our coal and offshore energy resources, our national "Hols" are coming to an end. With millennia of predominant self-sufficiency in energy disappearing, even if there is debate about how much can still be squeezed out of the UK shelf over the next couple of decades, we shall be approaching the scale of import-dependency of Japan, Germany, France and others. This has been one of the spurs to drive them "up" the adjustment process to generate tradable products. But Britain, having allowed the productive capacity of tradable value-added to run down, faces an acute problem in meeting the long-term costs. A vacuous exchange of simplicities will no longer suffice. And there had better be a better way than "too-little-too-late".

---

[1] David Marquand's *The Unprincipled Society* (Jonathan Cape) offers a stimulating account of the post-World War II political progression and recognises many of the key deficiencies in Britain's economic architecture compared to other countries. But the apparently shared "Keynesian" perspective of the neo-Socialists and neo-Liberals in the pre-Thatcher period was more the result of governments having to make knee-jerk responses against the inadequacies of industry and the financial community.

[2] Correlli Barnet's splendid account of British governments in the Second World War and immediate post-War periods, with breathtaking scholarship, does rather overindulge the verdict of stupidity, delusion and incompetence from hindsight. In fact, Ministers were just standard products of the British system struggling with the inertia of the self-same system. And we are going through a permanent replay.

[3] That the vitality of the debate over "protectionism" continues apace, in 1992 the *Nikkei Weekly* ran an article on Suzuki's worldwide car production, on the theme that the company had managed to achieve considerable scale by concentrating on secondary markets ignored by its larger Japanese competitors. It had opened a factory in Hungary, and the article reproduced a memorandum by the company to that Government on how to develop a national car industry:
The memo read: "The three keys to the success of domestic production of

passenger vehicles are: 1) restriction of imported cars, 2) restriction of imported cars, 3) restriction of imported cars."

Ironically, when Indonesia showed signs of wanting to develop its own indigenous car-manufacturing industry, by tying up one of its industrial groups with Kia three years later, including high protective tariffs against direct imports, and further price penalties for domestically produced foreign models, Japan was the first to complain about distortions of "free trade".

[4] "More Instruments and Broader Goals: Moving Towards the Post-Washington Consensus" and "Whither Reform? – 10 Years of the Transition" from *The Rebel Within* (Anthem World Economics).

[5] "As I read the comparison between this golden age (Mr Brown's speeches on "pluperfect Britain") in Britain and the grim problems that crowd in on eurozone economies, I feel that the only halfway adequate response is to send food parcels. The real figures, however, tell a different story." And he goes on to identify 5 EU member states that were wealthier than Britain, while UK productivity levels were lower than all other member states apart from Spain, Portugal and Greece, and the gap in productivity between Britain and France was growing. Four member states had a lower rate of unemployment than the UK, and the Chancellor of the Exchequer's claims that the eurozone was an "old inward-looking trade bloc" did not tally with reality. While the comparative trade balance figures were also less than glowing: the eurozone runs a trade surplus of about 1.1% of GDP compared with the UK which runs a deficit of 0.8% of GDP. Extract from *Guardian* (31.1.04) referring to a speech the previous day at Cambridge University.

[6] In an article *A Phoney Recovery* in *The Economist* (28.2.04) we learn, "The snag is that 'wealth' being built up is partly phoney. In a recent report, the Bank of England argued that rising house prices do not create genuine wealth in aggregate. Those who have yet to buy a home suffer a loss of purchasing power, so rising prices redistribute wealth, they do not create it. More serious is that the price of homes or shares can fall, while debts are fixed in value. In the long run, the only way to create genuine wealth is to consume less than income, and to invest in real income-creating assets."

[7] *Politicians should admit that choice has a price* (FT 30.6.04) by Philip Wright. "Choice" is a natural consequence of the belief in competition as the ultimate test of efficient prices. Yet it is one of the most striking differences between national systems: vividly depicted by Michel Albert in Capitalism against Capitalism (Whurr Publishers) in his account of Swiss insurance and banking, "I had always thought of Switzerland as the very incarnation of liberal economic philosophy and laissez-faire capitalism. Thus I was baffled when, to my question about the firm's approach to setting vehicle insurance rates, the managing director replied that there was no company policy in the matter – there never could be – because Swiss insurers had to comply with the law and offer the same rates.... Later, in the course of a business lunch, a Swiss banker told me that he was confident no

American bank would ever gain a significant foothold in personal banking in his country. I was intrigued: why not? Because, he answered, American banks are so obsessed with making constant personnel changes. "One simply can't imagine the Swiss entrusting their savings to people they don't know!"

[8] Lord May, previously Chief Scientific Adviser to the government, and currently president of the Royal Society remarked on the weakening flow of talent to create a supply of accomplished scientists and engineers (*FT* 3.3.04): "This is particularly true in the physical and mathematical sciences. According to the latest figures, the total number of A-level entries between 1991 and 2003 across all subjects in England, Wales and Northern Island increased by 7.4% – but there were falls of 18.7% in chemistry, 25.4% in mathematics and 29% in physics over this period."

PART III:

THEY AIN'T DAFT

But let's not toss all economics out with the bathwater. After all, as Robert Gilpin notes occasionally, rather in the manner of patting the head of the trusted St Bernard, economics has provided some "useful insights". The problem comes when trying to identify them. After all, Sun Tzu anticipated Schumpeter by a couple of millennia, indeed one could go even further back to Lao Tzu, "If you realise that all things change...."[i] It should be some comfort that the Treasury appears to have caught up.[1] While Sun Tzu's maxim, "Where the army is, prices are high; when prices rise the wealth of the people is exhausted. When wealth is exhausted the peasantry will be afflicted with urgent exactions" should also have come in handy to Mesrs Blair and Bush in contemplating the invasion of Iraq, but anticipated *The Cash Nexus*.[2]

And the average village chokra will have mastered "supply and demand" by the age of eight simply by observing the bazaar prices of bhutta and ghur depending upon the harvest. Even setting aside the institutions evolved in Lombardy and the Hanseatic League for handling trade finance, "bills of exchange" and "promissory notes" were part of China's littoral trade in the 15th century. And unsophisticated rural communities are capable of evolving effective mechanisms for "pricing" money.[ii] Nor is globalisation all that new, since even Adam Smith noted Japanese silver on sale in the streets of London.[3]

The elevation of platitude applies equally to other tenets of the scriptures – of course, "flexible labour markets" have always existed, and the formation of "companies", or "ordered communities"[4] has been a natural collective response down the ages to counter inevitable uncertainties; of course, the necessity for generating a "surplus" – "profits" – for future viability or sustainability is not unique to the conventional capitalist enterprise, but applies equally to subsistence farming, bazaar traders, and even state-owned undertakings; of course,

---

[i] *Tao Te Ching* translated Stephen Mitchell (Frances Lincoln) – Analect 74.
[ii] *Informal Finance* (Asian Development Bank/Oxford University Press).

"choice" is inherent in the human condition, going back to the Garden of Eden, and a natural response has been to create institutions and structures to create trust and confidence; and, equally of course, "competition" is natural, even if "co-operation" has been found to be often more effective in creating competitive advantages. So what's new?

There is, therefore, not surprisingly, and however much our economic theorists may claim an imperial monopoly on the constituents of capitalism, a very wide diversity in its national forms, to the point where it can be quite an exercise to disentangle the common threads.[5] Much of the fun, indeed, of time spent in international negotiating – however frustrating the immediate issues might be – is the sheer variety of ways in which societies have filtered these commonplaces into distinct national traditions, institutions and idioms. But if claims to monopoly of commonplace concepts are hardly justified, so equally are any pretensions to providing an effective approach to change and adjustment. Yet the claims persist, and to put the counsels from the British ivory tower into a real perspective, it is worth glancing at the underlying concepts of those who have coped with change rather more effectively.

Even though there have been passing fads to label different forms of capitalism "Rhineland", "collective", "organised", "developmental", etc,[6] there are inevitable variations between the national traditions and cultures that do not lend themselves to ready categorisation. If there is a bifurcation, it is one that distinguishes the "academic" mindset of Britain from the rest. The reaction of my erstwhile Treasury colleague to my recollection of Friedrich List – "Ugh. Protectionism" – is perhaps the neatest summary, where prejudice has distorted perception of the rationale behind List's approach.

COSMOPOLITAN VERSUS NATIONAL SYSTEMS

The contrasting alignments are highlighted by comparing key quotations:[iii]

"The taylor does not attempt to mend his own shoes, but buys them of the shoemaker. The shoemaker does not attempt to make his own clothes, but employs a taylor...

"What is prudence in the conduct of every private family, can scarce be folly in that of a great kingdom. If a foreign country can supply us with a commodity cheaper than we ourselves can make it, better buy it of them with some part of the produce of our own industry, employed in a way in

---

[iii] *The Unprincipled Society* by David Marquand (Jonathan Cape)

which we have some advantage." – Adam Smith, 1776.[7]

"[A] system of the private economy of all the individual persons in the country, or of the individuals of the whole human race, as that economy would develop and shape itself, under a state of things in which there were no distinct nations, nationalities, or national interests [is] ... not a scientific doctrine, showing how the productive powers of an entire nation can be called into existence, increased, maintained and preserved – for the special benefit of its civilisation, might, continuance and independence." – Friedrich List, 1841.[iv]

Apparently, Friedrich List (1789-1846) moved from embracing the Smith orthodoxy, before dismissing it as "cosmopolitan" in favour of the "national" bias as reflected in this quotation. His Damascus road was the spectacle of nascent German industries – still struggling in the aftermath of the continental wars and in a fragmented provincial structure – being "slaughtered in the cradle" by dominant British manufacturers. His "signature" quotation has, therefore, been:

"It is a very common clever device that when anyone has attained the summit of greatness, he takes away the ladder by which he has climbed up, in order to deprive others of the means of climbing up after him. In this lies the secret of the cosmopolitan doctrine of Adam Smith, and of the cosmopolitan tendencies of his great contemporary William Pitt, and of his successors in the British Government administrations.

"Any nation which by means of protective duties and restrictions on navigation has raised her manufacturing power and her navigation to such a degree of development that no other nation can sustain free competition with her, can do nothing wiser than to throw away these ladders of her greatness, to preach to other nations the benefits of free trade, and to declare in penitent tones that she has hitherto wandered in the paths of error, and has now for the first time succeeded in discovering the truth."

But, if largely suppressed by our prevailing orthodoxy, List had an adventurous life for an economic philosopher:[v] a public official; a tireless propagandist for such causes as the German customs union, and development of railways – today remembered as "Father of the German Railways"; and, travelling to America in 1825, he was known to its leading political figures, ran a German language periodical, and invested in a coal-mining venture in Pennsylvania, which had one of the first fixed rail transport systems in the country, but he had to sell out just before it hit

---

[iv] *The National System of Political Economy* by Friedrich List (Trans Sampson S Lloyd – Longmans Green 1885)

[v] *Friedrich List* by W. O. Henderson (Frank Cass)

the commercial jackpot.

Even before the spell in America, he was observing how Britain's dominance in industry was undermining the development of native German competitors, and wrote, "However much the world may owe to this economist (Adam Smith) in other respects, all his services cannot make amends for the enormous harm that he has done by persuading some of our capricious doctrinaires to accept the doctrine of so-called free trade. Adam Smith's fundamental error is that he ascribes to capital alone a productive power which, in fact, can be created only by labour in association with a large or a small amount of capital."

But America at the time was also embroiled in a debate harking back to Alexander Hamilton, Matthew Carey and Daniel Raymond, and mirrored by similar protectionists in France, on how far it should follow "prohibitions, tariffs and subsidies" to build up its own capabilities, and List entered this fray with pamphlets on *Outlines of American Political Economy* (1827). These pieces introduced many of the arguments that he was later to deploy in his 1841 *The National System of Political Economy*. Once involved in the tariff controversy, he inevitably became involved in the Presidential campaign in 1828, supporting the democratic ticket, and with the election of Andrew Jackson, he was rewarded with the appointment of American consul in Hamburg.

His overall rationale is set out in his 1841 work. Apart from being a good read, his heresy of advocating temporary protection to enable the nation to build up its "balance or harmony of the productive powers" and so enable it to engage in matching trade contests with some parity, rests on a distinctive rationale. At the inevitable risk of compression, his main building blocks were:

The primacy of knowledge/mental capital: "The present state of the nation is the result of the accumulation of all discoveries, inventions, improvements, perfections, and exertions of all generations which have lived before us; they form the mental capital of the present human race, and every separate nation is productive only in the proportion in which it has known how to appropriate these attainments of former generations and to increase them by its own acquirements...."

Productive power: "The power of producing wealth is (therefore) infinitely more important than wealth itself; it ensures not only the possession and the increase of what has been gained, but also the replacement of what has been lost."

Co-operation of productive powers: "The manufactory prospers so much the more in proportion as the commercial operations are divided, the

421

more closely the workmen are united, and the more the co-operation of each person is insured for the whole. The productive powers of every separate manufactory are also increased in proportion as the whole manufacturing power of the country is developed in all its branches, and the more intimately it is united with all other branches of industry."

Continuity: "...the least and briefest interruption has a crippling effect; a longer one is fatal.... Thus in a short time a complex combination of productive powers and of property becomes lost, which had been created only by the exertions and endeavours of several generations."

At the start of the 21st century, the Adam Smith quotation begs the question for Britain, "What advantages?", while List's arboreal metaphor suggests that this country has sawn off the branch on which it was perched while having lost the capacity to fashion ladders. Whereas List's emphasis on human capital, reflecting, as he acknowledges, a guild tradition going back to medieval times, is a remarkably perceptive depiction of the dynamics of adapting to shifting flows of knowledge.

LET'S NOT KID OURSELVES: AMERICA

A first hurdle to dismantle is the myth that the United States is some sort of free-market Elysium. A better starting assumption is that, apart from some similarities of language, the US is at least as foreign as France, Germany or Japan.

Hardly surprising since the newly independent America was the first developing country to confront the overwhelming dominance of British manufacturing and mercantile supremacy. Alexander Hamilton, perhaps the liveliest wire among the founding fathers – ADC to Washington, a hero of Yorktown, a leading hand in drafting the new Constitution, first Secretary of the Treasury, the formative spirit in setting up the new central bank – was acutely aware of his new country's dependence on British products during the war of independence; the crucial importance of a sound defence – especially naval – if the new nation was to develop real autonomy; and the rate at which technology was moving to make a predominantly agrarian state unviable.

England was attempting to prevent transfer of its leading technology, passing laws to outlaw the export of textile machinery, policing such contraband, and skilled mechanics were under threat of fine or imprisonment if they attempted to emigrate. While, before independence, British manufacturers of hats, nails, steel and gunpowder had obstructed American efforts to make comparable products. Against this, with

Hamilton's backing, deliberate attempts were made to entice British experts to America, to pursue industrial espionage, and to pirate technology, granting US Government patents to direct copies of British inventions.

In 1791, again with Hamilton's backing, a prospectus was floated for The Society for Establishing Useful Manufactures (SEUM), effectively the first "science park", to establish a range of model factories covering textile products, paper, furnishings, and even beer. The main inhibition was the "slender resources" available against the massive private surpluses behind such investments in Britain. Hence, Hamilton authorised government bonds to help raise the first $500,000 of initial capital. Perhaps as a presage of the future, there was a speculative bubble in bank scrip and fraudulent activities by several leading SEUM figures, from which the venture failed to recover.

If the first major government "intervention" was unsuccessful, Hamilton's *Report on Manufactures* submitted to Congress late that year, provided a textbook of measures that the Federal Government could take to stimulate industry. Whatever the attractions of the invisible hand – Hamilton had studied Adam Smith – he concludes his *Report*, "In countries where there is great private wealth much may be effected by the voluntary contributions of patriotic individuals. But in a community situated like that of the United States, the public purse must supply the deficiency of private resources." So, to counter aggressive European trade policies, he recognised that infant industries needed "the extraordinary aid and protection of government", including subsidies, tariff protection – albeit temporary in intention, incentives, technology acquisition and protection, regulation and inspection, development of infrastructure and "formation of arsenals".

If it hit controversy at the time, with opposition especially from the plantation and agrarian lobbies, *The Report* subsequently influenced Friedrich List, and provided the blueprint for America's post-Civil War industrial expansion. So, America became a dab hand at the use of protective tariffs to build up its domestic industry. A notable example was steel, where with the increase in demand for railroads and construction and under protective tariffs, its annual output increased from 1,485,000 tons against Britain's 1,790,000 tons in 1880-84, to 27,023,000 tons against Britain's 7,026,000 tons in 1910-14.[8] This scale dominance reached the point when, despite the formalities of neutrality, the Somme offensive of 1916 could be described, "Thus the battlefield of the Somme was drawn in steel: mountains of shells trained against underground fortresses of steel, the machines of Bethlehem versus the machines of Krupp."[9]

But just from personal brushes, during the farce of Britain's pretensions to a capability in rocketry, there was a final scene of scratching around to find something to do with Blue Streak, the half-developed remnant of an intercontinental missile mirage. An obligatory paroxysm in such Whitehall farces was a crawl across the Atlantic to see if there was some favour we could bum under "the special relationship". Well, Julian Amery went off on cue, and a meeting was duly arranged with some bureau chief in the State Department, very obviously a lawyer with the build of a healthy practice. The meeting lasted barely ten minutes, as, with virtually no pleasantries, he opened by saying that Congress had voted the massive appropriations for NASA and missile defence on the clear understanding that this would allow the US to secure the dominant position in commercial exploitations of space, and they would not contemplate opening the door to some outsider. Julian was a bit miffed, but I consoled him that this was the new Marciano style of diplomacy.

Subsequently, as we recalled earlier, as part of the Division negotiating offset sales for Skybolt, the US opening proposals were to buy British boot polish and laces, and we struggled to obtain a list of the Pentagon's forward purchasing programme against which British suppliers could offer competing equipment with some genuine technology content. Eventually, we demonstrated that the Jetstream – a product of the Handley Page design stable – was way ahead on performance for a Marine Corps communications aircraft order, despite ferocious lobbying from Beech and Cessna. When Skybolt was cancelled, so was the order for Jetstream, no messing about with the most competitive bid. And the head of the Marine Corps project office seemed genuinely sorry to leave his "beautiful bird".

Beyond anecdotes, there has been a continuing tit-for-tat about the commercial value of support provided to Boeing, GE and other aerospace companies under defence and other pretexts. But there is no shortage of material on the scale and range of US Federal R&D subsidies.[vi] And early US dominance in nuclear PWR derived from their nuclear submarine programme.[vii] When there have been occasional outcries that the US should have an industrial policy, informed opinion in the US itself has responded that they don't need one: they have the Pentagon. But historically it has always offered relatively massive procurement, R&D support and multi-sourcing from US industry in semiconductors, integrated circuits, computers and software,[10] not forgetting the massive post-war Federal subsidies towards biomedical research – "in 1965, the

---

[vi] *National Innovation Systems* edited Richard Nelson (Oxford)
[vii] *Beyond Engineering* by Robert Pool (Oxford)

Federal Government accounted for almost two-thirds of all spending on biomedical research." While the US recovery in semiconductors has been attributed to the SEMATECH consortium,[viii] and the National Nanotechnology Initiative was launched in the closing months of the Clinton Administration with a budget of $380 million, with an additional $3.7 billion added in 2003 by the Bush Administration. And toss in another $42m on hybrid battery research in the 2008 Budget.[11] Or, currently, the Pentagon is running substantial programmes on fuel-cell development to reduce battlefield dependence on oil, and enhanced security systems. Indeed, on some estimates, "the Pentagon's research and development budget may be as much as 70-80 per cent of all the globe's defence-related R&D."[ix] These programmes are bound to spill over into "non-military" applications, rather as the Silicon Valley phenomenon was a spin-off from research initially conducted under defence-related pretexts.

The Federal Government's involvement in infrastructure development goes back to the formation of the Corps of Engineers in the 19th century, and was given a major boost by "The New Deal". Even today, an informed commentator at a recent Conference remarked, "nothing moves without something from the Fed" – Federal Trust Funds – with frequent agency scrapping for modal funds. No sign that the US has bought into the absurdities of PFI/PPP, and, since the average citizen sees infrastructure as the most tangible return for paying Federal taxes, the trend was likely to be, given pressure on Federal budgets, for a reduced contribution with greater use of revenue bonds.

While the OECD "transparency exercise" revealed that the US at State level employed just as wide an array of "distorting subsidies" as any other country. And individual instances suggest levels of support that would have had problems getting past the Brussels competition directorate.[12] While, even in the sacred domain of capital markets, "more than a quarter of all loans in the United States either were intermediated by government or government-sponsored enterprises, or had government guarantees."[13] While the scale and alacrity of the Federal response to the "credit crunch" suggests that the traditional interventionist spirit has not declined.

So let's not kid ourselves. Even if there is enough exploitation of immigrant labour, profiteering from drugs and nabobism in Wall Street to delight exponents of the halcyon days of free trade, when it comes to fiddling the market for national advantage, the US is as venal as any, and

---

[viii] *The Productivity Edge*: Richard Lester (Norton)
[ix] *Power and Terror* by Paul Kennedy (FT 3.9.02)

probably more so than most. And Enron is emblematic of a more fundamental "crony capitalism" than exists in any of the countries who were arrogantly labelled as such. The issue is now one of "how crony" does capitalism have to be to work? And does the American model actually work?[14]

GERMANY

Even for one with a career interest in the relative performance of British firms against international competitors, Germany has always been a puzzle. It says something about our national industrial illiteracy that any attempt to isolate the country's distinctive industrial structures has to contend with mountains of material on Germany's post-1930s political history dominating bookshelves. Leave alone the absurd triumphalism of sections of the popular media and occasional leering remarks even from government Ministers. While the myopia imposed by our economic orthodoxies has been nowhere more constricting than in perceptions of Germany's industrial development.

Workaday contacts with German managers, covering a wide diversity of businesses from RWE (admittedly before they took on the motto of one of the world's leading water companies by their acquisition of Thames Water), KWU, Demag (in the days when, as a subsidiary of the "old" Mannesmann, it was one of the world's leading steel-plant contractors), Klöckner, and machine tool and forklift truck manufacturers, chemical plant contractors etc – have always left an impression of steady pragmatic professionalism, technical expertise, and focus on the minutiae of the business. In short, a preoccupation with "getting on with the job" without the "expectations" dimensions that seem to befuddle British managerial minds (the fact that such qualities should appear distinctive is its own commentary on the general quality of British senior management encountered over a career.)[15]

But depictions of the ethos and rationale behind notable German successes are difficult to come by since contemporary national preoccupations have shown progressively less interest in the evolution of other countries' industrial and economic progress. Perhaps as good a comparative insight as available came from a notable German banker, "When British managers describe their companies, they do so in the language of financial analysis, with precise figures on the development of profits, return on investment, the price-earnings ratio, and shareholder value. In Germany the situation is quite different: when one calls on a company, discussion tends to centre on products and turnover, market share, and the number of people on the payroll. Profits seem to be rather a subsidiary issue."[16] To grasp the eccentric commonsense behind the German relationship between finance and industry, we have to turn back the pages to the evolution of Germany as a State, and the dynamic thrust that took its industrial performance ahead of Britain in the 19th century.

Approaching German industrial history from the real-world deficit of a British liberal education, and a few years in Whitehall, demands a shift in perspective.[17] If the "unification" of Britain, which List had noted as a prerequisite to its industrial advance, had been accomplished over a few centuries of "blood and iron", the travails of producing a workable Federal system from the gaggle of 39 cussedly independent states left after the Napoleonic Wars, make the urge for reunification when the "Wall came down" in the 1980s entirely understandable. While the post-World War II creation of the European Union has been a doddle by comparison. But this history is still apparent in the fierce regional competition that persists even after more than a century of unification.

But to isolate, perhaps at the cost of truncating history a bit, the main quirks from the conventional "British" standpoint can be summarised:

– There had been industrial advances in the second half of the 18th century, if lacking the scale and mechanisation of Britain's revolution: a growth in textile and metal industries, new luxury goods such as silks and porcelain, and some technical innovations in fields such as water-pressure engines and new dyes, while there was a steady import of British expatriate expertise.

"....more rapid advances might have been expected in the early 19th century. But various other factors retarded industrial growth. The division of the country into numerous independent states – each with complete control over its own economic affairs – and the existence of numerous tariff barriers and river tolls restricted internal trade. At the same time foreign commerce was hampered by the high tariffs of neighbouring states such as France, Austria and Russia." The jerks and jolts of progress to create the Zollverein between the traditional jealousies of these states, and their concerns not to be dominated by Prussia, with Austria and other neighbouring states acting as complicating players did not achieve a full customs union until the 1870s. Intriguingly, List's "protectionist" message went largely unheeded, except in Austria, by the officials involved in the customs union negotiations, and the Zollverein tariff rates remained among the most liberal among leading countries. Indeed, it was only after the 1870s' bubble burst, and other countries began escalating tariffs that Germany responded.

– If there were a few notable entrepreneurs in the late 1700s, lacking the scale and liquidity of Britain's private surpluses from "plantation" and "mercantile" activities, "industrial progress was not hampered by any hard and fast adhesion to a definite line of policy in regard to the limits of public as compared with private enterprise. The rulers of the German states were expected by their subjects to take an active part in fostering the economic growth of their territories."

Hence there were some notable "official entrepreneurs", such as Christian von Rother, who in 1820 took over the Seehandlung, a Prussian state trading company with a diverse range of holdings in textiles, metals and engineering, chemical and paper plants, saw, flour and oil mills, and active in expanding trade even as far afield as North and South America, India and China. And Peter Beuth who took the lead in promoting technology, including establishment of the Berlin Technical Institute in 1821.

In practice, however, industrial investment across the country was stimulated from diverse sources: other than state ownership, the State also co-operated with private firms by providing subsidies, factories, and guarantees of interest on shares. The State also took on the provision and maintenance of main roads, rivers and canals. Across the diversity of states, there were nationalised coalmines, iron mines, furnaces, salt works, medicinal baths and spas, porcelain factories – most famously Meissen, postal services, canals, railways and armaments factories.

– The rise of joint-stock banking[18] created a form of industrial finance more closely integrated to the needs of developing industry than the historic aloofness in the City. Influenced by the French Credit Mobilier, beginning with the reorganisation of the Schaaffhausen Bank in 1848: "Few people realised at that time that this was a new type of financial institution and that it heralded a new era in the history of banking. While English bankers considered long-term involvement in industry to be unsound banking practice, those responsible for running the new credit banks (Kreditbanken) in Germany were directly concerned with promoting the establishment of new manufacturing enterprises."[19] Their growth and expansion through initially regional consortia evolved to the nine Berlin Grossbanken, most linked to a group of provincial banks. And the leading ones set up subsidiaries or "communities of interest" arrangements in Paris, New York, Vienna, Amsterdam and London, with a steady spread to South America, including Chile, Bolivia and Peru (even a branch in Cuzco), and the Near and Far East, including Calcutta, Singapore, Japan and several locations in China.

The banks would commonly lead in promoting shares for new

enterprises, act as proxy holders of private shares, and be represented on Supervisory Boards: to quote one contemporary commentator, "the banks attend an industrial undertaking from its birth to its death, from promotion to liquidation, they stand by its side whilst it passes through the financial processes of economic life, whether usual or unusual, helping it and at the same time profiting from it.... The industrial current account is the pivot of all transactions between bank and industry; promotion and issue transactions, direct participation in industrial undertakings, and co-operation in management through Boards of Supervisors, these stand in very many cases in a close causal sequence with bank credit."

The interrelationship between firms and their banks was capable of considerable innovation. For example, major rail and electrical companies evolved their own financial subsidiaries to take the lead in promoting investment to sell their equipment, bringing in their banks as the deal took form. And, if BOO/BOT is viewed as a recent mechanism, the pedigree goes back to the Berlin Municipal Electricity Works sponsored in 1884 by Rathenau, the driving personality behind AEG.

In promoting exports, German banks focused on the products of their clients and related national companies, where, if the trade finance techniques were similar to English foreign trade finance, the latter were ready to finance the commerce of other countries – including Germany.[20] While, "within a co-ordinated national system, the lengthy credit terms granted by Germans to customers in many markets where Americans and even British feared to trade except on a basis of cash against documents, puzzle and worry their competitors." But undoubtedly contributed to a more rapid penetration of German goods in overseas markets, "...and, judged on the whole, as a policy applied to the trade of a country which came late into the world's markets, it seems to have justified itself by its results."

– It is worth remarking that in the post-Napoleonic period (post-1807) up to the crisis of the 1870s, the dominant approach among the administrative bureaucracy was "liberal" under the influence of Adam Smith – with a motivation to "catch up" in industry and trade. But in the latter years of this period, tempered by a recognition that List's *National System*, "took the existing real conditions into consideration". But rumbling in the background, and influential among the "policy" bureaucracy, were some heavyweight philosophical canons. Hegel, drawing on his study of Adam Smith and other leading economic authors, and observing the social consequences of the Industrial Revolution, was sceptical whether "free markets" were capable of self-regulation without creating a destitute and unstable underclass. And he advocated social "states" organising themselves, beneath the bureaucracy as the "universal estate", into "corporations". In effect, devolved coalitions to provide moral cohesion against the consequences of market extremes. (Marx shared much of this diagnosis, but with rather different prescriptive consequences.)[21]

– As the country prospered, with the staggering growth in coal, iron, chemicals and rail investment, and increasing shares of world markets, there were inevitable tensions for greater private sector flexibility, and these reached their culmination in the post-unity economic bust of 1871-73. Helped by some sensational corruption cases, the "bust" could be blamed on reckless market speculation. This reinforced another remarkable feature of Germany's industrial evolution.

The German system had a diversity of corporate forms, and the major manufacturing, mining, shipping companies and banks "not only expanded, but drew more closely together in associations known by various names – interest groups, pools, rings, trusts, syndicates and cartels." The first cartels went back to a salt union in 1828, Prussian alum producers agreed an exclusive marketing deal with the Seehandlung in 1836, and in the 1840s a pig-iron association had been formed. But in the slump post-1874 more "children of the financial storm" were formed, with the total reaching 275 by 1900.[22] These trends were not, however, exclusively German: the impetus for setting up I.G. Farben, the largest chemical concentration, came from a visit by Carl Duisberg of Bayer to the US in 1903 when he studied the major trusts that had been developed there.

While the "consortium" approach was adopted by banks – going back to the Prussian consortium, which, led by the Seehandlung, placed state loans on the market to fund the military mobilisation for the Italian war of 1859. But, more focused on industry, the approach was applied to the overseas development of railways, and in Germany's nascent colonial empire.[x] But the banks participated in establishing mergers, rationalisations and cartels in various industries, most notably the electrical industry.[23]

But, you ain't seen nothing yet. The number of cartels rose from 353 in 1905 to a German government estimate of 3000 twenty years later, of which 2500 belonged to the sphere of industry, while the rest was distributed among wholesale and retail trades – even if several were

---

[x] *The German Colonial Empire 1884-1919* by W. O. Henderson (Cass)

probably equivalent to "trade associations".[xi] Far from the abhorrence of British economic theologians, their German opposite numbers, such as Gustav Schmoller, "did not dislike" the revival of a system of organisation which certainly bore more resemblance to their own favourite field of study, i.e. paternal and governmental industrial organisation in the time of mercantalism, than that of the "Manchestertum" and *laisser faire* of the 19th century. He expressed the view (in 1905) that cartels meant the beginning "of quite a new order of public life", with more resemblance to "medieval ideals than to the 19th century worship of freedom of trade." While other theological voices cried for "the replacement of free competition by a principle of mutual agreement", "a higher stage of economic evolution" en route to "organised capitalism", and that "the much admired system of free competition was most likely to end in "anarchy".

And the system continued to show advantages, as the German coal-mining industry advanced more rapidly with mechanisation (by 1928 77.7% of German coal was machine cut, compared to 21% in Britain); German steel output increased from 12 to 16 million tons between 1913 in 1929, while Britain's output increased from 7.6 to 9.6 million tons; retaining a leading position in the international chemicals market; in electro-technical products, having achieved 50% of world trade by 1913, it still held to 29% in 1928; while in the new mechanisation, auto and aviation industries Germany was among the pacesetters. Indeed, there were various British reports advocating some such association structure for fragmented British industries.

– Less readily discernible in the literature is the ethos and skeins of values necessary to make such a "co-operation of productive powers" function. The "benefits" of such associations were their own incentive not to be disruptive unless the inevitable tensions proved intolerable.[24] There was legislation against the abuse of economic power, and a Kartell Court. Their influence was apparently passive as a deterrent against abuse, with no sensational cases of monopoly exploitation, so that the durability of an association depended heavily upon public tolerance. Moreover, Germany has traditionally been "highly regulated" by British standards, and participants were bound to be meticulous in compliance, and comport themselves professionally to be "fair" and ensure their "reputation".

Consequently, the peculiar disciplines of co-operative association, like those between banks and corporate players, derived from a mutuality of

---

[xi] *Industrial Germany: a Study of Its Monopoly Organisations and Their Control by the State* by Hermann Levy (Cass, 1935)

431

interest, where dialogue, frank interaction, and responsible networking are high quotient values.

– As an evolutionary outcome of this process, the major concerns such as Siemens could have an awesome structure of cross-relationships built up through a series of associations, including sales and pricing coordination deals with AEG, the other main electrical group, either by direct mutual understandings – often the outcome of a fierce tussle over patents; through "confidential conventions"; or via joint ventures such as Telefunken and Osram (see chart below of the Siemens Koncern in 1928). A meter quota allocation cartel was formed in 1925, ownership of the leading battery manufacturer was shared, and Siemens did not hesitate to join forces if advantages, particularly technical or in regulating the market, could be secured. The group retained its essential form through the post-WWII deconcentration measures, and in 1966 the three main elements of the company merged to form Siemens AG. It follows that there are still a number of those untidy conglomerates that hold to the notion that diversification is a hedge against fluctuations in different markets.

Just as a quick update. Siemens had sales in 2007 of £66,359m and currently employs 420,000 people in more than 190 countries. Despite a series of management scandals and the global downturn, the German conglomerate boosted its sales by 5% with a 43% rise in operating profits in the first quarter of 2009. While their competitors, General Electric and Philips, suffered declines in sales and profits. Within an organisational overhaul focusing their business into three main sectors – healthcare, industry and energy – the group is gearing to take advantage of global green infrastructure investments, and exploit its relatively sound finance business. Its new President, Peter Löscher, apparently an adept skier, sums up the management priorities as: "Speed, speed, speed, speed, speed, but also continuity." (*FT* 18.5 .09)

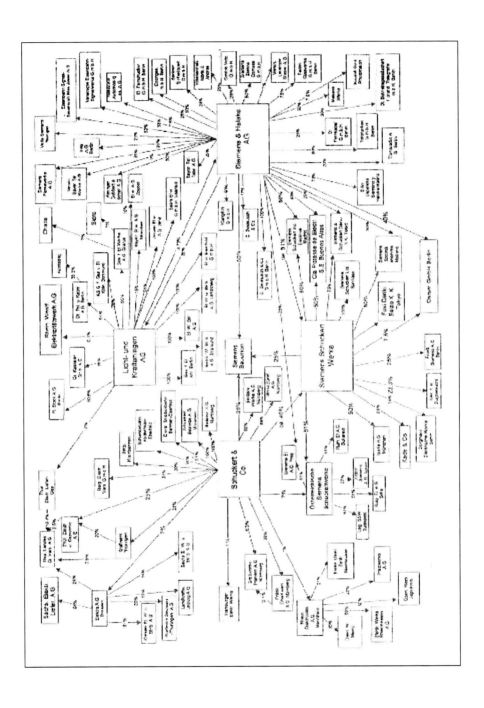

– At the other extreme, Germany has retained a strong corps of tightly controlled, usually by family or trust ownership, smaller regional companies. Many have survived through three generations of ownership, and built up international competitive strengths.[xii]

– Even if the "social market" concordat negotiated by Ludwig Erhart[25] might have struggled with a strong "cartel lobby", and eventually secured formal legislation, with a revitalised Federal Cartel Office, by 1978 there were still 266 registered cartels and by 1985, 241. Yet it would be rash to see this as a triumph of Anglo-Saxon liberal economics. For, as in the case of Japan's zaibatsu, old habits die hard: and the idiom of dealings with "mutual advantage" will have continued, even if some of the formal trappings are less evident. Accounts of modern German management confirm that professional networking and stability of relationships are still dominant, with established "institutions of co-ordination".[26]

– While the state, whether Federal or Lander, has not withdrawn from industry: on the contrary, the KfW, originally set up as a conduit for Marshall Aid, raising funds on the back of Federal guarantees, functions as a development agent for smaller companies.[27] And the state banks have also maintained a close interest in their business communities. While the heritage of Peter Beuth continues, with the country maintaining a high commitment to technology and innovation through tiers of agencies, such as the Max Planck Institutes, National Research Centres, Industrial Research Institutes, Fraunhofer Centres, Blue List Institutes and universities with their AN-Institutes.[28] With the inevitable consequence that the country has a high rating in patent awards, and an industry that is stimulated to hold its international position.

After its "miracle" phase in the 1950-70s, and a leading driver in the formation of the European Union, latterly British economic pundits have tended to berate the country's "sluggishness". Such criticisms ignore the massive costs of reunification – well over €1.25 trillion since 1980, with subventions of some €90 million a year to the East. If anything, confirmation of the inherent robustness of the system, despite recognition of the need for "reform", which has persistently held the country's leading position among the world's exporters.

[xii] See *The Mittelstand* in *Juggernaut*, and *Hidden Champions* op.cit.

[1] "Rapid technological progress and strong competition in global markets mean that the profitability and competitiveness of different industries are continually evolving." *Flexibility in the UK Economy. March 2004.* But, Pavlov immediately kicks in, "Flexibility in labour, product and capital markets is critical to ensuring that firms and individuals can adapt to these changes and thrive in a globally competitive environment" – the same response that has persistently led to the nation "opting out" of the evolving integration of knowledge.

[2] *The Cash Nexus*, a 500-page erudite tome on the funding of Britain's military and naval power since 1700, by Niall Ferguson (Allen Lane).

[3] On the global significance of the silver trade *China and the Manila Galleons* by Dennis O. Flynn and Arturo Giraldez (*Japanese Industrialisation and the Asian Economy* (Routledge))

[4] I was reliably informed by the wife of a senior manager in Itochu – in Japan, mothers have a special role in teaching children the language – that the ideographs that make up the Japanese for *Kaisha*, the term for a Japanese company, break down to mean "a protected meeting place".

[5] *The Capitalist Revolution* by Peter L. Berger (Wildwood House) is probably the standard attempt to elucidate common propositions. Yet the economic imperialism continues, evidenced in even the casual aside: "...the prosperity achieved by South East Asian economies that followed a broadly capitalist model...." is tossed into a routine book review of *Fundamentalist World* by Stuart Sim (Icon Books) – *FT* 8.4.04, where "broadly" covers an array of institutions, regulatory systems and transactional modes of a kind and diversity way beyond the mind-set of the author.

[6] *Capitalism against Capitalism* by Michel Albert (Whurr Publishers) probably started the fashion.

[7] *An Inquiry into the Nature and Causes of the Wealth of Nations* by Adam Smith. Of course, implicit in this quotation is that different nations will possess their own "advantages" which allow them scope to compensate for purchases from a "foreign country". Given Britain's relative superiority at the time, he did not seem to bargain for a situation where observation of his teachings would leave Britain's tradesmen bereft of advantages to match those of "foreign countries".

[8] See Bernard Elbaum in *The Decline of the British Economy* (Oxford). This increase was a function of scale, innovation in removing bottlenecks and increasing efficiency. But the levels of investment required would have been more hazardous if competition from Britain and Germany had been allowed on equal terms. But a more extended account of the role of the "state" in American industrial development is given in *The Myth of Anglo-Saxon Capitalism* by Richard Kozul-Wright in *The Role of the State in Economic Change* (Oxford). While in an entertaining tiff in the correspondence columns of the *FT*, Robert Wade recalled (*FT* 26.8.05), "And historical evidence on the rise of the currently

developed countries shows that a substantial level of protection need not prevent rapid economic development. The US itself is the 'mother country and bastion of modern protectionism', said economic historian Paul Bairoch; its tarrifs on industrial goods amounted to 37 percent of import value as late as 1925."

The tradition carries on, though the Bush Jnr. Administration's introduction of steel tariffs in 2002, ironically, was a defensive manoeuvre to shore up a failure of US companies, with the odd exception of such undertakings as Nucor, to adjust to the technology advances and rationalisation pursued by others.

A recent comprehensive biography of the extraordinary career of Alexander Hamilton by Ron Chernow is published by The Penguin Press. As a sideline, the American equivalent of Listian industrial policies is labelled "Hamiltonianism" in *End of the Line* by Barry C. Lynn (Doubleday), an account of recent trends in American industrial history.

[9] With the dénouement, "Five months after it started, the machine clicked off, destroyed by its own nihilistic power. The armies could give no more. British and French losses at the Somme later were put at 614,000 men, the vast bulk British, and German casualties at 440,000. Over the same period (June 24 to December 1, 1916) Bethlehem Steel sold arms totalling $23,267,135.18 to the British and French governments, according to the records of J.P. Morgan & Company." From *Sparrows Point* by Mark Reutter (Summit Books), an outstanding account of the origins, rise and decline of the steel plant, its management and workers, that became a major component of Bethlehem Steel.

A sad irony is the sale of Sparrows Point to Severstal, Russia's biggest steel maker, as a consequence of an antitrust ruling following the merger between Mittal Steel and Arcelor (Severstal buys US mill from ArcelorMittal: *FT* 22/23 .3 .08). The readiness to sell this industrial icon contrasts with the protectionist spirit that has debarred China's companies acquiring US oil and electronics switching companies, and Dubai taking over P&O's US ports.

[10] *Paths of Innovation*: Mowery and Rosenberg (Cambridge). But a false "typology" of the US as an exemplar of "capitalism" is a natural component of economists' special pleading. For example, *European corporatism needs to embrace market change* (*FT* 24.1.07) ostensibly summarises Edmund Phelps, a Nobel laureate, who apparently argues that a central distinction between "capitalism and corporatism" accounts for the laggard performance of the European economies more recently compared to the US. Capitalism is defined as "a system of free enterprise that embraces and motivates entrepreneurship", while corporatism is "a system in which businesses have to negotiate change with the government and "social partners" with the "shortcoming... the continent's corporatist economic system (or systems), a system constructed of big unions, big employer confederations and big banks, all mediated by a big public sector – a system that had been built up starting in the 1920s on the belief that it would be better than capitalism." It is mute whether this is an adequate definition to embrace the German Mittelstand, Italian small firms, France's lively private retail and luxury goods etc. But argues that because of such corporatism, "remarkably,

the information technology revolution is the first since the Industrial Revolution in which none of the big European economies plays a leading role."

This gave rise to a pointed response, *Post-war industrial policy set stage for US progress in IT* (*FT* 26.1.07) that big European economies did not play the leading role in the information technology revolution, but that was not due to "corporatism" as Prof Phelps argues. It was the result of American industrial (essentially Defence Department) policy operating over five decades of history.

"Coming out of the Second World War, the UK and US were on an equal footing with regard to IT (Turing v von Neumann, Colossus v Eniac). Knowledge of valves versus tubes was the same on both sides of the pond. Then macroeconomics and policy weighed in. The British did not have the resources to keep up, and the Continent at that stage was out of the game. Largely through public (read Defence) support of leading corporations the US took three big steps: development of programming and computer systems for national security purposes (concentrated on IBM), transistors (Bell Labs), and creation of the Internet (initially for the military in the Pentagon's Advanced Research Projects Agency Network, Arpanet)... Prof Phelps ignores history. Industrial policy sets the stage for corporate structure and responses, not the other way round." If playing the "typology" game, the US was "picking winners" as avidly as any other "corporatist" country.

[11] *Economist Technology Quarterly* (13.3.04) – incidentally, Japan had identified nanotechnology as one of the four fields for research-funding priority in 1996, with a budget allocation for 2004 of $890 million, a 5% increase over the previous year, and a series of applications research (*Japan Today* – April 2004). At about the same time (*FT* 2.4.04) a Commons inquiry was critical of the relatively low level of support provided by the UK. Some bright analyst commented, "Commercialisation is only just being explored. The big issue is getting academics talking to industrialists talking to venture capitalists talking to the City, and finding the right people to facilitate that." What would you expect? The costs of facilities to fabricate and process at these micro dimensions comes in very big bucks of billions of dollars, even for companies which have been engaged in comparable areas of engineering for decades. Disclosure of the support for hybrid battery technologies was the article *Bush pressed to support hybrids* (*FT* 26.3.07).

[12] *Toyota* by Reingold (Penguin) describes the support provided, with glowing self-congratulation, by Kentucky to the company's new plant in Georgetown, which would certainly have had a rough ride through Brussels.

[13] Joseph Stigltz's contribution *From Miracle to Crisis to Recovery* in *Rethinking the East Asian Miracle*(Oxford)

[14] One of the mysteries of current economic debate is the purported strength of US productivity, especially as it is flogged around in Britain as some metier to which other nations should aspire. The report of the MIT Commission on Industrial Productivity, published as *Made in America* in 1989, after a detailed

audit of eight principal industries, paints a dismal picture of "a serious productivity problem" mirrored in "sluggish productivity growth and by shortcomings in the quality and innovativeness of the nation's products". With "weaknesses... deeply rooted... the way people and organisations interact with one another and with new technology... the way businesses deal with long-term technological and market risks... human resources... rigidities" – all starkly reminiscent of the pleas from NEDO and other studies of the UK.

Richard Lester, Executive Director of this study, and Director of MIT's Industrial Performance Centre, revisited this terrain in *The Productive Edge* (Norton) in 1998. This study, with a lucid introduction to the inherent difficulties in measuring productivity, remarks the auto-industry as having absorbed lessons from Japanese manufacturers; the rise of such technological-driven producers as Nucor and Chaparral in steel; the resurgence of the semi-conductor industry, with SEMATECH having contributed an improved focus; deregulation of energy markets; the US role in the rising mobile phone/wireless IT arena; changing attitudes to personnel practices; increasing openness to co-operation; and a lively venture capital industry etc. The conclusion seems to have been a qualified optimism that underlying shifts promised a new trend of productivity improvement.

Well, as ever, subsequent events have tended to squash the cherries. US auto-manufacturers have seen a continued decline in their share of even their own markets, with Toyota vying to take the leading slot in the world league; all the US steel producers, including Nucor, lined up to support the Bush import tariffs; while semiconductors is a major battlefield as rising Asian producers vie with each other and tussles even at the custom-end of the market are becoming more fraught; Enron and California have not been the best exemplars of efficiencies from deregulation; and the mobile-phone scene is a struggle where US producers have shifting prospects.

Ever since, indeed, the pundits have had a grand time debating the reality or otherwise of the US productivity scene. As stock markets ballooned in the late 90s, the grand pretext was that this reflected the greater efficiencies of the new economy and wider applications of IT. But a running serial of "corrections" would cite *a spanner in the productivity miracle* and *the miracle of the late 1990s was not quite so miraculous* (*The Economist* 11.8.01) with the glowing 3.4% average annual productivity growth shaved down to 2.5%, as against the Federal Reserve's parading a 4% growth in 2001; or John Kay's *Alan Greenspan has endorsed an overstatement of US economic performance comparable to Enron accounting methods* (*FT* 01.3.02); or the failure of "productivity growth" to show up in company results (*The Economist* 11.5.02). While the debate around Robert Solow's, "You can see computers everywhere – except in economic statistics" (*The guru of profitless computing – FT* 28.6.01, occasioned by Paul Strassman's *The Economics of Information*) still rumbles on.

If ever there was a candidate for mumbo-jumbo, this is it. And it is hardly surprising that the Treasury should take unto itself pretensions to deal with productivity. But with "Privatisation of British Rail" on their pennant, the Treasury is an international laughing stock, while any suggestion of competence in "efficiency" and "productivity" is absurd.

[15] If actual examples are needed, some are well-documented in *Hidden Champions* by Hermann Simon (HBS Press), in *Juggernaut* by Philip Glouchevitch (Simon & Schuster), and in Peter Marsh's periodic portraits in the *FT*.

[16] A rare pleasure was to have listened to Ellen Schneider-Lenné, one of Germany's outstanding Rhinemaidens, then head of Deutsche Bank's London office, whose sad early death deprived their country of one of its most balanced and assured advocates. Out of several seminar presentations, most striking was her input – from which the quotation comes – to a NEDO-organised conference on *Capital Markets and Corporate Governance* (Clarendon Press Oxford), an early prototype of what has now become a major international industry, and in Britain evolving into another national ritual rivalling the maypole. After some berk from the National Westminster had done a piece on risk-management, concluding that so long as we were lumbered with the current national system, there was no point in considering alternatives, and then sugared off, Ellen then gave a clear account of the German approach. She potted many of the misconceptions, but with the message, "...German banks tend to seek a more stable relationship with the customer, and vice versa," "...it is in the interest of the companies themselves, their employees, and the community where the company is located," "...a firmly established co-operation between bank and customer has proved its worth particularly in such periods of increasing economic difficulty," and, "...Banks must continuously demonstrate efficiency, especially in the sensitive area of the terms and conditions applied to contractual relationships."

But most vividly, in the discussion session – not fully reported in the published proceedings, when challenged on the dominant power of the "house bank", she responded wearily, "I am on the main board of Deutsche bank, and head of the London Office. But every few weeks I have to return to meet a company that put its current account with Deutsche when I was a local manager. Otherwise, they would move their account to another bank." When was the last time a senior British banker visited a client? 20 or 30 years ago? Ever?

Another of her gems was, "In most countries, a fall in house prices is welcomed as a sign that the builders have improved their efficiency. In Britain, it's a national economic disaster."

[17] The standard work is *The Rise of German Industrial Power: 1934-1914* by W.O.Henderson (University of California Press).

[18] A convenient survey is *Joint Stock Banking in Germany* by P.Barrett Whale (Cass)

[19] "The original statutes of the Bank für Handel und Industrie, for example, empowered the bank (Article III K)
"To bring about or participate in the promotion of new companies, the amalgamation or consolidation of different companies, and the transformation of industrial undertakings into joint stock form; also to issue or take over for its own

account the shares and debentures of such newly created companies." (Ibid. p 12)

[20] And they haven't changed much since. During the sovereign debt crisis in the 1980s, British banks accounted for 17% of the problem loans to Brazil, when Brazilian imports from Britain were no more than 1.4% of their total imports.

[21] From *The Institutional Embedding of Market Economics* by Gerhard Lehmbruch in *The Origins of Nonliberal Capitalism* (Cornell University Press) pp 48 ff. The quotation is from Rudolph Delbrück (1817-1903), "who became the chief architect of Prussian economic policy and of the integration of Germany from the latter period of the Zolverein (German Customs Union) and during the first phase of Bismarck's leadership in the inaugural, liberal decade of the newly established Reich."

The article's summary of Hegel's orientation is, "Being sharply opposed to the romantic Conservatives, Hegel considered not only the French Revolution and the rule of rational law but also the market economy as irreversible achievements in the history of mankind. A basically liberal persuasion was thus an important component of his thought. But he shared Steuart's doubts about the capacity of markets for self-regulation and believed it necessary to check their disruptive tendencies and to correct market failure. The unequal distribution of wealth was in Hegel's eyes an inevitable outgrowth of the natural inequality of human capacities in civil society. But the example of England demonstrated to him that capitalist industrialisation resulted not only in the increasing accumulation of wealth but also in augmenting the dependence and deprivation of the working class and letting many of them – through no fault of their own – sink below the level of subsistence required for the dignity of being a member of civil society. Thus, in spite of its excessive riches, society was unable to control the excess of poverty and the resulting generation of a 'rabble' that had lost its human self-respect and lacked the incentives for work.

"Yet as concerned as Hegel was about these dilemmas resulting from capitalist industrialisation, he had no adequate solution. His programme remained limited to the idea of correcting market failure by a mix of administrative regulation (*Polizei*, in the older sense of the term) and self-regulation. For this the social classes ('estates') of agriculture, crafts, and merchants should organise themselves into 'corporations', which would provide to the individual the social recognition by members of other classes that he needed for his human dignity. The bureaucracy, as the 'universal estate' by virtue of education and universalistic ethos, should assume a central role in mediating social conflict and promoting the public interest. But though Hegel was aware of the social problems associated with the formation of a class of proletarians, the latter was not included in his pluralistic system of 'estates' and 'corporations', and obviously it had not yet occurred to him that the working class might be mobilised for collective action."

[22] "A number of the cartels were 'horizontal cartels' linking firms making the same products, but there were also 'vertical cartels' uniting firms engaged in different stages of production from the raw material to the finished article.

440

Among the larger cartels were the Rhenish-Westphalian Coal Syndicate, the Steelworks Union, the German Potash Syndicate, the Siemens-Schuckert group of electrical companies, the AEG and the Dye Cartel (I.G. Farben). The State – the Reich and the Federal States – favoured the development of cartels in the interest of industrial efficiency. The law regarded a cartel agreement in the same light as any other commercial contract. In 1910 the Prussian parliament passed laws setting up a 'compulsory cartel' of potash firms when it seemed inevitable that there would be cutthroat competition in the industry if the existing voluntary cartel was not renewed.

"There were four main types of cartel agreements. First there were compacts to share the market by which certain regions or customers were allocated to particular cartel members. Secondly there were agreements that fixed prices for sales at home and abroad. Thirdly there were agreements fixing the total volume of production of cartel firms, with a quota of the output allocated to each member. Finally there were agreements to share profits in accordance with a predetermined formula. Some associations were content to try to achieve only one of these objectives while others were more ambitious and sought to achieve several objectives at the same time." (*The Rise of German Industrial Power* – p 178)

[23] There has been some debate on the extent to which the banks might have driven such combinations. "A bank doing business with a number of similar industrial undertakings might be expected to encourage them to co-operate rather than to engage in wasteful competition; and it is sufficiently certain that many fusions and working agreements which were desirable on technical grounds were promoted in this way." On the other hand, the formation of alliances and cartels inevitably involved tensions between the banks of the various corporate members, and the tendency was apparently, "The banks had first to let the industrial development take its own course; the process of concentration had first to create a situation in which the interests of their industrial customers were so clear that the banks were thenceforward both in the position and under a compulsion to formulate a definite policy in relation to it. But this does not mean that the banks had no part at all in the development. At a very early stage they helped to prepare the way by encouraging fusions between individual undertakings and so reducing the number of competitors. Throughout their attitude was sympathetic, even while it remained passive. Finally, once the plans for combination had reached a certain stage and were within measurable distance of fruition, the banks gave active support to ensure their success." (*Joint Stock Banking in Germany* p 64)

[24] A fair summary of these advantages is: "...economies in the different spheres of such combinations, i.e. in buying materials, plant, stores etc, in making, selling and knowledge.... This especially applies to a better and steadier supply of material, unification of buying departments and staffs, bulk instead of detail purchase, greater opportunity for comparison and selection, cheaper credit and better discounts, standardisation of materials, standardisation of product, specialisation of product, improvement in plant, use of by-products, equalised distribution of work, quality, transport economies, unification of selling

departments and staffs, extension of export trade, collective advertising, lower costs of distribution, fewer middlemen, interchange of data and experiences, standardisation and interchange of costings, collection and dissemination of trade statistics, promotion of scientific and technical research, concerted action and common representation in legal matters, collective promotion of problems, improved opportunities of acquiring patents and of entering into new processes of production at first hand, etc, etc.....cartels and trusts may be regarded as effective instruments in carrying through rationalisation....protecting the interests of the smaller and less efficient undertakings against powerful partners, thereby acting more in a spirit of 'co-operation' and backing what might be called 'gewerblicher Mittelstand' (industrial middle class) than making their aim the utmost possible realisation of economic principles..... Where scientists remain in mutual touch with each other, there's a constant possibility of suggestions and a certainty that one will not be obliged to sit for years on an invention, only perhaps to learn that another firm has been able to make more progress on it in the meantime. This certainly acts as an incentive and is leading the scientific work in industry from the beginning to untilled fields promising success." (op cit p 201ff)

[25] An absorbing account is contained in *Freedom with Responsibility* by A.J.Nicholls (Oxford).

[26] The section on "Business and business people" in *The Business Culture in Germany* by Collin Randlesome (Butterworth Heinemann) is a good thumbnail sketch. While *Business, Government, and Patterns of Labour Market Policy in Britain and the Federal Republlic of Germany* by Stewart Wood in *Varieties of Capitalism* ed. Peter Hall and David Soskice (Oxford) is a broader comparison between the patterns of relationships within industry, and how they influence contrasting Government policies.

[27] Useful outlines of the KfW are contained in *Industrial Banking and Special Credit Institutions* by Yao-Su Hu (PS I Study No 632), and "Business and enterprise" in *The Business Culture in Germany*.

[28] A detailed account is provided in *Resilience in German Technology Policy* by Rebecca Harding (Industry and Innovation, Vol 7, Number 2, 223-243).

LIST'S FIRST DISCIPLE: JAPAN

If material on Germany's industrial evolution is elusive, Japan has been inundated by a proliferation of commentaries: hysteric, academic and pragmatic.[1] If anything, the country's traditions, ethos and aesthetic are so fascinating in themselves as to divert from the ferocious pragmatism that characterises their approach to industry and commerce. Within this bibliography it is a challenge to isolate the idiom revealed during the British motorcycle industry collapse. And this was only the most recent manifestation of Japan's relative commercial prowess, having overtaken Britain as the world's largest textile producer in the 1930s – earning the reputation of "Manchester of the East", and supplanting this country as the leading shipbuilder in the 1956. If bottling Japan is impossible, at least it should be possible to identify some of the distinctive elements that have contributed to its success, and how these differ from the orthodoxies of this country.

Transitions from feudal and agrarian to industrial societies are usually measured in historical phases of centuries, but the State-engineered transformation following the Meiji Restoration in 1868 must be among the most rapid achieved anywhere. The elisions of tradition, institutions and social attitudes with adjustments to "modernity" are complex, and a fascinating field of scholarship in itself. But there were underlying structures evolved during the "seclusion" of the previous couple of centuries that provided a foundation for rapid subsequent change and industrialisation – a tradition of artisan and craft industries at provincial and village level in metalworking, ceramics, textiles, husbandry etc that still persists,[2] while "Dutch Knowledge" of the West had been absorbed for more than a century through Nagasaki.

The decades immediately preceding the overthrow of the Shogunate had revealed an increasing vulnerability from Western imperialism: the defeat of China in the Opium Wars (1839-42); attention from Western trading and naval vessels, culminating in the "Black Ships" (1851); and the "Unequal Treaties" forced on the country after 1857. These reinforced the drive for "rich nation – strong army". And the comprehensive nature of the social change pursued to fulfil this vision was staggering[3] – "when Japan was actually confronted by foreign power in the mid-19th century,...

national unity became the most urgent concern, and it was to be sought by two means: political power must be retrieved from the scattered provincial domains and concentrated in the national government and national objectives must attract the commitment and support of the population. For the first time, the common people were called upon to join willingly in the national enterprise."[i]

Whilst there had been outward missions from individual provinces and students sent to study abroad, with the shift in focus these increased in numbers and a wide range of foreign experts were brought into the country – some "1000 Western experts per annum were engaged either by the government or by the private sector" for the first two decades of the Meiji era.[4] And the same ferment of ideas occurred in alternative approaches to economic management. Among the factional cliques of the leading Meiji bureaucrats there were conflicts between the advocates of "Enlightenment" and of protectionist nationalism:[ii] "The former based their economic policy on English free-trade liberalism; in their view public enterprise should be limited to the provision of goods and services in railways, education and mining. The latter, on the other hand, threatened by the power and advanced technical capacity of the West, saw it as imperative that the government protect all of the nation's economic activities for the sake of economic growth."

It was on the initiative of the former that the Ministry of Industrial Development was formed in 1870: this gave priority as "target industries" to "railway development, for which technology, tools and machines had to be imported, and the development of mining, principally coal and iron ore, which were viewed as essential infrastructure for other industries to develop. It also established public model enterprises and plants in such strategic sectors as steel, shipbuilding, textiles and machinery", when the anticipated private enterprises failed to materialise and under increasing balance of payments pressures. The Ministry of Home Affairs, established in 1873, primarily focused on modernising agriculture through Western expertise to replace imports and expand exports, and also founded model cotton-spinning and silk-reeling factories.

It says a lot for the perceptiveness of Japan's overseas researches that "In the official announcement explaining the purpose of the establishment of the ministries, there was an interesting shift of attention from English models and economic theory to the more mercantilist and technocratic practice of continental Europe. The government stated that it was only in

---

[i] From *Governing the Japanese Economy* by Kyoko Sheridan (Polity Press).
[ii] Kyoko Sheridan Ibid. Page 29

England that industrial activities and development were left to individual entrepreneurs. Elsewhere in Europe such activities were all supervised by integrating the major ministries and departments so that the government could guide their development through an integrated public programme."[5] But following a developing programme to build railways, to extend mining, and after the first tranche of model factories, pilot plants extended to ships, weapons, machines and machine tools, motors and general machinery.

A prime mover in the Home Ministry was Okubo Toshimichi, who established its Industrial Promotion Bureau, and he argued strongly for government intervention in industrial development: "In general, a nation's power depends on the prosperity of its people. The prosperity of the people in turn depends on their productive power. The amount of production is determined largely by the industriousness of the people, but more fundamentally it is dependent upon the guidance and encouragement of government officials... Okubo considered free trade a metaphor for Western hegemony and a device to perpetuate the Western powers' domination of the newly industrialising countries. What he witnessed was gunboat diplomacy and domestic industries too weak to compete with Western economic powers under laissez-faire policies. In order to develop domestic industry, he believed, it was necessary to cut back on Japan's large volume of foreign imports. Okubo's goal, however, was not economic autarky but rather to follow the example of England, the prototypical trading state. Okubo argued along classical mercantilist lines that as a nation gains political power it increases its trade surplus. The crucial variable was how the state chose to manage international trade. Okubo argued for protection by citing the example of England: its rise to world power was attributable to seventeenth-century mercantilist policies such as the Navigation Acts, which built up the merchant marine to world dominance by preventing unlimited importation of foreign goods. Only after achieving a dominant global position did England turn to free trade."[6] Neat enough to suggest a few hours with *The National System of Political Economy*.

If protective tariffs might have been one of the theoretical instruments to foster "infant industries", Japan's freedom to set tariffs were constrained "when it signed the 'unequal treaties' with the West between 1857 and 1868. These treaties limited Japan's tariffs to 5% until 1899 and only permitted selected increases after that. Immediately after 1868 a flood of imports, unchecked by tariffs, created economic havoc. The price of both rice and gold soared, and Japan faced a balance-of-payments crisis because it desperately needed imports of raw materials and capital goods to industrialise. In the early Meiji period Japanese leaders tried desperately to increase tariffs, but the Western powers, led by Britain, refused."

This put greater pressure on finding other mechanisms to nurture nascent industries: apart from model factories, there were direct export oriented programmes for handcraft goods, silk and tea, including support for merchants and a direct export firm; subsidies to encourage business and heavy sales taxes on imported goods; and a start on the process of regulatory controls, that evolved into the complex and measured structures of administrative guidance. It would certainly be over-egging to put this practice down to textbook protectionism, since tiers of coalition structures were an element of the country's traditional governance mechanisms and an essential instrument to enforce a social transformation, which extended even, for example, to the introduction of a national standard of time.

Intriguingly, partly because the initial model factories were not entirely successful since technology had to be adapted to indigenous attitudes and capabilities, with tensions between their role as public technology showpieces and the necessity to generate profits, but also because a lively group of new businessmen had emerged, most were "privatised" at knock-down prices within a decade. But privatised not into the fee-efficient financial markets of Thatcherite practitioners a century later, but where there was a strong regulatory context: "in contrast to the neoclassical economic assumption that industrial structure is a consequence of competition, Japanese bureaucrats saw industrial structure as something to be managed purposely and saw competition as a tool of industrial policy."[iii]

An early concern was that the Japanese people "vied with one another in commerce in isolation with no thought of banding together cooperatively," a not unreasonable concern when there was an acute scarcity of almost everything. If the Japan Spinners Association was the first, in 1884 a Standing Rule on Trade Associations was promulgated to organise producers and traders and encourage the formation of trade associations in order to control "excess production" and inspect the quality of export goods.

The tension between the "Enlightenment" and "Nationalist" factions was resolved in a "coup" in 1881, when the former lost their position in key offices, and industrial policy moved to a Germanic bias of protectionism and nationalism. This shift was extensive: for example, the Tokyo Imperial University, intended as the training ground for future

---

[iii] *Planning for Change* by John Vestal (Oxford)

generations of bureaucrats, had its Political Economy syllabus shifted to the Faculty of Law and remodelled on the German Historical School, with texts drawn from List, Roscher and others, while most English, American and French lecturers were replaced by German. And this bias was reflected more widely through the developing education system – German models were adopted also in the legal and healthcare systems, and supplanted the French as military advisers.

The success of this modernisation was remarkable: evolution of an effective managerial class; engineering and technical training structures; workable institutions; and in competitive performance taking the nation to world ranking by 1914.[7] In the imperial-machismo ratings of the day, Japan's success in the Russo-Japanese War (1904) signalled its arrival.[8] And it was the "-ism" of imperialism that was the less fortunate extension of "strong nation – strong people" into "self-sufficiency".

The recovery post the "Pacific War" is the second occasion when Japan has made an extraordinary transition. And again there was a carry-over of structures from earlier industrialisation, and the militarism era preceding the War, that elided with changes introduced under the Occupation, such as the foundation of trade unions. But the underlying tradition of coalition structures continued – there were some 20,000 "associations" in existence in the 1970s. Whilst regulatory multi-tiered coalition systems have been subjected to continuing criticism, both from within the country and from the international community, it has a sticky endurance: less autocratic than the stereotype of "picking winners" of pop-economics jargon, in practice these are consultative groupings of "informal quasi-voluntary jawboning and finger-pointing" supported by common values of enhancing the fortunes of all members, equity of treatment, and avoiding the instabilities of "excessive competition". But some industrial examples are illustrative:

– After having built up shipbuilding capacity – with planned coordination of subsidies, tariffs etc – to become a leading manufacturer by the early 50s, there was a domestic recession in 1953-4, and enhanced exports was the only means of sustaining the industry. The bureaucrats seized on controlled sugar prices as a less "blatant" way of subsidising export prices, which were reduced by 20-30%.[9]

When, however, the oil crises of the 70s reduced world demand for ships extremely sharply, there was a ferocious battle for orders, with continuing international allegations of dumping, subsidies, rigging etc, which led eventually to the OECD Guidelines on reducing capacity in 1976. Whatever may have been the norm for implementing OECD dictats, the need to reduce surplus capacity was indisputable. Under the Depressed

Industries Law (1978), the Ministry of Transport drew up a stabilisation plan with consultation including shipbuilders, representatives of trade unions and bankers envisaging a 35% scrapping of capacity. Implementation was through a special Association for the Stabilisation of Specified Shipbuilding Industries to purchase surplus yards and associating land funded by government, shipbuilders and bankers. A first priority for shipbuilders whose land or facilities were purchased was to assign funds to cover retirement pay for those who could not be readily employed by surviving yards. The interactions were indisputably complex, and depended upon a shared community of interests and values that had been established in the norms of prior networks.[10]

– The application of "controlled competition" in the successful evolution of Japan's computer and electronic communications industries has been very thoroughly presented by Martin Fransman.[iv] While a similar rationale, adapted in recognition of the different technological interfaces and corporate players, is being pursued to build up competences in nanotechnology. For example, the current MIRAI project for next-generation microchips embraces 25 companies. While for G4 mobile phones, the range of collaborative research is being extended to South Korea and China, since standardisation of codes within major markets will be crucial for success.

There are a miscellany of examples of measures to retain international market share, and manage an orderly reduction in capacity over the years calibrated according to the condition, structure, prospects and future technological evolution of particular industries.[11] The sheer versatility of ruses has been remarkable – including the Bicycle Rehabilitation Association (JBRA), which creamed off a percentage of revenues from bicycle racing to fund R&D for machine tools – some ¥5 billion in 1976; supported "collusive bidding", especially in power generation projects;[12] a battery of subsidies and tax incentives for exports and overseas investment at various times; and integration of overseas aid and support for rationalising capacity in aluminium, wood and pulp, and iron ore/steel. All have depended on consultation and compliance by a coalition of interests, and indeed occasionally such measures have failed to command support of key players – notably Sumitomo stuck out against efforts to limit steel capacity, and Honda refused to go along with measures to limit the number of motor vehicle producers.

– Japan's ambitions to return to the aircraft industry goes back to the formation in 1953 of the Jet Engine Consortium comprising Mitsubishi

---

[iv] *Japan's Computer and Communications Industry* by Martin Fransman (Oxford)

(MHI), Kawasaki (KH I), Fuji (FHI) and IHI, and the First Aircraft Production Law in 1954. This might have seemed farfetched at the time, with earlier production facilities having been closed down by the Occupation, and a "Peace Constitution" that effectively ruled out development of military aircraft. This was a major handicap since invariably technical and performance advances fed from military requirements and research to civil applications. And aerospace is an extremely costly industry in terms of research/development/certification, with heavy front-end investment for production. And prospects for generating significant sales were restricted by the Japanese Defence Forces as effectively the sole customer for military products, and a limited array of domestic airports for civil aircraft. Yet another constraint was the special defence relationship with the US, and requirements for interoperability. The US encouraged technology transfer through licensed production with increasing local content, until in the 1980s, as Japan's technological competences developed, the US shifted to seek more bilateral co-operation – culminating in the protracted negotiations over the FSX fighter development in the mid-80s, when Japan was focused upon a predominantly national aircraft, whereas the US on a virtual off-the-shelf buy, but conceding to an F-16 redevelopment with a minority of the development and production.[13]

In this situation, co-operation in sharing out available work was the only option: in commercial transport, MHI, IHI and FHI divided the airframe structures among themselves, with each having its own niche specialty e.g. Kawasaki in helicopters. On engines, IHI emerged as a specialist for large aero engines, earlier having shown considerable verve in taking on production of the Japanese engine for the first nationally produced trainer, with smaller engines the preserve of MHI and KHI. This sharing process "combined inter-firm co-operation with a transfer of manufacturing practice from other areas of their corporate business, enabling economies of scale even with low production rates. Thus, the spin-on of manufacturing and management practices became more important to the airframe business than the spin-off from high-tech aerospace to other business areas."

Attempts at wholly domestic aircraft had not been notably successful: the YS 11, begun in 1958, was a small twin-turboprop civil airliner, which, if sound in engineering, was not focused on a market segment, and, despite offering finance terms with a period of credit exceeding the certified life of the aircraft, was concluded in 1972, with most of the 180 aircraft produced used on domestic services. While the Asuka project for a domestically developed vertical-take-off transport had to be curtailed.

Where the approach was distinctly successful was the grouping of manufacturers into consortia for international collaboration: in aero engines with Rolls-Royce, Pratt & Whitney and GE on military programmes, with the result that the industry, with IHI as the leader, has achieved a competitive level of technology. On airframes, apart from acting as parts suppliers, the industry has collaborated with Boeing on the 767 (15% of production), the 777 (21%, and a larger share of design and marketing),[14] and a prospective 35% for the 787, the provision of carbon fibre for which Toray is building a US production plant (*Nikkei Weekly* 3.5.04/12.7.04); and 15% of whichever of the chosen GE or Rolls-Royce engines is selected by customers. While ANA was the first launch customer with options on 50 aircraft.

Meanwhile, MHI has announced the development of a wholly domestically developed civil airliner, aimed at taking full advantage of the latest systems and materials technology – announced, ironically, the same day as BAE declared it was withdrawing from civil aircraft manufacture in Britain. And a modest research funding has continued over the years on power-plant options for a future supersonic airliner.

While there has been a steady programme to evolve a space launcher/satellite capability, entirely funded by the government, but, having reached the potential for commercial activities, has been transferred to a consortium headed by MHI.

– Yet the real conundrum is how, within this apparently hyper-regulated system, there have emerged such staggering entrepreneurial successes as Honda, who openly bucked the system by going into cars, and, most recently, in developing its own jet engine in co-operation with GE, despite not being part of the aerospace industry club. But a string of other names could be added: Sony, Sharp, Canon, Fanuc, Seiko Epson, Kyocera, Rohm, Amada, Okuma… that have developed largely outside the regulatory sphere, as well as the stalwarts of Hitachi, Toshiba, Toyota, Toray… with a heritage many decades old. And the extreme competitive wars raged in specific product areas – motorbikes, calculators, cameras, copiers, air conditioners, white goods, mobile phones, and in every passing consumer fancy.

– So, within an undisguised "national" envelope, there is intense domestic competition among companies, dynamically focused on growth, and as a consequence the sphere of these contests spreads into international markets often setting the tempo that others have to match. But just a stab at some of the elements that should be replicable without recourse to cop-out arguments of "culture", "Confucianism", and so on.

– Having evolved from a historic origin of "scarcity" and "catching-up" manufacturing plants have a tradition of "developing" products and improvising with available skills and expertise.[15] This tradition has led to the widespread focus on developing a broadly skilled workforce cycling through different functions, with strong "incentives" to enhance individual expertise.[16] This, within a context of "care",[17] stimulates discrimination and positive feedback for adaptation to "increasing returns".[18]

– Part of the internal corporate tacit bargain is that, in return for such commitment and creative focus on "specific" advantages, those responsible for the conduct of the business will adapt and expand its activities to secure its future.[19] One of the most striking symptoms of this dynamic is the remarkably high percentage of national R&D funded by the private sector: historically above 80%. If anything, marked by increasing intensity as Japanese companies have evolved from followers to leaders, and by the latest trend of "black boxes" of tightly protected proprietary knowledge and binding key suppliers even more closely.

– Transaction efficiencies between assemblers and suppliers are stimulated by a common interest in growth: for "off-the-shelf" components, life is as tough as anywhere, only more so; but this carries the incentive to evolve to become sources of specialist design and innovation. As such relationships develop, "Self-interest and a recognition of interdependence as the best means to promote self-interest offer the only persuasive explanations for the social dynamism that underpins the Toyota production system.... Pursuing the twin objectives of individual profit and group reciprocity, companies exhibit high levels of adaptation and adjustment to market circumstances and technological change."[v]

– This form of network relationship evolves through direct face and "iterative" exchanges, and, with increasing feedback if mutual advantage is reinforced, demands less reliance on the formalities of "contracts":[20] instead, there are disciplines of "ostracism" against opportunistic behaviour. This networking structure has also contributed to the evolution and persistent adaptation of the unique general trading companies, which have been re-inventing themselves, some over centuries.[21]

– As an exemplar of List's "co-operation of productive powers" Japan comes close to a new model. "Competitiveness emerges as a network-enabled capacity activated by the ambitions and initiatives of countless corporate managers in countless institutional settings. Competitive strategies and cooperative structures thread through the Japanese enterprise system with a subtlety, resilience, concurrence, and ambition....

---

[v] Mark Fruin on the dynamism of the Toyota group Ibid. Pp 292-3.

The Japanese enterprise system is an interorganisational innovation of local design, major proportions, and global significance."[vi]

After its sustained economic expansion since the 1950s, there was, a perhaps inevitable, outbreak of "irrational exuberance" in the late 80s as property values escalated to extraordinary levels, and a subsequent bursting bubble with its attendant bad loans. Yet, like Germany, the resilience of the essential structure is attested by continuing investment in research and new capacity, often abroad, with significant restructuring among leading companies, repair of balance sheets, and the rise of a new generation of focused companies in advanced components for the rising disciplines of optics, mechatronics, and nano-products. While the national drive for technology and innovation, drawing on traditional structures, puts Japan among national leaders.[22]

---

[1] To adopt this general classification, a few favourite examples:
Hysteric: *The Japanese Conspiracy* by Marvin J. Wolf (Empire Books); *Trojan Horse* by Barrie G. James (W. H. Allen); *The Threat of Japanese Multinationals* by Lawrence G. Franko (John Wiley)
Academic: *The Rise of Modern Japan* by W. G. Beasley (Weindenfield and Nicholson); *The Political Economy of Japan* (2 Vols) Edited Banno Junji (Oxford); *The Japanese Achievement* by Hugh Cortazzi (Sedgwick & Jackson)
Pragmatic: *Kaisha* by James Abegglen and George Stalk Jr (Harper and Row) is an essential introduction, as also James Abegglen's other perceptive studies from his first eye-opener, *The Japanese Factory* (1958). On the development of Japan's distinct corporate patterns, *The Japanese Enterprise System* and *Knowledge Works* by Mark Fruin (Oxford): all are vivid and thoroughly researched introductions.

[2] *The Japanese Experience in Technology* by Takeshi Hayeshi (United Nations University Press); *Technology and Industrial Development in Japan* by Hiroyuki Odagiri and Akira Goto (Oxford); *The Technological Transformation of Japan* by Tessa Morris-Suzuki (Cambridge).

[3] A fascinating depiction of the crosscurrents and turmoil of the time is vividly depicted in *The Roots of Modern Japan* by Jean-Pierre Lehmann (Macmillan). But the sheer scale of institutional change ranged from a Central Bank, a Constitution and commercial code, land reform and break-up of old privileged classes, physical transport infrastructure and building up a military capability, and not just a declaration of universal primary education in 1872, but a superstructure of technical and engineering training.

[4] A lively account of this band of technology adventurers is in *The Imported*

Pioneers by Neil Pedlar (Japan Library). But the classic first-step in the Listian development model is an initial period of openness to secure leading technologies: "...In her case (Venice), as in that of the great kingdoms at a later period, freedom of international trade as well as restrictions on it have been beneficial or prejudicial to the power and prosperity of the State at different epochs. Unrestricted freedom of trade was beneficial to the Republic in the first years of her existence; for how otherwise could she have raised herself from a mere fishing village to a commercial power? But a protective policy was also beneficial to her when she had arrived at a certain stage of power and wealth, for by means of it she attained to manufacturing and commercial supremacy."

"The island kingdom (Britain) borrowed from every country of the Continent its skill in special branches of industry, and planted them on English soil, under the protection of her custom system."

It is worth speculating on the future development of China, as the country is going through this phase of importing technology on a massive scale, with already some signs of developing its own "champions" in motor vehicles, computers, and even declared ambitions for a nuclear power generating capability.

[5] And so it has remained for the best part of a century and a half: apart from periods of wartime command – usually very inefficient, "industry" has not figured in the Whitehall departmental nomenclature until the 1970s, and even then only on the "Through the Looking Glass" fantasy that there is some "perfect market" justifying government action only when there are "failures", "imperfections", or whatever.

[6] Quoted from *The Rise and Development of the Japanese Licensing System* by Yul Sohn in *Is Japan Really Changing Its Ways?* Edited: Lonny Carlile and Mark Tilton (Brookings).

[7] *The Origins of Japanese Trade Supremacy* by Christopher Howe (Hurst & Company) – a gem of a study tracing the rapidity with which imported models, from heavy naval guns to cotton spinning techniques, as well as traditional products were enhanced to an internationally competitive level.

[8] *The Origins of the Russo-Japanese War* by Ian Nish (Longman) is a standard introduction, while *The War of the Rising Sun and Tumbling Bear* by Richard Connaughton (Routledge) slants towards some of the absurd errors perpetrated in this conflict.

[9] The export market was seen as "the only channel of rescue, but the price-cost situation was not exactly favourable while outright subsidy would have been too blatant. Thus recourse was made to an administrative measure of allocating import permits of sugar to exporting shipbuilders. Since available foreign exchange was scarce at the time, importation of sugar had to be severely restricted, causing unusually high prices of sugar in the domestic market. Variables involved in the equation in the minds of MITI officials at the time were: (a) the needed margin of subsidy for making Japanese ships competitive

abroad; (b) the retail price of sugar which its domestic market could bear; and thus (c) the premium which its importers could earn. What was done then was to estimate the aggregate amount of (a) and divided by (c) to reach at the figure of 'needed' imports of sugar, and to allocate import permits to that amount to exporters of ships. Export prices of ships could thus be lowered by 20 to 30 percent; and the 'hidden' subsidy by this measure is said to have amounted to 10 billion yen in a little over one-year. This sum should be contrasted with the annual budget of 500 million yen of the Japan External Trade Organisation at around that time." *Japan's Capitalism* by Shigeto Tsuru (Cambridge), page 101.

[10] Summarised from a presentation on *Government and Shipbuilding: Japanese Policy for a Declining Industry* by Akira Morita at a conference at Brasenose College, Oxford in March 1988.

[11] *Japanese Industrial Policy* by Ira C Magaziner and Thomas Holt (PSI Report No: 5 85). For a more rounded account of the phases of "policy" see pages 278ff of *Growth through Competition, Competition through Growth* by Hiroyuko Odagari (Oxford).

[12] Clyde Prestowitz in *Trading Places* (Basic Books) notes that in a series of projects involving hydro generators, the three Japanese companies had won in a sequence of buggins turn bids, where each took it in turn to put in a markedly lower bid. This compares with research done by NEI on bidding patterns for a series of replacement coal-fired power stations in Australia where a similar sequence occurred. Such a device is inevitably difficult to counter since the practice only becomes evident well after the event.

[13] The revised 1989 introduction to *Trading Places* contains an entertaining account of the FSX saga.

[14] A summary account is given in "Co-opetition in the Japanese Aircraft Industry" by Sigrun Caspary and Toshihiro Nishiguchi in *Knowledge Emergence*, edited by I.Nonaka and T.Nishiguchi (Oxford).

[15] A full depiction of this feature is to be found in the treatment of "focal factories" in *The Japanese Enterprise System* by Mark Fruin (Oxford) – "A basic definition of such factories is a production site with appended planning, design, development and process-engineering capabilities, plus an ambition to accumulate, combine, and concentrate experience for the propagation and improvement of products and processes."

[16] Kazuo Koike has undertaken a number of studies of skill-formation, and "Learning and Incentive Systems in Japanese Industry" in *The Japanese Firm*, edited by Aoki and Dore (Oxford) illustrates the incentive effects of grading according to skill attainment. And the dynamic consequences are clearly set out in "Skill Function" in Hiroyuki Odagiri's *Growth through Competition, Competition through Growth* (Oxford).

[17] "Care" in the sense employed by Ikujiro Nonaka in *Knowledge Emergence* (Oxford), "High care organisations are characterised by employees who help each other, are accessible, have 'attentive inquiry', high degrees of tolerance, and share collectively in the same value for care," pp 30 ff.

[18] A typical example is an audit by a Toyota team of a Seven-Eleven store. Seven-Eleven, a leading Japanese convenience store chain, is itself a high innovator in retail efficiencies being among the first to exploit "point-of-sale" data, feedback from employees and delegated purchasing (see *Knowledge Emergence* p 21 ff). So no slouch. Yet the Toyota team identified 500 examples that time/waste/surpluses could be improved (*Nikkei Weekly* 7.6.04). Yet this is but one example, of which many more are illustrated in *Kaizen* by Masaaki Imai (McGraw-Hill), and by the approach of companies like Canon – "the goal of increasing productivity by 3 per cent per month throughout the organisation – which they achieve without laying off a single permanent worker." From *Canon Production System* (Productivity Press).

[19] From a starting premise, "the firm should be viewed primarily as a collection of human resources," it follows, "growth creates opportunities to utilise the firm's human resources fully and to enrich and expand them, because only a growing firm can create challenging jobs that free the workers to expand their knowledge and experience." (Odagiri Ibid.) But an approach expressed in the typical trading-company middle manager's remark, "We have to change. Otherwise, how can we look after our people?"

[20] "Instead of fixed-price contracts of a lengthy duration, there is a mutually understood dependence of one company upon the other, and this is expressed in the tightly coupled transactions that bind company to company rather than in tightly worded contracts of good-faith performance." Mark Fruin Ibid. P 274.

More generally, "According to a study published in 1987, 71% of the commercial contracts made by Japanese companies were concluded only orally. In Japan, Western societies are sometimes called *keiyaku no shakai* (societies of contracts), while Japanese society in contrast has been termed *mokuyaku no shakai* (society of tacit agreements)," and the number of lawyers and their involvement in ongoing commercial relations is remarkably low by Western standards – *Japan: Economic Success and Legal System*, edited Harald Baum (de Gruyter). Lee Iacocca once remarked of Japan, "They've got about as many lawyers as we've got sumo wrestlers," and on latest figures the total pool of licensed lawyers is no more than 20,000 against a population of 127 million. Even though steps are being taken to increase output, and reforms being introduced to lift many of the restrictions on foreign law firms practising in Japan, this is prompted by the increasing international concerns of business to have "one-shop" expertise in such areas as patent protection, corporate alliances, cross-border transactions etc, "but there are areas in which international firms are unlikely to try to muscle in, such as domestic corporate transactions" (*The Japan Journal* July 2004). Whatever the cultural dispositions against open contentious litigation, the approach of "keeping the lawyers outside the room" has a significant payoff in improved transaction efficiencies, time saved and abortive costs. So whatever the trend for change, it would be surprising if they were foolish enough to allow these to impinge on the pattern of daily inter-company exchange.

[21] The Sogo Shosha are a topic of study in themselves, and have played a key role in the country's development from its earliest move into textiles, securing raw materials, new technology, and acting as secondary banks for the growth of smaller companies. And they are continuously evolving, effectively reinventing themselves. Samples of the available literature are: *The Invisible Link* by M.Y.Yoshino and Thomas B.Lifson (MIT Press); *Sogo Shosha* by Y.Kunio (Oxford); and *General Trading Companies*, edited by Shin'ichi Yonekawa (United Nations University). From personal experience, as an adviser to one of the leading Sogo Shosha, their most striking feature is the sheer rounded talent of their people: it is as if the premier output from our leading universities, instead of being funnelled towards City accountancy, law and investment firms, were put to use contributing to genuine value-added. While "supply chain management" has become one of the recent management fads, the Sogo Shosha (and other Asian traders) have been practising this art for a century or more.

[22] A balanced and lucid appraisal of Japan's evolving dilemmas is *21st Century Japanese Management* by James Abegglen (Palgrave-McMillan). In particular, whereas general commentators have viewed a "lost decade" from the early 1990s, in practice this has been a period of largely successful retrenchment and readjustment from the era of very high growth to a more mature economy. With Japan retaining a dynamic research and development drive, and pursuit of enhancements to remain ahead of rapidly developing local neighbours and moves among established industrial countries. Having largely escaped the travails of finance stemming from the US sub-prime crisis, the country is re-emerging as an exemplar in popular commentary. For example, *Japan,s Business Renaissance: How the World's Greatest Economy Revived, Renewed and Reinvented Itself* by Mark B. Fuller and John C. Beck (McGraw Hill).

ALL LIST'S CHILLUN: SOUTH KOREA AND TAIWAN

There is such a vast repository of studies on the development of the fast flyers among the Asian economies, not least because of proximity in time and unprecedented growth rates, that there is no shortage of material to illustrate the constituents of their distinct approaches.[1] But the next generation of List's progeny arose through tough "mentoring" and emulation rather than doctrinal study, though it has been remarked that copies of List are available in paperback in South Korea. Both South Korea and Taiwan were subject to decades of colonisation by Japan, and a Japan that was in its most autocratic-state mode. For Korea this was perhaps the sharpest jolt from its "hermit" tradition, even though they could boast a history of technology going back to the first iron-hull ships. Formosa (Taiwan) had historically been a predominantly agricultural island with not always harmonious links to mainland China.

Both could identify a range of inheritances from Japanese occupation, even if the colonial idiom was one of enclaves owing allegiance to centres of authority in Japan: a banking system, essential infrastructure, rigorous labour conditions, and a corpus of locally developed managerial expertise, though there were inevitable variations depending upon local resources, and the role of the territories as "Go" clusters in Japan's imperial ambitions.

Korea was regarded as a supplier of cheap rice, logging, fish and mined minerals, while Japan's Oriental Development Company took over previously government-owned assets. Education improved mainly through foreign missionaries, and with local managerial positions confined to "sergeants", with all the resentful animosities that result. But the Japanese experience allowed South Korea readily to adapt their inherited institutions. For Taiwan, the southern climate focused development on food processing, notably sugar which accounted for 70% of manufacturing gross value in the 1930s, but with a traditional bias towards small business units.

Both nations became "front-line" in the Cold War, most dramatically South Korea as a result of demarcation following the ruinous Korean War. But Taiwan as the flagship outpost of the erstwhile Nationalist China Government (KMT). This prompted large aid flows, both financial and in technical assistance, from the US. And under this US guidance, there was major land reform in both countries that dispersed ownership more equitably. But both were also among the world's poorest nations with Per Capita GNP in 1950 of $876 in South Korea and $922 in Taiwan.

Another quirky similarity is that both countries had an ex-military leader as head of government during their grounding periods of post-Pacific War growth. After the croquet-playing Syngman Rhee was toppled following student riots in 1960, Chang Kyong in turn was ousted by General Park Chang Hee in a military coup in 1961. Through such organisations as the Economic Planning Board, monthly Export Planning Conference chaired by General Park, and the presence of erstwhile military staff in the government administration and company managements, the approach to "nation building through export promotion" was conducted in effect through a Presidential "general staff", with five-year plans and operational targets. If tough justice prevailed, General Park could rely upon a traditional sense of national loyalty.

When General Chiang Kai-shek took the seat of China's Nationalist Government to Taipei in the late 1940s with a coterie of followers and the choicest of national treasures, he had a trickier hand because the mainlanders were only some 15% of the population, with inevitable tensions between the Kuomintang (KMT) ruling class and the indigenous population: a tension still being played out as the Democratic Party, with its roots in the traditional indigenous population, has been tussling for power with the KMT – the latter just gaining election again, but a jockeying reflected in vacillating policies towards China. And deliberate policies were pursued (enforced) for universal education and spreading the use of Mandarin as a national language. There may have been a similar top-down autocratic drive as in South Korea; also with periodic national plans, and following a similar progression from import substitution to export stimulation, and from textiles, leather goods etc to high-tech electronics, but these took a different pattern.

For all these combinations of circumstances, the orientation of both countries was undisputedly, if not indeed ferociously over-compensatingly nationalistic. For the KMT in Taiwan there was the added spur of their national economic guru, Sun Yat Sen, whose thought had been driven by the motive of finding a response to China's dose of British "free trade" in the Opium Wars, and whose *Three Principles* put "nationalism" as the first.

Within this common "national" drive, however, the models were rather different: General Park was influenced by the pre-War system of Japan, with the *chaebol* evolving as the equivalents of the post-Meiji *zaibatsu* –

large diversified family-controlled business groups whose heads functioned in close proximity to the apex of political power: Mitsui, for example,[i] acted as Japan's primary government procurement agency and its finance department functioned effectively as the national central bank. But whereas the *zaibatsu* had a banking/finance function at their core, the General Park variation was to retain tight control of the banking system, in practice using credit rationing as an essential lever to coerce performance.

In Taiwan, however, the KMT arrived initially as effectively a foreign power (following, indeed, on a period of repression by the Nationalist Government before its leadership had to flee across the Straits). This imposed a power-clique in government, with a continuing need to convince a larger community of its legitimacy by mixtures of repression, coercion, education and sustaining economic growth. It took time, even under US pressure, for the technocrats to gain influence in government. Given this fissure in social structure, and the political traditions of mainland China, tight control of the banking system was also seen as essential, but initially the State's direct industrial investment was focused on the capital-intensive, upstream and high-risk sectors such as steel, shipbuilding, heavy engineering and construction, aluminium, electric power, petroleum and chemicals, fertilisers, sugar, tobacco, bus transportation and airlines. In effect, the "State" became a diversified conglomerate with extensive affiliate links.[2] On the other hand, if just as aware as South Korea that its prospects for rapid economic development lay primarily in exporting, the main driving force was through various support measures for smaller companies, many, notably in textiles, drawing upon managerial expertise imported from mainland entrepreneurs. These followed the progression from initially low-cost suppliers to predominantly American companies to become OEM businesses of increasing technical sophistication as they mastered commercial skills and new technology.

Therefore, both countries went through planning cycles, initially import substituting then progressively to enhance the volume and technical level of exports; both employed a wide repertoire of leverage/inducements through subsidies (intermediate assets and "getting prices wrong"), regulation and tariff controls etc; and both inherited cultures with distinct patterns of hierarchy, codes of obligation, and idioms of relationships more tolerant of informal business deals. All these are amply explored in the available literature. So, rather than catalogue these, it might be worth focusing on how they followed the essential Listian prescription.

---

[i] *Mitsui* by John G. Roberts (Weatherhill)

For sure, we can look forward to further esoteric alchemaic econometric modelling,[3] purporting to analyse inputs to Total Factor Productivity, the influence of "openness to trade", or, no doubt in due course, the contribution of tea consumption, all on questionable hypotheses,[4] and in support of the thesis that all these countries did was "to get the basics right" without any significant – or despite – a strong participation by the State. But undeniably these countries achieved spectacular increases in income[5] – probably unprecedented since Japan's post-Meiji modernisation, reductions in poverty, with relatively egalitarian distribution, and with sustained economic and export growth. Underlying this performance was a more remarkable, if less remarked, enhancement in technical and managerial skills to absorb knowledge across an increasingly wide spectrum, and development of the capabilities to create Adam Smith's "advantages" through innovative expertise and research. In effect, from "the accumulation" of knowledge, to the capacity "to increase these attainments" by their "own acquirements" – the crucial transition from "buying" to "making".[6]

But for a real take on their performance, Adam Smith's devotees have to admit the presence of "national purpose"; within regulatory and formal authority structures, the dynamic influence of "coalitions" across the boundaries of the State, finance and "business"; a dominance of "informal" skeins of interaction to disseminate knowledge and experience; and without the transaction inefficiencies of unnecessary legal mediation. And yet no lack of native commercial flair.

Both certainly received aid from the US, and from Japan under reparations. But given their destitution in the 50s and lack of virtually all resources, both countries had to adopt co-ordinated campaigns, achievable only through the co-ordination of a central authority to build up their *skills competences*, from primary education through the range of expertise and technologies, in order to "appropriate" knowledge across the spread of industries necessary to establish a national capability. Both achieved rapid rises in the social coverage, and up the levels, of education – particularly demanding when the dominant language for technologies and skills were "foreign" i.e. English or Japanese – by targeted programmes. If initially relying on third countries, notably the US, for their tertiary education, both have now evolved universities and technology institutes of world ranking.[7]

Technology transfer was absorbed and disseminated through diverse interfaces. Secreted behind the formal devices of licensing – where both Governments took steps to enhance the leverage of their companies, regulated joint ventures/alliances, and import of expatriate experts, etc are tiers of less formal media. To identify just a few of the main sources

– Reverse engineering, disparagingly dismissed by orthodox commentators as mere copying, is in practice a dynamic source of "free" knowledge: and devotees of Adam Smith have persistently failed to recognise what can be derived by passionate, creative, and technically competent brains behind "hands" (arguably, the "patents" game, as currently played by "fast following" companies and countries is to reverse engineer, and then add sufficient refinements/enhancements that are themselves patentable, and so set up a defence against claims based on the original patents).

– Demands for "local content" in purchases or inward investment. Now the norm in power/rail infrastructure, vehicles and domestic appliances, but especially in the technologies associated with defence equipment. Whatever may be the international trade rules, invariably the situation will offer the buyer leverage that few sellers are in a position to resist.

– An initial focus on specialist original equipment manufacture (OEM) as a subcontractor/supplier to more "advanced" producers can, again given motivation and creative minds, evolve technology, commercial and marketing expertise to become an original design manufacturer (ODM), moving up the tiers of technology competence, in turn increasing their absorptive capacity.

– Such informal flows as Taiwan's deliberate "reverse brain drain" in targeting nationals who had developed expertise in the US, especially in electronics and IT; Korean companies' deliberate enticement of Japanese managers to "moonlight" in their plants at weekends (now, indeed, with Japanese managers joining Korean companies as they have achieved leading-edge status); or diffusion through the internal company structure of the *chaebols*, or from government-owned businesses to their suppliers in Taiwan.

To encourage the transition to leading-edge products, both Governments supported targeted R&D, research centres and networking institutions. Notably, Taiwan's science park at Hsinchu was set up by the government with tough screening tests on admittance, and has earned the title of the Silicon Valley of Taiwan.[8]

– *Managerial expertise* was accumulated through managing heavy capital and plant investments, initially with foreign inputs, but evolving to self-sufficiency; gaining expertise in process and continuous manufacturing, and in international marketing, distribution and finance; and, latterly, through outward investment flows.[9]

But cutting, for a moment, to what was going on at the time in Britain, still engulfed in its historic myopic fog, the drive of these countries to international competitive clout went entirely unnoticed. Until, just as in the face of Japan's motorbike manufacturers, British producers collapsed against the contested dynamism of these new arrivals. Notably, while Korean and Japanese yards battled it out for shipbuilding orders, under-cutting and out-producing British builders, we witnessed the picaresque local amateur dramatics in the late-60s of politicians and trade unionists with megaphones atop cars on Clydeside, attempting caricatures of Leninist posters, totally oblivious to the real causes of the industry's competitive collapse. And whose hysteric antics inhibited any rational approach to devise a potentially viable response. That there were more successful responses is attested by the survival of Dutch, German, French, Italian and Nordic yards, while, after decades of political helter-skelter, there remains a single symbolic crane on the Clyde in remembrance of a "smokestack industry".

While, after an abortive thrust in cars into the US, Korean brands entered the UK market from the mid-70s to further reduce the dwindling share of BL/Rover in its native market. And, in overseas capital plant orders, Korean companies in the late 70s suddenly broke in with prices 40% or more below competitors.[10] And laggard British companies have not been the only sufferers: when Japan had achieved seeming dominance in memory chips to the point where the US was demanding "voluntary restraints", while these were being negotiated, Korean firms leapfrogged into the lead, and have carried this challenge into flat-screen devices, mobile phones etc.

Taiwan's advance has been less visible, discernible in the 60s/70s as producers of textiles, leather goods, sewing machines, bicycles etc, but with the first intimation of future trends as the source of low-priced tape Walkmans – recalling that the initial price of the Sony original was more than £100. But the shrinking British machine tool industry, having failed to keep up with the increasing precision, speed, automation and flexibility of leading Japanese and German producers, suddenly confronted low-cost competition in the more mundane products in which they had been stuck. The real impact, however, lay in the componentry for analogue TVs, portable radios, in which Taiwan producers were establishing dominance, leading on to becoming the main source – albeit with much of the actual production spread into China and other low-labour costs countries – of some 80% of the content of PCs and laptops irrespective of the brand label. But also capable of leapfrogging, as in its rapid ascendancy in semiconductor fabrication and design, and a competitive position in the rapidly evolving flat-screen market, illustrate. But these are industrial fields out of which British industry has opted, without any competitive counter and without any theatrics.

– *Expanding productive powers*: reverting to the world where self-indulgent amateur dramatics counts for nought compared to sustaining the drive to higher value-added activities and enhanced living standards, if Korea and Taiwan had shared this dynamic, the corporate structures that they evolved were rather different.

With the notable exception of POSCO, which has remained predominantly focused on steel products, Korea's choice of finance-rationing with incentives to build up dominant family-controlled groups – the chaebol – encouraged them to take on rapid growth, diversification and high levels of debt. Their evolutionary pattern was a "stepping-stone" logic of moving across interfaces of related activities[11] leading to some 30 main groups, but with half a dozen gaining international brand recognition – Hyundai, Samsung, Daewoo, Lucky Goldstar, Kia, Sunkyong etc – though embracing a broad diversification of activities. One consequence was that smaller companies, unless tied into one of the main groups, invariably had to fend for expensive credit in the "kerb market", and few could gain significant international presence.[12] By the late-80s, however, there was concern at the dominance of the chaebols – with some scandals tossed in, and with the prospect of the Uruguay Round (finally concluded in 1993) reducing the scope for supporting "infant industries", permissible under the previous GATT regime, deliberate efforts were made to ease the path of small firms with slow and mixed results.[ii] And an effort was made to rationalise the chaebols by restricting them to a limited range of specialties, though in practice there was still a compression of focus among the leading groups, and they still retained – certainly by British standards – a widely diversified range of activities.

Perhaps this extrovert and adventurous style of development is a reflection of national temperament – a Korean academic once characterised his fellow countrymen as "the Italians of Asia".[13] Taiwan's corporate community, by contrast, has managed to remain almost invisible. Even the sheer scale of the KMT's corporate holdings have barely attracted notice, while of their leading companies, only Evergreen and Acer have approached a significant brand identity internationally.

While Taiwan had its "private" diversified groups that evolved by a "stepping-stone" logic – Reuntex, Far Eastern, President and Evergreen, alongside the state enterprises, smaller companies followed the distinctive

---

[ii] See chapter on *Developing Local Enterprise* in *Korean Enterprise* (ibid.)

familial/paternalistic style of the "Chinese business": tight cash-control, informal and rapid transaction efficiencies, and the leverage of ostracism.[14] It was in stimulating the initiation and upgrading of electronic producers that the State has played a distinctive role: investment in central R&D institutes, with spin-offs to exploit particular technologies; conditions imposed on inward investment to secure technology and managerial skills; direct investment in key facilities, notably TSMC in semiconductor fabrication; disciplined incentives and subsidies; and stimulating the formation of vertical and horizontal networks of interfacing firms.[15] The results have been startling, ranging from a shift of 1% to 60% of world's CD-ROM output in six years, to the evolution of leading enterprises such as Acer; "Lite-On Technology", a member of the Lite-On Group and currently the world's fourth largest computer monitor manufacturer, with annual sales of $820 million; Winbond, the world's tenth largest producer of memory ICs, with sales of $457 million; Delta Electronics, the flagship of the Delta Group and the world's leading producer of switching power supplies (SPS) with sales of $399 million; Macronix, the world's seventh leading maker of nonvolatile memory products, with sales of $370 million; Primax Electronics, the world's leading producer of handheld scanners, with sales of $337 million; and Siliconware Precision Industries, the world's third largest independent IC packager (after Anam Industrial of South Korea), with sales of $268 million.[16] Just for starters. While others have followed a path of cross-national diversification.[17]

In clocking up 6%-plus growth over a few decades, both countries were helped by a benign international trading scene – not least the limitations of the Anglo-Saxon economies in countering the type of competitive threat they posed. But the financial crisis in 1997, triggered by devaluation of the Thai baht, and the resulting flight of hot money from neighbouring economies, posed a sudden dilemma. The repercussions in the two countries were very different.

The chaebol had evolved with an expressly expansionist objective on the back of preferential state-backed credit. Undisciplined, beyond a certain point, this can place the state in a double-bind, especially when these large enterprises are direct major providers of employment and welfare. This had hampered earlier attempts to restructure the chaebol. It is arguable that some had become so seriously over-geared with debt that their future would in any event have been precarious, but with the increases in interest rates demanded by the crisis (and the IMF) the six main chaebol were forced to confront radical change.[18] Most spectacular was the collapse of Daewoo, with accusations of corruption involved as well, whose founding President, Kim Woo-Chong, had been an iconic figure: a Spartan lifestyle, surviving on negligible sleep, and notoriously having turned around the bankrupt Okpo Shipbuilding Company's yard, with direct hands-on management. And he had expanded the group across a diversity of products and extraordinary geographic compass.[19]

The straightened circumstances gave the reforming Kim Dae Jong government the leverage to strong-arm rationalisation through a new Financial Supervisory Commission, but also with incentives such as reduced export-related taxes, deferred capital gains and corporate taxes, and reduced individual taxes. As a result, the surviving Big Five reduced gearing to below 200%, with the number of affiliates dropping from 252 to 165. There were severe social implications, with factory closures and rationalisations, involving a 10% reduction of the Big Five's labour force. There were inevitable work disruptions, leading eventually to reconciliation that enhanced the role of labour representation.

Taiwan's structure was more resilient against the "contagion" stemming from the crisis.[20] From their initial period of taking over government control, the KMT had taken control of the financial system, and, mindful of the unrest that had been stimulated by high inflation and that had contributed to the rise of the Communist Party in China, had followed a tight monetary regime: with relatively high interest rates contributing to price stability and simulating high private saving rates; and, by taking over the capital-intensive/higher-risk industries, the state bureaucracy was relatively immune from influence from major private interest groups.

Historically, whereas Korean companies would have debt-equity ratios (in percent) in the broad range of 360-450 in the preceding decades, the corresponding ratios for Taiwan companies were 75-120. But with a private corporate sector dominated by the high-savings, tight-cash, and familial financial support style of the Chinese business, between 1971 and 1994 Taiwan financed its entire gross capital formation out of domestic savings. While Taiwan's export success achieved among the highest per-capita foreign currency reserves. Consequently, Taiwan was the least damaged of the Southeast Asian economies. It was, however, given the predominance of IT-components manufacturing, badly hit by the bursting of the IT bubble, and in 2001 suffered the only year of negative growth in 50 years. But the country has continued its remarkable "invisible" growth,[21] building up its stash of foreign currency holdings to $239 billion by mid-2004 (Economist 15.1.05).

After the jolt of '97, South Korean companies have shown a dynamic resilience – Samsung and LG Electronics have become highly competitive brands, while Hyundai and Kia, albeit with shifts in ownership shares, are competing in vehicle markets, and the country remains a leading shipbuilder.[22] And the country has become a leader in broadband and wireless connectivity.

Yet, despite ups and downs and differences of cultural mix, both countries are exemplars of a focused "national" approach to accumulate "all discoveries, inventions, improvements, perfections, and exertion of all generations," with a determined drive to build up technical and professional competences; to establish systems to create "productive powers"; and to sustain the continuities for growth and "producing wealth".

Their supreme accolade lies in not just appropriating "attainments of former generations", but "to increase them by (their) own acquirements". This is reflected in the patents granted by the US Patents and Trademark Office – generally accepted as a surrogate measure of national innovative qualities – where both surpassed the UK between 1980 (Patents granted: UK-2,416; South Korea-10; Taiwan-69) and 2001 (Patents granted: UK-2,695; South Korea-3,538; Taiwan-5,371).

---

[1] Of the vast bibliography, *Asia's Next Giant* by Alice Amsden (Oxford), predominantly focusing on South Korea, and *Governing the Market* by Robert Wade (Princeton) on Taiwan are the best starting points for a more realistic view of their particular idioms of economic development. If the authors appear to be adopting a somewhat combative style, this reflects the struggles of permeating the "neo-liberal" doctrinal dominance of the World Bank, and other international agencies, with some injection of reality. A struggle reflected in the ambiguities, and occasional double-speak, of the World Bank study *The East Asian Miracle* (Oxford 1993).

Of others, it is always refreshing to have an insider's viewpoint, and *The Rise of the Korean Economy* by Byung-Nak Song (Oxford) has a mass of valuable comparative data, and useful chronology, with less of the conventional economics baggage. Equally interesting is the lively account of the internal dynamic idiom within an evolving chaebol in *Making Capitalism* by Roger Janelli/Dawnboe Yin (Stanford). Similar material on Taiwan is more elusive, but *Flexibility, Foresight and Fortuna in Taiwan's Development* by Steve Chan and Cal Clark (Routledge) is a stimulating analysis, with plenty of useful data, on the failure of different economic development theories to match the reality of Taiwan's outstanding performance.

[2] As late as 1994, concerns were being voiced about the scale, influence and lack of transparency of the KMT's business empire (*The Money Machine* in *Far Eastern Economic Review* 11.8.94). In this account, "With investments in more

than 100 companies, the Kuomintang's (KMT) corporate holdings are staggering. They range from nearly bankrupt firms in the textile and pharmaceutical businesses to hugely profitable oligopolies in the finance industry. Close ties to the government and state-run corporations are clearly a boon: party-operated enterprises enjoy privileges denied other private-sector firms. And KMT companies don't have to pay for inefficiency and often sloppy management. Most importantly, these businesses make the KMT the richest ruling party in the non-Communist world. They will contribute almost all of the more than US$450 million that the party will spend this year." Under the new Chairman of the Business Committee, Mr Liu Tai-ying – a Cornell contemporary of the Party Chairman, Mr Lee Teng-hui – measures were in hand to rationalise, including some privatisation, and improve the efficiency of this sprawling empire. In 1991, its assets were variously valued at NT $112 billion – NT $500 billion (approx US$3.7 billion – US$19 billion), and its activities ranged as far afield as Hong Kong, Indonesia, Vietnam, Singapore, North Korea, Russia and Japan.

[3] Typically the incomprehensible chunks of special pleading in *The East Asian Miracle* (World Bank, Oxford).

[4] See Joseph Stiglitz' charming dissection of the inadequacies inherent in such mystic accounting in *From Miracle to Crisis to Recovery* in *Rethinking the East Asian Miracle* (World Bank, Oxford).

[5] 2003 GDP Per Capita ($ at PPP) were 17,580 for South Korea, and 24,500 for Taiwan. As illustrative of the relative advance/decline convergence, the corresponding figure for Britain was 27,490.

[6] *The Rise of the "Rest"* by Alice Amsden (Oxford) is an outstanding essay on the successful policies applied by the East Asian countries in completing List's "national" vision of evolving the capabilities to "appropriate" and then to "increase (knowledge) by its own acquirements".

[7] Both countries have justifiable pride in their educational attainments. In the case of Taiwan, Robert Wade offers a useful summary in *The State-Market Dilemma in East Asia* (*The Role of the State in Economic Change* (Oxford)), "One of the most striking things about Korea, Taiwan, and even more Japan, is the increase in the ratios of skilled to basically skilled to unskilled people in the labour force over the past forty years. This is measured not just in terms of level of education obtained, but also in terms of the content of the education: a high proportion of the total is in engineering and science. In a population of 20 million, Taiwan's junior colleges have produced over 20,000 engineering diploma holders a year over the 1980s, the universities another 10,000 bachelor-level engineers a year (nearly twice as many as the USA in relation to population). About a quarter of all university graduates since 1960 have been engineers (law graduates, 1.2%). Science and engineering students together accounted for over one-third of post-high-school graduates during the 1960s, and over a half by the 1980s." Not many Balliol double-firsts in this lot.

While Byung-Nak Song (ibid.) has an understandable glow in his summary,

"In terms of education, however, Korea is far ahead of Taiwan and at a level equal to some industrialised countries such as the United Kingdom, France and West Germany. Indeed, in terms of the proportion of the population aged 20-24 enrolled in higher schools, Korea ranks higher than Taiwan, Japan, West Germany, France and England."

[8] The Hsinchu Science Park currently has some 380 companies, employs 110,000, and produces some $31 billion worth of high-tech goods a year. So successful that the Taiwan government has set up two further science parks in 1996 and 2002 on land previously owned by the Government's Taiwan Sugar Corp. After vetting, prospective clients are granted favourable loans and services are fast-tracked. Dominated by electronics and IT, with incumbents ranging from Corning to TSMC and United Microelectronics, the aim is to extend into computers, telematics, and biotechnology. (Taiwan's new science parks adding to island's global high-tech – *Nikkei Weekly* 21.2.05)

[9] The adventurous spirit to invest abroad has been striking: from the 70s, Korean companies would appear in relatively unexploited countries, such as Turkmenistan and Kazakhstan, and were among the first non-Soviet companies to invest in Eastern Europe. Taiwan's overseas investment has been much less visible, but with rising domestic labour costs, relaxation of capital controls and fiscal incentives, capital flows around Southeast Asia took off (*Taiwanese Firms in Southeast Asia* by Tain-Jy Chen (Edward Elgar)). But by 1997 Korea's overseas investment was running at more than $4 billion annually, and Taiwan's at $5 billion (Table 8.6 in *The Rise of the "Rest"*).

[10] This, less remarked, sudden catch-up took existing contractors by surprise. Particularly in Saudi Arabia and elsewhere in the Gulf, the story went that, to coincide with delivery of the main fabrication units, three Boeing 747s would arrive, disgorge several hundred Korean workers and equipment, who would build a tented city, complete the foundations and erection, pack up the tents, dust off the desert, and leave by another three Boeing 747s.

An insight to this was gained when participating in a management course at Templeton College. One student was a mature and charming Korean official, who said that he was from the Department dealing with Overseas Construction. Apparently, as tension on the border with North Korea diminished, there was less demand for national service conscripts; so, young Koreans coming up to their compulsory national service were offered the option of taking part in overseas projects. After training, and paid at conscript rates, they provided qualified cheap labour for Korean contractors and established skills and experience that could be immediately applied when their compulsory service was over.

This is an interesting subset of the "skills" gains from compulsory national service, which would provide qualified technicians and supervisory staff for careers in industry after their compulsory stint was over. One of the unwritten analyses is the extent to which similar technical training provided a temporary "skills" solution to the engineering and electronic industries in Britain. Sadly, perhaps, relieving these industries of the pressure for establishing their own "skills" development structures.

[11] There are several accounts of the evolution of the chaebol in *Asia's Next Giant*, and *Korean Enterprise* (HBS). Among the neatest is that of the Lucky Goldstar group, currently identified with an aggressive marketing move into mobile telephones under the smiling brand of LG (LG rises without trace in 3D market: South Korean group now second largest producer of the latest mobile phones – *FT* 12.10.04; Sheer adrenalin for LG Electronics' image: Sponsorship of action sports has helped a gutsy LGE breakthrough the brand barrier – *FT* 16.12.04). The then Chairman's account of its evolution runs, "My father and I started a cosmetic cream factory in the late 1940s. At the time, no company could supply us with plastic caps of adequate quality for cream jars, so we had to start a plastic business. Plastic caps were not sufficient to run the plaster-moulding plant, so we added combs, toothbrushes, and soap boxes. This plastics business also led us to manufacture electrical and electronic products and telecommunication equipment. The plastics business also took us into oil refining which needed a tanker-shipping company. The oil-refining company alone was paying an insurance premium amounting to more than half the total revenue of the then largest insurance company in Korea. Thus, an insurance company was started. This natural step-by-step evolution through related businesses resulted in the Lucky-Goldstar group as we see it today. For the future, we will base our growth primarily on chemicals, energy, and electronics. Our chemical business will continue to expand toward fine chemicals and genetic engineering while the electronics business will grow in the direction of semiconductor manufacturing, fibre optic telecommunications, and eventually, satellite telecommunications." (Harvard Business School 1985).

It is worth noting that, if all these ambitions have not materialised, the *FT* remarks that, "LG's handset business benefits from the powerful global marketing and distribution network of the wider LG Electronics company. LG is the world's largest producer of microwave ovens and air-conditioners, and owns half of LG Phillips, the second largest maker of liquid crystal displays used in flat-screen TVs and monitors.

"Handsets account for about a third of LG's sales, which amounted to $17.6 billion last year. A further third comes from other consumer electronics and household appliances, with the remaining 40 percent generated by flat-panel displays." (*FT* – 12.10.04).

Beyond electronics, however, the group embraces 39 subsidiaries and 39 joint-venture partners. While to vie with the drive of other chaebol into semiconductors, it established a range of alliances for access to relevant technologies embracing Hitachi, Siemens, Olivetti, Zilog, Fairchild, AT&T, AMD, and Motorola.

[12] After many years of keeping an eye open for smaller Korean companies, the only example in the archives is Romanson, a watchmaker notable for the Eleve brand (*Far East Economic Review* – 16.7.98). Its top-end watches are assembled and inspected in Switzerland, allowing them to carry The "Swiss Made" marker.

And other models import Swiss and Japanese micro-movements: 10% of turnover and 20% of staff effort go on R&D. The family-owned company began in 1988, and achieved a breakthrough by exporting through free-trade zones in the Middle East.

[13] Just sticking with our case of Lucky Goldstar, the appointment of Park K.C. to become an Executive Vice-President of LG in 1993 followed his 10 years with IBM in developing liquid crystal display (LCD) technologies, where "he felt that IBM was slow to put money into new technology development", and "disillusioned by the timidity with which the company invested in the future". Commenting on his new company's commitment to innovation, Park observed, "If we (LG) decide we need it, bang! – We go in. That's the way it has to be. No nonsense. That's what really excites me about Korea" (*Korean Enterprise* page 23).

[14] The extent of this traditional style, and its interplay with "colonial" powers goes back a long way – *Chinese Business Enterprise in Asia*, Edited R.A. Brown (Routledge): keeping heads down, ever watchful for threats and inside-tracks, learning from interaction with the "dominant" European traders and manufacturers, and remarkably fluid in crossing national boundaries – see accounts of the Wing On Company Group, and the Kin Tye Lung companies; but liable to twists of familial structure and allegiance. The more recent evolution of this style is delineated in Gordon Redding's *The Spirit of Chinese Capitalism* (de Gruyter). And the dynastic tradition persists – the founders of three of Taiwan's major companies retired: Taiwan Cement, Evergreen and Acer, each with companies extending beyond the original business, and management passed on to relatives (*Nikkei Weekly* 31.1.05).

[15] The range of the Taiwan government's palette of measures is lucidly depicted in Prof Alice Amsden's *Beyond Late Development* – co-authored with Wan-wen Chu (The MIT Press). In summary, virtually a handbook for late-developing nations.

[16] *The Rise of the "Rest"* page 195. For an update, the *Nikkei Weekly* (21.12.05) reports (Taiwan PC-takers star behind scenes) that in notebook computers, Taiwanese firms have evolved effectively an OEM (original equipment manufacturing) economy, where "in unit terms, Taiwan notebook makers have rapidly expanded their share of global production and are thought to account for more than 80% of all notebooks made in the world in 2005." Their major OEM manufacturers like Quanta Computer Inc., Compal Electronics Inc., Wistron Corp., Inventec Corp., and ASUSTeK Computer Inc., provide the bulk of notebook computers for retail giants like Dell, Hewlett-Packard and Acer, and significant elements of the content of other brands.

The elusiveness of their competitive advantage behind brand names disguises, for example, that Quanta's shipments in 2005 were some 17 million notebooks, nearly 30% of global demand, and a larger presence than Dell with a market share of 20%. Behind these Taiwan firms is a cluster of production facilities around

Shanghai, with Quanta's subsidiary rated as the second largest exporter by China's Ministry of Commerce in 2004.

[17] Rarely do we have a vivid account of this style of diversification, but Alice Amsden's summary of Pacific Electric Wire and Cable group (PEWC), which was established in 1950 is exemplary: "PEWC had entered into a technical collaboration agreement with Sumitomo Electric Industries Ltd Japan in 1960, invested in a Singapore cable company in 1967 and a Thai cable company in 1971, it established an R&D Laboratory and began to manufacture aluminium wire and cable in 1977, and was the first in Taiwan to manufacture core optical fibre cable in 1983 (the year in which PEWC founded the Pacific Laser Electric Optics Company). After 1986 internationalisation and diversification went even further with the appointment of a salaried president (Pacific Electric Wire and Cable 1995). PEWC founded a joint venture with Sumitomo Electric (Sumi-Pac Electro-Chemical Corporation) in 1987; founded the Pacific Yoshida Engineering Company in 1988, a joint venture with Japanese engineering companies to make machinery to manufacture cable; founded Pacific Securities with other local companies, the Greenbay Entertainment Company and the Pacific Southwest Bank in Texas, all in 1988; established a construction company with Sumitomo Electric in 1989; founded the Hotel Conrad Hong Kong with Swire Properties and Hilton Hotel in 1989; moved old plants in Taiwan to another site to build an 'intelligent' high-tech industrial community in 1989; established additional joint ventures to produce electric wire and cable in Thailand and Hong Kong; reinvested in the Winbond Electronics Corporation in 1990 (Taiwan's 67th ranking company in 1997); founded Taiwan Aerospace Corporation with other local enterprises and invested in Taiwan Cogeneration Corporation with Taiwan Power Company and Communication Bank in 1991; established Fubon Life Insurance with the Fubon group and established Chung-Tai Telecommunication Corporation with Walsin, Hua Eng, and the Tatung group in 1992; established Open Systems Software as a joint venture with Hewlett-Packard Delaware Corporation also in 1992; established an investment company with Sumitomo Electric, signed an agreement with the US-based Motorola and Iridium for joining 'Global System-Iridium Project' in 1993 (a project that failed); founded the subsidiary Pacific Iridium a year later; formed a joint venture with Raychem International Manufacturing of the United States to manufacture electrical wire especially for use in aerospace, marine transport, telecommunications, and rapid transit systems in 1994; and in the same year invested in Mosel Vitelic, a US-based specialised semiconductor producer in Taiwan.

"Throughout this later period, PEWC's assets and return on sales both rose, driven by diversification and telecommunication services, a 'strategic' industry (Pacific Electric Wire and Cable 1994). Despite all these diversifications, moreover, PEWC was nowhere near the top in Group size. And diversification on the part of Taiwan's business groups increased their overall share in GNP: the share in GNP of the top 100 business groups rose between 1986 and 1996 from 28.7% to almost 44.2%." (*The Rise of the "the Rest"* pp274)

---

[18] For fuller treatment, see *The Miracle As Prologue: the State and the Reform of the Corporate Sector in Korea* by Meredith Woo-Cummings (*Rethinking the East Asian Miracle*).

[19] By 1996, the Daewoo Group encompassed heavy industry and shipbuilding, construction, motor vehicles and components, electronics and electrical, telecommunications, hotels, finance and trading, with a geographical spread of manufacturing sites covering Algeria, Belgium, China, France, Hungary, India, Indonesia, Iran, Kazakhstan, Libya, Mexico, Myanmar, Pakistan, Philippines, Poland, Romania, Russia, Sudan, Taiwan, United Kingdom, United States, Uzbekistan and Vietnam.

[20] The contrast is explored by Phillip Hobson Park in *A Reflection on the East Asian Development Model: Comparison of the South Korean and Taiwanese Experiences* in *The East Asian Development Model*, edited by F. Richter (Macmillan Press).

[21] For example, to give a few quick snapshots of its dynamism:

– As an exemplar of the notable individual entrepreneur, virtually any laptop computer – Dell, Apple, Compaq, and even Toshiba – "there's a fighting chance" it was made by Quanta Computer (Face Value: His high-tech Highness – *The Economist* 13.7.02), albeit that much of the content is increasingly being outsourced to China.

– The flow of foreign direct investment to China has been between $2-4 billion since 1996, and the list of China's 200 top exporters in 2003 is headed by Hon Hai Precision Industry (exports worth $6.4 billion), Quanta ($5.3 billion) and Asustek ($a 3.2 billion), with another 25 on the list.

– While the world market shares of Taiwan producers was Wireless LAN, 85%; Notebook PCs, 64%; ADSL, 62%; Cable modem, 52%; LAN switches, 41%; PDA, 41%; CD/DVD/RW, 40%; PC Camera, 36%. (Economists Survey – Dancing with the enemy 15.1.05). Or, calculated differently, Motherboards, 80%; Notebook PCs, 70%; LCD monitors, 68%; Optical disk drives, 30%; and Desktop PCs, 25% (Nikkei Weekly 6.12.04).

– Taiwan's leading chip foundries – Taiwan Semiconductor Manufacturing Co. (TSMC) and United Microelectronics Corp (UMC) – have moved rapidly from being bulk producers of chips on assignment from chip designers, to the leading edge of 90-nanometre processes close on the heels of Intel, Samsung and Toshiba (*Nikkei Weekly* 20.9.04).

– The Taiwan government's "Challenge 2008" vision calls for an increase in R&D from 2% to 3% of GDP within six years, focusing on digital technology, software and biotechnology, using low-interest loans and infrastructure investment as stimulants. Apart from expansion of its science parks, leading IT companies are expanding their R&D facilities in the country drawn by high technical and scientific skills and expertise, and the familiarity of Taiwanese companies with local markets in China, "as many as 20 foreign companies, including Dell, IBM, Sony and Alcatel, have opened a total of 23 R&D bases in Taiwan since 2002", while of "300 Japanese-affiliated companies with bases in

Taiwan, 55.8% of respondents said they plan to increase or begin their R&D and product-planning activities in Taiwan." (*Nikkei Weekly* 6.9.04)

– While the country still retains its flair for coming out of the left field, with a special yacht-manufacturing zone, and out of 651 yachts of more than 80 feet ordered in 2004, 39 were built in Taiwan (Taiwan rides the tide in luxury yachts – *FT* 31.1.05).

[22] Typical of the post '97 transformation is Samsung, which has leapt to among the leading digital brands. A brief portrait (*FT* 9.3.05) recalls the company's origins in the 30s as a small dried-fish and fruit export company, with the formation of Samsung Electronics in 1969 through a joint venture with Sanyo. Still diversified around 27 subsidiaries and active in 63 businesses encompassing insurance, petrochemicals (with joint ventures with BP and Dow – *FT* 3.12.04), glass to amusement parks.

But in electronics, it manufactures not only increasingly high-end products in TVs, mobile phones and consumer devices, but also a wide range of components used by its rivals – a world leader in memories – with a third of world DRAM and SPAM chips and a fifth of world flash memories; and the largest producer of thin-film LCD screens. An earlier appraisal (*FT* 6.9.04) notes four design centres in London, Tokyo, San Francisco and Seoul, a consequence of the drastic reconstruction involving a cut in workforce by a third, sale of unprofitable businesses, including its venture into cars, substantial debt reduction, and a decision to shift focus away from volume and market share to higher value-added. This coincided with the rise of digital products where the field was relatively "a blank canvas".

Korea, however, has its own "fast followers", such as Pantech (*Nikkei Weekly* 4.10.04), which beat Samsung to introduce camera-equipped handsets and is toughing it out to lead in camera functionality.

...AN' MO' CHILLUN

The crescent of Southeast Asian coastal nations from Burma around to China all began the latter half of the 20th century thrust into "independence" from Japanese and European imperial overlords. This laid the essential foundation of a "national" aspiration to follow a Listian template, albeit that each has its own distinct cultural mix.[1] There were inevitable variations in political focus, such as the reclusive approach of Burma, and a continuing shadow of the Cold War bearing down on sources of economic influence – and aid. But it did not need Dr Mahathir's "Look East" declaration to focus attention on the demonstrably more successful development models just around the corner than those offered by conventional economic orthodoxy.

The three leading fast developers – Malaysia, Singapore and Thailand, followed by Indonesia and latterly Vietnam, have adopted the essentials of the Listian approach:

– Crucially, all conceived of "the State" as playing a key role in national development with some permutation of "Development Plans", "Industrial Investment", "Industrial Development", "Industrial Finance Board/Unit/Agency/Bank/Corporation" in their institutional structures; all employed some of the panoply of incentives, regulation, tax breaks, "zones" for export and research; and all envisaged the State as a coordinator "of productive powers" through demanding "reciprocal" performance obligations within periodic planning horizons to establish legitimacy and a common purpose.

– All gave high priority to education, with an initial emphasis on primary literacy and numerical competence, and technical/engineering /sciences in secondary and tertiary education, if initially having to rely on foreign centres for the first few decades. But with a clear purpose of enhancing their capability to "accumulate" and exploit past "discoveries".[2] And no one dealing with their officials could fail to be impressed by their technocratic competence.[3]

– Natural resources/advantages were taken as a starting point: Malaysia moved from a tin/rubber economy under the British Empire, adding palm oil and cocoa, with diversification of ownership; while

Thailand has maintained a steady agricultural base, moving from its traditional predominance of rice to maize, sugar, soya, coffee, palm oil etc, and expanding fisheries and livestock husbandry. From this base, both applied "import substitution" and "export drives" as the underlying objectives in their national contexts – national enterprises in basic industries were supported: petrochemicals (Petronas/PTT), cement, autos (Proton/Siam Motors), pulp and paper etc, drawing upon alliances with major international companies. But, taking advantage of increasing aid flows, especially from Japan as its scale of assistance to the region overtook flows from the US, with linked incentives for inward direct investment.

A measure of success has been the share of manufactures in their total exports: over 1970-95, these rose from 4.7% to 73.1% in Thailand, and 6.5% to 74.4% in Malaysia. With some surprising outcomes: Malaysia became a leader in electronic components (a trade balance rising from $1.424 million in 1970/74 to $18.4 million in 1990-94), while Thailand has earned the title of "the Detroit" of Asia, with virtually all the world's major manufacturers having facilities there, and some 2000 different companies involved in auto-related parts, machining and materials (with the total of auto-related exports on track to surpass ¥1 trillion ($8.5 billion) in 2006, with completed cars and auto parts reaching $4.4 billion in the first half of the year). While both have moved into higher value-added activities, and into the "make" dimension: in the case of Malaysia through development of its "multimedia corridor" and links with MIT, and in Thailand as companies have developed their affiliates, like Honda's Marujun, as part of their ASEAN/China networks.[4]

– Singapore, not always highlighted as one of the "tigers", is an exemplar of what can be achieved by judicious government involvement with effectively no natural resources beyond the qualities of its people:[5] without an agrarian or primary resource base, the city built on its entrepot role as a regional distribution centre,[6] and moved into financial services drawing on the strengths of its hub location.

If features of its social dirigisme have occasioned comment, through investment in infrastructure and continuous enhancement of skills and competencies, it has focused on establishing a conducive environment for inward investment – notably as the leader in achieving a "wired-up" economy. And, if a guiding light is to be sought, the City-state seems to have swallowed the Prof Porter "cluster" textbook, moving progressively from high-tech components, IT systems, and latterly into nanotechnology, biotechnology and medicine. Leading international companies in these fields number in the business directory, and with the joint development of an enterprise zone on the Indonesian island of Bintan it has secured a hinterland beyond its confined boundaries for related investment.

These countries have all enhanced GDP per capita, survived the 1997 financial crisis – with Malaysia sticking two fingers up to the conventional "globalisation" ethos by introducing capital controls – and a growth rate bouncing along at 2.5%-7%. It is a constant source of interest to observe how their enterprises are cropping up in the western capital markets game.[7] While the surge in China's growth has opened options for these "lesser tigers" to become involved. For example, Singapore has gained status as a model for controlled urban and technology development. But, if the resurgence of China has been grabbing the headlines, the parochialism of our high priests of policy, largely through reliance on the limited OECD range of data, has seriously underscored the growing impact of these countries for some time

REAL INVISIBLE HANDS

A remarkable feature of these countries, which also seems to have eluded the World Bank's study of the East Asian Miracle, is the prominence of ethnic Chinese businesses, often starting from relatively unremarkable activities – marketing agricultural produce, funding for small farmers, even developing a second-hand bicycle market. These businesses have evolved through informal familial networks, with a history of operating "invisibly" at tiers below those controlled by ruling imperial elites. In the "independence" era, many have evolved into diversified groups, taking advantage of the financial services of Singapore and Hong Kong, and increasingly acting in liaison with other groups and sources of technology from Japan and advanced Western economies. This style creates a dynamic and fluid idiom for "the co-operation of productive powers" where trust in crucial relationships reduces transaction costs, shared participation in major investments spreads risk, and such networks have been increasingly spreading across national boundaries since the 1960s. Even if their internal structures can be byzantine, this is no more than some of Europe's historic familial groups. But an adaptive business system that emulates the efficiency and learning gains of the Korean and Japanese groups, and the historic "combinations" structures of German industry. If there was a historic tendency for hereditary dissensions to introduce instability at points of generational change, the best have embraced professional technical and business expertise from leading countries in bringing up their rising generations, or increasingly brought in non-familial managerial talent.[8]

The elusiveness of this style of capitalism should not detract from recognising its increasing influence: with getting on for some 60 million in the Chinese diaspora, their aggregate turnover is comparable to the GDP of a medium-sized country like Spain. While their role in China's recent development has been substantial: from 1979 to 1991, the overseas Chinese – huaqiaos – accounted for nearly 75% of all foreign investment in China, including the migration of Hong Kong's manufacturing industry 50km up the road to Guangdong as the basis for the province's extraordinary development. By 2003, it was estimated that 80% of the stock of foreign direct investment in China is held by ethnic Chinese from the diaspora.[9]

CHINA'S MIRRORS

Despite enough entry visas to qualify as "an old friend", having earnestly received wisdom from foreign office sinologists, and shared impressions with experienced managers from Japanese trading companies, one is even more loath to add to the rising mountains of punditry on China, with barely a day passing without some new volume of interpretation. And it does not lack for advice from financial and economic commentators in the world's press. Yet its rise post-1978 has been so spectacular that it is now described as running the world economy.[10] Without having the Olympian viewpoint of *The Economist*, there seem to be a few fundamentals that condition the country's approach:

– Simply by virtue of its sheer size and diversity, the crucial dilemma posed for its rulers over centuries has been to counter the tendency for regions and provinces to pursue their own autonomy, at extremes by internecine strife. The squabble between Shanghai and Nanjing over the entrails of MG Rover was at least a commercial battle, as compared with the odd few thousand lives lost in "uprisings" in the past. This inherent tension demands some central authority, whether an Emperor and mandarinate, or "the Party".[11]

– China has inherited acute environmental constraints, exacerbated by the actions of past regimes: erosion, water control and availability, and latterly pollution, not least from the exploitation of its vast coal reserves to meet the energy demands that come with industrialisation and aspirations to Western lifestyles.[i]

– Both historically and by virtue of regional planning policies, the coastal provinces had an industrial structure more conducive to lighter

---

[i] See pp 361ff in *Collapse* by Jared Diamond (Penguin).

industry and access to international markets. If there was an imbalance in industrial structure, China has been a prototype of development in the IT era, where mobile telephony/computers have allowed more rapid information transfer than available to previous developing nations.

Yet, whatever label China gives to its progress since 1978 – something like "The Great Leapfrog" perhaps, as distinct from the 1958 "Great Leap Forward" that was less than nationally efficient, it has managed to go through the Listian chronology at breakneck speed.[12] The tradition of State control has not been without advantages. Sure, the State-Owned Enterprises (SOEs) with heavy managerial bureaucracies and over-manning by international standards, have posed a special challenge since they embraced social and welfare roles for their employees. But the Confucian respect for learning has carried through,[13] and current estimates are that China has 17 million university and advanced educational students, producing 325,000 engineers a year.[14]

If establishing national competences is an essential first step to "appropriate the attainments of former generations", as in List's prescription, by opening the national market to inward investment, initially with the usual "enterprise zone" inventory of incentives, the world's leading companies have been hurling know-how into the country. Apart from the learning and expertise built up by these new facilities, covering virtually the full range of manufacturing, electrical and IT products, the opportunities for learning via imitation and reverse engineering have risen in parallel.[15]

At the visible level of institutional change, China has a tier of "registered" groups, which acknowledges them officially and entitles them to preferential treatment: in 2000, there were 2655 such registered groups. Their parentage stems from a variety of agencies, notably the previous State Owned Enterprises, but also through transforming ministries and bureaus into business groups via holding companies – among these China Petroleum and Chemicals, China Nonferrous Metals, China Aviation Industrial, and the State Power Corporation as the largest. This process extended to provincial governments, and since their formation in the 1990s these groups have evolved through M&A, joint ventures and spin-offs. And steps had been taken to stimulate competition by breaking up erstwhile monoliths in fields such as aviation and telecoms. This evolutionary process is still underway.[16]

If the internal workings and peripheral activities of these "registered groups" is opaque, the most astounding transformation, even surprising China's leaders, has been the dynamism of rural enterprises developing from the commune and brigade-owned factories set up in the 1970s for manufacturing and servicing agricultural machines. With the reinstatement of the family financing system in 1978, the real value of agricultural output increased 6%, generating the savings that provided the initial capital for take-off of rural industrialisation. The number of rural enterprises increased from 1.52 million in 1978 to 20.15 million in 1997, by then predominantly privately owned; with financing primarily from household savings and borrowings from the informal financial market; encouraged by "entrepreneurial" provincial, urban and district authorities; with foreign direct investment (FDI), predominantly from "Great China" – the overseas Chinese – reaching $US 64.4bn by 1997; and cumulatively accounting for nearly half of China's exports.[17]

If a triumph of the informal idiom of capitalism, also a tribute to the natural verve and dedication of its people when allowed to flourish. There is a natural tendency, especially where alternative sources of finance are limited, for China's businesses to plough back returns from their rising exports into developing their own activities: if some of this investment is less than efficient by Anglo-Saxon models, it does feed into creating a dynamic competitive market.

China has had no shortage of successful Listian development models from its neighbours. For example, the first foreign language translation of the history of MITI was into Chinese. And its central officials are practised at evaluating how such models could be applied, and we should not underrate the accumulation of knowledge of international techniques and know-how, including through the return of expatriate experts and scientists.

Even so, by virtue of the sheer scale of its modernisation challenge and historic predominance of agriculture, the bias is likely to be towards the "Taiwan" model, with the State taking on the capital intensive/infrastructure obligations while supporting, with inducements and backing-finance, whether through state or local authorities, the development of a lively corporate sector. And, as in Taiwan, the distorting mirrors of interacting informal networks, with "constellations" spreading out from SOEs and regional groups, will befuddle the inexperienced new arrival.

From both perspectives, foreign companies attracted by the lip-smacking prospect of a billion-plus consumers, can expect pressures for increasing technology transfer, local content requirements, and local autonomy: and a strong continuing State role in key sectors – nuclear power, telecoms, transport infrastructure, aerospace, metals and processing industries, being but the most obvious.[18] While, just following business headlines, the State is showing a greater international profile in securing international energy and raw material resources.

If the ultimate Listian test is the enhancement of knowledge "by its own acquirements", there is evidence of growing scientific and leading-edge innovative flair, not least in IT software and biotechnology, with "high-tech zones" attracting research centres from a range of international players including GE, Intel, Siemens, Alcatel, Fuji Heavy, Roche and GSK.[19]

Such dynamism, even if unorthodox by Anglo-Saxon prescriptions, defies punditry.

AN' STILL MO' CHILLUN

The surge of nationalism following "independence" from old empires is still being repeated: the states of Eastern Europe freed from Soviet dominance, the separate states following the break-up of Yugoslavia, and the diverse kingdoms of Asia Minor now involved in a new "Great Game" in playing off the major powers for access to energy sources. If they have not all reached for their copies of Friedrich List, it is inevitable that, albeit within a new shifting international context, they too will have a strong "national" bias in their economic and social choices.

Perhaps the odd-one-out in direct Listian lineage is India: after having inherited a political, legal and administrative system as a heritage from the Raj, it moved initially in the direction of high-regulation and controls. Inevitably, not dissimilar to China, for a country of such scale and such acute levels of poverty, this pattern of centralised controls was an essential expedient to contain tensions. Sadly, this had the impact of restricting the natural talents – intelligence, adroitness, wit, and charm – of so many of its people. Now, these are being given fuller rein, with outstanding results. If, again like China, this shift is welcomed by economic pundits as the fruits of "liberalisation", the country still faces massive problems which are bound to demand a tempered policy approach. But, as a native Indian by birth, this new expression of natural flair is long overdue.

---

[1] There is a plethora of studies on the development progress and cultural interactions of these countries: for example, *Thailand's Industrialisation and Its Consequences* ed.Medhi Krongkaew (St Martin's Press). And there are short-cut overview works that analyse these distinctive patterns, and the special social and ethnic influences that distinguish them. Apart from the two World Bank studies already referred to – albeit the first on the East Asian Miracle demanding a high dose of anti-doctrinal immunisation, other suggested samplers are:

Business Systems in East Asia by Richard Whitley (Sage Publications).

Culture and Economy – the Shaping of Capitalism in Eastern Asia ed. Timothy Brook and Hy V. Luong (University of Michigan Press).

The East Asian Development Model ed.Frank-Jurgen Richter (Macmillan Press).

And there are also useful analytic essays on the region in *The Role of the State in Economic Change* ed.Ha-Joon Chang and Robert Rowthorn (Oxford).

[2] Table 8.13 in *The Rise of the "the Rest"* is a useful comparative survey.

[3] An amusing anecdote comes from the reaction of the Thai Board of Investment to the imposition of American-trained economists foisted on them by conditions imposed with US aid, "officials in the Board of Investment complained of constant criticism from 'pure economists'... who misunderstood the real world." Taiwan had apparently suffered a similar quandary and put their imposed economists to the job of presenting the country as a haven for small entrepreneurs. And with some success, obscuring the substantial holdings of the KMT government.

[4] *Nikkei Weekly* 11.7.05, with a fuller update in the *Nikkei Weekly* 4.9.06: this highlights increasing levels of investment by Toyota, Honda, Nissan and GM, with corresponding increases in export volumes in future.

[5] "After Singapore seceded from Malaysia in 1965, Lee Kuan Yew's government made the decision to achieve economic growth through foreign investment and foreign technology-driven industrialisation, with state-owned companies participating as joint-venture partners whenever possible." – *Culture and Economy* Page 166.

[6] The intense regional rivalry between governments can be illustrated by the race to develop port infrastructure. For many years, the Port of Singapore Authority (SPA) enjoyed a dominant reputation for the slickness of its systems and its efficiency, perhaps to the point of becoming complacent. But this was shaken by the Malaysian government developing a new container port at Tanjing Pelepas with aggressive pricing to attract major freight lines away from Singapore. With the massive increase in China trade, and inter-regional shipments, the battle of transhipment hubs involving also Hong Kong, Taiwan and the new portage in China is reaching epic proportions, with the prospect of a new generation of "megaships" adding to the mix. Apart from tightening its own costs, SPA has moved aggressively into investing in other ports in Europe, Asia and China to follow the growing trend for direct shipping (*FT* 15.12.04).

[7] A continuing interest in flicking through business journals is spotting the activities of major, but in British perceptions largely invisible, enterprises from these countries:

– We learn (*FT* 19.7.05) that Genting, "a Malaysian leisure group", has a 20% stake in Stanley Leisure, and 29% in London Clubs. This has become a prominent issue as Stanley has plans to expand, including development of the first UK regional super casino.

– Temasek, the Singapore state investment company, has been on a shopping spree around Asia in telecoms, banking e.g. taking a stake in Minshung Banking (*FT* 23.11.04), China's largest private bank; going for a stake in China Construction Bank (*FT* 20.6.05); and developing shopping malls in China, with the sale of its stake in the Raffles hotel chain to provide resources for future expansion (*FT* 20.7.05). Its acquisition of a stake in Standard Chartered Bank (Temasek stake secures StanChart's independence: *FT* 28.3.06) was noted as only the latest element in its expanding interests in financial services, currently estimated at US$20bn (Temasek adds strength to regional portfolio: *FT* 29.3.06). With indications of growing concern among Asian governments at Temasek's continuing expansion – its takeover of Shin Corp, the Thai telecoms group, in particular having triggered a political crisis (Predator plots a course across Asia: *FT* 7.9.06).

A convenient update (Temasek evolving into a global investor – *Nikkei Weekly* 3.10.05) points to further steps to increase its capital, "The company issued US $1.75 billion worth of 10-year dollar bonds on Sept. 14, and plans to ultimately raise US $5 billion over the medium term… Temasek is expanding its overseas investments not only in neighbouring countries like Indonesia and Malaysia, but also in the new economies of Brazil, Russia, India and China, the so-called BRICs nations."

[8] There is a rapidly growing literature on the Chinese diaspora, but perhaps the breakthrough study was Gordon Redding's *The Spirit of Chinese Capitalism* (de Gruyter), written from his then vantage point of the Business Centre at the University of Hong Kong. This explores their characteristics of internal organisation, business focus, and strengths and vulnerabilities, with examples drawn from the Philippines, Taiwan, Hong Kong, Indonesia, Singapore, Thailand and Malaysia. An interesting historical background is offered by *The Encyclopaedia of the Chinese Overseas*, Edited Lynn Pau (Archipelago Press, Singapore), a publication of the Chinese Heritage Centre.

Apart from the examples cited by Gordon Redding, a helpful portrait of one such family group is *Robert Kuok and the Chinese Business Network* by Heng Pek Koon in *Culture and Economy* op. cit. But among the most affectionately vivid is *Li Ka-Shing* by Anthony B.Chan (Oxford). Drawing out some of the characteristics of this idiom:

– On "transaction speed", the apocryphal example is Li Ka-Shing requiring "a mere seventeen hours to buy Hong Kong Electric", the power generator on Hong Kong Island, which came on the market when Jardine's Hong Kong Land was in trouble, though he subsequently remarked: "Take away the eight hours of bedtime and the whole process actually took nine hours."

But from personal observance, I was privileged to be one of the only four *gwilos* – the others being David Wilson*, then Political Adviser to the Government, Peter Thomson from the embassy in Beijing and the Hong Kong Trade Commissioner – in Hong Kong's first commercial delegation to Guangdong in 1981. The rest of the delegation was composed of thrusting local businessmen, all probably billionaires by now, one would guess. The itinerary included visits to a string of factories, all at the time in the category of "Soviet-primitive". Yet, it required only a quick sketch of the dimensions of a metal-pressing, machined component, switch device, or whatever, an exchange about price/volume of order, an initialled card, and "My man will be along tomorrow to complete the details", for a deal to be concluded. And some of our delegates were turning over half a dozen such tricks an hour. This was before mobile phones, so the potential trick-speed now must be measured in seconds.

– "Combinations" through informal networks are by their very nature elusive. But the biography of Li Ka-Shing, apart from its account of an extraordinary personality – having attended a meeting where he called on DTI's Secretary of State, perhaps also one of the most self-effacing – is an illustration of the idiom of developing a business through a series of opportunistic alliances, spreading risks and drawing in appropriate expertise, where integrity is an essential adhesive. Combinations of such groups build up gearing to take on liabilities that would be beyond the capacity of each individually. But the curious quirk of many of the major overseas Chinese houses is a penchant for hotel chains, but they all have "a diversified group" structure with byzantine ownership structures.

– Exploiting dual-systems: this structure of informal relationships functions in parallel with, and occasionally in a supporting role to, an increasing adeptness at playing the "capital markets" game. Again taking Li Ka-Shing as an exemplar, he creamed off nearly $20bn from selling Orange, its 2G telecoms operator. While bringing Hong Kong Telecom – once the jewel in Cable & Wireless's portfolio but also surely a continuing prize for Li Ka-Shing – into "the family" was achieved by a takeover through PCCW, a company run by No. 2 son, Richard Li: at the time, PCCW's financial structure was viewed as relatively weak, yet clearly there was a perception that the resources of the Li Ka-Shing Hutchinson empire were behind it. While the growth of Hutchinson has been spectacular, with 27 supermarkets and 100 drug stores in mainland China, and 3500 stores in Europe (*The Economist* 8.1.05). And its build-up by acquisitions/joint-venture developments in ports has accumulated over 13% of the world market with 35 ports in 17 countries (*FT* 15.12.04).

– Succession dilemmas: one of the most frequent tensions in dynastic businesses comes at generational junctures – notable examples would be Tata, where Ratan is staying on as chief executive into his 70s to sort out the succession, and Reliance, where there has been factional squabbling between brothers. Perhaps the most intriguing succession was Sir Y.J. Pao's World Wide Shipping, since he had three daughters and no sons: onlookers expected a replay of King Lear, but the eldest daughter had married Helmut Sohmen, who turned out to be an outstanding custodian despite hailing from landlocked Austria (*FT* 25.10.04).

An update on the impact of the 1997 financial crisis on these groups is provided in *Business Groups in East Asia* ed. Sea-Jin Chang (Oxford). One of the attractions of these essays is that they are mostly compiled by native commentators, with a historic scope reaching back before the financial crises of the 90s. The striking message is the resilience of these group structures: some, particularly in Indonesia and South Korea may have collapsed from unsustainable debts, yet elements were taken up by other more viable groups; the passing of political leaders severing the links of patronage can have a major impact; the more viable groups, despite government efforts to rationalise them, have a rugged persistence; and in Taiwan, least affected by the Asian crisis, but responding to pressures for greater liberalisation, the native business groups have attained an even higher influence in the economy.

[9] The persistence of ties between the overseas Chinese community and the provinces in terms of their family and origins has been superbly documented in *Overseas Chinese Business Networks in Asia* by Michael Backman, a study commissioned by the Australian government. Setting out the diversity of provincial clan societies and clubs in South Asian capitals, and their continuing links, even before 1979, it is a compendium of network contact information.

[10] *How China runs the world economy* (*The Economist* 30.7.05). The summary reads, "Everyone knows that most TVs and T-shirts are made in China. But so, in some ways, are developed countries' inflation rates, interest rates, wages, profits, oil prices and even house prices – or at least they are strongly influenced by what happens in China." In which case, the condescension of China attending the G8 confabs by invitation is all the more blatant, and the patient forbearance of China's delegates the most striking instance of stoicism. Even though one suspects a glint in their eyes as they look forward to comeuppance for the lectures and hectoring that they have to suffer.

[11] "Empires wax and wane; states cleave asunder and coalesce" is the opening line of China's 14th century historical narrative *The Romance of the Three Kingdoms,* echoed, 120 chapters later, in the closing lines, "States fall asunder and re-unite; empires wax and wane." The sagas of the "warring states" are imprinted in popular memory, while the Taiping Rebellion is a vivid reminder of the human cost of "cleaving asunder" (*God's Chinese Son* by Jonathan Spence (Harper Collins)). And more recent history is a vivid pointer to national vulnerability when the country is divided.

The maxim from *The Romance* should resonate with Britain's imperial history. But a more direct parallel lies in the continuing tensions in the governance of India under the Raj, which required a mandarinate, the Indian Civil Service, backed by military force: in more honest accounts of the Raj, there was barely a day unaccompanied by some repressive display of force somewhere (*Raj – The Making and Unmaking of British India* by Lawrence James (Little, Brown and Company)).

This inherent tension makes forecasting China's future problematic, and a non-committal tone of speculation concludes John Gittings' account *The Changing Face of China* (Oxford), drawing upon several decades of close familiarity, or as close as Western observers can expect to get: but a fascinating account of the doctrinal tensions beneath the Marxist overlay, where Confucianism and the ideas of SunYat Sen remained components of continuing schismatic shifts and debates.

A balanced and vivid insight into the human dimension of China's transformation is offered in *China Shakes the World* by James Kynge (Weidenfeld & Nicholson). It also offers a contemporary variation on the opening line of *The Romance*: "When reform is too fast there is chaos. When reform is too slow there is stagnation", a maxim propounded by Cao Siyuan, one of China's dogged reformers attributed with having played a key role in devising the country's first bankruptcy law.

[12] Let's just recall List's "teachings of history" based on Britain's early industrialisation, "...having attained to a certain grade of development by means of free trade... they sought, by a system of restrictions, privileges, and encouragement, to transplant on to their native soil the wealth, the talents, and the spirit of enterprise of the foreigners." (*The National System of Political Economy* ibid)

[13] My most vivid reminder was being put up in the Commercial Counselor's Lodge of Hong Kong Island after a stint of negotiations in China. He was having a Scottish dancing evening, and the last thing one could face was the noise and spectacle of Britain's answer to the dervishes, so a room out of earshot with a bottle of Scotch seemed the surest retreat. The room already had an occupant of like mind, someone from the British Council, who confirmed that he too had just spent a few weeks in China. He recounted that, even in relatively small urban and village areas, it was common to find class sizes of 120-130 of 13-year-olds learning A-level maths.

[14] The figures are drawn from *China Inc.* by Ted C. Fishman (Simon & Schuster).

[15] Complaints about piracy are legion: among the best illustrations is that Honda were finding its motorbike sales undermined by cheap Chinese look-alikes, so it established a facility in Vietnam to produce its own cheaper look-alikes. But to illustrate the sophistication to which piracy can extend: Sony has been engaged in a five-year investigation of piracy of its PlayStation games console. This apparently "unearthed a web of at least 10 subcontractors' with a production capacity of 50,000 units a day for PlayStation consoles and controllers, as well as 'modifying chips'." Among the chain of subcontractors was "a prison in Shenzen" (*FT* 22.12.04).

[16] For a more thorough account, see *Chinese Business Groups: Their Origin and Development* by Donghoon Hahn and Keun Lee in *Business Groups in East Asia* ibid.

[17] Again, the rise of the rural enterprise economy in China, if spectacular in impact, has the elusive quality of the informal style of capitalism. Among the most authoritative and balanced accounts is *Chinese Rural Industrialisation in the Context of the East Asian Miracle* by Justin Yifu Lin and Yang Yao of Peking University in *Rethinking the East Asian Miracle* (World Bank). China's economic census in 2005 indicated that the number of private enterprises had increased to more than 30 million (*FT* 26.8.05).

[18] A neat potted account of the "infant industry" approach is China's intention to develop its Liquid Natural Gas (LNG) carrier industry. "At China's state-owned Hudong Zhonghua shipyards near Shanghai, a liquefied-natural gas carrier with its trademark camel-like humps is taking shape.... Officials at Hudong are keen to play down the significance of the deal, signed in August, to build five LNG carriers. 'We have no technological edge at all over shipbuilders in Korea and Japan,' said a Hudong official, who asked not to be named. 'Our success was the result of strong backing from the government.

Few doubt that China is already on track to eclipse Japan and to become a formidable long-term competitor to South Korea.

In the short term, Chinese market share will receive a boost from a policy dictating that new LNG import contracts include provisions for ships to be built in local yards. It coincides with a strategic decision by China to develop an advanced shipbuilding industry to go hand-in-hand with a navy capable of projecting power into the oceans of the Asia-Pacific now controlled by the US and its allies.

But Chinese companies are increasingly able to win contracts on their own terms. Labour-intensive manufacturing gives them the flexibility to make customised ships, an important advantage over the Japanese, where the process is fine-tuned and largely inflexible. Yet cheap labour is only part of the story.

"China is investing [during the present boom] what it takes to match the Koreans," says Mr Batra (a director of Drewry, the shipping consultants and brokers). "In my mind, it is only a question of money, and the will to do it. And in every case, China has shown that they have the money, and definitely the will." (*FT* 17.12.04)

China seems to have even skipped through Britain's old Navigation Acts. But for a really comic aside, the same edition of the *FT* included a piece by their resident economic guru, Samuel Brittan, entitled "There is no such thing as the state".

But how about civil nuclear energy:

"Super-efficient nuke reactor set for trial
October 5, 2005 – China Daily
Author(s):Fu Jing

Chinese scientists are planning super-efficient nuclear reactors that can maximise uranium burn-up and minimise waste in the generation of electricity.

If the first experimental reactor, set to be in operation by 2010, is successful, the technology could help relieve China's uranium supply problems as the country accelerates nuclear power plant construction. China Academy of Atomic Science President, Zhao Zhixiang, said a team of scientists has already mapped a detailed plan to speed up research and utilisation of the so-called next-generation fast reactors. The new reactors are expected to burn 60-70 per cent of their uranium fuel - a conventional reactor consumes only 0.7 per cent of the uranium it is fed.

"This kind of reactor can greatly improve the efficiency of fuel burn-up, and we are trying our best to put the experimental reactor into use over the next five years," Zhao said.

Current reactors are only able to harness the power of 0.7 per cent of the radioactive isotopes found in natural uranium. In the fast reactor, the process is optimised so that more of the previously untapped isotopes can be used to generate electricity, burning-up fuel at least 60 times more efficiently than in a normal reactor.

"We will have no concerns over fuel supply if such reactors are used to generate electricity commercially," Zhao said.

China started research into fast nuclear reactor technology in 1995 and invested 1.38 billion yuan (US \$170.2 million) into the construction of the experimental reactor.

"I hope an experimental reactor with a capacity of 200,000 kilowatts can be put into use by 2010," Zhao said. He added that construction of the reactor is close to completion but did not identify the site of the project under the High and New Technology Research and Development Program of the Chinese Government. He also said plans for a fast-reactor prototype are expected to be included in the country's medium-and long- term science and technology development blueprints.

The prototype reactor, with a capacity of 600,000 kilowatts, will be constructed and put into operation by 2020, Zhao said, adding: "After that, we will consider commercial operation of the reactor."

As China's economy keeps developing rapidly, demand for power also keeps increasing. To meet its growing energy demands, China has mapped out a national plan to increase nuclear generating capacity to 36,000 megawatts by 2020, up from 8700 megawatts today. The proportion of national power output supplied by nuclear energy is expected to rise from 2.3 per cent now to 4 per cent.

A senior official from the National Development and Reform Commission told China Daily that the country will have an even more ambitious plan to generate nuclear power after 2020.

"All the plans urged our researchers to develop our own core technologies for the reactors," said the official, who declined to be named. "And I personally believe the fast reactor will play a leading role during the 2040-50 period in China's nuclear plant construction."

Apart from fast reactor research, China has also made a breakthrough in gas-cooled nuclear reactors, which can generate considerably higher temperatures than conventional nuclear reactors, leading to a high power generating capacity. Using helium as a coolant, the reactor, mainly developed by researchers from Tsinghua University, is also able to shut down and cool automatically in an emergency. Senior State Council officials have called for early commercial application of China's first gas-cooled nuclear reactor to help restructure China's energy supplies strategy.

Most of the nuclear reactors currently in operation in China rely on technology imported from France and Russia."

[19] Just as samplers of China's intent to evolve its capacities for a leading role in new technologies:

– Founder Holdings Ltd:

"The company virtually owns the market for Chinese-language electronic publishing systems, both inside China and just about anywhere else in the world where Chinese newspapers and magazines are published and read. Founder has staged rapid growth with its proprietary technologies and own-brand products, and has established a solid foothold in Japan. The firm is now looking towards its ultimate goal of making a name for itself in the markets of the West.

Global share 90%

Cheung Shuen Lung, the company's president, speaks proudly of Founder's accomplishments. "We hold around a 90% share of the Chinese newspaper market worldwide". Founder's systems for editing, publishing and printing newspapers and magazines are found everywhere among the 2000-odd companies that make China's newspaper industry, and they are also commonplace among print media for ethnic Chinese readers in Hong Kong, Taiwan, Southeast Asia and beyond.

The firm's parent company, Peking University Founder Group Corp (Peking Founder), was established in 1988 as a wholly owned subsidiary of Peking University. Peking Founder is a wide umbrella organisation that covers companies for everything from PC manufacturing to pharmaceutical production, but at the core of the group sits Founder Holdings, which oversees all the IT operations of the group.

Dreaming big

Founder Holdings operates out of Hong Kong and has a number of subsidiaries, including a business for newspaper editing systems and one for banking systems. Its sales of HK 2 billion (US 257 million) for the year to December 2004 accounted for only around 10% of total Peking Founder group sales, but the parent company nevertheless considers the IT business its core operation.

Cheung recalls the dream of company founder Wang Xuan: "First we will make a success with the Chinese language, then we will enter the Japanese market, which is 10 times larger, and eventually we will do printing software for the West." For Cheung, the most important thing about Peking Founder is that it was spawned from the Chinese character-processing technologies of Peking University.

When Founder entered the Japanese market in 1996, it instructed its research and development group in China to focus their efforts on publishing systems for the Japanese language. Now many companies in Japan use Founder systems, including Nikkan Sports Printing Co, a number of major newspaper companies and magazine publisher Recruit Co. Founder's experience building a wealth of systems for the global Chinese-language market gives it the ability to quickly customise systems for clients in Japan. "Japanese companies are extraordinarily demanding, so every single project is a challenge for the R&D team," Cheung said.

Ticket gates, maps

Last September, Founder partnered with Omron Corp. to begin a business around automatic ticket gates systems for subways in China. This is a market that is huge and growing, as more large cities in China draw up plans for subways. Founder has also linked up with Japan's map publisher Shobunsha Publications Inc. to develop digital maps for China." (*Nikkei Weekly* 25.7.05)

– Lifesciences Investment: "Medical and related biotechnology research is among its top scientific priorities. In fact, China is developing a large population of researchers working in the life sciences. In biotech alone, the country boasts fifty thousand research scientists, with another forty five hundred graduating from universities every year. China also works hard to attract Chinese scientists who have been trained and have worked abroad. The Shenzhen biotech corridor is one example of a local government luring scientists to private enterprise, but across the country there are similar efforts to attract foreign-trained scientists into Chinese academia. China offers returning scholars high positions and salaries commensurate with what they were making abroad.... The country is pouring no less than $600 million a year, much of it aimed at a rapidly growing market." (*China Inc.*pp224ff)

The report of a DTI-sponsored mission on stem cell research concluded that the region's researchers had "powered ahead" recently to match – and sometimes surpass – their counterparts in Europe and North America. "Researchers in China, South Korea and Singapore are as talented as their UK counterparts," the mission's report said. "They are probably better funded and equipped. The perspective is more long-term in all three countries.... The challenge to western pre-eminence in stem cell science from China, Singapore and South Korea is real.

"Where stem cell research in China is unique in our experience is in the drive to the clinic. There is much less resistance than will be met in the West to pursuing experimental therapies into clinical practice". (*FT* 6.1.05)

– "Gendicine is the only gene therapy in the world to have received regulatory approval, after it was authorised by China's State Food and Drug Administration. The drug was developed by Peng Zhaohui, a Chinese scientist who founded SiBiono, a private company, in 1998 after his return from the US, where he was a visiting professor at the University of California.... Dr Peng points out that human genes cannot be patented. The crucial p53 gene that Gendicine uses for its therapy is thought to be a fault in more than half of tumours, and has been widely studied. The tricky bit is engineering a virus that can deliver the gene to the tumour safely. SiBiono holds a Chinese patent for this process and for the drug and has applied for international versions.

Dr Peng opened SiBiono's laboratories in Shenzen with seed money from Beijing's science and technology fund. The company has since received about $40m (£21m) in this state aid and more than $60m in private investment from the domestic pharmaceutical industry. The company is using the funds to build a new facility with the capacity to produce 150m doses of Gendicine a year, equal to $581m to $968m in annual sales, with the help of New Brunswick Scientific, a US supplier of laboratory equipment." (*FT* 1.4.05)

– Huawei's international expansion: when Huawei turned up as a potential buyer of Marconi, commentators were nonplussed by its corporate status. Typical were comments in *The Guardian* (9.8.05), "Huawei, based in Shenzhen, was founded in 1988 by Ren Zhengfei, a former officer in the People's Liberation

Army. It is not a publicly quoted company and its ownership structure remains unclear, but given its success in securing a favourable $10bn (£5.6 bn) from the China Development Bank last year (as reported by the *FT* 3.1.05, this was a $10bn credit line, intended to help the company compete with rivals such as Ericsson, Cisco Systems, and China's ZTE Corp), the assumption among analysts is that the Chinese government has some form of stake... as one telecoms insider who has visited Huawei's Shenzhen facility put it: 'They can employ more research and development PhDs per pound than any company in the Western world.'"

THE OLD GUARD

The conventional jargon is to refer to a "European" style of capitalism, which is no more than to say "them's different". For, across old Europe, there are probably as many variants on the capitalist theme as there are countries, and each with a distinct idiom:[1] a mixed gouache depending upon national circumstances and resources; patterns of regional devolution; trade, guilds, crafts, ownership, cooperative and labour networks; and national support systems of education, finance and infrastructure. Yet there are certain qualities that they share and underlie this perceived distinction.

In pursuing industrialisation in the 19th century, none had the same advantages of private accumulation from "the plantations" as Britain had enjoyed in the first industrial revolution. Notably, all accepted "the state" as a player/guarantor of the investment/risks inherent in catching up in the capital-intensive chemicals, metals, railway and electrical industries. And, while the traditional corporate structures had been family oriented with "protection" via devices of differential voting rights, cross-ownership, cross-representation on supervisory boards, holding companies etc, many in these and related industries were also drawn into the evolving cartel structures of the European market.[2]

Even Holland, which historically had a "capital market" before London, also had a strong tradition of inter-linked boards and a government that could not avoid involvement since typically 30-40% or more of public expenditure was devoted to keeping the country physically afloat. At the other extreme, the Sociéte Générale of Belgium was in effect a comprehensive State Corporation. In between, there has been scarcely a variant of the permutations of relations between state and industry that any developing country, confronted by outrage from liberal economic theorists, could not point to as precedents, including family dynasties that wield "distorting" influence with Wallenberg and Agnelli at the top of the list.

After the Portuguese, Spanish and Dutch pursuit of Empire had run out of "stretch", apart from a few pockets around the globe, the only serious contender to Britain in the "acquire lands" business was France, whose West Indian colonies were more productive and competitive than those of

Britain, and evolved a distinct Creole culture. But even France, after the wars of 1793-1815, expulsion from Saint Domingue, conceding the Louisiana Purchase and withdrawal from Mexico had to yield the palm of "free-trade imperialism".[3] And Britain became the prime spokesman of "free-trade" hypocrisy – but not to say that others entirely gave up the "acquired lands" game, such as France's colonisation of Indochina, the Dutch in Indonesia, Russia's expansion eastwards, and the general scrum in the scramble for Africa. Until World War II marked the final play of the "acquired lands" business.

OUR FRENCH COUSINS

For some reason, the French seem to have attracted an undue share of ire from the dogmatic wing of the liberal economic fraternity. This has latched onto "the national champions" tag – despite some of their major firms being leading contributors to British employment and exports.[4] From fairly continuous involvement with the French, apart from a natural intelligence, wit and sophistication, their most refreshing quality is a total absence of dogma, rather a professional pragmatism. What probably gets up these pundits' noses is that despite their engaging scepticism of economic dogma, France has performed remarkably well in the post-World War II era, and, in some fields, done so precisely by ignoring the sacred shibboleths of economic theory.[5]

France has had quite as exciting a history as any,[6] and has its own roster of notables in science,[7] and, indeed, philosophy and economics (apparently, the term *laissez-faire* was coined by Thomas Le Gendre (1638-1706), who appropriately owned vast interests in Africa and the New World). But, more recently, Jean Monnet was one of the founders of the European project. With a developed system for educating engineers, technologists and commercial disciplines well in advance of Britain by the late 19th century: indeed, the London School of Economics was "intended as a mixture of the political and commercial *grandes écoles* of Paris".[i] While the country was an early leader in several industries, such as aviation, motor vehicles (Renault taxies were among the first in London), cinematography etc.

Historically, France has had a dynamic private tradition[8] –Saint-Gobain tracing its history back to 1665 maintained its predominant family tradition through its growth through merger in the late 19th century, as did

---

[i] See *Management and Business in Britain and France*, ed. Youssef Cassis, François Creouzet, Terry Gourvish (Oxford).

the early auto-pioneers of Citroen, Peugeot and Renault, the aerospace leaders of Breguet, Potez and Gnome & Rhone, while Rhone-Poulenc was a leader in chemical processes. The 1930s Depression, Occupation and post-war stringencies enforced rationalisation, with inevitably increased involvement of the state, including, for example, SNECMA absorbing the old Gnome & Rhone. On the other hand, the French retail sector has remained stolidly private, including major international players such as Carrefour and Casino.

Yet, the "state" has historically been viewed as a guarantor of the nation's well being: one recalls an eminent ex-Minister heading one of their corporations, summarising, "the French love the State, but hate politicians". And, reflecting their national pragmatism, from the 20s the Société d'Economie Mixte was formulated whereby the government would have a joint venture stake, and applied particularly to infrastructure developments. But the device was used to create Air France in 1935, bring arms industries under national control in the 30s, and to create the national railway company in 1938[9] – the French are adept at the "mixte" approach, including "credit mixte" in support of their aggressive overseas sales drives.

Particular ire is inspired by their support of "national champions".[10] This line of criticism ignores France's unabashed immodesty in admitting the role of "the state", but also their pragmatic recognition of the nature of modern manufacturing; the post-World War II pressures to rationalise and establish internationally competitive enterprises; and the technocratic expertise that underlay the success of this approach.[11] The French will listen politely to criticisms, but point, with a shrug, to industries where the system has been successful, even if admitting that electronics/computing has been a weakness, though many others, including Britain, have not been notably more successful.

---

[1] There are several readily available commentaries, even if no direct personal contacts have allowed, of the cultural variations in economic components between countries – *The Seven Cultures of Capitalism* by Charles Hampden-Turner and Fons Trompenaars (Doubleday), covers the main European countries, with a wryly detached commentary on the quirks of the British system. And *Business and Politics* by Graham Wilson (Macmillan) is a handy reminder of the widely differing interfaces between the state and business in Europe, which, despite "globalisation" and the endless preaching of the OECD, World Bank etc, retain a remarkably sticky resilience.

A gem is *European Business Systems* ed. Richard Whitley (Sage) with contributions on Holland; the strikingly distinct Danish evolution of farmers cooperatives/railway towns, with its strengths in foodstuffs (and latterly biotechnology), and the "bottom-up" evolution of garment and furniture complexes; the vertical integration from forest and mineral industries followed in Finland and Sweden, extending into strengths in electronics and IT (though not the outstanding emergence of Nokia from the forests of Finland); and posing the contrast between this pattern of industrial evolution compared to the wool industries of Australia and New Zealand, where despite being the world leaders in the raw material, under imperial dominance neither evolved the higher-value processing industries (comparable to Britain's destruction of the Indian cotton industry, noted by List) since this was reserved for the metropolitan economy.

While *Country Competitiveness*, ed. Bruce Kogurt (Oxford) has a range of vignettes covering France, Germany and Italy (and, incidentally, the best summary of the evolution of the Toyota production system, by Mark Fruin).

[2] *Family Capitalism*, ed. Geoffrey Jones and Mary Rose (Cass), contains some useful illustrations of the family business evolution and its response to pressures, with examples from Britain, US, Holland and France.

[3] An account of the distinctive French approach to "acquired lands" is given in *The Construction of the French Colonial System* in *The Making of New World Slavery* by Robin Blackburn (Verso).

[4] The list can be readily compiled beginning with the obvious names of Lafarge, Michelin, Dowty-Meco, Peugeot, while Renault/Nissan's plant in Sunderland is rated the most efficient in Europe, and Saint-Gobain's plate-glass plant at Eggborough in Yorkshire won the Best Factory Award in 2005 (*FT* 21.9.05).

[5] It does not take a visitor long to identify the development of TGV system, aerospace, space technology, road network, and civil airport development. But perhaps outstanding has been France's development of a nuclear power industry: just to cite a US commentary:

"Of all the mistakes the US nuclear industry made in the 1960s and 70s, the single most damaging was the failure to settle on one or a few standard designs for nuclear plants. Standardisation maximises learning. It allows people to learn from others' experience as well as from their own. But the utilities never saw any need for it.

Why not? For one thing, utilities were accustomed to custom-building their fossil-fuel plants, and it had never been a problem. Also, no part of the utility industry was really conscious of how much something cost. The utilities themselves, as regulated monopolies, got paid according to their expenses – as long as the cost of a generating plant wasn't unreasonable, the utility was allowed to set its rates to get a reasonable return on its investment. and the companies that build plants for the utilities – including nuclear plants – generally were paid on a cost-plus basis. Perhaps if the utility industry had been more cost conscious, it would have been more interested in standardisation as a way to keep down costs.

Finally, since nuclear technology was changing so rapidly during the 1960s and 1970s, with the designs steadily improving, there never seemed to be a good point at which to stop and standardise.

As it was, the utilities ordered each nuclear plant as a custom unit, and the sizes of those units increased yearly throughout the 1960s and into the 1970s – 300 megawatts, 600, 900, and eventually as large as 1200....

By contrast, the French nuclear industry did standardise, and it avoided many of the problems that plagued the US industry. Throughout the 1960s, France began construction on only a few units, all of them gas-graphite reactors developed by the French nuclear industry. In 1969, President Georges Pompidou decided to switch technology from the homegrown reactor to US-designed light-water reactors. Five years later, after the Arab oil embargo, the French national programme took off, ordering 16 reactors in 1974 and another 12 in 1976. By this point, the French had a decade of US experience to learn from, and they took advantage of it.

France's one utility, the state-owned Electricité de France (EdF), decided that all its reactors would be based on a single design licensed from Westinghouse. One company, Framatome, would build the pressurised-water reactors, while another, Alsthom-Atlantique, would have a monopoly on the steam turbines paired with the reactors. EdF itself would design and build the remainder of each nuclear plant. Under this arrangement, the French nuclear programme maximised learning. Not only did it benefit from any of the mistakes made by the US program in the 1960s and early 1970s, but also focused its own experience by standardising everything it could. This included the reactors and turbines, the plant designs, the control rooms, and even the construction procedures and contracts. Framatome did increase the size of its reactors, but, unlike its American counterparts, it did so slowly, taking the time to learn how its reactors performed before changing them significantly. Its earliest reactors, first sold in 1970, were 900 megawatts. From there Framatome moved to 1300 megawatts in 1976 and finally to 1450 megawatts in 1987.

The care and caution paid off. The French nuclear programme has been one of the world's most economic. It's plants cost $1 billion to $1.5 billion apiece – about $1000 per kilowatt, or about what the most economical American plants cost and half the average cost of US nuclear plants. EdF has consistently built plants in six years or less, much more quickly than most American utilities, which has also helped keep costs down. And once the plants opened, they are very reliable, ranking among the world's best in the percentage of time they are available to generate electricity." *Beyond Engineering* by Robert Pool (Oxford).

Needless to say, Britain made the wrong choice of technology, sticking with AGRs. But also had these built by different consortia, none of which still exist. And the same policy of custom-design and competitive tendering in coal-fired power stations has meant that of more than 60 built in the post-war period, only two are arguably the same. While Britain has no manufacturing capability for boilers and turbines left.

[6] In many respects Britain has had a relatively quiet time: Simon Schama's

Citizens (Allen Lane) is an extraordinary account of what a real revolution actually involves. And if the subsequent Napoleonic sweep of imperial ambition was not entirely successful, the old guy left a permanent legacy in the Civil Code, which has served as a model beyond national boundaries, and other legal codes for a unified system.

[7] Flick through any account of scientific development, and the names Amontens, Ampère, Bèmont, Biot, Bouguer, Carnot, Coulomb, Curie... will fall out.

[8] *The Large Family Firm in Twentieth Century France* by Emmanuel Chadeau (*Family Capitalism* op. cit.). But the categorisation of firms need to take account of other quirks: Michelin, still a private company, has the legal status as a *société en commandite par actions* – a French limited partnership by shares – providing "a rock-solid defence against hostile takeover" (*FT* 6.10.04).

[9] Covered more fully in *Sixty Million Frenchmen Can't Be Wrong* by Jean-Benoit Nadeau and Julie Barlow (Robson Books), an entertaining survey of the distinct characteristics of the French by two Canadian authors, probably as good a perspective from which to make cross-cultural comparisons.

[10] As a recent carbuncle of this old complaint, the *FT* Leader "Fortress France talks of raising drawbridge" (31.8.05) occasioned by the announcement a few days earlier by France's industry Minister "that the government was developing a list of "strategic" sectors to be declared off-limits to foreign bidders" confirms that picking old sores is still a preoccupation of theorists.

[11] To give full credit to the French, they have been implementing "supply chain management" long before it became a theme in the guru management jargon, except they use the term "filière". The "national champion" – whether in nuclear power, aerospace, space technology, shipbuilding etc – is the apex of a linked chain of suppliers, and, as was vividly illustrated by hassles over allocating key components and technology of Concorde, the objective is to ensure that the essential links in the chain are within national control. The viability of the structure depends on the continuity of orders flowing down to suppliers, and the role of the "national champion", with the repertoire of state support, is to secure sufficient orders from international markets to keep this continuity going. A formula that would not come as a surprise to the top management of Toyota.

PART IV:

GET OUT THE SHOVELS

The credentials for this quick Cook's Tour around industrial development history are impeccable. Schumpeter apparently concluded, "if, starting my work in economics afresh, I was told that I could study only one of the fundamentals fields of economic analysis, [economic history, statistics, or theory] but could have my choice, it would be economic history that I should choose." Yet the school of "we're all intellectuals, really," and the "Balliol's buggered us" tradition would not take even a cheap bucket-shop package. Instead, stalwart denial is the conditioned reflex: even an erstwhile Director General of CBI can declare, to punditry applause, "it feels right that if companies are locked in ever more global competition, so too must countries be. But this assumption is almost entirely wrong.... it is in fact close to impossible to apply the term "competitiveness" to nations."[1]

For an update to the new millennium, we need look no further than the declaration by Gordon Brown, when Chancellor of the Exchequer, that "my visits to Asia, especially to China, have convinced me that Asia is in no doubt that it is in a race to the top – investing in technology, innovation, science and skills..." (*FT* 9.9.05). This might, might, be symptomatic of a twitch slightly different from traditional reflexes, since presumably his utterance reflected some input from the plume-wielding scribes of the Treasury. And his subsequent visit the following month to Beijing to chair the G7/G20 Finance Ministers meeting should have revealed the pathetic level of UK exports to China compared to Japan, Germany, France, Italy, Taiwan and South Korea. For his sentiments have been repeated by various British commentators down the decades for at least the past 150 years with, instead of "Asia", from the mid-1800s "America and Germany"; post-World War I "Germany and Japan"; and post-World War II "Germany, France, and Japan". And every declaration accompanied by continued British atrophy.

So, "What's new?" There has been a "race to the top" going on for at least two centuries. And the supreme historic irony is that Britain, clinging to the "free trade" and "markets" guff of its days of imperial supremacy, has never learned to compete against other nations, initially compelled by

Britain's dominance to adopt a "national" focus in evolving their "productive powers". And whose success prompted emulation from other rising industrial nations. But, over time, this country has simply failed to evolve the breadth of technocratic competences and expertise to think coherently in these terms, leave alone develop the repertoire of institutions and social infrastructure to exploit the nation's potential. Set aside the macho national spin in which politicians are prone to depict their self-proclaimed successful management of Britain's economy, but revisiting the main countries covered in our Cook's Tour through the patents granted by the US Patent and the Trademark Office, taken as a broad surrogate measure of the effectiveness of national innovation efforts, even by 2001 the UK (2,695) had been surpassed by South Korea (3,538) and Taiwan (5,371), while still lagging behind France (4,041), Germany (11,260), Japan (33,223) and the US (87,670).

Moreover, like all glib political analogies, the Chancellor's metaphor of "a race to the top" carries false connotations. There is no "top". Recalling Sochiro Honda's maxim, "There is no end to technology", the leading competitors are continuously pushing the "top" higher so that "catching up" becomes pursuit up an increasingly more demanding slope.[2] And unsurprisingly, it is the country that has "caught up" successfully twice, currently surrounded by the most aggressive pursuers, and in closest proximity to the "threat" of China that has most assiduously mastered this lesson. According to Nikkei's annual survey of the research intentions of Japanese companies, 304 major companies plan a combined $94.1 billion in their R&D budgets in financial 2005, "up 4.9% from the previous year's final figures, marking the sixth straight year of growth."[3]

A rationale of "diminishing returns" and "wait-and-see" is not going to encourage British industry to achieve anything like this momentum in "the race". Moreover, for decades, whereas in Britain (and the US) the government has accounted for 70% or more of national R&D, in Japan the private sector has traditionally been the predominant R&D investor. All their recent Nobel Prize winners, for example, have been company employees. One consequence is that, with the virtual disappearance of a tier of mid/large industrial companies, the UK is even less equipped to engage in this race against competitors who are raising the thresholds of competitive technologies.[4]

It's always tempting to engage in that favourite national pastime, "It's some other bugger's fault". But, instead of apportioning blame in a traditional buck-passing debate, a more fruitful slant is to query, "Who is there who can absolve themselves from contributing to national decline?" And, by our peculiar perverse logic, it is invariably those with the highest professed motives and a self-proclaimed excellence as among "the best" who have the strongest grounds for exempting themselves from absolution.

THE UNRIVALLED SERVICES OF THE CITY

While Germany was evolving a banking system and co-operative structures to support and spread risks for the industrial investment to gain a leading position in the "Second" Industrial Revolution – chemicals, heavy engineering, and electric power – during Victoria's reign, and while America and Japan were evolving with their own blends of trusts and confederations, the spirit of the City of London's elite was summarised, "I mean never to have anything to do with industrial undertakings in the sense of lending our name".[5]

The network of financing structures that had supported Britain's success in leading the "First" Industrial Revolution had been undermined by the aggregation of financial clout in the City. And, as the City became the "strongbox" of the world, protected by marine dominance, appropriate "private" finance to match these foreign upstarts could not compare with the returns from mercantile and overseas finance.[6] The champions of this era of "gentlemanly capitalism" have also disappeared: most spectacularly Barings, whose apogee lay in the "informal empire" pursued in Latin America i.e. finance as an alternative to territorial conquest, but whose name is now lost somewhere in the American Midwest. But elsewhere a few scattered remnants and relics may still be seen, like the musty panelled BALSA boardroom hopefully still tucked away in one of Lloyds Bank's buildings.

Even if the power plays and jockeying with other nations for imperial supremacy preoccupied the nation's ruling elite, it would be only balanced to acknowledge that the Empire was not entirely without its industrial impact:

– Maintaining Britain's maritime supremacy led to a relatively large and continuing flow of orders on the shipbuilding industry, accounting from the days of timber for befuddled tourists looking vainly for Sherwood Forest as the national woodland was plundered, but then leading to several industrial clusters of steelworks, fabrication and shipyards to build naval and merchant ships. But other clusters evolved for military vehicles, motorbikes, equestrian husbandry, military uniforms and kit, and so on. Even though there were some major outfits, notably Vickers, none had the network support structures of the leading German and Japanese companies. And by the First World War both these countries were vying with Britain in international significance.

– If by no means as "protected" as foreign opinion was prone to argue, the Empire, even when there were no formal "protective" regimes, still retained a bias for British-produced goods – language, legal codes, financing sources, familial linkages etc.[7] Indeed, foreign companies like Colt, Siemens, Bosch etc invested in Britain to gain access to imperial markets in the 1870s, as indeed did Ford and General Motors after the First World War when "imperial preference" was introduced.[8] In the longer term, this might have been a mixed blessing, since German management will invariably argue that it was only the existence of an effectively captive Empire market that allowed British industry to get away with such deplorable products for so long.

– And there were some notable successes from the combination of these factors: for example, Babcock & Wilcox in Scotland was originally a licensee of the US parent's technology in combustion boilers. And from the plant in Glasgow it exported widely both within imperial markets and as far afield as Europe and Latin America.[i] While the far-flung geographic spread of the Empire instigated the need for communication links with companies like Cable & Wireless evolving on the network of wireless and undersea cable links that were developed.

– Less remarked[9] was the group of "export houses", operating primarily in the Empire, but also extending agencies and offices to Latin America, China and non-empire territories of Africa. If not the broad supply-chain managers of the Japanese general traders, nor with the same links as between German banks and their companies, they did offer a conduit with a local presence and expertise for British goods to be exported. Names such as Anthony Gibbs, Dalgety, Guthries, Ralli Brothers, and Duncan Fox are now mere echoes, and even the residual rumps of Harrison & Crossfield, Booker McConnell, Inchcape and Jardines have contracted out of their erstwhile pre-eminence, with Swires, Lonrho (a few scandals later) and the remnants of the United Africa Company, now within the Unilever empire, as shadows of this once-British world presence. Today's trading intermediaries who will know "how the local action works" are to be found among Japan's Sogo Shosha, local offices of German and Italian chambers/trade associations, and the informal networks of China's overseas diaspora.

– Yet, despite orders from "maritime supremacy" and "empire", Britain never developed corporate enterprises of the "scale and scope" of the leading German *Koncerns* nor the major corporations of America, nor,

---

[i] *The Babcocks & Wilcox Company* by Kristine Bruland in *From Family Firms to Corporate Capitalism* (Oxford).

of more recent evolution, the combinations under the structure of the *zaibatsu* in Japan. Even ICI, Britain's champion, did not rate against the DuPonts or IG Farbens.

– All the old industries of steel, shipbuilding, coalmining, and the more recent leading-edge sectors of vehicles, aviation, telecoms etc were exploited, often relying on licensed foreign technology. In a fragmented corporate structure when orders were readily available these might have offered a simulation of competition, but suffered the vulnerability that once the flow of comfortable orders declined, or against more aggressive international competitors, these "contested clusters" reverted to gaggles, each lacking the scale and accumulated expertise of competitors from other climes.

– World War II had the dual effect of perpetuating this industrial gaggle, since provisioning had to employ the existing suppliers without scope for pursuing the niceties of their relative competitive competences. And the old rumbles of labour disaffection, strikes and shoddy quality persisted. But native scientific ingenuity, under the stimulus of military demand, led extraordinarily to leading competences in electronics, computing, pharmaceuticals, aerospace and nuclear technologies. Hence the paradox at the end of the war of scientific excellence – as remarked by Peter Drucker, but with the traditional failings of corporate fragmentation, and an industrial financing structure not much advanced since the 1880s.

Which is where we came in. Seduced by our own propaganda of achievements in these areas, the "white heat" trumpeting of these offering "comparative advantages" was a natural consequence. A diminishing *sotto voce* political theme – "Britain is a great place to do research" its most recent refrain – ever since. But such declarations were, and still are, wholly oblivious to the prerequisites of sustaining competitive and stable corporate structures, of appropriate financing and of skilled and creative people at all levels of the enterprise. And transformations in the managerial mindset and sullen "bunker" labour attitudes were crucial if these advantages were to be translated into lasting competitive strengths.[10] To the extent that no serious or cohesive steps were taken to realign these antique polarities of conflict, any subsequent efforts to evolve globally competitive businesses were probably doomed from the start.

ANYONE FOR CONSOLIDATION?

Instead, industry went through a continuous process of "consolidation". To left-leaning governments this embraced a mixture of ideological frustration in "nationalisation" pantomimes, and a reliance on the limited mechanisms of gentlemanly capitalism, for example, through the Industrial Reorganisation Corporation, or through stimulated/supported rationalisations. Without repeating the saga of the computer industry's "consolidation" into ICL, then sold to Fujitsu, a miscellany of other ancient lays would run:

British Leyland was itself the creation of a government supported "consolidation", which after dismemberment as bits like Jaguar and Land Rover were flogged off, left the residual lump of MG Rover to be broken up in 2005 – and the remnant "consolidated" with Nanjing (another "consolidation" through the Chrysler rescue passed further remnants onto Peugeot-Citroen);

BAe is the rump of the "consolidated" aircraft industry: the multitude of aircraft companies were progressively merged into the British Aircraft Corporation and Hawker Siddeley, and these then "consolidated" into BAe. Some, like Fairey and Hunting, diversified out of reliance on aerospace;

The 600 Group is the only British machine tool survivor, as the lineage of Alfred Herbert, BSA, Kearney Trecker Marwin, Colchester et al have disappeared or "consolidated". (Mazak's plant at Worcester is the dominant facility left in this country);

The names of Decca, Plessey, AEI, Thorn, STC, etc, all at times strutting their claims of excellence in electronics, have "consolidated" down to Marconi as the last straggler, finally "consolidated" into Ericsson's.

And similar "consolidation" recitals could be given for textiles, chemicals, shipbuilding, diesel engines, and power generation, to cite only the most obvious. If the superficial merits were building structures of increased "scale", from which economies were assumed naturally to spring, and securing a future under better management – the mainstay route in the IDU "rescues", the outcomes were, measured on a world scale, marginal producers or extinction.

A Panglossian spin on this process is depicted by Geoffrey Owen* in *From Empire to Europe* (Harper Collins), much as one would expect from an ex-editor of the *Financial Times*, who concludes, "there is no evidence that industry... was damaged by excessive takeover activity".[11] Yet just totting up the rough number of mergers and acquisitions in even the limited number of sectors that he covers, presumably with assistance from the *FT* research department, gets to a figure close to 200. If a good yarn of contests between inflated egos, there are sadly few survivors.

The collapse of the motorcycle industry was just another typical example of "consolidation" of remnant companies into NVT. But it was unique in avoiding a further misapplication of resources through being subjected to an authoritative appraisal of the industry's capabilities against the competitive demands set by international leaders. We need hardly remind ourselves that the levels of investment, innovation and productivity among British manufacturers were woefully inadequate. And there is ample evidence that had a similar international benchmarking being applied to other industries – as again we repeated for Sunderland Shipbuilders – before expensive juggling of company paper and management, the outcome would not have been dissimilar.[12] The obvious corollary is that, changes in ownership, and new names on the bridge, are pointless if the engine room isn't working.

Whether this "takeover activity" was "excessive" demands some comparison against other systems. Revisiting our Cook's Tour destinations, the tradition in the main European countries,[13] and among Japan and other Asian countries is for stability in corporate ownership. Indeed, these systems could be depicted as expressly designed to inhibit "unwelcome" takeover activity. And even the United States has its own panoply of protective devices.[14] While "damage" can readily be measured by the contribution of "enormous disruption" through takeovers towards Britain's companies' history of losing market share and retreat to collapse against competitors with more sustained and supportive ownership structures.[15]

Hardly surprising that a new takeover code for Europe should have encountered opposition since the process of drafting began in 1989, and it eventually emerged, to the chagrin of the British financial market liberalists, in a form that allows anti-takeover obstacles to continue.[16] While in Japan, if, under badgering by the US, the use of company shares in mergers and acquisitions is to be permitted for the first time, the authorities have allowed enough grace for companies to install protective devices.

Meanwhile, in New Labour's Albion, the nearest approximation to an industrial policy is a "car boot sale", with progressively more of "British" industry falling under the control of foreign "national champions" – Lafarge, Saint-Gobain, EDF, Renault, Siemens, Deutsche Post, Bosch, Skanska, Ericsson, Cemex, Dubai Ports World, Sulzer, Tata and Finmeccanica, have been added to the roll of Toyota, Honda, Denso, Hutchinson, Linde, Peugeot and BMW as providing the bulk of the country's tradable value-added. The aggregate statistics can be impressive, as in the UNCTAD (United Nations Conference on Trade and Development) Report on foreign direct investment in 2005, where Britain led the international league by a mile – with capital inflows of $219bn

(£122bn). Evidence, as politicians are wont to plead, of Britain as a "great place to do business". For everyone, it seems, except British-owned companies, as actual investment in the economy as a share of national income in 2005 was the lowest on record.[17]

ATTRITION BY M&A

Beneath the glittering parade of takeovers, with its pantomime of strutting heroes and cheery-chappy commentators that passes for "business" in our national setting there has been a disastrous skewing of managerial perspectives. Rarely remarked, or indeed wilfully suppressed, there have been only occasional desperate voices, such as the introductory essay to DTI's 2003 R&D scoreboard:[ii] in reviewing the total investment (R&D plus Capex) and acquisitions spend of 79 UK companies between 1997-2001, the study "identified a total of 684 acquisitions where the consideration has been disclosed. A further 308 acquisitions were also completed in this period...." But setting the latter aside, "total acquisition spending was equivalent to 209% of total investment" (excluding the two largest mergers of GSK and AstraZeneca, the ratio was still 153%). On a comparison with the US – with a larger sample, but generally regarded as the nearest analogue to the UK's market system – where UK companies averaged 9 acquisitions per company, the US average was 3. The 2004 Report makes a plaintive repeat, with a cautionary comment, "that major acquisitions are associated with lower shareholder returns for the acquiring company in two-thirds of cases and for some years afterwards" – in fact there is no shortage of commentators critical of the real merits of takeovers even on the criteria of "shareholder value" on which they are based – the only sure bet is that shareholders in the target company will gain through the usual bid premium.[18]

A more vivid study was a comparison of company attitudes to innovation in Germany and Britain,[iii] which noted "the sheer scale of R&D performed by (German) industry is staggering compared to Britain", but also the staggering survey conclusion "the technology-based British firms expected use of mergers and acquisitions as a source of technology to increase substantially in future", whereas "German firms in the survey emphasised their total commitment to building up capabilities over the long-term, through investment in R&D and training."

[ii] *Acquisitions and Investment in Organic Growth in the UK and USA* by Brian Harding.
[iii] *Attitudes to Innovation in Germany and Britain: a Comparison* by the Centre for Exploitation of Science and Technology (CEST) (1991).

CORPORATE INGESTION AT WORK

After decades of exposure to "the bubbling bid broth",[iv] with British companies the most exposed to acquisitive manoeuvres and the diversion of managerial focus to this charade, it is hardly surprising that investment, notably in R&D, should have lagged at abysmal levels for so long.

Out of the clatter of corporate "consolidation", perhaps the emblematic exemplar of the "British model" has been the saga of Marconi.[19] If an iconic name in the development of wireless telegraphy, the company was bundled into GEC as a consequence of the various takeover rationalisations that created this conglomerate headed by Arnold Weinstock*. Setting aside the acquisitions that ranged from Avery (weighing machines), Metrocam (rail/underground rolling stock) to Yarrow (naval shipbuilding), in electronics this process went back to the takeover of AEI in 1967, following the merger of Sobell into GEC, and snaffling English Electric from a putative bid by Plessey the following year – which included Marconi and Elliott Automation in the package. To this were added bits from the break-up of Plessey, and the remnants of Ferranti. This agglomeration of businesses was subsequently "restructured" with the disposals of the power-generation and rail businesses through a merger with Alsthom in 1989, and the disposal of the heavy defence industries – notably shipbuilding where VSEL had been added to the portfolio – to British Aerospace. Ostensibly to "reposition" to a "more tightly focused" international group "centred around" leadership positions where "our electronics expertise and systems integration capability can be better exploited".[20]

Inevitably, a key element of this "repositioning strategy" was "an acquisition program aimed at developing a leadership position in our chosen sectors". And taking Weinstock's famed "cash mountain", the proceeds of disposals, and with further borrowing, GEC Marconi blew £12 billion on a takeover spree in the US (There had been an earlier expedition through the acquisition of A.B. Dick that had not delivered the expected gains of entry into office computing). If customary in City annals to blame top management, they were egged on by shareholders – for whose value the company is avowed to strive – pushing the company's market capitalisation to £35 billion. But the whole pack of cards collapsed in 2000, and, after sundry financial reconstructions, the dregs of Marconi were sold to Ericssons in 2005 as a knockdown job-lot.[21] At the time of Arnold Weinstock's (by then Lord Weinstock) death, the shares, once worth £12.50 at their peak, had fallen to 4p.

[iv] The depiction by Lombard (*FT* 23.11.05).

If a certain poetic justice in the spectacle of an agglomeration built up by acquisitions, finally been brought down by acquisitions, the process could not on any yardstick be depicted as remotely "efficient". Apart from shareholder funds washed away, the whole saga of misapplied resources and management focus involved the annihilation of swathes of industrial competences and potential – those workforces and managers rarely mentioned in financial commentaries, beyond a shrug that these "resources" will naturally move to other more profitable uses. But a worthy commentary on the fallibility of "mergers and acquisitions as a source of technology".

The ingredients that go into this broth of corporate ingestion are a goulash of financial practices misaligned to contemporary industrial demands:

– *The British Clearing Banks*: no hope of our clearing banks picking up the baton of those local sources of finance that supported Britain's rise as an industrial power, a style of "neighbourhood/relational term finance" demanding a continuing dialogue between the sources of finance and those with a view to the future of the business, and a style still dominant at the grass roots of many countries. Nor any likelihood of moving toward the "house bank" traditions of Germany, Japan and other continental countries. Rather, since finance became agglomerated in the City, the "arm's-length (nose-held)" ethos of the late 19th century persists, as our banks skulk behind their "fixed and floating charges", pocketing the gratuitous gains from "leading and lagging" changes in interest rates, and, to the steady stream of complaints from consumer bodies, screwing their own clients. The "credit crunch" has its own poetic justice as the banks pursued as the ultimate device of making money out of "fantasy" assets, except that the collateral damage will be felt by clients and the wider economy.

Whatever their self-proclaimed accomplishments, the "credit crunch" comes only as a climax to the recent history of our banks, in pursuit of the safest way of maximising returns, having explored almost every conceivable way of losing large sums of money – periodic property booms, sovereign debt fiascos,[22] costly flirtation with investment-banking following "Big Bang", etc. But nothing that could not be rectified by the occasional write-off, and recovery through the extra margins that can be tucked away under the high interest policies adopted by the Treasury and the Bank of England.

The Marconi-equivalent among our banks was perhaps Midland Bank's acquisition in the mid-1980s of Crocker, a Californian bank that had stashed up a heavy portfolio of Latin American debt. It turned out that

Midland could have done virtually anything better with the money, including burning it. But it allowed the Hong Kong and Shanghai Bank (HSBC), another old Imperial warhorse, to pick up entry to the British high street retail market by acquiring Midland for a knockdown price. Where Midland led, others followed, with the Royal Bank of Scotland achieving a pinnacle of self-destruction with its acquisition of ABN Amro, with a scale of losses that threw itself into majority state ownership.

Yet behind this facade of "a proper concern for depositors", it was not infrequent to hear British companies mutter that our clearing banks were a bigger threat to their survival than their international competitors.[23]

– *Capital Markets*: beneath enough esoteric tomes on financial economics to bury any mediaeval monastery, including encryptions by the odd Nobel laureate;[24] beneath the flow of megabucks sloshing around capital markets; beneath the headline jousts of takeovers; and beneath the cheery-chappies proffering themselves as commentators on "business", "the contributions of capital by shareholders" to the investment demands to sustain "real business" is negligible – "in contrast to the standard description, stock markets are not a major source of capital financing for industry and large stock-market economies do not raise more equity finance for their industries than small."[25]

In practice, as repeated studies have confirmed, the dominant source of funds for capital investment, research and innovation – around the world – is retained earnings. Despite a plethora of debate to justify different dividend policies, UK companies had been paying out higher proportions of earnings as dividends than most other countries – "dividend payment levels of UK firms were around three times as high as those of German firms", and causing "the level of dividends in the UK to be high and inflexible in relation to that in countries in which investors are more closely involved....".[26] Even, as a marked contrast with the US, usually labelled as similar to the UK, Microsoft only began making dividend payments at all in 2003.

But a peculiar feature is that the disjunction between UK companies and their shareholders apparently requires the former to engage in "signalling", through, amongst other "benchmarks", the prospective levels of dividend payments against "expectations".[27] In a less fantastical context than the City, even semaphore would offer a more effective form of communication.[28]

A root cause lies in the ethos of shareholders: even if collectively some institutions may have very substantial proportions of issued stock, spreading holdings around in "diversified portfolios, each holding in a particular company is carefully judged to avoid any necessity or obligation to become involved in the real business". In effect, carrying on the tradition of "functionless rentiers"[29] going back to the "slave/plantation trades" where, if ownership of the "estates in Antigua" gave title to the proceeds, this carried no obligation nor the least concern as to how these proceeds were achieved. And, in the stock-market world of "liquid markets" with the added comfort of the freedom to "exit" by selling, if by any whim, proceeds are not sufficient. Or, in more recent practice to "lend stock" to hedge funds and others, to the point where accurate ownership of shares can become a matter of dispute.[30]

Against the sanctions implicit in this "discipline", whereby "property rights as well as equity claims to earning streams can be traded" and which "solely reflect the interests of shareholders", company managements become complicit in the expectations charade, especially in the game of devising impenetrable reward mechanisms for themselves, including the safeguard of rewarding failure.[31] Comparable only to the remuneration packages of plantation stewards and slave-trade captains. (Forget the convenient jargon of "stakeholders" since none – employees and suppliers – have the sanction of "exit" without damaging their own interests.)

The dilemma of reconciling the interests of "investors/shareholders" who have no interest beyond financial returns, the task of managing the businesses over which a company has custody, and the scope for participants to "play the system" for individual gain[32] – as exemplified by the Enron era scandals, backdating of share options etc, has spun off an entirely new industry of "corporate governance". Marked by successive reviews under whatever convenient figureheads were to hand – Cadbury, Greenberry, Hempel, Myners and Higgs – while the fundamental irreconcilabilities, and easy rewards for participants under the status quo, will keep this industry going long after the Hobbits. So far, little to show beyond a bit of pretentious manicuring.[33]

– *Termism*: No shortage of critical texts on the malfunctions that can flow from granting pre-eminence to the demands of "functionless rentiers", the maximisation of shareholder value.[34] And the more "active" the investors, the more the pressure is applied towards the "rentier" performance demanded by shareholders.

The consequential influence, however, on managerial ethos, and ultimately on competitive industrial performance, has been less remarked. The response from foreign companies – German, Japanese, French etc – to a query about how they view their British counterparts will cluster around "finance-driven companies". The most obvious symptom is the predominance of accountants or ex-bankers, in the top echelons of management, whereas elsewhere the norm will be experienced engineers or production managers/scientists. More insidious is the paralysis induced by an almost religious devotion to "discounted cash flow", which translates into such dicta as "we'll only go ahead if there is an IRR (Internal Rate of Return) of at least 28%," or "we're expected to get our money back in three years."[35]

A substrata of this bias were the, even occasionally heated, debates in the 1980s over the "short-termism" of City investors. If now comfortably buried below the threshold of public debate, partially because the number of companies with anything other than a "short-term" perspective have disappeared and partly through increased subservience to the myths of the City, the issue has not evaporated.[36] And the persistence of this ethos over decades is amply evidenced by the extinction and relative competitive position of British companies against international competitors.

Another substrata is the "equity gap" to finance the initial development of smaller companies – originally designated the "Macmillan gap" when first flagged up in the 1930s. Apart from some relief from the Small Firms Guarantee Scheme, reliance is still placed on those "distinctly unadventurous" City venture capital funds.[37] For, over decades the bulk of "venture funds" has been predominantly devoted to Management Buy-Outs (MBOs).[38]

For "termism" infects the venture-fund business as much as any other, since many are offshoots of City players, and are looking towards realising gains, on a suitably discounted calculation, for their "investment" with "exit" via an "initial public offering" (IPO) of shares on the stock market or on the "small caps" market within a few years. And just as liable to "bubbles" – Biotech, dot-com etc – with attendant scandals.[39] Unless the initial owners take deliberate steps, this process simply puts the business prey to the whims of "functionless rentiers":[40] not a context to provide appropriate finance to develop the business to international scale.

The shady domain of "analysts" and "research", with their own mysterious remuneration mechanisms, are also subject to the ruling "rentier" ethos. Not for them a genuine context of the demands imposed by international competitors, rather "sectoral" criteria and bogus ratios. While the Investment Relations (IR) charade is a game of promoting comfortably attainable expectations.[41]

But the consequences of overbearing "finance" on company behaviour extends beyond the obvious mechanisms of the City. A peculiarity of British companies, despite campaigns for "alternative dispute resolution", is their proclivity to call in lawyers – not just when the scale of risk is "betting the house" or in international projects where a safe "arbitration" mechanism is desirable, but even for relatively mundane activities. This drive to pretend to cover liabilities in legal verbiage, and the contest to shift liability on to someone else's books, inhibits British companies from the collaborative and networking options more comfortably pursued by the cooperative patterns of commercial relationships elsewhere.[42]

Despite a long-established tradition of periodic bouts of "irrational exuberance",[43] of which the telecoms/dot-com collapses were but the most recent, the myth of "efficient markets" is still peddled.[44] And advocates readily drop into an absurd anthropomorphism, "markets look behind..." "perhaps the market is looking ahead...", "markets are sometimes wiser..." etc etc.[v] Opening the door to the daily diet of our cheery-chappies proclaiming, "the market has caught a cold from Wall Street...", "the market has been taking a breather...", "suffering a bit of indigestion…", "the market seems to be looking over its shoulder...", and so on.

Out of the melange of activities embraced by The City – insurance, metal and commodity exchanges, maritime brokerage etc – there may be some national gains, though none have been immune from episodes of controversy. But, by any measure of "revealed comparative performance", the City has not contributed appropriate finance nor disciplines for British-quoted companies to match their international rivals. Genuinely "long-term" shareholders (or bankers) might be expected to invest some effort to apply constructive pressure on a company to give priority to the demands of sustaining skills, expertise, research, innovation, product renewal, market presence and organizational evolution necessary to advance against leading players in its businesses. If only. Despite occasional voices calling for shareholders to exercise such a role,[45] any move in this direction strays into the uncomfortable domain of "functions" where some commitment is required beyond pocketing "dividends" and exploiting opportunities for "exit", before commuting back to their contemporary "Mansfield Parks".

---

[i] *JUST CAPITAL-The Liberal Economy* by Adair Turner (Macmillan). Even though he does go on to glance at "Which capitalism is best", the simplest challenge is, "Then why has Britain not evolved any companies to match such

---

[v] See *Market Assessment of Company Performance* by Paul Marsh in *Capital Markets and Corporate Governance* op. cit.

enterprises as Siemens, Toshiba, Hitachi, NEC, Fujitsu, Sony, Honda, Toray, Samsung, Lucky Goldstar, Lafarge, Saint-Gobain or Hutchinson Whampoa and so on, all of which have characteristics reflecting the societies and traditions in which they evolved? Or, just as pertinent, why does it remain inconceivable that Britain ever could? Or, why has Britain opted out of new technologies while these other enterprises have taken the lead?"

A comment high on the economics bollocks register. Up there in fairy lights alongside, "There is no such thing as the state" (Samuel Brittan, *FT* 17.12.04): another typical example of Pavlovian denial, and, as already noted, an amusing instance of that journal's propensity to have editorial columns contradicted by their own correspondents – in the same edition was a report from their man in Shanghai, "China aims to challenge South Korea's lead in shipbuilding... in the short term, Chinese market share will receive a boost from a policy dictating that new LNG import contracts include provisions for ships to be built in local yards. It coincides with a strategic decision by China to develop an advanced shipbuilding industry to go hand-in-hand with a navy capable of projecting power into the oceans of the Asia-Pacific now controlled by the US and its allies."

[2] A view of technology repeated by a more recent iconic tyro, Mike Lazaridis, co-founder of RIM, the firm behind the BlackBerry. "You can never invest too much in basic research", but with the sensible caution, "You don't go from the laboratory test tube straight to someone's garage and then on to success – that's a fable. You've got to have all the parts in place, including efficient mechanisms to train young people who will transfer new scientific knowledge to industry, as well as companies that are ready and receptive to employ and empower that talent." (*The Economist Technology Quarterly* 23.9.06). Could be a brief description of Honda.

[3] To summarise the results of the review (*Nikkei Weekly* 22.8.05) in more detail:

"Japanese companies are boosting spending on basic research to better arm themselves against tougher competition from a mid- to long-term perspective.... According to the survey of 304 major companies, 47% of them will strengthen basic research in fiscal 2005, surging from the 31.9% that did so in fiscal 2004.

A growing number of Japanese companies are investing hefty sums in what they see as priority areas – environment, nanotechnology, fuel cells and genetic engineering – expecting that basic research in these areas will bring them an important edge that should play a major role in their operations a decade ahead, rather than next year.

The Nikkei poll showed that the companies plan a combined ¥10.26 trillion ($94.1 billion) in R&D budgets in fiscal 2005, up 4.9% from the previous year's final figures, marking the sixth straight year of growth. More than 70% of the respondents plan to raise R&D spending in fiscal 2005.

By sector, food, pharmaceutical and biotechnology firms predict the sharpest expansion (9.3%), followed by materials maker's (7.5%), far outpacing the information technology sector (2.6%).

'Getting prepared for intensifying competition' topped the list of purposes for expanding R&D spending, at 43.8%, followed by 'entering/developing new businesses', at 32.5%. The proportion of firms that cited preparing for stiffer competition was particularly high in the automobile (70%), medical/biotechnology (61.5%) and information technology (58.5%) sectors.

Among the more striking sectoral results were:

The annual survey found that one in nearly 4 major domestic firms plans at least 10% increase in R&D investment in fiscal 2005 from a year earlier. Especially aggressive are food, pharmaceutical and biotechnology companies. Among drug makers, industry leader Takeda Pharmaceutical Co. as well as Eisai Co., Sankyo Co. and Daiichi Pharmaceutical Co. will boost R&D by about 10%. Ajinomoto Co., the largest food processor, will raise it 10%.

Materials makers also project a sharp expansion. Sumitomo Chemical Co. will raise research spending by 22.7% to ¥96 billion ($880 million), mainly to study new materials.

In contrast, the IT industry, which accounts for nearly half of all private-sector R&D investment, plans a modest 2.6% rise. Sanyo Electric Co., which is working hard to revamp its operations, and Nippon Telegraph and Telephone Corp, whose 6-9 telephone service is reeling from the spread of Internet Protocol telephony, even plans to cut research spending. Fujitsu Ltd and NEC Corp, which both have a longstanding ties with NTT, plan either very small R&D increases or none at all.

An exception in this sector is NTT DoCoMo Inc, which plans a more than 7% expansion to ¥109 billion. The spending will focus on upgrading third-generation cellphone services and developing a fourth-generation phone capable of transmitting data at speeds comparable to fibre-optic networks.

The companies in favour of applied research that could immediately lead to tangible businesses are now attaching more importance to basic research that would underpin their businesses many years ahead... In particular, 65% of machinery makers, engineering firms and shipbuilders, will expand basic research in a bid to cultivate new businesses. in the areas of information technology and materials, where innovations are constantly altering the market landscape, over 50% of the firms plan to expand basic R&D. The findings indicate that as the economy recovers, companies have regained enough confidence to launch research projects that would support their long-term business strategies."

A broadly contemporaneous snapshot of Britain's level of R&D is provided by the 2004/5 DTI R&D Scoreboard, which "gives the top 750 UK-based companies [including foreign-owned subsidiaries]... with R&D totalling £17 billion". Of this the "foreign-owned subsidiaries" account for nearly £5 billion. And a subsequent update, "Spending on R&D decreases by 3%," (*FT* 26/27.11.05) suggests that the trend is for further decline, "Business spent £13.5 billion on R&D, a fall of 1%, from £13.7 billion the previous year, according to the Office for National Statistics. Stripping out the effects of inflation, spending was down by 3%." This prompted the Conservative spokesman on trade and industry (David Willetts) to remark that the government's strategy was not working. "These figures showing an absolute fall in R&D spending are very bad news," he said. "It is more evidence that we aren't investing for the future."

[4] A valuable appraisal of the patterns of R&D investment of leading international companies comes in the Booz/Allen/Hamilton *Resilience Report* (12.5.05), "Money Isn't Everything". Drawing on data from the top 1000 international quoted companies, the study disposes of direct correlations between scale of R&D investment, ratios of R&D against turnover etc and commercial success.

Among the threads that the study suggests as indicative for successfully capturing research and innovation, two are particularly relevant to the failings of British industry:

"Size matters – Scale leads to advantages. Larger organisations can spend a smaller proportion of revenue on R&D than can smaller organisations, and take no discernible hit." And the essential ingredients of "creativity, analysis and disciplined management" and "good cross-functional capabilities" can often be found in circumstances where "incumbency has a big advantage". And these will also have a greater proclivity to have evolved effective "innovation processes: the way a company generates, selects, develops and commercialises ideas."

Secondly, "Spending more does not necessarily help, but spending too little will hurt."

Against Britain's industrial decline, the moral is that, first, with sadly few exceptions (e.g. Rolls-Royce), where there were businesses of international scale, they spent "too little" on R&D compared to major international competitors, and failed to achieve the same dynamic "innovation processes". Secondly, part of this failure must be attributable to demands from shareholders that disregarded the competitive necessities imposed by leading competitors from other countries, and a preoccupation among corporate leadership of the apparently easy mechanisms of using company paper in the M&A game.

[5] The signature quote from David Kynaston's *The City of London (Vol 1: A World of Its Own, 1815-1890)* is: "It was a catastrophic start for the industry, as those public companies (including Brush, but not Hammond) that had survived the rollercoaster of 1882 found themselves for most of the rest of the century hobbled for capital and having to pay out unrealistically high dividends in order to prevent a complete collapse of confidence on the part of an already deeply sceptical stock market. This was disastrous, for by this stage in its economic development, starting to be caught up by Germany and the United States in terms of its mature industries, Britain should have been looking to the new industries – above all, electrical engineering, chemicals and in due course motor cars – in order to regain its unquestioned industrial ascendancy. All three of these new industries were high-tech and capital-intensive, so there could be no question of relying on traditional forms of self-finance and local finance. In other words, the role of the London capital market was pivotal. The point, however, was not so much *total* supply of funds that it did or did not channel into these new industries, but rather whether it was capable of effectively applying the element of long-term, disinterested discrimination. The experience of the 'Brush boom' suggested that, in terms of the crucial latter service, there was ample room for improvement.

"Perhaps one could not have expected otherwise from the City in 1882. There were still very few industrial securities quoted on the Stock Exchange; an inevitable concomitant of this was poor marketability; not helped by the Committee's determination to preserve the monopoly rights of jobbers; and in the admonitory words of Erasmus Pinto's *Ye Outside Fools! Glimpses inside the Stock Exchange* (1877), 'Take no shares in industrial companies, unless fully acquainted with the concern'. A further discouragement until the turn of the century was the legal restriction on underwriting industrial shares, though O'Hagan among others was finding ways round the problem by the 1880s. Symptomatic of – and perpetuating – the Cinderella status of the Miscellaneous market (as the Stock Exchange's industrial department was called) was the reluctance of the leading merchant banks to sponsor domestic industrial issues, a reluctance attributable partly to their risky reputation and partly to the small and therefore unprofitable size of most of the issues. 'I never mean to have anything to do with industrial undertakings in the sense of lending our name', Everard Hambro asserted in 1882, and with a few notable exceptions it was an attitude that would persist among the City elite for the best part of half a century... So, the City's treatment of British industry was left for the most part to the tender mercies of an assorted band of company promoters. Some, like O'Hagan, were more or less honourable; most were not; and the results were well-nigh disastrous."

[6] *British Imperialism* (2 Vols) by P. J. Cain and A. G. Hopkins (Longman) is an impeccably thorough account of the pre-eminent interests of finance in the British brand of imperialism.

[7] The conventional economic history account of the glorious era of "free trade" is a shade partial. After the flurry of legislation in the mid-1800s to repeal the Corn and Navigation Laws and to cope with the stirrings of colonial autonomy, there was indeed a period when UK/Empire tariffs were relatively low. A blow-by-blow account is given in *The Fall of Protection 1840-1850* by Bernard Holland (Porcupine Press). But prompted by continuing high American tariffs and the post-1870s rise in European tariffs, there were increasing pressures at the turn of the century led by Joseph Chamberlain, over which he resigned, for "imperial preference", even if it was left to his sons to secure these with legislation in 1919 and in 1932.

[8] See *Britain and the Multinationals* by J. M. Stopford and L. Turner (Wiley): one of the historic lessons is that no company has invested in Britain for its national market alone, but rather to gain access to imperial markets, the EU or to take over British companies that have a market presence outside the country.

[9] Save for Geoffrey Jones' superb obsequies in *Merchants to Multinationals* (Oxford), with its conclusion, "The demise of so many of the old British trading companies was curious given that the world political economy appeared once again to offer prospects for their skills, as economies were liberalised and opened to foreign trade and investment. In part firms fell victim to their failed attempts to diversify into regions and industries where they lacked expertise. The fate of

particular firms rested in part on their main host regions. Jardine Matheson and Swire's, most obviously, continued to draw enormous advantage from their position in Hong Kong, while – conversely – UAC's fate was all but sealed by the decline of the West African, and especially the Nigerian, economies from the 1970s.

"However the ultimate arbiter of the fate of the diversified trading companies in the late twentieth century was the British capital markets. The capital markets which had made the creation of the diversified business groups possible before 1914 were to prove their nemesis in the 1990s. It was the declining share price of the publicly quoted firms which led to their ultimate demise as diversified trading companies, while it was the family control of Swire's and Jardine Matheson which ensured their survival."

[10] The self-destructive play of these opposites is comprehensively catalogued in Correlli Barnett's *The Pride and Fall Sequence* (Macmillan).

[11] Not that the *FT* is an entirely unbiased commentator, well illustrated by Lombard's regretful survey, "More a merger murmur than merger mania" (31.12.04) sadly reporting that, even though 2004 had seen £108 bn values of M&A, the number of deals was "relatively low at 2198, only 86 ahead of last year. You have to go back to 1997 for a significantly worse number. And the value is a fraction of the heady record of £ 313.6 bn in 2000. More a merger murmur than a merger mania." The year 2000, of course, was the height of the IT/dot.com boom which eventually wiped out £bns (or $trns) of shareholder value.

[12] Archivists will readily find press references to Ford executives remarking on "Soviet-style" factories after they took over Jaguar in the mid-80s, an investment from which it is inconceivable that the company will ever gain a sensible return. Especially when it had to throw another £1bn into the Jaguar black hole (*FT* 23.12.05). Ford executives must have drawn a deep sigh of relief to dispose of Jaguar, with Range Rover, to Tata in May 2008.

While there were studies that showed a similar discrepancy in UK performance: for example, in steel, "with the intensification of competition in the 1970s,... Japanese capabilities posed a serious competitive challenge by this time; in 1975 a Japanese worker required 6.2 hours to produce a tonne of raw steel, a German worker 8.9, an American worker 10.5, a French worker 12.1, and a British worker 17.4" (Esser and Fach in "The Steel Industry" in *Industry and Politics in West Germany: toward the Third Republic* (Ithaca).

British Steel is an ironic example where nationalisation was probably an appropriate solution: it undertook, particularly under the Chairmanship of Monty Finniston* a massive modernisation investment programme, inevitably chalking up heavy losses, but putting the company in a position for privatisation: and, for a time, subsequently its Chairman, Brian Moffatt*, could claim it was "the low-cost producer". The subsequent saga of "rationalisation" into Corus, with Tata again coming to the rescue, continues the driving force of investment bankers' "fees" in Britain's industrial evolution.

---

[13] *The Control of Corporate Europe*, ed. Balca/Brecht (Oxford) is a comprehensive account of the European systems of corporate governance following the disclosures of corporate holdings brought to light by new EEC transparency requirements. In itself, a very useful survey of the byzantine variations of differential voting rights, cross-holdings, voting control structures etc that have evolved in different ways among European countries.

[14] Apparently "most S&P 500 companies (in the USA) put a variety of anti-takeover devices in place at the beginning of the 1990s... ranging from external control provisions (like poison-pills and blank cheque preferred stock), through internal control provisions (like classified boards and supermajority amendments), to state anti-takeover laws (like freeze-out or control share acquisition laws)." *The Control of Corporate Europe* Ibid pps 285ff. More recently, John Plender has remarked in the context of moves among European countries to create, or extend, "shark repellents" against aggressive takeovers (Europe feels the toxic effect of corporate nationalism – *FT* 6.4.06) that it is the continuing use of such devices in the US that was seized upon as the pretext to avoid a more liberal takeover code in Europe, "What we are now seeing, then, is an incipient process of convergence on the high-toxicity US system. Indeed, it was precisely because the Germans and Swedes could point to this protectionist element in the US capital markets that they were able to knock the stuffing out of Europe's takeover directive and cross-border market in corporate control. On both sides, protectionist pots have been calling kettles black."

[15] Even Geoffrey Owen cites the boss of Glaxo commenting on the "the enormous disruption inherent in mergers and acquisitions".

[16] For example, "Watered-down EEC takeover directive is a missed opportunity for open markets" (*FT* 20/21. 12.03).

[17] Of the total inward investment, $156.7bn was accounted for by the larger acquisitions of UK companies (*FT* 25.1.06), while the comment on the relatively low level of investment in the real economy was made in the following edition of the *Observer* (29.1.06). Reinforced a week later in the *FT* (3.2.06), "The share of business investment in nominal gross domestic product is at its lowest since records began in the 1960s."

[18] A conveniently caustic reminder comes from John Kay, "Why many mergers are a triumph of hope over experience" (*FT* 15.11.05). For those of a more scholarly disposition he advocates a perusal of *The finance literature on mergers* by D.C.Mueller in M. Waterson (ed) *Competition, Monopoly and Corporate Governance* (Elgar). This review, in a volume of otherwise esoteric essays, is a stunning sceptical analysis of studies of the value of M&A reaching back to the 1950s, following the varying fads of their time: from "conglomerates", "synergistic gains", "replacement of defective management through the market for corporate control", "surplus cash-flow", "managerial hubris", etc.

About the only constant is significant gains for the target shareholders, since, as an inducement for the majority to give up their shares, a premium over the pre-merger price usually needs to be paid. As such studies accumulated, the gains for acquiring companies appeared even more problematic, for example "aggregate losses to acquiring companies' shareholders exceeded the gains in wealth of the targets". While, as M&A waves tend to be driven by the optimistic hysteria of stock-market booms, those made near the peak will more assuredly leave the acquirers' wealth most seriously dented (Marconi again!). But taking a performance window pre- and post-merger, only a relatively small proportion could genuinely be claimed to be wealth creating for the acquirer, and prospective gains perceived at the time of a merger can be judged as problematic at best.

Not least of the causes for the recurrent failure of takeovers is the, often underrated, clashes to reconcile different management traditions: recall again the boss of Glaxo on "the enormous disruption inherent in mergers and acquisitions". Second, no mergers and acquisitions occur without relatively astronomic fees to advisers/lawyers/investment banks, of which there are a plethora of examples, which account for virtually all the "bonuses" in the City. If these may help to keep house prices in Kensington and Chelsea beyond the average citizen's reach, for the companies concerned they can be a major drain on cash flow: for example: EMI paid some £50 million in fees even though its merger with Bertelsmann was called off, and M&S paid fees of £40 million in defence, even though Philip Green did not proceed with his takeover. In "successful" takeovers, the cash-flow penalty of the new business will be the cost for both contestants, and hence any prospective "synergies" have to overcome this immediate cash penalty for the resulting business. While straightforward flotations, such as QinetiQ, can put £100m into the pockets of "advisers" (*Observer* 29.1.06).

[19] There are several accounts of the rise and fall of GEC. But since the company's evolution was so intimately tied to the eccentricities of its chief executive, among the more balanced and racier accounts is *Arnold Weinstock and the making of GEC* by Stephen Aris (Aurum).

[20] From the statement by George Simpson – GEC Marconi's managing director – in 1997 following his strategic review. Of course, "a strategic review", rather like "we timed our rights issue well", has become a signal of imminent disaster.

[21] A summary of the Marconi collapse is given in the chapter on *City Scandals and Calamities* in *The City* by Richard Roberts (Economist).

[22] As old habits die hard, when the Brazilian debt crisis blew in the late-80s, British banks were responsible for 17% of the country's problem loans, while UK exports to the country amounted to only 1.4% of its imports.

[23] Not always whispered, as this sentiment was brazenly pronounced at a CBI Conference on Bonding: the speaker went on to describe devices, such as leaving his client with a signed "open-dated" cheque instead of requesting his bank for the requisite bond. The occasion was also an illustration of the craven attitude of much British management, since, when provoked by the criticism that "for the banks to charge a premium on a guarantee that is secured against a company's

assets (i.e. without taking any risk) is the nearest thing to money for old rope", no other companies present took up the challenge.

[24] The collapse of Long-Term Capital Management (LTCM) depicted in *When Genius Failed* by Roger Lowenstein (HarperCollins) is a superb account of the economist's ultimate alchemaic dream of a formula that converts everything to gold – except for a hole in one of the assumptions that nearly brought the world financial system to collapse. Saved only by a surreptitious panic operation of "Western crony capitalism" (John Plender – *FT* 4.10.98).

[25] Colin Mayer's probing contribution *Stock-Markets, Financial Institutions, and Corporate Performance* to the seminar *Capital Markets and Corporate Performance* (Oxford). A collateral account based on US corporate experience, "Throughout the twentieth century, corporate retentions and corporate debt, not equity issues, have been the main sources of funds for business investment." *Contests for Corporate Control* by Mary A. O'Sullivan (Oxford).

[26] Colin Mayer op. cit. For an update, a NikkoCitigroup comparison of average dividend pay-out ratios quoted the UK at 52.8%, Germany at 30.6%, the US at 26.5%, and Japan at 21.1% (*FT* 29.3.07).

[27] The interplay of the "expectations" game, with all its mutual back scratching, conflicts of interest, and misaligned incentives is elegantly depicted in *The City – inside the great expectations machine* (*FT*-Prentice Hall) by Tony Golding, himself an ex-investment banker.

[28] The best brief summary of this fantasy-world is John Plender's trenchant "Capitalism's revolution from above" (*FT* 1.11.02), including:

"Expectations are manufactured in the City of London in the same way that Detroit makes cars or Paris produces haute couture. It is all designed to satisfy the fund managers' demand for certainty and to manage their hatred of bad news....

It is little wonder that chief executives rush into injudicious takeovers. For in this world takeovers are never injudicious, because they are a way of keeping expectations up and reality at bay. And there is always a handsome pay off if it all turns sour.

It would be unfair to blame the fund managers for perverting the system, for the penalties and rewards in their world are similarly simplistic. Pension fund trustees unquestioningly accept the benchmarks of fund management performance recommended by a narrow group of consultants. and many trustees measure the performance of fund managers on an even shorter-term basis than fund managers assess industrialists.

Yet that cannot disguise the absurdity of the outcome. The cost of capital is now being set in an Elysian fantasy world where all the actors assume the economy is imbued with ineradicable stability and chief executives are endowed with godlike prescience and power. Corporate earnings growth in perpetuity provides the motor for the fiction's plot. But nobody – trustees, fund managers, analysts, industrialists – will opt back into the real world until it impinges forcibly on them [, as at BP]. Objectively, it is crazy. Or maybe life is a dream."

But this fantasy goes to the extreme where even "measures of value" become mere ciphers:

"Data mining is the key technique for nearly all stockbroker economics. There is no claim that cannot be supported by statistics, provided that these are carefully selected. For this purpose, data are usually restricted to a limited period, rather than using the full series available. Statistics, it has been observed, will always confess if tortured sufficiently.

The greatest single triumph yet achieved by data mining is the invention of the bond yield ratio. This claims that equities can be valued by comparing bond yields and earnings yields. These ratios showed a strong correlation in the US from 1977 to 1997. But the exact opposite relationship ruled from 1942 to 1968. It is, of course, possible to use all the available data, thereby flattering the prejudices of economists but offending the key principle of data mining. If this is done, it shows that there is no relationship at all between bond yields and earnings yields.

Readers can, nonetheless, be confident that the use of the bond yield ratio will not disappear simply because it cannot be supported by either theory or experience. Claims based on data mining are not discarded simply because they do not work. They are just put into the pending tray with the standard excuse that "the relationship has broken down". While this cannot be logically distinguished from "there never was a relationship", it has two great advantages. First, it sounds a great deal better and, second, it demands less effort to reuse old nonsense than to invent new follies.

Nonsense about value comes in many other forms...." (There is little value in broker economics – Andrew Smithers – *FT* 4.1.06).

[29] A pithy bull's-eye phrase quoted in *End of the Line* by Barry C. Lynn (Doubleday). The disjunction between shareholders and their companies is no better exemplified than in the practice of stock-lending/forward-selling which has reached the point where, "management has no way of checking whether the fund can in fact vote the shares or not" i.e. "The rapid growth of derivatives markets and practices such as stock lending make it harder for companies to discover the identities of their owners" (*FT* 18.2.06).

[30] Reaching the point where we even hear "Concern in US over 'empty voting'" (*FT* 6.10.06), remarking on studies by University of Texas professors identifying instances "in which what they call 'empty voting' or 'hidden [morphable] ownership' of shares either clearly or likely impacted a shareholder vote." Leading one commentator to conclude "These practices, while making sense from a market perspective, undermined the most fundamental assumption in corporate governance, which is that share ownership and economic interest and voting rights all go together."

[31] "a multiplicity of scarcely comprehensible share option, incentive and bonus schemes...." John Plender op. cit.

[32] Not least in the fees of investment banks, which have attained a special

Elysium entirely insulated from the dynamics of competition by which the rest of the world functions. Savaged accurately in *The Greed Merchants* by Philip Augar (Allen Lane).

[33] An entertaining account of the byzantine diminishing circles of the dispute is given in the section on *Debates on Corporate Governance* in Mary A. O'Sullivan op.cit. But "activism" has taken on a whole new meaning, from special interest groups using a bundle of shares to establish a platform for complaint, to "hedge funds" and "private equity groups" applying pressure, invariably with a bias "to shoot for short-term gains, without regard for the effect on the company in the future" (Fruitless? Activist shareholders could be losing their ability to shake managements – *FT* 11.1.06). Yet, in the area of the most persistent criticism – boardroom remuneration – no discernible impact appears to have been made.

[34] A fair example is the anthology compiled by Joel Bakan in *The Corporation: the Pathological Pursuit of Profit and Power* (Constable) and its accompanying film now widely viewed through TV and DVD.

[35] An actual quotation from a GEC manager, stated in all seriousness, and prefaced by, "We are not short-term". On the other hand, there were many in that company who were engagingly self-deprecating about the "cash disciplines" of its distinct managerial style.

[36] Unsurprisingly, the "short-termism" debate has receded: Prof Porter's essay on *UK Competitiveness* is studiously economically correct, "The City of London is one of the most competitive financial services clusters in the world... it's equity markets in particular are highly rated, although there is anecdotal evidence of companies going private to avoid the markets short-term scrutiny". And later, in reviewing the potential causes for low investment in capital and innovation, there is a nod towards "the UK's equity based financial markets structure that, it is argued, favours a short-term management outlook. There is clear evidence that the value of financial assets can be mispriced for extended periods of time. There is, however, no systematic evidence that ties this to management behaviour. The anecdotal evidence of firms going private to enable more long-term strategies indicates that this might be the case, but it also indicates that companies have a choice and that there is no determinism."

An equally likely scenario is that the British companies who were so outspoken in the early 90s, like Dowty (quoted in *City State*), no longer exist. While perhaps the most penetrating study of the topic was by the Innovation Advisory Board (DTI) in 1990, *Innovation: City Attitudes and Practices*, largely researched and put together by John Chapman, another in the band of officials who was restive under the prevailing orthodox market ethos of DTI: he took the trouble to interview fund managers on the extent to which a company's R&D investment influenced their views, with responses universally clustering around, "Sod all!" If anything, evidence of a "long-term" perspective lies not in "the average period of holding shares is five years" – conveniently averaging high rates of "churning" against the stable holdings in major companies like RTZ,

Shell, BP etc, but whether shareholders have been urging their companies to protect their future prospects by investing comparable levels in R&D as their international competitors. Yet, Britain's abysmal level of corporate R&D and decline in world markets has continued unabated.

Or perhaps just exhaustion, as more fully explained by Tony Golding:

"The experience of this period (the 1990s recession) – and the public discussion of 'short-termism' – persuaded shareholders and companies that much was to be gained from a regular and open dialogue, without the intervention of a securities firm (with a different agenda). Management began to reveal its longer-term plans and targets to its shareholders. It did not take long for these to be translated into self-generated performance benchmarks ('promises') against which they could be measured, just as the institutions are themselves judged.

What of 'short-termism' now? Since the early 1990s the issue has virtually disappeared from public view. Rarely does a business leader make any comment on the timescales of institutional shareholders. Does this mean that 'short-termism' never existed? Or that the institutions have adjusted to industrial horizons? The truth is that it did and still does exist, although in a modified form. Its influence has been tempered by increased liquidity constraints and a considerably more constructive and understanding relationship between industry and its institutional investors.

Ironically, fund managers would, in an ideal world, like to take more short-term bets but are inhibited by limited liquidity. To an extent then, the bigger fund managers have become longer term by default. It would be wrong, however, to take this argument too far. External pension fund managers, unit trust and unit-linked managers are under constant and intense pressure to maximise current performance. The current quarter is what matters, perhaps the next quarter, certainly not next year's equivalent quarter or the one two or three years hence. Confronted with the prospect of an uplift in the value of his portfolio from a bid, or a decline in performance as a company reports a short-term blip in an upward trend, the gut reaction of a professional fund manager will be to go for whatever enhances or protects his current performance figures. He may, in the event, be swayed by other considerations but the initial reaction will be the bird in the hand. 'Short-termism' lives on but perhaps not in quite the same form as it did before."

The rising ascendancy of private-equity offers only a variant of short-termism, illustrated by the management attraction that "their success and financial reward will depend on managing heavily indebted companies owned by aggressive funds whose goal is to sell it at a much higher price within a few years." If, apparently, a relief from "the tyranny of quarterly earnings" and cumbersome board structures, this "greater long-term flexibility" is questioned as "their true horizon is three to five years." (Life on the other side – why private equity is luring top talent: *FT* 22.12.06).

A faint whisp of protestations past lingers in the Engineering and Technology Board report *SET (science, engineering and technology) and the City: Financing Wealth Creation from Science, Engineering and Technology* of 4.12.06 (*FT* 5.12.06) that concludes, "All the evidence cited calls into question the commitment of the major financial institutions to technology stock and suggest that nothing less than a fundamental change in investment attitudes will reverse these trends" pitched in terms of "the paradox which threatens the future of the UK economy." And the report covers well-trampled ground: the private sector has to match public investment in science and engineering; government procurement should be angled to support emerging technology-based companies; and active support of capital markets is essential to grow emerging companies into world-class enterprises. And nothing less than a fundamental change in investment attitudes will reverse these trends. Cor! We've had this a few times before, with recommendations on discrimination in favour of small firms, tax incentives for venture capital, and a few changes in the structure of consultative committees. Yet another prance around the maypole.

[37] See Richard Roberts op.cit. pp 147-9. While evidence of the persistence of "the equity gap" is reflected in the correspondence pages of the *FT*, for example "Venture capital trusts are the only credible means to tackle 'equity gap'" (*FT* 21.1.06), where pleading the merits of Venture Capital Trusts (VCTs), it is remarked, "In absolute terms, there are almost no other sources of capital for equity investments of less than £5m. The departure from the market of 3i a few years ago, and the desire of most private equity firms to run ever larger funds, has meant that VCTs are the only credible funding vehicle addressing the 'equity gap'". Surely, for a shortcoming that has been remarked for eight decades at least, it might have been possible for a solution to have emerged by now?

[38] This bias is understandable since the MBO involves a business with an established track record and managerial experience, particularly the "public to private" deals. But with the increasing numbers of "private equity" houses, and the scope offered to leverage debt, the MBO has become a major activity (Record £25 billion in 2005 with MBOs set fair – *FT* 3. 1.06). On the other hand, whether this activity is conducive to sustained focus on evolving the business, rather than "squeezing out" surplus costs before returning for a higher market quotation, must remain mute.

[39] A useful survey of how the US venture capital industry evolved from spin-offs from labs backed by government subsidy to "vulture capitalism", where "the typical IPO of the last decade (1990s) proved to be at best a mediocre investment, and at worst an outright wealth destroyer" is provided in *US Corporate Responses to New Challenges* in *Contests for Corporate Control* op. cit.

[40] There is an understandable reluctance among institutional investors to become holders of shares in smaller companies since, "With small companies accounting for only a few percent of the market, no balanced or UK Equity fund manager, benchmarked against the All-Share, is going to allocate a significant proportion of his portfolio to an in-house small Fund, particularly given the extra layer of cost involved." Moreover, "The small company problem is further compounded by the way the securities business works, dominated, as it is, by investment banks with high cost structures. Stockbrokers rely on transactions to generate revenue. Limited liquidity means few transactions. They cannot justify spending time on

companies in which there is little trade. Consequently, many small and mid-sized companies have only a few analysts following them."

"Through a perfectly rational sequence of decisions, balanced or UK Equity fund managers can end up with either no small or even midcap stocks in their portfolios – on the basis that they are not worth the bother – or with larger stakes than they would wish in illiquid small and medium-sized companies. This is not because they dislike the idea of investing in small companies. Many would welcome the opportunity to "spice up" their portfolios, to do something a bit different. But that is not what the business is about in today's world. They are boxed in, prisoners of circumstance." Tony Golding op. cit.pp 181ff.

[41] The liaison system between companies, analysts and financial journalists is "a ménage à trois that works because everyone gets something out of it", where "the name of the game is managing estimates to a number that can be modestly exceeded". Tony Golding op. cit. pp 203ff.

[42] Typically, the British brand of Public Private Partnerships, or Public Finance Initiative, activities will typically have legal/consultancy fees well above 20% of costs: a novel variant of "outdoor relief".

[43] The standard account is Charles Kindleberger's *Manias, Panics and Crashes* (Wiley).

[44] An entertaining tour through the diminishing circles rationale of the efficient market hypothesis (EMH) is contained in Mary O' Sullivan op. cit. pp 169ff., with the succinct quote from Prof Fama, "Market efficiency per se is not testable".

[45] Allen Sykes has been arguing, with other critics of the separation between finance and management, for mechanisms to restore "committed and knowledgeable long-term shareholders" – *Proposals for a Reformed System of Corporate Governance to Achieve Internationally Competitive Long-Term Performance* in *Capital Markets and Corporate Governance* op. cit. A theme that he develops further in *Capitalism for Tomorrow* (Capstone).

OH WOT A LUVELY TREASURY

All states have a custodian of the national treasure, but only Britain would have stuck it in the cellar of a Viceregal Lodge in a latter-day Whitehall Raj. Aloof, disinterested, uninformed, palisaded against rioting mobs, and protected by the hussars and Camel Corps of other Departments against the merest encroachment from the real world.[1] Handing out moneybags is accompanied by trammels of ballsaching bureaucracy: the endless pursuit and refinement of "criteria", with its recent elaboration of "targets", "tests", and "league tables" as measures of devolution; and "value for money" assessments that range from questionable to downright manipulated.

If the City is a dysfunctional source of finance for industry and imposes debilitating benchmarks for management, its natural synergetic companion is the Treasury. Sir Richard Wilson – then Cabinet Secretary – confirmed in his meditations to the Prime Minister in July 1998 "a weakness in looking ahead to future opportunities and threats": setting aside the banal management-speak, admission of a shortcoming stretching back over the years that has rolled into the perennial excuse of "decades of under investment". A failing that leads inevitably to sudden calls for "emergency" funding, equally inevitably increasingly large to make good historic shortfalls, and pushing governments into panic reactions – the national health service, railways and the London Underground but the most obvious recent examples, with others such as coping with London's sanitation, and meeting the "energy gap" still to come. In practice, a consistent strategy for "the orderly management of decline": except the "orderly" seems to have got lost.

There may be, assuming "world enough and time", a perverse enjoyment in the metaphysical exchanges and linguistic gobbledygook of dealing with the Treasury. An enjoyment emanating most likely from reading Lewis Carroll in early youth. Even if many of the exchanges would be regarded as pure fantasy in other countries. For example, "displaced concreteness" might be comprehensible, and in certain restricted contexts, actually meaningful. But apparently the game goes on, as we see references to "reputational externalities" in the rationale for the London Underground PPP.[2] And, to be fair, there is a caste, typically among the Oxbridge output, with a natural affinity to the comforts of acrostics and juggling numbers to suit the Treasury's web-weaving.[3] On the other hand, the staff effort to match these demands could require a quarter of the direct efforts of departmental personnel, and a diversion of a substantial element of effort elsewhere: creating an ever-increasing tension between calls for "smaller government" and the rising nugatory efforts to match the Treasury's stipulations. While the outcome of the Treasury's budgetary system is prone to perverse results.[4]

One of the mysteries of the British system is how the Treasury has managed to keep its vestments of purdah, or monastic cowls, even when at the centre of economic disasters. Its calculations and procedures for dealing with Parliament are so opaque as to require a subtlety in deciphering small print as to be beyond the reach of all but a few specialists. While the charge of multiple counting in budgetary statements, doctoring statistical material, in order to cast an opaque cloud to suit its purposes has led to public outcry, and the setting up of a UK Statistics Authority.[5] Yet within Whitehall, it calls the shots even though other Departments are left to keep a straight face in public.[6] This insulation has led to a peculiar amalgam of ignorance and arrogance.[7]

One of the oldest of Departmental criticisms is "Treasury 'reasons' are not worth considering at all... Reasons founded on entire ignorance... nothing can be more useless and absurd". Still valid, since ignorance is a precondition for maintaining the surrogate reality where the precepts of economics can be argued as relevant.[8] How else such claptrap as, "We are acting on behalf of the taxpayer and consumer"?

Ask not for what public services the consumer has to thank the Treasury, but this takes us back to the benches at the Chester Miracle Plays in tights, codpiece and bare bodkins.[9] The paranoid presumption is that others do not equally share these concerns, even if with a rather closer appreciation of what the consumer actually demands. How many generations of civil servants have identified the necessity for investment to maintain and improve health services; rail, road and air transport infrastructure; water supply and drainage systems; educational services...? Only to be met by Treasury responses that insult the intelligence of those actually in contact with the reality of such services.[10]

The extent to which the Treasury has been "captured" by the City in the past couple of decades is among the more opaque interfaces of contemporary Britain: for, it seems, we are fortunate in having anyone left in the Treasury, as staff are liable to "leave in droves to make fortunes in the City".[11] The converse is a process of reverse osmosis as the Treasury imposes across Whitehall the ethos and practices of the City. Obvious examples are the flow of public to private sales/buyouts – all contributing to the bonus packages of investment banks/lawyers/accountants (including presumably swathes of ex-Treasury officials); the City's "benchmarking" conventions, reflected in the plethora of "targets";[12] the vast expenditures on consultants;[13] and the variations of public/private partnerships.[14] Many of these manoeuvres driven less by genuine objectives of "value for money" – the fallacy of "risk transfer" spectacularly blown by the disaster of the British Rail privatisation – than hook-or-by-crookery to get spending out of the PSBR.

The Treasury is also the prime mover of the ultimate inertia machine. Look out for "review", or even more ominously "fundamental review", as pretexts for ensuring protracted lapse times before anything is done. Such exercises are usually conducted with a Treasury participation of fresh-faced novices, either from Universities or City outfits with no real-world experience. "Let's start from first principles" has been the driving force for decades of reinventing the wheel, while continuity of investment and management are undermined. The end product being, "constipation by review". But a gimmick only applicable in a setting without common aspirations.

By such devices, and normal purse-strings control, the sway of the Treasury's myopia extends over other Departments: hence the rote repetition of "free trade" – despite this happy condition never having existed,[15] and "flexibility".[16] If "insulation" has been the buttress against any awareness of the realities of industry, it has erected an even more impenetrable barricade against any awareness of the political economies of those around our Cook's Tour, all of whom have distinct national idioms, met by the traditional terms of ignorant dismissal – "socialist" or "corporatist".[17]

If financial markets are erected on the basis of "money is commerce decontaminated"[18] this is matched by the function of economics as the foundation for the surrogate reality within which the myopia of the Treasury functions – an edifice of some 150 years antiquity.[19] But the Treasury's essential quality, also shared with the City, is near contempt for any acknowledgement of responsibility for cock ups, leave alone even a modest apology.[20] Instead, we have been treated to the spectacle of "the best Chancellor for a century" every couple of decades: Roy Jenkins (export-led growth); Nigel Lawson (blowing the North Sea bonanza); and Gordon Brown (fantasy-fed and import-led growth). As a small consolation, for Whitehall watchers, one of the delights of New Labour has been how the Pooh-Bah aspirations of the Treasury to be "Lord-High Everything Else" has brought its dabbling increasingly into the public spotlight and displayed for all its comprehensive incompetence, instead of its traditional posture of skulking behind other Departments .[21]

If it seems a bit grumpy to kick the Treasury arse, it has a natural complement in the sect of "mad scientists" who were only too ready to offer politicians fantastical schemes to feed their "imperial" and "world-power" visions. These gave us the mountain of abortive aerospace prototypes, most glaringly the sleek form of Concorde, and the decision to opt for AGR nuclear stations rather than PWRs, compounding the error by insisting upon different design variants and consortia for each station.[22] Equally products of the same basic myopia.

If consolation is to be sought, it lies in the guarantee that Britain will never have a democratic deficit so long as the Treasury continues its detached existence. For no government can survive beyond a few elections with the Treasury in its key role, without rendering the economy in a state of popular revolt. The corollary is that leading political parties can maintain a steady flow of vacuous verbiage to spin out time before their next "buggins turn".

Value for Money in Other Climes

As a footnote on other perspectives, at a seminar on the theme of "project evaluation" merchant bankers, consultants and accountants had given their usual scintillating accounts of risk analysis, cash-flow sensitivities, securitization of future cash-flows, discounting, optimal organisational structures and so on. A distinguished silvery-haired member of the audience, after sitting silently through these presentations, remarked, "If these procedures had been applied in the twelfth century when some farmers started to recover land from the fens, we wouldn't have Holland." He was Tjebbe Visser, then Director General of the Dutch Ministry of Construction, whose budget customarily accounts for 25-30% of GDP.

Not bad as a bit of "increasing returns". And the same issue of "goods" beyond the conventional value analysis is raised by the Roman investment in roads connecting distant parts of Britain, ostensibly to allow movement of troops to control the country, but which has served as a key element of transport infrastructure for centuries since. Or the development of India's railways, also partially motivated by the need to ensure rapid military deployment, but, as a side effect, an essential component of the country's development ever since. In conventional economic discourse Holland is merely an "externality", or perhaps the accumulation of a series of "externalities".

But is money an adequate measure of value? Translating such components of value as safety, environmental consequences, stability of performance and externalities like "Holland" into monetary equivalents can lead to Byzantine reasoning. While "money" as a currency of measurement lays the process open to "accountancy" rationalisation – discounting, originally pursued as a methodology for comparing investment options, if adopted as an absolute measure effectively institutionalises "diminishing returns".

---

[1] Apparently, in preparing for the Fundamental Expenditure Review, the Treasury were surprised at the feedback from other Departments of the latter's view of the Treasury, "aggressive, rude, arrogant...", while Alan Bailey* – an ex-Treasury Deputy Secretary – on becoming Permanent Secretary at the Ministry of Transport is reported as saying, "It is difficult for people in the Treasury to realise how sheltered they are from the constant pressures of public accountability, to which those in spending departments are exposed." He might also have mentioned the Treasury's immunity to the pressure on those who actually deliver public services on the ground. From *The Secret Treasury* by David Lipsey (Viking) (p 179).

An equal source of aggravation is the convention, springing from the principle of unified Cabinet responsibility, whereby Departmental officials have to implement and defend the consequences of Treasury machinations – however crazy: and observing blank expressions of incredulity and stupefaction among those outside the Whitehall system is part of the normal daily round.

David Lipsey's book, well received among the coterie of economic plauditors, is a delightfully double-edged read for those in the real world who may want an insight to the detached, and, some might conclude, demented, world of the nation's economic management. But it offers a fair account of Treasury mores, since the author seems to have been granted access to many of its acolytes, and for the purpose of this chapter will be quoted without repeating references. But perhaps the most galling feature of this tome is the praise of Treasury officials "hard work" regime. As nothing to the extra workload burdens they lumber – often at short notice – across all other Departments.

[2] Quoted from an outburst by Bob Kiley, when London Transport Commissioner (*Guardian* 2.5.01), who obviously suffered from the disability of thinking that his actual experience of running underground systems was of the least concern to the Treasury. To play the Whitehall game, he should instead have enquired whether there were not also compensating "disreputable externalities".

[3] Lipsey gives a useful summary of the bureaucratic variations from the Public Expenditure Survey Committee (PESC) established following the Plowden Committee in 1961, with Program Analysis Review (PAR) cycles, Fundamental

Expenditure Reviews coming on the scene in the 1990s, and the current variation of Comprehensive Spending Reviews. With their accompanying "Star Chambers", EDX Committees and variations thereafter. While, beneath this shifting mountain of bureaucracy, the nation has been subjected to a continuing series of 5th form test tube economic experiments: "displacement", "crowding out", "Laffer", "monetarism", and "shadowing". Not to mention EuroPES, a device to net off any receipts from EU programmes against approved spending – despite EU funds being intended to be additional to national budgets, and interminable debates (and consequential disruption) on "national test discount rates". All without the slightest regard for the sheer waste of effort involved.

Typical of the Treasury's cavalier attitude to other people's time was their insistence on "discounting" the forward estimates on Concorde, when the results would do no more than demonstrate that a disastrous outcome of several £100ms in losses would be calculated to "several several £100ms" at current prices. But an exercise that, given the range of financial flows involved in the project, took three busy staff out of real work for a couple of days. But other departmental officials could multiply examples by the score.

And it doesn't seem to have improved. Michael Bichard*, in his farewell interview, "A tireless crusader for hands-on experience" (*FT* 3.7.01) remarked, "I am regularly told that for the Treasury [management experience] is not necessary. And I say it is *more* necessary, because they are setting the targets and challenging departments about whether things are working. I think that you need management expertise to do that." Not, of course, if "cultivated ignorance" is an essential prerequisite to maintaining the fantasy of economics in support of "detached aplomb".

[4] Again typical, a system based on "cash budgeting" is peculiarly bad at coping with sudden increases (or decreases). One's first encounter with this quirk was in my first appointment in Trunk Roads, Division where, in the mid-fifties the government suddenly realised that the nation's roads were falling below even adequacy and introduced a sharp increase in expenditure both for starting the new Motorway network, and to upgrade existing roads. Given the sheer practical constraints on schemes that could be rapidly started and responsibly monitored, these were not going to mop up the available annual budget. Rather than forego funds unspent at the end of the year's budget, the wheeze of "bottlenecks" was invented whereby sums – of the order of £200,000 i.e. below the threshold for seeking approval as a distinct "scheme" – could be spent on short stretches of road of 4-5 miles, providing these were not contiguous. Drivers on the A1 for the subsequent four decades will have undergone the experience of the road changing character every few miles, punctuated by roundabouts, between "bottlenecks" since the gaps were not filled in before the budget was subjected to the next panic cut. This experience was only terminated in the 1990s as the whole route was brought to Motorway standard.

But the "cash budgeting" obsession has claimed many more spectacular disasters. Again Departments could compile an Almanac, but none more stupid than the sad travails of London Transport when they were expected to meet the escalation in costs on the Jubilee Line from their usual "cash" allocation, to the direct detriment of funds available for maintenance and improvements elsewhere. This stashed up investment requirements to a scale that the Treasury could only duck by the byzantine PPP arrangements.

[5] Even with legislation on the table, there is still a call for "the Treasury must make the necessary concessions" to increase "public trust in statistics". (Not lies but statistics – *FT* 8.1.07). And, even with a new UK Statistics Authority, there are still lingering doubts as to how far it can insulate itself against Treasury intrusion. Yet it might be too discriminatory to focus just on the Treasury, for, like many organisations relying upon economic modelling on inadequate data, there is the inevitable temptation to pursue "policy-based evidence-making", a delightful phrase pointed at the World Bank by Aid Agencies (Ideology that may be driving the bank: Letters, *FT* 27.12.06).

[6] Perhaps the sharpest public critique has come from Philip Stephens in what most civil servants would regard as the Treasury's house magazine, the *Financial Times* (Troubling times for the top man at the Treasury – 6.9.05). Among the choice extracts are, "The august institution.... has long been the most arrogant and aloof of government departments. Its cast of mind defies the historical record. The past half-century, after all, is littered with economic misjudgements. Harold Wilson's devalued pound. Tony Barber's boom and bust. James Callaghan's supplication before the International Monetary Fund. Nigel Lawson's miracle-turned-mirage and John Major's humiliation on Black Wednesday are among moments that leap from recent history.... No matter. Nothing rattles the Treasury's unwavering self-belief. I remember being told by a former permanent secretary that its foremost talent was a capacity to execute perfect U-turns while insisting that it was travelling in a straight line.... The irony is that the Treasury has never been good at making policy. Its role is to count the beans rather than spend them. So recent forays beyond that remit have not all been unalloyed successes. Costly public/private sector partnerships to modernise the London Underground, renationalisation of Railtrack and the administrative chaos surrounding tax credits for working families come to mind... is so widely mistrusted within and outside government. A measure of opprobrium is an inevitable price of holding the purse strings. But the disquiet goes beyond that. The Treasury answers to political masters; but it once contrived to draw a moderately clear line between serious policy and political expediency."

In normal language, "perfect U-turns" translates into, "totally unscrupulous". For example, having denied proposals for private funds to be employed in transport infrastructure under the pre-Gorbachev rationale of the Ryrie Rules – "The Treasury had traditionally imposed strict limits on public use of private money. Under the Ryrie Rules, it was easier to get camels through the eyes of needles than private-public projects past Treasury scrutiny. For example, private finance could only be used if it could be shown to be cheaper than funding the same project from public money. This was so even if there was no public money available, so that the alternative to private finance in practice was delaying or ditching the project altogether." Yet, the Private Finance Initiative, the converse of this rationale, became seamlessly attractive through its convenience to provide finance off-balance-sheet against restrained borrowing limits. In fact, the only occasion when one consciously broke the unwritten rule of not denouncing in public the Treasury, came at a Civil Engineering EDC where the industry challenged the Ryrie Rules and both myself and a colleague from the Department of Environment turned to our Treasury companion with the remark, "You're on your own, mate."

[7] The arrogance seems to stem from an extraordinary self-aggrandisement – "The Treasury does have extremely good people", except "It's male dominated; it's public school dominated, it's Oxbridge dominated", recalling the antique excellence of the "Balliol double-first".

Yet, in the experience of most working Departments, the Treasury also maintains a press gang to commandeer, on their own unique criteria, from the dumbest reaches of the population. Maybe this is from the same source. But recorded on files around departments are occasions when the cost of exchanges with the Treasury exceeded the sum in dispute: one vividly recalls a struggle over £80,000 for new fire-fighting clothing before the sale of Hurn Airport to the Bournemouth authority that dragged on for several months, consuming vastly higher sums in bureaucratic exchanges, when it was clear that the government had no option but to meet this cost.

[8] Ignorance remains, of course, an essential prerequisite to sustaining the doctrinal adherence to economics. The passage from my farewell note that somehow got leaked to the *Financial Times*, and which has prompted many civil service colleagues to commend others to read, seems even more apposite today and runs:

"But the myth carries on. Sir Robin Butler, who hasn't strayed too far from the environs of Great Russell Street and so probably is another reasonably representative nice Treasury chap, remarked in a lecture on the new agency approach for Whitehall "...whether the business is in aircraft or toffee apples, waterproofs or widgets. For them all there is, at the end of the day, the same bottom line. They can all be equally tested by the return which they make on the assets of their shareholders and obliged to change if the trend is in the wrong direction". And, he goes on, "in some areas, of course, the services provided by Government.... are or can be subject to similar market pressures." But then, of course, there is a good deal that is of a social interest, subtlety, and political character beyond such testing. Maybe he was just reiterating a standard Treasury brief. But if such crashing condescension goes down okay with a British audience, in Frankfurt or Osaka these remarks would probably gather no more than the polite applause accorded to a talking polar bear. For the view of business, the role of shareholders and common purpose between public and private sectors is rather different in the more competitive industrial economies. The point is not to have a poke at doughty Treasury warriors, but rather to point out that the "market efficiency" myth is used as a convenient pretext to pretend that there is some "invisible" mechanism to create order and a sensible use of resources, where patently there is not. And such effect as there is does not produce the dynamics for competitiveness compared to other countries – in any field of industry and commerce.

Such allegiance to a "market efficiency" totem probably needs a structural anthropologist to work out. But a large part of the blame must lie in the fact that we still have an education system optimised on the output of instant anachronisms. For these, economics appears to provide, if not perhaps an "opiate", at least a surrogate reality, with a comfortable algebra whereby events can be assumed to follow similar general patterns, sufficient to ensure the minimum contact with reality. There is, indeed, a striking synergy between the "cult of the amateur", whereby cultivated ignorance is a positive virtue to maintain that detachment of mind necessary to consider the high abstractions of "policy", and the notion that there is a self-regulatory system that by and large ensures the common good in the rather grubby commercial world without sullying the purity of those dealing with principles. Taking a macro-view, perhaps "policy" formulation as practised in Britain is a nigh-perfect fusion between the pretensions of those who purport to do it and the delusions upon which such pretensions necessarily depend."

[9] Let's just juggle. How many Producers are not also Consumers and Taxpayers? How far does the Consumer's capacity to consume and pay taxes derive from employment by a Producer or service activity dependent on a Producer? On what is the Consumer to exercise his function satisfactorily if not to enjoy the choices offered by Producers? And so on. In practice, a nonsense argument depending on fallacious exclusive terminology. And consuming doesn't generate any exports.

[10] A frustration most elegantly expressed recently by Baroness Onora O'Neill in her essay "A View from "Near Abroad" in *Changing Times* (OCSC 2005).

[11] "Agency capture" is a technical term for situations where undue influence is exercised by one agent over another, thus, in theory, upsetting the functioning of "markets". In the special pleading of the Treasury this is apparently termed "producer capture", and is a core component of the self-proclaimed "institutional *raison d'etre* to protect the common weal against vested interests". "To Treasury man, the outside world is a dangerous place, full of people who want to grab the taxpayers' money or use the state's power for their own purposes. It is better to keep a clear head and avoid their blandishments."

Such arrogance, however, conveniently overlooks the "vested interests" buzzing around the City, all focused on squeezing as much as they can from whatever source, not least the taxpayer.

There is apparently a suppressed recognition of this skewed ethos, in the words of one wise mandarin, the Treasury "should try to distinguish between producer capture and recognising that producers, too, have hearts. Without meaning to, the Treasury does things that are very harmful to producers, simply because it has never understood how these people tick" – there is more than a suggestion that the "blandishments" of City interests may indeed influence the Treasury in its exercise of regulatory functions over financial services. Witness

Don Cruickshank's outrage that his proposals to police payment systems networks among banks (in his report on *Competition in UK Banking*) were frustrated (How bank reform was sabotaged: *FT* 22.2.05), where he concludes, "The banks do not just rely on the power of the senior civil service to look after them. They practise what the Japanese call *amakudari* – descent from heaven – whereby top bureaucrats on retirement land jobs in the industries for which they were responsible. Indeed, the civil servant responsible for the banks while I was doing the review went to Royal Bank of Scotland shortly thereafter. It does not look or feel right. It is not right."

[12] As an antidote to the trend of targetry, *The Audit Society* by Michael Power (Oxford) offers an Orwellian warning of the dangers of ingesting the matrices of financial markets: if no substitute for a reading of his experience-based argument, just a couple of cautionary extracts from the concluding section:

"The question which must be brought back to the surface in every particular case is whether the tail may be wagging the dog and, in the process, whether audit provides deluded visions of control and transparency which satisfy the self-image of managers, regulators and politicians but which are neither as effective nor as neutral as commonly imagined. Against official images of a technical fix I have counterpoised the possibility that audit emerges more as a new form of image management. Rather than as a basis for substantive change, it is a practice which requires social trust in the judgments of its practitioners and which is only superficially empowering to the notional publics which give it its purpose. And when audit fails, or is presumed to fail, strategies exist to insulate it from radical inquiry about its role and operational capability. Worse still, audits may turn organisations on their heads and generate excessive preoccupations with, often costly, auditable process. At the extreme, performance and quality are in danger of being defined largely in terms of conformity to such process....

Finally, the way societies call individuals and organisations to account says much about fundamental social and economic values. Power is this ability to demand accounts, to exercise control over performance, while at the same time remaining unaccountable. Such accounting arrangements are necessarily contingent and varied, ranging across formal and informal, financial and non-financial, detailed and aggregated measures of performance. Auditing operationalises a balance of liberty and discipline which is not shaped simply by objective economic necessity or commonsense. Rather, even in its most mundane techniques, it reflects a complex and not always consistent constellation of social attitudes to risk, trust, and accountability. The motif of the audit society reflects a tendency for audit to become a leading bearer of legitimacy and this must be so because other sources of legitimacy, such as community and state, are declining in influence. So the audit society is a symptom of the times, coincidentally a fin de siècle, in which a gulf has opened up between poorly rewarded 'doing' and highly rewarded 'observing'."

Judging by his views subsequently (reported in the *Observer* 12.5.02), his worst fears have been realised as the "audit explosion" has "extended its purview from cost control to broader evaluation of almost any kind of performance". The article recalls an *Economist* survey which identified a total of 600 targets against which public services had to perform "from hospital waiting times to literacy to crime clearance rates – all for which figures have to be collected internally, to be monitored and audited externally."

Consequently there has been a continuing chorus of complaint. Again, a persuasive series of Reith Lectures by Baroness Onera O'Neill (*A Question of Trust* (Cambridge)), pointing up the nonsense of routine matrices applied to genuinely demanding professional tasks (and contrasting this with a corresponding failure to regulate the press). This gave rise, amongst other commentaries, to a perceptive critique by Michael Prowse (Topsy-turvy culture of accountability: *FT* 30.6.02), "Why have British governments imposed on public sector professionals a singularly burdensome form of regulation (and one with few parallels in the developed world), while acquiescing in any amount of misrepresentation, distortion and deception by powerful elements of the print media?

"The answer, as so often these days, lies in the uncritical adoption of free-market doctrines by governments of both right and left. This has had the effect of elevating to the status of a universal truth a certain narrow type of accountability that markets, when properly competitive, can guarantee....

"Academics, teachers and doctors, by contrast, are unaccountable *by definition* because they do not sell anything to anyone and so are not subject to market disciplines. Since they do not have to respond to consumers' shifting preferences, there is no alternative but to invent surrogates for market pressures, such as endless performance targets, audits and reporting requirements.... the things that are truly valuable can be appraised neither by markets nor by the facile methods of the management consultants who have taken over Whitehall."

For Treasury-watchers, Simon Jenkin's *Thatcher and Sons* (Allen Lane) offers a delightful summary of the "manic" approaches to targetry, exaggerated reliance on consultancies, and questionable devices to pursue "value for money" in the post-Thatcher years.

[13] The literature on the dubious value of consultancies is extensive. If Carol Kennedy's synopsis, *Guide to the Management Gurus* (Business Books Ltd) is a convenient entry into the lexicon of jargon, *The Witch Doctors* by John Micklethwait and Adrian Wooldridge (Heinemann) is a cautionary introduction to the quicksands beneath the cloaks of the avowed profession. While *Rip-off* by David Craig (Original Book Company), if prone to ramble, is an entertaining firsthand account of some of the ruses and scams employed in what has become a soft public-sector market in Britain. While his succeeding account in *Plundering the Public Sector* is an even more vivid account of actual examples exploiting the naivety of Whitehall in coping with the conmanship of the British private sector. Other commentators have remarked on the ominous presence of "McKinsey man" among the corps of special advisers, a presence not reflected in any improvement in performance.

The surrender of competence to "consultants" has an august tradition in the literature on industrial decline: "This reliance on market mechanisms for coordination was reflected in the importance of the consulting engineer, whose baleful influence on innovation and export performance was cited by a number of authors.... The institution of the consulting engineer provides an excellent example of the effects on corporate organisation of exclusive reliance on contractual arrangements in the innovation and design processes." (Industrial Research 1900-50, by D.C.Mowery in *The Decline of the British Economy* op. cit. 189ff).

The pervasive spread of the "consultant" may owe something to the generous tax treatment for avowedly commercial services – a convenient shelter for bombed-out ex-managers, but goes back to the special "division of labour" between "abstract thinking", "doing" and "making", on a declining scale of class status. "The English attachment to pure science was in keeping with a longstanding set of class values whereby abstract or classical subjects were a mark of status superiority for the upper classes. It was, in the words of one critic, 'fashionable to direct the intellect into useless channels'" (W.H.Bailey, *Journal of the Society of Chemical Industry*: 1896, cited by Julia Wrigley in *Technical Education and Industry in the 19th Century* in *The Decline of the British Economy* op. cit.). And nothing seems to have changed since.

The pursuit of "policy" divorced from the practicalities of "delivery" is probably the purest diversion of "the intellect into useless channels". But worse, to become involved in the real management of "doing" is far too demeaning, so that "the consultant" becomes a convenient transitional object to reach to "the practical" without the nausea of direct involvement – irrespective, of course, whether the consultant is genuine or up to the job.

Sadly, for the rest of us, the Treasury has been hoist on its petard – or tripped over its tangled knickers, or knackered itself on its knotted jock-straps, or whatever – in its reliance on a "fiscal target" without probing the sustainability of the revenue stream from the boom of 1998 to 2000. As John Kay has pointed out (Labour's affair with bankers is to blame for this sorry state: *FT* 25/26.4 .09), "The reasons targets do not work are evident from any study of the failure of planned economies. You can require people to meet goals, but that is not at all the same as encouraging them to meet the objectives behind the goals. By emphasising targets you undermine both their motivation and their ability to achieve these more fundamental underlying goals. In a delicious irony, a major victim of this process would be the Treasury itself. ... We now know that many of the banking profits of that period were illusory. But they generated substantial revenues from corporation tax and income tax on bonuses. The real funding gap was wider even than it appeared."

[14] There have been some astonishingly naïve slip-ups (or deliberate omissions) in the early PFI's – notably in missing the scope for the private interests to refinance their borrowings once the "risks" of construction had passed. Not entirely inadvertent, it seems, from the PAC's inquiries into the Norfolk and Norwich University Hospital PFI, where the private consortium was offered an open book for gratuitous gains through refinancing – "The Treasury had guidelines specifically saying there should be no refinancing clauses. It was a lure to get the

private sector involved.... Ultimately it all stems from Treasury guidance. It was the Treasury prohibiting refinancing clauses" (*Guardian* 9.5.06). Eventually, we have the Treasury owning up, "The position of the Treasury at the time was that to encourage entrance into the market, we would not include refinancing or gain-share clauses" – not us lot now, Guv ("How any hospitals and the prison service were barred from making gains in early refinancing deals" – *FT* 28.1.06). And, unsurprisingly, the genuine "value for money" remains unproven – see, "Sector opaque as ever on value for money" in the survey "Uncertain destination: will private finance for public projects soon run out of road?" (*FT* 8.2.06). And in several instances, especially among Health Trusts and Education Boards, the penalties of extra interest payments are beginning to become significant financial burdens.

While the National Audit Office has noted that the cost to the public sector owing to delays in tendering was "at least £63m", with the full figure undoubtedly much higher after it examined a sample of projects that closed between 2004 and 2006. PFI projects were taking on average almost 3 years – 34 months – to tender, when the norm should be no more than 18 to 24 months; one third of projects had only two groups willing to submit detailed bids, compared to one in six projects previously – hence making the public sector vulnerable if a bidder pulled out; negotiations to finalise the deal with a preferred bidder were getting longer, on average over a year, and in some cases as long as five years; and that in a third of projects the public sector changed what it wanted significantly during preferred bidder negotiations, on average altering contract values by 17% (*FT* 8.3.07). By any standards, a sad commentary on the "efficiency" of this British technique of financial engineering.

A charmingly wry comment on the characteristics of the PFI approach comes from Franciseo Fernández Sáinz, the head of the military transport aircraft division at EADS, responding to questioning by the Commons Defence Committee on delays to the contract for the air tanker order by the RAF, "It is an expensive way.... but it is difficult to say to a country that this is wrong or this is not right." And when pressed on how the costs of PFI compared with a straightforward acquisition, he replied, "I cannot answer this question... It is a good business for banks and lawyers, that is for sure."

Despite the claim that this is a technique "invented in Britain", it is worth recalling that "consortia" between manufacturers, banks and local authorities were applied in Germany in the late 19th century, particularly in the investment phase of introducing the "new" technology of electrical power. And almost certainly without the bureaucratic and legalistic waste of resources of its British variant.

[15] Not that there ever was any chance of the state of "greatest liberty" being achieved: even Adam Smith was far from sanguine about this condition being attainable judging by the catalogue of instances of counter-tendencies e.g. confederations, labour unions, apprentice training, the Corn Laws, intervention of governments, to the point where having a pint in the local is an excuse for plots to be hatched "against the public interest". While the myriad of literature on "how to

do business..." in China, India, Japan, South Korea, and virtually every European state suggests that "language" and "culture" could be added to the list of obstacles.

[16] The old hollow rhetoric continues, "The UK economy... needs to focus on high value added business, where skills, productivity and flexibility are at a premium" (Gus O'Donnell* "The Relationship between Economy and the State" in *Changing Times* (OCSC)). Not yet out of the "...men, like other commodities" rationale. And still without recognising that "flexible labour markets" misses the "increasing returns" from "flexible labour" within the community of enterprises oriented towards long-term success.

[17] Symptomatic of this myopia was a remark by Geoff (James)Littler*, a doughty senior Treasury official, on return from his first visit to Japan – "God. They're interventionist". Prompting speculation on what he thought had been going on for the past century.

[18] A useful phrase from Alistair Mant's *The Rise and Fall of the British Manager* (Macmillan), quoted in The *Seven Cultures of Capitalism* (Platkus).

[19] A significant feature of the essays in *Changing Times* ibid. lies in its starting point with the Northcote-Trevelyan reforms of 1854, as though the world had not changed since then. In perhaps the quote of the century, the then Permanent Secretary of the Treasury, and subsequently Head of the Civil Service, boldly declared, "The fundamental skill set for this new administrative cadre however revolved around the policy advice and consigliore function. What would nowadays be called 'delivery' skills were confined largely to the military and colonial services." The frankest admission yet that "policy" has been an ethereal exercise in verbal sophistry divorced from any awareness of practical delivery. And conversely that the reality of implementation has been inadmissible to the dream world of "policy". But bluntly, any "policy" that does not embrace "delivery" must be spurious.

[20] And this quality seems to rub off on Chancellors, witness the *Economist*'s quip about Gordon Brown, "who doesn't do modestly" (1.10.05). Even when clobbered by the National Audit Office for "acting like chief executives looking only to boost their short-term share price", singling out for criticism Gordon Brown's pet schemes – tax credits and pension credits. The former had created "chaos and confusion" because of a "failure of imagination and sociological competence," while the latter represented "a terrible waste of resources" (*The Economist* 29.7.06). But was there ever a Chancellor who did "do modestly"?

[21] Hence the splendid outburst, "The Treasury Trabant has run out of road" (*FT* 12.2.08). This highlights "the Treasury's capacity to separate its lofty self-regard and status from its record", and its recent mode of having "ruthlessly amassed the responsibilities of several other departments – and then made a hash of them." The list skims through "the half-baked part-privatisation of the London Underground"; "the Treasury's tax credit scheme... still costing £1bn a year in

overpayments and fraud" – with only £2bn (recovered) of the £6bn overpaid since 2003; and "The price of Empire-building has been neglect of the Treasury's core responsibilities. The dithering over the future of Northern Rock has spoken to the weakness of the oversight of financial markets, the backlash over changes in capital gains tax to the incoherence of tax policy, the Inland Revenue's loss of personal data of 25m recipients of child benefit to managerial chaos."

On top of this, a range of self-erected "strategic objectives" most within the purview of other departments, and occasionally tipping into the absurd: apparently these include "higher productivity in other (yes other) European economies" – the suggestion that the Treasury had the remotest acquaintance with "productivity" would come as the proverbial bolt from the blue for generations of civil servants, apart from the obvious evidence that this country has fallen behind other major European economies.

[22] If confirmation were needed of the synergy between zany scientists and the Treasury, "The UK Advanced Gas-cooled Reactor programme has resulted in a series of reactors that are unique to the UK. The variety of designs and limited number of reactors built has made it challenging to encourage the UK supply chain to invest in the facilities and staff required to support long-term operation and maintenance. There is no global market to support these UK specific reactor designs and many of the original equipment manufacturers have ceased trading. This has resulted in increased costs of ownership and operation, as additional skills need to be developed and retained in-house by the operator. Selection of the standard international reactor design would have given access to both international operating experience and a secure global supply chain for long-term support." (Andy Spurr, Deputy Chief Nuclear Officer, British Energy – quoted in IBM Business Consulting Services' report "An evaluation of the capability and capacity of the UK and global supply chains to support a new nuclear build programme in the UK" 2005).

THE POLITICAL CAVALCADE

To assign the Treasury a higher role in industrial decline than politicians is a nice call. With its hypocritical presumption of resisting "producer capture" – despite being in thrall to the City – and the surrogate reality against which government activities are assessed, the country has suffered a unique miasma of impotence. Politicians, however entertaining, have rarely had the nous or inclination to challenge this dogma – save in the zany escapade of Tony Benn and the extreme left, the dodgiest basis on which to mount any challenge. Mostly just preoccupied with other "matters of state", or just too bored. The most lethal combination, as Lord Roll concluded, has been Ministers who fancy themselves as literate in economics being appointed to the Treasury, where they are absorbed into the prevailing sludge. However glittering the resulting boom, the inevitable subsequent bust has rendered Britain's economic progress comparable to early attempts to conquer Everest.

In the immediate aftermath of World War II, those countries on our Cook's Tour circuit were focusing their efforts to rebuild, or create, their industrial capabilities, with governments invariably taking a central role – encouraged by the necessity to allocate Marshall Aid funds or aid provided in support of Cold War alliances (Britain's Marshall Aid instead was devoted to reduce national debt). All had a sense of national purpose that commanded public consensus. Whether building on historic traditions, institutions and network structures or driving from a minimum inherited base, such as South Korea and Taiwan, to build up native skills and technological competences.

Meanwhile, in Britain the political caste laboured under an enormous jumble of baggage. The overhang of Empire,[i] with its "fighting retreat" from territories before wan ceremonies of pulling down the Union Jack; sporadic gestures to compensate by edging towards Europe; and preoccupations with the nation's "place in the world", after being one of the Big Three during the War, tenuously hanging on to pretensions of a leading role in the Cold War. But against an undeniable US dominance that

---

[i] Among the various accounts of "Empire" in its dying years, *A Fighting Retreat – the British Empire 1947-97* by Robin Nellands (Hodder and Stoughton) is a vivid survey.

continuously stretched the resources necessary to sustain British pretensions. Domestically, the common priority was the welfare reforms following the Beveridge Report, and such contacts with industry were confined to occasional leisurely sessions with the barons. And a special British piquancy in the soap opera of personality clashes, intrigues, scandals and posturing reflected in the reams of commentaries, autobiographies, biographies, diaries, memoirs, and cheered on by the media hangers on.[ii]

So far as there was a government interest in industry, this was focused through perpetuation of the Ministry of Supply on those – aerospace, naval, defence electronics and army weaponry – that supported the Cold War role. But, just as in the aerospace industry, without recognising the imperatives of evolving commercial markets. Elsewhere, for the first decade after the War, as industries in countries involved in the hostilities recovered, British companies had a relatively easy run, particularly in Imperial markets. Consequently, with no previous interest in the industrial evolution of other countries, and the classical Oxbridge education that barely recognised industry as a normal human activity, the inexorable drift was continued myopia of what was going on elsewhere when there were matters of post-imperial import and international stage-strutting to take the attention.

The Suez Crisis in 1955/56, triggered by Colonel Nasser's coup and nationalisation of the Canal, his government's developing relations with the Soviet Union, and then the actual invasion of the Canal Zone grabbed all the headlines. But unnoticed beneath this hurly-burly was the rise of Japan's shipbuilders to overtake Britain as the leading maritime producer in 1955. If the Suez Crisis is regarded as the turning point when Britain's Imperial jodhpurs fell around the knees, the withering of the shipbuilding industry was a rusty template of decline replicated subsequently with variations across swathes of other industries.

The shipbuilding industry had several common national traits – a fragmented structure, with baronial yard owners and a tradition of labour disputes, even during the War, over demarcations (more guilds than building a mediaeval cathedral, to recall Correlli Barnett's depiction), hours, overtime rates, or whatever.[iii] This concoction, where each faction believed itself to be a special case with special entitlement to continue their antique practices without change, was least fitted to cope with falling sales, loss of market share, contracting utilisation, rising costs, demands for lay-offs, feeding back into historic unstable labour relations. And

---

[ii] Entertainingly catalogued in *Never Had It so Good* by Dominic Sandbrook (Little Brown).
[iii] A wistful obituary is provided in *The Rise and Fall of British Shipbuilding* by Anthony Burton (Constable).

pressures increased as South Korean, European and Latin American yards increased their investment and efficiencies, and as the market fell sharply in the aftermath of the "oil shocks" of the 70s.

Over three subsequent decades, this special blend of decline was carried through with the inevitable "Committee", with its chairman immortalised by its title – "The Geddes Report"; the inevitable calls for collaboration; inevitably ineffective "consolidations"; rising political temperatures as Ministers became dragged in – "the Clyde running through my office"; sporadic efforts to stimulate investment by selective assistance; nationalisation, with the high farce of "hybridity"; privatisation, and finally a few yards hanging on to sporadic naval orders and special projects.

This turmoil, however, missed out entirely on the crucial investment and organisational structures necessary to face up to rising competitors and to handle the new generation of container ships,[1] bulk carriers or cruise liners. Missing out also on the fundamental changes in working practices and supplier relationships that were enhancing the efficiency of Japanese, and then South Korean, shipbuilders. And the beriberi of decline spread to suppliers – steel, motors, pumps, valves, steering gear etc, and in turn through the component supplier network, leading to further layoffs and pretexts for militant action. And so on.

Beyond the imperial/Cold War industries, awareness of the interdependencies of industrial structures only permeated slowly into the political consciousness. Despite the birth of the Ministry of Technology in the 60s carrying over the "white heat" rhetoric, look not for the technocratic focus being applied elsewhere. For the British mindset was a blend of the antique Oxbridge programming of "parsing the gerund and a smattering of Adam Smith", and attitudes scarred by memories of unemployment lines in the 30s: for the generation of political leaders of all parties up to the mid-70s, this was a continuing legacy leading to an overriding concern with "employment" but tipping into a defensive attitude towards Trade Unions, opening the way to the surge of the extreme left. Toss in periodic bouts of "going for growth"[2] – the Maudling/Barber/Lawson booms – so that the process of stop-go became an ingredient of decline. The slopping around of these traits in the parochial national bucket, with the later addition of Thatcherism, underlay Keith Joseph's melancholy shake of the head, "Britain is the only country that politicised industry". And the outcome of this historic sludge created "The British Disease" – extravagant pay demands, strikes, stoppages, breakdown in supply chains, ludicrous pay settlements, high inflation, loss of market share, contraction, consolidation, layoffs, strikes, stoppages....

Within this mock-heroic there was a mythical episode derided by subsequent commentators as "corporatist". With rising trade deficits, continuing labour breakdowns, high inflation, and increasing competitive performance of other countries, it dawned on Ministers in the 60s that the wheels were coming off the economic hackney carriage. And after one of the regular doses of "stop" – Selwyn Lloyd's "little budget" in July 1961, which included increasing purchase tax to 10%, bank rate raised to 7%, cutbacks in government spending and a "pay pause", the brilliant solution of a National Development Council was propounded, for "a joint examination of the economic prospects of the country stretching five or more years into the future.... Above all, it would try to establish what are the essential conditions for realising potential growth. That covers, first, the supply of labour and capital, secondly, the balance of payments conditions and the development of imports and exports, and thirdly, the growth of incomes. In other words, I want both sides of industry to share with the Government the task of relating plans to the resources likely to be available."[3]

Wow! A typical recognition of "both sides of industry", repeated running down the years in political rhetoric, still evident in the continuing tetchy exchanges between the CBI and TUC, and underwritten by the mantra of "flexible labour markets". To the point where "both sides of industry" should rank high on the epitaph of British industry. But hardly likely to rattle the china in the teahouses of Asia. If the formation of the NEDC (The National Economic Development Council, as it subsequently became labelled, with a supporting staff comprising the Office, hence the variant NEDO) was a typically lame national reaction to the inescapably better performance of France, with its structures of "indicative planning", and the "consensus" style of Nordic countries. That the furthest reach of the political telescope was near Europe – ignoring the steps being taken in Japan, South Korea and Taiwan, or even among the German Lander Governments – was only further illustration of the traditional myopia.

But the NEDC was bound to fail. The "barons" of industry, no more than the "barons" of the Trade Unions, were incapable of delivering cohesion among their respective cohorts. Even after the Chequers meeting of November 1975, where there was apparent agreement on both sides to work together under NEDO with the more active application of "selective assistance" to stimulate laggard investment, continuing distrust between "both sides of industry" inhibited the consensus necessary to overcome the general failings that had been laid bare by the analysis of the collapse of the motorcycle industry.[4]

Yet it would be unfair to blame only the arrogant "baronial" outlook of the two "sides". For there was elsewhere, not least in Whitehall, a vacuum in knowledge of the real prerequisites for industrial advance in the international context of evolving technologies and processes. A failing conditioned by the output of generations of "well-rounded amateurs" from the best of British education.[5] Among politicians, the only partial exception to the convention of relying on advice from "the barons" was the oddball approach of Tony Benn at the Department of Industry, when, from whatever mixture of motives, he enjoyed the populist practice of whipping around among "the workers": but again with no appreciation of the necessities to meet the demands of international competition. As the collapse of the motorcycle industry illustrated in neon lights. For a time there was even some effort to bridge the gap through demands on DTI staff to monitor actual activities in companies receiving "selective assistance", with several becoming interested in the new production practices/processes evolving among leading competitors and increasingly adept at questioning antique managerial/worker attitudes in British companies.

That commentators should have labelled these lame attempts as "corporatism" betrays a complete failure to observe how other countries were focusing their national efforts, and equally betrays the total absence of those technocratic competencies necessary to run such systems effectively. Nor, if the release of animal spirits from market liberalisation since the 1980s, heralded by the same commentators, is there any evidence that the "market" has been any more successful in evolving competitive British enterprises: indeed, it could be argued, this period has seen an even more disastrous decline in the country's industrial capabilities.

For, behind the political strutting and pseudo-economic jargon, the advent of Mrs Thatcher as Prime Minister coincided with the first significant landings of oil from the North Sea. And, for all the triumphalism of the Thatcher years in "defeating the miners" and "curing the British Disease", it was only in practice to replace this malady with "variant Dutch disease" – "When a country strikes hydrocarbons, a sudden inflow of dollar-denominated revenues often leads to a sharp appreciation in the domestic currency. That tends to make non-oil sectors like agriculture and manufacturing less competitive on world markets, thus leaving oil to dominate the economy."[6] An effect amplified by the high interest rates pursued by the new Tory government in the early 80s, which resulted in closure of some 20% of manufacturing capacity: just when many firms were waking up that there were other ways than "piecework".

Yet the British variant has a number of distinguishing features. Firstly, the very limited duration of "the inflow" of revenues and domestic supplies of oil and gas. These may have underwritten the politically expedient tax cuts of the Lawson years, supported the "defeat of the miners", indirectly – as revenues dipped for a time – stimulated the "privatisations" to make up the PSBR, and for a time allowed moderate gas prices following privatisation of the Central Electricity Generating Board (also uniquely enabled by the CEGB having erected a comprehensive national grid). This euphoria carried over into New Labour, and supported the dream economy of higher growth than European neighbours. Continuing the tradition of "hip pocket" economic policy carries with it the inevitable corollary of an aversion to raise direct taxation – hence relying on fiscal drag as inflation reduces the real value of previous tax thresholds. But, as the scope for privatisations has passed its peak, squaring the dilemma of meeting public expectations raised by electoral promises by variations around the theme of "private funding", lays government increasingly open to being screwed by the private sector. "They are not long, the days of wine and roses", however, and the country is left confronting increasing dependence on volatile international energy prices, with a stunted national coal industry and negligible residual competencies in all aspects of thermal or nuclear generating plant.

But, second, the uniquely British accomplishment is to move from energy surplus to confronting an "energy gap" within just over 25 years, when the situation had been predictable for most of this time, without the merest twitch of a muscle. Such "detached aplomb" could derive only from centuries of imperial dominion.[7] A natural complement to "detached aplomb" is imperviousness to absurdity: to pretend to have a decisive role in tackling the world's greenhouse problems, when the country accounts for no more than 2% of noxious emissions,[iv] has the reputation of "the dirty man of Europe", and when China is increasing its power generation capacity by the equivalent of the UK's total installed capacity every 18 months – predominantly coal-fired, with India also pursuing ambitious plans for increasing coal-fired capacity, only continues the great tradition of national hubris.

Whether standing idly by, with practised "detached aplomb", while the nation's assets are flogged off is an effective cure for the withdrawal symptoms of "variant Dutch disease" must be mute. But to attempt some exoneration of the political clan, by comparison with their counterparts in other countries, Ministers have to put up with enormous Parliamentary noise and constituency obligations as distractions from acquiring any professional competence in their briefs. And hardly surprising that the rhetorical hoopla to meet "party" demands can generate some weird anomalies. None more so than to proclaim submission to "markets" while banging on about "sovereignty". For finance has no allegiance beyond

---

[iv] *Our Energy Challenge*: DTI Energy Review Consultation Document (January 2006).

increasing its own gains, illustrated vividly by City traders hurling themselves to exploit the collapse of Sterling on "Black Wednesday". Or bringing the nation close to ruin in a heedless pursuit of profits.

Despite the tomes accumulated by political commentators, however "challenging", in effect playing their supporting roles in the charade, for a neat summary of the British political cavalcade two less august observers have stuck in memory. The first, one of the "cops behind the Chair" – policemen stationed at the House of Commons entrance "behind the Speaker's Chair", who were traditional custodians of messages, and a useful source of tips on horses and the stock market,[8] whom one had known over a few decades of hanging about waiting to go into the Officials Box for statements, questions, and debates running into the small hours – when asked what had been the main changes in politics from his vantage point, responded, "Before Wilson, it was all gentleman. After Wilson, it was all deals." The second, from an even more surprising source, is Gore Vidal's depiction of British politicians in a Sunday Times piece during the Thatcher years as "interchangeable careerists": all the more apposite as the political parties fall over each other to capture "the middle ground," all reciting the same "Blue Peter" and "hip-pocket" economic jargon, yet with ever-more frantic protestations disguising a complete lack of perception of national failings, leave alone any realistic concepts of how these should be mitigated.

---

[1] *The Box: How the Shipping Container Made the World Smaller and the World Economy Bigger* by Marc Levinson (Princeton University Press) is a scholarly account of the evolution of the container revolution, drawing a fillip from the logistic demands of the Vietnam War, and the subsequent shifts in the dominance of terminals. But less on the industrial impact, as dominance shifted to Asian producers who undertook the scale of investment necessary for this new generation of vessels.

[2] One of the myths of economic management has been that a bout of stimulated growth is not only good for the punters (voters), especially just before general elections – probably Chris (Lord) Patten's most eloquent contribution to political debate was not anything he wrote or said, but occurred while at the dizzy heights of chairman of the Conservative Party during the 1992 election when his response to a TV commentator's question on the most important electoral issue was to pat his hip-pocket. But also, apart from hip-pocket economic policy, it was assumed that growth would stimulate industrial profits and so increase industrial investment. Not until pigs can loop-the-loop in wineglass formation. Nothing of competitive investment levels ever transpired from these bouts of "go". And even

during the recent "Brown boom" economic commentators have been puzzled at the apparent decline in investment despite relatively high economic growth. Will they never learn?

[3] *Never Had It so Good* op. cit.pp344ff, which includes an amusing account of the assemblage's first session: "Most of its members arrived at the first meeting panting for breath; in an unpromising omen, the lift in their building on the Embankment had broken down. They were a distinguished bunch: among those at the table of the first meeting were the bosses of Dunlop, Boots, Ferranti, the British Transport Commission and the National Coal Board, as well as the heads of the Transport and General Workers, the Amalgamated Engineers, the National Union of Railwaymen and the TUC."

[4] Not to mention other futile attempts by governments over the years to bridge the divide – the Wilson/Castle struggle to establish "In Place of Strife", and all the variations in "pay policy" – entertainingly summarised in *Incomes Policies in Britain since 1940: a Study in Political Economy* by Brian Harrison in *From Family Firms to Corporate Capitalism* (Oxford).

[5] One of the more charming admissions of this lopsided upbringing comes from Gus O'Donnell*: recall again "In the early Northcote-Trevelyan era reform was undoubtedly needed to end cronyism and nepotism, and to create a meritocracy. The fundamental skill set for this new administrative cadre however revolved around the policy advice and *consigliore* function. What would nowadays be called "delivery" skills were confined largely to the military and colonial services." (The Relationship between Economy and State in *Changing Times* (OCSC)). There you have it. Our only chance to achieve the competences for "delivery" is to summon up the sepoys and coolies.

[6] *The curse of oil – The paradox of plenty* (*The Economist* 24.12.05). A typically condescending criticism of the "wasted wealth" of hydrocarbon revenues in many developing countries. And, obviously, no recognition that a similar impact could occur in Britain. With all the concern about "sovereign funds", PricewaterhouseCoopers have calculated that Britain could have built up a £450bn sovereign wealth fund had it not spent its North Sea bonanza on politically expedient tax cuts and higher public spending (*Guardian* 1.3.08). So, not only did Britain suffer the exchange rate penalties, but blew the revenue gains.

[7] Perhaps the best corrective to "detached aplomb" is Norman Dixon's *On the Psychology of Military Incompetence* (Pimlico), which illustrates the peculiar British mindset that has historically contributed to the saga of military cock-ups. But equally applicable to failings in British leadership elsewhere in industry and economic management – the boneheaded response to the ERM crisis was comparable to Lord Haig in the First World War.

[8] Sadly, those paragons of "Cops behind the Chair" no longer exist, apparently having been excised in some Parliamentary efficiency drive.

MANAGERIAL VACUUM

Oh those proud top managers who pay themselves several times more than their international counterparts who run businesses several times larger. A constant theme in the annals of Britain's industrial decline is the failure of management,[1] and one of the standard DTI (presumably now BERR) briefs recycled with every new Ministerial appointment goes, "Britain has some of the best companies in the world, but the management of too many has a long way to go to match the best", or, in less politic language, "most are still thickies by international standards". Even if, with each repetition, the number of companies genuinely qualifying for "best" has narrowed to those with continuing slugs of orders from government – aerospace and pharmaceuticals, and to those still hanging on to a post-imperial international position – the oil majors, RTZ, Unilever, Tate & Lyle and HSBC the most obvious, but with fading memories of Bookers and P&O as reminders that even these are vulnerable.

Without reiterating international comparisons, underlying the continuing failure of management is a myopia reacting to a composite of dynamics and pressures: a traditional preoccupation with "class", perhaps reflecting a carry over of the owner/slave rationale dating from the earliest origins of the British brand of capitalism; a failure to recognise the demands for upgrading skills, whether among operatives or among themselves; latterly, the convenience of stock-market devices and allegiance to "shareholder value" to jack-up remuneration packages, but more destructively as a substitute for the real management of organic evolution achieved by competitors;[2] an attachment to formal contractual relations to "cover the arse" of management against inevitable risks and unforeseen events – with the failure of other British companies to perform among the main concerns; and a continuing failure down the years, and more marked in recent decades, to match the research, development, investment and market expansion of international competitors.

Among the "thickies" we should not exclude the nation's brand of trade unionists. For the persistence of tensions within companies, compared to the mechanisms and traditions in other countries to achieve a greater cohesion of purpose, has been a large chunk of grit to slow competitive adjustment – even to the point where, if, for every demand to increase skills, there was the threat of an automatic demand for increased pay, the weakness of skills fell further behind competitors. To the point where the CBI, TUC, Institute of Directors, Chambers of Commerce, and those multitudinous trade associations down to the bottle-top manufacturers, have served only as voices for convocations of thickies. Joined in harmony, this bunch has performed as a national bleating chorus.[3] Allied to a corporate scene – as always with a few exceptions – of unstable ownership and closures, flowing from a preoccupation with mergers and rationalisations, the remaining companies with genuinely competitive legacies have declined.

Consequently, we are confronting a vacuum of "legacy" from decades of management sacrificing their options for growing their businesses to the "short-termism" of shareholders, and surrender to the M&A bias of the City's financial jugglers. More fundamentally, if the jargon of management consultancies/academia has latched on to "knowledge" and distinctions between tacit/explicit,[4] in Britain these distinctions in the practical application of knowledge are lost behind the education system's priority for "posh" knowledge – academic tags that ensure students enrolment into careers in law, accountancy, economics etc where the necessity to foster these practical qualities are deliberately bypassed, and "skills" all-too-readily dismissed as plumbing and bricklaying. Despite the occasional rhetorical political flourish about "skills", lacking the tradition of crafts of other leading nations and the demand-pull of companies pursuing these process disciplines, the predominance of thickies will continue.

---

[1] Just flicking through the earlier bibliography should be sufficient, but there are recent variants such as *Blunderboss* by Roger Trapp (Capstone) and *Business Blunders* by Geoff Tibball (Robinson) that maintain the tradition. But a particular favourite to illustrate the persistence of these traits is the passage:

"The finding that Britain has been deficient in human skills would not have surprised the numerous critics who for more than a century now have condemned the country's educational system for its failure to turn out a work-force with the capabilities that modern industrial life demands. Already in 1868 Lyon Playfair, a chemist trained on the continent and head of the science section of Britain's Department of Science and Art, was insisting that "the crying want for this country is a higher class of education for the foremen and managers of industry." One year later J. Russell, in his Systematic Technical Education for the English People, observed that "the English people do not believe in the value of technical education". Since then, lamentations about British attitudes to education and to adequate facilities have formed an enduring refrain in the debate about the nation's declining economic prowess. Sixty-four years after Russell, A. Abbott could conclude "it is not generally believed that technical education can play a most important part in the struggle to increase national well-being." Sir Bryan Nicholson of the Manpower Services Commission, speaking in 1986, gave this argument its most trenchant expression. "We are," he concluded, "a bunch of thickies." *The Decline of Industrial Britain 1870-1980* Op. Cit.

[2] One has become cautious of the conventional British management jargon of "organic growth" having heard over the years aspirations of "we're going for organic growth" flowing glibly from senior managers in Dunlop, NEI, Dowty and a score of others that no longer exist. One can only assume that British management draws its inspiration from growing rhubarb.

[3] Invariably, at DTI reunions, qualms about the dilapidated state of British industry are liable to be greeted by the response that industry richly deserves this abasement given the amount that successive governments have done to satisfy the continuing chorus of bleats. Yet with negligible gains in terms of industry's international competitiveness.

[4] The seminal work on this theme was *The Knowledge-Creating Company* by Ikujiro Nonaka and Hirotaka Takeuchi (Oxford) which explored the approaches to innovation pursued by a variety of Japanese companies through integrating internal expertise and sensitivities to market demands. As a survey of creativity, rather more a source of academic references than practical application among British companies.

PART V:

AND NOW THE BULLDOZERS

FIND THE FUTURE

Going back to Eric Roll's account, after our modest biographical and scholarly route, a résumé of our industrial decline in the 20th (and 21st) century could be sketched as a bunch of mostly well-intentioned duffers struggling with the demands of a changing international context with a mental apparatus – derived from traditional education, social ethos and institutional structure – devoid of the mechanisms to appreciate the dimensions of the challenge leave alone the practical competences to respond. But with a dash of our indomitable tolerance of farce and cock-ups: perhaps an overhang of the "blitz mentality", as successive generations of "leaders" plod along in the same old footprints and with the same blundering myopia.[1] No surprise that the nation has gravitated to Friedrich List's canny forecast, "it is possible for a nation to possess too many philosophers, philologers, and literati, and too few skilled artisans, merchants and seamen. This is the consequence of a highly advanced and learned culture which is not supported by a highly advanced manufacturing power and by an extensive internal and external trade; it is as if in a pin manufactory far more pinheads were manufactured than pinpoints." Bang on! No neater summary of our national condition than a lack of productive power and a surfeit of pinheads.[2] Time may have shifted some of the contenders for pinhead and pinpoint status, but the disjunction between guff-peddlers – "We're all intellectuals, really" – and contributors to tradable value-added still stands.

What he could not have foreseen was the blend of froth that has achieved this condition of vulnerability in such a short period. Passionate protestations of all varieties of convictions have flowed down the gutters of recent political history. Vast tracts, carrying over from tutorial essays in our premier centres of higher education, ostensibly on "policies", yet all divorced from the nausea of actual "delivery". Svelte City rats scuttling around hip-pocketing exorbitant fees in a corporate ingestion system that has seen native industries "consolidated" into oblivion, or near obsolescence. And a managerial ethos more intent upon matching these bulging "hip-pockets" than competing in international markets. Mixed into this froth have been dollops of fantasy, farce, bedlam, bullshit, sanctimonious dogma and arrogant hubris, with an accompanying chorus of outrage, flippant political rhetoric, glib chat-show chatter, academic mutual wanking, and astounding international posturing.

Many commentators are resigned to this blend of vapid myopic decline as irreversible, and see the only prospective comforts in the increasingly byzantine special pleading needed to avoid confronting the necessity for change. At its most subtle in those texts and lectures under the pretext of "change" that leave the essential institutional structure unchanged. Still, it is difficult to write off all hope that such national stupidity is not amenable to illumination, when almost daily the fragility of this archaic mixture becomes more apparent, and it must surely occur to enough people that our system is just not delivering for the nation at large.[3]

How?

How to answer such queries, usually well-intentioned, from foreign colleagues, frequently confronted in one's official career and subsequently, as "What's happened to the London underground?",[4] "Why are there problems on your railways?", "Why are your roads so congested?", "Why does your water distribution seem to have so many leaks?", "How can you have a drought with all your rain?". Just for starters. The only comprehensive response is to admit, with the best of effortless shrugs, that Britain is unique in not having to worry about the future. Despite countless submissions to "policymakers" over the years pointing to the urgent need for capital and maintenance spending on the Underground and rail. Despite continuous studies, dating back to the 60s, predicting that the growth of road traffic would exceed forecast capacity. Despite it being obvious for decades that the country could not rely upon the engineering foresight of our Victorian forebears for water and sanitation systems. And the same ingredients account for the "energy crisis" as the country becomes increasingly reliant on imported energy, as old CEGB power stations come to the end of their useful life.[5] Or the spectacle of the government hurling funds into the NHS, without provision for accommodating the service workers necessary to make the health service function. Or more generally while allowing house-price inflation to take off, fail in providing proximate accommodation for the police, fire service, and teachers (*Guardian* 29.7.06).

It would not have demanded "Soviet style" planning to anticipate the dimensions of these future demands, and to take timely steps to neutralise the "British" delay in confronting failures in national services. Just the normal coherent application of "consistent policies" pursued by every country that has advanced its economy. But sustainability, in any sphere, by "revealed comparative performance" apparently lies beyond the reach of this systemic impotence.

Fruitless to debate which, which combination, or whether all the national players can claim the greatest credit for this malaise. For any future vision for this increasingly backward island, we have to look outside these ossified institutional relics. Governments have persistently failed to look much beyond their electoral horizon. The Treasury, the ultimate custodian of the national purse, similarly has a forward horizon limited to Public Expenditure cycles – and the period that seats can be kept warm, before its officials can exit to sinecures in the City. While industry is largely in thrall to the "short-term" expectations of shareholders, and academia seems so wrapped in parroting the prevailing consensus that it would be more than their prospective knighthoods were worth to stray beyond the limits of tolerable criticism. In practice, by proven performance, none can be relied upon to take a view beyond the convenient "chat-show" dimensions of a myopic present.

Nor does harking back to the past help much: maybe George Brown's ill-fated Department of Economic Affairs (DEA) might have provided a structure for looking beyond the immediate political and expenditure horizons. For all the Treasury's euphoria at its demise, that Department has signally failed in what other nations would regard as the basic "policy" function of funding continuing maintenance and capital expenditure with some "foresight" of future demands. Nor would it be feasible to contemplate such a fundamental constitutional shift as establishing a *"Conseil d'État"* that has contributed to France's ability to sustain major investment programmes in transport and energy infrastructures.

Causes for the electorate's disillusion are wide and various, but one component for sure is the instability and resulting lack of confidence in the provision of such public services. Even if the general populace's familiarity with Thomas Hobbes is not what it used to be, there is an undeniable common perception that taxes are paid to ensure the integrity of these social essentials. The dilemma is to find a mechanism that opens a perspective of 20-30 years, the timescale for effective infrastructure investment, but beyond the horizons of immediate political preoccupations and the studied bookkeeping disinterest of the Treasury.

Look not for the technocratic competences to emulate the structures built up since Meiji Japan, or in the "rise" of South Korea, Taiwan and other later arrivals. That would be entirely beneath the dignity of engineering on the "Balliol" template to produce masters in the dialectic of "policy" devoid of concerns for delivery. If we have no Napoleons in sight, the French system does at least offer a pointer to get over our entrapment in the short term. An obvious immediate candidate for reviewing longer-term demands might be the National Audit Office, which has inched its traditional retrospective view of Departmental performance to a focus on more current activities. And by common consent it generally does a good job. But it would be a substantial additional task to take on this forward view, and would suffer from the weakness that it reports to Parliament.

The Privy Council, however, even without a revolution to transform it into an equivalent of the Conseil d'État, has retained an honorific role – whether its members are still entitled to chunks of the Royal venison. When popular reference is made to a "Privy Council" solution, the implication is a view from "the great and the good" untrammelled by party-political haggling. So, it's halfway there. What remains is for it to build up its capability to take on this wider review function: drawing upon the best technocratic expertise, uninhibited by Treasury dominated Departmental mouthpieces, and probing the dimensions of issues and programs in a perspective beyond administrative/political horizons. One assumes that the monarch would not be averse to having material to hand to quiz her/his Ministers on where they think they are taking the country. The political factions would then be charged to find the measures to take forward a constant program "in the national interest". Any outcry against the legitimacy of such an outfit could be countered by the argument that its legitimacy lies precisely in the failure of the country's current political/governance system to provide the essential fundamentals for a modern functioning economy.

Nothing better illustrates the need for such a Privy Council function than the recently formed Infrastructure Planning Commission. Intended to reduce the procedural delays that have traditionally bedevilled public service projects, the Commission's formation was triggered by potential investors in future nuclear power stations identifying uncertainties in the planning process as a constraint against formulating viable projects. Setting up the Commission was proclaimed as evidence of the government taking "the long view" of the country's energy needs.

It has, however, been obvious for over three decades that further nuclear generating capacity would be needed as part of the investment to replace the old CEGB's nuclear and coal-powered stations. Mrs Thatcher's government cancelled plans for building Sizewell C, a nuclear plant to follow on the expertise gained through the B station, and with the privatisation of CEGB its plans for further coal-fired stations were shelved. The future operational life of the remaining stations, even assuming they were "sweated out" has been predictable, while, with the rundown of the coal industry and falling North Sea gas output, increasing reliance on imported gas has been inevitable.

Apparently, 2020 is the earliest that the first of the new nuclear stations could come on stream, about the same timeframe for the current North Sea fields to become exhausted: dependence on foreign sources of energy will therefore increase still further. This prolonged indecisiveness has spanned governments of both main parties. An authoritative Privy Council should have prompted a timely consensus many years before such a vulnerable energy situation became inevitable.

---

[1] A succinct "academic" survey of this national confusion is provided in the concluding essay, "The State and Economic Decline" by P. A. Hall in *The Decline of the British Economy* op. cit. Notably the conclusion:

"This analysis suggests that the state is not primarily responsible for Britain's economic decline. But it is not an innocent bystander. If the principal causes of economic decline lie elsewhere, successive British governments did little to address them. There were alternatives. The French experience in the post-war period suggests that the state can transform the operation of its economic system, but first it must transform itself. The British have found that difficult because institutional rigidities affected the actions of the British state, just as rigidities influenced the operation of the British economy.... The very stability of the British political system, so long a valued asset, has become something of a liability in an era of rapid economic change. The consequences have been grave because economic failure in the modern age is also political failure. After several decades in which politicians claimed credit for every economic success, electorates have begun to hold them responsible for every economic failure."

The essay is also notable for a balanced account of the period depicted in fantasy as "corporatism":

"State intervention (of this sort) can take many different forms, however, and it is important to distinguish those in which the government enforces reform on particular firms and industries from those in which state-supported schemes are essentially directed by the private sector. The striking feature of British intervention has been its reliance on the latter. With the exception of an occasional nationalisation, compulsory schemes have been avoided in favour of an approach that has been highly consensual, or "quasi-corporatist" to use Samuel Beer's term..... Under the Conservatives in 1970-4 and Labour in 1974-9, industrial policy reverted to its normal course, marked only by larger sums paid for declining sectors. After an abortive switch to investment allowances, the Industry Act of 1972 restored a system of subsidies, but almost all went to regional development grants or the industrial bail-outs of British Leyland, Rolls-Royce, and Cammel Laird. The industrial policies of the Labour government were very similar. Only one of the "planning agreements" that the 1973 program advertised as a scheme for imposing investment plans on industry was ever negotiated; and the National Enterprise Board became little more than a source of capital for ailing firms whose redundancies the government was unwilling to tolerate. The "new industrial strategy" of November 1975 created thirty-nine sectoral working parties (SWPs) operating by consensus at the sectoral level, much like the state-sponsored cartels of the 1930s.

What were the effects of this pattern of industrial policy? In political terms the answer is clear. Despite the growth of the state apparatus and the nominal extension of intervention, British policy tended to reinforce the power of private sector actors vis-a-vis the government. The result was "less the domination of public over private powers than their interpenetration leading to the creation of a broad area of shared authority..... most studies of post-war policy conclude that insufficient resources were devoted to the problem, that policy was not sustained enough to produce results, or that it had very little impact on the investment and allocation decisions of private sector actors. Although British policy cushioned the impact of contraction in declining sectors, it seems to have had little effect on the most serious problem underlying poor economic performance, namely, productivity. Only in the one period when industrial policy veered towards dirigisme, under the labour government in 1964-70, did the growth of the capital-labour ratio and output per person begin to approach continental levels. The experience of other nations, such as France and Japan, suggest that in order to tackle underlying productivity problems Britain would have needed an industrial policy based less on voluntarism and more on rationalisation enforced directly by the State."

[2] *A National System of Political Economy* op. cit. A useful template to apply to any TV chat show of politicians and celebrities is to enquire of each, "Is he/she a pinhead?" But a natural consequence of the fashion "to direct the intellect into useless channels".

[3] Given recent performance by government in implementing the recommendations of its own "Reviews", it would be more than trite to attempt a list of specific changes. As, for example, in the concluding section of Barry C. Lynn's *End of the Line* (Doubleday) pp256ff, setting out a prioritised sequence of steps for the "noninterventionist" United States, such as "Use antitrust power to ensure that no global lead firm controls more than a quarter of any American market", "Limit how much of any key input any industry, as a whole, can source from capacity located in a single foreign nation", "Require firms to double-or even triple-source all components and all business-process services, in real-time, from suppliers in two or more different nations", "Require managers to make public their sourcing and supply-chain relationships, to enable investors to shy

from firms that take unnecessary risk", "Enable workers to more effectively counterbalance the power of shareholders by giving them an absolutely equal right to act collectively within the US economy", and "Professionalise management of the US corporation by compensating top management only in salary and not in stock or stock options", just as a few examples. This would require a regulatory framework of a scope and rigour to make Sarbannes/Oxley mere kindergarten finger wagging.

[4] Almost impossible to credit from a present vantage point, the London underground had an iconic status around the world in the 1930s. But now dwarfed by more modern systems in other capitals, or, indeed, Hong Kong and Singapore.

[5] The phasing out of the old CEGB-built coal and nuclear power stations has been predictable, within the timeframes of major investment in energy, since the 1980s. Prior to "privatisation" the CEGB, operating in a Cold War context, had maintained "security of supply" as a prime responsibility, regularly retaining a 20% surplus capacity. And, prior to privatisation in the 1990s, had already awarded initial contracts for two new coal-fired stations to take over as its oldest plants had to be withdrawn. With privatisation, these contracts were cancelled. But the surplus capacity, with assets being sold-off at knockdown prices and relieved of debt, contributed to British privatisation avoiding the disaster of California's energy privatisation.

That it should be 2006 with the government's consultation paper "Our Energy Challenge" published in January, confronting the complete closure of the old CEGB stations, with the exception of Sizewell B, around 2015 before a serious attempt to confront the issue is but the latest, and clearest, example of this perpetual failure of public policy. To suggest that it is an incidental consequence of Britain's "Variant Dutch Disease" distracting attention from a basic national need is hardly a valid plea in mitigation.

A side effect of industrial decline is the obsolescence of much accustomed jargon. When a leaked report by the Nuclear Safety Directorate indicated cracks in the graphite bricks of the UK's older nuclear power stations, even if concluding "a large release due to failure to shut down on demand" was not "a likely scenario" (*Guardian* 5.7.06), there was an accompanying piece "Bad news at a crucial time for industry". Those damned "producers" again, being frustrated from pushing their evil stratagems for profiting at public expense. But we ain't got a nuclear "industry" anymore: the major elements of pressure vessels, steam turbines, high-pressure pipe work, customised sensing and control systems, and design competences based on evolving technologies and expertise can be realistically sourced only from outside the UK (See the evaluation of the capability and capacity of the UK and global supply chains to support a new nuclear build programme in the UK by IBM Business Consulting Services, 2005). Indeed, the available range and scale of construction skills have withered, or are questionable. While there is no university faculty that has sustained a significant competence in nuclear science and engineering.

In these circumstances, for all the debate over nuclear power, there are probably more natives involved in the lobbying industry on behalf of foreign operators and manufacturers than will be involved in the construction and operation of any nuclear power stations eventually built. In "The powerful business of promoting a nuclear future" (*Guardian* 11.7.06) Terry McAllister provides an entertaining account of the manoeuvres of PR specialists around the lobbying industry including Andrew Brown – the brother of Gordon Brown – moving to EDF from Weber Shandwick, the Nuclear Industries Association picking up personnel from British Nuclear Fuels Ltd (BNFL) and DTI, with other lobbying outfits like Bell Pottinger, Financial Dynamics, Martin Adeney Associates, Sovereign Strategy, Brunswick and sundry lobbying groups including Transatlantic Nuclear Energy Forum and, supported by the trade unions, Nuklear21 and Nuclear Workers Campaign.

DISPELLING THE CLOUD OF UNKNOWING

The UK's noxious emissions account for "only about 2% of total global emissions" – a percentage bound to diminish further as China, India and other countries invest heavily in new coal and gas-fired power generating capacity. But given the dodgy basis of the usual run of economic data, 2% is probably as fair a measure of the country's present relative global economic significance.

If only this was matched by a similar balance in Britain's economists' emissions. We should be so lucky. Totting up the output in our daily press, journals, among commentators, "policy" advisors, published tomes, and with "economists" up there with "philologers" among List's "pinheads", we must be vying for 20% of global economists' emissions. Maybe, indeed, a new formula: the performance of economies is inversely related to the number of economists in their employ. But this legion is probably the most intractable obstacle to following Dr Johnson's precept.

If all these emissions were in the mode of the mediaeval scholars – and, for sure, a fair proportion are esoteric disputations on the inadequacies of the traditional canonical teachings in coping with the realities of the world, fine. But sadly there remains a corpus of practitioners who still find it congenial to pretend the ancient scriptures still have some relevance. And nowhere more than in a Treasury-dominated Whitehall, where apparently there are now some 800 disciples spread around Departments – a modern variant for a non-thought-police. (As a source of future staff savings, that's 794 posts that could be demolished without any detriment to the public weal.)

This inertia-induction mechanism fits naturally into a bureaucratic game of "criteria" and "targets". On arrival in the Industrial Development Unit, absorbing the intricacies of the legislation was followed by a glance at the "criteria", which included the mystic phrase, "correct market imperfections". Of a practical slant, and recognising that the Unit's appraisal staff came from the "horny-handed" private sector, one inquired of our philosophers what this meant: for there must presumably have been some notion of "perfection" towards which corrective measures were to be directed. No reply. One suspects because they knew all along, as has now been generally admitted, that the conditions for "perfection" are so nebulous as to make the concept worthless.

This excursion into high metaphysics was curtailed by the cascade of corporate kippers landing on the Department's doorstep. Wherever "perfection" may lie, it could surely not be among the gaggle of buffoons, knaves and trolls that paraded as leading figures of management and finance. But this garbage reappeared at a seminar on supporting capital goods exports when Ian Byatt*, then one of the Treasury's red-hot economic enchiladas, declared, "the market is only moderately imperfect". Set aside the logical robustness of the proposition, but it denoted a viewpoint where, whatever evidence to the contrary, "the market" retained its sanctity as a pretext for avoiding any direct involvement in the real economy.

This trail of garbage has now morphed into, "only soundly based policies that correct for market failures".[i] Whether any interrogation is applied to identify the conditions for "market success", or, indeed, whether such a phenomenon actually exists, seems questionable: and probably just as fruitless. This new slant derives apparently from "developments in the way economists think about economic growth" – Wow! As we observed in going over the dilemma of adjustment, this revolutionary insight flows from a realisation that over five decades actual economies have behaved entirely contrary to the standard cant.[1] The vaunted productivity gains from this formulation are barely evident. And with probably less than half a dozen managers in our companies having the faintest clue what this gobbledygook means, it is hardly surprising that DTI should be dismissed as "a joke" in need of "a complete cultural transformation" by one of the country's award-winning companies.[ii] A transformation presumably attempted by abolition, and replacement by a Department titled BERR, though how far this new fashion-change eschews comedy remains unproven.

This type of linguistic wrangling, if confined to these shores, does not prevent the daily stream of cringe-inducing sanctimonious clichés peddled by politicians: demonstrating a myopia that ignores the passage of centuries in determining cultures and institutions very different from this country. Their readiest excuse is that they are simply reciting briefs from the "surrogate reality" of their officials. So let's take a typical "officials paper", drafted in the vein of a second-year essay, arguing the standard liberal menu – a Treasury paper presented while the UK held the EU Presidency.[2]

It contains the stunning platitude, "In a world of rapid change,

---

[i] DTI Prosperity for All – The Strategy: analysis (Sept 2003).
[ii] *FT* 30.6.06

technologies arrive and quickly become out of date. Companies rise and fall..." The first proposition entirely misses the interactive and feedback process whereby the stock of knowledge is enhanced.[3] While the second, if apparently a truism from watching the round of mergers, acquisitions, spin-offs and "consolidations" of the City, rather misses the presence, among the leading corporate citizens of its audience, companies with a legacy getting on for a century or longer: Solvay, Ericsson, Maersk, Saint-Gobain, Siemens, Lafarge, Bosch, BMW, Bayer, BASF, Akzo Nobel, MAN, not to mention the scores of third-generation mittelstand and Italian family firms. If the gaze were to be lifted further, the list would be multiplied by the addition of Mitsui and the zaibatsu-heritage companies, Seiko etc,[4] and Tata among a rising new generation in Asia. All with aspirations to be around for the next century, and longer.

The most ostentatious manifestation of this myopia inevitably comes from our politicians, who are continuously self-duped into utterance when humble silence would be more appropriate. Out of this cloud of unknowing, we hear that the nation's future is to be cast adrift into "free trade and open markets". Even attaining some mystic nirvana where the country is beyond "economic nationalism" – echoed, presumably with an eye on the bread-and-rations knighthood that goes with the job, by a Director General of the CBI.[5]

Set aside that "free trade" has never existed beyond a pretext to enhance imperial ambitions, nor indeed attainable even in theory. But in the decades of increasing liberalised trade in the latter half of the 20th century it has been the most regulated and "national" motivated nations that have been the main beneficiaries – in Europe, Germany and France, elsewhere Japan, South Korea, Taiwan with Malaysia, Singapore and China rising. This is not to begrudge their success, but to query why the country most given to preaching should have performed so poorly, despite an initial advantageous position. If anything, "open markets" also has equally perverse outcomes: despite official declarations (and financial commentators) deploring "national champions", Britain has become predominantly an outpost of other countries' champions – Siemens, Bosch, BMW, Finmeccanica, Renault, Volkswagen, Ericsson, Lafarge, EDF, Airbus,[6] Toyota, Sharp, Honda, Maersk, Hutchinson, Tata, Dubai Ports etc – are now more significant participants in the economy than British "national" companies in their respective fields. While foreign "champions" are dominant in the City and in power generation/distribution. Elsewhere, a significant international trend is for governments to take an increasingly circumspect view of foreign ownership of domestic companies – with China following the sceptical crowd.[7]

Yet the 5th form economics textbooks chime on – "Across the world, we are seeing not only the impact of terrorism and the geopolitical uncertainty on our economies but also a surge of protectionism. Whether it is called 'populism' in Latin America, the promotion of 'national champions' in Europe or 'nativism' in the US, the same sentiments are sadly fuelling isolationism in parts of the world, anti-Americanism in others and anti-globalisation forces almost everywhere.

"These are now magnified by one of the most ominous summer setbacks – the damaging collapse of the world trade talks. We must all wake up to the reality that, without the forward momentum a new trade agreement would give, we risk rolling backwards to the age of beggar-thy-neighbour protectionism and the further threats to stability that would flow from it," our Chancellor of the Exchequer drones on.[8] Full marks. Immaculate stuff. Except these ringing calls ignore a couple of centuries of economic history: for, when was there not a time when nations ambitious to achieve sustained growth in order to improve the lot of their people did not pursue "economic nationalism"?[9] And banging on about "trade" is a bit quaint, when the Chancellor's own country has had such an abysmal, and worsening, recent performance. Even to the point of attaining a Gilbertian paradox whereby the world's most loquacious advocate of "free trade" has attained among the world's worst trade performances.

What is inexplicable to spectators is the persistence of this cant, despite a rising tide of commentaries exposing its limitations; the direct evidence from the success of countries that have evolved enterprises within their own very different national institutions and traditions;[10] and the relative decline of Britain's significance. The influence of ego-tripping can never be excluded from the native political species, and, with actual impact on the international scene diminishing, maybe there's a temptation to compensate with purist rhetoric, even if singing from a dog-eared hymn book. To find the repository of these verses, we have to return to the "Balliol's buggered us" syndrome, where economics carries the gloss "leave it to the City" as one of the strands whereby the elites perpetuate themselves and offers the stock ticket to make progress to senior functionaries and accolades. And by the sheer multitude of passage, over the decades we have got stuck in Lord Roll's "Pavlovian" rut. And bleating on about "markets" may also explain why we have such an inept elite, whose converse with reality is driven by avoidance at all costs.[11]

In 1930 Keynes recalled that the dominant influence of the British economy, especially given its massive exports of capital, was so great in the latter half of the 19th century that the country could determine credit conditions around the world by varying its internal holdings of gold. "This power to call the tune, coupled with certain other characteristics of the period... put Great Britain in a position to afford a degree of laissez-faire towards foreign lending which other countries could not imitate." Included in the "certain other characteristics of the period" were supplies of cut-price legions of sepoys and mercantile dominance. Consequently, British economists and policy-makers "attributed the actual success of laissez-faire policy, not to the transitory peculiarities of her position, but to the sovereign virtues of laissez-faire as such. That other countries did not follow her example was deemed – like their bias towards protective tariffs – to be an indication of their inferior political wisdom.[iii]

Easy incantations of "free trade" jargon ignore the evaporation of these "characteristics" and scratch on like old Imperial 78 records. Apart from its increasingly vacuous arrogance, "free trade and open markets" are now the exclusive refuge of those who have no direct experience of real trade, and, indeed, hold out a comfortable condom to prevent any such contamination. For, even disregarding the legitimacy of countries protecting vulnerable indigenous communities and their nascent industrial capacities by tariffs and quotas, every nation has its distinct culture, language, conventions, regulations, transactional customs, interlinking – often informal – networks of commerce, and social hierarchies. Outside the imposed structures of Empire, trade has always had to accommodate itself to these national contexts. And, despite the dire predictions of the consequences of failure to complete the Doha Round of WTO negotiations, until the catastrophic side effects of the credit crunch, world trade was growing at an annual clip of around 4%.

Mentioning "costs", it seems to be a presumption of the brand of cant preaching against "producer capture" that industry carries costs – presumably subsidies. Just following this rationale, the Pavlovian production line is sustained only through university economics faculties funded by the taxpayer, and by the flow of "studies" commissioned on a multitude of vacuous "policy" pretexts: an infinite maw, since the country has not had a single sustained policy in half a century. Particularly now that "economics is bollocks" has been outed in our serious journals,[12] looking forward to the country's essential future capabilities, this must be a gross misallocation of resources when faculties for sciences, maths and languages are being closed. Rather, terminate "economics" faculties, save where they can earn an honest crust, and reallocate the funding to studies more likely to contribute to the creation of tradable value-added. Otherwise the nation is doomed to an ever-increasing trade deficit. But

---

[iii] "*A Treatise on Money* by John Maynard Keynes (New York: Harcourt, 1930)."

apparently, not such a novel idea, since a former chairman of the US Council of Economic Advisors has suggested that, given the low useful output of economists, less money should go into their research, and he compared them to over-subsidised dairy farmers.[13]

---

[1] A typical quote, "Traditional schools of economic thought – which stressed the importance of capital accumulation – suggested that there was little that Governments could do to raise the long-term rate of productivity growth. However, in recent years developments in the way economists think about economic growth have highlighted the important role of 'externalities' in the growth process. This 'new growth theory' suggests the government can have a positive effect on both the level and rate of productivity, and thereby prosperity, if policies seek to correct for *market failures*..." Aghion, P., and Howitt, P., *Endogenous Growth Theory* (1998)"

To explain, "Economists frequently state a particular action is 'endogenous', meaning that the action can be explained by an individual's self-conscious effort to promote his or her economic interests. For example, if a scientific discovery were motivated by a desire for profits rather than being due to intellectual curiosity, one would say that the cause of the discovery is endogenous" (Robert Gilpin op. cit.). If that helps. To which he adds the quip that Einstein's Theory of Relativity is exogenous, as distinct from endogenous, since it arose not from his daily employment in the Austrian patents office.

[2] Global Europe: full-employment Europe (HM Treasury: October 2005).

Apart from the howlers mentioned, another typical Martian-based perception is, "Trade in services has also intensified and there has been a shift in the composition of global FDI, with the service proportion growing from just a quarter in 1960, to around two-thirds in 2002. And with the services sector accounting for over 70 per cent of GDP in advanced economies but only 20 per cent of global exports, given technological advances, there is clear potential for continued rapid expansion of services trade," though recognising "India has shown dramatic growth in exports of services."

The artificial distinction between products and services is not so simplistic. From aero engines and machine tools to lifts and seals, manufacturers are offering lifetime servicing as part of the product sale, even to the point where this is becoming a norm. And many "tradable services" are directly tied to trade in products – shipping and airfreight; trade finance, insurance and logistics; design and other consultancies etc. Consequently, the scope for increasing services trade is closely tied to the origin of products. Moreover, just skimming *The World Is Flat* by Thomas Friedman (Farrar, Straus and Giroux) the scope for Indian, and other developing country, service industries to move into higher-value-added activities is evolving rapidly.

[3] The conventional "waves of destruction" view has been covered already. But a

convenient résumé of recent work on the evolution of technology is contained in the section on "Innovation and Governance" in Mary O'Sullivan's *Contests for Corporate Control* (Oxford), summarised as "cumulative, collective and uncertain". And "an intricate mixture of new knowledge, applied knowledge, and techniques were integrated together by institutions and organisations to realise the potential of this knowledge" is the depiction in Douglass North's *Understanding the Process of Economic Change* Ibid.

[4] As further evidence of the freakish outlook of the Treasury, a survey by Prof Toshio Goto found 3,113 Japanese firms with a history of more than 200 years, 1,500 German and 300 in France (*Nikkei Weekly* 19.5.08).

[5] This gentleman even distinguished himself by criticising a visiting French Minister for his Government's steps to restructure Alsthom. If not common courtesy, even a modest appreciation of how the French system actually functions should have tempered his remarks. If the French are in the midst of competing for nuclear power stations and TGV systems in China and elsewhere, they are not going to permit lack of confidence in a prime supplier to yield a card to competitors. And he might also have spared a thought for the Royal Navy's submariners, who rely upon Alsthom steam turbines to keep moving.

[6] A process depicted in a study by Breughel – a Brussels-based think-tank – "'National champions' becoming European giants" (*FT* 3.7.06).

[7] Provoking a paean against "misplaced fears that foreign takeovers threaten national economic sovereignty", in "The strange paradox of economic nationalism" (*FT* 10.8.06), though the author rather blows the argument with the concession that "defence contracting may generally qualify" as "as of strategic importance". The US, for example, has used "defence" as a pretext for massive subsidies to aerospace, rocketry, computers, software, semiconductors, new materials, batteries, power generation, nanotechnology etc. All of which has placed their industries with an "advantage" against companies from other countries, many of whom have felt compelled to "defend" their domestic industries with similar devices.

[8] Article in the *FT* 29.8.06, "Tough choices that safeguard stability". It's not often that sympathy for the IMF can be evoked. But apparently our Chancellor has badgered its Managing Director into putting "trade and globalisation at the top of the agenda". Yet, let's recall that just the day before, the same journal had recounted the outcome of a Central Bankers' jolly at Jackson Hole, "But figures showing the human costs and benefits of globalisation, which cannot be adequately captured by mainstream economic data, are some way off. Debate on the pros and cons of globalisation looks set to continue in largely evidence-free fashion."

[9] "The sustained orientation of economic activity to growth, the characteristic 'spirit of capitalism' which makes modern economy modern, owes its existence to nationalism. In general, this 'spirit of capitalism' is the economic expression of

the collective competitiveness inherent in nationalism – itself a product of the members' investment in the dignity or prestige of the nation." From Liah Greenfeld's *The Spirit of Capitalism* (Howard University Press) page 473, a follow-up to her *Nationalism*. If my Cook's Tour seems a bit cursory, Prof Greenfeld offers a far more rigorous and erudite stay in Britain, Germany, France, America and Japan in the periods before their "takeoff", and Holland as an anomaly where, despite an embarrassment of riches, it failed to achieve sustained growth. She offers the comforting prospect, "The foreseeable future of nationalism looks bright. We still live in the social world created by a national consciousness – it cannot be otherwise. For the same reason, the future of economic growth looks bright...."

[10] The most recent trend for the economic fraternity is to acknowledge that there are no neat nostrums or menus to deliver sustained economic growth, as spelt out by the World Bank Growth Commission's report (May 2008): rather more realistic than the rank dishonesty of its earlier report on the East Asian Miracle. The old orthodoxies are left to scrabble around for common denominators that can be salvaged (typical *One Economics Many Recipes* by Dani Rodrick (Princeton)), or pros of "engaged government" and the cons of policies to be avoided, but leading to the lame apologia, "There is much for economics to be humble about. But humility should not be mistaken for total ignorance" (Martin Wolf: *FT* 4.6.08).

[11] A suitably irate outburst is *Britain's Power Elites* by Hywel Williams (Constable).

[12] Following on a fairly heretical article in the *Financial Times*, "Baroque fantasies of a most peculiar science" by Philip Ball (*FT* 30.10.06), Paul Ormerod followed up with a rejoinder, "Shun the rational agent to rebuild economics" (*FT* 6.11.06). Choice quotes are, "In limited circumstances, the conventional economic view of rational behaviour is a good one. But most of the time it is a poor approximation, sometimes very poor. Its use can give seriously misleading views of how the world actually operates.... The problem, and it is a very big one, is that most economists continue to act as if very little has changed and that the rational agent postulate remains generally valid.... The textbooks used to instruct most students have, if anything, gone backwards in recent years. Aimed at the mass market of US community college students, they have dumbed down the subject to a terrifying degree. Even the material presented to strong students is replete with 'theorems' and 'lemmas' based on postulates of behaviour that have been discredited empirically within economics itself."

[13] "Gregory Mankiw of Harvard, and also a former chairman of the Council of Economic Advisors, suggested that, given the low useful output of economists, less money should go into their research, and he compared them to over-subsidised dairy farmers" (*The Origin of Wealth* op. cit. p22).

THE PATH OF INNOVATION AND DISCOVERY

Just as the combination of systems, institutions and networks to secure sustained growth have proved proof against developmental experts, the magic has been even more elusive in this country, despite our high density of economists. Instead, a recurrent cycle of booms and busts, with each cycle ratcheting down the country's capabilities. Since Lord Young's bold prediction in 1988 that we confronted only "temporary" periods of trade deficits, the subsequent two decades have seen a steady deterioration to some £100bn a year. And when once a deficit of a few £ms could threaten the survival of governments, today billions of pounds flow by without the slightest political comment. With no signs of improvement in prospect.

A PERPETUAL SLIPPERY SLOPE

As a résumé, if imperial preoccupations and uninterested finance, compared to the combinations of state and financial systems of the US, Germany and Japan, dropped Britain out of the second industrial revolution in the latter half of the 19th century, a similar combination of attitudes has relegated national capabilities to marginal significance in however many revolutions there have been subsequently and however many other countries have evolved their capabilities – nuclear energy, computing, diversifying electronic applications, new materials, micro-manufacturing, and even aerospace and pharmaceuticals/biotechnology have experienced a declining world share.

Augmented, in recent decades, by a confluence of economics snake-oil from academia sponged into politics, the civil service, and the City; of distracted political factions dreaming up instant menus of "policies" when not engaged in mutual, and internal, Punch and Judy contests,[1] with barely more than a dilettante glance at international commerce; of financial services that have perpetuated the "functionless rentier" tradition of the plantation and slave trades, and a developed ingestion system to pursue mergers and acquisitions of fanciful "synergies" with no concern for the demands posed by the competitive idiom of international "real" markets or moving into pure fantasy in generating debt without assets; the rise of "private equity" set upon profitable "exit" as soon as debt burdened balance sheets can be juggled; and of managerial attitudes going back to the comfortable business of imperial days, and the post-war buggins turn public ordering, but only too ready to pocket the easy returns of the stock market "expectations game".

A lot of Pavlovian conditioning perhaps. But a "senior common room" vision that robustly ignores the realities of actual wheeling-and-dealing. No better exemplified than in the grandiloquent political guff of Britain leading the way in "globalisation" and deploring symptoms around the world of "economic nationalism". For, whatever may be said about Britain's past imperial jingoism until the end of the Second World War,[2] its persistent propaganda contributed to the national fervour – and indeed the substantial accumulation of fighting capability[3] – that carried the country through its part in the hostilities. With the dissolution of Empire, this sentiment has attenuated into a typically febrile "British" debate about "Britishness" and a maelstrom of disputation about multiculturalism. It is as perhaps a faded remembrance of "world significance" that we are expected to swallow this hollow flow of sound bites about embracing "globalisation".[4] But look out. "Globalisation" has given the economist clan even greater scope to pontificate on dodgy data. And for "policymakers" a further excuse, now that "the invisible hand" has transpired to be no more than a weird Scottish joke, to invoke some heavenly force that justifies "sitting on hands".

THE PERSISTENCE OF NATIONALISMS

Yet, by comparison with this saga there are some simple lessons from the economic traditions of other nations. For, beneath the supercilious verbiage of "policy" in this country there is a real world of sweat and effort: OK, things have changed a bit since Marco Polo brought noodles back from China, and mega-containerships, air freighters, and international IT networks have increased the scale and speed of cross-national transactions. But at the level of direct wheeling-and-dealing, it is still necessary to strike mutually agreeable compromises between the customs, conventions, aspirations and social values on either side. If you like, Adam Smith's "propensity to truck, barter and exchange" continues, except now far more complex with differing languages, technical sophistication and complex finance. And the national traditions illustrated in our earlier Cook's Tour continue to influence these: entirely consistent with Liah Greenfeld's summary, "Nationalism was the ethical motive force behind the modern economy of growth." If anything, the trend for nations to attempt to exact maximum leverage from their "national advantages" has increased – Russia's gas/oil resources and aluminium dominance, Brazil's timber, iron ore and agriculture strengths, Venezuela its oil,[5] China its massive potential market and growing accumulation of foreign exchange reserves and the rising significance of "sovereign funds" fed by oil and raw material revenues. Just for starters. Augmented by a growing appreciation of the practices of international business, picked up by the myriad of developing country students on MBA courses around the world, to add to their native acuity and spirit.[6]

Inevitably, therefore, "nationalism" is bound to continue as a constant driver in the evolution of "real globalisation" – some, surely, prudently pursuing a course of "free trade-free growth" as in the past.[7] As the relative success of those countries that have prospered without reference to the tenets of naïve economic orthodoxy proffer increasingly attractive models. Consequently, in the frame of the real world, the fevered bleat of senior British Ministers against "economic nationalism" is plain crazy.

WHERE'S YOUR VALUE-CHAIN?

A few pages further on in the dog-eared British hymnal there now seems to be universal unison on "going up the value chain, investing in high technology and high skill jobs".[8] The trouble is that on all evidence of recent industrial history, this appears just another instance where rhetoric has far outstripped reality as the country has fallen off comparisons of innovative capacity.[9] If anything an even more urgent reminder for immediate closure of economics faculties in favour of enhanced funding of applied sciences and engineering.

The flag-waving of "support for science" is being hauled up again. Yet again. For it has been an intermittent constant since the "White Heat" days of Harold Wilson.[10] This may reflect "knowledge" having only recently become a respectable term in economics theology.[i] On the other hand, to complete the quotation underlying the title of this section, "there is no path which leads more rapidly to wealth and position than that of invention and discovery" goes back to Friedrich List in 1841: Germany, and the disciples on our Cook's Tour, have been pursuing this motto as a constant constant for more than a century. And by any measure of national economic comparison, this continuity has paid off.

WHAT ABOUT THE OTHERS?

By contrast, a survey into British university and business links in 2003

---

[i] See the note on Knowledge and the Wealth of Nations. op. cit.

apparently remarked on the anomaly, "the UK's citation rate in academic papers is 58 per cent higher per capita than Germany's; yet that country makes 230 per cent more patent applications per capita than the UK."[ii] This should at least call into question whether the pursuit of "citations" is a valid measure of scientific attainment, or merely an intellectual substitute for mutual masturbation. The answer to the quandary, very obviously, lies in the research investment, and resulting patent applications, of Bosch, Siemens, BASF, Merck, Hoechst, BMW, VW, Daimler and the multitude of smaller specialist companies, compared to the abysmal R&D and innovation investment of UK companies with their tradition of looking to M&A as a source of innovation – German companies registered 4,838 US patents in 2005 compared to 775 by British companies.[11] For, as a growing weight of studies confirm, the mysterious process of "technology fusion" arises from entities that have a legacy of sustaining their levels of competitive technology, sensitised to the potential of new technologies to advance their product offerings, and have built up a portfolio of skills in devising efficient ways of incorporating new technologies into their production processes as part of their heritage; and networks for creating market opportunities.

A sad consequence of Britain's self-delusive myopia has been to sever contact with, leave alone to evolve an effective riposte to, the dominant idiom of international competition. Going back to the motorcycle saga, the striking difference between Honda and its British competitors lay in the high levels of R&D coupled with a competitive drive for efficiencies and market success by the Japanese producers.[12] Just to take an update from Honda's 2005 Annual Report, this combination has achieved annual sales of 10.5 million motorbikes alone, and the company employs more than 137,000 around the globe. According to the *Financial Times* Global 500 on 2005 figures the company had a market value of $56.7 billion and a turnover of $73.6 billion – not bad considering it was incorporated in 1948 with a capital of ¥1 million (at ¥360 to the $, just under $2800),[13] but now ranking third behind Toyota and Daimler (General Motors and Ford no longer figure) in the auto sector. Its R&D outlay in 2005 was £2.3 billion, registering 822 US patents, with activities ranging from clean power units, robotics, new materials, and a jet engine and light executive aircraft. And an aspiration to achieve global sales of 18 million motorbikes and 4.5 million cars in 2010.

This idiom, with individual variations in products, internal routines and systems, has also paid off for many other Japanese companies that have grown over the same period. The Global 500 includes our old chum from

---

[ii] *FT* 31.9.06

leading the development of flat screen LCD technology, Sharp, with a market value of $19.6 billion and turnover of $21.6 billion, though extending the reach of its technology into a leading position in solar panels, mobile phones and other electronic products. Sony, another of the post-War generation that began with less than a couple of dozen employees, despite its recent problems, has a market value of $46.3 billion and sales of $55.9 billion. Of the same vintage are Canon ($58.6 billion market value and $31.9 billion turnover), Fujitsu (market value $17.4 billion and turnover of $40.6 billion) and its offshoot Fanuc (market value $23 billion and turnover of $2.8 billion), Komatsu (market value $19 billion and turnover $12.2 billion), Nintendo (market value $20.1 billion, turnover $4.39 billion), and a group of companies that have grown to prominence in the digital electronics era – Kyocera (precision ceramics), Hoya (optical applications) and Shin-Etsu Chemical (silicon and PVC products).

The growth of these companies over the past five decades has been largely free of the dreaded "interventions" of MITI.[14] Of course, there's more to it than throwing money at R&D. Just to jot down some of the main common constituents for the dynamic amalgam that has generated this clutch of "champions": a national education system that demands a uniform high proficiency in maths and sciences; an artisan tradition, often identified with geographic communities; a corporate tradition of paternal/familial values, where "to look after our people" is a dominant concern; a sharply contested local market;[15] consequently a pragmatic focus on improving production efficiencies and quality, and developing internal skills to match, and lead, others in the same field; a continuing evolution of captured, and exploration of new, technologies; "surpluses" deployed first to support these demands, but secondarily to foster an enterprise role in its local communities and to provide due compensation to shareholders; and in a corporate, and social, network of obligations and trust where resort to formal contracts/litigation is an unfavoured option. Also striking in the Global 500 list is the rise of companies from other once-designated "developing countries" – LG Philips, Samsung, China Mobile, Wipro, Infosys, Tata Consultancy Services, Hon Hai Precision Machinery, Taiwan Semiconductor Manufacture – most growing on digital-related products and software. But also sharing, from glancing around during our Cook's Tour, very similar national ingredients.

INDUSTRIAL ISOLATION

Whether economics can, or ever will, model the diversity of positive feedback in these interactions, these companies have an unassailable comparative advantage. As do those German companies just instanced. As do those foreign "national" enterprises making up an increasing share of this country's productive activities. They none have their primary listing on the London Stock Exchange. No point discussing "short-termism", "misaligned incentives", "compliance culture", or the other traditional tags of debate. The City, with its baggage of "disciplines" is by revealed comparative performance the worst funding agency for developing and sustaining businesses in the international competitive arena. If anything, recent gimmickry for extracting value exploiting "the wonders of leverage and the art of extracting cheap money from bankers", "the real joy of private equity: the so-called "dividend recap", a dividend-for-debt-swap", and "credit derivatives" makes the system even less supportive of the continuity of investment and of the risk tolerance necessary to sustain businesses that have to compete in "real" markets.[16] Especially when, quite apart from companies evolved in other capitalist cultures that have buried their erstwhile British competitors, the competitive scene is augmented by new denizens from nations whose businesses are evolving into world-players. Bluntly, Britain's financial services are incompetent to perform the funding and supporting role to evolve enterprises to match the rhetoric of "high-value-added high-skills" opportunities.

Yet, let credit crunches and bailouts come and go, don't look for any magic wands to change the City. Any more than admissions from economists that they have been peddling garbage. Or from the Treasury over their cock-ups. For the "Balliol" ethos is all-pervasive. And, in any event, there are too many stashing away too much easy money to tolerate any interruption to their activities, above all from the happy condition of "functionless rentiers"; when "share price", despite its subservience to many variables outside managerial control, becomes a determinant of management remuneration; or when, through the practices of share lending, the link between economic ownership and voting power is becoming even more tenuous.[17]

Despite reams of critiques, financial services remain an introverted system of mutually supportive complicities. And there is no shortage of economic gurus to argue either that the relative decline of industry, with its corollary of a relative increase in "services", is "desirable" or "inevitable", or that we are entering a "post-industrial society": despite modern society becoming increasingly dependent on the products of industry. We used to hear passionate arguments that "shareholders" included funds who were custodians of the nation's pension savings, now reduced to a modest whisper as the City has ruined all trust in saving and despite a trend to withdraw from UK equities for a more balanced mix of assets against longer-term commitments. On the other side of the street, however, a new gaggle of cheerleaders have emerged through the thirst for funds to satisfy the ambitions of the new London Mayor's office, and the rising rateable value of properties in Chelsea, Battersea and Kensington with their ripple effect across valuations in other London boroughs. And where would political parties look for funding outside City patrons?

SLIPPING FASTER

Returning to our audit of national obsolescence, the country's industrial impotence derives, as our earlier explorations suggest, from a variety of causes for which there is no one ultimate villain. To go further in analytic deconstruction for an underlying dynamic would deduce a highest common factor of fundamental national stupidity,[18] perhaps as an extension of that "absentmindedness" whereby apologists claim Britain gained its Empire. This impotence continues to undermine national resolve, most vividly depicted by the failure to achieve the creativity and continuity demanded for successful exploitation of increasingly rapid, and interacting, technological change.

So persistent a failure of the country's institutional, corporate and financing systems that stupidity is the only possible excuse for such inertia: not only in advancing the technological strengths that derived from the rush of "war-innovations", but in sustaining a leading edge as new flows of innovations have followed. And the aversion to confronting this reality is typically reflected in even government publications, such as the 2006 R&D Scoreboard, which – despite an obsession with "league tables" in virtually every other sphere of national life – conveniently ducks the inevitable question of where the UK stands in international comparisons: taking its own data as the raw material, we can go further than our earlier references and compile a fuller league-table on relative national performance in securing US patent registrations:

US	Japan	S. Korea	Germany	Netherlands	France	Taiwan	UK
26,397	18,803	5,473	4,838	2,575	1,298	804	775

Or to make a comparison of the relative UK/Total patents in different sectors: Aerospace and Defence – 180/1859; Automotive – 0/326; Automotive Components – 48/2913; Chemicals – 117/2325; Electronic and Electrical Equipment and Leisure – 31/14,526; General Industrials – 0/7399; Healthcare – 33/570; Household Goods – 45/572; Personal Care – 0/594; Pharmaceutical and Biotech – 220/2441; Software and Computer Services – 5/14,387; Technology Hardware – 62/22,219; Telecom Services – 34/604.

There may be a queue of apologist caveats over the relative value of individual patents; variations in the resources and time demanded to secure registration; differences in commercial value and the demands for achieving successful exploitation; degrees of protective value; and so on.[19] Yet such patents represent potential commercial knowledge that the company concerned sees genuine value in placing in the protective patents architecture, or to retain leverage to trade for other competitive know-how. And US registrations, as the most dominant arena, are generally accepted as a first indication of the potential gains from research, effectively a measure of the "D" achieved from "R" in R&D.

The only fields where UK companies have a significant percentage are defence/aerospace and pharmaceuticals: the two areas that have enjoyed continuing government patronage. Elsewhere, there is a sad before-and-after comparison of a negligible presence in those fields where British industry enjoyed a comparative lead in the post-World War II period: general industrials – power stations, railway motive units and rolling stock, machinery, control systems, materials etc; electronics; and computing applications. While these latter, measured by the sheer volume of patents, are the technologies showing the most dynamic evolution. Significantly, the 2007 R&D Scoreboard omits the section on US patent registrations, presumably out of sheer embarrassment.

If Britain has now become the laggard, the US and Germany have maintained their commitment to the leading edge of technology, albeit with differing interactions between state, academia and industry, and varying effectiveness of transformation into market success. Most striking has been the historic growth of Japan and its leading enterprises, from a situation of massive "imports" of technology and expertise following the Meiji Restoration, replicated after the Pacific War by scrupulous acquisition of leading technology – "For $17 billion they bought the lot"[20] – to the point where many of their companies currently find themselves in the uncomfortable position of leading in their product areas. And just as Japan has "caught up" with erstwhile leading industrial powers, South Korea and Taiwan have learned the lesson, with others on our Cook's Tour following suit. So there is every chance that Britain will lag even further behind "the rest".

WHITHER CONTINUITY?

Friedrich List's concern over breaching continuity was that, "in a short time a complex coordination of productive powers and of property becomes lost, which had been created only by the exertions and endeavours of several generations." His perception was perhaps better than he knew, since recent studies of the components for innovative success recognise that continuity is a crucial component in "knowledge creation" through "the mobilisation and conversion of tacit knowledge". "Knowledge creation is a never-ending process that requires continuous innovation" within an organisational structure where "fields of resonance" can be stimulated and perpetuated.[21]

Consequently, since corporate destabilisation has been a perennial outcome of the country's political vacillation, the theoretical dominance of "flexible labour markets" and "liquidity" of capital markets, and managements aligning their objectives to "shareholder value", List's maxim is probably the best epitaph to Britain's industrial decline. And a complacent institutional structure that will inhibit all attempts to achieve the magic goal, usually trotted out at TUC conferences, of "British knowledge creating jobs for British workers" – present signs are not hopeful.[22]

WHENCE CO-OPERATION?

A prevailing weakness of British industrial effort has been a myopic preoccupation among corporate managers in fighting, even unto death, to pursue their immediate "bottom lines", either by confining their own involvement to as narrow a risk-free range of tasks as feasible, or shunting risk onto others via legal instruments. Whether these latter are as reliable a firewall as pretended, or merely a pretext to ensure future legal wrangles, excuses are lined up – the short-term expectations of shareholders; the attitude of clearing banks to contingent liabilities; lack of trust in other British companies to perform, or to move beyond their immediate "bottom line" perceptions; the need for let-outs against these, or any other potential changes; and so on. But evidenced in the historic failure of any "British" consortium to win, or successfully perform, overseas projects; a reluctance of companies, even of the relative scale of once mighty GEC and Hawker Siddeley, to move beyond the comforts of providing equipment to order, or effectively sticking as subcontractors; and an inability to pursue the dynamic interactive links with suppliers to create the flows of innovative products that characterise international competitors; down to the absurd margins demanded for alleged "risk", and legal/consulting fees in PFI/PPP contracts.

But, hooray! The advent of the Internet made "networking" impossible to ignore, and the success of the Dell-model of "modular" subcontracting, has brought tribes of consultants on "supply chain management" and "outsourcing" swinging down from the trees. Yet, if breakthroughs in the British industrial scene, elsewhere old hat – for example, in the German cooperative tradition, the "group" orientation of Japanese industry – where their general trading companies have been managing supply-chains for over a century, or the French "filière" approach to building national industrial competencies. All structures where these new technologies and practices augment established relational industrial connections. While the "arm's-length"/"shareholder value" of the British tradition remains an endemic weakness in exploiting these opportunities.

Yet List viewed the "co-operation of productive powers" in a broader context, recall, "the productive powers of every separate manufactory are also increased in proportion as the whole manufacturing power of the country is developed in all its branches, and the more intimately it is united with other branches of industry." Yet again, perhaps, an early intimation of one of the current economic fashions – the dynamic merits of industrial "clusters". But Britain, with the dissipation of its industrial capabilities, has lost so many "branches" that it becomes almost impossible to conceive of "co-operation" in such a national context.

As a vivid counter example, whereas flogging-off the remnants of Rover to China marked the effective end of a national motor vehicle industry, in anticipation of Toyota overtaking General Motors as the world's leading car manufacturer, the Nikkei ran a series of articles on the extent to which Japan's auto industry had contributed to sustaining the economy during the decade of "deflation".[23] In brief, the presence of leading assembly companies continuously pushing to upgrade their performance, quality and appeal contributed to leveraging advances across an array of industries – steel and materials; rubber compounds; electronic applications to enhance traction control, engine efficiencies, system response, and driving aids; improved precision, speed and flexibility of machine tools; and sustaining mercantile freight carriers. A hinterland of dynamic interaction only feasible if the driving brains and intentions are retained in a stable national community. And a similar analysis could surely be done for other auto-producer regions surrounding BMW, VW, Daimler, Citroen, and Renault. Other industries will be surrounded by their hinterlands of interactive chains – Nokia in Finland, shipbuilding in South Korea, nuclear power in France, electronics/IT in Japan, Taiwan and South Korea etc.

Similar skeins of supplier/client linkages underlie the industrial structures in other fields of industrial activity – power generation, rail transportation, road infrastructure, public services such as hospitals, stadia etc, where it is common practice in other countries for operators and suppliers to maintain a continuing dialogue: feeding back to suppliers any weaknesses or areas for performance improvement, and from the manufacturers modifications offering enhancements, with each undertaking complimentary development work when needed. Hence, the Shinkansen train has gone through a series of upgradings, and the same pattern of progressive improvement would be common to France, Germany, Italy, Sweden and elsewhere.

In Britain, even in the era of nationalised utilities, each – CEGB, National Coal Board, British Gas and British Rail – retained technical centres with their own research programmes. But all were inhibited from establishing continuing cross-feeding development relationships with suppliers by a national dogmatic predisposition to believe that "competition" was a prerequisite for "efficient" public purchasing. Matched, partly as a reflection of this same national mindset, by British companies' reluctance to invest in research unless sure of gaining an early advantage beyond waiting for the next inevitable "buggins turn" order, relying instead on "customer specifications" from the utilities deriving from the latters' experience and research.

NOT ME, MATE

The peculiar British propensity for fragmentation reflects the very different trajectory of industrial evolution compared to the "late starters". Reinforced by a context of "Empire" the dominant tradition was for export houses, based on local connections in overseas markets, to suss out opportunities as these emerged for power generation, railways, traction and rolling stock, river shipping, textile and metalworking machinery etc. And then, through their British contacts, tie up deals with any of the variety of national producers. Even if not as overtly protectionist as many critics have argued, common legal conventions, sources of finance, and language, customs and support organisations inevitably made the UK the base for securing orders in imperial markets – going back to Siemens' investment in Britain in the late 19th century and US car producers in the 1920s.[24] It is arguable that despite many of the inherent weaknesses of this relatively fragmented structure,[25] it was ironically an advantage during World War II when rapid innovation and improvisation were the order of the day – and when national defence provided a source of finance where immediate tangible results took priority over haggling on price.

Still, if these characteristics may have contributed to a loss of international competitiveness in several "new" industries from the late 19th century, they were equally incapable of capitalising on the temporary advantage of the immediate post-World War II period, when Britain still had a residual Empire market, and while – apart from the United States – industries in other countries faced major reconstruction. The "British shambles" was progressively overtaken by the "miracles" of European countries as their traditional "corporate" institutional bias provided a better discipline in labour demands and a surer basis for investment to modernise their industries. In parallel with British industrial fragmentation, at the end of the War there were a multiplicity of employers organisations (1900) and trade unions (700) defeating all efforts for national coordination.[iii]

Rather than confront the inevitable major unemployment and labour unrest of this fragmentation being worked through by competitive attrition, governments chose the "consolidation" routes of nationalisation, or through induced mergers arranged by the "gentlemanly capitalists" of the City. There may have been periods when nationalisation achieved enhanced output, efficiency and investment, for example in coalmining. But elsewhere, especially in facing rising international competition from Europe, and then Japan and South Korea, the process of burying hatchets, paying off the dog-eared, the lack of consistency in labour relations, reorganisation costs, and managerial changes diverted resources and focus from the real investment and disciplines necessary to keep pace.

Not the least of the hangovers from earlier fragmentation lay in managerial attitudes and basic competence. Going back to the ancient family outfits running the mines, the desultory shipyards, steel plants and manufacturing companies, the dominant ethos was a baronial grandeur, irrespective of the size of the patch over which it was exercised. Implanted into the gene pool of British management, industry has suffered from successive generations of arrogance, irrespective of the viability of the underlying business or whether it rated in international markets. In general, the degree of arrogance was inversely related to the company's prospects. And, fatally, this was matched by the sullen and obstructive attitudes among labour representatives, creating a uniquely British synergetic bond. The dynamic clash between all these various factions stood no chance against the more focused and cohesive structures traditionally evolved in other countries, and, reinforced by financial institutions immune to the demands of a competitive industry, relative –

[iii] *The European Economy since 1945* by Barry Eichengreen (Princeton University Press) page 123ff.

and now absolute – decline was probably inevitable. And with all the participants priding themselves that they were superior.

Consequently, where are Britain's managerial heroes who have carved out enterprises with the resilience to grow internationally across generations? Very scarce, as the usual suspects skulk off to secret retreats clutching their swag from massaged incentives, share options and undisclosed pensions, without much thought for the business beyond their tenure.[26] And/or to be deftly recycled into comfortable seats where an exalted record of playing "the expectations game" is a useful badge of glory.[iv]

GOT ANY BRAKES?

Industry has no lack of pundits, academics and self-styled gurus, whose publications festoon from the sky purporting profundities on competitive diagnostics and remedies: even advising countries like China struggling with their unique development contexts.[27] With the accumulated vacuum from traditional decline, British companies are scant among exemplars.[28] And offer even less prospect that any fundamental changes will work their way through corporate finance departments bowing to the "expectations" of rentier shareholders.

Elsewhere, despite the pontifications of British commentators, new enterprises are emerging among the later-late industrialising countries modelled on their immediate predecessors on the development slopes, and many indeed exploiting new opportunities opened up by the ease and speed of international commerce.[29] It's a fair bet that just as Britain's capacity to evolve viable international companies has been superseded by European and Asian late-starters, the British model has even less prospect of standing up to the new tempo of competition. Especially when, again, others enjoy the comparative advantage of not being subject to the complicit ingestion of "shareholder value" regimes pursued by the City, reinforced by the economic fraternity's sleight of verbiage that "markets" are a source of efficiency: only sustainable if competitiveness in "real markets" is excluded. Hardly surprising, really: among Adam Smith's more perceptive, if meticulously ignored, insights was the inherent competitive fallibility of the joint-stock company.[30]

With national competences in many fields atrophying, any prospect of future development through "knowledge industries", apparently "broadly defined to include high-tech manufacturing, education and the creative

---

[iv] "Old chief executives never die, they land new jobs" (*FT* 24/25.6.06)

and cultural industries"[v] has a high component of fantasy. By any measures the nation's capacities for stimulating talent, the scope and range of education, mechanisms for realising potential, and drive lags the idiom of developed nations intent upon sustaining their traditional strengths and emerging countries motivated to match their erstwhile "leading nations". If, as is argued by some, "China's place in the world economy is, increasingly, as a dependent part of the supply chain rather than as a player in its own right",[vi] then Britain can only respond, "Join the club" – except that China is intent upon elevating itself from this dependence.

So, with institutional and financial incentives that have served only to stimulate industrial decline, and peculiarly resistant to change, the national hackney carriage is short of brakes, leave alone any gears to reverse these dysfunctional characteristics. To be fair, there is the occasional native voice of protest pointing the way back to a more sustainable corporate system. For example:

"It is impossible to forecast variables like volumes, competitive pricing, raw material costs, interest rates or currencies three or five years out. What is very easy, however, is to appreciate that speeding up a process, reducing waste, eliminating direct labour and improving tolerances and reliability will enhance both the products and their manufacture, as well as the experience of the end user. These benefits will be long-term and valid, irrespective of the output, exchange rate, raw material costs, and all the other variables."[31]

"Building a business is hard work and requires commitment to see through the ups and downs of commercial life. It is a frame of mind that seems less and less in evidence as executive incentives are skewed towards quick rewards and career progression."[32]

Yet these are mere echoes of a truism that goes back to Friedrich List's insistence upon continuity, and grasped intuitively in the economic development of all successful nations. Even Britain at one time. And borne out by the dynamic evolution of innovation – once laundered of the economist's overlay of "waves" – as a continuous process of "internal growth" whereby a legacy of distinct capabilities are created from accumulated experience and feedback. As distinct from "external growth" by M&A. If companies that have evolved from a tradition of "internal growth" engage in M&A, it is from the basis of their established expertise in particular technologies and processes that, if synergy is meaningful, can be applied to enhance the performance of the new enterprise.[33]

---

[v] *The Writing on the Wall* by Will Hutton (Little, Brown).
[vi] Ibid p116

Consequently, the mindset and disciplines of "internal growth" have been, and remain, the origin of international corporate success. This implies a continuing drive for innovation, and the relative performance of UK and competing international companies is a commentary on the extent to which managerial focus has been diverted to "shareholder value" and the false growth offered by acquisition not based on an established legacy of specific capabilities.

IS BRITAIN A DEVELOPMENTAL STATE?

Reeling off comparisons of relative national capabilities, not least in the "knowledge industries" puts Britain behind erstwhile developing/emerging countries: to the point where, as a contrast to "emerging", Britain rates a new category of "submerging". And the impetus of inertia seems as dominant as noted by Eric Roll – the same old financial institutions and conventions, obsolete economic nostrums, rutted political rhetoric etc. Sporadic belated "initiatives", ever more impotent, hold little hope of achieving the sustained evolution of capabilities to match either the historic, or new, momentum of other countries. Symptoms, to back up the prospect of achieving "unremarkable mediocrity" flow daily out of the headlines – typically, "Cost of sick leave has risen to over £13bn, says CBI"; "Pay puts quality of academics at risk"; "Staff training given low priority"; "Britons admit to aimless surfing"; and "Science graduate shortage threatens nuclear industry" (10 April 2007); following on the UNICEF report that the UK shares with the US the distinction of being the worst two industrialised countries in which to grow up.[vii] Or, "Universities forced to teach students the maths" (25.4.07). Or, "Business reluctant to make skills pledge" (21.5.07). Or, "Shortage of skilled staff in London worsens", "Warning over lack of experts", "Working days lost to strikes soar" (12.6.07). Or, "Crossrail delays threatened London's prosperity", "Labour blamed over fall in rates of start-ups" (7.8.07). Or, "'Crumbling' transport links hitting business" (13.8.07), "Rising building costs threaten projects" (14.8.07). Or, "Britain slips down the global league table of graduates" (19.9.07). Or, "Skills expert warns of "gap" with EU and US" (14.10.07). Or, "Academia fails to foster start-ups" (12.11.07). Or, "UK pupils fall behind in the league table for science" – remarking on the OECD's Pisa ranking of 15-year-olds' learning attainment in science, where the UK rates 14 behind Finland, Hong Kong, Canada, Taiwan, Estonia, Japan, New Zealand, Australia, Netherlands, Liechtenstein, Korea, Slovenia, and Germany

---

[vii] "Child poverty exposes the Anglo-American model" (*FT* 2.4.07).

(30.11.07). Or, "Standards in maths and reading fall" – commenting on the 2006 Pisa rating where the UK scores were no higher than the OECD average (5.12.07). Or, "Germans shun investing in UK" (5.12.07). Or, "Social mobility is still at 1970s levels" (13.12.07). Or, "Civil engineers see risk to public works – Skills shortages fuel £8bn in extra costs" (17.1.08). Or, "Migration fears risk adding to skills shortages" (8.4.08). Or, "Apprentice scheme fails to fire enthusiasm" (1.6.08). Or, and so on.

Ironically, one of the clearest examples of the country reverting (advancing) to the practices of "late industrialisers" is defence procurement. On the one hand, the Ministry of Defence has an interest in sustaining the country's capabilities in key technologies and achieving better product performance and lifetime costs. On the other, native industries have competed/rationalised themselves close to oblivion leaving only a handful of relatively significant companies – BAe Systems, Rolls-Royce and GKN, with an array of relatively vulnerable small suppliers and subcontractors. The response is for MoD to "look to create long-term partnerships with a combined approach towards initial purchase and 'through life' equipment maintenance" (*FT* 2.4.07). "Partnerships" may be modish management/political jargon, but reflects the normal pattern of industrial evolution in Germany, Japan, France, South Korea, Taiwan etc, who began their industrialisation with very few effective companies on which to develop. Typically, one of the immediate "British" responses was for Smith's to sell off its aviation interests to GE of the US. Still, who knows, perhaps we shall see "golden shares" taken by the main prime-contractors in more vulnerable key suppliers, and the evolution of "group" structures similar to those that have been the basis of German and Japanese industrial development.

Yet in the impetus behind education, skills development, and pursuit of global markets the UK lags even the most recent batch of "rising" economies of South Korea, Taiwan, China, India, Singapore and Malaysia. And the pace of change is such that even glib catchphrases begin falling into obsolescence – "outsourcing" is but the latest, where Embraer, the Brazilian aircraft manufacturer, effectively "reverse outsources" specialist manufacture and major systems to Japan, US, UK as well as components to Asia; or, as the Indian IT outsourcing and generic drug companies build up matching competences in client markets, initially the principals in commissioning their "outsourcing" business;[viii] or, the recent trend for "industrialised" country retailers "outsourcing" the sorting, labelling and distribution for their "home" retail outlets; or, to

---

[viii] "India's IT groups start to move to near sourcing" (*FT* 2.11.06), and "A new twist in India IT outsourcing" (*FT* 31.1.07).

reverse the conventional wisdom on the pre-eminence of "brands", component and contract suppliers in Taiwan, Japan and South Korea can vie for the title of "the largest company you've never heard of" by virtue of being common suppliers to HP, Dell, Apple, Sony, Toshiba etc effectively "outsourcing" to the latter the costs and risks of "brand" battles.

In this dynamically turbulent international setting, there are few, if any, universal maxims for companies to establish a sustainable future. Beyond perhaps a few basic building blocks: a continuing questioning of "Why do we exist?".[34] If a shade too much in a philosophical vein for the taste of traditional British management, the response can only be eclectic and company-specific.[35] Second, a vision embracing both "survival" and "advancement" through inbred expertise, and pursuit of new horizons of knowledge.[36] And, third, an acute awareness of the increasing threat of "instant reverse engineering" by aggressive new competitors.[37] These qualities create and flow from the company's heritage of cumulative expertise and a focus on capabilities that allow it to exercise leverage in competitive contests. Honda's survival in a context where "there are no constant conditions" remains as good an exemplar as any.

These qualities derive from a settled view of purpose – continuity, and the capacity to evaluate and absorb evolving technologies and skills – and co-operation. Despite all the panegyrics about globalisation, and the trend for companies to "distribute" their R&D around the globe, the location of "the driving purpose" remains crucial. For responses to the fundamental question about direction, and decisions on the allocation of resources that result, are inevitably centred on where this corporate nucleus resides. And, sadly, it is just these qualities that are undermined by the undue focus on sterile "shareholder value", dishing out dividends to manage "expectations",[38] and the accountancy acrobatics demanded by the City. Equally, all the rhetorical aspirations about the country moving to higher-value-added activities hinge on the existence of enterprises that possess these qualities.

Recalling hours chairing "sifting meetings" for Queens Awards, and borne out by years of subsequent awards, there is no lack of innovative flair among a diversity of companies. Yet a prevailing weakness has been to evolve the drive and continuity of purpose to match their counterparts in other countries. Sure, our politicians will remark at the drop of a hat, "small firms are the backbone of the economy". But the same could be said of Germany, Japan, US or elsewhere, except that UK small firms' advocates flounder against the question, "Why can't we have 'some small firms' like Sony, Honda, Nokia, Bosch?" that have evolved by dint of focus and technology into major enterprises.[39] Conversely, even in those ancient times when there were arguably "large" British companies – GEC, Hawker Siddeley, Plessey, ICI, Courtaulds etc, none was significant by comparison with leading international competitors – GE, Hitachi, Toshiba, NEC, BASF, Hoechst, Du Pont, Toray etc, and steadily lost comparative global position with the continuing fugue of take-overs, mergers, sell-offs, and break-ups. This lack of company scale matters when the levels of investment – and preceding R&D – to keep pace with the leading edge is rising: just as examples to hand, upgrading a plant for next-generation flat-panel TVs or to process 300mm-diameter silicon wafers for semiconductor manufacturing can run to $2.5-5.0bn a throw, and of the order of $8-16bn for a 450mm-diameter wafer factory.[ix]

You might have thought that Britain's authorities confronting their own depleting range of internationally competitive industrial enterprises and the corresponding attrition of skills, expertise and supporting infrastructures should have naturally thought to apply lessons from the repertoire of approaches successfully adopted by other countries. Not likely, with a parochialism approaching a national "attention deficit disorder" Britain has never learned to compete – save for the exceptional circumstances of war. Rather, the tempo of pink gins on the veranda is more compatible with incantations of choice quotations from the turgid prose of an eccentric Scotsman, writing at the height of the surpluses from the plantation and slave trades, as a substitute for thought or involvement in reality. So, even when such desultory efforts have been made to emulate the French "indicative planning" of the 50s/60s, this was from the surrogate reality of ancient economic dogma.

To reverse continuing decline demands a shift in fundamental attitudes far more demanding than just turning over a page of history. Even assuming a sharp reorientation of educational incentives from primary through to university towards skills, engineering and sciences, there still remains a dearth of immediate career opportunities that can be offered only by viable growing companies within this country.

---

[1] There is an etymology to be updated on "policy". Originally a term implying general principles or objectives that have an enduring value, reflecting, perhaps, a time when the world moved slowly enough, or at least communications in a far-flung empire were protracted enough, to permit an elaborate process to refine such principles. Even if real application was secondary, or incidental. While it traditionally carried a "class" connotation, implying a mystical activity suitable

---

[ix] *Nikkei Weekly* 23.4.07 and 26.5.08.

only for "fine minds" i.e. with Liberal Arts degrees from Oxbridge, where practice in tutorial sessions was a suitable apprenticeship. Since the stipulation from Ministers for "two-page summaries", the capability to do 5th form précis has been added to the necessary accomplishments. Within the British public service, this distinction underlay the class designations between "Administrator" and "Executive". Now, as the world has become smaller and faster, and as the functioning of Whitehall becomes a secondary offshoot of the corporate governance industry, apparently it is proposed that "encouraging Ministers to concentrate on policy will promote better policy-making in Whitehall. For one thing, it should allow Ministers and their advisors to concentrate more fully on policy assessment and development." This would leave Departments to be run on an analogy with the corporate governance principles of the private sector, and Permanent Secretaries under comparable "disciplines" (*Whitehall's Black Box* by Guy Lodge and Ben Rogers – IPPR 2006). Given the source, it is difficult not to read into the conclusions that "policy" has effectively become a market commodity, open for the multitude of "advisors" to bid for depending on their political inside tracks.

[2] It has come in for some revisionist bashing, such as, *The Scandal of Empire: India and the Creation of Imperial Britain* by Nicholas Dirks (Harvard University Press). Not entirely fairly, since most recent commentaries on "Empire" have admitted the corruption of the East India Company, and the "spin" associated with such episodes as "The Black Hole of Calcutta" and the massacre at Cawnpore. On the other hand, America was also a beneficiary of the early imperial adventures – the Yale brothers were among the East India Company's shady operators, and Elihu Yale, after a spell as Governor of Madras, was dismissed with his brother for irregular activities, which by the standards of the time must have taken some doing, and went on to found a college in 1718 subsequently honoured with his name (*The Honourable Company* by John Keay (HarperCollins).

[3] Admirably chronicled in *The British Empire and the Second World War* by Ashley Jackson (Hambledon Continuum).

[4] "Globalisation" has arrived as an economist's wet dream, and the term was probably invented by the clan as a pretext for continuing output of guff on fallible data. A self-revealing admission is "Globalisation is a big word but an old idea, most economists will say, with a jaded air. The phenomenon has kept the profession's number crunchers busy, counting the spoils and how they are divided. But it has left the blackboard theorists with relatively little to do" (*The Economist* 20.1.07), though the article suggests that the "theorists" are beginning to sense an opportunity to dream up a "new paradigm".

But, aside from the natural evolutionary interaction of technologies impacting on industrial development and trade, the term was given a whole new meaning in post-Cold War triumphalism – the brief age of "the end of history" – where the presumption in an ideological frenzy was that an Anglo-Saxon style of capitalism would sweep the world. This gave rise to entertaining counterblasts like John

Gray's *False Dawn – the Delusions of Global Capitalism* (Granta) that twigged the fallacious determinism underlying this Utopian fantasy. But then came the 1997 Asian financial crisis, where the ideologues displayed just how destructive they could be when unleashed: the theme of Joseph Stiglitz's *Globalisation and its Discontents*. Since when, as the developing group of China, India, Russia, Brazil and others have started to exercise their clout, and the Doha round of trade talks ground into inertia, there are even cheers of applause, such as *The Collapse of Globalism and the Reinvention of the World* by John Ralston Saul (Atlantic Books). Yet by typical sophistry, economists prattle on "globalisation lives" (Martin Wolff: *FT World Economy Supplement* – 13.9.06), or "After all, globalisation is unstoppable...." (*The Economist* 20.7.06). Sure. But in a form influenced by the havoc wrought by economists as China and India hold on to control of their currencies – recalling that this insulated them against the 1997 Asian financial crisis, or developing countries stashing up foreign exchange reserves – recalling that Taiwan, with the largest per capita foreign exchange reserves, also managed to ride this crisis.

[5] A trend, even reported in daily journals, is for countries with substantial indigenous resources – Russia in energy and aluminium, Brazil in soya and bioethanol output, Venezuela in oil and gas etc – to deploy access to these as part of their international diplomatic hand. While the global distribution of energy reserves suggests this trend will continue, with the state-controlled oil and gas reserves of Saudi Arabia, Iran, India, Venezuela, Russia, Dubai and others vastly exceeding those of the main commercial "sisters" such as Exxon, BP and Shell ("Oil's Dark Secret" – *The Economist* 12.8.06). The converse is the aggressive drive from resource-deficient countries to gain access to resources, deploying a variety of inducements (The Ugly Face of China's Presence in Africa – *FT* 14.9.06). While the scale and diversity of "unlisted enterprises", many "state owned", in the *FT's* roll-call (15.12.06) suggests that "States" are far from being non-participants in their domestic and international markets.

[6] India has a clutch of software enterprises, such as Wipro, Infosys and Tata Consulting and generic drug firms, Dr Reddy's and Ranbaxy, that are moving up the value chain and into international markets. And the old "family dynasties" of Mahindira, Birla, Reliance, and Tata have upgraded their traditional businesses to take on international markets. While China, if the takeover of IBM's laptop arm is the only high-profile international move, has many rapidly evolving businesses. Just for examples to hand, Hondra, as its name implies, began manufacturing Honda counterfeit motorbikes. But when it came under pressure, reading the counsels of Jack Welch of GE fame, went for diversification into buses, mineral water, paint thinner, imported wine, newspapers, duck-down jackets and football team ownership. Or Haier, best known for consumer electrical products, also embraces insurance, pharmaceuticals, personal computers, mobile phones and a chain of noodle restaurants among its 86 products. (*China Shakes the World* op. cit.)

Or the Wahaha Group, began by a school business official in 1987 to market a herbal children's tonic, expanded via taking over vacated factories and marketing in non-urban areas, a joint venture with Danone, selling a Coke alternative, and a line in children's clothing in association with a Paris design studio, to the point in 2005 of having 70 subsidiaries employing more than 10,000 with nearly 900 having advanced degrees. (*One Billion Customers* by James McGregor (Free Press)). Even if relations with Danone have subsequently come under strain, to the point where the French company has launched a $100m lawsuit in the US (*FT* 12.6.07). Or, with a somewhat different pedigree, Hauwei Technologies, started in 1988 with a $9 million state bank loan as a venture based on the technical research facility of the People's Liberation Army. 2006 revenues have climbed past $11 billion, with more than 60% from overseas (*FT* 3.1.07). Or the remarkable Mrs Cheung Yan who has built up Nine Dragons on the basis of recycling packaging from the US and elsewhere into the largest paper producer in the world with an annual capacity of 5.4m tons, with further capacity due next year, having made Mrs Cheung "the wealthiest self-made woman in the world" (*The Economist*: 9.6.07).

[7] The title "Economist" covers a broad range: for example, Takahiro Fujimoto, author of the best available account of the development of Toyota's production system, referred to earlier, enjoys the title of "a professor in the Faculty of Economics, University of Tokyo". While his British counterpart – shielded by a self-erected extreme aversion to contamination by contacts with reality – is still reciting Adam Smith's account of a pin factory.

[8] David Cameron's pronouncement while on a visit to Delhi in August 2006.

[9] On the "innovative capacity" measure developed by Professors M.E. Porter and S. Stern as "a country's potential – as both an economic and political entity – to produce a stream of commercially relevant innovations" between 1995 and 2005 the UK failed to register in the top 10, behind Japan, Finland, Switzerland, Denmark, Sweden, USA, Germany, France, Norway and Canada.

[10] "We have a good economic record, but the next stage will be about fostering public and private investment in science, skills and infrastructure; energy security and sustainable growth; streamlining planning and stimulating private enterprise to give us a knowledge-based, high-value-added industrial and science base" – Tony Blair when Prime Minister (*Guardian* 27.6.06). The obvious contrast lies in the continuity of other countries' pursuit of these aims, as distinct from the rhetorical gimmickry of "stages".

[11] DTI – The R&D Scoreboard: October 2006, Vol 2 page 220ff. Other comparisons cited will draw on the information in this convenient ready reckoner.

[12] Just to recall, Honda had 1700 staff engaged on R&D and design, compared to a total of 100 employed on similar activities by all British manufacturers: this led to Honda having introduced 5 new models in the crucial big bike segment in the previous five years, whereas British manufacturers had reduced their models from 8 to 3, with a single engine upgrading. Allied to this high investment in R&D,

Honda demonstrated its ability to exploit advances in production efficiencies: again the comparison was between UK companies' output per man year of 10-18 bikes and Honda's 106 bikes and 21 cars per man year.

[13] It is also worth recalling the scene in August 1949 when, after making clip-on bicycle engines, the company's first prototype motorbike was completed. A celebration party was held the office, with all the desks pushed into one corner. President Honda and his 20 employees had reason to be satisfied as they drank home-brewed sake and ate sardines and pickles. Someone said, "It's like a dream!" And Honda shouted, "That's it! Dream." And the company's first motorbike was the "Dream Type D". The company's advertising motto, "The Power of Dreams" harks back to this original inspiration. The 2010 expectation was pronounced at a Global Management Forum (*Nikkei Weekly* 11.12.06) by President Takeo Fukui, with the further comment, "We aim to be the leader in every area of environmental technology. Our alternative energy development efforts include mass production of solar panels and, in biotechnology, producing ethanol from straw."

[14] Of these, Fujitsu's position in computing is partly derived from the "controlled competition" approach adopted by the Japanese government in the 1960s and 1970s. And Komatsu also benefited – as depicted in a famous HBS case study – from temporary tariff protection, but with the express condition that these would be withdrawn after a set period when the company would be expected to fight its corner.

[15] Life at the top is never easy: Shin-Etsu Chemicals may be the world's leading producer of silicon wafers with 31.7% market share, but Sumco and Komatsu Denshi, the second and fifth largest silicon wafer manufacturers are due to merge, with their combined market share rising to 30.8%. Shin-Etsu's response is to invest another $1 billion to raise output of 300mm wafers to 1 million a month from its current level of 700,000 per month. According to the company, "Demand for semiconductors and wafers used to come mainly from the PC industry but since about 10 years ago demand has increased from a broad range of products including games and mobile phones. Recently, there has been growing demand from vehicle manufacturers as well, as their vehicles use a lot of semiconductors too." (*FT* 21.9.06) While Fanuc is finding its position as the established leader in computerised machining systems coming under pressure from Yaskawa Electric, whose approach to application-optimised production has increased its global share for multi jointed robots to 20.2%, surpassing Fanuc. (*Nikkei Weekly* 18.9.06)

[16] From an entertaining tongue-in-cheek piece by John Plender, "Private equity firms could do wonders with Microsoft," suggesting that the techniques of "leveraged buy-outs" could extract vast value from Microsoft's "inefficient" balance sheet, albeit gutting the effectiveness of the business (*FT* 18.8.06).

[17] Let's recall again the report on "Concern in US over 'empty voting'" (*FT* 6.10.06), where the practice of lending shares has led to a situation where "the

basic legal and economic underpinning of the public corporation had been washed away. The link between economic ownership of shares and corporate voting power had been severed." With the study giving examples "in which hedge funds borrow shares just before a shareholder vote, vote the shares, then return them to the lender, never taking an actual economic interest in the company." And there was a vivid example in the last minute rush to find out who owned what shares in the Mittal takeover of Arcelor.

[18] Through much of Britain's imperial past, stupidity has been a national comparative advantage. Typically, during the Indian Mutiny there would be a fortress captured by a few thousand hysterical mutineers, and some Colonel Anstruther-Grey or another would turn up with a relief column. On a quick appreciation of the situation, he would command, "Bring up my Highlanders!" And a few hundred ill-shaven, scruffy figures in weird skirts would shuffle forward. "Charge!" he would shout. And off they went. The incumbents of the fort, on seeing this gaggle, would conclude that they were confronting a foe even crazier than they were. And prudently fled.

And we have even had epic poems lauding this strain of stupidity. In response to "Charge those Russian guns!" any other nation's contingent of light horse would have speared the subalterns and sugared off.

Mentioning this thesis of national stupidity to a French civil contractor, he responded, "Mais, vrai! It is the same in France. All those young men who followed Napoleon." Then, after a pensive pause, he added with a sigh of regret, "Ah stupidité is no longer enough."

On a national balance of subsequent stupidity, the French have managed a good record free of this mindset in energy, transport infrastructure, and sustaining their major companies in international markets. In contrast to the perpetuation of this underlying mentality on this side of the Channel. But their greatest advantage has been to avoid the stupidity of the brand of economics that has permeated the British decision-making process, for stupidity correlates closely with pretentious ignorance. Even to the point where leading economic figures question the essential precepts of "traditional economics" – Joseph Stiglitz's conclusion, "Anybody looking at these models would say they can't provide a good description of the modern world", or Alan Greenspan, "We really do not know how [the economy] works.... The old models just are not working", having earlier noted, "A surprising problem is that a number of economists are not able to distinguish between the economic models we construct and the real world." (*The Origin of Wealth* op. cit. p 22).

Perhaps the surest symptom of historic stupidity has been the failure of economic dogma to acknowledge that "manufacturing" and "services" are complementary – only reluctantly admitted to be "interdependent" by *The Economist* in October 2005. Maybe it will not be long before there is also a recognition that "consumers" and "producers" are also complementary, even if also a bit late in the day: even *The Nikkei Weekly* can offer a gentle philosophical homily, "If Bohr's philosophy is followed, newly hired workers would recognise themselves as members of the society with dual but mutually complementary properties – consumer and producer – rather than labelling themselves as members of only one of the two groups" (16.4.07).

[19] Perhaps the key caveat is that the list does not do justice to countries with rising levels of R&D effort: notably India's generic drug producers are committing increasing resources to evolve their own patentable innovations. While China's R&D capabilities have expanded rapidly, to the point of investing $136 billion in R&D, exceeding the $130 billion being spent by Japan in 2005 (China overtakes Japan for R&D – *FT* 4.12.06), while 77,395 scientific papers were cited in patent applications in China (Chinese science citations go beyond bicycles – *FT* Letters 8.12.06): according to the OECD, "In the last decade, R&D has more than doubled as a share of the country's gross domestic product. China has also just overtaken Germany in terms of patent filings to stand fifth in international rankings (The dragon's lab – how China is rising through the innovation ranks: *FT* 5.7.07).

[20] James Abegglen's colloquial summary of, "This massive transfer of technology from the United States and Western Europe in fact provided the technological bases for nearly all of Japan's modern industries. Without this critical technology transfer, no amount of capital and labour could have moved Japanese companies to their present competitive positions so rapidly. Yet the cumulative cost of all that transfer over a period of more than 20 years has been only $17 billion, a fraction of the current annual US research and development budget." (*Kaisha* op. cit.)

[21] The recognition of "tacit" knowledge as a source of creativity – even if the distinction between "tacit" and "explicit" is traceable back to M. Polyani writing in the 60s – to be exploited as part of effective management really begins with Ikujiro Nonaka and Hirotaka Takeuchi's *The Knowledge-Creating Company* (Oxford). The more illuminating and balanced since the authors had both done stints in leading US universities, though much of their case material draws upon Japanese companies.

[22] The "flat-panel LCD" syndrome continues, even when another potential $billions innovation comes out of Cambridge's Cavendish Laboratory (University Centre paves way for plastic microchip: *FT* 3.1.07). Plastic Logic, a university start-up, is pursuing a development, "by using a cheap and simple set of processing operations to build up layers of circuitry on plastic 'substrates' – the material on which circuits are formed – rather than silicon wafers used in conventional microchips, the developments promised to slash the cost of making semiconductors." The potential cost-savings in manufacturing semiconductors and other applications has attracted $100m of investment, and the venture is due to be building a factory in Dresden to come on stream in 2008 producing "flexible control circuitry for large displays the size of a piece of paper that can hold large amounts of information – equivalent to thousands of books". If "the displays will most likely be made by other electronics companies, with Plastics Logic providing the crucial control circuitry and possibly licensing its designs", the

immediate employment gains will be in Saxony, primarily because "the city's strong traditions – dating to a time before the Berlin Wall fell, when it was a leading centre in micro-electronics research for the whole of the Soviet empire." But what of the locations once the centres of the British electronics industry? Why have they not also survived?

Moreover, the consortium backing the venture includes BASF and Intel, with Siemens and Dow Chemical among its shareholders. This structure will virtually guarantee that the value added from applications and derived uses will be secured by non-UK companies (*FT* 4.8.08). In the case of "flat-screen LCDs" the failure to pursue applications from the original patent occurred when there were major British companies in related technologies: this time, the excuse is that there are no longer significant companies in related technologies left.

Consequently, if the evolution of e-paper/polymer materials in future electronic and industrial applications is bound to be a contested arena, again, despite this breakthrough, the vacuum of British industrial capability will almost surely mean that the main "applications" gains will be taken elsewhere.

[23] The Co-operation of Productive Powers

The decision by Peugeot in April 2006 to close their factory at Ryton, Coventry (a heritage of the disposals following the Chrysler rescue in the mid-70s) had the routine response of trade union outrage – if historically a weak diminuendo compared with the strident days of the British Leyland collapse, the flurried rush by Ministers to the site – though not the pre-Election galaxy that responded a year earlier to the collapse of Rover, with the usual dose of current government reassurances that this was a consequence of globalisation, which had also attracted investment into the country from leading world companies. The Prime Minister under challenge at Questions, recalled current British car output being greater than in the 1970s, and mumbled that they were contributing exports of some £10 billion (In fact some 1.6 million cars were produced in 2005, compared to some 2 million in 1970 – *The Economist* 22.4.06). It was for the Lex column (*FT* 21.4.06) to recall "investment per employee has almost halved over the (past) decade and Britain's trade deficit in motor products ballooned from £5bn to £12bn in 2004".

Concentrated on producing a single model, the 206, that was due to be phased out, with production of a successor, the 207, due to begin production at a new plant in Slovakia, and relying on imports for 75% of its main components, the closure of Ryton was inevitable. Apart from some remaining "cottage" niche companies, like Morgan, Aston Martin, TVR – now also closed – Caterham etc, that struggle unless picked up by a larger international player, such as Lotus, the bulk of Britain's car industry is made up to varying degrees of outrider production units that are linked into the parents' supply network, which may involve sourcing from as far afield as Indonesia and Brazil. And the very specialist niche of Formula I stables, heavily subsidised by sponsors. While there are British component firms, like Smiths and GKN, and some overseas companies like Honda, Nissan and Toyota have taken steps to improve the quality of UK suppliers, they are inevitably in competition with established parent suppliers, such as Denso and Bosch, who have also set up outrider units in this country.

Behind the comforting totting up of total finished car production, the British car industry exemplifies the withering of interdependent networks of activities that are generated by a vibrant national industry. To illustrate such a dynamic "co-operation of productive powers", we therefore have to look elsewhere. Perhaps reflecting a modest triumphalism as Toyota comes up to overtaking General Motors as the world's leading car producer, the *Nikkei Weekly* has run pieces underlining the interdependence between the technologies behind the success of Japan's car producers: worth quoting in full.

"Auto industry sits atop tech chain

Demand for advanced parts prompts suppliers to create cutting-edge innovations

Japan's automobile industry is in high gear, having surpassed its US rival in terms of total worldwide output. Meanwhile, Toyota Motor Corp. may overtake General Motors Corp., the global market leader, in terms of production this year. Having expanded their pace of technological innovation to cover everything from electrical machinery to basic materials, automakers are sitting at the top of a comprehensive industrial chain.

Delphi Corp., the largest US manufacturer of auto parts, filed for bankruptcy last autumn with an array of Japanese companies, including NEC Electronics Corp. and Matsushita Electric Industries Co., on its list of creditors.

The former GM unit boasts expertise in electronic parts, with the creditor list illustrating the support of major Japanese electrical machinery manufacturers. US semiconductor sales have doubled in the past decade while Japan has been on the decline from its one-time status as a chip giant. That is not the case, however, in regard to the category of chips for cars.

The number of semiconductors used in one car has jumped to around 70 from just under 15 about 15 years ago. The distance between the automobile and electronics industries is narrowing rapidly.

Evolution is accelerating. NEC Electronics is working on a safety technology that uses semiconductors to enable the instant analysis of images taken by cameras installed in vehicles and the issuance of warnings to drivers. "An image processing market will start up in five years," said Yoshiro Miyaji, general manager of the firm's automotive systems division. Once the technology is adopted, the company is expected to win a steady stream of orders as new models are released.

Japan's automobile industry has two main attractions for peripheral industries. First is its large-scale and comprehensiveness. With domestic shipment value projected at just over ¥40 trillion ($350 billion) and worldwide shipment value at ¥200 trillion, the domestic auto industry influences a significant number of industrial categories, from chips and basic materials to transportation and other services. Its multiplier effect is huge.

Machine tool orders

Of domestic orders for machine tools, about 20% are from the auto industry. "Actually, 60-70% are for the auto industry (indirectly)," said an official of the Japan Machine Tool Builders' Association. With regard to orders from other industries, many customers of the companies that place orders for machine tools are automobile-related firms.

Second is the auto industry's role as the driver of technological innovation. If Silicon Valley can be likened to a sacred place for the information technology industry, the comparable site for Japan's auto industry may be the Chukyo region in central Honshu, where Toyota is headquartered.

Nippon Steel Corp. has dispatched engineers to Toyota to jointly develop new steel products. The purity of the constituents of electrical steel sheet used in the motors of gasoline-electric hybrid vehicles was improved drastically to efficiently turn electricity into automotive power. "Our close relationship is supporting the technological innovation of Japan," said President Akio Mimura of Nippon Steel.

Co-operation with a singleness of purpose also benefits steel makers. High-performance electrical steel sheet is used in refrigerators and air-conditioners as well as automobiles, causing a trickle-down effect.

Technological innovation in the global auto industry has been concentrated in Japan since the latter half of the 1990s, including the world's first mass production of hybrid-engined cars and fuel-cell electric vehicles.

Foreign firms are also heading for Japan. US chemical giant DuPont set up a new research-and-development base in Nagoya last autumn, and General Electric Co will open a technological centre for automotive materials in Mooka, Tochigi Prefecture, this year.

The head of marketing to automakers at the plastics division of GE is stationed in Japan, not in the US. Mark Kingsley, general manager of global marketing, GE Plastics, Automotive, takes it for granted that he leads the firm's global business from Tokyo, saying Japan has every element necessary for technological innovation, including cash-rich automakers and demanding consumers.

Service sector

With the failure last spring MG Rover Group Ltd of the UK, there are no longer any British-owned automakers. The UK, which in the 1970s boasted the second-largest auto industry in the world, is now a mere shadow of what it used to be. The British mass media has said there is no need to worry about the lack of a locally owned automobile industry as the ratio of service-oriented businesses to the overall economy has risen. But is this really true?

UK shipping companies, which once controlled the oceans of the world, were purchased by foreign capital and disappeared. In contrast, despite passing through a long shipping slump, Japan emerged with three major shipping companies intact. Automobiles decided the outcome of their struggle. "The reason why we could maintain our international competitiveness was the steady growth of Japanese car exports," said Akimitsu Ashida, president of Mitsui O.S.K. Lines Ltd.

Development power creates iPod economy

Steel wire developed by Hitachi Metals Ltd originally as material for piston rings for automotive engines is used for small bearings incorporated in the iPod portable digital audio player. The bearings shoring up magnetic heads in hard disk drives need to be made of material of a high degree of purity that causes little friction, because lubricating oil cannot be used and the bearings must not make any noise.

After a lot of searching, Apple Computer Inc of the US spotted the steel wire as an ideal material for one of the key parts for its innovative portable audio player. Hitachi Metals controls 25% of the global market for the steel wire, which is highly durable but hard to process, by devising a system to instantly fine-tune design.

The auto pyramid has also interfaced with the iPod economy in another area as an increasing number of cars are equipped with audio systems that can play music stored on the iPod. Some analysts forecast more than 30% of new cars offered in the US this year will be compatible with the iPod.

Super-large press

Meanwhile, the auto industry has played a role in the sophistication of Japanese manufacturers' technologies in various sectors. For example, Komatsu Ltd, a major construction machinery maker, has succeeded in developing a servomotor-powered super-large press machine with a maximum capacity of 4000 metric tonnes, 2.5 times that of existing models, at the request of Toyota.

Unlike conventional press machines, the servomotor model is capable of subtly adjusting speed and force, and it can easily mould high-tensile steel sheet. But the machine is difficult to control. To overcome the shortcomings, Komatsu, together with Toyota, came up with technology to simultaneously control a number of motors. The press machine, which took a year to create, and which is used to mould steel sheets into large panels for car bodies, has no rivals, company officials claim.

Nippon Paint Co has developed, jointly with Nissan Motor Co, a new paint which can automatically cover scratches on car bodies typically left by washing. "By striving to respond to requests from automakers, we have amassed technological prowess to an extent that we are able to meet any request from our customers," said Junji Yokoi, director of the firm's technology planning R&D division.

Technological innovation at industrial machinery makers and material producers, which comprise the lower layers of the auto pyramid, spurs a virtuous circle by helping upgrade the quality of Japanese automobiles, which in turn prompts further improvements in technologies at related manufacturers.

Home court advantage

Nippon Steel President Mimura argues that domestic blast furnace steel makers like his own can fully display their competitive edge only in Japan. The steel maker's strength stems from close ties with domestic car companies with which the company regularly holds meetings of top executives to discuss technology. The company supplied 30% of its fiscal 2004 domestic shipments totalling 20 million tons to automakers, surpassing the 26% for the steel industry as a whole.

Last August JFE Holdings Inc opened within its Steel Research Laboratory a customers' solution laboratory where auto-related advanced steel materials and processing technology held by the group has been gathered. The new lab in Chiba Prefecture has created steel sheets that, despite lacking reinforcement, can be used as car doors that do not dent. It aims to have the sheet adopted by automakers for their new models in 2008.

There is a drawback to such cosy relations between carmakers and their suppliers, however. Koji Sakate, vice president of the Japanese unit of A T. Kearney Inc, a US management consulting firm, warns against the practice of Japanese suppliers, pushing ahead with technological development at the request of automakers even when it is uncertain that the initiative will profit the suppliers, or to accept automakers' demands to substantially cut prices. "You never see this sort of thing taking place in the West," he said.

The closely linked technology chain bolsters the competitiveness of Japanese carmakers while benefiting a wide range of industrial sectors. But if the structure has given rise to a myth among suppliers that they will not suffer as long as they follow the lead set by automakers, as Sakate points out, that is a potential problem. Parts suppliers need to mine their own resources in the search for the second and third iPod economies." (*Nikkei Weekly* 16.1.06)

While the auto-industries' pressures for reliability and precision push performance for springs, screws and fasteners (*Nikkei Weekly* 13.2.06), stimulates applications for new dye-sensitised solar panels (*Nikkei Weekly* 8.5.06), and, as a further example, watchmakers like Citizen and Seiko are leveraging their precision machining technologies for auto applications such as components for anti-lock brakes, airbag ignition systems, and electronic components for locking and safety systems (*Nikkei Weekly* 13.2.06).

Similar networks have evolved in Germany, France, Italy and in nascent form in China. With culture, language and decades of expertise, matured through developing trust and mutual confidence, such networks inevitably develop an exclusive character. And over time, as the gains of cooperative participation over the losses from maladaptive/opportunistic behaviour become apparent, the coterie quality becomes more entrenched. Consequently, extremely difficult for newcomers to break into, leading to outcries over "protectionism", "collusive behaviour", and "non-tariff barriers". But, in practice, an entirely natural process of industrial evolution within a national/regional context.

The absence of a comparable interdependent industrial structure in Britain is reflected in the classic disruption between technological discovery and exploitation. Despite the much-self-proclaimed "cluster" of design/manufacturing studios for Formula 1 racing – each depending on sponsorship contributions, or finance as part of the development activities of major auto manufacturers, in themselves they are not economically viable – any technology of application to vehicles in the commercial market is siphoned off to the development programs of the international car manufacturers.

Reverting to the pretext for the Nikkei article, rarely a week passes without reference to the depths of GM's miseries – "Even during American's Great Depression, General Motors eked out profits. Today's cocktail of uncompetitive labour agreements, spiralling health care costs and superior rivals sounds less calamitous, but has brought the company closer to the edge than the 1929 Crash.... Even if GM pulls off the costs, there is another challenge: revenues. Too many of its vehicles sell for less than those of its rivals, the legacy of a volume-focused strategy to cover fixed costs. True, GM is raising revenue per unit built, but it will take time to assess the success of GM's pricing strategy" (*FT* 1.5.06).

Behind this situation is a protracted history of declining world and domestic US market share, losses in production whereas competitors – especially the Japanese producers and BMW – have been declaring record profits, and a failure to keep pace with new customer-oriented models introduced by foreign rivals. Attributed causes for this collapse have been various – "unaffordable promises which successive waves of managers have made to meet the living and health-care costs of workers in their retirement"; an unfocused model policy that has lagged the innovation of competitors; the series of international joint ventures/mergers ranging from South Korea, Japan and Europe, now being largely unscrambled; failure to implement the lessons of evolving production and supply processes, despite Toyota having set up a joint factory, NUMMI, to help transfer know-how; and, "Investors who fret about GM's decline tend to forget that they, too, have had a hand in this. Under pressure from shareholders, the firm paid out billions in dividends and share buybacks that it sorely needed for investment" (*The Economist* 15.10.05).

These factors have been operating for several decades, while relative decline from apparently unassailable dominance to near-failure has occurred. By contrast, Toyota, which in the 50s and 60s was a predominantly domestic producer, little-known beyond Japan, has focussed on evolving its own distinct regimes for quality and efficiency, embracing its domain of suppliers. The feedback from this evolving expertise has led to a steady increase in market share with opportune and well targeted products; investment in new plant extending from UK, France, Thailand, Poland, Russia, China, Canada and, most notably, in the US where it continues to increase capacity; a steady commitment to research and innovation has created a stream of challenging models ranging from the up-market Lexus to the more "freaky" Scion – marketed via the Internet in California (*FT* 1.5.06); and the lead in hybrid applications. While it has taken over GM's stake in Fuji Heavy Industries (the manufacturer of Subaru cars) to help ease GM's financial pressures, and in Isuzu with an eye to the latter's expertise in diesel power systems.

As for its network of suppliers, the views of Mr Koji Sakato must have been quoted with a touch of irony. For all the companies mentioned – Hitachi, Nippon Steel, NEC, Matsushita, Komatsu, Nippon Paint, JFE etc – are all competitive over a range of products, and whose involvement in the auto industry is part of a process of dynamic cross-reinforcement, where they draw advantages from being in the demand pull of different flows of product evolution. If anything, reverting to the GM case, it is an open question whether the company or Delphi is leading decline. Exacerbated by rises in oil prices leading to falls in demand for the "gas-guzzlers", once the dominant profitable segment of the US market.

For an update on Toyota, the *Nikkei Weekly* R&I analysis of 1.5.06 is a neat summary:

"Toyota group firing on all cylinders
Carmaker accelerating investment in R &D, global operations
Full-line automaker Toyota Motor Corp. is expanding its business bases in

major markets around the world.

Toyota maintains excellent cost competitiveness as a result of its joint cost reduction efforts with affiliated auto parts makers as well as its long-time cost improvement activities, and also has an advantage in environmentally advanced technologies, including hybrid engines.

Although its capital investment and research-and-development expenditures are swelling with its expanding global production capacity, the company is maintaining and developing a very strong financial position, with the net financial assets of its automobile production and sales division amounting to about ¥2 trillion ($17.4 billion), supported by its high ability to generate cash flow..." while its sales in 2005 reached ¥20.7 trillion, and net profit ¥1.3 trillion.

The stark opposite trajectories of Japan's car manufacturers and suppliers and of GM and its American subcontractors might suggest some contrast in the effectiveness of their respective styles of capitalism. Yet, despite a grudging acknowledgement of Japan's "recovery", apparently it's "corporations waste capital", whereas "If Japan's were truly a reformed economy, in which management was forced by shareholders to achieve a globally competitive return on capital...." (Japan's failure to reform has not prevented its recovery: Martin Wolf – *FT* 8.3.06). Presumably his model is General Motors.

By contrast, Hiroshi Okuda, chairman of Toyota, and in his capacity as head of the Keidanren, the country's main business federation, seems to applaud the capital allocation of his country's firms, "Japan should be a country based on science and technology. The major factor behind the economic recovery was that Japanese companies patiently continued research and development activities to boost their competitiveness during the previous lengthy period of economic stagnation. Japan must not lag behind the ongoing global trend toward focusing on scientific technologies." (*Nikkei Weekly* 17.4.06)

On revealed comparative performance, which view carries more conviction? Apart from the British experience of having lost the capability for a genuinely dynamic network of "cooperative productive powers", it must remain questionable whether any management "forced by shareholders to achieve a globally competitive return on capital" will be able to match the innovative and market drive of unreformed nations. While, beneath the picture of overall "car production" lies a vacuum in supporting industrial infrastructure. For much the same structures underlie BMW, Honda, VW etc.

[24] Remarkably, the excuse of the loss of empire as a route to "reaching scale in global enterprise" seems to have hung on, judging by the justification of Amersham executives for selling out to GE (Donald Brydon – *FT* Letters: 16 February 2007).

[25] Debate about the inefficiencies of the UK's fragmented industrial structure go back to Alfred Chandler's analysis of the growth of the large American corporation, articulated in *Scale and Scope: the Dynamics of Industrial Capitalism* (Cambridge MA). Not uncontested, given the persistence of family and dynastic undertakings, and taken up, for example, in *Family Capitalism*, ed.

Geoffrey Jones and Mary Rose (Cass). While the persistence of these dynastic enterprises over generations is illustrated in *Family Capitalism* by Harold James (Belknap Harvard), and the European sagas of the Wallenberg, Bouygues, Michelin, Agnelli, Merck etc businesses, with the continuity of Tata and other Asian groups prompt the view "The pendulum swings back to family values" (*FT* 1.2.07).

[26] A typical aside, "When asked if Smiths Group would still be in existence in five years, Keith Butler-Wheelhouse, chief executive, said: 'I can count on that [it going out of existence] not happening in the next two years, after that it will be somebody else's problem' arose following Smiths' sale of its aviation interests to GE." Of course, no reflection on Mr Butler-Wheelhouse, who seems a suitably excellent fellow ("Sigh of relief over Smiths' GE deal – Speculation of breakup starts" (*FT* 16.1.07))? But a handy contrast to the declared purpose of Honda's move into aviation to preserve the long-term future of the company.

[27] A glance along the "management" shelves of any bookstore will cast up a sparkling array of quick solutions: "Blue Ocean Strategy", "The Innovation Wave" – liquid is apparently a good image; "Built to Last", "Built to Change" – bricks and mortar have an instant appeal; and other variants of "excellence", which have a currency limited by the failure rate of icons; or the touchy-feely variations of "Emotional Intelligence", "Think, Play, Do". Over time, enough bandwagons for a score of Hollywood musicals (or John Wayne Westerns) – Re-engineering, Social Capital, Complexity, Disruptive Innovation, Knowledge.... In practice, going over the biographies of successful companies, there is a total absence of evidence that their achievements have derived from perusing any such texts.

While, apparently, nowhere has been more vitiated by economic dogma than professed managerial training. In the tiff following the late Sumantra Ghoshal's assertion that, by virtue of the influence of economics, the way MBA students are taught has freed them "from any sense of responsibility" for what they do in their subsequent business careers, *The Economist*'s bouncy defence ran "As long as schools are teaching academic degrees (and, after all, the letters MBA stand for Master of Business Administration), they have to teach the most compelling business theories around. It may be a pity that these are mostly to be found in economics. But that is the fault of other disciplines for not coming up with ideas to rival, for example, agency theory or the maximisation of shareholder value."

Going to Ghoshal's case (*Sumantra Ghoshal on Management* (Prentice Hall)), his main thrust is that economics' pretensions to "a science" are inappropriate to management where "imagination or will" are components of an "intentional" idiom of performance. Typically, for example, "employees are not 'factors of production,' as in neo-classical economics, nor 'strategic resources,' as in much of the currently popular management literature, but they are 'volunteer investors'." The concept of "labour" as a "factor of production" may hark back to Adam Smith's "commodity" valuation of "men", but that this should figure in any purported account of managerial functions is astounding in this day and age, with the rising dominance of enterprises where employees are sources of expertise, feedback and creativity for "increasing returns" to create higher-value activities.

Ghoshal is criticised in some quarters for fairly questioning the inappropriate assumptions of economics, yet failing to provide a countervailing theory. His summary, "Just as shareholders invest financial capital in a company in the expectations of both income and capital growth, similarly employees invest their human capital in a company, with exactly the same expectations. The company's responsibility to employees, therefore, is both to ensure competitive remuneration and to continuously add value to them by enhancing their repertoire of useful knowledge and skills. The employees' obligations, in this new relationship, is to continuously learn, in order to protect and improve their human capital, and to use their expertise and their entrepreneurial capabilities to create new value and thereby improve the company's competitiveness and performance." This account would reasonably cover effectively all leading international companies, the likes of Toyota, Honda, Siemens, BMW, Samsung, or Embraer – just as a broad field of examples, none of whom would attribute their achievements to "administration" or "theory" in *The Economist*'s sense of these terms.

Who needs theory? All these rising successes would point to Ghoshal's depiction, and suggest that their best means of fulfilling their responsibility to employees is to be more successful than their competitors. For there is no lack of authoritative voices questioning whether management is compatible with, or irreparably undermined, by being treated as an academic discipline. To pose a question that was unanswered in an *FT* Internet debate, "How many MBAs are employed by GM and Ford, compared to Toyota, Honda and Hyundai?" The answer might have suggested that the prevalence of MBAs among company managements was inversely related to their competitive success. Enron and Anderson offer cautionary exemplars.

Pre-eminent among the sceptic voices is Henry Mintzberg, for example *Managers Not MBAs* (Prentice Hall), and typical of his critique, "MBA programmes are not solely responsible for all the dysfunctional aspects of managing we now see around us, from the exaggerated executive compensation schemes and the sales strategies and mergers to the scandals of dishonest corporate behaviour, all indicative of a demise of leadership. A hyped-up business press and questionable consulting practices have contributed, too. But they have done so in conjunction with the educational programmes, which have both legitimised and encouraged some of the daily behaviours they should be challenging.

"Destruction is so much easier than construction. It takes nine months to grow a human being and a moment to destroy one, years to build a great organisation and months to run it down, centuries to establish a democratic society and decades to undermine. Leadership is an old phenomenon; the managership promoted by the MBA is a rather new one. In my opinion, it has contributed to what will be described here – and I have chosen the word carefully – as a pervasive corruption, from education through management to organisations and into society." Crisply summarised, "Courses and MBA programmes that claim to create leaders all too often promote hubris instead. No leader was ever created in a classroom" (*FT* 23.10.06). Or, as Anita Roddick, founder of Body Shop, put it fairly bluntly, "Don't get a business degree, get angry" (*FT* 15.11 .06). Mintzberg's approach is to combine the academic with real corporate experience, and one of the heartening developments is the evolution of various forms of "corporate universities".

Phil Rosenzweig must also figure high in the debunking/commonsense league (*The Halo Effect* (Free Press)): after demolishing the preconceptions touting the validity of many journalists and guru commentaries, he returns to the ground laid out since Sun Tzu of individual businesses confronting their own distinct "situations" of technology shifts, evolving competitors and changing markets, where "strategy" lies in perception of these trends and openings to exploit them, coupled with the skills and competencies to "execute" more effectively than competitors.

By contrast, *The Economist*'s semantic juggling that "Administration" belies an academic focus on "theory" is roundly disproved by corporate performance in real markets, and even the British civil service has dispensed with the formality of an "Administrative" class. For some fields of employment MBAs may offer a filtering mechanism – *The Economist* cites investment bankers as being particularly attracted to MBAs, and there is an alumni network effect, for good or ill. The qualification has an appeal, however, for myriads of foreign students to gain the rudimentary commercial alphabet, though how far they swallow prevailing "theory" remains mute.

[28] Under the ominous title, "You've Never Had It so Good", *The Economist* ran a special report on Britain (3.2.07). After a natural eulogy to the development of London as a financial centre, under the heading, "From wonks to widgets", we learn that "Britain still makes and exports things. Manufacturing has grown steadily, if less rapidly than services. For a smallish post-industrial country, Britain has a surprising number of giants", and goes on to cite Vodafone, whose UK-content of turnover would be pushed to get to 2%; GSK in pharmaceuticals, which has evolved under the favourable procurement patronage of the NHS; Rolls-Royce, the country's inadvertent "national champion", also partially shielded by defence procurement; and JCB, even if much smaller than major international rivals like Komatsu and Caterpillar, it survived through the 80s – to quote its chairman Sir Anthony Bamford, only because it was not quoted. Despite all the self-congratulation about, "we'll live by our wits", there is recognition of a dearth of talent, and the necessity for British companies to recruit engineers abroad, while the country's education and skills attainments continue to lag even emerging countries.

[29] The cited literature, and occasional press articles, offer examples aplenty of businesses, both from developed and emerging economies, that have achieved international prominence. Often in surprisingly short periods of a couple of decades – Nokia, in mobile phones; Mittal, in international steel production; CEMEX, in supplying concrete to global markets; Dassault Systems, in business

process/design software; or Taiwan Semiconductor Manufacturing Company, in fabricating silicon wafers and chips for a large number of independent designers – just to pick some of the most obvious.

Taking advantage of such recent publications as *The Emerging Market Century* by Antoine van Agtmael (Simon & Schuster), a striking feature of the past few decades is the geographic spread of these new international competitors:

Argentina: Tenaris has evolved a competitive international network for on-time delivery of high-quality seamless steel pipes to rival global leaders such as Sumitomo Metals and JFE.

Brazil: Petrobras has become the leading Latin American oil company, with 89% of its resources offshore, and a leader in deep-water drilling; CVRD is the largest and lowest-cost producer of iron, but also a leading producer of manganese, copper and nickel; Embraer has evolved to a leading regional jet manufacturer, "outsourcing" fabrication to Japan, and engines and components from US, UK and Europe; Aracruz Cellulose, now a leading pulpwood producer with 98% of its output going to the global market; while Brazil is the leader in sugar-based ethanol for use in "flex fuel" vehicles.

India: Plenty enough has been written about the rise of India's software companies – Infosys Technologies, Tata Consulting, Satyam, Wipro, or rising drug development companies –Ranbaxy, Dr Reddy, but there is a growing presence of the traditional "family dynastic" companies – Tata has expanded in steel through the acquisition of Corus, expanding also through the purchase of Jaguar and Range Rover, but also in commodities like tea distribution, and has plans to develop low-price cars; Reliance, despite internal feuding, is moving into a dominant position in oil refining, retailing, mobile phones etc; and Mahindra has improved its quality and product standards to rival international competitors. While, its entrepreneurial spirit can yield sudden successes – Mittal in steel, and Suzlon in wind turbines whose acquisition of Repower Systems makes it the world's fourth largest (*FT* 28.5.07).

Mexico: Apart from the remarkable international expansion of CEMEX, Modelo is the origin of the Corona beer brand, and America Movil, Telmex and GrupoTelevisa have a rising global position in telecommunications and media.

South Africa: Going back to the period of anti-apartheid sanctions, Sasol developed the existing technologies for converting coal and gas into oil and its derivatives, and is expanding its activities globally enhanced by increasing costs and rising scarcity of accessible reserves of oil.

South Korea: Following the rationalisation of the main chaebol groupings, Samsung Electronics has leveraged a shift from commodity electronics and memory chips to a leading global position in specialised semiconductors, mobile handsets, TV screens, and digital media, albeit still part of the Samsung group. Similarly, LG is moving to an international position in digital consumer products. While Hyundai motor, having absorbed Kia, has been one of the fastest-growing manufacturers in recent years, and Hyundai Heavy Industries retained its leading position in shipbuilding and heavy industry. And POSCO remains among the leading steel manufacturers.

Taiwan: Remarkable for its "invisible" companies from Yue Yuen, a world leader in shoe production, to a range of companies in computers and electronic components, like Hon Hai, Acer/BenQ, High Tech Computer and Qanta, which have moved progressively from commodity component and subassembly suppliers to evolving their own distinct products. While Taiwan Semiconductor Manufacturing has become the largest fabrication foundry.

[30] "To buy in one market, in order to sell, with profit, in another, when there are many competitors in both; to watch over, not only the occasional variations in the demand, but the much greater and more frequent variations in the competition, or in the supply which that demand is likely to get from other people, and to suit with dexterity and judgment both the quantity and quality of each assortment of goods to all these circumstances, is a species of warfare of which the operations are continually changing, and which can scarce ever be conducted successfully, without such unremitting exertion of vigilance and attention, as cannot long be expected from the directors of a joint-stock company." (*The Wealth of Nations* vol II) On this basis, Adam Smith would have viewed the collapse of the British motorcycle industry, and, indeed, most other manufacturing, as inevitable.

[31] *Entrepreneur fires broad attack on manufacturers* (*FT* 19.1.06), a summary of Edward Atkin's address to the Institution of Electrical Engineers (Mr Atkin had presided over the growth of Avent, one of the world's biggest manufacturers of babies bottles and infant feeding products), where he goes on to point out, "As soon as financial criteria become the main method used for evaluating investment opportunities, the company is almost certainly doomed. Companies subject to the control of investors through a stock market flotation are more likely than private entrepreneurs to be swayed by short-term financial considerations, which are likely to deflect them from decisions linked to building up a global brand on the back of innovative and competitive products."

[32] *Why values must still matter to tomorrow's companies* (*FT* 31.1.07) by Stuart Hamson, chairman of John Lewis Partnership, commenting on the rise of private equity funds, recalled the origins of the Tomorrow's Company initiative, and their interim conclusion in 1994 on "the incredible wastefulness of business structures based on conflict rather than constructive relationships. The shibboleth of 'shareholder value' – regardless of the significance of other stakeholders – was eroding performance."

[33] Not the simplistic alternatives depicted by *The Economist* (21.1.06), "In essence, there are two ways of achieving top-line growth: companies can buy it through mergers or acquisitions, or they can generate it internally. To do the second, they need to innovate." Marconi remains the classic example of attempting growth through "bolt on acquisitions" without an established tradition of "internal growth". Nor are these modes readily interchangeable, as implied in Stefan Stern's article *Ignore the sweetener of yet another deal and go organic* (*FT* 9.1.07) – ignoring the British tradition of pursuing organic growth on an analogy with cultivating rhubarb – for, internal growth is, as Stuart Hamson remarks, "a frame of mind".

Perhaps the best unremarked business study is *Growth through Competition, Competition through Growth* by Hiroyuki Odagiri (Oxford), which illustrates the development of the codes, incentives, competitive tensions and ethos for successful "internal growth", combined with a sharp critique of the "external" approach of growth by acquisition.

[34] See the introductory essay in *Knowledge Creation and Management* ed. Kazuo Ichijo and Ikujiro Nonaka (Oxford).

[35] A lively account of the diversity of corporate approaches in the current international scene is offered in *How We Compete* (Doubleday) by Suzanne Berger and the MIT Industrial Performance Centre. A source distinguished by a proven track record of pragmatic analysis largely unencumbered by economic theorising.

[36] See Kazuo Ichijo's essay on *The Strategic Management of Knowledge* in *Knowledge Creation and Management* op. cit., which instances Sharp's drive to advance its LCD development and retain its leading position.

[37] A surprisingly neat summary comes in an article on Sulzer Pumps, a subsidiary of the Swiss group, that retains its leading role as a specialist pump producer (Quality marks manufacturing revival: *FT* 23.11.06). The article offers a quick menu on "How Britain can beat China", as follows:
– Constantly innovate, stay ahead of the competition
– Create production processes that are hard to replicate
– Exploit skills and knowledge not easily transferred
– Make customised products – avoid commodities
– Offer services as well as products
– Operate flexibly to meet customers' needs

[38] Whereas UK companies already have the highest distribution of post-tax earnings, the bias elsewhere – and particularly in China – is to retain earnings to develop the business (Invest without rest – why China steadily ploughs back the profits: *FT* 18.7.06).

[39] Corroborated by, "British hi-tech companies tend either to stay small or, when they get to a certain size, throw in their lot with a big international company..." (Memo to boards: think before you sell out – *FT* 15.2.07).

PART VI:

A MAJOR OVERHAUL

Where now? Take your pick. Sticking Humpty Dumpty together, forging a new axle for the hackney carriage, plugging holes in the old steam boiler, or any selection of images to depict the challenge of correcting the accumulated blundering of the "British way". Hardly sustainable save as a source of "innocent merriment" for international observers. Yet skeins of parochialism from traditional programming persist despite all the evidence of decline. And significant change must traverse chasms hollowed out by the flow of "path dependencies" and deserts of vast pomposity.

SAVED BY THE CRUNCH?

Having drifted so far up the creek on the fantasy of a "service economy", other countries have been steaming purposefully to keep in the mainstream. Even worse, as the tide of lax credit runs down, not only up the creek bereft of paddles, but the keel is beginning to scrape. Rudderless navigation and powerless flapping without paddles must begin to be noticed as having limited virtues.

To change the metaphor, when Her Majesty the Queen bowled her fast leg-stump yorker at the London School of Economics in October 2008 by querying, "Why did nobody notice?", there was much shuffling of feet both immediately and in subsequent ruminations among devotees, with the conclusion, "Many saw a piece of the jigsaw but very few practitioners of the dismal science covered themselves in glory" (*FT* 16.12.08). Come off it. "Unsustainable" has been a constant refrain in World Bank/IMF/OECD/Bank of England reports and among commentators for several years. More likely, the reason for shifting footwork was to evade the supplementary fast-kicking bumper, "And why did nobody do anything about it?"

Look at the skeins of complicities tied to the status quo: just as Thatcherism itself derived from a naive economics dogma, so there continues in the groves of academe comfortable sinecures peddling "efficient markets", "bounded rationality", and modelling founded on "other things being equal" etc; while increasing reliance on services was the celestial path delineated by economics mystics; others pumping out "financial economics" in the guise of "finance and profits theory", "risk management", "value-at-risk", "probability distributions", etc in business schools; swathes of consultants and analysts drawing comfortable screws from rehearsing prevailing jargon; credit rating agencies and auditors who readily countenanced dubious valuations; lords of private equity, investment bankers, brokers and dealers condoning "leverages" on fantasy assets; regulators lounging on "light touch" disciplines; and officials, advisors and politicians pretending competence in managing the economy declaring "the longest period of sustained growth" since Hengist and Horsa. All closeted against the impact of this delusional fabrication on the humdrum of everyone else's daily existence. And all protected by the convenient rhetoric that the pursuit of "self-interest" must, by definition be in the public interest. While, after all, "there is no alternative". For all the comforts of this undeclared conspiracy, the rearing head-high bumper must be ducked by all conceivable postures of denial.

THE UNHOLY ALLIANCE

This permeation of mediaeval scholastics across national governance and finance is a uniquely "British" accomplishment, unreplicable elsewhere, disseminating from the Oxbridge economics faculties – and their lesser clones, and the City. Together, a lethal cocktail.

The tradition of "trade-offs in realism"[1] has nowhere been better exemplified than the fantasy of "a modern service economy".[2] It has been obvious outside the cloisters for centuries that there are no services that can function without implements or mediation of manufactured products, as much as manufacturing is unsustainable without allied services. Apparently, breaking out of decades of miasma *The Economist* had come around belatedly to recognise the blindingly obvious – "neither manufacturing nor services is inherently better than the other: they are interdependent".[1] If a breakthrough in canonical rote learning, recognition of this mutual dependence has yet to overcome tempestuous headwinds of special pleading for financial services, where tax-fiddling is the acme of "services" value-creation.[3]

Among many historical ironies is the dismal performance of the City in providing finance on terms to match those available to enterprises in other genuinely industrial countries, and then claiming that Britain's industrial

---

[1] *The Economist* (1.10.05)

decline is part of some evolution to a more elevated "service economy" where "higher-value R&D, design and marketing" are inclined "to stay at home".[ii] Even if true, Britain's "home team" is sorely depleted, with only a handful of companies ready to apply the resources and ingenuity to secure US patents, and in many fields either barely or not registering at all. In practice, however, these activities cannot generate a continuing value stream in isolation: they have to be directly applied to products, processes or projects, and even then comprise only a relatively small element of the totality.

Not to underrate the native innovative flair and suppleness among the new generation of industrialising nations, "R&D, design and marketing" have also shown the same tendency to be located where the right brains are to be found, assisted by software developments that facilitate "business systems outsourcing" (BSO),[4] or for functions such as development and marketing being devolved locally for rapid response to distinct national market demands. Crucially, this "academic" jargon ignores entirely the "knowledge" created by feedback within the actual process of manufacture. And lookout for vacuous semantics in pursuit of Britain as "a knowledge-based powerhouse".[5]

Taken to its natural outcome, such "services" in which the country pretends to superiority, without the manufacturing capabilities to exploit them, will become increasingly dependent on foreign supply. Rising trade deficits not only reveal this trend, but will inevitably continue as the proportion of "services" that are "tradable" fails to keep pace with ever greater dependence on imports. Particularly as a large element of "tradable services" is directly linked to merchandise trade – logistics, shipping/air freight, supply-chain coordination, warehousing, product servicing etc, and is inevitably dictated by the preferences of the manufacturing originator.[6]

The same *Economist* article harks back to the origins of the peculiar British fantasy: "People always resist change, yet sustained growth relies on a continuous shift in resources to more efficient use." Underlying the bland prescriptive arrogance is the same simplistic approach examined in the section on "The Adjustment Dilemma". But, even in these generalised terms, Britain stands as perhaps the worst exemplar of this precept: not only a negligible position in creative innovation in sectors from which British companies have largely exited – even those where contemporary rhetoric once proclaimed, "Britain leads the world", but an equally minimal position in IT and Software, Electronics etc to which "resources"

[ii] *The Economist* op. cit.

should have been shifting on the "efficient use" hypothesis. For, in practice, "resources", which, within the dumb conventional jargon of ubiquitous "commodities" – like "men", presumed to slosh about like water or olive oil in buckets, or whatever may be the analogy built into economists' models, is a misleading catch-all term. If it plays neatly into the naïve, and convenient, belief that "exit" allows "resources" to float in a "a continuous shift" to higher value-added, it bypasses the essential prerequisites for exploiting such a "shift" in an established heritage of skill sets, competencies, assets and processes which in turn make calls on finance, managerial expertise, and creative dynamism.

THE VALUE OF CONTINUITY

By proven historic performance, qualities entirely lacking in the institutional structures of British industry. Instead, nothing grows. In contrast to the priority on "continuity", "mental capital", and "co-operation" in the national traditions encountered in our brief Cook's Tour: where the evolution to higher-value added derives from "internal" "resources" of skills and experience. Again, rather than the dumb conventional simplification of a "core competence", this pattern of corporate development builds up an envelope of expertise to absorb and exploit relevant technologies as these evolve.

Taking forward our earlier glance at Honda, it is impossible to disentangle the contributions of "R&D, design and marketing" to their products, while the range of "expertise" covers, just as a quick outline, combustion chamber geometry, fuel systems, hydraulics, metal and other materials, electronics, catalytic chemistry, sensors and control linkages: and all integrated, drawing in the expertise of suppliers, to provide the performance and aesthetics to be attractive against market competitors. And, as the company has developed into a worldwide producer, extending disciplines of production processes and techniques to guarantee quality among diverse cultures.[7]

Within this complex are activities that would be classed as "R&D" that would fail the usual "rate of return" criteria of UK "shareholder value" companies. Their ASIMO humanoid robot, seen in a vivid TV advert touring the Science Museum, however valuable as a marketing device is many years away from fully fledged commercial application: yet its demands for sensors, materials, control systems and integration exact levels of expertise that are applicable to Honda's other products.[8]

The sustained feedback of experience over time accumulates a legacy of expanding depth and range in the envelope of expertise. These "internal resources" are applied to exploit new technologies, to update existing products, and to explore other options where the company's accumulating heritage can be applied.[9] Consequently, such a focus of expertise opens opportunities for new products and processes to be pursued applying "resources" to higher-value activities: in Honda's case, motorbikes still involve competitive model changes, as do its cars, but the range of activities extends to powerboats and other power products, and developing new lines of business in aero engines and light jet aircraft, solar panels etc.

If citing Honda is to pitch the bar high, its essential qualities are shared by a host of internationally competitive enterprises, whether German, Japanese, Nordic, Asian or, indeed, major US leaders such as Microsoft – which only began paying dividends a few years ago.[10] But with extremely rare, and diminishing, British warriors daubed in shareholder-value-woad still standing. Still, not to worry. This is yet a further instance where by natural superiority, "Britain leads the world" – "Just as Britain led the world into industrialisation, so now Britain is leading it out".[iii] *The Economist* again: for all its earlier breakthrough into reality, dumb dogma has persisted. If hardly an adequate summary of the very different paths of industrialisation followed by other countries, often in aversion to the social consequences of the British model, they are hardly likely to follow this British subaltern's wave to advance from atop the parapet.[11] Instead, having suffered over centuries the barrage of sanctimonious lectures of British commentators, they will be more inclined to relax in their trenches sure in the knowledge that they have not only "caught up" but "far outstripped" the khaki imperial preachers. Just look behind you. No one's following. Bluntly, the notion that German, Japanese, French, South Korean, Taiwanese, or indeed any other, companies are going to dispense with their legacies of competitive advantage is plain crazy.

FRAGILITY OF FINANCE

Can anyone take such academic hubris seriously? For, as Britain has inexorably lost its capabilities for innovation and productivity, the widening discrepancy between the nation's true weight and the prize-fighting classification at which flailing political punches are purportedly thrown has become inescapably apparent. Beneath our comforting flow of GDP figures over the past decade, there has been a collapse in education, skills development, engineering, sciences, managerial competences; creaking infrastructure, terrorism, street violence, social fragmentation, community disruption, growing dependence on imports of energy,

---

[iii] *The Economist* 23.6.07

foodstuffs and consumer products, and absence of any national vision. As is borne out in virtually all international comparative measures.

The length and depth of the post-credit-crunch downturn is anyone's guess. Comforting notions of "the cycle" leading to an inevitable upturn may turn out to be another of those vacuous assumptions on which economists' prescriptions are based. Japan suffered a "lost decade" in getting over its property-boom/credit-crunch crisis, despite having a string of companies at the leading edge of a wide range of products and a booming Chinese market next door with the US still in consumer frenzy. At the very least, it should have been apparent that putting too many national eggs into the fragile basket of the City was ever a dodgy heritage.

It would not take much for a few of its slippery denizens to diversify more of their activities to Dubai, Hong Kong, Singapore, Shanghai or other financial centres closer to the loot deriving from energy surpluses and export success. And, like a mackerel well, the spiral will follow the few fish at the bottom. All that is needed is a period of wobbling confidence to get a few lead mackerels to scratch around elsewhere: within the realm of reasonable surmise, given the national record of prevarication in infrastructure investment, the London Underground – even as Crossrail eventually emerges from its decades of review – could be undermined by increasing demand, continuing delay in upgrading, and a failure to cope with rising ambient temperatures – after all blocks of ice cannot be a permanent solution to hot summers, even if the Underground is not submerged by a failure to enhance flood defences as the Thames Barrier comes under pressure from rising surge levels. Toss in threats from terrorism, gang culture moving just a couple of miles into luxury dormitory areas, and advances in information/computing technologies, and the aggregate would be enough to stimulate the footloose mackerel princes of finance to find other tax havens with more clement conditions.

Despite its vulnerability, the cry is on for "Saving the system" (*The Economist* 11.10.08) or keeping "the UK a world leader in financial services" (*Guardian* 20.10.08) with aspirations for a typically "British" scenario of sticking with the Duke of Wellington's precept "in the same old style", reinforced by decades of *burrah sahibs* pontificating the same old garbage,[12] and sycophancy from political parties for donors playing speculative games in "business services" in esoteric jargon in the "onshore tax haven of the City", whose performance is measured in equally speculative statistics (see "Wot's Going On?"). "CDOs, CMOs, CPDOs and a host of other acronyms"[iv] may become yesterday's jargon, but the

---

[iv] "Of Humpty Dumpy walls and falls" (*FT*fm 6.8.07)

tricksters will still have scope to arbitrage through and around whatever regulatory hurdles are raised. This vision would also preserve the comforts of those sponging off the speculative swarm, leaving, in this scenario, aspirations for life-chances for the rest of the nation dominated by the ancillary services to feed consumer demand and the housing market, to the extent that these revive with the rising levels of private debt to sustain them.

INCOMPATIBLE ASPIRATIONS

Besides, there is an acute danger of rhetorical knickers-twisting, as "leading the world" out of industry conflicts with the political paean that Britain can "lead the world" in skills and sciences. For, the latter demands a tier of viable and dynamic companies to offer career opportunities and attractive salary incentives to encourage the rising youth to devote the extra effort to gain more demanding professional and technological qualifications. And, however many scientists clocking up citations, or Nobel prizes, in academia, whether their attainments reach applications in the real world depends upon viable enterprises to develop them into marketable products. No chance if the only options are retailing, estate agents, solicitors' offices and finance-related services.

As some consolation, however, this "leadership" out of industry is not quite as distinctive as the proclamation might suggest. The rising "capital inflows" that have prevented the current account deficit moving more rapidly towards infinity has largely comprised a "car boot sale" of British companies under the rubric of "free and open markets". If virtually denuding the FTSE 100 of manufacturing companies, this has been compensated by most being flogged off to companies from other national traditions uninhibited by the dynamics of decline imposed by British shareholders: Saint-Gobain, Lafarge, Linde, Cemex, Ferrovial, Nippon Sheet Glass, Tata, Heidelberg Cement, Iberdrola, Holcim, Akzo-Nobel and others. Probably the first contribution of British shareholders to the long-term sustainability of the businesses in which they have had a stake.

These new immigrants add to an already large foreign ownership of native industries: Siemens, Bosch, EDF, SABIC, Nissan (Renault), Toyota, Honda, Sharp, Hitachi, BMW, Volkswagen, Sulzer, Alsthom, Komatsu, Mazak, Denso, and others, also from capitalist idioms different from the sterile British variety. And to this should be added the long list of US companies that have been in this country for decades: IBM, GE, Dupont, Proctor & Gamble, and so on. In aggregate, this "foreign" contingent sustains many thousands of higher-skill jobs, and are the main source of exports, substantially larger than those of the hyped "knowledge industries".

The resulting paradox of contemporary industrial Britain is that such few businesses that still survive under the mantle of City shareholders struggle on with relatively low investment and "deficits in innovation, skills and management practices",[13] whereas from the real world of competitive international commerce are subsidiaries from radically different industrial traditions: over the years studies have consistently identified higher levels of investment by foreign subsidiaries than their native counterparts. One of the clearest symptoms of this bifurcation is the persistent bleat by British companies about the "skills deficit", continuing a paper trail going back at least to the mountains of verbiage generated by the National Enterprise Development Office. Sure enough, British companies' stereotyped response to the government's call to sign up to a "skills pledge" was that it was "unhelpful and patronising"[v], masking the old excuses that those who invested in skills training ran the risk of having their trainees pinched by other companies only too ready to "free ride".

None of the foreign companies in Britain need persuasion of the importance of recruiting and retaining their own skilled members, nor the advantages of a constructive relationship with local communities to help achieve this. And their concerns must have been one of the prime movers in stimulating the government's realisation of the chronic weakness in skills training. Yet a growing reliance upon foreign industrial investment and productive capabilities is a mixed blessing. If it puts more native employment beyond the whims of the City's "functionless rentiers" influencing managerial decisions, the facilities in Britain are part of an international network subject to strategic considerations deriving from national corporate headquarters elsewhere. Thus UK facilities will be subject to comparative assessments of prevailing economic conditions – for example, exchange-rate volatility – and availability of skills and expertise against other locations for access to the parent company's target markets. While UK suppliers will be competing against the parent companies' established networks of "home" sources. The 2006 R&D Scoreboard draws some consolation from foreign-owned companies accounting for 22% of the R&D of the UK's 800 companies, and that in some instances the levels of R&D in the UK exceed the intensity of the parent company's home facilities.[vi] Even here, however, there is the caveat that commercial applications from such UK R&D is absorbed as part of the technology streams of international product development and production networks dictated by the parent companies, which will generate value-added activities for the parent across its operations, well-

---

[v] "Business spurns 'patronising' government skills drive" (*FT* 15.6.07).
[vi] 2006 R&D Scoreboard, Volume 1: Section 9.

beyond the UK. A continuing dilemma will be to retain these foreign enterprises and encourage them to expand their facilities as technologies advance.

This evolving industrial structure has given us a steadily declining international position in innovation and in commercial applications of technology. And a corresponding atrophy in the mechanisms for renewing scientific and skills competencies, seeping through the skein of interdependencies to a reduced take-up of relevant subjects in schools and universities, closure of faculties, inadequate numbers of specialist teachers and lack of investment in quality laboratories. Notwithstanding a rising clamour from industry and calls for government measures, yet again barely changed over the decades since the annals of NEDO, and the reluctance of industry to commit to enhancing skill levels.[14]

Whatever the response to the arm waving for "golden carrots", the linchpin in the chain of supply is the number of potential employers who can offer exciting career prospects to reward students for the extra application demanded of technological subjects. For some commentators, any reference to "more than 2.4 million" of specialist employees needed over the next decade will surely be greeted by cries of "Soviet-style planning". But this country is leagues behind the focused application followed by the rising economies of our Cook's Tour – Taiwan, South Korea, Singapore and China, while similar concerns are already being pursued vigorously in the real industrial economies of Germany, Japan, France and the Nordics. Except that they have long-established institutions to renew their technological capabilities, and a solid bedrock of industrial companies that have been around long enough, and with the ongoing development activities, to hold out the prospect that they will still be around long enough, to offer exciting careers.

Given the inevitable wastage of students in the course of their studies, constraints of quality teachers and facilities, the diminishing range of native companies geared to sustaining themselves in the international market, and the technological and industrial illiteracy of politicians and Whitehall, the prospects of attaining "more than 2.4 million" is somewhere in the realm of aerobatic porkies and felines in Hades.

TOWARDS SUSTAINABILITY

It is debatable whether the UK's future as a significant industrial nation is recoverable. So long since the country has had businesses gaining international market position that memories have become dimmed to traces of industrial archaeology. While institutional structures have become ossified to accelerate decline: for example, the "short-termism" of Britain's "functionless rentiers" – and the concomitant trend of British companies distributing higher dividends from post-tax earnings than competitors – has been remarked for decades,[15] without any serious attempt to correct this bias which has continued to undermine national creativity and talent to match other countries. Attempts to modify the system, however well argued, collapse against comfortable special pleading and self-referential argument.[16] The necessity for government to re-capitalise the banks is dramatic evidence that the theology of "shareholder value" has broken down, with shareholders unwilling or unable to exercise custodianship of management.

In the face of blank astonishment from foreign colleagues at the country's industrial apathy, the only response is to suggest a narrative of Britain's history that puts the role of finance into its persistent and dominant role:[vii] the earliest "acquired lands", plantations and the associated slave trade, provided the "private surpluses" and demand that contributed to finance the "industrial revolution";[17] a fair share of the surpluses flowed into the "merchant banks" who subsequently exploited "Empire" for its mercantile gains; hence the "freetrade imperialism" of the East India Company's commercial buccaneering, the exploitation of the tea/opium trade, "capture" of South Africa's mineral resources etc; in effect, the quick buck, irrespective of how, was the dominant motivation, building up to the City as the "strongbox of the world"; "industry" did not rate unless it could offer rapid and sure returns to compare with those from other activities. The shady figures behind "hedge funds" and "private equity" stashing away their margins irrespective of the consequences for others are simply the contemporary exponents of an ancient tradition.

None of the European late-starters – with the partial exception perhaps of France – suffered from the same early "advantages" and consequent primacy of "finance". Instead, industrial development required risks to be shared with a wider community, including the State, and focused on building up national capabilities. Typically, for example, German banks focused their finance on their domestic charges, while Britain's finance houses would chase any source of returns. The Great Exhibition in 1851 provided clear evidence that other countries had closed, or surpassed, any British technical advantage. Thereafter, the provision of capital for the "new" heavy industries of chemicals, steel and electricity, for which the narrow return perspectives of City finance, were inadequate against the structures of European, US, and latterly Japanese industry. Sure, there were still native innovations, but, save where government finance was

---

[vii] Taking the lead from *British Imperialism* op. cit.

called in under military exigencies, the prevailing ethos stemming from City finance houses was the curse of "making assets sweat": leaving only islets in aerospace, defence and in supplies for the National Health Service. Consequently, this combination has persistently failed to evolve enterprises with an internationally sustainable drive.

The world has unfortunately kept up its habit of changing. Just as the proclamation of Britain "leading the way" to a "services" economy is simply crude special pleading for continued generous allowances for finance, so too other countries have retained the essential structures and priorities of their industrial evolution. The former continues as a driver of obsolescence, and the latter as a source of stimulating native creativity and competitiveness.

In keeping with this changing world, the domain of real business is distinctive in its sheer diversity: from the major diversified groups of General Electric, Siemens, Samsung, Tata, Toshiba etc to a myriad of smaller firms ranging across the mittelstand, small focused enterprises of Japan, Taiwan and Italy, to the urban/village enterprises of China. And embrace every variation of state, local government and family networks of mutual support. Out of this mêlée, companies can come "from nowhere" to take leading world positions in less than a decade – Nokia, Lenovo, Acer, Mittal, Embraer, Nine Dragons… Viewing this dynamic scene from the perspective of "this scepter'd isle" any British companies that might have evolved into major groups have long been scrambled out of existence by consolidation, while there is scant evidence of contenders for the fast growth route to international pre-eminence, and a diminishing band of stable mid-tier companies, as the pressures for "shareholder value" impel their break-up. The only hope of a viable industrial future is to offer companies a route to evolve free from the travails of myopic and disinterested shareholders and arms-length banks in order to compete against international enterprises that do not suffer these constraints.[18]

BUILDING BLOCKS – NEW PADDLES FOR OLD

If the undertow of the nation's drift up the creek has drawn upon myopia, complacency, disinterest and arrogance, the institutions of academia, Whitehall, Parliament and the City have only been paddling to push the vessel of state further and faster.

That the academic fantasy of a "service-led" economy is unsustainable is beginning to permeate with Sterling's persistent fall against the Euro and Dollar, and when the current account deficit hit 5.7% of GDP, we heard, "Sterling's hitherto sustained strength had fooled people into believing 'you can run the economy permanently on the back of consumer spending and rising land prices'."[19] This fantasy fugue may be a natural corollary of the prattling on about "markets" and the totem of the City as the "world's leading financial centre", but it has persisted so long that there has been an attrition of industrial capacity. That manufacturing accounts for 10% or 12% of GDP is less significant than the resulting depletion of the industrial infrastructure in ranges of technology and process accomplishments necessary to sustain internationally competitive enterprises – recall our quick glance at the Japanese auto industry.

In simple terms, the rising trade deficit reflects the country's inability to generate exports sufficient to counter the rising dependence on imports of energy, foodstuffs and essential products such as flat screen TVs, mobile phones, computers/laptops, DVD players etc. That it has been rising incessantly despite the glories proclaimed of national accomplishments in "services" underlines that any hope of "services" reversing this trend are illusory. Taking the objective of increasing UK tradable value-added,[20] a national SWOT matrix (a rudimentary management concept for totting up Strengths-Weaknesses-Opportunities-Threats) yields only a few scant lines under "S" and "O" and jammed-up boxes under "W" and "T". Ask anyone to try. And their universal response will be that "no one would start from here". In such a quandary, we cannot duck that our national systems, so long a convenient script to lecture others, are obsolete. Nor, fail to concede that others have evolved structures and institutions more resilient and effective at sustaining themselves against the demands for change. So let's have a shot at outlining a few of the areas where "modernisation", or new paddles, is most called for.

Technocratic Competencies

While Britain was stuffing its elite with Herodotus, the other baggage of Classical "Greats" and "useless" knowledge to produce "fine minds" to run the Empire – even up to the late 1950s possession of an "O" level in Latin was a prerequisite for Oxbridge entry, irrespective of subject to be studied – Germany, France, Sweden, Japan and the first generation of "late industrialisers" were pushing sciences and technology mastery as the first step in their efforts to develop their economies. The pattern has been followed by the next-generation of successful modernisers of East Asia – South Korea, Taiwan, Thailand, Malaysia, Singapore... and currently China.[21]

As the globe has turned, Britain has brought itself to an advanced level of technological illiteracy. Not just in skills and technical capabilities, but embracing a wilful ignorance of the commercial idiom of other countries, and reaching its apogee in political and intellectual pretensions mostly drawn from the surrogate reality of academic economics.[22] This "amateur" tradition offers infinite scope for farce in the spectacle of its politicians and commentators, barely able to pass the proverbial test of changing light bulbs or bicycle wheels, expounding on the importance of skills and sciences. Behind the *Yes, Minister* comedy is the dark side of an absence of no-nonsense professional practicality: recent examples aplenty in the vast sums spent on consultants of dubious value; a privatisation of power generation that put future investment and security of supply into commission; a crazed break-up of British Rail, and an ersatz replica in the London Underground PPP; PFI's of perverse consequences and a vast overhang of government financial commitments; a tax-credit system so erratic as to induce anxiety rather than comfort; a "flog it" gullibility in privatisation, such as QinetiQ and Actis; and a public administration ground down by a mound of counterproductive targetry. All the consequence of the fundamental British bumbledom incapable of the resolve and timely action to tackle basic social necessities. This dithering propensity, if a natural part of the nation's self-deprecating modesty and daily grist for commentators, just ain't a sensible way to run a railway, leave alone a country.

Nothing more typifies the "amateur" spirit than the British fashion for sporadic "initiatives" in virtually every sphere, but most destructively in education for sciences and skills: each occasion preceded by glowing declarations about laying the foundations for "the future of the economy", but displaying the very lack of continuity that has distinguished the approach in advancing economies over the past century and a half.[23] But also lacking the fundamental changes that would achieve a genuine longer-term shift out of the traditional "technological illiteracy".

A primary function of the revamped Privy Council, or equivalent, would be to replace the futureless and visionless sporadic jerk idiom of the traditional political approach with a consensual legitimacy that can attempt some adequate provision for approaching cycles of technology and change. A continuing part of this role should be supporting mechanisms to assess trends in technology – as Japan, US and others do, and as Britain's system has been peculiarly unwilling to attempt, and identify fields of science/engineering to which priorities should be applied (the jargon of "benchmarking" or "markets" suffer from the common ailment of continuously running behind the game). Such a framework would give industry and other participants some sense of direction that they can pursue with government support – and demands from government an entirely new repertoire of competencies from the "cultivated ignorance" necessary to sustain orthodox economic dogma.

With an educational system geared from its earliest levels through to tertiary to the priority of "useless" knowledge, and producing the raw materials for the "amateur" spirit, secondary education seems to be in its customary "review" state. But whether by baccalaureate or other adjustments, there should be a stipulation that maths <u>and a science</u> at GCE Ordinary Level, or equivalent, should be a prerequisite for all university entrance (a less "useless" stipulation than the ancient reverence for classics). At least "the intellectuals", even those pursuing "Mickey Mouse" degrees, in future might have the rudiments of technical literacy.

"Skills shortages" is a global phenomenon: many countries are confronting the "greying" problem of an increasing proportion of their populations reaching retirement age, with a corresponding reduction in projected young people coming into employment; and contending with rapidly evolving and interacting technologies. This country's couple of centuries of inattention has led to a cavity where there should be a bedrock of established engineering and skills training and development – apparently a major educational innovation is the creation of "maths champions" in primary schools. Whereas countries that have consistently taken "productive power" seriously have not only a better educational foundation but also enterprises that have a heritage of competencies and an orientation to secure their long-term futures. Instead of relying upon "flexible labour markets", these enterprises have an established tradition of networking with their educational sectors at secondary and tertiary levels, and increasingly in primary education – compare the efforts of German, Japanese, South Korea and Taiwan companies to cultivate and secure their future skills forces with the spasmodic and rare steps taken by their British counterparts.

The decline of industries weakens demand-pull from enterprises with a future vision for quality employees. A further depletion in demand-pull from a perspective of continuing sustainability has been an indirect consequence of the "privatisation" mania of the 80s and 90s. Where once there were "public utilities" with the prospect of a stable interest in sustaining their design, operating and maintenance disciplines, these have been replaced by private operators who may be motivated by short-term profits before selling out, or subsidiaries of international groups who will have evolved their own national recruiting structures.

If the national fixation on fragmented "competition" has sacrificed the effectiveness of continuity in many fields, the production of "instant anachronisms" for Whitehall and the City is probably the only sphere where continuity has been sustained: those bank grandees whose admitted contribution to the "credit crunch" was having no clue what they were buying or selling, as much as Treasury officials hardly competent to put together and run a Hornby train set privatising a rail system – the myopic comforts of dogma remains a common denominator. To curtail this flow would demand desperate measures: in the absence of a suitable strain of myxomatosis, perhaps debarring ex-top civil servants/financiers /politicians from taking leading university appointments, so breaking the breeding lineage.

Pragmatically, however, the origins of virtually all government cock-ups lies in the myopia of failing to reach out from the Viceregal Lodge of Whitehall to sustain a genuine professional dialogue with the real world, with all too many of its liveried hierarchies earning the sobriquet of "prats", or something similar, from those wrestling with reality. To confront the next century, leave alone catch up with the last one, demands a concerted shift from the rounded amateur to the competent technocrat, equipped to engage in the consultative networking to match the idioms of development set by the rest of the world. Nations will have evolved their own patterns of "bureau pluralism", very different from the customary British bureaucratic mode of "consultation" via committees with transitory Ministers in the chair, where none of the participants can deliver the performance of their constituents. The official participation cannot consist of amateurs sitting on hands coddled in obsolete economics nostrums and setting "targets" or "objectives". Rather, direct knowledge of the relevant technologies, industrial infrastructures and global competition contexts should be contributed, and demanding conditions applied with professional appreciation. At least, Departments should have the professional expertise not to rely on outside consultants, or at least have accumulated sufficient know-how to avoid being conned.[24]

To get to there from a tradition of "instant anachronisms" and producing *burrah sahibs* demands national reengineering towards a technical standard of commitment and tailored internal training to provide the level of competence with which they and the rest of society can confidently interact. There have been reviews of the civil service aplenty, but under senior echelons who have been programmed by tradition to preserve the territory of cultivated ignorance at its core. The ideal should be an expert agency capable of technically unimpeachable advice for Ministers, but equally one competent to lead in practical application.

Beyond this move to enhance technocratic competence, the rhetorical flourishes about leading the way in globalisation should at least be matched by a general education in the development of other countries. For all the fuss over "Britishness", and arguments for enhancing the place of national history, a dominant national trait has been insularity, and one that the country can ill afford as its status and influence diminishes. And anticipating comments on the creation of a "merchanting" capability, a language, particularly Asian, should be reinstated among the list of compulsory subjects.

Company Evolution

Whatever the golden eggs laid by the City goose,[25] providing appropriate finance for industry in a perspective of international competitive performance has demonstrably not been among them. When the Chancellor in his 2007 Pre-Budget Report declared in bold terms that the boost for innovation is aimed at "helping ensure British research and industry are brought closer together to develop the new products and services the world wants to buy," there is absolutely no track record of such an achievement through the nation's existing financial services.

Whatever the detritus and misery from the "credit crunch", one certain consequence will be a vast increase in the number of tomes, yardage of commentaries, and piles of profundities on the analysis of risk, uncertainty and stability. And guidebooks on the appropriate attire, posture and facial expression for senior management of our banks in holding out their platinum begging bowls to the Bank of England.

There has never been any such complexity in the treatment of companies by British banks and shareholders in the City. The traditional banking approach rests on the presumption of complete security through a charge on fixed assets and a "floating" charge over all other receivables with priority over all other claims: this has allowed them to adopt a studiedly "arm's-length" relationship to the company, and limiting their exposure to the distressed value of the assets in the event of break-up. "Risk" is shuffled off as a responsibility of shareholders, who, because of their exposure, are expected to exercise responsibility for the conduct of the company through a management answerable to them. Banks like this model, because they can argue that "risk" so far as the future of the companies concerned lies outside their purview – in situations of company difficulties, try persuading banks to convert debt to equity!

As for "shareholders", perhaps in ancient times when the business derived from a family initiator, and holders of the equity were committed to its future, this model may have applied. But with the evolution of external "shareholders", it's not too much of a caricature to conclude that "risk" translates to guaranteed profits within 3 to 4 years, preferably in the form of cash dividends or proceeds from share sales, without regard to longer term or collateral consequences. Management is permitted almost any excess in remuneration packages, so long as they meet these "expectations" irrespective of the international competitive scene.

While for smaller companies, the "equity gap" is a theme that was popularised on "78" records in the 1930s. That "The Lost Equity" has been playing unchanged through the eras of LPs, tape and CDs, and currently a popular TV parlour game *Dragons' Den*, without any improvement in our "products the world wants to buy", puts it high on the chart as an anthem to industrial decline. Such sheer sterility over such a long period is yet another symptom of myopic parochialism. In practice, by comparison with the systems evolved elsewhere, British equity – with its bias of "one share, one vote" enhancing the influence of "functionless rentiers" – has been poisonous for generating internationally sustainable businesses.[26]

In a context where the commercial scene is characterised by an array of different competitive contests for products, technologies and services, each posing a distinct existential challenge, it is hardly surprising that a stereotype of "shareholder value", a priority of "dividends for shareholders", "share prices compared to indices" etc has proved so destructive of national competencies. Instead, going back to basics, the main source of "equity" i.e. funds for investment in research, new plant, or driving for new markets where there are higher risks of not yielding early profits – for companies across products and nations, has been "retained earnings" i.e. the surplus generated by ongoing commercial activities after interest, depreciation, the taxman and other charges.

Recalling earlier examples, when Sharp evolved flat-screen LCDs, the financing came from the returns on their range of products in handheld calculators, microwave ovens and consumer electronics; or Toray, developing carbon-fibre, was drawing upon returns from its position in artificial fibres, synthetics in blends of textiles etc; or Fujisawa's focus on production efficiencies and driving for market share as a means to exploit Honda's technical flair. Nor have these companies remained static – as any British companies that might have had the competences to take forward these technologies have slithered into oblivion. Sharp is still pursuing enhanced precision, speed and visual qualities of its flat-screen TVs, with applications for handheld games, laptops and evolving its own line in mobile phones, securing a leading position in solar panels etc. Toray has become the leading producer of composites for the Boeing 787, and is exploring applications in motor vehicles, while taking a lead in nano-fibres – with applications from all-weather clothing to quick-drying bikinis – filtration membranes and other products such as high-performance reflecting film for LCD televisions and treatments for hepatitis C. Honda, still producing enhanced offerings in motorbikes and cars, has developed its own jet engine and small jet aircraft.[27]

These examples could as readily have been among continental and some US companies. But with a cycle of decades between laboratory breakthrough to significant commercial products, the process demands financial investment in an environment of relevant, motivated and evolving expertise. On the other hand, with the progressive decay of a stratum of British companies offering these qualities, the old adage that Britain has a reputation for invention but a failure to exploit this commercially will surely continue.

Britain's venture capitalists have a distinctly unadventurous track-record: historically the bulk of their transactions have been in "buy-outs", where chunks of established businesses are purchased, preened and dolled-up for flotation or trade-sale within 3 to 4 years for the best screw that they can get. Its performance in taking "British research" into the realm of what "the world wants to buy" has been miserable beyond a mere few. Analogies with the US are a blend of the fanciful and hopeful since there is no comparison in the massive scale of Federal funding for research, especially through the Pentagon and NASA; the US still retains a hinterland of industries interacting in application of technologies; and a tradition of private wealth going into ventures that do not necessarily move into early stock-market flotations (the dot-com boom, with the vast write-offs in its collapse, was in practice an aberration from the traditional approach). The latest example where Britain's leadership has led to sod all in major commercial success is biotechnology, "While there are some very strong companies developing – including Oxford BioMedica, Acanbis and Protherics – the sector is really in dire shape," and "the sector is shrinking as private biotech companies are bought by cash-rich pharmaceutical companies, most of which are based abroad."[28]

Endless repetition of "The Lost Equity" has also masked the dysfunctionality of British banking in supporting industrial evolution. The unique British convention of a "fixed and floating" charge reflects the primacy of finance in traditional priorities. This contrasts with Germany and Japan, where – apart from security against specific assets purchased by a particular loan – the banks rank behind trade creditors, reflecting a bias towards the sustainability of businesses in supply chains.

Here, far from the days of Britain's industrial growth when finance derived from local sources with concern for neighbouring social and employment implications, banking and finance has gravitated to the City. Retail banking – providing local services – has been a diminishing element of banking activities with shrinking local networks and more distant bureaucratic managerial interest in local businesses, compared to playing with paper through such devices as "structured investment vehicles" (SIVs): if often just another avenue for losing money, recompense is readily attainable from leading and lagging interest rates and other charges on normal domestic and business clients. While sitting on their "fixed and floating" charges, banks are free to maintain their sterile risk-free tie on companies without involvement in their ongoing prospects.

From the heights of imperial dominance that had never addressed the essentials for creating and sustaining viable industrial enterprises, despite a steady flow of comparative commentaries over decades on the relative success of others,[29] the residual institutional structures in Britain have fallen into obsolescence – not fit for purpose, in current jargon. For, at a fundamental level, British "capitalism" has become dislocated from the essential purposes of such a system. Today, "investment" has come to mean buying shares looking to "revenues" from a dividend-stream or gains from selling the shares at an opportune time. Or, indeed, from "lending shares" for short selling. These imply no more than a transitory or superficial interest in, or, in co-operating in short selling complete disregard for, supporting the underlying business of the company in confronting its competitive challenges.[30] In its original formulation, and as still applied in most other countries, "investment" means providing funds for the essential capital, research and non-variable costs of the business, with "revenues" deriving from the success of the company's management in exploiting its capital and human resources of which "shareholders" take a slice to the extent that they have supported the company. One recalls the account of a senior Vice-President of the Industrial Bank of Japan, Mr Ishihara, on Japan's aversion to aggressive takeovers, "We respect the human quality of companies", and a vivid contrast is the normally brief company profile in the *Financial Times*, concentrating on financial measures, and the depth and range of similar analyses in the *Nikkei*.[31]

There is therefore a major job of rehabilitation to restore the functioning of "British capitalism" to the mode of supporting productive tradable value-added activities. If anything from a worse starting point than other countries that have developed their industrial finance from scratch. Though the brave gesture of the government having a slug of equity in some banks would offer a point of leverage to discover "real" banking as pursued elsewhere. Picking around the alternative structures evolved elsewhere, there are plenty of potential models: France, Germany, Japan and the Nordics, or even among the rising "rest".[32] Bearing in mind, always, the proviso that one element of the structural mix cannot be isolated from others.

Industrial Investment Bank

Virtually all industrialising nations began with the disadvantages in "catching up" of a lack of private surpluses, as had been enjoyed by Britain's early industrialisation from the slave and plantation trades, and a relative weakness in market outlets, compared to the markets generated through Britain's "acquired lands" and maritime dominance. Their industrial development inevitably took a course of greater reliance on domestic banking finance and involvement of the State.

Even though models could be found in most European countries, among the more recent was the KfW (Kreditanstalt für Wiederaufbau) established in Germany in 1948, initially to mediate the allocation of Marshall Aid. Its role as a development bank has expanded into the provision of overseas aid, but domestically it has provided long-term loans alongside existing banks to support German companies growth without recourse to the stock markets. Operating with a Government guarantee it has a triple-A rating in raising finance.

In mechanical terms, a government-backed investment bank to provide loans for 12 to 15 years on state borrowing, or concessional, terms to stimulate longer-term growth on an analogy with KfW should be relatively simple. Particularly as objections in principle should be muted by the rescue of Northern Rock and the stakes taken in other banks: the obvious difference would be support for an institution focussed on the positive priorities of enhanced real investment and sustained viability as against bailing out bust retail banks. Where previous attempts "to support industry", such as the Industrial Reorganisation Corporation (IRC), the National Enterprise Board (NEB) and Selective Assistance, were based on the presumption that "the disciplines" of City banks and shareholders would contribute to evolving competitive enterprises, in practice they have militated only to a progressive loss of companies with any durable international presence. Consequently, a prime objective for a corresponding British institution, let's call it the IIC, even if working in parallel with existing banks, should be to insulate the enterprise from the debilitating influence of our traditional financial mindset.

Thereafter, analogies become more difficult to draw. For IIC loans could be subordinated to normal loans from our clearing banks, with conditions limiting the interest rates charged by the latter to avoid "free riding". But, whereas KfW could rely on a range of mediating banks which had a continuing interest in the enterprise to be supported – "good old-fashioned banking", Britain has not enjoyed such financing institutions for a couple of centuries. That mythical figure of the "local branch manager" with good neighbourhood networks and the source of friendly advice for local business has long passed into Dodo-land.

There may have been some moves to encompass a more "term lending" approach, essentially lending against the future prospects of a business. And the practice of pop singers and football clubs to float "bonds" against future earnings has developed. Yet the overhanging "floating charge" still inhibits finance being crafted against the longer term growth of the business.[33] In short, security against specific assets funded by loans, fine. But the "free ride" of stipulating a charge over other assets should be disallowed as a condition for joining with IIC loans and banks would stand behind suppliers and trade creditors in terms of security i.e. comparable to practice in Germany and Japan. Irrespective of the presence of an IIC, there is a strong case for the government through its ownership stake in banks to realign this approach towards industry, especially towards companies with a potential to exploit an international edge in technology: no doubt this would be greeted by howls from the banks, but it would compel them to take a closer and sustained interest in the development of the business. An alternative might be to allow a "floating charge" providing the bank has not less than 5% of the company's equity – again requiring a more direct involvement for having such a decisive role in the development of the business.

The IIC would also serve as some protection against the other "Death Star" of British industrial endeavour: the dominance of "shareholder value". There are mechanisms already available to insulate businesses against these: private ownership, trust ownership, protection by differential voting rights etc. To avoid demands from shareholders undermining the scope of the business to invest for growth, associated with IIC's loans should be a stipulation that no more than 30% of shares will be publicly owned voting stock.

Such insulation would carry several gains: the flexibility to allocate shares with greater recognition of those who contribute to developing the business; involving the workforce via such devices as trust funds financed by a share of profits that could also pay out bonuses according to the performance of the business; and, to reinforce mutual dependencies, encourage cross-shareholdings with key suppliers without concern for traditional shareholders' bleats about "pre-emption rights". At the same time, management could focus on the longer term development of the business without diversion from bogus incentive schemes linked to share prices, nor the pressures of performance measurement against analysts' largely self-developed "indices".

Unburdened by these constraints, the business can focus on the challenges, growing in intensity and diversity, of meeting competition in international markets. This would include comparable horizons for product development, sustaining expertise and skills to adapt to exploit these, laying down options for the future evolution of the business, and establishing the essential continuities for growth. Maybe we might even see British companies with the dynamism and durability of the Hondas, Sonys, and BMWs.... And perhaps even the evolution of "diversified groups" – a stable component in successful economic development elsewhere.

We even have a few surviving examples of this architecture: as various as JCB, Renishaw, Ove Arup and John Lewis. An essential function of the IIC would be to offer an alternative source of finance for corporate growth without recourse to the sterile pattern of "venture capital/flotation", and subsequent speculative buying and selling of shares. The fundamental caveat, and dilemma, for this evolutionary path are the same: the managerial pool that has any perspective to build and sustain internationally sustainable businesses is meagre. While the up-and-coming generation passing through the technocratically deficient national education system, with the dominance of "finance" in academic business training, is a continuing failing. The same dearth of horizons militates against the run of clearing banks playing an effective role in developing businesses, and equally serious in finding appropriate skills and personnel for the IIC. The "fees to flotation" mindset of the private equity/venture capital barons is unlikely to be a source of guidance for our future Hondas, Sonys, BMWs....[34] To suggest that these tyros have a higher growth perspective than listed company shareholders is to take barely a minimalist benchmark.[35]

Drawing together business expertise with this time horizon may well demand recruiting from foreign sources, or conceivably establishing a joint venture with other countries' industrial development organisations. For it'll take some time for the stark realities of the international scene to permeate through to the output of our educational system.

A Path to Tradable Value-Added

If British industry is scarcely marked by sustained advances in international markets, its most consistent activity has been to sustain the volume of bleats through representational mouthpieces. The numbers of variations around "bottle-top manufacturers associations" may mercifully have declined, but in compensation the volume of vacuous special pleading is now concentrated in such organisations as the CBI, Institute of Directors, British Chambers of Commerce, Engineering Employers Federation, Societies for Chemicals et al, Institutions of Engineering (various) etc. The current burden of bleats clusters around pretensions that the managerial elite should be absolved from the nausea of paying taxes, while expecting governments to fund increases in transport infrastructure and skills; complaints against EU standards for the treatment of temporary employees; dubious allowances for R&D; with further menus due every couple of months.

If there are fewer tinkling prancers, the maypole is by now rattling and wobbling, and surely in need of attention from Eastern European welders. Not least of the corrosive influences has been the consistent failure of industry to improve its international standing in response to all efforts by governments to respond to these bleats down the years. The system has the advantage for government in ensuring enough discordant views, or enough clustering around prevailing political rhetoric to be logged hopefully against future honours nominations, to allow governments to do whatever they want to do anyway.

To be fair, this guff generation system has been matched by a distinctly imperial approach to trade from successive governments. After all, the "fat cats" can be expected to look after themselves, though currently few would meow louder than kittens in any international breeders contest. While smaller companies deserved a leg up by alerting them to "opportunities" through an information network fed by the "outposts" of commercial staff in embassies abroad, even if this data flow was openly available to all competitors from other countries and despite the understandable frustration of overseas officers at the lack of response by British companies. And augmented by occasional, and diminishing, support of "stands" at trade exhibitions, and equally occasional Ministerial visits to "bang the drum".

With a steadily declining share of world trade, this pretentious morass has little to show beyond ineffectiveness. Taking a realistic glance at how trade has actually been conducted, in the halcyon days of Empire, when Britain originated 20% or more of world exports, "market share" had been gained through "acquired lands" with a British elite in administrative control and dictating investment and commercial practices, protected by maritime dominance and the resources of Empire to provide military manpower. Beneath this, the trading structure was underpinned by a wide diversity of "export" and "merchant" houses that mediated between British suppliers and local needs. Direct contact with native agencies and customs, financing the production and transporting local commodities and products to British and other markets, they also imported British products, financed local production centres etc. And the network extended beyond the territorial Empire to China and Latin America.

The decline of Empire led to a withering of these mediating links.[viii] So British industry lost a large, if not entirely protected, at least comfortable market, and the network of local links that facilitated trade into foreign markets. If the US, both within the American continent and in its imperial aspirations, followed the British model, and France retained its metropolitan (franc) overseas interests, other countries evolved their industrial development and international market penetration with their own distinct networks – Japan through its trading companies, Germany via overseas banking networks and the traditional international orientation of its companies.

At the most basic level, with a generally open trading system and the flattening trends of globalisation, it is questionable whether any business can have a sustainable future entirely within its national boundaries: this applies even to those with relatively large "home markets" like the US, Japan and Germany, but even more so for a relatively small British market. And for all the new dimensions of the Internet, and the new freedoms and reduced costs of travel and logistics, external markets demand a continuing and adaptive local presence.

Already established multinationals will over time – probably many decades – have learned this and built up their local presence. For British companies that are subsidiaries of foreign multinationals, they will be supplying within the structures of their parent organisations: if this may have reduced the need for establishing independent sales networks, they will be subservient to the parent's priorities and global market intentions. Similarly, companies that are international component suppliers to distinct industries will also have an established range of clients: yet also with hazards as clients are increasingly compelled to spread their global reach and open opportunities to alternative suppliers.

For small companies to widen their market presence, there is an added pressure: time. Technologies are evolving quicker, the cross-feed and feedback from innovations multiplying, and new challengers arising in almost every product field. Even if a new gizmo is evolved, it is only one sale and an air journey away to stimulate a competitive pirate version. Consequently, the capacity to move rapidly to achieve an international market position is all the more demanding. This in turn puts an onus on the merchanting role.

Sadly, one that the country has allowed to dissipate. Not to belittle the efforts – and inevitable frustrations – of staff in the commercial sections of overseas posts. But beyond fields where governments have a customer

---

[viii] *Merchants to Multinationals* op. cit.

relationship with producers – notably defence sales, and at one time power generation, mining and rail transport, and where long-term credit is a key component in the mix (France being the current leading player) – a diplomatic tag is not the best entry to the highways, byways and alleyways of local commercial networks. Rebuilding a merchant capability is among the most crucial underlying problems for a country that has permitted its trade to fall into rising deficit. And the skein of talents necessary cannot be assembled quickly.[36]

A prerequisite is a clear-out of the redundant pontificators, most of whom have no, or scant, direct experience of trade beyond Dover, and whose protestations to government have been steadfastly ignored for decades. Attrition has happily disposed of most of the battalions of "bottle-top manufacturers associations" and their ilk. But it would be beyond the ingenuity of Mr Dyson to devise a suitable vacuum cleaner to suck up the remaining bits-and-bobs proponents of vacuous protestations. Instead of this gaggle, arguing in the wilderness, a more credible voice for industry would be achieved if the remainder were amalgamated into one – again models in Germany, Italy and elsewhere are available. Yet, left to themselves, the attractions of mayoral chains and picking up honours on the cheap are formidable and the pleas accompanying continuing loss of international market share will continue.

Always assuming a government concerned at an inexorably rising trade and current account deficit – even if a cast of mind ignored in Britain for several decades, a single source of bleating should save many hours of officials' time ploughing through guff. This could readily be achieved by Government stipulating that it will receive representations from only one industrial trade body: leaving the CBI, EEF, British Chambers of Commerce, Institute of Directors and the other bits and pieces to sort out a mutual agreement. Some incentives could be offered:

– it should be compulsory for all companies operating in Britain to be paid-up members, with subscription rates based on the numbers of UK employees; and

– an annual subvention from Government would be justified as a recompense for reducing the abortive effort in dealing with the previous gaggle.

More taxing is the conversion of such a body from a bleet machine, preoccupied with protecting the remuneration systems of top management, regurgitating received dogma, and in the expectation of honours falling out of a slot machine. A genuine role for such a body in supporting the international growth of industry, and to contribute real substance to any advice it might give, would be achieved by taking over the trade promotion function from government. Putting trade promotion into the domain of commercial functionaries who should have a direct interest and array of capabilities to service British companies would place the merchanting role where it should rightly belong, though clearly there would still be a need for a few related staff in overseas posts. And the onus for maintaining local teams expert in the language, commercial regulation and networks would lie with this trade body. The very formation of such an entity, with growing experience of the realities of trade, would enhance its input into government policies.

But let's not get too prescriptive. These lines of action are merely indicative of the sheer scale of change to put the country in the starting blocks to evolve sustainable businesses to compete for tradable value added in international markets. There may, just may, be other avenues: for example, having expanded overseas, banks might use their local presence to support their UK client companies to link into overseas commercial networks, but this would imply a tradition of industrial banking that they would have to learn from scratch, apart from the discomfort of leaving their desks.

For a society that over decades, and one could reasonably suggest over centuries, has failed to give sustained attention to the growth of enterprises to match competitors nurtured in other countries, all the more taxing. Repetition of phrases from the junk-fiction of conventional economic text books may make for easy rhetoric, but offers no way out of a rising trade deficit. And other countries, including the US in the tradition of Alexander Hamilton, have inherited structures that allow co-operation between the state and industry. Consequently, Britain has a unique challenge in building the infrastructure and ethos to be competitive. Instead of an idiom of piffle and tiff politics, where the party complexion of government is immaterial as all avert their eyes from fundamental change, with debate essentially dictated by the social flotsam and jetsam of national decline, a cohesive approach is called for: underpinned by an effective Privy Council/Conseil d'État function where trivial party differences are relegated behind national purpose.

---

[1] "Walras's willingness to make trade-offs in realism for the sake of mathematical predictability would set the pattern followed by economists over the next century" *The Origin of Wealth* op. cit. p33.

[2] "The strong pound: Ten year strength of sterling speeds transition to services" (*FT* 17.5.07) "The strong pound helped speed a far-reaching move from manufacturing to a service economy... it is hard to imagine a similarly fortunate set of circumstances for the UK: a swift transition to a modern service economy, with cheap trips abroad thrown in."

Typical of the habitual trait of "economics" to make it up as it goes along. The accepted developmental theology is "a well-trodden ladder from agriculture through manufacturing to services" (Avoiding the rush – For countries to climb the economic ladder they need strategies to get around China – *FT* 14.6.07). The implication being that "services" represents some evolutionary advance beyond "manufacturing". Yet is this, or was it ever, borne out by real economic history? Even in the period of Adam Smith and the Industrial Revolution, the major generator of "private surpluses" was the slave/plantation trades: if involving "manufacturing" in the products exchanged for slaves and in the process of harvesting and producing sugar, the "wealth-generation" was still dependent on the "services" of redoubtable navigators and plantation managers. And, carrying on into the age of manufactures, sustaining production of cotton and machinery demanded overseas sales and all the "services" of shippers, merchant houses, finance and insurance. Not to mention the massive profits from the opium/tea trades in the latter 18th and 19th centuries.

Even if this "ladder" simplification is special pleading for financial services, it is questionable whether "spread betting", "tax fiddling", "scams", "flogging dodgy policies", "SIVs", etc represent the highest creative aspirations of the human condition. Of course, "services" also embrace a mass of even less glamorous activities – call centres, take-away pizzas, checkout counters, drug and human trafficking, gun-running, and so on. But what happens when others climb the ladder to be as effective at "services"? And what is the evolutionary step beyond "services"?

From a more realistic perspective, other nations might view an environment to stimulate the creative potential of all their people as a desirable objective. This implies a continuing presence of industries to exploit the shifting dynamics of technology, and a balance between manufacturing and services to reinforce each other, and, indeed, in this age of biotechnology, between agriculture and services.

[3] Typical of recent "authoritative" commentaries, "Tax crackdown sparks alert for new fraud scams" (*FT* 1.6.07), or "Tax loopholes leave private equity investors to clean up" (*FT* 11. 6.07): the latter with the illuminating conclusion, "Time and again, a tax break that is big enough to make a difference to the behaviour of entrepreneurs and investors ends up being exploited in a way that was not intended." And, for what? A senior partner in Alchemy Partners comments, "As an industry we are only barely able to demonstrate that we are superior to managing companies compared to public markets" (*Guardian* 12.6.07).

[4] As a vivid example, design of the Boeing 787 Dreamliner, with manufacture spread internationally but including, Kawasaki, Mitsubishi Heavy Industries and Fuji Heavy Industries, has "done away with almost all blueprints, not only at the

design stage, but also on the factory floor, 'by employing the CATIA software developed by Dassault Systems'". (*Nikkei Weekly* 14.8.06).

[5] Taken from the article "How Britain rates as a knowledge-based powerhouse" (*The Economist* 4.8.07). Despite recognising the endemic discrepancy between Britain's high rating in published scientific papers and its abysmal record in securing patents "for turning scientific discoveries into new products and services", this is partly excused by "an economy that has switched a long way from manufacturing to services".

"Yet the City of London invests heavily in computer software and is heaving with innovation, notably in derivatives", drones on *The Economist*. A standard complaint, however, from bankers has been that many innovations offer advantages only for "the next deal" since they can be readily emulated by competitors. And whether such innovations are necessarily benign remains moot in the playing out of the "credit crunch": for example, "For some, the rapid and dramatic unravelling of the sub-prime lending industry has echoes of the costly savings and loans crisis of the early 1980s – a meltdown that also had its origins in financial market innovation and inadequate supervision...." (Payback time – As subprime bites, US investigators look for culprits (*FT* 9.8.07)). Or, to quote John Plender, "There has been a systemic deterioration in credit quality as a result of financial innovation" ("We need more than a US rate cut to resolve the crisis" *FT* 18/19 .8 .07). Or, yet another financial commentator, "The accelerated pace of financial innovation and the ever-proliferating complication of modern financial instruments seem to defy the ability even of the products' designers to fathom what is going on. And the new instruments are often thinly traded, if at all, so values are guessed by simulation or calculation, not in the market. Sophisticated investors are left poorly informed about the risks they are bearing; unsophisticated investors have not got a clue. Desirable as fuller disclosure by hedge funds and private equity firms may be, it is hard to believe that it will be enough. In other words, financial innovation itself is the problem" ("The next financial crisis starts here": Clive Crook, *FT* 93.8.07).

Grasping for fig leaves, *The Economist* proclaims "Britain is a software-savvy country, spending £23 billion ($42billion) in 2006 - worth 1.75% of GDP, one of the higher levels among advanced countries." Sadly, there is no evidence of this savvy leading to US patent registrations in "Software and Computer Services". And the piece concludes on a sombre note, "But Britain's poor record in basic schooling should puncture any premature celebration. A well-educated and highly skilled workforce is vital in adopting new technologies and innovative practices. It is hard to see how Britain can score top marks as a knowledge-based economy as long as so many of its youngsters fail to make the grade."

Of course, skewing the sample to cover only "advanced countries" ignores the rising competence in software disciplines and innovation of India, Singapore, China and others. And the article also ignores the growing dynamic interactions between software development and innovations in the hardware elements of computing/communications technologies, where Britain is also extremely weak.

But for common sense, no better than the seasoned wisdom of J.K.Galbraith,

"Financial operations do not lend themselves to innovation. What is recurrently so described and celebrated is, without exception, a small variation on an established design.... the world of finance hails the invention of the wheel over and over again, often in a slightly more unstable version." *A Short History of Financial Euphoria.*

[6] To take a typical month, in July 2007 the trade figures for May were published by the Office for National Statistics: give or take subsequent amendments, the deficit in goods was £6.3bn, the smallest gap since October 2005. The breakdown was imports of £24.5bn, exports of £18.2bn, with £2.8bn surplus on trade in services, leaving a total balance of trade deficit of £3.5bn. For all the high-flown rhetoric about "services", their contribution to total exports is less than 20%. And with increasing dependence on external sources of energy, the prospect of "services" generating increasing surpluses to match this trend must be pie in the sky.

[7] Honda is raising the local content of its China operations to 90% by 2008, ahead of other foreign car producers (*Nikkei Weekly* 11.6.07).

[8] Like taking a lead in developing a 3-D chip fabricated from stacking three different types of chip to achieve greater speed and lower power consumption "as part of the effort to develop high-performance chips for its Asimo robot" (*Nikkei Weekly* 11.2.08).

[9] In the latest jargon, "evolutionary learning" (*Evolution of a Manufacturing System at Toyota* (Oxford) by Takahiro Fujimoto op. cit.). This presupposes an organic capability to evolve, a quality almost extinct among British-owned companies.

[10] Business evolution reflects national traditions, which, as we have noted, may vary significantly from the accepted stereotypes of the current UK model. The lineal development elsewhere has a fascinating diversity: Philips, the Dutch electronics group, derives from a family business begun by Karl Marx's maternal uncle; Seiko Epson traces itself back to the Hattori family, a 19th century timepiece manufacturer; Toyota is a spin-off from Toyoda Spinning going back to the age when Japan was the "Manchester of the East"; Saint-Gobain goes back to Royal foundation in the 17th century, with a widening diversity of products ever since; BMW has evolved from a leading aero engine producer in the First World War and in the early days of commercial aviation – the origin of its distinctive logo, through motorbikes to cars; Fujitsu – and its spin-off Fanuc – go back to a joint venture with Siemens before the turn of the 20th century; Sharp derives from an early 20th century entrepreneur who produced the Eversharp propelling pencil, but now with a product range embracing mobile phones, LCD television, solar panels, and a variety of electronic language gizmos; and so on. Such enterprises naturally evolve through the "forbidden" pattern of diversification: Haniel, typical of the German "family groups", goes back more than 250 years, began from fresh food storage but currently covering a range of pharmacies, retail, wholesale, hygiene, and construction materials; other "continental" odd-balls would include

the Agnelli and Wallenberg groups, but a common pattern elsewhere, such as Tata, Samsung, Mitsui in their differing national contexts; and it is often misleading to be led by a brand name which may be the most prominent activity within the group e.g. Noritake, generally viewed as an up-market brand of chinaware, is part of the Morimura group, which has a wide range of interests in industrial ceramics. In fact, Honda is a relatively new kid on the block, like Sony, Nokia, Acer, Mittal and Hyundai, who have come to international prominence from relatively small origins.

[11] For an immediate riposte, "A country that abandons its factories is a country that has lost its identity" – Nicolas Sarkozy (*FT* 25.6.07)

[12] Let's recall that the essential quality of the *burrah sahib* in his original Indian Civil Service guise was that he could not be wrong: any admission of error by the Government of India, or the ICS, would have brought the edifice of the Raj crashing down. This has been perpetuated to a national apotheosis as some Treasury berk, after education in economics at Cambridge, volunteered an "efficient" privatisation of British Rail, that actually created a shambles with costs running to billions of pounds – and a few mortalities and injuries – to rectify: for this service, he is awarded a knighthood and, via Rothschilds, a sinecure in one of the nation's leading banks. Similarly, a benighted ex-Treasury Permanent Secretary in the Home Office, after presiding over the department being reduced to "not fit for purpose", finds his natural niche in the Bank of England.

[13] LSE Centre for Economic Performance: UK Productivity during the Blair Era (June 2007). The study's stark conclusion is that over the past decade "output per hour worked in the UK is still about 13% lower than Germany's, 18% below the US level and 20% below France."

[14] Typical has been the CBI's umpteenth call for special measures, variously reported on 13.8.07: "CBI seeks bursaries to boost science and engineering studies" – "more than 2.4 million employees with engineering and technical skills are needed by 2014. Science and engineering businesses are already facing a recruitment crisis with industrial, energy and utility companies expecting a shortfall of up to 80% this year".... "Since 1984, the number of students taking physics A-level has slumped by 57% and the take-up of chemistry has dropped by 28%"... "The Royal Society of Chemistry said a quarter of labs were unsafe or unsatisfactory, suggesting much of the £200m allocated by the government to raise standards remains unspent".

And yet, a study by the LSE's Centre for Economic Performance suggests that "in 1992 one in five male graduates was in non-graduate work. By 2006 this had risen to just over one in three", and even in maths and sciences 19.5% were not adequately employed (Rise in graduates overqualified for their jobs – *FT* 24.11.07).

[15] Let's just recall, "Since World War II, the UK has developed a most efficient system for encouraging and collecting personal savings on a massive, continuous

and long-term basis, but this does not seem to have benefited the productive sectors of the economy... (Notably) the contractual savings between individuals and insurance companies and pension funds. In 1981 for example, the net inflow of funds into these institutions from the UK household sector came to around £13bn, which represented about half of households' total gross savings, and about five per cent of the gross domestic product (GDP), a colossal amount by any reckoning. What could be more suitable for financing industrial investment? Yet despite the earlier admiration of foreign observers, there is no doubt that very little of this found its way as fresh money into the UK industrial and commercial sectors. The total net inflow of funds into these sectors, as measured by the intersectoral flow-of-funds statistics, was £2.2bn in 1981; total capital issues by UK industrial and commercial enterprises were £1.7bn in the same year. Although the insurance and pension funds devote around 20% of their money to purchasing UK company securities, much of this consists in the acquisition of existing paper, the household sector having been a net seller. Unlike in Germany, Japan or France, there is no mechanism whereby the institutions' funds can be made available, on a massive scale, to industry. Nor do the major banks, the London clearing banks, have an industrial banking tradition. The result is that, in terms of final uses of the funds, household savings go mainly to finance house purchases, consumer credit, the government, nationalised enterprises, and overseas investment, private sector enterprises trailing behind all the rest." *Industrial Banking and Special Credit Institutions* (PS I Paper No 632, October 1984). A few booms and busts, bubbles and bursts, and credit crunches later, the levels of national savings that find their way into industrial investment are, if anything, even lower.

The tendency for British shareholders to squeeze higher dividends continues: over the period 2003-6, British companies paid out an average 43.7%-78% of net profit as normal dividends, compared to 33.3%-42.2% in France, 35.8%-43.6% in Dow Jones industrials, and 32.6%-35.8% in Germany, with the comment: "There's a strong German tradition of keeping dividends steady and reinvesting profits in the company" (*FT* 7.5.07).

[16] Typical is the fate of Will Hutton's *The State We're In* (Jonathan Cape), which, as a diagnosis of failings was eminently sound – and became a surprise bestseller. But he suggested that a better balance between "stakeholders" was a route to enhance performance: hopeless, for sadly all too many British top-management there is only one "stakeholder" for whom they give a shit – "shareholders" whose connivance is essential to allow exorbitant top management "performance incentives".

[17] "We have seen that the pace of capitalist industrialisation in Britain was decisively advanced by its success in creating a regime of extended primitive accumulation and battening upon the super-exploitation of slaves in the Americas... What it does show is that exchanges with the slave plantations helped British capitalism to make a breakthrough to industrialism and global hegemony ahead of its rivals. It also shows that industrial capitalism boosted slavery. The

advances of capitalism and industrialism nourished, in fateful combination, the demand for exotic produce and the capacity to meet this large-scale demand through the deployment of slave labour." *The Making of New World Slavery* op. cit.

[18] For a quick reprise a conveniently timed comparison is offered by the *FT*'s Lex column – usually a self-professed voice for the City's myopic vision, remarking on the future prospects of the Smiths Group (14.9.07). Smiths Industries had been one of the rare successes of British industry, having evolved steadily under Roger Hurn* by exploiting cross synergies in avionics and health systems. It became Smiths Group after taking over TI Group – in more halcyon days Tube Investments – itself a typical consolidated agglomeration of other British companies, notably bits and bobs of Dowty. This followed the well-trodden path of "consolidation to extinction", as companies dished out exorbitant dividends to meet "expectations" of City investors, and merged as an alternative to collapse – with a lucrative trail of fees for investment bankers, but inadequate investment to match international competitors.

Dogged by a share performance lagging the FTSE All-Share index, after sale of its aerospace activities to General Electric, Lex's attention focuses on the medical equipment and industrial seals businesses that "now need more investment" and concludes that for the Chief Executive "due to step down next year, a break-up could be a parting gift to shareholders". Adding, of course, to the silvery trail of investment bankers' fees, and the usual British corporate denouement of final break-up following on GEC, Courtaulds, ICI etc. A line of speculation taken up again when a joint venture with General Electric on security detection systems was dissolved (*FT* 20.9.07).

The same week as the Lex article, *Nikkei Weekly* (10.9.07) summarised an interview with Osamu Suzuki, Chairman and CEO of Suzuki Motor. The company evolved from a textile machinery manufacturer (like Toyota) founded in 1909, through a post-World War II move into motorised bicycles, motorbikes, small engine products, and light cars: rather than slug it out with larger car manufacturers, the company has focused on the smaller car segment, including four-wheel drive, and pursued markets that larger companies have tended to eschew – India, Pakistan, China, Eastern Europe, with manufacturing facilities in China, India, Pakistan, Hungary and plans for a new plant in Russia. Apparently, "On page 2 of Suzuki's training manual is the commandment not to compete head-on with the large carmakers", according to Tatsuo Yoshida, auto analyst at UBS in Tokyo. With the markets in which it has traditionally been strong coming under pressure, its model range is expanding into larger and more varied types.

In the interview, Mr Suzuki remarks that while domestic sales of mini-vehicles shrank by 4.5%, sales of their compact cars increased, while exports grew by 20% in volume and more than 30% in value. Other points touched on in the interview were:

– a projection for the current year's net profit could not exceed a 1% increase because "we need to take into consideration such factors as high materials prices, research and development expenses, depreciation and other costs. An unexpected

rise in such costs could offset the benefits gained from the weak yen."
    – a dividend ratio of 10%, lower than other companies, is justified on grounds "it would be a kind of bogus dividend if we simply compare ourselves to other firms and pay a larger amount than we can afford. Our operations in developing countries account for a significant portion of Suzuki's total business, which means we face relatively high risks. That is why we need to increase internal reserves."
    – in response to rising competition in India: "We will use our full strength to compete against them by exploiting our advantage as a pioneer in the country. With its comparatively strong brand recognition and extensive sales network, our Indian operation is growing steadily."
    – on the rationale for the planned manufacturing plant in Russia, "Although we are not a pioneer in Russia, we want to use in the country the expertise we have gained in emerging economies elsewhere. In India, we benefit from what we have done there for the past 25 years. So we would like to continue making such preparations for future global business." [It is reported in the same edition that the company plans to export low-priced compacts to Russia from its manufacturing base in India, starting around 2010. Suzuki's sales to Russia were 16,000 vehicles in 2006, 60% more than in 2005, shipped from Japan and Hungary. The new factory in St Petersburg, due to start in 2009, will produce Grand Vitara sport utility vehicles with a 2.0 to 2.7-litre engine and the SX4 compact sedan with 1.5 to 2.0-litre engines. Subcompacts with 1-litre engines would be exported from India, where production is scheduled to start next year.]
    – the justification for purchasing shares in Nippon Steel and JFE Holdings (another leading steel producer) in cross-shareholding arrangements, "We are clients of both steel makers, and deepening relations with them by holding shares in each other can help us secure a stable supply of steel products. All three of the firms were seeking to increase the number of stable shareholders, of which Suzuki does not have many. The idea was not brought up by anyone in particular, but arose as something hoped for by all parties."
    As a contrast in corporate visions, whereas one is focused on judicious growth with investment to expand market position and retaining reserves against potential risks (when did any one of the constituent companies in Smiths Group ever have a dividend as low as 10% of post tax earnings?), and a concern to avoid being diverted by erratic shareholders; the other is caught up in pressures from cash-hungry shareholders. Whereas Suzuki, whether in its original specialisation in loom manufacture, or when it moved into motor vehicles, must have been dwarfed by most of the august companies vacuumed up into the consolidation lineage of Smiths Group, the latter's sales in the year to July 31 2007 were £2.16bn (*FT* 27.9.07) compared to Suzuki's $26.7bn! Or, as another symptom of the future orientation of the two businesses, Smiths Group invested £ 143.6m in R&D in 2005/6 (presumably before selling its aerospace interests to GE) as compared to Suzuki's equivalent investment in R&D of £428.85m.

[19] A comment by Martin Weale, director of the National Institute of Economic and Social Research (*FT* 14.1.08). A bit late, mate. The same eminence had

pronounced only a few months earlier, "Most people would say it was a good thing that we switched to services early; that we didn't make the mistake of hanging onto manufacturing at all costs like Germany and Japan" (*FT Magazine* 3/4.6 .07). And what's wrong with Germany and Japan: while the UK was registering a current account deficit of 5.7% of GDP, they were managing corresponding surpluses of 5.6% and 4.8% respectively. And where's the cost in evolving companies of the quality of Toyota, Honda, BMW, Siemens, Toshiba, Hitachi, Sony, Matsushita...? And, after all, bailing out the financial sector can cost a bob or two.

[20] "Tradable value added" is an old-fashioned concept going back to the days when governments were concerned about the trade balance: essentially a measure of the output from UK assets in goods and services that are sold in international markets. Rather different from the conventional "Valued Added" data in the government's (BERR) Annual Scoreboard. The 2008 edition has the glowing tribute, "I am pleased that this year's Scoreboard shows that the Value Added by the top 800 UK companies increased by 9.6% over the previous year amounting to some £646,342 million. It is also pleasing to see that the UK leads the way in Europe accounting for 22.7% of Value Added amongst the top European 750 companies; Germany is in second place with 19.7% of Value Added."

Yet out of the top fifty European companies by Value Added, the UK's list is Royal Dutch Shell, BP, HSBC, Vodafone, Royal Bank of Scotland, Barclays, Glaxo SmithKline, BHP Billiton, BT and HBOS. While the German entries are Daimler, Deutsche Telecom, Siemens, Volkswagen, Allianz, Deutsche Post, Deutsche Bank, Robert Bosch, BMW, E.ON, BASF, Deutsche Bahn, ThyssenKrup, and RWE.

It would be prudent to set aside banks from these ratings, since subsequent events suggest that they must have been engaged in value destruction on a massive scale. However, just taking these examples to illustrate the discrepancy between "Value Added" and "UK tradable value added", BHP Billiton is a UK company solely by virtue of the venue of its listing, and only a negligible proportion of its activities are in this country: being primarily involved in raw materials development elsewhere, notably Australia. If anything it's UK tradable value added is marginal or negative. Similarly, Shell and BP have their main activities elsewhere, and since the run down of North Sea output are also predominantly importers rather than exporters.

Also problematic is Vodafone, whose main activities are operating mobile phone systems in other countries, either through acquired networks or joint ventures: in the UK it is one of several operators, but also an importer of systems and mobile phones (for example, as ZTE, a Chinese manufacturer, proudly announced in *The Economist* (21.6.08), "ZTE supplied high-performance, customised handsets to Vodafone, fulfilling their strict requirements for design, features, parameter, quality and materials. According to Vodafone's specific requirements, ZTE's industry-leading research and development group carefully created and tested the product. Today, two tailor-made models are sold all over the world through Vodafone. A total of 6 million handsets that support 34 languages were delivered in half a year." (A glance at ZTE's website reveals that through "locked up" shares the Guangdong authorities retain a controlling protective stake in the company) Again, the net UK tradable value added is marginal or negative. Conversely, BMW originates significant UK tradable value added by virtue of its Mini and Rolls-Royce plants, though hardly enough to offset imports of components and other BMW models.

German companies, however, as indicated by its trade surplus, plainly generate more national tradable value added than the UK's, as the country suffers a significant trade deficit. This is but one of the caveats against such cross-country analyses based on financial data: notable are among other dodgy assumptions in this exercise is the use of "average cost of employment of each person employed" as a measure of "skill intensity": this instantly places "general financial" in the "high skill" category, whereas actual performance leading up to the credit crunch, and subsequent bailouts and begging bowls, rights issues and emergency refinancing suggest a distinct lack of skills despite high levels of remuneration.

[21] "No matter how hands-on a political leader (Korea's Park Chung Hee, for one), most left industrialisation to professional civil servants in government bureaucracies and professional managers in private firms. Most professionals were no-nonsense engineers." *Escape from Empire* by Alice Amsden (MIT Press).

Inevitably, there will be insufficient engineering places in Britain, in which case prospective recruits to the civil service should be enrolled in faculties abroad – most of the major engineering schools offer courses for English speakers to attract students from other developing countries. And a broadened horizon before joining Whitehall might also contribute to a greater awareness of reality. In terms of internal staffing policies, professionalism also implies a rigorous and focused apprenticeship with all the interests involved, including where feasible corresponding expertise in other countries.

John Bourn with a long experience, as head of the National Audit Office, of the vagaries of Whitehall performance is sharply sceptical: for example, "Public servants are popularly supposed to be risk-averse. The opposite is the case. They take the most colossal risks without knowing the risks that they are running." Following on from, "The whole culture of the senior civil service needs to be changed…. At the moment they are given to those best at helping their Ministers get through the political week. Changing this would produce a new breed of civil servants who would concentrate on securing successful public services. It would alter ambition and behaviour right down the line." (Whitehall urgently needs to reform its culture: *FT* 14.5.08). Maybe a little too simple, as there are many a shambles created following "private sector" alledged expertise and advice tendered to Ministers by their coterie of experts. But a fair critique of the "we're all intellectuals really" school.

[22] Otherwise how come the earnest Sir Keith Joseph, whose "reading list" must have been a compendium of academia's "most useless knowledge" and with

fluency in French, including Proust in the original among his bedside reading, had no clue of how the French system functioned?

[23] The latest proclamation was "A £1bn government program to boost business innovation and applied research over the next three years...., along with a campaign to improve science teaching in schools" (PM pledges £1bn boost for innovation: *FT* 6/7.10.07). Coupled with this was another "£8m over the next three years to double the number of science and engineering clubs in schools from 250 to 500 by April 2009."

Accredited physics, chemistry and maths courses will be introduced to retrain teachers, with a £5,000 incentive. Included in the package is "better targeted support for early stage hi-tech companies." While to help them attract equity finance, a scheme will be established to channel initial "proof of concept" funding through regional development agencies. And better use of public procurement will be made "to drive innovation", and more money provided to "business facing universities".

[24] Just imagine a Treasury with some capability to have the semblance of a real dialogue with actual people, rather than a hermetic can of wankers' ejaculating targets.

[25] Beyond tax returns to the Treasury, so far as the general citizenry are concerned, the eggs have a distinctly addled aroma: they will readily recall pensions and endowment mortgage mis-selling; dodgy products such as precipice bonds, payment protection insurance, and split capital investment trusts; and the latest round of the credit crunch with its reduced and more costly credit for the public resulting from the City's innovation in financial products.

[26] An amusing commentary is the decision by the EU's single market directorate to drop its campaign for "shareholder democracy" pushed by the advocates of the British "one share, one vote" school of corporate governance, because studies had shown that there was no obvious added economic value in companies where shareholders had a voting weight commensurate with their stake (*FT* 4.10.07). Hardly a blinding flash of illumination, if the dismal performance, including disappearance, of British companies subject to the principle of "one share, one vote" was set in the scales against European companies that employ such "control enhancing mechanisms" as priority shares, multiple voting rights and ceilings on voting rights. If this discourages share purchases by "functionless rentiers", so be it.

[27] To put Honda's evolution on a comparative scale against British industry, from its initial flotation for ¥1m (when the ¥: $rate was 360:1) i.e. $280,000, its market value in 2006 was nearly $64bn, achieved while resolutely steering clear of acquisitions. This would put it as the 15th largest British company, some twice the size of BAe Systems and some four times the size of Rolls-Royce.

[28] After the glamour of university spin-offs a decade or so ago, with high-profile big bucks for academics, there has been "a string of high-profile drug failures,

share prices have plunged and there have been almost no public listings." While various commentators remark, "The UK has always laboured under the yoke of not having enough venture capital around and not having the people prepared to take risks", "The trade sale route should be seen as a sign of the strength of the UK in terms of science. But it is a short-term fix that does not necessarily fit with creating a sustainable sector", and "The UK's most prized biotech assets are being sold off to foreign companies because we cannot afford to retain them. That is not acceptable. The foreign companies get the UK science and labour force. The early-stage investors make money. But this is short term. The UK loses the ability to develop a greater labour force and profit from potentially blockbuster drugs." (British biotech struggles with the quickening onset of decline – *FT* 23.6.08).

[29] To cite a couple of more frequently quoted examples:
"To sum up... the radical fault of our system lies in the fact that our financial... institutions are out of touch with our industries, with the natural consequence that these industries, or the majority of them, are defective in their organisation and equipment." (The Financing of Industry and Trade in *The Economic Journal*, December 1917)

"British companies in the iron and steel, electrical, and other industries must meet in the gate their great American and German competitors who are generally financially powerful and closely supported by banking and financial groups, with whom they have continuous relationships. British industry, without similar support, will undoubtedly be at a disadvantage. But such effective support cannot be obtained merely for a particular occasion. It can only be the result of intimate co-operation over the years during which the financial interests get an insight into the problems and requirements of the industry in question and the industrial interests learn the value of the support which financial interests can give.... We believe it not unfair to say that certainly in American and German banking circles, and possibly in French also, there would be found many more men with an intimate knowledge of the problems of industry than in England." (Macmillan Committee on Finance and Industry, 1931)

[30] The practice of borrowing shares and then selling them in the expectation that the price will fall so that a profit can be realised by buying them back before returning them to the lender is a technique of some antiquity. But the practice has risen in the past decade through the activities of hedge funds, "with long/short funds accounting for more than 40% of the total \$2800bn invested in hedge funds" (Negative sentiment – Short-sellers are under ever closer scrutiny: *FT* 29.6.08). The point of controversy arose through suggestions that the activities of short-sellers were undermining the rights issues being pursued by some banks to restore their balance sheets. The Financial Services Agency stipulated rules for disclosure of a net short position of at least 0.25% of the outstanding stock of a company. This occasioned protests from prominent hedge funds, but also some critical analysis of the practice itself.
The justification for short selling is the view that it helps to create liquidity

and maintain market efficiency. The counter concerns have been to question the attitude of shareholders who lend their shares towards "obligations" of ownership, and the impact on managers of the perception "that their companies' shares are not merely an asset to be bought and sold, but also a handy device for high-speed financial engineering (Short-term owners who leave the C-suite bitter: Stefan Stern, *FT* 24.6.08). While the creation of "a kind of financial black hole" involving share-loans "believed to exceed a stunning £7.5 trillion" comes in for even sharper criticism by Will Hutton (As we suffer, City speculators are moving in for the kill: *Observer* 29.6.08).

That it should have been a hiccup in banks' rights issues that had occasioned this debate, and not the progressive dismantling of British companies under the mantle of "efficient markets" as they have failed to match international competitors in "real markets" suggest a misplaced priority accorded to the former and lack of regard for the latter. It is significant that countries where shareholders are expected to maintain a genuine supportive interest in the progress and sustainability of companies in whom they have a stake have either disbarred or restrained the practice of short-selling – notably Japan and Germany.

[31] A quaint example of Britain's corporate financial idiom is the *FT's* comment on the prospective impact on Rolls-Royce of an economic downturn (Rolls-Royce shares in danger of tailspin: 5.7.08). "The stormy business outlook suggests that the shares' present tailspin could soon accelerate, leaving shareholders trapped in the mangled wreckage."

The commentary acknowledges, "Rolls-Royce's order books were looking healthy enough earlier this year. Also, the company has plenty of work lined up servicing and repairing engines that it has already sold. However, demand for air travel is likely to weaken sharply as the world economy falters, causing airline companies to cancel orders for new aircraft, and hence for the Rolls-Royce engines that power many of them. At least the company is wearing a decent financial parachute: it was sitting on a cash pile of almost £900m in February."

Taking a comparative view of the company and its markets, they should appear more robust than many other sectors such as banking, housing, construction or retail. But, we go on, "Even so, having hovered around their 200-week exponential moving average for some 16 weeks, Rolls-Royce shares have since dropped decisively through that level. They may now have fallen into their monthly Ichimoku cloud, deepening the gloom. Because the shares have fallen so hard lately, their MACD momentum oscillator is displaying an oversold reading only seen once since the aftermath of the September 11 terrorist attacks.

"As a result, the shares may well be overdue a corrective bounce at least to their 21-day exponential moving average (EMA), which sits at 364p today, and perhaps even to the 21-week EMA at 410p. Applying an Elliott-wave interpretation, however, it seems unlikely that any rally will mark the start of a new bull market. Instead, investors should brace themselves for a further descent. Unless the bottom of the monthly Ichimoku cloud (currently 279p) provides the floor, Rolls-Royce could easily drop to 268p, a support level dating back to the late 1990s.

"In the longer term, Fibonacci relationships between the waves suggest that a drop to as low as 194p would not be surprising. To reverse the downtrend, getting back above the 21-week EMA is essential."

The horror is that there may be analysts and fund managers, whose actions might influence the company's shares, who may actually be influenced by this garbage. Whether the company itself understands this gibberish, or has to employ someone who does, this is a diversion on which neither of its major competitors have to waste resources – both GE and Pratt & Whitney are subsidiaries of larger groups. Nor can one envisage Honda, or any others aspiring to enter the aero engine market, being similarly afflicted.

This may be a jolly bit of waggery for those "in the club". But otherwise garbage of dubious merit.

[32] An entertaining compendium could be compiled of development banks around the world, SNCI in Belgium, CN and Caisse des Dépôt et Consignations (CDC) – still active in corporate restructuring, in France, IMI in Italy, ICC in Ireland, DH in Holland, with a variety of special agencies for smaller firms. Looking at the "late industrialisers", Japan had the IBJ and Shoko Chukin Bank, and all variety of state-backed financing institutions have been established in Taiwan, South Korea, Malaysia, India etc, well catalogued in *The Rise of "the Rest"* op. cit. As noted earlier, Temasek, the Singapore government investment fund, has followed a wide-ranging spread of international interests from banking, telecoms to a leading shareholder in Neptune Orient Lines (NOL), a leading freight carrier (NOL is weighing up anchorage in Hamburg: *FT* 1.7.08). While China is evolving its own variations through the residual party governance structures.

[33] A banner under which Britain's banks have explored virtually every conceivable way of losing money – property speculation, sovereign debt, off-balance sheet "structured investment vehicles" etc. And all with the comfort of having government as a backstop against incompetence, "No industry has a comparable talent for privatising gains and socialising losses. Participants in no other industry get as self-righteously angry when public officials – particularly, central bankers – fail to come at once to their rescue when they get into (well-deserved) trouble.

"Yet they are right to expect rescue. They know that as long as they make the same mistakes together – as "sound bankers" do – the official sector must ride to the rescue. Bankers are able to take the economy and so the voting public hostage. Governments have no choice but to respond." (Why regulators should intervene in bankers' pay – *FT* 16.1.08)

[34] Revealingly, a CBI study of the reaction of companies to the pre-Budget proposal to raise capital gains tax (CGT) in year three from 10% to 18% suggested "almost half of the UK's estimated 650,000 small and medium-sized businesses could be put up for sale before April to escape the Chancellor's 'swingeing tax grab' on entrepreneurs" ("Rush to sell firms" before CGT change – *Observer* 25.11.07). Not many nascent Hondas, Sonys or BMWs in this lot.

[35] Research on the performance of buy-out firms suggest that their returns, measured even on conventional investment criteria, "under performed the benchmark S&P 500 share index by 3%, after fees charged to investors" (Doubt cast on buy-out firms' huge profits – *FT* 23.11.07). With only a modest consolation that "private equity firms were longer-term investors than many listed company shareholders".

[36] From direct experience of working within a Japanese General Trading company, just a rough sketch of the inventory of competencies to function effectively as a trade intermediary: continuing trust relationships with local networks of commercial influence; fluency in the language, local regulations, power structures and customs; product/process specific technical knowledge to secure the confidence of partners to a transaction, and covering the range of products with potential in a particular market; possession, or expertise in, the appropriate logistics and financing of supply and support; and, the tactical experience and prowess to match manoeuvres by competitors. Even then, creating such an entity would lack the judgment and vision of enterprises that have evolved these qualities over many decades. So, if we cannot create a mercantile enterprise overnight, our purported business schools might focus on these areas of expertise, rather than the sterile niceties of corporate finance.

CODA

Acknowledgement of the skewed deficiency of the economy is becoming inescapable, even to the diehards of the "service-led economy" school: "When a country does not really make anything, watching its property, retail and financial sectors implode, prompts the question: what's left?".[i] And we are even offered a recipe; "Manufacturers are less vulnerable to the effects of slowing demand than in the 1990s. Mass-produced, price-sensitive components account for a smaller part of output. Many more companies are involved in high value-added research and development, design and marketing.

"During the past decade, as the service industries boomed, manufacturers cut around 1m jobs. Their productivity has risen as a result. The need to adopt global sales strategies and turnout goods with fewer people means producers are fitter than before the last recession... Manufacturers drive skills development, support supply chains and create wealth. Yet their share of GDP has fallen from 19 to 14% since 1995. Strongly branded US firms focused on technology and overseas markets have benefited from the weaker dollar. Similar growth in the UK could offset the effects of a financial services and consumer-led downturn.

"Just as ministers have striven to preserve the City's competitiveness versus other financial centres, they now need to respond to competition from foreign manufacturers. More generous incentives for training and research and development make sense. A broad-based economy with thriving exporters is a realistic goal".[ii]

Or even, "The idea that Britain's economy can rely solely on finance – exporting banks and importing goods – is surely dead".[iii]

A bit of a change from "Britain leading the way out (of industrialisation)", but Lord Roll's "inadequate clinical observation and analysis" still persists. The fantasy of a window box treatment of industry

---

[i] UK not OK: Lex (*FT* 9.7.08).
[ii] "Manufacturing a recipe for resilience – The UK must nurture what remains of its industrial base" (*FT* 9.7.08).
[iii] "The return of the "real" economy – Successful economies need finance and manufacturing" (*FT* 31.12.08).

"nurtured" by sprinkling "more generous incentives for training and research and development" simply fails to address the reality of British industry in an international context. However many UK companies are "involved in high value-added research and development, design and marketing" comparative data on R&D investment and patent acquisitions suggest that their performance in most sectors is relatively modest, if not abysmal, by international comparisons. The comparative competitive dynamism of foreign companies springs from more fundamental causes than a sprinkling of government incentives: as barely needs repeating, it derives from a continuing sense of purpose that has longer horizons and embraces wider interdependencies than allowed by this country's financing institutions. And be careful about knocking "mass produced" components, when in engineering at micron precision levels even capacitors and screws can be high value-added.

Underlining our critique, however, is perhaps a vision of resurrecting another mythical figure – "the pragmatic Englishman" as against the present capture by a sect of mediaeval scholastics. The challenge confronting the nation in resuscitating this creature is a reorientation to drop outdated dogma and preconceptions and create a genuinely adaptive capability to respond to a rapidly changing world. To delineate the main themes:

– Among the intellectual regalia to be dismantled are the stereotyped tramlines of economic orthodoxy dunned into student brains by academia. Whatever the merits of "efficient" markets – setting aside whether this condition is actually attainable, their impact in this country have been totally ineffective, if not destructive. How this "bollocks" has persisted, and indeed even gained dominance, demands guidance from the works of Claude Lévis-Strause.[1] An undertow of "markets" has been bubbling along in the Treasury and among officials in the "trade" fraternity for years. Despite the lack of any evidence of its efficacy, the jargon was a useful device to perpetuate the Raj tradition of sanitised aloofness from any contact with reality.[2]

In effect, the old aloof imperial strut – mouthing "free trade" and "open markets" oblivious to how the rest of the world was evolving – has persisted far beyond the point of striding with stately jodhpured gait beyond the cliff edge until, poised like the classic cartoon character, there is only thin air beneath our feet. And the future rate of descent is entirely out of national control.

Yet, elsewhere out there beyond Dover, beneath the veneer, and verbiage, of "globalisation", the world is ineluctably nationalistic. And has been for the best part of a couple of centuries.

The essential qualities of countries that have industrialised successfully are close involvement of the State as regulator; custodian of education, infrastructure, concessions, guarantees, and subsidies; and stimulating through direct relationships the evolution of their companies as innovative and dynamic competitors drawing upon national artisan, social and cultural traditions. In contrast to the contemporaneous British bias over this period towards "Empire" and priority for the spoils of wealth harboured in the City. Fair enough, the collapse of "Empire" was inevitable, but far from heightening any sense of the need to match the idiom of other countries that were adjusting successfully, Britain has never learned to compete. A Pavlovian hangover of the education and class ethos of the days of "Empire" has contributed to our unique "deindustrialisation".

– At the level of real international commerce, Adam Smith's view that it was "a species of warfare" has proved remarkably accurate. And just as perceptive was his assessment that "the joint stock company" – at least in its British variant – is the least effective formation for this style of conflict. For, whatever may be the travails flowing from "the credit crunch", the toxic contribution of the City to the real economy has been the run-down of British industry: the dominance of "rentier" shareholders whose attitude to the enterprise ostensibly in their charge is reflected in pressures for dividends irrespective of whether funds would be better deployed in matching the development and market thrust of international competitors; pursuing gains through devices such as lending stock for short selling, debilitating mergers and acquisitions, demergers etc; and inhibitions, if only to make life easy for analysts, against the evolution of diversified business groups that have been dominant agents in the evolution of economies elsewhere.

– We are coming up to another of our periodic "white heat" moments, though "technology" has gone up-market to "knowledge". Whatever varieties are encompassed by this latest version, in practice this country has always had a flair for coming up with bright innovative ideas. And in university laboratories and research centres this tradition may well be still alive. However, to transform "knowledge" into tradable value-added products and services demands mediation by commercial enterprises with the resources, competences and orientation to take on competition in international markets. Just where we have lamentably failed – and the saga of British innovation being exploited by others is bound to continue without "radical" changes.

– Consequently, and crucially, along with dispelling the inane dogma that pretends "efficiencies" are to be secured primarily by transactional contests on price, to introduce institutional and policy changes that stimulate the more enduring efficiencies of continuity and co-operation: beneath the inevitable maelstrom of punditry about repairing the functioning of financial markets, Britain still confronts the rudimentary task of establishing a system of corporate funding to encourage national enterprises to evolve the continuity, innovative flair and diversity to match competitors from other climes, and to modify its kindergarten belief in competition to enable such enterprises to develop. Without such a shift, all the guff about "activism", "route maps", "intervention" or "strategy" can be junked – after all, many £ billions have been hurled at British industry over recent decades in all varieties of "incentives" to negligible effect in evolving enterprises with a competitive international presence.

If our Cook's Tour may have missed the usual tourist and gap-year sights, it might at least offer a basis to meet one of Sun Tzu's preconditions for success – "Know your enemy". Our trip through Whitehall, the City and managerial qualities might contribute pointers to the second of the old sage's preconditions – "Know yourself". The suggested lines of change in the previous section are aimed at evolving a corporate finance structure that might stimulate the development of enterprises that can be credibly pitted against competitors in international markets. More widely, however, honest introspection should be added to Lord Roll's list of national failings. Probably the most tenacious of the Raj traditions, where the chosen elite presume their own undisturbed perpetuity, from which they can command any number of "reviews" of everything but themselves. Pavlovian reinforcement sustains this fantasy.

Now that, beyond any peradventure, the City's contribution to the national weal is a busted flush, it must be within the bounds of wild surmise that some questing spirit may query what should be done to resuscitate the nation's competences to evolve internationally competitive industries. Our past history is no guide. Okay, Britain might have initiated industrialisation in the 18th century, but dominance shifted to the US, Germany, France and then Japan, while today the template for aspiring "catch-up" countries, as also for old drop-out lags like the UK, is probably Taiwan's ascendancy to a leading position in semiconductors/electronics. Whatever, if ever, the rubric that filters through the standard political dogma of our times, in response to an ever-worsening trade deficit, "route maps",[3] "visions", "long-term perspective" etc, this will demand a competitive level of technological prowess, sensitivities to commercial relationships, awareness of the international idiom of competition, openness to genuine dialogue for consultation with business interests, and confident relations to pose the right – not necessarily polite or uncritical –

questions. Taking Prof Amsden's lucid survey of the palette of measures and steps to stimulate networks of related technologies[iv] pursued by the Taiwan government, there is nothing in the track record of politicians, Whitehall, the City or industrial management that suggests the technocratic competence to compete: in effect, our current caste of *burrah sahibs* lacks the nous to hack it.

The main Pavlovian constriction has been the aspiration to divine detachment: to be fair, this long predated Lutyen's Secretariat buildings in New Delhi, harking back to Sir Charles Trevelyan, of doughty East India Company stock, who shrugged aside the plight of the Irish peasantry during the 1840s potato famine, "...the greatest improvement of all which could take place in Ireland would be to teach the people to depend on themselves for developing the resources of their country." Today, appropriate distance is maintained by "radical" measures like the pursuit of "competition" and "choice", under the mantle of cash budget allocations, against "targets" and "incentives": all irrespective of their suitability to the organisation or activity.[4] To the extent that these mimic the performance stipulations of City finance, this is to adopt probably the most sterile model worldwide.[5] Saddest of all, these zombie formulae militate against the basic quality that distinguishes the more successful examples – whether of commercial enterprises or public services: continuity. The continuity that stimulates the internal "positive feedback" of creativity within an organisation oriented towards enhancing performance by "increasing returns" to sustain itself into the future.

Transition to such an idiom of capitalism from the current short-term transactional shareholder-value brand is a genuinely "radical" challenge. More than tweaking some of the accepted financial structures of the City, it demands a reorientation of education at all levels towards technical competences, with a coverage embracing management, finance, public administration and politicians. No mean task against centuries of Pavlovian reinforcement. In the annals of other countries' successful development, there are concepts like "national purpose" – rather more forceful than the British laid-back "consensus", where there is a shared dynamic readiness to defer immediate satisfaction for building long-term capacities. Strutting on thin air may offer some immediate self-satisfaction for politicians, economic commentators and others jockeying for position in our national Gymkhana, but carries diminishing persuasiveness.[6] And in the 21st century, the country faces climbing back up the cliff against others who have assiduously applied themselves to reaching, or staying at,

---

[iv] See *Beyond Late Development* by Prof Alice Amsden and Wan-wen Chu (MIT press) op. cit.

the top. Or, catching-up with the caught-ups.

To speculate on immediate future prospects, with the rundown of industry, the trade deficit, proudly excused in 1988 by Lord Young as a "temporary" consequence of successful high growth, has risen to more than £100bn in just two decades. This has put continuing pressure on Sterling's exchange value, with recent significant falls against the euro, dollar and others. In Blue Peter theory, this is supposed to make British products and services more competitive in international markets. After decades of depletion, however, and relative loss of market share; with many inputs "outsourced" to previously "cheap" production locations, devaluation increases the cost of these components as well as raw materials; the high import content of products made by foreign subsidiaries will also increase in cost; the resulting rising costs of "essential" imports such as flat-screen TVs, mobile phones, computers etc i.e. precisely those product areas that British industry has vacated; and exacerbating the national cost of imported energy. Blue Peter theory is likely to be proved wrong. Having allowed the collapse of so many industrial infrastructures, and with a financing system unattuned to industrial development, the country is hard-wired for continuing decline. And the country faces the prospect of a continuing cycle of rising trade deficits, pressures on Sterling, and further consequences for inflation and rising costs of such facilities as power stations, railway rolling stock and other capital goods where the main sources of supply are foreign. The comfortable mumbo-jumbo of "markets" proclaimed in the sunny *maidans* of unsustainable growth is transforming into a dirge as twilight darkens.

---

[1] The leading proponent of structural anthropology, whose key works were *Totemism* and *The Savage Mind*: the reverence accorded economics carries echoes of Hopi, Navajo, Dinka, Polynesian and other primitive thought structures.

[2] There must be many historical analogies to national complacency deriving from periods of dominance, going back to Rome, Byzantium and the moguls. A pertinent and ironic instance of the symptoms of a once "top dog" nation accumulating blindness towards what is going on beyond its immediate sphere of authority is the perspective of the Quin dynasty at the close of the 18th century, "These three broad patterns of foreign management – with the north-west, the missionaries, and the south – shared some fundamental Chinese premises of great importance. At their root was the assumption that China was the "central" kingdom and that other countries were, by definition, peripheral, removed from the cultural centre of the universe. The Chinese, therefore, showed little interest in

precise information or detailed study of foreign countries."

On this analogy, Britain with its preoccupation of empire, despite its global reach, was more concerned with avoiding this fragile structure toppling over, primarily by military/maritime/financial leverage. How other countries mobilised their national resources to counter this imperial dominance, save when it came to direct military confrontation, did not register as a matter of concern. So, just as the Quin were left inadequately prepared for the unscrupulous drive of European merchant venturers in the 19th century, and latterly Japan's imperial ambitions, Britain's institutions are outmoded against the new styles of commercial competition. And, most serious, the production line of duffers who were dispatched to screw up far-flung corners of Empire now have only the limited channels of government administration and the City in which to exercise their "useless" knowledge. (The account of the Quin comes from *The Search for Modern China* by Jonathan Spence (Norton): out of the mounting volumes on China, still among the most eloquent, balanced and engaging accounts of the strands leading into contemporary attitudes and thought.)

[3] The term used by Sir John Rose, chief executive of Rolls-Royce, in his call "Britain needs an industrial route map" (*FT* 23.4.08). To where?

[4] The absurdities perpetrated in the naïve belief that economic activity can be ordered on the same principle as buying pairs of socks defy cataloguing. As a typical example, the destructiveness of this dumb approach over time can be illustrated by the power-generating industry. Prior to privatisation, the CEGB had commissioned some 70 power stations since World War II, and, under the convention of seeking competitive bids, there were only two pairs of station that were arguably the same. In the case of nuclear stations, each was an individually distinct design. None of the British contracting companies now survive. Over the same period, the French had commissioned some 50 stations on a single evolving design, with the same suppliers, who still exist.
But in the past couple of decades we have witnessed a series of defective applications of "competition" – privatisation of British Rail, the defunct PPP for the London Underground, naive PFI's that allowed scope for refinancing and tax haven fiddles, collusive bidding etc. None contributing to evolving British enterprises with global presence or leadership.

All deriving from a primal misreading of Adam Smith, who envisaged competition as a device to avoid exploitation of a largely uneducated public (and landowners too dumb to know where their self-interest lay). He never addressed a situation where the client will be as professionally equipped with technical expertise as the supplier, and entirely capable of ensuring reasonable terms of sale.

[5] John Seddon is among the pragmatic critics of this dysfunctional managerial idiom: for example, "It is an unquestioned assumption that organisations must be managed by financial information from the accounting system. As these budget-based measures cascade down the hierarchy, the successive levels of management and, finally front-line workers, become engaged in 'making their numbers'. The

budget or target becomes the purpose. Managers and workers know what they have to do to meet it and how they are going to be judged. To question the basis for a target, if it occurs to anyone to do so, might be seen as a sign of weakness.

"Perhaps because managerial roles are created by the same logic, targets prevent managers from seeing the consequences of their actions. Their preoccupations are with the function they preside over, not the flow of work from and to the customer. In most organisations the cycle of management activity is: plan the budget, cascade the plan and associated functional numbers, monitor performance against the plan. As everyone makes their numbers, the organisation fulfils the plan, and all is well. Not so." (*Freedom from Command & Control* (Vanguard Education Ltd)).

[6] With John Maynard Keynes now all the rage, less remarked among his insights was his diagnosis of the vacuous arrogance of Britain's elite who "attributed the actual success of laissez-faire policy, not to the transitory peculiarities of her position, but to the sovereign virtues of laissez-faire as such. That other countries did not follow her example was deemed – like their bias towards protective tariffs – to be an indication of their inferior political wisdom." (Ibid)

Lightning Source UK Ltd.
Milton Keynes UK
25 October 2010

161843UK00002B/146/P